Applied Artificial Intelligence

A Sourcebook

Applied Artificial Intelligence

A Sourcebook

Editors
Stephen J. Andriole & Gerald W. Hopple

McGraw-Hill, Inc.

New York St. Louis San Francisco Auckland Bogotá Caracas
Lisbon London Madrid Mexico City Milan Montreal New Delhi
Paris San Juan São Paulo Singapore Sydney Tokyo Toronto

FIRST EDITION
FIRST PRINTING

Library of Congress Cataloging-in-Publication Data

Applied artificial intelligence : a sourcebook / editors, Stephen J.
Andriole and Gerald W. Hopple.
p. cm.
Includes index.
ISBN 0-8306-8263-5
1. Artificial intelligence—Handbooks, manuals, etc. I. Andriole,
Stephen J. II. Hopple, Gerald W.
Q335.A672 1991
006.3—dc20 91-30241
CIP

For information about other McGraw-Hill materials, call 1-800-2-MCGRAW in the U.S. In other countries call your nearest McGraw-Hill office.

Acquisitions Editor: Larry Hager
Book Editor: Sally Anne Glover
Director of Production: Katherine G. Brown
Book Design: Jaclyn J. Boone
Cover Design: Greg Schooley, Mars, PA TPR4

Contents

Acknowledgments

This sourcebook has been several years in the making. In some respects, a sourcebook of applied artificial intelligence could not have been compiled ten years ago; the range of successful applications was just not broad enough. Today we can point to a variety of spectacular successes (and some notable failures), and chronicle progress in a way that, hopefully, lends itself to introspection and imitation. Neither of these noble goals would be possible if it were not for the work of the contributors to this sourcebook. The first and foremost acknowledgment thus goes to the professionals who have successfully applied artificial intelligence.

We would also like to thank Orlando Petrocelli for his guidance and patience, and the editors at TAB/McGraw-Hill—especially Sally Glover—for so professionally engineering the production process. An undertaking of this size requires an enormous commitment; TAB Books has made a major contribution to the field via its commitment to this sourcebook of applied artificial intelligence.

About the editors

Stephen J. Andriole is Professor of Information Studies in the College of Information Studies at Drexel University in Philadelphia, PA, where he directs the Center for Multidisciplinary Information Systems Engineering. He is formerly the George Mason Institute (GMI) Professor of Information Technology, and Chairman of the Department of Information Systems & Systems Engineering (ISSE) at George Mason University (GMU), the state University of Northern Virginia.

Since 1979, Dr. Andriole has served as the President and Chief Scientist of International Information Systems (IIS), Inc., a company he founded. IIS specializes in requirements analysis and rapid prototyping, and has perfected several techniques for modeling and validating user requirements. The company also specializes in multidisciplinary systems engineering solutions to complex analytical and computational problems.

Dr. Andriole is also formerly the Director of the Defense Advanced Research Projects Agency's (DARPA's) Cybernetics Technology Office (CTO), where he was also a Program Manager. As Director of CTO (in 1978 and 1979), Dr. Andriole managed a $25 million program of research and development that led to a variety of important technological advances in the broad-based information sciences. CTO supported the MIT-developed Spatial Data Base Management System (SDMS), one of the earliest applications of the desk-top metaphor; the office also supported the design and development of video disk-based surrogate travel systems, training simulators, and direct manipulation interface devices. CTO also supported the development of Yale's SAM natural language understanding system, and a variety of decision support systems for option generation, resource allocation, and forecasting.

Prior to joining DARPA, Dr. Andriole spent the years immediately after graduate school in industry (Decisions & Designs, Inc.), where he designed and developed interactive systems for a variety of clients. Many of these systems were based upon decision theoretic principles, especially Bayes' Theorem, rational choice modeling, and utility theory. Some of the tools designed and applied in those days included simple decision trees, influence diagrams, Bayesian hierarchical inference structures, and multi-attribute utility assessment models. These and other models and tools were incarnated in computer software and linked directly with analysts faced with complex problems.

Dr. Andriole's research has focused on the design and development of various problem-solving systems, as well as the processes by which such systems are implemented. He has perfected the design and development of "storyboard prototypes" for user requirements validation. He has introduced the formal "requirements conference" as a means to forge consensus among system users and designers. A recent book on these and other design concepts—*Storyboard Prototyping for Systems Design: A New Approach to User Requirements Analysis*—published by QED Information Sciences, Inc. in 1989, suggests how the methods can be used to model software systems before programming begins.

Dr. Andriole has also conducted research in interactive systems design and development, analytical methodology, applied artificial intelligence, and user-computer interface technology. Some of his publications in these and related areas include *Interactive Computer-Based Systems Design & Development* (author, Petrocelli Books, 1983), *Microcomputer Decision Support Systems* (editor and co-author, QED Information Sciences, Inc., 1985), *Applications in Artificial Intelligence* (editor and co-author, Petrocelli Books, Inc., 1986), and *Defense Applications of Artificial Intelligence* (co-editor and co-author, Lexington Books, Inc., 1988). He has recently authored a new book for AFCEA International Press entitled *System Design Principles for the 90s* (1990). This book analyzes why we have had so many problems fielding cost-effective systems, and proposes a number of multidisciplinary information systems engineering-based solutions.

Dr. Andriole has also conducted research in defense command and control (C^2). He is the editor and co-author of *High Technology Initiatives in C^3I* and *Advanced Technology for C^2 Systems Engineering* (AFCEA International Press, 1986, 1990). He is also the co-editor and co-author of *Principles of Command & Control* (AFCEA International Press, 1987). His work in the area has concentrated on information processing, user computer interface technology, decision support systems, and life cycles for cost-effective C^2 systems design.

Dr. Andriole is the author, editor, co-editor and co-author of over 25 books and numerous articles, book chapters and technical reports. He has recently contributed to special issues of the *IEEE Transactions on Systems, Man & Cybernetics* and *Defense Analysis*.

He is a contributor to the long-running series in *Advances in Computers*, as well as the *Encyclopedia of Computer Science & Technology* (for Marcel Dekker, Inc.), the *McGraw-Hill Yearbook of Science & Technology*, and the *McGraw-Hill Encyclopedia of Science & Technology*.

He is a member of the Institute for Electrical & Electronic Engineers' (IEEE's) Computer and Systems, Man & Cybernetics Societies (where he also serves as an SMC Administrative Committee Member and Associate Editor of the SMC Society's *Transactions*), the American Association of Artificial Intelligence (AAAI), the Association for Computer Machinery (ACM), and the Armed Forces Communications & Electronics Association (AFCEA).

Dr. Andriole received his B.A. from LaSalle College in Philadelphia, PA, in 1971 in Liberal Arts, and his MA and PhD (in 1973 and 1974) from the University of Maryland (College Park, MD) in Quantitative International Relations.

He is listed in numerous directories of "Who's Who," is the recipient of the Defense Meritorious Civilian Service Award, and is a Charter Member of the U.S. Senior Executive Service. Dr. Andriole was born in 1949 in Philadelphia, PA.

Gerald W. Hopple—until his untimely death in 1991—was an Associate Professor of Information Systems and Systems Engineering at George Mason University in Fairfax, Virginia. Dr. Hopple joined George Mason in 1988 after serving as Senior Scientist at International Information Systems, Inc., Defense Systems, Inc., and the Battelle Memorial Institute. He also served on the faculty of the Defense Intelligence College and the University of Maryland.

He had conducted extensive research and managed a number of projects in the areas of cognitive psychology, decision support systems design and development, and knowledge-based systems engineering. Dr. Hopple was the author, co-author, editor and co-editor of over ten books, including *The State of the Art of Decision Support Systems* (QED Information Sciences, Inc., 1988) and *The Military Intelligence Community* (Westview Press, 1987). He had contributed papers to numerous edited books and had published numerous articles in a variety of journals, including the *International Studies Quarterly*, the IEEE *Transactions on Systems, Man & Cybernetics*, and *Large Scale Systems*. He is a co-editor of the first *Encyclopedia of Military Intelligence* (Garland Publishing, 1990).

Dr. Hopple specialized in analyses of cognitive information processing and how such requirements can be converted into applied systems concepts. His work in artificial intelligence is extensive. He is the co-editor and co-author of *Defense Applications of Artificial Intelligence* (Lexington Books, 1988). He designed and developed several large object-attribute-value knowledge bases for tactical planning. He also applied artificial intelligence to logistics planning problems, among others.

Dr. Hopple was a member of several professional societies, including the Armed Forces Communications and Electronics Association (AFCEA) and IEEE's Systems, Man & Cybernetics Society, among others.

He received his MA and PhD from the University of Maryland in 1974 and 1976.

Introduction

Stephen J. Andriole

Applied artificial intelligence (AI) is many things to many people. To those who labor in the public and private sector laboratories, applied AI often includes any research with even indirect relevance to real-world applications. Those in the systems trenches often define "applied" only in terms of debugged operational systems. As always, accuracy lies somewhere in the middle. While it might be hard to determine the relevance of basic research in uncertainty management, it is just as hard to field an expert system without committing to one (or several) of the multiple approaches to inference-making under conditions of uncertainty.

There is a basic-to-applied continuum that must be respected. At the same time, there are apparent disconnections along the way that account for perceptions of irrelevance and cost-ineffectiveness. This large volume attempts to bridge the gap between basic and applied research by focusing on the research progress that has been made—and translated into applications—over the past twenty years. This is a "sourcebook" of applied artificial intelligence. It deals with tools, techniques, methods and approaches as they have been applied to the design and development of knowledge-based systems. It deliberately avoids the controversial issues in basic research. It grants the existence of enormous problems and challenges, that there are many who still believe that the only real applied possibilities lie in deductive inference-making in well-bounded domains. It acknowledges the false starts, the hype, the aggressive research agenda, and misguided private and public funding programs that have taken us farther than anyone imagined possible. It assumes that progress in complex research areas is never linear, and that the march toward multidisciplinary applications is never easy.

Like many fields of inquiry, AI has experienced an imbalanced evolution. There are basic and applied areas in AI that have received far more attention (and funding) than others. It is safe to say that more of the applied funding has been targeted at the development of expert systems than at natural language, image processing or robotic systems. Such relationships are redressed over time; already we have seen some impressive results in natural language processing that will no doubt trigger larger investments. There are some obvious—and serious—missing links, such as the lack of design, development or validation metrics. Yet there are some striking successes in domains with specific characteristics. There are many deductive diagnostic systems working today. There are now graduate programs producing students in AI, though most of these scholars are more interested in basic research than applications. There are corporate centers of excellence, however, training professionals in AI and championing—where appropriate—the application of AI.

The distinction between basic and applied research is perennially blurred. Applications are understood differently in the management information systems (MIS) world than in "other" worlds. MIS assumes that systems will work nearly all of the time, are relatively easy to use, are documented, and maintained by people with real budgets. Those who build "prototypes" for the military, for example, define applications somewhat differently. This latter group sees applied AI as the next step beyond basic AI. There are changes afoot, however, changes that led to the compilation of this volume.

As you review the table of contents, you will notice that the book is organized around some key areas: the basic technology (Part I), the processes by which knowledge is acquired, represented and implemented (Part II), current application areas (Part III), and some insight into where we are now and where we're likely to go in the future (Part IV). The purpose of the book is not to get everyone up to speed in AI and then present some prototypes. Rather, the hope is that those who read this sourcebook will already understand basic knowledge engineering concepts and are more interested in how all this "stuff" can be applied to their specific problems. Part I of the book presents an overview of the technology, as well as some thoughts about the current state-of-the-practice. Part II presents some ideas about how to get knowledge out of domain experts, how to represent it, how to engineer it, and how to select among competing "shells" and programming languages.

Part III presents selected case studies from a multitude of substantive areas, ranging all the way from airline to legal applications. Part III is a tour de force of applications in artificial intelligence. It is intended to be suggestive of how expert and other knowledge-based systems can be used to solve complex analytical problems; it is also intended to demonstrate where knowledge-based systems can have the most impact—and where they will likely fail.

Part III also summarizes progress to date. The articles in Part III together constitute an applied snapshot of where we are at a particular point in time. No doubt the picture will change over time. New domains will become amenable to the tools and techniques of AI, and other once promising ones will be considered just too hard. AI is currently shaking itself out. Some of the older start-up companies are no longer with us. Sales of those that have survived have been unpredictable. Some of the hardware vendors have not fared well as knowledge-based programming environments migrated to not-so-special architectures. Yet many of the companies and government agencies that waited a bit before leaping into the technology have scored some impressive successes.

It is now time to acknowledge the role of AI vis-a-vis other problem-solving disciplines. Once upon a time, over-eager proponents of the technology felt it could replace just about every other applied solution; today, "systems engineers" have given AI a place in the general analytical methods inventory, a place alongside some of the "older" yet tried and true methods.

Part IV of the book deals with some nagging issues about the ultimate power of AI, and introduces the next promising technology for intelligent computer-based problem-solving—neural network modeling. But make no mistake about the new technology; it is not here to compete with "conventional" AI; rather, it is intended to work with conventional expert systems, to extend their range, and contribute to the larger effort in intelligent systems engineering.

Applications in AI are expanding; at the same time, the range of problems to which AI is considered appropriate is narrowing. More applications in "good" areas are occurring, while the community is beginning to understand why some problems are unsuited to AI. Parts II and III of this sourcebook provide insight into the process by which appropriate domains are identified.

We are also witnessing the "greening" of AI via its integration into larger systems with other methods. New fields of inquiry like expert databases and intelligent query systems design and development are emerging as quickly as mergers can be engineered. This is an enormously important and natural evolution for AI; in fact, arguments can be made that the very survival of AI largely depends upon the extent to which it can cooperate with other problem-solving tools, techniques, methods and systems.

This book is perhaps as much a feasibility study as anything else. The applications reported here are the result of countless person-hours, dollars, meetings, and expectations. There have clearly been some spectacular successes (just as there have been some noteworthy failures). The sourcebook skips most of the controversy and distills the applied essence of AI down to its most diagnostic properties. Hopefully, the effect is coherent and useful.

Part I

The state of the practice

There is considerable debate about the current state of the practice of artificial intelligence (AI). Many in academia believe that the field is too young for complex applications, while just as many in industry believe that the technology has already lingered too long in the ivory tower.

It is safe to say that we now have a strong sense of the kinds of problems to which AI is best applied. We know, for example, that problems characterized by enormous uncertainty, unboundedness, and a lack of human expertise usually make poor candidates for AI. But we also know that well-understood problems that are primarily deductive are often quite amenable to AI.

The first part of this book provides insight into the basic concepts of AI, the essential building blocks. It is included because many readers do not have a deep understanding of the technology, and because it is necessary to develop an understanding of AI prior to proceeding through the rest of the book.

Note the use of the phrase "state-of-the-practice." The emphasis here is on how AI can be applied to real problems, not on promises made by AI gurus or futurists. Hence, Part I does not address the "state-of-the-art" or the "state-of-the-expectation." The four papers in Part I present the building blocks, but they also provide an evaluative context. Papers appear that provide some "lessons learned," as well as insight into how to validate knowledge-based technology.

The first paper in Part I is "An Overview of Intelligent Systems Technology," by Paul Lehner. If you are basically unfamiliar with AI, intelligent systems, and knowledge engineering, take some time to study Lehner's paper. It provides an introduction to the technology and catalogs some of the more famous tools, techniques, methods, models and systems. Lehner's paper will permit you to understand, appreciate and critically assess the applications in AI presented in Part III of the book.

V. Daniel Hunt's paper will provide insight into the evolution of AI. It is important to remember that AI is an extremely young applied field of inquiry. Hunt looks at AI's short applied life, and interprets many of the events that led to successes and failures. Hunt's paper is about AI as a field (where Lehner's paper is about AI as a technology). The two papers complement each other nicely.

Bahill, Harris, and Senn provide some thoughts from the applied trenches. Their lessons learned are representative of experiences that many practitioners have had over the past few years. There is, as they say, what you can read about how to do something, and then there is what you learn from actually doing it. Bahill and his colleagues provide a little of the former and a lot of the latter.

O'Keefe, Balci, and Smith provide details about how to know if your expert system is any good. Knowledge bases are not validated in the same way as conventional databases or algorithms. Because of their nature, knowledge bases are more difficult to size, measure, and evaluate. The last paper in Part I helps identify the steps necessary to validate the performance of expert knowledge-based systems.

Taken together the four papers provide the tools to understand AI, assess AI tools and techniques, appreciate the knowledge engineering and expert systems design and development processes, and understand how to validate expert knowledge-based systems. Part I also sets up the rest of the book. After reading the papers in Part I, you will be in a position to critically assess the applications in AI that comprise the bulk of this sourcebook.

1

An overview of intelligent systems technology

Paul E. Lehner

Editors' note *Paul Lehner's overview is comprehensive. He deals with the fundamentals of intelligent systems technology in a tutorial way. He describes how expert systems work, how knowledge can be represented, how to reason under uncertainty, how natural language systems work, what computer vision is (and is not), what intelligent instructional systems are, and the hardware/software environments in which knowledge-based systems can be designed, developed, and tested.*

This paper should certainly be read by those basically unfamiliar with AI, though even those who practice the technology might well find his presentation useful. Once this long tutorial is studied, much of the rest of the book will become self-explanatory. (Reprinted from Artificial Intelligence and National Defense *by Paul E. Lehner (TAB Books, Blue Ridge Summit, Pa., 1989). References to chapter numbers and part numbers refer to those in the original book.)*

1.0 Basics of expert system technology

Of the various types of AI systems, *expert systems* have received the most public exposure. Expert system technology is widely perceived as the AI technology with the most potential for the development of near-term applications. Literally hundreds of efforts are ongoing to attempt to exploit this potential.

Expert systems are computer-based consultants that provide advice to users in real-world complex problem domains. For example, one of the first expert systems to gain significant notoriety was MYCIN (Shortliffe, 1976). MYCIN provides expert advice to medical doctors on the diagnosis and treatment of various types of bacterial infections. It is considered an "expert" system because its procedures for diagnosing and recommending treatment are modeled after the procedures and decision-making heuristics employed by human experts (viz., experienced doctors). Emulating human expert behavior is often considered a defining characteristic of an expert system.

In this chapter, a basic introduction to expert system technology is provided. An extensive introduction can be found in Hayes-Roth, et al. (1983).

1.1 How expert systems work

Expert systems are usually composed of two components: a *knowledge base* and an *inference engine*. The knowledge base is a database or set of databases that contain encoded problem-solving knowledge derived from human experts. The inference engine is a software package that functions to apply the encoded domain knowledge to problem-specific data to generate problem-specific recommendations. Figure 1-1 contrasts this approach with that of traditional programming where all procedures, algorithms, heuristics, rules, etc. needed for problem-solving are directly coded as software.

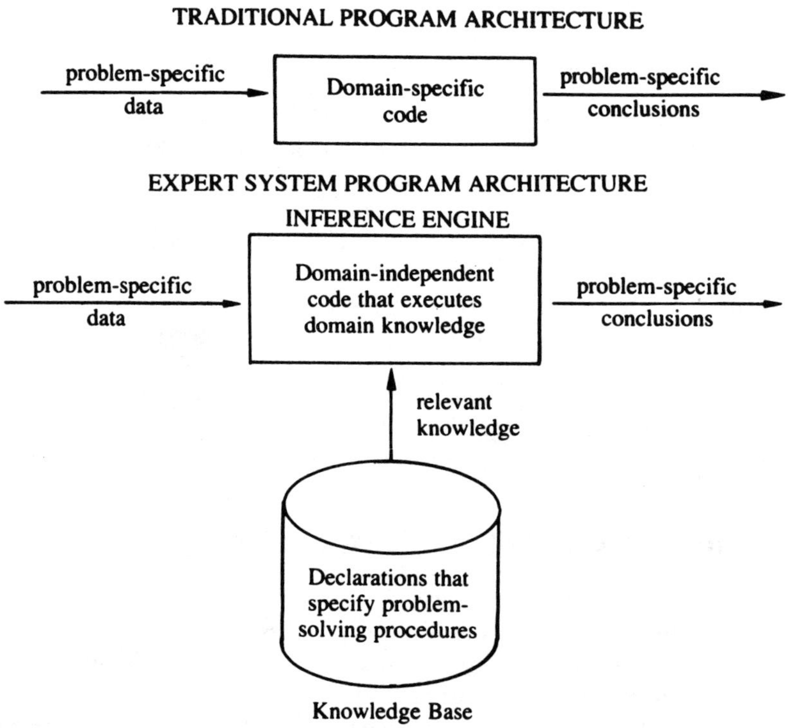

Fig. 1-1. Traditional vs. expert system software architecture.

Frequently, expert knowledge is encoded in a knowledge base in the form of a set of IF-THEN declarations called *production rules*. These IF-THEN expressions are designed to provide a flexible approach to specifying situation-action pairs (that is, expressions that specify the action to be taken whenever the situation is believed true).

Figure 1-2 shows some examples of production rules from three well-known systems. These examples point out several features of the production rules that may be in a knowledge base. First, the complexity of these rules can range from a single IF-and-THEN clause to a complex combination of interrelated clauses defining the IF or THEN expressions. Second, the THEN expression can incorporate any of a variety of "actions," including estimates of the degree of belief that a hypothesis is true, suggesting to the user that he or she perform some action, or even automatically invoking a routine to perform some action (e.g., an automatic display command). Third, the THEN expressions of some rules may correspond to the IF expressions of other rules, thereby making it possible to create hierarchies of rules. These rule hierarchies, when represented graphically, are called *inference networks*. Figures 1-3 and 1-4 show several rules and their corresponding inference networks. Expert systems often consist of hundreds of rules combined into complex hierarchical networks.

SYSTEM: RI (configures VAX systems)

IF:
1) The current context is assigning devices to Unibus modules, and
2) There is an unassigned dural-port disk drive, and
3) The type of controller it requires is known, and
4) There are two such controllers, neither of which has any devices assigned to it, and
5) The number of devices that these controllers can support is known

THEN:
1) Assign the disk drive to each of the controllers, and
2) Note that the two controllers have been associated and that each supports one device.

SYSTEM: MYCIN (medical diagnosis)

IF:
1) The site of the culture is blood, and
2) The identity of the organism is not known with certainty, and
3) The stain of the organism is gramneg, and
4) The morphology of the organism is rod, and
5) The patient has been seriously burned

THEN: There is weakly suggestive evidence (0.4) that the identity of the organism is pseudomonas.

SYSTEM: PROSPECTOR (mineral exploration)

IF: There is hornblende pervasively altered to biotite

THEN: There is strong evidence (320, 0.001) for potassic zone alteration.

Fig. 1-2. Sample production rules.

IF: The exhaust is smoky, and
The car is backfiring, and
There is a lack of power,

THEN: The carburetor fuel mix is too rich.

IF: There is a lack of power, and
There is a gray deposit on the spark plugs, and
The engine overheats,

THEN: The carburetor fuel mix is too weak.

IF: The carburetor fuel mix is too rich, or
The carburetor fuel mix is too weak,

THEN: The carburetor fuel mix needs to be adjusted.

Fig. 1-3. Sample production rules.

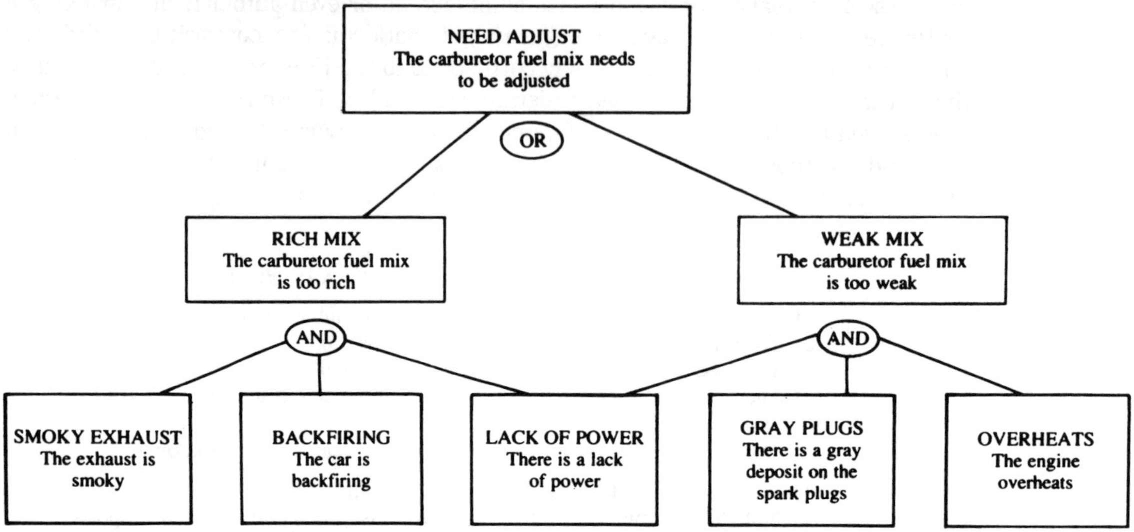

Fig. 1-4. Sample inference network.

The inference engine of an expert system performs a simple but very basic function. It applies the procedures implied by the rules in a knowledge base to specific problems. Consequently, the terms "rule applier" and "rule interpreter" have also been used to refer to inference engines. A simple inference engine might be one that performs the following steps:

1. Search all clauses in the rule hierarchies to identify the *primitive* clauses, that is, IF clauses that do not correspond to THEN clauses in other rules.
2. For each primitive clause, ask the user if it is true or false.
3. For each THEN clause in the rule base, calculate if it is true or false and report the result to the user.

1.1.1 Alternative control strategies

The simple inference engine described above is theoretically sufficient for processing rule hierarchies of any size. However, as the number of rules in a rule base increases, the behavior of acquiring all available *evidence* or primitive values would become very inefficient, as well as frustrating to a user if he or she must enter all the data. To efficiently manage the application of domain knowledge to specific problems, inference engines apply a *control strategy* that carefully controls the order of rule activation.

One common strategy is to select a *goal hypothesis*, usually a top level hypothesis in the rule hierarchy, and to chain down the hierarchy one rule at a time to identify intermediate and primitive clauses that impact the selected goal hypothesis. The expert system then gathers data about evidence items specifically related to the goal hypothesis of interest. The medical diagnosis system MYCIN, for instance, considers only one type of bacterial infection at a time. It queries the user about relevant patient symptoms and test results until it acquires enough data to either accept or reject the diagnosis before it goes on to the next one. This approach of managing the utilization of rules is called a *goal driven* control strategy, inasmuch as it selectively pursues one goal at a time. It is also sometimes referred to as *backward chaining* or *consequent reasoning*.

A *data driven* control strategy is one in which rule activation is controlled by data available and not by the pursuit of particular goals. In the data driven approach the expert system awaits the input of new data. When new data is entered, the inference engine scans for rules that are impacted, applies the impacted rules to generate whatever conclusions it can, and then resumes waiting for input.

A data driven strategy is appropriate for situations where data becomes available intermittently over time, or for rule hierarchies in which there are relatively few primitive clauses with a large number of goal hypotheses. The goal driven strategy is appropriate for situations where the number of goal hypotheses is small relative to the number of primitive clauses.

Figure 1-5 shows a simulated session with an expert system executing the rules in FIG. 1-3. Note that this expert system uses strictly Boolean logic, and applied a goal driven strategy to select which rules to test.

SYSTEM: **Currently trying to determine if the carburetor fuel mix needs to be adjusted.**
SYSTEM: **Is the exhaust smoky?**
USER: No.

SYSTEM: **Is there a lack of power?**
USER: Yes.

SYSTEM: **Is there a gray deposit on the spark plugs?**
USER: Yes.

SYSTEM: **Does the engine overheat?**
USER: Yes.

SYSTEM: **Given the above evidence, conclusions are that the carburetor fuel mix is too weak. The carburetor fuel mix needs to be adjusted.**

Fig. 1-5. Sample consultation session with an expert system.

1.1.2 Reasoning with uncertainty

In most realistic domains, inference and decision-making occurs in the context of considerable uncertainty about the status of the problem being addressed. For an expert system, this implies that the status of the primitives will not be known with certainty. To deal with this problem, developers of expert systems generally incorporate some mechanism for incorporating degree-of-belief considerations into the rules. Rather than have rules that are strictly IF-THEN expressions, expert systems often include functions for calculating the "degree" to which the THEN conclusion is believed as a function of the degree to which the IF expression is believed. That is, rules of the form:

IF A is believed with degree X
THEN Conclude B with degree of belief f(X).

Various types of mathematics are used for calculating belief values. Bayesian techniques, based on probability theory, are the most popular. These techniques assign likely estimates to the various possible conclusions from which the probability that each conclusion is true can be derived. Mathematics from Fuzzy Set theory are sometimes used to calculate degrees of membership to a set or class. Evidential Reasoning techniques provide a mathematics that can be used to generate a non-probabilistic estimate of the degree of support for or against a conclusion. It is often the case that the equations in an expert system are not based on any theory at all, but rather reflect the ad hoc formulas that appear the most representative of how human experts assess a degree of belief in a conclusion.

1.1.3 Alternative approaches to representing knowledge

In the above discussion of how expert systems operate, it was assumed that knowledge was encoded in a knowledge base in the form of production rules. This is not always the case. As AI has matured, other approaches to *knowledge representation* have been developed. Some of these alternative approaches are briefly summarized below.

Production rules As noted above, production rules are a series of IF-THEN expressions that specify the relationships between various situation-action pairs. Figure 1-6 shows a small rule base which will be used for comparison purposes.

```
   IF:  has feathers,
 THEN:  animal is a bird.

   IF:  flys and
        lays eggs,
 THEN:  animal is a bird.

   IF:  animal is a bird, and
        can't fly, and
        color is black and white, and
        can swim,
 THEN:  animal is a penguin.
```

Fig. 1-6. Comparison rule base.

Predicate logic Some expert systems have been built around the use of predicate logic formalisms for representing knowledge. In this approach, a set of predicates and the logical relationships between them are specified. These relationships correspond primarily to the typical AND, OR, IF-THEN, etc. expressions most people are familiar with. In this approach, the inference engine for applying knowledge may be much different than the production rule approach wherein an IF-THEN expression is processed by examining if the conditions under the IF part are true. If so, the THEN portion is processed. In the predicate logic approach, an [IF A, THEN B] expression translates into its logical equivalent [NOT(A) OR B], where the order relation (i.e., test A first) is lost. As a result, a predicate logic system could use the evidence "B is false" to conclude that "A is false," or it could use evidence that "A is true" to conclude that "B is true." Most expert systems built outside the U.S., particularly in Europe and

```
(OR NOT (HAS_FEATHERS)
    ANIMAL_IS_BIRD)
(OR (NOT (AND FLYS  LAYS_EGGS))
    ANIMAL_IS_BIRD)
(OR (NOT (AND ANIMAL_IS_BIRD
              CAN'T_FLY
              COLOR_BLACK_AND_WHITE
              CAN  SWIM))
    ANIMAL_IS_PENGUIN)
```

Fig. 1-7. Predicate logic equivalents of comparison rules.

Japan, use this approach. Figure 1-7 shows predicate logic equivalents to the rules in FIG. 1-6.

Semantic networks Semantic networks are declarative representations that define concepts and objects in terms of relationships with other concepts and objects. Concepts and objects are described as nodes in a network where the arcs are labeled with types of relationships (e.g., a-kind-of, a-part-of). Semantic networks are sometimes embedded in systems that also have other knowledge representation techniques. The well-known geological analysis system PROSPECTOR, for instance, uses both semantic networks and production rules. Figure 1-8 shows a semantic network representation of the rules in FIG. 1-6.

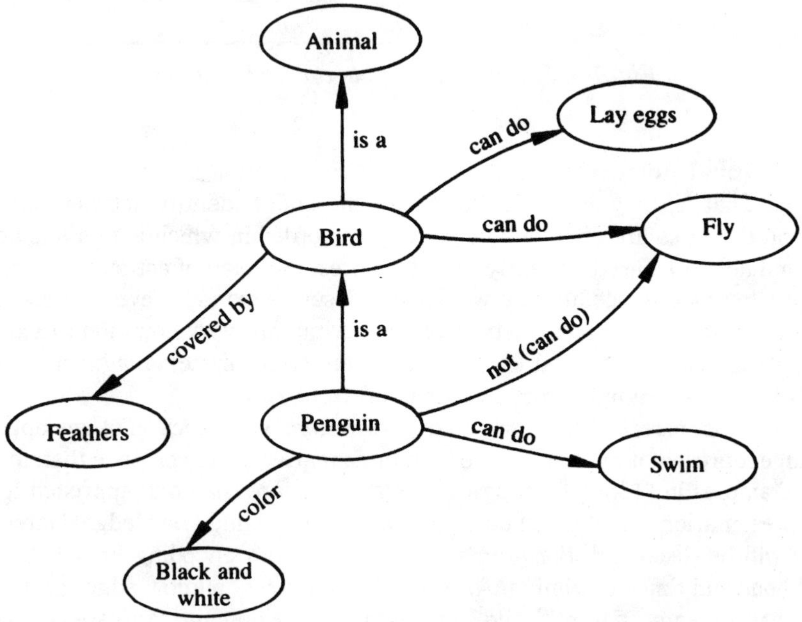

Fig. 1-8. Semantic network equivalent to comparison rules.

Frames Frames are static structures for describing various conceptual and physical objects. Within a frame there will be a set of slots that identify the dimensions by which an object can be characterized, and a set of attached procedures for filling those slots. Frames are usually organized by some higher order relationships that specify how various frames interrelate. Frame-based representations are becoming very common in AI-based decision support systems. The primary advantage is that they merge into a single framework both declarative knowledge, such as found in semantic nets, with procedural knowledge, such as found in production rules. Figure 1-9 shows a frame-based representation of the rules found in FIG. 1-6.

BIRD
type of: Animal
covered by: Feathers
travels by: (Flies = default)
offspring by: Lays eggs

PENGUIN
type of: Bird
travels by: Swims
color: Black and white

Fig. 1-9. Frame equivalent to comparison rules.

Procedural networks Procedural networks define a partial order of actions over time. That is, they are networks where the nodes identify actions that may be taken, and the links are directed and specify the order in which action should occur. Procedural networks are frequently used to represent a plan of action (see Chapter 3). *Scripts* are template procedural networks that describe standard event sequences that frequently reoccur. Procedural networks and scripts are very common in expert systems that deal with mechanical, electrical, and electronic system diagnosis and repair. Figure 1-10 shows a sample procedural network.

For the most part, in developing an expert system, the selection of one approach to knowledge representation over another is more a matter of convenience than feasibility. As the examples in FIGS. 1-6 through 1-9 illustrate, more than one approach to knowledge representation can often be used to represent the same knowledge content. However, as will be discussed, the process of obtaining and encoding knowledge can be quite tedious and time-consuming. As a result, selection of a knowledge representation format that appears "natural" and appropriate for a domain can save a substantial amount of time over the duration of an expert system development project. Indeed, expert system developers often switch knowledge representation schemes midway through such projects. This can usually be done without too much difficulty.

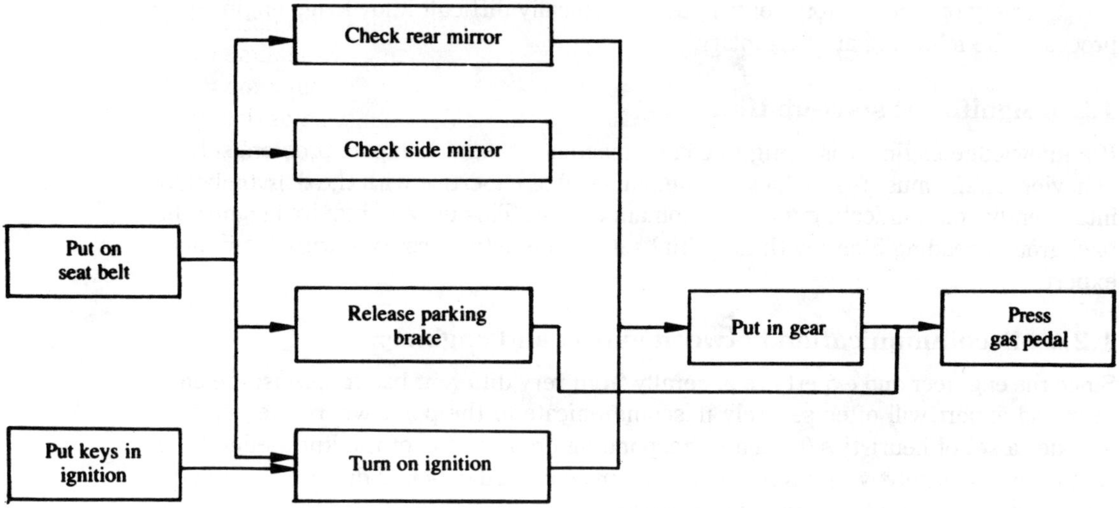

Fig. 1-10. Procedural network for starting car.

1.1.4 Summary of expert system processes

There are a number of dimensions by which expert system software can vary. These variations are largely independent of knowledge content. That is, for a given knowledge content, any of a variety of expert system software packages can be developed to execute that content. Selection of a control strategy, equations for probabilistic reasoning, knowledge representation schemes, etc. may determine the *efficiency* of the execution of the knowledge, but often do not impact the *feasibility* of developing the expert system in the first place. The major feasibility issue revolves around the ability to define the knowledge content. Difficulties in the process of extracting and encoding knowledge and other general limitations of this technology are discussed in following sections.

1.2 The problem of knowledge engineering

Expert systems can be described as computer-based consultants that emulate human expert reasoning in a problem domain. The process of extracting and encoding domain knowledge held by human expertise is called *knowledge engineering*. Given the state-of-the-science in AI today, knowledge engineering remains a time-consuming and labor-intensive process wherein an AI technologist, called a *knowledge engineer*, must repeatedly interview one or more human experts over a long time period (often years) to extract the heuristics to be encoded in the expert system knowledge base.

Knowledge engineering is essentially a process of instruction. The knowledge engineer must not only learn how the expert solves problems, but must learn it to such a level of detail that he or she can in turn provide precise instructions for a *tabulae rasa* machine. This is not an easy task inasmuch as human experts are often unaware of their own internal reasoning processes. Comments such as, "Once I understand the situation, the course of action is obvious," are common.

A variety of other factors contribute to a typically difficult knowledge engineering process. The following are exemplary.

1.2.1 Significant start-up time

If a knowledge engineer is going to code a machine to exhibit expert problem-solving behavior, he/she must first achieve a minimal level of expertise with the domain before intelligently communicating with the domain expert. This usually requires significant background reading along with an initial set of interactive sessions with the domain expert.

1.2.2 Miscommunication between expert and engineer

Since the engineer and expert are generally from very different backgrounds, the engineer and expert will often severely miscommunicate to the point where the engineer encodes a set of heuristics (with a corresponding organization of the knowledge base) that is on an entirely wrong track. Once the miscommunication is discovered, a major rework of the knowledge base is often required.

1.2.3 Limitations on availability of human experts

People who achieve the classification of "expert" are by definition very good at their job. They are usually much in demand and very busy. Interactive sessions with an expert must be planned long in advance and are generally infrequent. This problem compounds the previous one inasmuch as infrequent knowledge engineering sessions result in infrequent opportunities to correct miscommunications. This combination often produces very significant time delays.

Various estimates have been put forth for the amount of knowledge engineering it takes to build an expert system, with some ranging as high as two person-weeks per rule. While this situation is improving with experience, the process of encoding domain knowledge remains today much more of an art than a systematic science.

1.3 Limitations of expert systems technology

Potentially, expert system technology provides a powerful set of tools for developing systems that can generate expert advice to users for solving important and complex problems. Unfortunately, while the potential is there, a number of practical difficulties exist that have resulted in relatively few successful applications of this technology. As has been noticed by many scientists, these difficulties significantly limit the types of problems that current expert system technology can successfully address. The following, drawn from Gevarter (1985), represent a typical characterization of these limitations.

- *Narrow domain of expertise*. Because building and maintaining large knowledge bases is difficult, only a few expert systems have been developed that cover a significant range of knowledge.
- *Limited knowledge-representation languages*. Certain kinds of knowledge, particularly those without immediate IF-THEN consequences, can be quite difficult to represent efficiently with current knowledge representation techniques.

- *Limited and stylized languages for input and output.* Users must describe problems in a strictly defined formal language. Explanations of outputs are limited and very stylized (e.g., rule traces).
- *Laborious construction.* At present, a knowledge engineer must extract knowledge from a human expert and laboriously build it into a knowledge base.
- *Need for a single expert to serve as "knowledge czar."* Expert system developers are currently limited to their ability to maintain consistency and resolve conflicts among overlapping items in the knowledge base. Thus, though several experts may contribute to a project, one expert must maintain absolute control to ensure the quality of the knowledge base.
- *Fragile behavior.* Most systems do not deal with problems at the boundaries of their knowledge. Furthermore, they generally do not have the necessary knowledge built into them to identify problems beyond their capacity. Consequently, even some of the best systems generate clearly false answers for problems outside their knowledge base. Even within their knowledge domain, they can be misled by unusual cases.
- *Knowledge engineer must operate the system.* Often, only the builders of an expert system or others with similar experience can effectively operate these AI systems. Questions to many of these systems must be carefully framed to extract reasonable solutions. Most system developers have not constructed friendly interfaces for their programs.

1.4 Tools for building expert systems

A number of systems have been developed that are designed to support the process of expert system development. Most of these systems are problem-independent tools for expert system construction. The primary component of most of these tools is a generic inference engine that could, in principle, be applied to any of a variety of problem domains by entering domain-relevant knowledge into the knowledge base. Example systems of this type are listed in TABLE 1-1. The systems listed in the figure were all advertised in the Winter 1986 issue of *AI Magazine*. They represent only a small subset of a broad variety of software systems that provide expert system developers with an up-front rule application capability.

Despite the fact that a plethora of generalized inference engines exist, it is not at all clear (at least to this author) how much they contribute to the expert system development process. Even for a relatively small expert system, with say 200 to 300 rules, the most time-consuming aspect of development is the knowledge engineering process. The incremental cost of building a new inference engine that is tailored to the requirements of a problem domain is usually small relative to the knowledge engineering investment. Consequently, if a developer is oriented toward developing more than a small demonstration system, then budgeting the resources to develop a tailored engine may well be worth the investment.

On the other hand, if a small, proof-of-principle demonstration is desired, or if the system builder is very uncertain of the knowledge base requirements of the problem domain, then using an available general inference engine should significantly reduce the start-up cost of exploring the problem domain.

Table 1-1. Some expert system development tools

Expert System Development Tool	DEVELOPER OR DISTRIBUTOR
GURU™	Micro Data Base Systems, Inc.
Rule Master™	Radian Corporation
OPS5 +	Artelligence, Inc.
KES II	Software Architecture and Engineering, Inc.
The Knowledge Workbench™	Silogic, Inc.
Personal Consultant™	Texas Instruments, Inc.
Exper Facts™	Exper Ielligence, Inc.
EXSYS	EXSYS, Inc.
ES/P ADVISOR	Expert Systems International Ltd.
KDS	KDS Corporation
OPS83	Production Systems Technologies, Inc.
DAISY	LITHP Systems
XSYS	California Intelligence
TOPSI	Dynamic Master Systems, Inc.
Expert Edge™	Human Edge
S.1 and M.1™	Teknowledge, Inc.

Another class of tools for supporting expert system construction provides direct assistance to the knowledge engineering process. These tools fall into three broad categories. The first category are tools that perform *internal rule checks*. For instance, a good rule base is noncircular in its reasoning (e.g., A→B, B→C, and C→A do not all occur), consistent in its conclusions (e.g., A→B and A→Not(B) are not both members), and nonredundant (e.g., A→C is not a member if A→B and B→C are members). Systems which check new rules against these criteria provide some feedback on the quality of the organization of a rule base. Several expert system development tools (e.g., EMYCIN) have feedback capabilities of this type.

A second category of knowledge engineering tools provides some *objective feedback on rule quality*. For instance, some systems maintain a library of test cases that permit a knowledge developer to assess the impact of new rules against these test cases. An example of this type of tool is discussed in Lemmer and Mitchell (1984; see Chapter 7 for summary), where the system they describe allows users to develop computer vision rule bases by testing proposed rule sets against a variety of images to determine if it is sufficient for detecting a searched-for object.

A third category of knowledge development tools performs *automatic rule generation*. Some systems, for instance, allow users to specify instances of a concept from which the system abstracts a set of rules for identifying future instances of that concept. The derived rules are usually much simpler in form than the complex rule hierarchies a knowledge engineer working with a domain expert may generate. The ACLS

(Analog Concept Learning System) described in Chapter 6 provides some automatic rule generation capability.

1.5 Summary

Expert systems are widely perceived as the most practical and useful type of AI systems. As will be seen in Part II of this book, the expert systems are being developed that address problems in virtually every area of military decision-making. This is true despite the fact that many of the system development difficulties noted in Sections 1.2 and 1.3 often resurface.

Also, there is a key difference between the expert systems that are envisioned for our national defense and "traditional" systems such as MYCIN and PROSPECTOR that provide the foundation of expert system technology as it exists today. Whereas these traditional systems were all stand-alone systems, the expert systems envisioned for national defense are generally designed to be embedded in larger systems. In many cases, the role of the expert system is to be an *intelligent interface* between these larger systems and their users. At this point, it is premature to discuss the difference between stand-alone and intelligent interface expert systems and some of the unique technical problems associated with building intelligent interface expert systems. This discussion is found in Chapter 11 after examples of national defense applications of expert system technology are presented in Chapters 7 through 10.

2.0 Natural language processing

Within AI, natural language processing refers to machine understanding of a language that people use during the course of normal discourse. The field of research in machine-based natural language understanding involves several areas. A first-level decomposition that will be reflected here is the understanding between written text vs. the understanding of spoken speech. Written text understanding requires a machine with lexical, syntactic and semantic knowledge relevant to processing the language. An understanding of spoken speech requires this same knowledge, along with a perceptual processing capability sufficient to translate auditory sensory information into a form essentially isomorphic to written text.

A general introduction to AI techniques used to interpret individual sentences is in Section 2.1. Longer forms of discourse are examined in Sections 2.2 and 2.3. A more extensive introduction to national language processing can be found in Harris (1985). The chapter on natural language processing in Rich (1984) also provides a good introduction.

2.1 Understanding individual sentences

Processing single sentences requires two types of activities: interpreting the individual words in a sentence and integrating the individual word interpretations into a structure that represents the overall meaning of the sentence.

Interpreting individual words in a sentence requires that the machine, at a minimum, have access to a dictionary or *lexicon*. Unfortunately, most languages have many words with multiple possible meanings. A "diamond," for instance, can refer to a baseball field, a precious gem, or a geometrical shape. A bat can be for playing baseball or a type of flying mammal. The process of identifying a single interpretation for a word, when multiple interpretations are possible, is called *lexical disambiguation*. The disambiguation process is based on information from the rest of the sentence, where hopefully other words have been assigned precise meanings. ("Pick up your bat and play ball.") Lexical disambiguation is therefore the process of using understood parts of a sentence. As a result, it is often embedded within the broader sentence interpretation process.

As stated above, sentence interpretation is a process that involves integrating the individual word interpretations into a structure that represents the overall meaning of the sentence. There are two general forms of this type of structural analysis: syntactic analysis and semantic analysis. *Syntactic analysis* refers to the transformation of a word sequence in a structure that characterizes how the words relate to each other. *Semantic analysis* is the process of assigning meaning to the structures and substructures that (usually) were created by the syntactic analysis. These two forms of analysis are discussed below.

2.1.1 Syntactic analysis

Syntactic analysis involves a process called *parsing* for determining the underlying structure of a sentence. Sentence parsing requires a well-defined *grammar* that characterizes the set of possible structures for strings in the specified language. Once a grammar has been defined, a parser can assign a structure to any sentence that is grammatically correct. The resulting structure is often referred to as a *parse tree*. Figures 1-11 and 1-12 show a simple grammar for a subset of English and a parse tree based on this grammar. Note that each decomposition of a node in the parse tree is consistent with the grammatical rules shown in FIG. 1-11.

S → NP VP
NP → ADJS N
NP → the NP
ADJS → ADJ
ADJS → ADJ ADJS
VP → V
VP → V NP
ADJ → old|new|small|big
N → bicycle|boy
V → broke|fixed

Fig. 1-11. A simple grammar for a fragment of English.

Although the examples in the figures make parsing look straightforward, it can be a very complex process. Sentences are often structured such that early parts of the sentence can only be parsed after the rest of the sentence is parsed. Consider the sentence, "Have the students, who missed the exam, taken it today?" It is impossible to determine whether "Have" is an auxiliary or main verb until sentence parsing gets to "taken it today?".

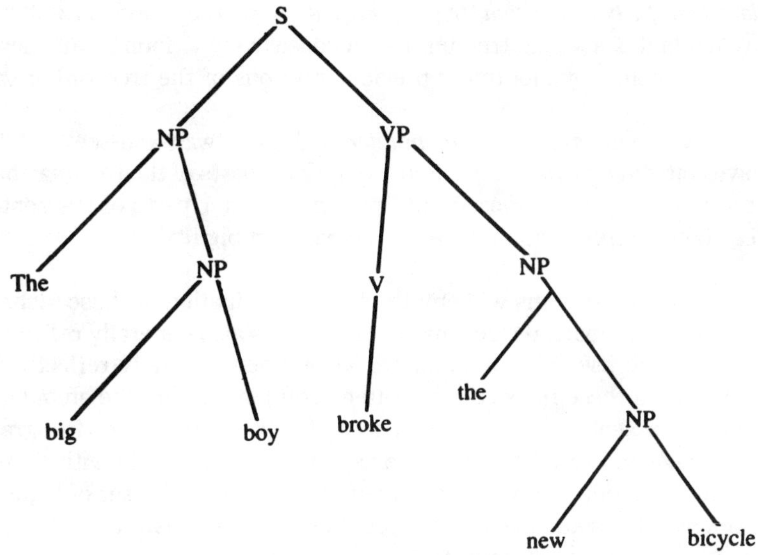

Fig. 1-12. A sample parse tree.

To handle complex sentences such as this, natural language parsers generally employ some type of search mechanism to control development of the parse tree. Parsers differ in whether they use a top-down, bottom-up or combined approach to searching through the space of possible parse trees. In the top-down approach, the parser begins with a start symbol and applies the grammatical rules recursively until the parse tree decomposition results in terminal nodes that correspond to the specific components of the sentence being parsed. In the bottom-up approach, grammatical rules are applied backwards. This process starts by matching the postconditions of some of the grammatical rules to the sentence components and then recursively builds up higher levels of the tree until a single tree is found. A third approach is to combine bottom-up parsing with top-down filtering. In this approach, the parse tree is actually generated bottom-up, but as various nodes are added, top-down techniques are used to determine whether the evolving tree will ultimately be consistent with the grammar.

In addition to the search mechanism, a natural language parser requires a mechanism for handling ambiguities. For instance, the sentence that began with "Have the students . . ." has the embedded ambiguity of whether or not "Have" is a main or auxiliary verb. Techniques for parsing ambiguous words include the following:

- *Keep track of all paths*. Have the parser build a parse tree for all possible interpretations of the sentence as it is unfolding. This process continues until all but one parse tree has been rejected as invalid.
- *Follow best path and backtrack as needed*. Here the parser builds a single parse tree until it is complete, or until a word is found that is inconsistent with the tree as it is being built. Once an inconsistency is found, the parser backtracks to an earlier word, finds a new interpretation for that word, and continues as before.

- *Follow best path and patch tree as needed.* Like the previous approach, this approach builds a single tree until an inconsistency is found, but then resolves the inconsistency by modifying previous portions of the tree rather than backtracking.
- *Record ambiguities and resolve them later.* This is a "wait-and-see" approach that involves building partially specified trees. Early parts of the tree may have nodes that are not fully decomposed until parsing of latter parts of the sentence provides enough information to resolve the early ambiguity.

Most natural language systems will employ some combination of these techniques.

In addition to grammatical rules, natural languages also generally reflect a number of restrictions on the use of its grammar. That is, they generally reflect a restricted grammar. Exploiting these restrictions is often useful in limiting the amount of search required to parse a sentence. A common way of representing both the grammatical rules of a language and restrictions on the use of that grammar is with *transition networks*. Such networks identify for any element of a sentence the set of legal forms for the next element of the sentence, i.e., the set of legal transitions. Figure 1-13 provides a simple example of a transition network.

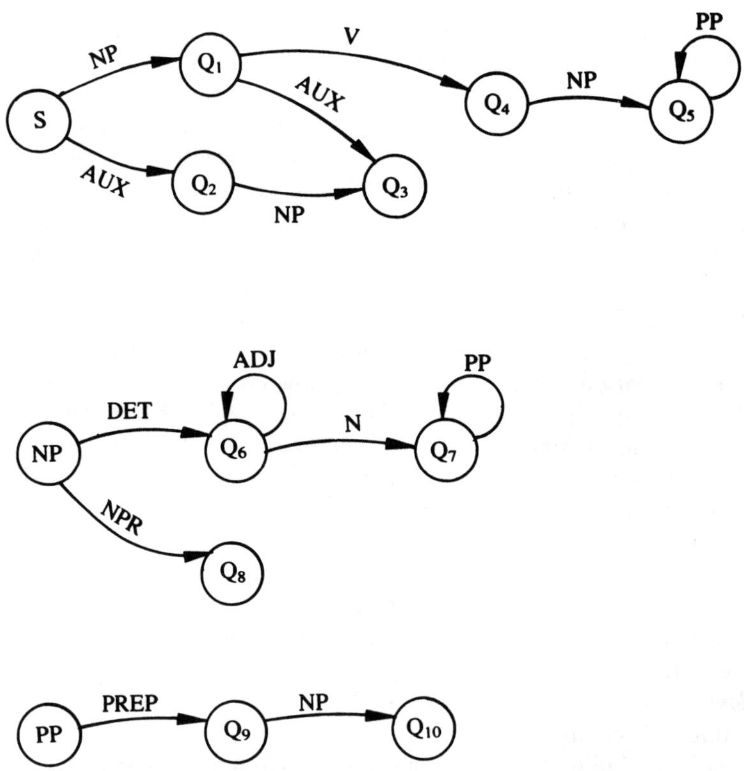

Fig. 1-13. Sample transition network.

2.1.2 Semantic analysis

The goal of semantic analysis is to determine the meaning of a sentence. Although it might at first appear that semantic processing can only occur after the syntactic structure of a sentence is uncovered, it is often the case that finding the correct syntactic interpretation depends on the semantics of the sentence. As a result, natural language processing systems often combine both syntactic and semantic analysis into a single common process. Two common approaches for combining syntactic analysis are (1) utilization of a semantic grammar and (2) the use of case grammars.

A *semantic grammar* is context-free wherein the elements and rules of the grammar reflect both syntactic and semantic relationships. Figure 1-14, for instance, shows a simplified semantic grammar drawn from the LADDER system described in Chapter 9. Note that the elements of this grammar incorporate semantic categories, rather than just syntactic categories like noun and verb phrases. Since a semantic grammar is defined in the same way as a purely syntactic grammar, syntactic parsing techniques can also be used to generate parse trees based on the semantic grammar. Once a parse tree is so generated, it will show the relationships among the semantic elements of a sentence and thereby provide a complete interpretation of that sentence.

S → what is SHIP-PROPERTY of SHIP?
SHIP-PROPERTY → the SHIP-PROP | SHIP-PROP
SHIP-PROP → speed | length | draft | beam | type
SHIP → SHIP-NAME | the fastest SHIP2 |
the biggest SHIP2 | SHIP2
SHIP-NAME → Kennedy | Kitty Hawk | Constellation | . . .
SHIP2 → COUNTRYS SHIP3 | SHIP3
SHIP3 → SHIPTYPE LOC | SHIPTYPE
SHIPTYPE → carrier | submarine | rowboat
COUNTRYS → American | French | British | Russian | . . .
LOC → in the Mediterranean | in the Pacific | . . .

Fig. 1-14. Parts of a semantic grammar.

One disadvantage of the semantic grammar approach is that the number of rules in the grammar may be prohibitively large for even very limited domains of discourse. This is because all acceptable relationships among various semantic elements for the domain of discourse must be represented in the grammar. Furthermore, even when an extensive semantic grammar is generated, its size will result in a lengthy and expensive parsing process.

Case grammars provide an approach to sentence interpretation that translates the results of a syntactic parse into a deeper, more semantically-oriented structure. Figure 1-15 exhibits several examples of case grammar interpretations. Note that these interpretations all revolve around verbs and the relationship of those verbs to their arguments. Listed in FIG. 1-16 are some of the semantic categories (i.e., deep cases) that are found in all case grammars.

Sentence parsing with a case grammar operates in a manner similar to the syntactic parsers discussed previously. However, since case grammars have a very detailed

SENTENCE	CASE GRAMMAR INTERPRETATION
TOM broke the bicycle.	(BROKE (AGENT TOM) (OBJECT BICYCLE))
JOHN went to the store.	(WENT (AGENT TOM) (GOAL STORE))
Bob gave Mary a ring.	(GAVE (AGENT BOB) (BENEFICIARY MARY) (OBJECT RING))

Fig. 1-15. Examples of case grammar interpretations.

Agent	— instigator of action
Dative	— entity affected by action
Instrument	— object used to cause event
Factitive	— result of the event
Location	— place of event
Source	— starting location of a movement
Goal	— ending location of a movement
Beneficiary	— the benefactor of the event
Time	— time of event occurrence
Object	— entity changed on/acted upon

Fig. 1-16. Some common elements of case grammars.

and explicit representation of how verbs may relate to their arguments, this knowledge is used to guide the parsing process. In particular, once the verb of a sentence is isolated, it is used to predict which noun phrases will also occur in the sentence, and the relationship of each phrase to the rest of the sentence. This added knowledge about semantically meaningful relationships limits the syntactic parsing process to only exploring syntactic structures that are consistent with the case grammar.

A third approach to semantic analysis is through the use of the *conceptual dependency* representation. This approach is similar to that of a case grammar in that it provides an underlying semantic representation that is independent of the structure of the original sentence. However, the conceptual dependency representation is a much deeper and lower level representation than that of a case grammar. This deeper level is achieved by defining a set of very primitive actions that, when taken in various combinations, correspond to the intended meaning of most verbs. For instance, the word "gave" would require the following conceptual dependency elements to be included:

```
                                                  to
              P              O             R          [Receiver]
[Giver]      <->    ATRANS   ->   [object] ->
                                                      [Giver]
                                                  from
```

The symbols in this example have the following meanings:

- Arrows indicate the direction of the dependency
- Double arrows indicate a two-way link between actor and action
- P indicates past tense

- ATRANS is one of the primitive acts used by the theory to indicate transfer of possession
- O indicates the object case relation
- R indicates the recipient case relation

Figures 1-17 and 1-18 provide a brief description of some elements of the conceptual dependency representation and the use of that representation for the deep semantic interpretation of some sentences.

PTRANS	Transfer of location of an object
ATRANS	Transfer of a relationship (e.g., give)
PROPEL	Apply physical force to an object
MOVE	Self-movement of a body part (e.g., throw)
MTRANS	Transfer of information (e.g., tell)
MBUILD	Build new information (e.g., conclude)
SPEAK	Produce sounds
ATTEND	Focus sense organ (e.g., watch)
INGEST	Ingest an object into body

Fig. 1-17. Some primitive actions in conceptual dependency.

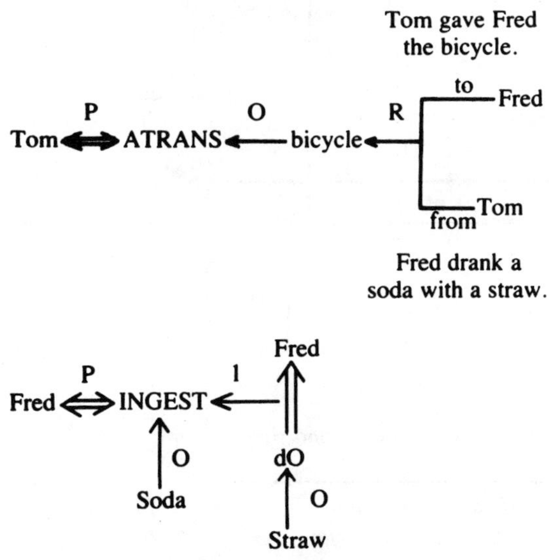

Fig. 1-18. Two examples of conceptual dependency representation.

2.1.3 Pragmatic analysis

In addition to a strictly syntactic and semantic analysis, sentence interpretation often requires some form of pragmatic analysis to determine *why* a sentence was generated. For instance, "Do you know what time it is?" is clearly a request for the time. A strict syntactic/semantic analysis approach would not normally reveal such an implicit request. Understanding the pragmatics of a sentence usually requires understanding the broader context that a sentence is within, either as part of a collection of sentences or as part of an interactive dialogue. These topics are covered in the following two sections.

2.2 Understanding multiple sentences

Sentence understanding involves generating a structure representation that shows the relationships among various parts of the sentence. The same is true of understanding a collection of sentences. For instance, paragraph understanding can also be done by generating a structure that represents the paragraph elements and their interrelationships. Three types of structures commonly used for understanding written text are semantic networks, goal structures, and scripts/schemas.

Semantic networks characterize relationships between words. Such networks provide a convenient mechanism for representing the contents of declarative sentences. In addition, semantic network representations of the relationship between objects in a domain of discourse can effectively assist sentence understanding. Once a sentence has brought into "focus" specific elements of a domain of discourse, then future references to those elements can be understood quickly (see FIG. 1-19).

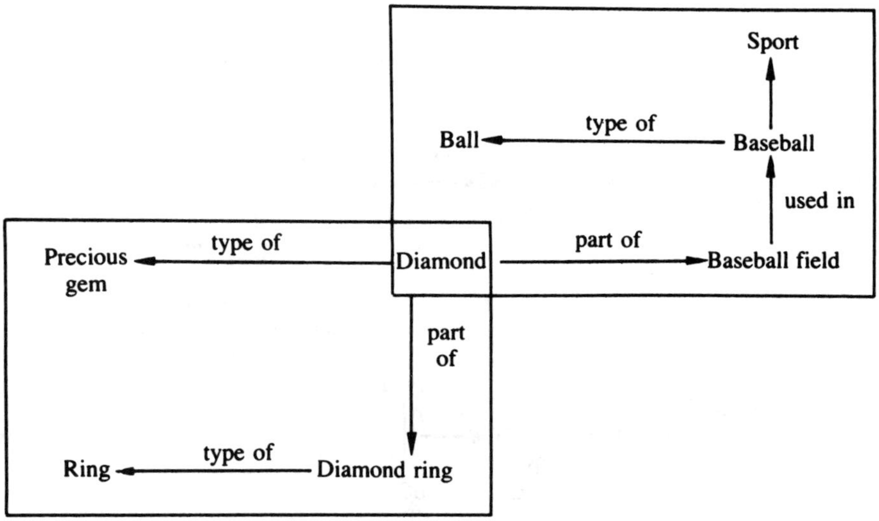

Fig. 1-19. Example of semantic network focusing. The interpretation of "Diamond" depends on the space in focus.

While semantic networks provide a good background representation for understanding texts dealing with events and physical objects, they do not provide a sufficient structure for understanding stories that deal with human actions and motivations. Interpreting this type of text requires an understanding of the goals of the actors and their plans for achieving those goals. Consider the following story:

Fred was hungry. He asked a man where the nearest restaurant was.

To understand this story, one needs to recognize that the primary actor had a goal of obtaining food, and a plan for achieving that goal, viz., go to a restaurant.

One approach to representing goal structures is found in the story understanding system PAM (Planner Applier Mechanism). PAM incorporates a knowledge base of goals and goal-seeking actions represented as conceptual dependencies. It performs story understanding by first passing a text to the conceptual dependency parser, and then using the resulting representation to identify goals and goal-seeking actions embedded in the story. When all the actions in a story can be explained by a consistent set of goals and goal-seeking actions, then the story is considered to be understood (see Wilensky, 1988).

A third approach to text understanding is based on the observation that many event sequences frequently reoccur. For instance, the basic sequence of events that occurs when one goes to a restaurant is static. A *script* represents a pattern of events that will typically occur in certain contexts. Scripts are frame-based structures that contain slots that identify the elements of a stereotypical event sequence (Schank and Abelson, 1977). Once a script has been identified as appropriate for a segment of text, then it can be used to understand meanings in the text that were not explicitly stated. Consider the following story:

> John went out to lunch. He sat down at a table and called the waitress. The waitress brought him a menu, and he ordered a hamburger. Afterwards, John went back to work.

While to a human reader this story is perfectly simple, to a machine there are many gaps. The following are some questions that might be asked. Why did the waitress bring John a menu? Did John eat anything? What did he eat? Did he pay for lunch? Questions like these cannot be understood without a fuller understanding of what normally occurs when one goes to a restaurant. Applying this general knowledge to a specific story is done by (1) identifying a relevant script, and (2) filling in the script slots with the specifics of the story. Slots defining events that are not filled-in are still assumed to have occurred, just the specifics remain in doubt. For the example given above, mapping the text segment to the restaurant script can then be used to more fully understand the text and answer the above questions.

Note that having a script that describes the normal course of events in certain contexts can also be used to detect and understand abnormal occurrences. Consider the following story:

> John went to a restaurant. He was shown to his table. He ordered a large steak. He sat there and waited a long time. He got mad and left.

To understand why John got mad and left, it is necessary to understand that the normal event sequence is to order a meal and then be served that meal. Consequently, a script-based test understanding system, when given a text segment such as this, would be able to correctly answer the question, "Why did John get mad and leave the restaurant?"

2.3 Carrying on a dialogue

Given that we have a machine that can understand natural language text, the next step would appear to be a machine that can carry on an active natural language dialogue. As with everything else, dialogue understanding poses some interesting and unique difficulties. These include the use of indirect speech acts where people say less than they really mean, implicit presuppositions where people ask questions that presuppose incorrect facts, anaphoric references that require interpretations based on an earlier portion of the dialogue, and the frequent use of fragments that do not represent grammatically correct sentences. These difficulties are further compounded by the fact that most dialogues represent a mixed initiative (Carbonell, 1970), where the topic and focus of conversation frequently shifts, and the control of these shifts can occur by either party.

Dialogue understanding systems use one or more of the following techniques to handle these difficulties:

- *Dialogue goal understanding*. Each utterance generated by the user must be interpreted in terms of the purpose of the act (answering a question, requesting information, issuing a system command, clarifying a previous utterance, etc.). A dialogue understanding system must be able to recognize implicit goals and respond accordingly.
- *Maintain current focus of dialogue*. Dialogues involve frequent changes of topic with little warning. Dialogue understanding systems must be able to maintain and represent the current focus of conversation. One technique for doing this is the use of focus spaces in semantic networks. These spaces isolate subsets of a network that represent the present domain of the dialogue and the set of objects and events relevant to the present focus.
- *Model each participant's beliefs*. Frequently, dialogue participants differ on underlying assumptions and beliefs relevant to a conversation. Indeed, many dialogues can be characterized as attempts to reconcile different beliefs. To handle this aspect of interactive dialogues, machines must have some model of both the machine's and human's dialogue-relevant beliefs. Semantic networks, for instance, can be used to represent the space of all dialogue relevant beliefs, while focus spaces can be used to represent the subspace of machine and user beliefs.
- *Understand shared rules of conversation*. In a dialogue with two cooperating parties, certain rules of conversation may be assumed to be valid. For instance, if A makes a request of B, then it is a sincere request. That is, (1) A wants B to do the request, (2) A believes B can reasonably do the request, (3) A believes B would be willing to do the request, and (4) A believes B would not have done the requested action anyway. A great deal of implicit information can be drawn from the common rule that requests will be sincere.

2.4 Summary

The value of a natural language processing system is that it provides the opportunity for user/computer dialogues that are in terms and references familiar to the user. Presumably, this dialogue is about something of interest to both the computer and human, which in most applications implies that natural language processing systems provide some type of interface between the user and a computer-based system or database computer. The development of natural language interfaces is consequently the primary application of this technology to date. Examples of this type of application in the national defense arena will be discussed in Part 2.

3.0 Basic concepts in computer vision

Computer vision is a complex and diverse research area oriented toward the processing and interpretation of two-dimensional images. For our purposes, an image can be defined as a two-dimensional function $f(x,y)$ that specifies the value of each point (x,y) in an image. Each (x,y) point in the image is called a *pixel*. The range of the $f(x,y)$ function differs with the type of image. In *monochromatic* black-and-white pictures, the function specifies the level of gray intensity. For panchromatic color images, the function describes a vector of color intensities. In some cases, the function can also specify a distance value for each point. The task of a computer vision system is to "understand" the scene depicted in an image; that is, to identify the objects embedded within the image.

Computer vision research is not unique to AI. Several research fields claim computer vision to be within their purview of interest. While the techniques from these research fields overlap, frequently borrowing from each other, each has its own orientation and goals.

One category of vision research techniques (from Cohen and Feigenbaum, 1982) involves signal processing, image classification, and image understanding. These are described by Cohen and Feigenbaum (pp. 127-128) as follows:

- *Signal processing*. Signal processors transform an input image into another image that has desirable properties. For example, the output image may have a better signal-to-noise ratio or may be enhanced by emphasizing the details to facilitate human inspection. The content of the image is often irrelevant. *Image processing* and *picture processing* are the most common terms for this class of processing. As well as digital techniques, optical techniques and electric video-signal techniques can often provide very fast throughput.
- *Classification*. Classification techniques classify images into predetermined categories. Character recognition is a typical example. Often, a predetermined set of future values is extracted from images, and the decision of how closely an image "fits" a class is made on the basis of statistical decision methods applied to the multidimensional feature space. There is a large body of theory for designing optimal decision rules. These methods are usually called *pattern recognition* or *pattern classification*, although the word "recognition" is used only for historical reasons.
- *Understanding*. Given an image, an *image-understanding program* builds a description not only of the image itself but also of the scene it depicts. In AI vision research, the term *scene analysis* was often used to emphasize the distinction between processing two-dimensional images (as in pattern classification)

and three-dimensional images (as in pattern classification) and three-dimensional scenes. Image understanding requires knowledge about the task world, as well as sophisticated image-processing techniques.

AI has focused primarily on the problem of machine understanding of images, and has consequently borrowed from the other two classes of techniques as needed to assist the understanding process. A brief overview of image understanding technology is provided below.

3.1 An overview of image-understanding techniques

Broadly described, image understanding involves two basic steps: *segmentation* and *interpretation*. *Image segmentation* is the process of translating a "raw" image into an intermediate representation that describes the lines and regions within that image. *Image interpretation* is the process of examining the regions in a segmented image to identify the objects in that image.

Image segmentation is the process of extracting lines, edges and regions from an image. Although a large number of very specific techniques have been developed to support this process, all are based on a search for adjacent pixels that have either contrasting or similar values. *Edge detection* generally proceeds as follows. At each pixel location, the local area around that pixel is explored to determine whether it may be an edge. It is classified as a possible edge if there is a sharp difference between the value of the pixel and its neighbors. Assessment of a "sharp difference" can be done by computing the derivative, or by comparing the local pattern of pixel intensity with that of an edge template.

Once edges have been identified, they must be grouped into meaningful lines. *Line detection* is done by tracing the detected edges according to some set of rules. The edges of an image generally have gaps, sudden curves, multiple forks, false edges, etc. As a result, it is often difficult to follow a meaningful line, and the corresponding set of rules for handling these difficulties may be quite complex.

Once lines and edges have been found, the image must then be segmented into *regions*. Regions are areas, surrounded by detected edges, that have pixels of similar values. The objective of the segmentation process is to translate an image into a set of separate regions that correspond to the objects and object-derived features (e.g., shadows) in the scene depicted by the image. Higher-level image understanding and object identification can then proceed. Unfortunately, despite a great deal of research in this area, segmentation procedures will generally only produce a crude approximation to the true regions of an image. For instance, to detect all the edges in a region, a low threshold is used, but this will often result in a number of false alarms of spurious edges also being detected. Line-tracing algorithms will often separate a single line into two separate lines or merge two distinct lines into one. As a result of errors such as these, the regions defined in an image will be either over- or under-divided. The surface of an object in the scene will often be divided into multiple regions in the segmented image, while at the same time, distinct surfaces from several objects may be merged into a single region.

Figure 1-20 shows a typical example of a segmented image. As can be seen, trying to identify the objects based only on the information in FIG. 1-20 is far from trivial, yet this is exactly what image understanding algorithms must do. The image in the figure was a picture of an urban area complete with numerous buildings and city streets.

Fig. 1-20. A computer-segmented image.

Once a segmented image has been generated, the computer vision system must interpret it. The approach generally taken is to examine the regions in the image to determine whether they match features from one of a predetermined set of possible objects. In effect, to limit the search space of possible interpretations, AI vision researchers have relied heavily on the development of models that guide what the image interpretation mechanism expects to see.

Developing models to guide expectancies has an added benefit. Namely, if the vision system has some idea as to who it expects to see, then the parameters in the segmentation process can be tuned to maximize the probability of detecting the edges, lines and regions of the expected object. As a result, not only can the interpretation process be controlled by a top-down model, but the low-level image processing techniques can be controlled as well.

3.2 Two examples of vision systems

Provided below are two examples of vision systems. The first provides an instance of how a vision system can exploit world knowledge to focus visual information processing. The second is an example of a general system that can be adapted to a variety of image understanding problems.

3.2.1 Using world knowledge to constrain search

As noted above, if a vision system contains a model of the world it is trying to perceive, then it is possible to use that knowledge to control the image interpretation process by looking for expected features. A classic example of this approach is found in Waltz's algorithm (Waltz, 1975) for interpreting simple blocks world images. Consider the line drawing in FIG. 1-21. Drawings such as this reflect lines that may be obtained from the segmentation of an image of several blocks. The goal of Waltz's algorithm is to identify the objects in that image, viz., the blocks.

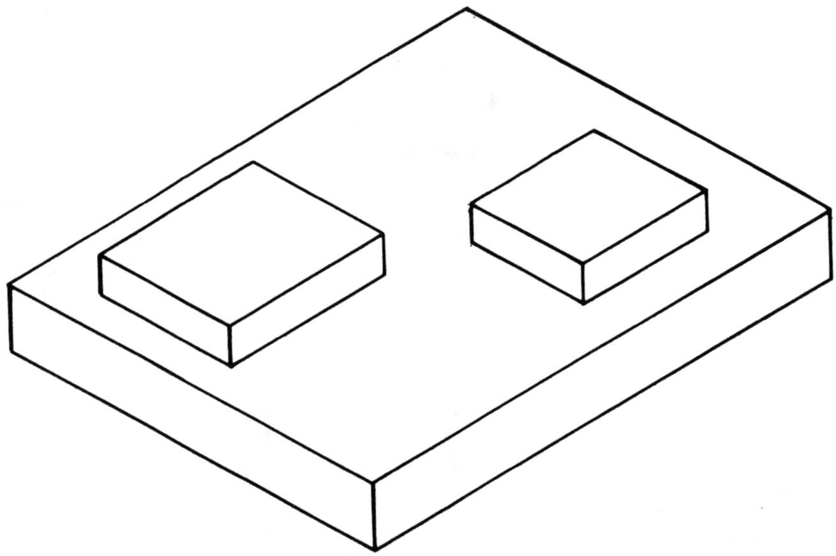

Fig. 1-21. A simple segmented blocks world image.

To interpret images, such as in FIG. 1-21, Waltz performed a detailed investigation of the possible line types that might bound an object in a line drawing. If one ignores shadows and object imperfections, there are only three types of lines possible. These include:

- Obscuring edges that reflect a boundary between an object and another object or background;
- Concave edges that form an acute angle between two faces;
- Convex edges that form an obtuse angle between two faces.

The first step in interpreting a line drawing is to determine for each line in the drawing exactly which type of edge it is. Applying the labeling convention shown in FIG. 1-22 to our sample drawing, the labeling in that figure results. Once this labeling is

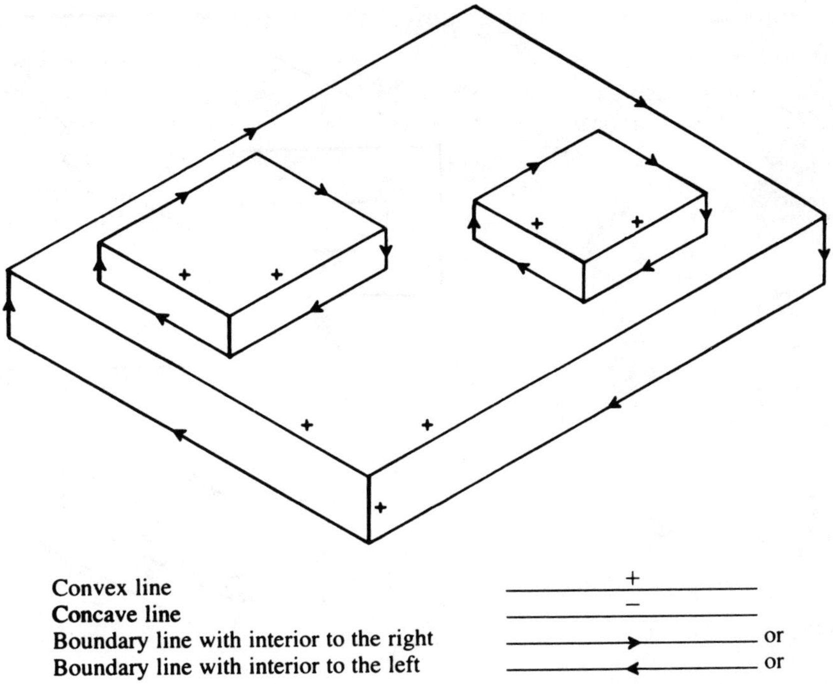

Fig. 1-22. An example of line labeling.

performed, it is a straightforward task to discriminate the block in an image. The goal of Waltz's program is to perform this labeling.

The key to Waltz's approach is the recognition of the fact that in the blocks world only a small number of possible vertice types are possible. If we examine domains where there are only trihedral vertices (vertices that join exactly three planes), then only four types of vertices are possible. These are shown in FIG. 1-23. In principle, there are 208 possible patterns of line labelings that can result from these vertices, of which only 18 are physical possibilities. These 18 are shown in FIG. 1-24.

Using the knowledge that only 18 distinct vertex labelings are possible, and that each line must be uniquely labeled, the problem of image interpretation and object extraction becomes a straightforward search process. Specifically, the goal of the computer vision system is to find a labeling of the lines in the drawing such that each vertex has a pattern of labels that maps into one of the 18 patterns. By looking sequentially at connected vertices (like connecting the dots), it is possible to quickly narrow down the possible interpretation of each new vertex examined.

Overall, Waltz's approach is a good example of how world knowledge can be used to limit the number of features a vision system needs to search, and as a result to quickly constrain the process of searching alternative possible interpretations of an image.

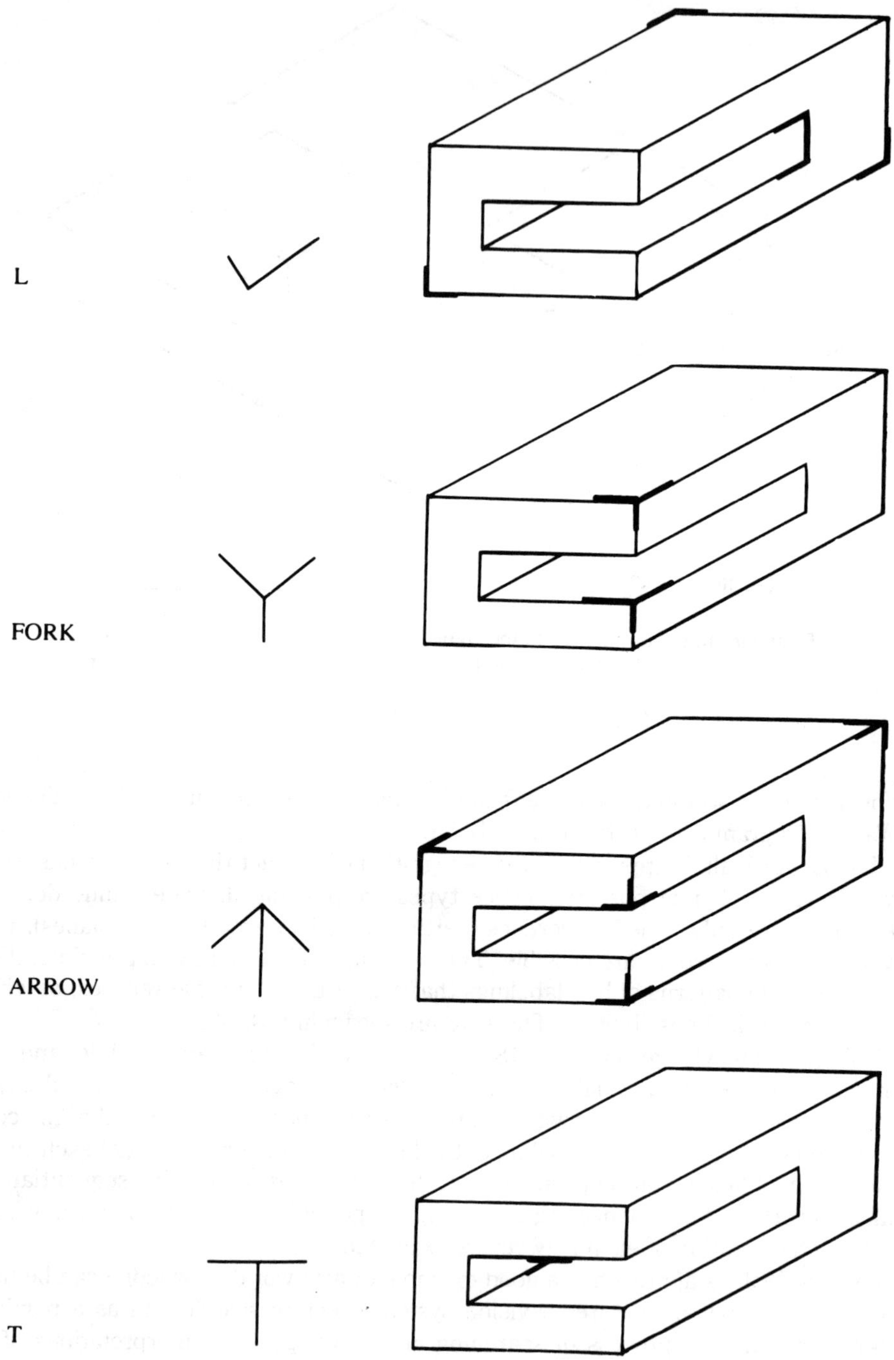

Fig. 1-23. The four types of trihedral vertices.

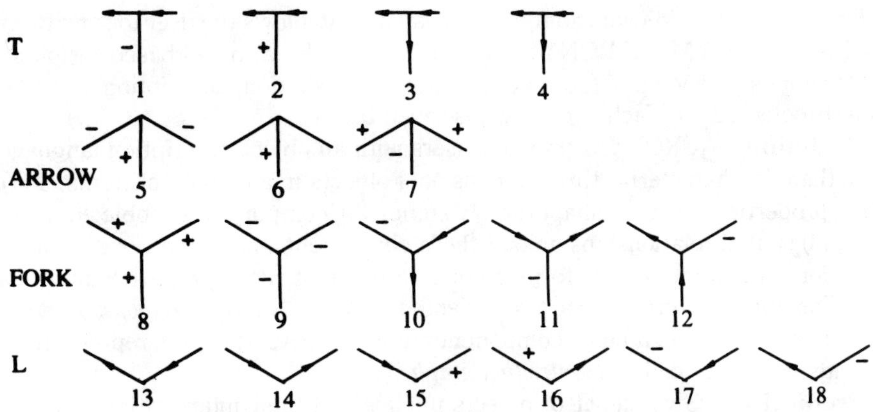

Fig. 1-24. The 18 physically possible trihedral vertices.

3.2.2 A domain-independent vision system

The program described above is highly domain dependent. That is, the program is only designed to solve problems within the blocks world domain. It exploits properties of that domain that may not be invariant for problems outside that domain.

A more domain-independent system is one that possesses a variety of procedures for exploiting perceptual capabilities, but allows the user to enter a world model; this world model represents a knowledge base of the objects found in a problem domain and the characteristics of the objects that may be found in a given domain. In this type of system, the world model is used to make predictions about what is likely to be observed, and then the perceptual capabilities focus on finding these anticipated observables. This process is iterative in that, as the perceptual system reports observations, these observations are matched against the present predictions and world model, and new predictions are made. This general process is shown in FIG. 1-25.

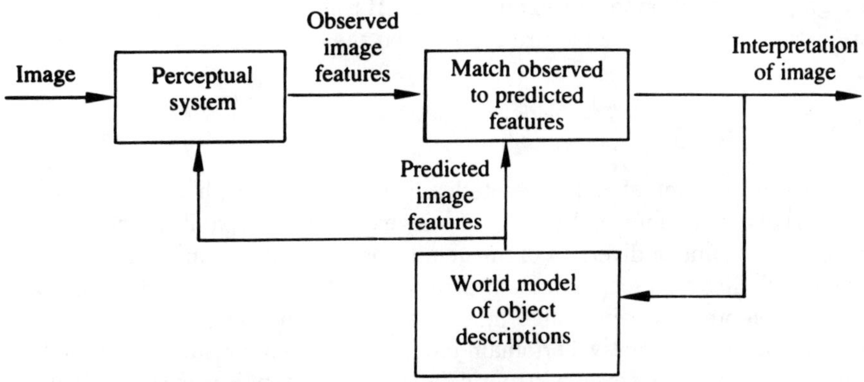

Fig. 1-25. Components of model-based vision system.

Perhaps the best-known example of a system that allows the user to specify a world model is ACRONYM. ACRONYM is considered to be a model-based vision system that decomposes vision into four parts: modeling, prediction, description, and interpretation (Brooks, 1981). Each is briefly described below.

Modeling ACRONYM provides users with an object description language that allows them to characterize three-dimensional objects in a domain of terms of (1) geometric properties such as shape and volume, (2) component subobjects within an object, (3) spatial relationships among these components, and (4) a series of algebraic expressions that allow a user to parameterize many of those properties and relationships. The object descriptions are represented in ACRONYM by an *object graph*, while algebraic relationships among components (e.g., relative size) are represented in an associated structure called a *restriction graph*.

Prediction Given a set of objects models and their interrelationships, ACRONYM applies some internal geometric analysis procedures to identify features of objects that will be invariantly observable if the object is present in an image. For the class of objects defined in an object model, ACRONYM attempts to extract a sufficient number of invariant features to uniquely discriminate objects in one class from other possible objects in a domain and to determine the position and orientation of an identified object. ACRONYM does not predict all features that may be observed as part of an object.

The product of this prediction process is a *prediction graph*. The nodes in a prediction graph are the object features that should be observable, while the arcs characterize the relationships among these features (distance, relative size, connectivity, etc.).

Description For a given image, ACRONYM applies some line-finding and segmentation procedures to identify a set of regions in a two-dimensional image. These regions are characterized in terms of their shape and relative location and orientation in the image. Region descriptions are maintained in a structure referred to as a *picture graph*. The picture graph characterizes the elements of an image in terms of the same features and variables as found in a prediction graph.

Interpretation In ACRONYM, interpretation is accomplished by matching the picture graph description to a prediction graph. If there is a reasonable match between the prediction graph and the picture graph, then the object is identified.

3.3 Summary

A considerable amount of military intelligence is based on photographic and other types of images. The range and variety of image collection capabilities that exist today can result in a volume of diversity of image interpretation problems that far exceed the capacity of existing systems, manual or otherwise. As a result, there is a natural interest in the development of automated image interpretation capabilities.

With the advent of relatively domain-independent systems such as ACRONYM, it is becoming feasible to develop generic image understanding systems that can be applied to a variety of problem domains. ACRONYM, however, was an experimental system. Work in this area has continued and has moved into the development of prototypes of operational systems. A discussion of such a system is provided in Chapter 8.

4.0 Other types of AI systems

Most applications of AI technology to problems in national defense involve the development of an expert system, natural language processing system, automated planning system and/or an automated image understanding system. Chapters 1 through 4 provide a general introduction to the basic types of AI systems that are of most interest to the national defense community and from the perspective of this community show the most potential for practical applications in the near term.

There exist, however, many other classes of AI systems and techniques that provide significant potential opportunities for national defense applications, but have so far received comparatively little attention. Some of these systems are briefly overviewed in this chapter.

4.1 Intelligent training systems

A general application area of AI techniques is in the development of intelligent systems for training and education. Training is a major expense in the military. As noted in Fletcher (1985), on an average day in 1983 about 214,000 active duty personnel, 40,000 National Guardsmen and Reservists, and 12,000 foreign military students and civilians were undergoing some type of formal training. The development of any techniques that could streamline or reduce the expense and time required for training would be of significant value. The applicability of AI to education and training problems are discussed.

4.1.1 Intelligent computer-aided instruction

Computer-aided instruction (CAI) is an educational technology oriented toward developing instructional programs that provide for the individualized tutoring of well-prepared course materials. While many CAI programs have been developed, most are limited to the presentation of standard instructional materials, or, if students consistently repeat certain errors, the presentation of standard remedial materials. As a result, the only aspect of instruction that is tailored to individual students is the order of presentation of the instructional materials and not the instruction itself. This limitation is an inherent result of the fact that CAI programs do not themselves have any knowledge about the domain in which they are providing instruction. This is unlike a human teacher who will understand (hopefully) the problem domain he or she is teaching. A good teacher, upon observing that a student is making errors, will engage in several cognitive processes that will result in providing the student with proper instruction. These processes include the following:

1. Determine the correct answer.
2. Think about the process required to generate the correct answer.
3. Identify the knowledge required to execute this process.
4. Hypothesize about what aspects of this knowledge the student is lacking. (This may involve trying to vicariously simulate the student's thinking.)
5. Select a strategy for instructing the student as to the required knowledge.
6. Instantiate the selected strategy with specific instructional materials that the teacher may generate on the spot.

Obviously, a teacher's cognitive processes for tailoring instructional materials to the student are considerably more sophisticated than the simple order and branching techniques found in CAI devices.

Intelligent computer-aided instruction (ICAI) is a research area devoted to the development of instructional systems that have a true knowledge base of their teaching domain. That is, they can, in principle, intelligently solve the same problems that they are trying to teach students to solve.

At first, it might appear that building an intelligent instructional system for a domain is a straightforward extension of the problem of building an intelligent system for solving problems in that domain. After all, if a medical diagnosis expert system can be built that emulates the reasoning of human doctors, it should be relatively easy to extend that system to teach medical diagnosis techniques. This turns out to be quite false. MYCIN, for instance, is an excellent program for diagnosing bacterial infections, but is not very useful as an instructional system even when adapted for this purpose (Clancey, 1984). The reason has to do with the types of knowledge that are required for proper instruction. These are discussed below.

Components of an ICAI system To emulate some of the techniques used by a good instructor, ICAI systems must have at least three separate "intelligent" components: a domain knowledge base, an approach to student modeling, and a teaching strategy. These are discussed below.

Domain knowledge base This component contains all of the knowledge in the ICAI system relevant to problem-solving in the instructional domain. This component is responsible for generating test problems and evaluating the correctness of the student's solutions to the problems. This component should be sufficiently expert in its own right to be able to solve the test problems.

To obtain the required problem-solving expertise, the knowledge base component of an ICAI system will generally reflect the same knowledge representation schemes found in other AI-based problem-solving systems. Semantic networks are sometimes used to represent facts, causation and relationships, scripts may be used for representing causality and temporal relationships, production rules are used to emulate problem-solving heuristics used by human domain experts, etc.

The knowledge-based expert component of an ICAI system is sometimes referred to as an *articulate expert* if it can explain the decision processes necessary to solve a problem in a way that is consistent with human problem-solving processes. Such articulation can be very difficult to program even in systems that emulate human problem-solving processes. The MYCIN system, for example, diagnoses and recommends treatment for bacterial infections using production rules that correspond to the same heuristics used by medical doctors. In research performed by Clancey (1984), it was discovered that the standard rule trace used by MYCIN to explain its diagnostic reasoning to doctors was not very useful for instructing diagnostic reasoning to students. Students indicated that the MYCIN rules were difficult to understand and remember and did not incorporate easily into their problem-solving processes.

In order to convert the MYCIN knowledge base into an articulate expert knowledge base, several enhancements and additions to the knowledge base were required. First, the control strategy for choosing and ordering which diagnostic rules to test at any given time had to be explained to students. (That is, MYCIN has embedded within its control procedures a general approach to diagnostic problem-solving. Since this problem-solving strategy was encoded into the MYCIN program, it was never declared explicitly in the rule base. Therefore, MYCIN was not able to articulate it to the students.)

Second, the MYCIN rules themselves were not self-explaining. These rules, in fact, were essentially summaries of a considerable amount of background knowledge and experience. In order to justify or explain MYCIN rules to students, elaborate justifications of the rules were required. Such justifications were needed not only to provide students with an understanding of why each rule exists, but also to provide necessary mnemonics for remembering the rule.

Third, MYCIN itself has no knowledge of the boundaries of its own knowledge base. That is, it contains no rules for differentiating conditions under which its diagnostic rules are appropriate from conditions under which they are irrelevant (e.g., it will never recommend that something other than infectious disease may be the cause of the problem). Consequently, knowledge needs to be added so as to instruct students as to the conditions under which what they are learning should or should not be applied.

Student models The objective of an ICAI system is to adapt to the instructional requirements of individual students. To achieve this objective, the system must have some knowledge of the status of the student's knowledge base. The purpose of the student modeling component of an ICAI device is to generate a representation of the student's understanding of the material being taught. The student model component is usually oriented toward generating and testing hypotheses that account for misconceptions and noncriterion performance in students.

The student modeling component can examine several sources of data to generate hypotheses about student misconceptions, including the student's (1) present problem-solving behavior, (2) historical problem-solving behavior, (3) responses to direct queries to the student about what he or she understands, and (4) a characterization of the learning material itself, such as its overall difficulty. Against this evidence, standard pattern recognition techniques can be employed to determine if the student's pattern of errors is consistent with a specific hypothesis regarding his lack of understanding.

The student model itself is a representation of the student's knowledge base. One approach to student modeling is the use of *overlay models* (Carr and Goldstein, 1977). In this approach, perceived student knowledge is matched against the domain knowledge base, and areas of student understanding are flagged. For instance, if the ICAI device has a knowledge base in the form of a semantic network, then individual arcs in the network are flagged as the student exhibits an understanding of the relationship involved. On the other hand, if a production system is used, then individual production can be flagged whenever the student exhibits problem-solving behavior that employs them.

An inherent characteristic of the overlay model is the implicit assumption that the student's knowledge base is a direct subset of the machine's knowledge base. That is, student errors are interpreted only as a *lack* of knowledge; the possibility that the student may have incorrect knowledge is not considered. As a result, an ICAI system using an overlay model will only provide instructional materials that attempt to fill in knowledge gaps. Correcting a student's incorrect ideas can only be an unplanned-for by-product.

Another approach to representing a student's knowledge base is in terms of a set of *bugs*, where a bug is defined as a deviation from his/her knowledge base. The bug model, while theoretically more complete, is also generally more difficult to implement than the overlay model. This is because the system must represent and detect knowledge structures other than the expert knowledge embedded in the ICAI knowledge base.

Tutoring approach Once an ICAI system has diagnosed a student's errors in terms of incorrect or missing knowledge, it must still provide instruction to correct his knowledge base. There are a variety of approaches/strategies to teaching which significantly differ in the type of instructional materials that they present and the procedures used to select what next to teach.

One approach is called the *Socratic method*. This method involves querying the student about his answers in a way that will encourage him to reason further about his own knowledge, thereby clearing up misconceptions. Shown in FIG. 1-26 is a sample interaction with the program WHY which teaches students about meteorology (Stevens, et al., 1978).

Another approach is that of *coaching*. In this approach, the student is involved in some problem-solving or skill-acquisition activity, such as in computer games. The system observes the student's behavior and at selected points interrupts his/her activity to provide new information or suggest new strategies. A coaching program must therefore identify and interpret student errors, select advantageous moments to interrupt the student's stream of activity, and provide advice that results in improved student problem-solving performance.

Summary of ICAI techniques ICAI systems provide the potential for intelligent systems that provide adaptive and effective instruction to students. As such, they represent a discipline of research that in the long run may greatly benefit instructional elements of a national defense system through both cost reduction and better instruction. However, this area remains largely a research topic.

TABLE 1-2, from Fletcher (1985), lists some recent ICAI systems. As can be seen in this figure, the instructional domains of these systems are very specialized and are of little relevance to national defense. The best potential in the near future for the development of practical AI-based instructional systems appears to be in the area of maintenance diagnosis and repair (Fletcher and Psotka, 1986).

4.1.2 Other types of training systems

In addition to ICAI applications, AI techniques can benefit training in other ways. Two that are frequently discussed is the use of AI for embedded training and the development of intelligent simulations. *Embedded training* refers to the development of training modules that could be incorporated into operations systems (e.g., tank artillery, communication systems, etc.). These modules would provide instructions to users of these systems on how to use the system, as well as on the problem domain for which the systems were developed. Embedded training systems would incorporate many of the ICAI

Do you think the Amazon jungle has heavy rainfall or light rainfall?

** Heavy rainfall

Why does the Amazon jungle have heavy rainfall?

** Because it's near the Atlantic

Yes, the Amazon jungle is near the equatorial Atlantic.
How does that affect rainfall in the Amazon jungle?

** The water in the current is warm

.
.
.

What happens after the mositure-filled air reaches the land?

** I don't know

Do you think the Andes mountain range has any effect on the rainfall in the Amazon jungle?

** Yes

How?

** The prevailing wind hits the Andes and the air cools

Do you think that any place with mountains has heavy rainfall?

** Yes

Southern California has mountains.
Why doesn't Southern California have heavy rainfall?

Fig. 1-26. Example of Socratic method from program WHY. Student responses are preceded by two asterisks.

techniques discussed above. *Intelligent simulation systems* would provide for simulation capabilities that would be dynamically adapted to a simulation as it unfolds. For instance, in a battle simulation, an automated adversary could "play red" and dynamically respond to the actions of the simulation user.

4.2 Machine learning systems

The concepts of intelligence and learning are highly intertwined. Indeed, in dictionary definitions, "intelligence" is often associated with the ability to understand (learn)

Table 1-2. Some ICAI programs

System	Subject Matter	Knowledge Base	Student Model	Tutor Model
SCHOLAR	South American geography	Semantic network	Overlay with importance weights	Socratic dialogue management
WHY	Causes of rainfall	Scripts	Misconception identifier	Socratic dialogue management
INTEGRATE	Symbolic integration	Self improving rule-based representation	Overlay	Reactive environment with advisor
SOPHIE	Electronic trouble-shooting	Semantic network with circuit simulator	Overlay	Reactive environment with guided interactions
WEST	Arithmetic expressions	Rule-based representation	Overlay	Reactive environment with coaching
BUGGY	Subtraction	Procedural network	Misconception identifier	Reactive environment with advisor
WUSOR	Logical relations	Genetic graph (network)	Overlay with familiarity weights	Reactive environment with coaching
EXCHECK	Logic and set theory	Rule-based representation with logic interpreter	Overlay	Reactive environment with advisor
BIP	Programming in BASIC	Rule-based representation	Overlay	Reactive environment with curriculum net and advisor
SPADE	Programming in LOGO	Rule-based representation	Overlay	Reactive environment with coaching
ALBEGRA	Applied algebra	Rule-based representation	Overlay	Reactive environment with coaching
LMS	Algebraic procedures	Rule and rule-based representation	Rule-based diagnostic representation	Reactive environment
QUADRATIC	Quadratic equations	Self-improving rule-based representation	Overlay	Reactive environment with advisor
GUIDON	Infectious diseases	Rule-based representation and meta-knowledge	Overlay with application probability	Reactive environment with structural interactions

Table 1-2. Continued.

System	Subject Matter	Knowledge Base	Student Model	Tutor Model
MENO	Programming in PASCAL	Semantic network	Misconception identification	Reactive environment with advisor
STEAMER	Steamship propulsion	Device model	Overlay onto device model	Overlay onto environment with advisor

things quickly or to perform other forms of *adaptive* behavior. Unfortunately, while the connection between intelligence and learning is quite reasonable, the ability to learn is not characteristic of most AI systems today. The knowledge base of an expert system, for instance, is usually a static structure that is only changed by a programmer or knowledge engineer. As a result, knowledge base development is a very time-consuming and labor-intensive task.

Machine learning remains very much a research field in AI, with relatively little to show in the way of applications. However, as an area of research it is very active (see Michalski, et al., 1983, 1986). A number of scientists are exploring automated and semiautomated techniques for developing a knowledge base that could eventually lead to the rapid development of expert systems and other types of AI systems.

4.3 Automatic programming systems

Automatic programming is the automated generation of software code. The goal of automated programming in AI is to allow nonprogrammers to generate code by having the machine translate user-specified functions into proper software that can execute those functions. It is not presumed a priori that user-functions are precise or well-defined. Rather, user specifications will be in a natural language or other imprecise form. Consequently, AI-based automatic programming systems generally work interactively with users to iterate through a series of software programs that represent successively better approximations of what the user wants coded.

This approach to automatic programming is somewhat different than that suggested by Martin (1982) and others where precise, graphic-oriented techniques are used to specify functions and to then automatically compile these well-defined requirements into code.

For the most part, AI-based automatic programming techniques are not widely used. One exception is in the development of natural language interfaces (NLI) where the goal of the NLI system is to provide an interface to one or more database systems. Generally, an NLI will generate a database retrieval program as the product of its natural language processing of user inputs (see examples in Chapters 6 and 7). Database retrieval is relatively simple, and is oriented toward one-time applications. That is, once the data retrieval is successful, the automatically generated program can be discarded.

Other areas of automatic programming involve the automatic development of software that will be used repeatedly, and consequently may need to meet stringent performance specifications (e.g., reliability, validity, processing speed, etc.). Research applications involve the development of repeated-use programs in such areas as robot planning (Sussman, 1975) and geological analysis (Barstow, 1984).

While automatic programming is not a major aspect of ongoing AI applications in national defense, it has been discussed as a possible key element of the Strategic Defense Initiative. (See Chapter 10 for a discussion.)

4.4 Nonmonotonic reasoning systems

AI systems for making deductions (e.g., expert systems) operate by accepting inputs on the status of primitives, and then performing some reasoning process based on those primitives to generate conclusions. Since absolute certainty about the status of primitives is rarely the case, estimates, guesses and assumptions must often be made about them. Consequently, a deduction may be based on any number of assumptions that may later be shown to be false. When this occurs, most AI systems can do little but restart the reasoning processes from scratch to determine if the previously generated conclusions are still valid.

Nonmonotonic reasoning refers to a logic for dealing with reasoning under assumptions (Doyle, 1979). Nonmonotonic reasoning systems provide a deduction mechanism that keeps track of assumptions and any intermediate or final conclusions based on those assumptions. Whenever an assumption proves false (or is simply no longer believed), the system will identify all consequences of that change. These consequences may come in a variety of forms: previous conclusions may now prove false, other conclusions that were initially based on the no-longer-accepted assumption may still prove true because of other logic chains, still other assumptions may be rejected by consequence (e.g., if A and B imply C, and C is known to be false and B true, then A must be false), etc. Nonmonotonic reasoning systems can operate either as independent systems or as adjuncts to other reasoning systems (e.g., an expert system using some other logic) to keep track of multiple paths to a conclusion.

While nonmonotonic reasoning will eventually be an important aspect of many AI systems, it is not now a major mechanism of ongoing AI applications in national defense. There is, however, a strong interest in this area by national defense sponsors of AI research.

4.5 Automatic theorem-proving

An important research topic in AI is the development of systems capable of automatically generating proofs of proposed mathematical conjectures given a set of well-defined axioms. Theorem-proving systems have been built in a number of areas of mathematics including calculus (Martin and Fateman, 1971), set theory (Bledsoe, 1971), and topology (Bledsoe and Bruell, 1974).

Various approaches to automated theorem-proving exist. *Resolution refutation* techniques provide a general mechanism for proof by contradiction that is theoretically guaranteed to find a proof if one exists, but is often infeasible in practical applications because of the amount of search required. *Rule-based deduction techniques* apply more heuristic approaches and principles to theorem-proving. These techniques are generally feasible, but are not by any means guaranteed to find a solution.

While systems for generating proofs of mathematical conjectures may not be of immediate interest to national defense applications, many of the techniques that have resulted from this work have been found to be useful in other areas. Resolution refutation techniques have been found to be a useful approach to intelligent retrieval from databases. Some automatic programming is based on theorem-proving techniques, as are some approaches to robotic problem-solving.

4.6 Summary

For the most part, the technologies described in this chapter are not sufficiently mature to support the development of practical application systems. However, the long-term prospects for applying these technologies are very promising. As AI researchers develop the capabilities for systems to adapt to a changing problem environment, keep track of their own assumptions, automatically generate software programs, etc., it is clear that these capabilities will be incorporated into many application systems.

5.0 Development environments for AI systems

With the explosion of serious interest in AI system development and applications, a comparable increase of options has appeared for hardware and software environments in which AI systems can be developed and delivered. Indeed, options are appearing so quickly that any attempt to document a comparative evaluation of these options would be useless. Such an evaluation would likely be invalid by the time it appeared in print. We can, however, characterize the option space, which is precisely what is done in Sections 5.1 and 5.2. Section 5.3 provides a discussion of AI on microcomputers. This somewhat specialized topic is included to provide the reader with an appreciation of the true requirements for baseline processing requirements in which AI system implementation and delivery can occur.

5.1 Language options for AI systems

Regarding programming languages for AI system development, three classes of options exist: (1) general AI languages, such as LISP and PROLOG; (2) specialized AI languages, such as the expert system development packages noted in Chapter 1; and (3) "conventional" programming languages, such as Pascal, C, Ada, FORTRAN, etc.

5.1.1 General AI languages

Although various general-purpose AI languages have been developed, LISP and PROLOG are, by far, the most widely used. LISP, invented in 1968 by John McCarthy, has been the computer language of choice for most research and development in AI (Barr and Feigenbaum, 1982). This has been particularly true in the U.S. Several important ideas behind the design of LISP have made it a useful tool for AI applications. LISP is a language designed for symbolic computation with the *linked list* as the basic data structure. It has a control structure based on function composition and recursion. An essential feature of LISP is that it allows for the representation of "code as data." That is, it provides the ability to interpret a LISP program as data, or data as a program.

The essential core of LISP can be defined by about 10 primitive functions, and the rest of the language can be defined in terms of these primitive functions. A LISP interpreter can thus be written in LISP itself and serve to define the language. It should be noted, however, that most practical LISP implementations include many built-in functions. As a result, several dialects of LISP exist that have significantly different features.

The extendibility of LISP, the elegance and simplicity of its representation and control structures, and the resulting powerful interactive debugging capabilities that are usually included in LISP implementations all make it an ideal language for rapidly testing ideas and developing prototype systems. The approach of using a flexible and extendible language for quick experimentation and cyclic development has been characteristic of AI research and system development. This development strategy is sometimes referred to as *iterative refinement*.

PROLOG is a programming language based on mathematical first order logic, and has been used in a number of AI research and application programs (Clocksin and Mellish, 1981; Clark and McCabe, 1982). It is very popular in the European AI community, and has been selected to play a major role in the development of the Japanese Fifth Generation Machine project (see Chapter 10).

PROLOG has built-in mechanisms for deductive inference and a uniform representation for the facts and rules that make up a knowledge base. New facts can be derived from existing facts and rules via the built-in backtracking and theorem-proving mechanisms. The extendibility and flexibility of PROLOG also makes it a powerful tool for describing and developing solutions for programmers and system developers by using the approach of iterative refinement.

5.1.2 Specialized AI languages

Another category of languages available for use in AI system development are the tools and languages specifically designed for certain classes of applications. Many of these systems obtain their specialization in part from the fact that they presume a specific approach to knowledge representation and utilization. Most of the expert system development tools noted in Chapter 1 assume a production rule representation of knowledge. On the other hand, languages and tools such as KRL, FRL and K:base assume a frame-based approach to knowledge representation.

All of these specialized languages are designed to help the process of knowledge-based system design and development. They generally provide built-in features and packages (e.g., rule editors) to aid system design and knowledge engineering. Also, they generally interface with other languages, and so can be used as subsets of more general systems.

5.1.3 Conventional languages

Conventional general-purpose languages, such as Pascal, FORTRAN, Ada and C have been around for many years. Although a number of AI-based programs have been written in these languages, they are relatively few in comparison to the number written in AI languages. Part of the reason for the lack of use of these conventional "procedural" languages is that of historical precedent—the first AI programs were written in languages such as LISP. Since then, most AI programs, and also work in AI programming environments, have been done in general languages.

One "problem" of conventional languages is that over the years they have become more specialized for dealing with number-crunching and database storage and retrieval, while most AI applications are oriented toward symbolic processing and recursive problem-solving. Conventional languages, however, tend to have faster throughput than comparable AI languages, and also have the benefit of many years of fine-tuning and efficient compiler writing. In addition, there are fewer hardware requirements and restrictions when using languages such as FORTRAN than with more specialized languages such as PROLOG or LISP. As a result, conventional languages are good for run-time applications, but are extremely weak in the development area. Many developers have adapted the strategy of performing research and exploratory development in an AI-oriented language, and then reimplementing the system in a conventional language. For some types of AI systems, where the technology is well understood (e.g., rule-based expert consulting systems), many developers have gone straight to conventional languages. Some examples of this are provided in Section 5.3.

5.2 Hardware options for AI systems

A variety of options exist for hardware environments in which AI systems may be developed or delivered. These options differ in a variety of dimensions, including their basic processing power, the degree to which they have specialized AI language processing capability, how advanced their graphic capabilities for system development are, etc. Provided below are some categories of options of AI hardware.

5.2.1 Multiuser general-purpose systems

Until the advent of LISP machines (discussed below), most AI research and development was performed in general "mainframe" environments (e.g., DEC 10) where the system hosted many simultaneous users performing a variety of different tasks. Since access to mainframe environments is usually readily available and inexpensive for single users, this is likely to remain a prominent option for AI system developers. However, two common weaknesses of this type of environment include a relatively slow response time for interpretive languages such as LISP when system use is heavy, and a limited number of graphics terminals, which implies development may have to occur on a standard text terminal. Both of these tend to slow up development time which may be problematic if a rapid prototyping approach to system development is used. However, if the AI system is to be embedded as part of a larger software system resident on this environment, then it is often desirable to stay within the same environment.

5.2.2 LISP machines

As noted in the section on AI languages, LISP is the most commonly used language for AI system development in the United States. To facilitate more efficient processing of this language, specialized LISP processors were developed. LISP machines are special-purpose AI development computers that are built around a LISP processor. They are normally single-user machines with high-resolution monitors and special input devices (e.g., mouse). In addition to rapid processing capabilities, these machines are characterized by having a host of software development tools to support AI system development, including extensive graphic tools for user interface development.

5.2.3 General single-user workstations

Powerful single-user workstations provide many of the same capabilities as LISP machines. These workstations often have the same hardware architecture as that of multiuser systems, but with a software and operating system environment oriented toward single users. As with LISP machines, these machines also typically include high-resolution monitors and special input devices. Also, because many have available one or more LISP dialects, AI system development tools are also available for these workstations.

5.2.4 Microcomputers

Microcomputer configurations (e.g., IBM PCs) have been used surprisingly often in AI system development, especially for expert systems. Microcomputer-based AI is a separate topic discussed in Section 5.3.

5.2.5 Parallel processing machines

Parallel processing machines represent a new type of computer architecture that will allow many simultaneous (possibly interrelated) processes to occur concurrently. In principle, these machines will have many times the processing power of more conventional architectures and are likely to become a primary environment of delivering AI and other types of systems in the future. In particular, if some of the ambitious goals of the DARPA Strategic Computing Program are to be met (see Chapter 10), then computers with extensive parallelism will become a common delivery environment.

5.3 Baseline requirements for AI system development

As noted previously, AI system development "traditionally" is done in LISP or PROLOG on either a mainframe or in a specialized LISP or PROLOG processing environment. The popularity of these languages and machines in AI has led many developers and sponsors to assume that these environments are essential for implementing AI systems. In reality, quite the opposite is true. While these powerful development environments are very convenient they are often not necessary.

In this section, AI work on microcomputers is explored. The goal of examining this somewhat specialized topic is to provide the reader with a sense of *baseline* hardware and language requirements for implementing many of the AI technologies discussed in previous chapters.

5.3.1 Expert systems

A number of different software systems have been designed for implementing expert systems on microprocessor-based computer systems. Many are problem-independent tools for building expert systems. They utilize a variety of inference mechanisms and knowledge representation schemes. Many are currently being used for a wide variety of expert system applications and are undergoing enhancements or improvements for future releases. They run on a variety of microprocessor-based computer systems, including the more popular personal computers with minifloppy or Winchester disk storage capabilities. Many of these systems can run on as little as 64K bytes of memory with small knowledge bases, but with more memory, larger knowledge bases are possible.

TABLE 1-3 shows some of the microcomputer expert system development tools available at the time of this writing. TABLE 1-4 lists some of the expert system applications that have been pursued using these tools. Note that AL/X, an expert system development tool that provides an inference engine, rule description language and consultation system capability similar to the well-known PROSPECTOR system, was the first commercially available inference engine.

Table 1-3. Some expert system development tools available for microcomputers

System	Developer	Hardware	Required Memory
ACLS	Intelligent Terminals Ltd.	APPLE II+ IBM PC	64K
AL/X	Intelligent Terminals Ltd.	APPLE II+ LSI 11/02 IBM PC	64K
APES	Department of Computing Imperial College University of London	IBM PC (any machine with Micro-PROLOG)	128K
DELTA	General Electric Research and Development Center	PDP 11/23	N/A
ERS	PAR Technology Corporation	IBM PC/XT	256K
GEN-X	General Electric Research and Development Center	IBM PC LSI 11	256K
K:base*	Gold Hill Computers	IBM PC	512K
M.1*	Teknowledge Inc.	IBM PC	128K
The Personal Consultant*	Texas Instruments Inc.	TI Professional Computer	512K
RuleMaster*	Radian Corporation	IBM PC/XT	512K
TIMM*	General Research Corporation	IBM PC/XT IBM PC/AT	640K

*M.1 is a trademark of Teknowledge Inc. K:Base is a trademark of Gold Hill Computers Inc. The Personal Consultant is a trademark of Texas Instruments Inc. RuleMaster is a trademark of Radian Corporation. TIMM is a trademark of General Research Corporation.

Table 1-4. Some microcomputer-based expert system applications

System	Applications
ACLS	Induction of rules for classifying chess and game positions.
AL/X	Oil production platform fault diagnosis.
APES	Determining eligibility for Social Security benefits; pipe corrosion diagnosis; suitability of sites for dam construction; care for terminally ill patients.
DELTA	Troubleshooting for diesel locomotives; plastic injection molding equipment; process controller designs.
ERS	Interpreting military sensor information; aircraft design for maintainability evaluations.
GEN-X	Troubleshooting for jet engines; industrial process control.
K:base	Financial analysis of interest rate swaps.
M.1	Various demonstration systems for the knowledge engineering tutorial T.1.
RuleMaster	Severe-storm forecasting; transformer fault detection.
TIMM	Financial analysis; personnel management; insurance underwriting for yachts; tuning the VAX VMS operating system.

5.3.2 Natural language interfaces

Natural language interfaces apply natural language processing techniques to provide users with flexible and easy-to-use information access and retrieval from one or more databases. Although various NLI systems exist, they all have in common some type of ability to automatically create a database access program to answer a variety of questions that can be input by the user in a natural language format. Figure 1-27 provides a short example of a session with the Advance Query Facility (Mah, 1980) which provides natural language access to several databases on Soviet aircraft.

Compared to the extensive work in microcomputer expert systems, the number of microcomputer-based natural language interface systems is small. The reason for this is not, as might at first be imagined, that microcomputers do not have the computational power necessary for this type of natural language processing. Rather, it is that the utility of developing such capabilities has in the past appeared somewhat limited. Since the goal of an NLI is generally to provide easy access to one or more databases, then implementing an NLI on a stand-alone microcomputer that does not contain any important databases has little value. However, the increasing power of microcomputers and the corresponding increase in the use of microcomputers for serious decision support applications is likely to result in a proliferation of important microcomputer-resident databases. This in turn may result in the development of a number of natural language systems for microcomputers.

```
"A Q F DEMONSTRATION"
"   VERSION   08-06-00   "

GRY>TELL ME ABOUT AIRCRAFT.

THIS IS A SOVIET FIGHTER AIRCRAFT DATA BASE, DERIVED
FROM UNCLASSIFIED PUBLICATIONS. IT DESCRIBES CREWS,
FUSELAGES, WINGS, ENGINES, ARMAMENTS, AND PERFORMANCE.

QRY>LIST FIGHTERS ORDERED BY NATO NAME.

ROLE       /NATO/ NAME
-----------------------------------------
F/B        FARMER          MIG-19
F/B        FARMER-C        MIG-19SF
F/B        FARMER-D        MIG-19PF
F/B        FARMER-D        MIG-19PM
FGA/T      FISHBED         MIG-21
FGA/T      FISHBED-C       MIG-21F
FGA/T      FISHBED-D       MIG-21PF
FGA/T      FISHBED-F       MIG-21PFK
FGA/T      FISHBED-J       MIG-21PFMA
FGA/T      FISHBED-J       MIG-21MF
FGA/T      FISHBED-K       MIG-21MF
FGA/T      FISHBED-L       MIG-21MF
AWF        FISHPOT         SU-9
FS/A       FLOGGER         MIG-23
FS/A       FLOGGER-B       MIG-23B
FS/A       FLOGGER-C       MIG-23U
F/B        FRESCO          MIG-17

QRY>WHAT ARE THE DIMENSIONS OF THE FARMER?
----------------------------------FT---------------FT---------------FT
MIG-19     FARMER     LH = 48.83       Ht = 13.19         Ws = 29.54
QRY>HOW MUCH DOES IT WEIGH?

                       WEIGHT
-------------------------LB
MIG-19     FARMER      19180

QRY>PRINT THE ARMAMENT OF THE FARMER.

-----------------------------------------------------------------------
MIG-19           FARMER            "CFON"          1 AA MISSILE ALKALI
                                                   3    CANNON
                                   "CFON"          4 AS ROCKET
                                                   2    BOMB
                                                   3    CANNON
                                   "CFON"          1 AS ROCKET
                                                   2    BOMB
                                                   3    CANNON
```

Fig. 1-27. Sample AQF session.

QRY>HOW FAST CAN IT FLY?

		SPEED MACH	FT
MIG-19	FARMER	0.50	80000
		0.60	70000
		0.75	60000
		0.97	50000
		1.24	40000
		1.32	30000
		1.09	20000
		0.84	10000
		0.66	0

QRY>THE FRESCO?

		SPEED MACH	FT
MIG-17	FRESCO	0-39	40000
		0-48	30000
		0-62	20000
		0-80	10000
		0-92	0

Fig. 1-27. Continued.

5.3.3 Machine learning

Even in the area of machine learning, there is serious on-going work using microcomputers. One system in particular, ACLS (Analog Concept Learning System), is a general system that allows users to generate classification rules from examples or cases of a rule application. These classification rules are essentially IF-THEN production rules that are often found in expert systems. ACLS provides a capability for describing the attributes of a classification problem and a set of examples that illustrate the application of an as-yet unknown classification rule, and from the examples generates a rule consistent with the examples. It therefore provides an effective tool of knowledge engineering. A marketed version of ACLS called Expert-Ease is available for microcomputers under the UCSD P-System Operating System, which is available for most microcomputers.

5.3.4 Summary of baseline requirements

Although the systems described represent only some of the work on microcomputer-based AI systems, it is clear from the variety of these systems that implementing AI capabilities—such as expert systems—on microcomputers is a serious option for users and developers of AI technology. Often, this option is not feasible, or if feasible, is not preferred. However, it usually deserves serious consideration. A detailed discussion of AI on microcomputers and the conditions under which they might be preferred to more powerful hardware environments is found in Barth and Lehner (1986) and Lehner and Barth (1985).

5.4 Summary

Overall, it is clear that the developer of an AI system has many options for the hardware and software environment in which to develop the AI system. There is no true "standard" environment for AI system development. Rather, the selection of an environment should be based on a serious evaluation of the specific requirements of the type of systems that will be implemented.

References

Alvey Committee, "A Programme for Advanced Information Technology: The Report of the Alvey Committee," HMSO, 1982.

S. Andriole, G. Hopple, J. Thompson, and H. Black, "An Intelligent Aid for Tactical Planning," *IEEE Transactions of Systems, Man, and Cybernetics*, November/December 1986.

A. Barr and E.A. Feigenbaum (eds.), *The Handbook of Artificial Intelligence: Vol. 1*. William Kaufmann, Inc.: Los Altos, CA, 1981.

A. Barr and E.A. Feigenbaum (eds.), *The Handbook of Artificial Intelligence: Vol. 2*. William Kaufmann, Inc.: Los Altos, CA, 1982.

D. Barstow, "A Perspective on Automatic Programming," *AI Magazine*, 1984, Vol. 5, No. 1, pp. 5 – 27.

S.W. Barth, H. Coyle, and D. Sobik, "User Guide for the Duplex Army Radio/Radar Targeting Aid (DART)," PAR Technology Corporation Report, 1984.

S.W. Barth and P.E. Lehner, "Artificial Intelligence on Microcomputers," in *Microcomputer Decision Support Systems*, ed. S. Andriole, QED Information Systems: Cambridge, MA, 1986.

H.J. Berliner, "Some Necessary Conditions for a Master Chess Program," *Proceedings of the Third International Joint Conference on Artificial Intelligence*, Stanford University, Stanford, CA, 1973.

W.W. Bledsoe, "Splitting and Reduction Heuristics in Automatic Theorem Proving," *Artificial Intelligence*, 1971, Vol. 2, No. 1, pp. 55 – 77.

W.W. Bledsoe and P. Bruell, "A Man-Machine Theorem Proving System," *Artificial Intelligence*, 1974, Vol. 5, No. 1, 51 – 72.

M. Bramer and D. Bramer, *The Fifth Generation: An Annotated Bibliography*, Addison-Wesley Publishing Company: Reading, MA, 1984.

R.A. Brooks, "Symbolic Reasoning Among 3-d Objects and 2-d Models," *Artificial Intelligence*, 1981, Vol. 16, pp. 285 – 348.

J.R. Carbonell, "AI in CAI: An Artificial Intelligence Approach to Computer-Assisted Instruction," *IEEE Transactions on Man-Machine Systems*, 1970, Vol. 11, pp. 190 – 202.

B. Carr and I. Goldstein, "Overlays: A Theory of Modeling for Computer Aided Instruction," AI Memo 406, AI Laboratory, Massachusetts Institute of Technology, 1977.

A.D. Christiansen, "The History of Planning Methodology: An Annotated Bibliography," *SIGART Newsletter*, October, 1985.

W.J. Clancey, "The Epistemology of a Rule-Based Expert System: A Framework for Explanation," *Artificial Intelligence*, 1984.

K.L. Clark and F.G. McCabe, "Prolog: A Language for Implementing Expert Systems," in *Machine Intelligence 10*, eds. Hayes, J.E., Michie, D. and Pao, Y-H., Halsted Press: John Wiley and Sons, New York, 1982.

W.F. Cloksin and C.S. Mellish, *Programming in Prolog*, Springer-Verlag, New York, 1981.

P.R. Cohen and E.A. Feigenbaum (eds.), *The Handbook of Artificial Intelligence: Vol. 3*. William Kaufmann, Inc.: Los Altos, CA, 1982.

R.J. D'Amore and C.P. Mah, "One Time Complete Indexing of Text: Theory and Practice," *Conference on Research and Development in Information Retrieval*, Cambridge, England, June, 1984.

J. Doyle, "A Truth Maintenance System," *Artificial Intelligence*, Vol. 1, No. 3, 1979.

R.O. Duda, P.E. Hart, and J. Gashing, "Model Design in the PROSPECTOR Consultant System for Mineral Exploration," in *Expert Systems in the Microelectronic Age*, ed. Michie, D., Edinburgh University Press, Edinburgh, 1979.

N.L. Dyer, F.K. Frantz, and M. Livingston, "AELASS: A Knowledge-Based System for Multisensor Surveillance Data Exploitation," *Proceedings of the Conference on Artificial Intelligence*, Oakland University, Rochester, MI, April 26 – 27, 1983.

C. Engleman, E.A. Scarl, and C.H. Berg, "KNOBS: An Experimental Knowledge-Based Tactical Air Mission Planning System and A Rule-Based Aircraft Identification Simulation Facility," *Proceedings of the Sixth Annual Joint Conference on Artificial Intelligence*, 1979, pp. 247 – 249.

E.A. Feigenbaum and P. McCorduch, *The 5th Generation*, Addison-Wesley: Reading, MA, 1983.

C. Fields, "The Strategic Computing Program: An Overview," *SIGNAL*, August, 1984.

R.E. Fikes, P.E. Hart, and N.J. Nilsson, "Learning and Executing Generalized Robot Plans," *Artificial Intelligence*, 1972, Vol. 3, No. 4, pp. 251 – 288.

J.D. Fletcher, "Intelligent Instructional Systems in Training," in *Applications in Artificial Intelligence*, ed. S. Andriole, Petrocelli Books, Inc.: Princeton, NJ, 1985.

J.D. Fletcher and J. Psotka, "Intelligent Training Systems for Maintenance," *SIGNAL*, 1986, Vol. 40, No. 10, pp. 89 – 95.

J.P. Flynn and T.E. Senator, "DARPA Navy Battle Management Applications," *SIGNAL*, Vol. 40, No. 10, pp. 59 – 70.

P.E. Friedland, "Knowledge-based Experiment Design in Molecular Genetics," Doctoral dissertation, Computer Science Department, Stanford University, Stanford, CA, 1979.

W.B. Gevarter, "Expert Systems: Limited But Powerful," in *Applications in Artificial Intelligence*, ed. S. Andriole, Petrocelli Books, Inc.: Princeton, NJ, 1985.

R.H. Granger, A. Meyers, G.B. Taylor, and R. Yoshi, "NOMAD: A Naval Message Understanding System," *Proceedings of the Conference on Artificial Intelligence*, Oakland University, Rochester, MI, April 26 – 27, 1983.

B. Hayes-Roth and F. Hayes-Roth, "A Cognitive Model of Planning," *Cognitive Science*, Vol. 3, 1979, pp. 275 – 310.

F. Hayes-Roth, D.A. Waterman, and D.B. Lenat (eds.), *Building Expert Systems*, Addison Wesley: Reading, MA, 1983.

L.R. Harris, "User Oriented Data Base Query with Robot Natural Language Query System," *Proceedings of the Third International Conference on Very Large Data Bases*, Tokyo, October, 1977.

M.D. Harris, *Introduction to Natural Language Processing*, Reston Publishing Company, Inc.: Reston, VA, 1985.

G. Hendrix and E. Sacerdoti, "Natural Language Processing: The Field in Perspective," *BYTE*, September, 1981, pp. 304 – 352.

G. Hendrix, E. Sacerdoti, D. Sagalowicz, and J. Slocum, "Developing a Natural Language Interface to Complex Data," *ACM Transactions on Database Systems*, 1978, Vol. 3, pp. 105 – 107.

JIPDEC, "Preliminary Report on Study and Research on Fifth Generation Computers 1979 – 1980," Japan Information Processing Development Center, 1981.

S. Kaplan, "Cooperative Responses from a Portable Natural Language Data Base Query System," Ph.D. dissertation, University of Pennsylvania, 1979.

C. Kelly, "Autonomous Robot Vehicle Program," *SIGNAL*, August, 1984, pp. 104 – 106.

P.E. Lehner, "Planning Under Adversity: A Computational Model of Strategic Planning in the Game of Go," Doctoral dissertation, Department of Psychology, University of Michigan, Ann Arbor, MI, 1981.

P.E. Lehner, J.R. McIntyre, L.A. Adelman, K. Gates, P.W. Luster, M. Probus, and M.L. Donnel, "Combining Analysis and Artificial Intelligence," *IEEE Transactions of Systems, Man, and Cybernetics*, SMC-15(14), July/August, 1985.

P.E. Lehner and P.E. Barth, "Expert Systems on Microcomputers," *Expert Systems: The International Journal of Knowledge Engineering*, Vol. 2, No. 4, October, 1985, pp. 198 – 208.

P.E. Lehner, "Adversarial Planning Procedures with Provable Properties," in preparation, 1988.

P.E. Lehner and D.A. Zirk, "Cognitive Factors in User/Expert System Interaction," *Human Factors*, in press.

J.F. Lemmer and B.T. Mitchell, "Interactive Aids for the Development of Computer Vision Rule Bases," PAR Technology Report, 1984.

C.P. Mah, "Advanced Query Facility," PAR Report No. 80-53, 1980, PAR Technology Corporation.

W.A. Martin and R.J. Fateman, "The MACSYMA System." *Proceedings of the 2nd Symposium on Symbolic and Algebraic Manipulation*, Los Angeles, CA, 1971, pp. 23 – 25.

J. Martin, *Application Development Without Programmers*, Prentice-Hall, Inc.: Englewood Cliffs, NJ, 1982.

E.D. McWilliams and G.L. Ricard, "Portable, Intelligent Simulation for ASW Training," in *Computer-Based Instruction for Military Environments*, North Holland Press: Amsterdam, to be published.

R.S. Michalski, J.G. Carbonell, and P.M. Mitchell, *Machine Learning: An Artificial Intelligence Approach*, Tioga Publishing Co.: Palo Alto, CA, 1983.

R.S. Michalski, J.G. Carbonell, and T.M. Mitchell, *Machine Learning: An Artificial Intelligence Approach: Vol. II*, William Kaufmann Publishers, Inc.: Los Altos, CA, 1986.

V.J. Pecora, "EXPRS: A Prototype Expert System Using Prolog for Data Fusion," *AI Magazine*, Vol. 5, No. 2, 1984, pp. 37 – 41.

J. Pitrat, "A Chess Program Which Uses Plans," *Artificial Intelligence*, Vol. 8, 1977, pp. 275 – 321.

W. Reitman and B. Wilcox, "Modeling Tactical Analysis and Problem Solving in Go," *Proceedings of the Tenth Annual Pittsburgh Conference on Modeling and Simulation*, Pittsburgh, PA, 1979, pp. 2133 – 2148.

E. Rich, *Artificial Intelligence*, McGraw-Hill: New York, 1985.

E.D. Sacerdoti, "The Structure of Plans and Behavior," Doctoral dissertation, Computer Science Department, Stanford University, Stanford, CA, August, 1975.

E.D. Sacerdoti and D. Sagalowicz, "A LADDER User's Guide," SRI International, Technical Note 163R, March, 1980.

R.C. Schank and R.P. Abelson, *Scripts, Plans, Goals, and Understanding*. Lawrence Erlbaum: Hillsdale, NJ, 1977.

E.H. Shortliffe, *Computer-Based Medical Consultations: MYCIN*, American Elsevier: New York, 1976.

J.R. Slagle and H. Hamburger, "An Expert System for a Resource Allocation Problem," *Communication of the ACM*, 1985, Vol. 28, No. 9, pp. 994 – 1004.

A.L. Stevens, A. Collins, and S. Goldin, "Diagramming Students' Misconceptions in Causal Models," BBN report no. 3786, Bolt, Beranek and Neumann, Inc., 1978.

G.J. Sussman, *A Computer Model of Skill Acquisition*, American Elsevier: New York, 1975.

D. Waltz, "Generating Semantic Descriptions from Drawings of Scenes with Shadows," in *The Psychology of Computer Vision*, ed. P. Winston, McGraw-Hill: New York, 1975.

D. Waltz, "Initial Language Access to a Large Data Base: An Engineering Approach," *Proceedings of the 4th International Joint Conference on Artificial Intelligence*, Tibilisi, Georgia, USSR, pp. 868 – 872.

R. Wilensky, *Planning and Understanding: A Computational Approach to Human Reasoning*, Addison-Wesley: Reading, MA, 1983.

D. Wilkins, "Using Patterns and Plans to Solve Problems and Control Search," Stanford Artificial Intelligence Laboratory Memo AIM-329, Stanford University, 1979.

D.E. Wilkins, "Domain Independent Planning: Representation and Plan Generation," *Artificial Intelligence*, Vol. 22, 1984, pp. 269 – 301.

W.A. Woods, "Transition Network Grammars for Natural Language Analysis," *Communication of the ACM*, 1970, Vol. 13.

P.R. Young and P.E. Lehner, "Applications of a Theory of Automated Adversarial Planning to Command and Control," *IEEE Transactions on Systems, Man, and Cybernetics*, November/December, 1986.

2

The development of artificial intelligence

V. Daniel Hunt

Editors' note *This paper briefly presents the key elements of AI, and then turns to a short history of the field. It is useful because it dates key events in the history of AI, marking its emergence as a bona fide applied discipline. Hunt concludes the paper by examining current AI technology and AI-related research and development programs, especially the Defense Advanced Research Projects Agency's (DARPA's) Strategic Computing Program. This paper is about the field itself, not necessarily about the technology. This paper first appeared in a special issue of* Signal Magazine *in 1986.*

Artificial intelligence (AI) is a term that has been historically applied to a variety of research areas concerned with extending the ability of the computer to do tasks that resemble those performed by human beings.

Elements of artificial intelligence

Artificial intelligence can be subdivided into several relatively independent areas. Some organizations are concentrating on the development of hardware systems used to run unique AI software. These systems include products from major main frame companies, such as Digital Equipment Corporation, to companies producing unique AI hardware systems, such as Sun Microsystems, Inc., Symbolics, Inc., and Xerox, and to low cost delivery systems featuring the IBM AT. Another major area of AI concerns the development of computer programs that can read, speak or understand language as people use it in everyday conversation. This type of programming is commonly referred to as natural language processing and voice synthesis. A major research activity is concerned with developing AI language programs that use symbolic knowledge to simulate the behavior of human experts. Another group of technologists is developing smart robots with machine vision systems and other improved sensors, and it is interested in developing visual and tactile programs that will enable robots to respond to ongoing changes as each takes place.

Expert systems are seen to be the first significant commercialization from 25 years of research in artificial intelligence. An expert system is an intelligent computer program that uses knowledge and inference procedures to solve problems that are difficult enough to require significant human expertise for their solutions. Knowledge necessary to perform at such a level, plus the inference procedures used, can be thought of as a model of the expertise of the best practitioners in the field.

The knowledge contained in an expert system consists of facts and heuristics. The facts constitute a body of information that is widely shared, publicly available and generally agreed upon by experts in a field. The heuristics are mostly private, rarely discussed rules of good judgment and reasoning that characterize expert-level decision making in the field. The performance level of an expert system is primarily a function of the size and quality of the knowledge base it possesses. AI researchers now understand this process well enough to be able to build operational AI systems for applications in narrow areas of specialization, for example, advising on repair of C^3I hardware systems or capturing the knowledge of an individual expert.

The historical record of AI is one of starts and stops, of progress and digression, of trying to create products that in some way simulate the thinking processes of a human; but unlike the human, AI can be in many places at the same time and will live for as long as its creators wish. That history, with theories of AI evolution, can be traced from the ideas of early pioneers to present and future systems.

The roots of artificial intelligence

The idea of automated intelligence has intrigued people for more than a century. One could conceive of AI as the culmination of the mechanistic paradigm of scientific thought that has been dominant since the time of Sir Isaac Newton. Some historians suggest that humans always have sought to represent and embody life and intellect in their artistic and useful creations. In the 1950s, John von Neumann expressed confidence that, within a short time, computing machines would equal or surpass human intellectual capabilities.

Improvements in the understanding of computation and knowledge organization, coupled with advances in computer speed and memory capacity made possible through improvements in electronics, have encouraged intermittent waves of optimism that super electronic brains would be available in just a few years. Often, these waves of optimism have ebbed in the face of a common problem. As the systems that researchers contemplate and build are required to deal with more information—because the situations in which they are required to operate become more realistic, more complex and unpredictable—the fundamental computational principles, methods, hardware and software that they have to work with will become less effective.

The age of activity and pursuit

The modern history of AI dates back to the 1950s. The difference between now and then is the tremendous expansion of information and the need for users to find new and better ways to access and employ this information.

Several occurrences in the early 1950s caused a major push forward. Alan Turing, a British mathematician, conducted experiments to determine the feasibility of machine intelligence. He first prepared arguments against intelligent machines and then refuted each of those arguments. He concluded that various machines already had imitated parts of humans, including the television camera as an eye, the microphone as an extended ear and servomechanisms as simulators of many of the human feedback systems. He argued that the brain of an infant was not unlike an unorganized machine waiting for general knowledge, routines and other information to make it whole. He was not misled by the differences that even he could see between the digital computer and human physiology, and he stressed their commonality. Finally, he concluded that insight into one surely would give insight into the organization of the other. During that same time, the computer was being converted from a room full of vacuum tube circuits into a transistorized system whose computational and storage powers were expanding almost exponentially with time.

The period from 1955 to 1960 was the formative years in AI development. For the first time, the few AI researchers that existed began to come out of the laboratories to explain their theories to the scientific and technical community. The technical community was looking for ways to access and manage the large amount of information that was being created by an unprecedented expansion in the technology bases of the world.

The term "artificial intelligence" was coined in 1956 by John McCarthy, a Massachusetts Institute of Technology (MIT) professor, to describe the subject of a conference on AI that he was organizing. This meeting, held at Dartmouth College in New Hampshire, brought together researchers in different fields whose common concern was the study of human and machine cognition. Among the researchers assembled at the Dartmouth conference were John McCarthy, Marvin Minsky, Nathaniel Rochester and Claude Shannon. The conference established AI as a distinct discipline and also served to define the major AI research goals: to design machines that think and to understand and model the thought processes of humans.

Thus, AI research is grounded in computer science and electrical engineering and also has its roots in cognitive psychology, linguistics and philosophy. There is an appreciation among many researchers that AI and expert systems are interdisciplinary studies born of the interaction of AI research goals and that the intersection of the separate disciplines constitutes what has become a core of concern distinguishing AI from other fields of science and engineering.

An AI program, dubbed the Logic Theorist, was presented and discussed during the Dartmouth conference. This first program using heuristic search techniques was developed by Allen Newell, Ray Solomonoff and Herbert Simon. They later went on to develop the General Problem Solver (GPS), which applied codified problem solving techniques to problems in different task environments. John McCarthy designed the LISP language in the late 1950s, which is an AI language used by many U.S. researchers.

The 10 years from 1961 to 1971 were filled with more research oriented seminars, new languages for evolving AI systems and still more computational capability coming on-line so quickly that it became hard to remain current with the state of the art. During this decade, development was redirected toward more realistic goals for AI. Stanford University, Carnegie-Mellon and MIT were the leading academic centers of AI research during this period. At the Stanford Research Institute, a robot was developed with sufficient intelligence to plan and carry out its task. In 1965, work began on DEN-

DRAL, the first expert system developed by Stanford Research Institute. The system analyzes information about chemical compounds to determine their molecular structure.

Joseph Weizenbaum created ELIZA, a psychology program that simulated the responses of a therapist in an interactive dialogue with a patient, to illustrate that natural language capability can make a computer appear to be highly intelligent. In another 10 years, AI was applied to more prototype scenarios with growing media attention. The age of the high technology specialist had arrived, taxing human capabilities so greatly that people were forced to become narrowly focused in their individual areas of specialty. At times, experts in the same knowledge categories were so specialized that they could not relate even to each other.

In 1970, Marvin Minsky became the director of the MIT AI laboratory that specialized in computer vision and included all aspects of robotics, expert systems, learning and intuitive reasoning, languages and computer architecture. Alan Colmerauer and his associates began the development of the PROLOG programming language, which is a symbolic AI programming language based on predicate calculus. PROLOG is the most popular language for AI research in Japan. The discovery of knowledge based systems resulted in the creation of MACSYMA, a system performing differential and integral calculus with symbolic input and output. MACSYMA has been used by mathematicians, engineers and scientists.

From 1971 to 1976, the Defense Advanced Research Projects Agency (DARPA) initiated basic research into speech understanding. Some of the programs developed included SPEECHLIS and HWIM. During this period, DARPA began an image understanding program that sponsored research into vision and image processing. William Woods of Bolt Beranek and Newman Corporation developed LUNAR to be used by geologists in the evaluation of material obtained from the moon's surface during the Apollo 11 mission.

An expert system called MYCIN was developed at Stanford University in the mid-1970s. This research system was designed to aid physicians in the diagnosis and treatment of meningitis and bacteremia infections. MYCIN often is spoken of as the first expert system. Other systems used many of the AI techniques associated with expert systems, but MYCIN was the first to combine all of the major features with the clear separation of the knowledge base and the inference engine. This separation led to the subsequent development of the first expert system building tool. After the developers completed MYCIN, they decided that they could remove the specific medical knowledge from MYCIN, hence Essential MYCIN (EMYCIN). The resulting shell consisted of a backward chaining inference engine, a consultation driver and several knowledge acquisition aids. This shell, or tool, then could be combined with another knowledge base to create a new expert system.

The 1980s still are unfolding, and the desire to capture an expert's knowledge continues with increased real world interest in applying AI technology. AI is being scrutinized more than ever as an aid in coping with the applications of information in the military, industrial and public sectors.

In 1980, XCON, the first commercially based system went into operation at Digital Equipment Corporation. XCON was designed to configure VAX 11/780 computer systems. From a customer's order, it decides what components must be added to produce a complete operational computer system and determines the spatial relationships among all of the components. XCON outputs a set of diagrams indicating these spatial relationships to technicians who then assemble the VAX system. XCON handles the configuration task by applying knowledge of the constraints on component relationships to standard procedures for configuring computers. The system is noninteractive, is rule based and uses a forward chaining control scheme. XCON was developed through a collaboration between researchers at Carnegie-Mellon University and Digital Equipment Corporation.

General Electric Company's Corporate Research and Development Division has applied expert system technology to the problem of troubleshooting and repairing diesel electric locomotives in railroad running repair shops. The DELTA/CATS expert system uses production rules and an inference engine that can diagnose multiple problems with the locomotive and can suggest repair procedures to maintenance personnel.

Another practical AI application is Prospector, which acts as a consultant to aid exploration geologists in their search for ore deposits. Given field data about a geological region, it estimates the likelihood of finding particular types of mineral deposits there. The system can assess the potential for finding a variety of deposits, including massive sulfide, carbonate lead/zinc, porphyry, copper, nickel sulfide, sandstone uranium and porphyry molybdenum deposits. Prospector was one of the first commercially successful expert system programs. It was used to find a molybdenum deposit in Washington state after other attempts had failed.

In 1981, Japan announced its intention to start a fifth generation computer system project, and in 1982 it launched its Institute for New Generation Computing, located in Tokyo. These efforts initiated a new international panic to implement AI technology. Fifth generation computers are seen as the next generation of computing machines, and it is assumed that they will be larger and faster and will incorporate fundamentally new designs. Parallel processing, capturing the ability of a computer to process several different programs simultaneously, is expected to result in a massive increment in computational power.

Since advanced military and space expert systems tend to be large and involve a substantial amount of processing, it is assumed that these types of applications of expert systems will not reach maturity until more powerful machines are available.

The Microelectronics and Computer Technology Corporation (MCC) located in Austin, Texas, was created as a private company with 20 participating corporations, including Honeywell, RCA and Eastman Kodak. The intent in setting up MCC was to develop advanced technology that all of the participants ultimately could use and market. Although no government funds are involved, MCC is considered the only operation in the United States that rivals the Japanese fifth generation project.

In 1983, the European community formed the European Strategic Program for Research in Information Technology (ESPRIT) to compete in the race for a fifth generation computer. ESPRIT is the common market's program for the development of new AI technologies; its structure is similar to Japan's fifth generation project in the scope of what it hopes to achieve.

In this time period, Golden Common LISP (GCLISP) was developed by Gold Hill Computers as a LISP development and training system for microcomputers. GCLISP created an inexpensive, yet powerful, AI programming environment and is the first implementation of common LISP on microcomputers, such as IBM personal computers.

In 1986, there was a move from expensive research oriented delivery hardware such as Symbolics, Inc., work stations, toward less expensive use oriented hardware based on a personal computer system. During this period, Intellicorp developed a knowledge engineering language called KEE for frame based representation. It supports rule based, procedure oriented and object oriented representation methods. Its principal characteristics include multiple knowledge bases to facilitate modular system design and forward and backward chaining for its rule interpreter. In 1986, KEE was made available for use on IBM AT personal computer systems.

Artificial intelligence today

The AI industry is now one of the fastest growing technology markets in the United States. Revenues for companies in the AI market exceed $700 million in 1985 and have been predicted to reach $1 billion in 1986. Various consulting firms predict that, by 1990, the size of the AI industry market will be more than $5 billion.

Growth of the entire AI market was spurred in 1986 primarily by military and corporate interest in expert systems and by continued use of artificial vision systems and smart robots in the automotive and electronics industries. Both voice recognition and natural language markets lag behind other technologies in technical advancement and commercial implementation, despite a large amount of attention and interest fostered in 1986.

As expected, 1986 did not produce many technical advancements and achievements for all fields of AI technology. It was primarily a year of prototype developments and new hardware and software product introductions—as well as active public relations marketing—on the part of AI companies. Notable events of 1986 included the introduction of major commercially viable expert system applications, increased work toward the creation of voice-activated typewriters and a range of new personal computer software products with embedded AI techniques. While 1986 was more oriented toward marketing and public relations, some important technical strides did occur. This is particularly true in the area of connecting and linking AI software and machines to more traditional architectures, especially within the realms of engineering design and data processing.

Other AI events to look forward to in 1987 are the demonstration of the DARPA/TI LISP chip, a computer terminal using voice recognition design to replace the typewriter, and more products with AI that contain expert systems and natural language techniques as a primary feature.

1987 will be the year of more integration of separate AI technology elements, including voice recognition used in conjunction with vision systems to control robots, intelligent systems for manufacturing process control, natural language features on voice systems and expert systems to determine grammar use in natural language. Several emerging fields of computer technology will be based specifically on AI, including the generation and maintenance of computer code for applications using expert systems; use of AI front ends for access to various databases; and increased use of AI in factory automation process planning.

The trend toward providing increased performance at lower cost will continue in 1987, with LISP machines and voice recognition boards as specific examples. This trend is leading toward the inevitable shakeout of the more than 300 companies involved in marketing AI technologies. Due to the failure to gain market share and to unprofitable operations, many companies that developed AI marketing/technical support staffs already have reconfigured their operations and moved from having separate AI centers to integrating AI into functional product requirement areas. In the artificial vision and expert systems markets, a large number of companies are selling similar products to too few customers. These two markets have attracted the major share of large corporation involvement.

The AI hardware market also is facing significant competition from established companies in the minicomputer and work station industries. As the trend toward less expensive delivery systems continues, traditional vendors of expensive research work stations will lose their market share. The most important aspect of 1986 will be further AI integration into mainstream computing, elevating it from fringe development status and increasing its commercial viability.

Government funding

The Department of Defense is the lead agency funding AI research. DARPA, which established the three university "centers of excellence" at MIT, Carnegie-Mellon and Stanford University, has been awarding contracts since the early 1960s and has proposed a significant expansion in its AI efforts. The Office of Naval Research (ONR) and the Air Force in particular is interested in AI techniques for image understanding. ONR and AFOSR funding is expected to remain stable in the near term.

The National Science Foundation (NSF) has been awarding grants for university and some industrial AI projects since the late 1950s. In recent years, the NSF AI research budget has remained stable at approximately $6 million annually. Two NSF directorates, Computer Science and Information Science and Technology, provide the bulk of these funds. A number of the awards are made jointly between these two divisions, with the NSF Office of Interdisciplinary Research, or with other programs within NSF.

Strategic computing

DARPA has embarked on a major effort to push the frontiers of computer technology and AI for application in future military systems. The Strategic Computing Program plans to spend $600 million over the next five years, above the past levels of funding, and spending will accelerate to unspecified levels as prototype development begins in the late 1980s. The project calls for the demonstration of significant military capabilities within 10 years. The major areas of focus are the autonomous (unmanned) vehicles; the pilot's associate systems to aid combat pilots in coping with the complexity of current and planned aircraft; and battle management under conditions of uncertainty.

Some of the goals of the Strategic Computing Program, particularly the vision system requirements for autonomous vehicles, have been described as ambitious. Some describe this program as unprecedented in the history of U.S. government funding of science and technology. Unlike the Manhattan Project or the manned moon landing mission, which principally were concerned with engineering problems, the success of the DARPA program requires basic scientific breakthroughs—neither the timing nor nature of which can be predicted easily.

It is expected that the Strategic Computing Program will approximately quadruple the annual federal funding of research and development (R&D) in AI and related hardware. This major increase in R&D funding will have significant and far reaching effects on the AI community and research environment. Undoubtedly, the increased flow of money will have some positive effects on AI research. In particular, the availability of funds for modern equipment should make university laboratory facilities comparable to increasingly well-equipped industry laboratories. The increased availability of graduate student financial aid in the form of research assistantships should draw in and help hold more qualified postgraduate trainees, thus expanding the potential faculty base.

The current imbalance in the supply and demand of AI personnel will continue, will most likely increase and may intensify competition among commercial, military and academic AI programs. Thus, some applied research, such as that toward intelligence database systems, computer assisted education and fundamental research that is unlikely to have high immediate military value, may be neglected.

The potential for AI growth is significant; however, the heavily funded government prototype systems must demonstrate success by being incorporated into functional application requirements.

3

Lessons learned building expert systems

A. Terry Bahill
Pat N. Harris and Erich Senn

Editors' note *Here, Bahill, Harris, and Senn share with you some lessons learned. The discussion revolves around two expert systems, Cogito, which provides advice about how to bring the UNIX operating system up on Digital Equipment Corporation's VAX computers, and the Data Communication Diagnosis system, which provides advice about how to connect a terminal to a computer. The lessons address the knowledge engineering process, how to select the "right" development environment and tool(s), how to assess user satisfaction with intelligent systems, and how to test expert systems to determine if they are doing what they are supposed to be doing. The paper is practical and a little introspective. (Reprinted, with permission, from the September, 1988 issue of* AI Expert. *©* *1988,* AI Expert. *All rights reserved.)*

We have made many expert systems. Two of our best are Cogito, which gives installation advice for bringing up the UNIX (Bell Laboratories) 4.2BSD operating system on a VAX (Digital Equipment Corp.), and Data Communication Diagnosis (DCD), which helps a person connect a terminal to a computer. This article will compare and contrast the development, tool selection, and testing of these two systems.

Background

Before Cogito was completed, two detailed reference manuals were used for UNIX 4.2BSD installation instructions. [1], [2] These voluminous manuals were difficult to use. In contrast, Cogito is easy to use because it filters the information and presents only relevant advice about the user's computer system. Cogito remembers data the user has previously entered and uses it to customize its response. Cogito is written in M.1 (Teknowledge Inc.), runs on a personal computer, and used *if-then* production rules to encode the task knowledge.

DCD is a knowledge-based system designed to help engineers connect a peripheral device (terminal or printer) to a computer, modem, or local area network. Most of DCD was written in OPS5, although parts were written in C and M.1.

Instructions for connecting peripheral devices to computers are contained in the reference and user manuals of the devices. Unfortunately, their usage is fraught with difficulty. It is not easy to collect all the relevant information for the two devices in question since this information is spread over several chapters (for example, pin connections are discussed in the hardware section and transfer parameters in the set-up section) in several manuals written by different companies. DCD had three specific requirements:

- Provide enough advice to people who have some previous computing experience but little experience in data communications so they can design a cable with a 25-pin connector on each end that can be used to connect a peripheral device to a host device
- Read in a description (name) of the devices and ask the user for values of parameters not stored in the expert system's database, provide a help feature to support the process of answering questions, and produce a sequence of instructions to help the user successfully interconnect the devices
- Derive an approximate solution even if some information is missing or the answers to questions are unknown.

Unfortunately, modern computer users are often overwhelmed with information. Expert systems can help reverse this trend. Voluminous data with many interrelationships presented over a short time span can overload the user. Data become useful information when the relationships between items are cohesive. Both Cogito and DCD eliminate extraneous information and relate relevant information, reducing the chances of user overload.

Creating the knowledge base

Our first expert system, [3] made in 1984, had a flat tree: every premise was tied directly to the conclusion. However, to emulate human input-output behavior, we believed that an expert system should have a bushy tree. We discovered that we had to invent intermediary conclusions if we were to mimic a consultation with a human. Furthermore, humans have a limited short-term memory, thus a solution going from premises to conclusions should follow a path of simple knowledge intermediates.

Of course, even with this hierarchy, the rules do not write themselves; the expert still had to add knowledge to get the rules. For example, the expert knew that pins 2 and 3 are used to transmit and receive data. So if pin 2 transmits data, pin 3 receives data.

The *if-then* production rules were derived from the hierarchy. The hierarchy helped make sure rules were not overlooked. For example, it was easy to check that each pin was contained in at least one rule.

This hierarchy was not very structured, but it still helped in writing the rules. Rules are easier to write in problem domains that can be structured more systematically with a technique that divides the problem space into a set of objects where every object has attributes and every attribute has values. This object-attribute-value ordered set is called an O-A-V triplet.

Typical usage of O-A-V triplets is: the object *has* an attribute and a value *is* an attribute. Another way of writing the O-A-V triplet is as a sentence ("attribute of object is value"); for example, "marking of coat is striped." This usage makes the construction of facts easy:

type of animal is mammal
category of mammal is ungulate
extremities of ungulate is hooves.

With such facts, it is easy to write *if-then* production rules, for example:

if composition of coat is hair
then type of animal is mammal.

if type of animal is mammal
and extremities of animal is hooves
then category of animal is ungulate.

if category of animal is ungulate
and marking of coat is stripes
then identity of animal is zebra.

A tree is seldom built all at one time; instead, branches are added incrementally. When a branch is added, sometimes something that is a value at one level becomes an object at a lower level ("mammal" is a value in "type of animal is mammal," but becomes an object in "category of mammal is ungulate").

In contrast, sometimes O-A-V triplets are linked together without an intervening attribute:

type of animal is mammal

marking of coat is stripes.

Teknowledge distributes a tutorial expert system, SACON, with their PC-based shell, M.1. The company has been refining SACON for 10 years. It is composed exclusively of O-A-V = O-A-V linkages. This implies that perhaps these are the best linkages for an expert system.

We have subsequently tried several other methods for constructing *if-then* production rules without forcing human experts to distort their reasoning processes to produce *if-then*-type rules. We have found the analytic hierarchy process [4], [5] helpful in constructing O-A-V triplets.

Selecting the proper tool

Consider the following analogy. A sculptor wishes to create an image of a dove, and has both marble and ice in which to carve. Although the mediums of ice and marble require different tools and speed of construction, the marble and ice doves are the same as the image within the sculptor's mind. The difference in mediums does not affect the result. Now suppose the sculptor wants to sculpt with iron rebar and a torch. This dove will not appear the same. In this case, the medium does affect the result.

Current expert system shells force a structure on the knowledge base that may be different from the expert's structure; for example, requiring the knowledge to appear as production rules, semantic networks, or frames. When an expert has trouble developing a rule that covers a certain situation, it is often said that the expert's knowledge is nonverbal and internalized. Alternatively, perhaps the expert cannot develop a rule that fits the situation because he or she does not think in terms of *if-then* production rules.

Cogito provided many examples of how humans are forced to fit their knowledge into the constraints of a tool. Cogito has many rules that might otherwise be simple lists. Furthermore, Cogito's problem domain is probably most suitable for a forward-chaining strategy. If the inference engine had been capable of extensive forward-chaining, the knowledge base could have been shortened. Thus, the tool used definitely affected the coding of the knowledge.

However, an engineer's job is to find and apply the best available tool to solve a problem. The tools available for Cogito were M.1 and OPS5. The decision to use M.1 was primarily based on the differences in rule implementations and ease of input and output. Cogito's rules are English-like phrases. OPS5 rules are reminiscent of LISP code; experts who are not familiar with OPS5 or LISP have trouble reading and understanding OPS5 rules. Rule readability is important so the knowledge engineer can verify with the expert that the intent of the rule is the same as the coded rule. With M.1, the knowledge engineer can concentrate on problem semantics and not on the syntax of OPS5 or LISP.

We selected OPS5 for DCD primarily because it used forward chaining, and this seemed the best type of inferencing when all the data are available at the beginning of the inferencing process. However, a subset of the problem (creating a cable plan) was also written in M.1, which gave us the opportunity to compare these two tools.

The quality of a system's user interface is crucial for a system's survival. M.1 has an advantage in this matter since it provides legal value checking, which is difficult and cumbersome to implement in OPS5. The human-computer interface of M.1 is better than that of OPS5, but this did not matter in our case since all the data were collected from the human expert before the inference process started using a module written in C.

The knowledge base contains the rules to solve the problem at hand. Rules written in M.1 are easier to read than those in OPS5. However, the easier rule syntax of M.1 is only an advantage for novice knowledge engineers. Based on our experiences, we think experienced programmers can write either M.1 or OPS5 rules with equal ease. On the other hand, M.1 is at a disadvantage because its conclusions cannot have values for several different expressions. This handicap is not shared by OPS5, where several different expressions can be in the conclusion of a rule, reducing the number of rules.

M.1 automatically handles the answer "unknown." In OPS5, we had to specify in each rule how "unknown" should be handled. The inference engine of M.1 uses certainty factors. OPS5, on the other hand, does not provide a mechanism that deals with uncertainty. Probability calculations can be done in OPS5, but this is cumbersome. However, DCD, like most expert systems, did not need certainty factors. In fact, in one of our expert system classes at the University of Arizona, Tucson, we found that only six of the 25 student-generated systems used certainty factors.

Quantitative selection

We have helped build over 80 expert systems for class projects, master's theses, and commercial ventures. We are often asked why we chose a particular expert system shell. Often our qualitative answers do not satisfy the questioner. Therefore, for the DCD project, we provided a quantitative answer to this question.

No one-to-one match exists between problems and software tools. However, conceptions of particular types of problems are the same for several different domains. These conceptions are commonly referred to as consultation paradigms. Examples of consultation paradigms are diagnosis/advice, planning, and design. Diagnosis/advice is the consultation paradigm used by DCD.

According to P. Harmon and D. King, [6] the shells the best suited for diagnosis/advice are M.1, S.1, and OPS5. Hundreds of commercially available expert system shells exist; we did not consider every one for DCD, but restricted ourselves to these three. The following discussion illustrates a technique and is not meant to advocate a particular shell.

To select the shell for our data-communication problem, we concentrated on the following criteria:

- Representation: The knowledge that enables us to solve data-communication problems must be formulated with *if-then* production rules. The inference strategy used should be forward-chaining since all necessary data are given at the beginning of the inference process. The tool to be selected must provide an approximate solution when some information is missing or the answers to questions are unknown.
- Implementation: When this project began, available hardware included several personal computers, many PDP 11s, and a VAX. Available software included OPS5, M.1, and ROSIE.
- Interfacing: Questions asked by the system should be displayed on a screen and answers entered on a keyboard. Solutions to a problem must be written to a data file. The knowledge base must be built and modified with a tool-independent text editor.
- Support: Documentation should be readable with easy-to-understand examples. References to past tool applications and their level of success should be available.

Many software packages that are commercially available (such as Expert Choice[4]) aid multiobjective decision analysis in the face of nebulous and uncertain data. We used the Multi-Attribute Utility Technique (MAUT), [7] sometimes called SMART, to choose among M.1, S.1, and OPS5.

User satisfaction

We found it easier to install a UNIX operating system using Cogito than the UNIX reference manuals because with Cogito the information presented to the user was tailored to the specific application. For example, in the disk-definition state, the file '/etc/fstab' must be created. Assume that the boot disk is a 'AMPEX 300M' connected to uba0 at drive 1. This implies that the disk address is 1. Also assume the user's name is 'Pat' and that Pat is ready to install 'fstab'. Since the instructions given in the manual are generic, the installer must relate the general instructions to the specific application.

Cogito has remembered information the user gave it a half-hour ago: that the user's name is Pat and the disk is an AMPEX 300M. Cogito has used this information to make its instructions specific. Cogito's instructions are personalized, relevant to the user's task, clear and complete.

This example illustrates that the manual's instructions are incomplete and rely on previous and implicit knowledge. The instructions are incomplete because the swap partition '/dev/up0b', must be added to the file. They rely on previous knowledge because the user must recall that the UNIX standalone disk name for a 'AMPEX 300M' is 'up'. They rely on implicit knowledge because the user must somehow know that the disk address of the partitions must be changed from '0' to '1'.

Testing

Testing Cogito was difficult. It was impossible to present the system with every possible combination of inputs and evaluate its outputs. The best test we devised was to let intended users try Cogito in many hypothetical situations. If the knowledge base was incomplete, then in some situations the advice given to the users should be incorrect.

Cogito was tested by the computer systems administrator and a professor of the Dept. of Systems and Industrial Engineering and the computer systems administrator for the Dept. of Computer Science at the University. All found Cogito's advice to be complete and correct.

In an effort to bolster our testing, we asked several nonexpert computer users to try the system. Their evaluations emphasized the difficulties they had using Cogito and making sense of its queries or output, and the extent to which they were able to fool the system with plausible (but nonsensical) inputs.

Recently, we gave Cogito a real test. Because of inadequate glue on the heads of our RA811 disk, we had to rebuild our operating system from the distribution tapes. Cogito helped us. We found a few omissions in Cogito's advice, but no mistakes, and completed the task in about 12 hours. It took us three months the first time we built the system, but we were way down on the learning curve then.

This experience has reinforced our belief that all expert systems are inadequately tested. No quantitative procedures exist for testing expert systems. Most tests merely involve running a few case studies; they do not exhaust all possibilities. For example, we are confident that Cogito works well for small VAX 750 systems, but we cannot be sure it will work as well for 730s or 780s.

We carefully planned our tests and evaluations for DCD. Because the DCD system was designed for users with little previous experience in data communication, we allowed juniors from our microcomputer class to test and evaluate it. Thirty-three student teams (two members per team) participated in testing and evaluation.

It is impossible to test all the combinations of problems likely to occur in data communication. Therefore, only two typical test cases were given. System users were asked to use DCD to:

- Design a cable that would connect a WYSE terminal to a VAX computer and to give advice about setting up the WYSE terminal to make the interconnection work
- Design a cable that would connect a WYSE terminal to the Sytek local area network and to give advice about setting up the WYSE terminal and the Sytek port.

We specified two major subtasks in the evaluation process. First, we focused on the accuracy of the system. Was the advice given by the system sufficient to make the interconnection work? This assessment was trivial since the advice given by the system resulted in go/no-go situations. Second, the students evaluated the quality of the human-computer interaction. Was the system easy to use? These evaluation criteria should be directly proportional to future frequency of use of the system.

All the undergraduate students accomplished the tasks with an average time of 20 minutes, suggesting that the accuracy of the system was 100%. The students rated the quality of human-computer interaction as "user friendly." As a further test of the DCD system, a selected graduate student tried to connect a WYSE terminal to the VAX computer and a WYSE terminal to the Sytek net using only the manufacturers' user and reference manuals. He succeeded after 1.5 hours—about three times longer than the undergraduate students who established the same connections by consulting the DCD system.

After this initial test, the DCD system was used by juniors at the University for five consecutive semesters. This continued usage proves its usefulness. However, DCD's usefulness is diminishing as our equipment changes, and none of our knowledge engineers have experience with OPS5 to update the knowledge base.

General-purpose testing

The most difficult aspect of expert system design is testing. The traditional testing method is to have a human expert run many sample cases on the expert system. This consumes a lot of the expert's time and does not guarantee finding all mistakes. Conversely, brute-force enumeration of all inputs is impossible for most systems. Therefore we have developed a general-purpose tool to help debug knowledge bases without the intervention of human experts. We have tried to make this tool generic so it can work on any knowledge base, no matter which expert system shell is used.

The first component of the tool is a simple spelling checker with a preprocessor that replaces hyphens, underbars, and parentheses with spaces and removes terms specific to the shell being used, such as *legalvals* and *automaticmenu*. The second component of this tool is designed for backward-chaining shells. It collects all terms that appear in the premises (the *if* parts) of the rules, and flags as potential mistakes those that do not also appear in the conclusions (the *then* parts) of the rules or in questions or goal statements. It also traces every term appearing in a premise to the conclusion of that rule, then to the premise of another rule, and so on until a goal statement is reached. If it does not reach a goal statement, then a rule is missing.

The third component of this tool, which is not yet completed, acts like Tieresias [8] in pointing out rules that do not fit the pattern established by the rest of the rules in the knowledge base. For example, when we ran this component on our animal-discrimination knowledge base, it said, "Rule 15 is suspicious, because most rules that mention the animal's fur also ask if it has spots. Rule 15 does not."

The fourth component comes into play at run time. The firing of each rule is recorded. Rules that never fire and rules that fire for all test cases are probably mistakes and are brought to the attention of the human expert.

Size

Cogito contains 800 rules, 200KB, and took 800 hours to build. DCD contains 60 rules, 40KB (plus an interface program and a large help file), and took 120 hours to build. To better understand these numbers, we performed statistical analysis of 25 simple expert systems written by students in partial fulfillment of the requirements of a course in expert systems in 1987. (We call these systems simple because they did not use external functions or special hardware.)

The average student spent 100 hours on the project: 15% of this time was spent learning the subject, 10% interviewing the expert, 60% developing and debugging the knowledge base, and 15% testing the system. The average knowledge base contained 150 rules and required 32KB. From these systems and from a less formal evaluation of 60 other student-generated expert systems constructed over a three-year time span, we concluded that the number of rules (or knowledge base entries) is not a good indication of the complexity of a system.

However, we also concluded that in routine expert systems, novice knowledge engineers consume three to four hours per kilobyte of knowledge base. Sophisticated knowledge engineers may expend as much as five to 10 hours per kilobyte, because they know how to collapse similar rules into more general expressions and might be using external functions.

Appropriateness

We used M.1 and OPS5. One is primarily a backward chainer; the other primarily a forward chainer. We do not think much difference exists between the two. For our problems, we could have made either type of chaining work. After learning each of these expert system shells, Senn remarked, "It's just another language."

This remark has another implication about the knowledge-transfer process. Expert systems have made one step forward accompanied, unfortunately, by one step backward. While expert systems permit a higher level of abstraction, they also demand that the knowledge base remains tightly coupled to the inference engine. Even though the knowledge has already been captured in Cogito or DCD, converting this knowledge to another inference engine would be difficult. A fundamental breakthrough occurred when traditional programming languages became independent of the processor; a similar breakthrough must be effected within the expert system realm.

How can one identify a task appropriate for a PC-based expert system? First, there must be a human who performs that task better than most other people. Second, the task's solution must be explainable by the human expert in words without relying on pictures. Third, the problem must be solvable in a 20-minute or even one-hour telephone conversation with the expert. If it would take a human two days to solve the problem, it is far too complicated for an expert system; if the human gives the answer in two seconds, it is too simple. Fourth, problems that involve determining one of many possible solutions are ideal candidates for expert systems, such as answering the question, "What disease does the person have?" Fifth, the problem must encompass uncertainty or inexactness in the data, or a diagram on paper would be superior.

The first four criteria help predict whether the expert system will be successful, whereas the fifth helps decide whether a complex expert system shell is needed or if some simpler tool would suffice. The animal classification system is an example of a problem domain that has no uncertainty or inexactness. This task could be performed better using a diagram than an expert system on a PC.

Given these criteria, giving advice for bringing up UNIX on a VAX computer was an inappropriate task for a PC-based expert system. It cannot be done in a one-hour conversation with an expert. We estimate that it would take an expert one or two days to do this task (it took us three months to do it the first time!). Cogito's 800 rules filled two floppy disks.

We succeeded in making an expert system that worked, but it was hard work. A more powerful tool (such as KEE [IntelliCorp], S.1 [Teknowledge], ART [Inference Corp.], or Knowledge Craft [Carnegie Group Inc.]) would have been more appropriate.

However, helping a person connect a terminal to a computer is an appropriate task for an expert system. In the future, we think most computer equipment manufacturers will have expert systems (interactive textbooks) to help their sales personnel install their equipment. This will insulate their research engineers from mundane questions and build confidence in the sales force, which will then be able to answer difficult questions about their product.

The two real-world expert systems discussed here were designed to perform certain tasks, and they did them; so they were successful. However, the more important aspect of these endeavors was that we learned a great deal about making expert systems. We learned that an expert system shell is not Merlin's long-lost magic wand. You cannot do things with expert system shells that you could not do in any other language; but you can develop a prototype a lot faster. We learned that expert systems can be made friendlier than conventional computer programs. But we also learned that testing and validating expert systems is difficult.

This research was partially supported by grant no. AFOSR-88-0076 from the Air Force Office of Scientific Research.

References

1. *UNIX Programmer's Manual Reference Guide.* Berkeley, Calif.: USENIX Assoc., 1985.
2. *UNIX Systems Manager's Manual.* Berkeley, Calif.: USENIX Assoc., 1985.

3. R. Moller, A.T. Bahill, and L. Swisher. "The Development of ESIAC, an Expert System for Identifying Autistic Children," in *Proceedings of the International Conference on Systems, Man, and Cybernetics*. New York, N.Y.: IEEE, 1985, pp. 875–878.
4. E.H. Forman and T.L. Saaty. *Expert Choice*. McLean, Va.: Decision Support Software, 1986.
5. T.L. Saaty and K.P. Kerns. *Analytic Planning: Organization of Systems*. New York, N.Y.: Pergamon Press, 1985.
6. P. Harmon and D. King. *Expert Systems: Artificial Intelligence in Business*. New York, N.Y.: Wiley, 1985.
7. W. Edwards, "How to Use Multiattribute Utility Measurement for Social Decision Making." *IEEE Transcripts on Systems, Man, and Cybernetics* SMC-7: 326–340, 1977.
8. B.G. Buchanan and E.H. Shortliffe. *Rule-Based Expert Systems*. Reading, Mass.: Addison-Wesley, 1984.

4

Validating expert system performance

Robert M. O'Keefe
Osman Balci and Eric P. Smith

Editors' note *O'Keefe, Balci and Smith discuss the thorny problem of validation in this important paper. They specifically address the questions of what to validate, what to validate against, what to validate with, when to validate, how to control the cost of validation, how to control bias, and how to cope with multiple results. The paper is reprinted here because it deals with a huge problem in a systematic way. (Reprinted, with permission, from the Winter 1987 issue of* IEEE Expert. *© 1987, IEEE. All rights reserved.)*

Most definitions of expert systems mention their ability to perform at close to human expert levels. Yet expert system validation—that is, testing systems to ascertain whether they achieve acceptable performance levels—has (with few exceptions) been ad hoc, informal, and of dubious value. This article seeks to establish validation as an important concern in expert system research and development. It discusses problems in expert system validation, and presents both qualitative and quantitative methods for validating expert systems.

Typically, engineers have validated expert system performance by running test cases through a system and comparing results (that is, the classification, final certainty factors, and advice given) against known results or expert opinion. These engineers calculate a percentage for the system's success rate and use subjective judgment to analyze and explain expert system failures where test results contradict known results or expert opinion. Examples of this simple approach range from MYCIN's early validation [1] to the recently reported validation of Emerge—a chest pain diagnosis system. [2]

However, this simple approach presents several problems. The final percentage obtained hinges on the choice of test cases, and its accuracy hinges on the number of test cases chosen. When we compare a system against the expert on whose knowledge that system was built, as happened with Prospector, [3] the so-called validation is of dubious value.

Since many expert systems began as research prototypes, validation has often been conducted to qualitatively measure system performance, as with Internist-1. [4] Or validation has simply been part of an overall evaluation to assess an expert system's value to a particular domain, as with the medical diagnosis system Casnet [5] and the auditing system EDP-Xpert. [6] However, since expert systems to be used on a regular basis—particularly in critical areas—must be validated carefully, the use of formal validation methods has increased in developing some implemented systems. Both a later validation of MYCIN, [7] and a validation of the chemotherapy adviser Oncocin (like MYCIN, developed at Stanford), [8] used formal methods backed by statistical tests. The VAX configuration system R1/Xcon also underwent some formal validation. [9], [10]

Verification, validation, and evaluation

We are concerned with validating performance only. Typically, validation is part of evaluation—a broader area seeking to assess an expert system's overall value. In addition to exhibiting acceptable performance levels, expert systems should be usable, efficient, and cost effective. Validation is the cornerstone of evaluation, since highly efficient implementations of invalid systems are useless.

Separating performance validation from other aspects of evaluation can be difficult. For instance, testing is difficult when users balk at using systems that fail to consider human factors; for example, systems with poorly designed interfaces. For this reason, developers must decide at the outset whether or not to separate validation. In ground-breaking applications particularly, an overall evaluation policy may seem more relevant—especially if it is determined at the start that a reasonable performance level will be difficult to attain.

Validation is often confused with verification. Simply stated, validation refers to building the right system (that is, substantiating that a system performs with an acceptable level of accuracy), whereas verification refers to building the system "right" (that is, substantiating that a system correctly implements its specifications). In modeling studies, nobody solves the *problem*—rather, everybody solves the *model* of the problem. Since an expert system represents human reasoning and knowledge, we must justify its representation level through validation.

The purpose of this article is twofold: First, we seek to establish validation and evaluation as important concerns in expert system research and development. Second, we wish to present both qualitative and quantitative methods of formal validation—some taken from other areas of computer-based model validation—that can be applied to expert systems. The work presented here draws upon our experience in (1) developing expert systems [11] and (2) using validation methods in computer-based modeling.

We will examine the problems encountered in validating expert system performance, address basic concepts fundamental to validation, review appropriate qualitative methods, and discuss the use of quantitative methods. We will close with our conclusions regarding the application of validation methods.

Validating expert systems

We have encountered the following major problems in validating expert system performance:

1. What to validate,
2. What to validate against,
3. What to validate with,
4. When to validate,
5. How to control the cost of validation,
6. How to control bias,
7. How to cope with multiple results.

We encounter all of these, to a greater or lesser extent, in validating any computer-based model. The next section discusses these problems and provides some guidelines.

What to validate We can validate any intermediate results, the final result (often called the conclusion), the reasoning of the system, or any combination of these three. [10] Since a poor reasoning process that provides a correct result cannot be scaled up to a larger application domain, or may give a different result when used with an extended knowledge base, we should validate the reasoning process. [12]

What to validate is intrinsically linked to what developmental stage we have reached. At any stage, if part of the system's performance can be measured for a given set of inputs, that part should be validated so as to catch errors as early as possible in the development life cycle. Typically, we may concentrate on validating the reasoning process early on in development, and only be concerned with validating final results when the knowledge base is more complete.

Furthermore, it may be difficult (or impossible) to classify the result of an expert system as right or wrong. In the following excerpt, Kulikowski and Weiss discuss Casnet's validation:

> Classifying conclusions as being merely correct or incorrect is an oversimplification. The program's conclusions are presented not as single unique diagnoses but rather as combinations of judgments about a patient's status.

In such cases, however, one can often get experts to classify intermediate results, conclusions, and reasoning into several categories. For instance, Hickam et al. had chemotherapy protocol experts classify the performance of Oncocin as ideal, acceptable, suboptimal, and unacceptable. [8]

What to validate against Expert systems can be validated against known results as well as against expert performance. For example, consider an expert system that predicts the financial performance of a company. Given the input conditions in 1985, the expert system can be asked (today, that is) to predict that company's known financial performance in 1986. Thus, validity can be assessed by comparing the system's prediction against the company's known performance. It's unfair to expect expert systems to perform at levels close to known results when human experts cannot perform at these levels. Expert systems should be validated against experts, although known results (when available) can provide a useful background for validation.

A problem with known results is that previous expert decisions may precipitate those results. Suppose that a bank uses a performance prediction when deciding whether or not to support company X financially. If an expert had decided a year ago that the financial position of company X would be poor in a year's time and thus implemented withdrawal of financial support, the present poor financial position of company X might be due in part to that previous expert decision.

What to validate with In an ideal world, many documented previous cases—representing work from a number of experts on a complete range of problems—would be available for use in validation. In the real world, unfortunately, only a small sample is available—a sample drawn from a single or a few experts. And, in extreme instances, no test cases are available.

Further, the choice of test cases biases the success of any validation. Any test case used in system development should be discarded since (supposedly) the system will have been altered to handle the case successfully. Numerous situations are fairly standard in many domains, and can be handled with limited expertise; for example, suppose we are developing a medical diagnosis system in a domain where 90 percent of the cases are standard and the other 10 percent require considerable skill. A 90-percent success rate for the expert system would not inspire confidence when validated against test cases.

For a fair cross-sectional system validation, test cases should be randomly selected using stratified sampling; that is, randomly selected within each identifiable result type. For instance, if an expert classifies a diagnosis as A, B, or C—and previous histories indicate that these classifications occur respectively 80 percent, 15 percent, and 5 percent of the time—then a collection of 200 test cases should include 160, 30, and 10 instances where A, B, and C resulted respectively. However, the value of a stratified approach is debatable. The ability to handle cases producing infrequent results is an expert trait; frequently, developers devote a disproportionate amount of knowledge and effort to such cases. In many instances, more detailed validation will require testing the system against a small number of obscure or complex cases—cases that even top experts find difficult—and qualitatively assessing how well the system handles these.

Obviously, the number of test cases used affects our confidence in the system. However, the law of large numbers simply does not apply here. The issue is not the *number* of test cases, it is the *coverage* of test cases—that is, how well they reflect the input domain. The input domain is the population of permissible input, [13] and should not be confused with the application domain in which the expert system operates. The larger the input domain, the more difficult validation becomes.

If no historic test cases are available, or if all of them have been used in developing the system, it may be possible to synthesize test cases by having experts randomly create some. But this is problematical because any set of synthesized cases is unlikely to represent a well-stratified sample. Moreover, since experts are unlikely to expend as much time or effort on synthetic as on real problems, their reasoning and the results may well suffer. In some instances, however, this may well be the only means of providing sample test cases.

When to validate Little agreement exists regarding when to validate expert systems. In the following excerpt, Bachant and McDermott relate the folly of expecting high performance from a system early in its career:

> To expect anything close to perfection during the first few years a system is being used (especially if the task is significantly more than a toy) is probably a very serious mistake. [9]

On the other hand, Buchanan and Shortliffe believe that

> . . . high performance is a *sine qua non* for an expert system and thus deserves separate evaluation early in a program's evolution. [14]

Although these two statements appear contradictory, we believe there is no contradiction. Typically, expert systems must exhibit acceptable performance at some early stage of development. But the level of acceptance may be different for differing systems: With a research prototype, medium performance plus indications that the basic approach is correct may be acceptable. As the system is extended, further validation may be necessary but such validation should concentrate on validating the extensions—indicating areas that need improvement or fine-tuning. With noncritical applications such as R1/Xcon, we can validate the system in the field as it's used. In critical applications where lives are at stake or where fortunes are at risk, field-testing is usually impossible (although in certain instances it may be possible to run an expert system in parallel with a traditional system).

How to control the cost of validation Validation can be time consuming and expensive. Assessing the amount of money and effort that should be applied to validation is difficult. We believe that validation costs can be controlled by designing formal validation methods that are integrated within the development process. Clearly, the value of validation links directly to (1) the value of a system to its users, and (2) the risk involved in using a poorly validated system. These ideas will be developed further in a subsequent section.

How to control bias Expert systems may be validated against experts whose expertise is biased when compared with other experts. When judging expert system performance, an expert biased against introducing computer-based systems may unfairly assess the system. Conversely, selecting test cases so as to guarantee good system performance exemplifies developer bias.

We can control expert bias by using blinded evaluation and cross-checking, both employed in Oncocin's validation. [8] When judging performance, experts should not be able to distinguish between human expert and program performance. Using statistical tests, bias between experts can be checked for, as we will discuss later.

Developer bias can be a more difficult problem. Even developers who are honest professionals may be unaware of their biases—while they validate their work thoroughly and objectively, they may be too close to the project to realize broader issues. We can minimize this problem by having a different team validate the expert system; that is, a team replacing the original developers.

How to cope with multiple results When validating an expert system with multiple results, a serious hitch exists—a hitch referred to as the *multiple-response* problem. We cannot appropriately test the validity of a multivariate-response expert system by testing the validity separately for each response variable. Shannon [15] illustrates this problem in validating simulation models. We must use a multivariate approach to incorporate the correlation among results and to test for overall system validity.

In a medical diagnosis system prescribing appropriate drug treatment, for example, two types of drug can be validly prescribed if each is separately considered as a treatment—yet that combination of drugs may be unacceptable. Hence, the overall system response is invalid.

Some basic concepts

This section introduces some basic concepts in expert system validation; namely, the acceptable performance range, input domain, validity testing, validation formality, and the expert system builder's/user's risk.

Acceptable performance range The validation concept should not be considered a binary decision variable in which expert systems are *absolutely* valid or *absolutely* invalid. Since expert systems are representations or abstractions of reality, we cannot expect perfect performance. The performance level acceptable to users is called the *acceptable performance range*, and should be specified during development. In some cases an acceptable performance range can be specified by a government agency, the project sponsor, or a third party.

Suppose that an expert system produces classifications A, B, C, or D. We may be able to specify an acceptable performance range in terms of each result's occurrence. For instance, we may decide that the system should always correctly classify A and B, but that some variation in classifying C and D is acceptable. Further, the probability of a particular incorrect classification may be vital; it may be vital that the system never produces B when the known result is A—that is, *Prob*(B | A) should be shown to be zero.

Frequently, the acceptable performance range will reflect the ability to perform at levels equivalent to human expertise. Bachant and McDermott pointed out that

> . . . the people who used R1 did not demand more of it than of its human predecessors. [9]

Thus, we may be able to specify an acceptable performance range with regard to the performance of human experts that the system models.

The input domain Developers should design an expert system for a specific purpose or application, and should assess system adequacy or validity only in terms of that purpose with regard to a prescribed input domain. An expert system can be valid for one input domain, and completely absurd for another.

Validity testing An expert system can only be tested for validity under a prescribed input domain and for an acceptable performance range related to the system's intended purpose.

Validation formality Validation can range from formal to informal. Formal validation (1) establishes when validation should occur within the development life cycle, and (2) identifies validation methods, input domain specification, the level of acceptance, and (where appropriate) the relevant application of statistical techniques. Informal validation—typically done at the end of development—employs ad hoc methods and is often an afterthought.

Most validation ranges between formal and informal, yet it is generally accepted that validation is too informal—that developers do not consider their approach to validation early enough, and hence do not build it into the development life cycle.

Builder's/user's risk Validity testing results in four possible outcomes (see FIG. 4-1), including type I and type II errors. Type I error results if system validity is rejected when it's sufficiently valid. Type II error results if system validity is accepted when it's invalid. We call the probability to type I error *builder's risk*, and the probability of type II error *user's risk*. Balci and Sargent have quantified these risks in using statistical hypothesis testing for the validation of simulation models. [16]

		State of the expert system	
		System is Valid	System is Invalid
Action	Accept as valid	Correct decision	System user's risk (Type II error)
	Declare invalid	System builder's risk (Type I error)	Correct decision

Fig. 4-1. Types of risk in validation.

Type I error unnecessarily increases expert system developmental costs; these additional costs may not be negligible and can precipitate abandoning systems that have taken much effort to develop. Type II error, on the other hand, has more dramatic consequences; for example, a medical diagnostic system that incorrectly diagnoses illness can cause patients to suffer through mistreatment. Therefore, we must minimize user's risk in critical applications. Objective consideration of these risk types, their relative importance, and the cost if each should occur, will help provide a basis for validation design.

Qualitative validation

Qualitative validation employs subjective comparisons of performance. This does not imply that such approaches are informal; we can design highly formal qualitative validation. Where appropriate, qualitative and quantitative methods can be combined. If expert system responses can somehow be quantified (that is, expressed in numbers), then we can employ quantitative (statistical) techniques.

This section reviews seven common qualitative approaches to validation, some of which have been used to validate expert system performance.

Face validation Face validation is a useful preliminary approach to validation. Project team members, potential expert system users, and people knowledgeable about the application domain—all using their knowledge and intuition—subjectively compare system performance against human expert performance. They assess at face value, with regard to a prescribed acceptable performance range, the results obtained from an expert system running under a given set of test cases.

A group of six experts validated R1/Xcon, reviewing its performance on fifty orders. [17] Perceived mistakes were rectified prior to installation.

Predictive validation Predictive validation requires using historic test cases and either (1) known results or (2) measures of human expert performance on those cases. An expert system is driven by past input data from the test cases, and its results are compared with corresponding results—either known results or those obtained from the human expert. Hudson et al. used this approach to analyze Emerge. [2]

Turing tests Turing tests validate expert systems against human experts by evaluating human expert performance and system performance without knowing the subject performer's identity. Assessments of system performance can then be compared with assessments of human performance. Such blind evaluation eliminates any pro or con computer bias—a positive side effect. If assessments can be objectively measured (for example, if experts can conclude that test cases were handled correctly or incorrectly, or can assess performance to be expert, good, fair, or poor), then statistical techniques can be used to test for variation between expert systems and human experts, and for consistency between experts.

Chandrasekaran recommends Turing tests for validating medical expert systems. [12] Such tests have been used to validate both MYCIN [7] and Oncocin. [8]

Field tests Field tests place prototypical expert systems in the field, and then seek to perceive performance errors as they occur. From the developer's viewpoint, this offers two considerable advantages: First, it places the burden of testing upon users. Second, acceptable performance ranges are obtained implicitly, since users may cease to report problems when acceptable performance ranges are reached. This may backfire, of course, with users reporting minor problems for the duration of system existence.

Field-testing is possible only in noncritical applications, where users can assess the correctness of expert system performance. Subsequent to its implementation, R1/Xcon underwent considerable field-testing. [9] Incorrect results can be easily observed with R1/Xcon, since the VAX configuration will either not fit together or not work.

Subsystem validation Subsystem validation requires that the expert system be decomposed into subsystems, enabling the performance of each subsystem to be observed under given input data. In this approach, subsystems are validated one at a time as they are developed.

Subsystem validation has three significant advantages: (1) Validation, incorporated within the development life cycle, is carried out along with development; (2) we can validate subsystems more easily since they are less complex and more manageable; and (3) error detection is much easier since errors are localized.

Disadvantages of subsystem validation are (1) it may not be possible to observe the input-output behavior of a subsystem, and (2) successfully validating each subsystem does not imply overall system validity since accumulated error tolerances can be significant in overall system performance.

In some instances, we might identify a subsystem in which all possible outputs can be generated for all possible inputs; for example, this could occur in production rule systems where a rule set applies crisp logical inference on a limited discrete input domain. If we gather user's judgments on a continuous scale and use them as certainty factors, we can simulate subsystem performance over the range of permissible input. Langlotz et al. provide a relevant example. [18]

Sensitivity analysis We perform sensitivity analysis by systematically changing expert system input variable values and parameters over some range of interest and observing the effect upon system performance. Consider a system that gives complete satisfaction (that is, if intermediate results, the final result, and reasoning are all assessed to be sufficiently expert) when dealing with case C. If C uses inputs (such as data and user's judgments) $i_1, i_2, \ldots, i_n$, then sensitivity analysis validation would involve altering each input and assessing the change in system performance. For instance, if i_3 is the patient's temperature and our satisfactory consultation case included a 101-degree temperature—and if, in addition, we know that temperature should have no effect on diagnosing this case—then altering i_3 to any other value (while leaving i_1, i_2, and $i_4, i_5, \ldots, i_n$ as before) should not alter intermediate results, the final result, or perhaps even the reasoning process.

To our knowledge, expert system developers have not used sensitivity analysis for validation—at least not explicitly. However, sensitivity analysis may be the most powerful qualitative method at hand: It is especially useful where few or no test cases are available. It is also highly appropriate for systems using uncertainty measures and requiring users to provide judgments for premise uncertainty, since these can be altered as desired and the effect on intermediate and final uncertainty measures can be examined.

Visual interaction Visual interactive validation provides visual animation of expert system workings and allows experts to interact, altering parameters as desired. In essence, we can view this as an environment for interactive face validation, subsystem validation, and sensitivity analysis. Visual interaction has been successfully employed in validating operations research models—particularly discrete-event simulations. [19]

This validation approach could apply to expert systems, particularly with the appearance of graphical interfaces to knowledge-based systems (Guidon-Watch, [20] for example). Experts studying the reasoning process, rules access, and uncertainty propagation can thereby validate the reasoning process.

Quantitative validation

Quantitative validation employs statistical techniques to compare expert system performance against either test cases or human experts. We will discuss the applicability of three quantitative methods: (1) paired *t*-tests, (2) Hotelling's one-sample T^2 test, and (3) simultaneous confidence intervals. We will then address consistency measuring between experts—an important issue when performing validation against multiple experts.

Quantitative validation methods generally fall into two categories: Either we construct a *confidence interval* for one or more measures and subjectively compare it with an acceptable performance range, or we use a formal *hypothesis test* to compare measurements with a predetermined acceptable performance range where the hypotheses are

H_0: The expert system is valid for the acceptable performance range under the prescribed input domain.
H_1: The expert system is invalid for the acceptable performance range under the prescribed input domain.

Paired *t*-tests Producing a single proportion as a performance measure has limited value. We can use a paired *t*-test more appropriately to compare the difference between observed results. We can measure the difference between expert system performance and human expert performance or known results by D_i where $D_i = X_i - Y_i$, X_i are system results, and Y_i are either known results or results from human expert performance. For n test cases, there will be n observed differences D_i to D_n.

This method covers many types of result. If final judgments are produced on a continuous scale (for example, as is -5 to $+5$ in Prospector), then X_i can be the system's judgment, and Y_i can be the human expert's judgment. If both known results and expert performance are known, we can have a third-party expert measure the performance of each on a scale of 1 to 10, under blind evaluation, and thus X_i and Y_i will be the absolute performance of the system and the expert, respectively.

For the differences D_i, the following confidence interval can be produced:

$$d \pm t_{n-1,\alpha/2} S_d / \sqrt{n}$$

where d is the mean difference, S_d the standard deviation, and $t_{n-1,\alpha/2}$ the value from the t distribution with n degrees of freedom. If zero lies in the confidence interval, then we can accept H_0.

Hotelling's one-sample T² test A previous section discussed the problems of multivariate responses. While a paired *t*-test is appropriate when systems produce a single final result, simultaneously applying a paired *t*-test to a number of final results is inappropriate since we can expect the final results to be correlated (see the previous section on multiple results). In such cases, Hotelling's one-sample T^2 test should be used.

Consider validating an expert system against human expert performance. We give each exactly the same input. Assuming that we have k responses (measurable results) as the expected output, we determine the differences between corresponding k paired responses. Repeating this for different input values, we construct k vectors of differences, one for each response. Then, the one-sample T^2 test is used to determine if the means of the difference vectors are significantly different from zero simultaneously (or jointly). This method has been used to validate multivariate-response trace-driven simulation models. [21]

Simultaneous confidence intervals To validate multivariate-response expert systems, we can construct simultaneous confidence intervals or joint confidence regions for differences of paired responses. Usually, we compare confidence intervals or regions constructed with a prescribed acceptable performance range. This method has been used to validate simulation models. [22]

Consistency measures If we wish to compare an expert system with multiple experts—or to compare multiple experts with a system in a Turing test—then consistency between experts (often called *interobserver reliability*) is a major consideration. The interclass correlation coefficient, a commonly used consistency measure, has been used to evaluate reliability between legal judges: If a judgment by expert i on test case j is denoted Y_{ij}, then a model for expert reliability is $Y_{ij} = \mu + E_i + \epsilon_{ij}$ where μ is the mean rating across all experts, E_i is the effect of the ith expert (that is, deviation from the mean μ), and ϵ_{ij} is the error term. From this model, we can produce and test a correlation coefficient. If Y_{ij} is a categorical variable (such as expert, good, fair, or poor), rather than a continuous variable, then we can use the kappa statistic to measure reliability. [23]

We can use a related statistic to compare joint expert agreement with system agreement. [24] This is appropriate in Turing tests, which aggregate multiple expert judgment; for example, where the system performs a task normally performed by related experts. Fleiss discusses other tests, including confidence interval approaches. [25]

As was once the case with knowledge acquisition, performance validation is seen as a black art. Yet few would disagree that expert systems should exhibit acceptable and reliable performance levels. Validation and evaluation—important concerns for most expert system developers—require considerably more attention then they presently receive. A recapitulation of useful guidelines for validating expert system performance follows.

1. We must validate systems only against an acceptable performance range for a prescribed input domain. Previous human performance indicates the acceptable range.
2. We should build validation into the development cycle. Often, we must carry out a cross-sectional performance validation prior to implementation, and specific validation tests as the system evolves after implementation.
3. We must consider the risks in using invalid systems (user's risk) relative to the risks in not using valid systems (builder's risk).
4. We must choose an appropriate qualitative method: Field-testing may be acceptable for noncritical applications. Turing tests are useful for comparing systems against experts in blinded evaluations, and can avoid pro- or anti-computer bias. Subsystem validation and sensitivity analysis are useful for validating specific areas of concern.
5. We must use quantitative methods where applicable. We must use them as informatively as possible; for instance, to produce confidence intervals rather than single-point estimates. We must be aware of the multiple-response problem, and use appropriate multivariate techniques.

Of necessity, most of this article has been *descriptive*. But expert system developers need a *prescriptive* methodology; that is, one explaining how to validate expert systems under certain conditions (such as consultative or real-time critical applications) and under certain constraints (such as funding and development time). At present, expert system validation experience is limited. A methodology, or methodologies, will evolve only in the light of future collective experience and critical appraisal of that experience.

Acknowledgment

We are grateful to John Roach for providing a number of useful comments.

References

1. V.L. Yu et al., "Evaluating the Performance of a Computer-Based Consultant," *Computer Programs in Biomedicine*, Vol. 9, No. 1, 1979, pp. 95 – 102.
2. D.L. Hudson et al., "Prospective Analysis of Emerge, an Expert System for Chest Pain Analysis," in *IEEE Computers in Cardiology*, IEEE Service Center, Piscataway, N.J., 1984, pp. 19 – 24.
3. J. Gaschnig, "Preliminary Performance Analysis of the Prospector Consultant System for Mineral Exploration," *Proc. Sixth Int'l Joint Conf. Artificial Intelligence*, Morgan Kaufmann, Los Altos, Calif., 1979, pp. 308 – 310.
4. R.A. Miller, H.E. Pople, and J.D. Myers, "Internist-1, An Experimental Computer-Based Diagnostic Consultant for General Internal Medicine," *The New England J. Medicine*, Vol. 307, No. 8, 1982, pp. 468 – 476.
5. C.A. Kulikowski and S.H. Weiss, "Representation of Expert Knowledge for Consultation: The Casnet and Expert Projects," in *Artificial Intelligence in Medicine*, P. Szolovits, ed., Westview Press, Boulder, Colo., 1982, pp. 21 – 56.
6. J.V. Hansen and W.F. Messier, "A Preliminary Investigation of EDP-Xpert," Working Paper 85 – 6, Accounting Research Center, Univ. of Florida, Gainesville, Fla., 1985.
7. V.L. Yu et al., "Antimicrobial Selection by a Computer," *J. Am. Medical Assoc.*, Vol. 242, No. 12, 1979, pp. 1279 – 1282.
8. D.H. Hickam et al., "The Treatment Advice of a Computer-Based Cancer Chemotherapy Protocol Advisor," *Annals of Internal Medicine*, Vol. 103, No. 6 (Part 1), 1985, pp. 928 – 936.
9. J. Bachant and J. McDermott, "R1 Revisited: Four Years in the Trenches," *AI Magazine*, Vol. 5, No. 3, 1984, pp. 21 – 32.
10. J. Gaschnig et al., "Evaluation of Expert Systems: Issues and Case Studies," in *Building Expert Systems*, F. Hayes-Roth, D.A. Waterman, and D.B. Lenat, eds., Addison-Wesley, Reading, Mass., 1983, pp. 241 – 280.
11. R.M. O'Keefe, V. Belton, and T. Ball, "Experiences with Using Expert Systems in O.R.," *J. Operational Research Soc.*, Vol. 37, No. 7, 1986, pp. 657 – 668.
12. B. Chandrasekaran, "On Evaluating AI Systems for Medical Diagnosis," *AI Magazine*, Vol. 4, No. 2, 1983, pp. 34 – 37.
13. W.C. Hetzel, "Principles of Computer Program Testing," in *Program Test Methods*, W.C. Hetzel, ed., Prentice-Hall, Englewood Cliffs, N.J., 1973, pp. 17 – 28.
14. B.G. Buchanan and E.H. Shortliffe, *Rule-Based Systems: The MYCIN Experiments of the Stanford Heuristic Programming Project*, Addison-Wesley, Reading, Mass., 1984.
15. R.E. Shannon, *Systems Simulation: The Art and Science*, Prentice-Hall, Englewood Cliffs, N.J., 1975.
16. O. Balci and R.G. Sargent, "A Methodology for Cost-Risk Analysis in the Statistical Validation of Simulation Models," *Comm. ACM*, Vol. 24, No. 4, 1981, pp. 190 – 197.
17. J. McDermott, "R1: The Formative Years," *AI Magazine*, Vol. 2, No. 2, 1981, pp. 21 – 29.
18. C.P. Langlotz, E.H. Shortliffe, and L.M. Fagan, "Using Decision Theory to Justify Heuristics," *Proc. AAAI 86*, Menlo Park, Calif., 1986, pp. 215 – 219.
19. P.C. Bell, "Visual Interactive Modeling In Operational Research: Successes and Opportunities," *J. Operational Research Soc.*, Vol. 36, No. 11, 1985, pp. 975 – 982.
20. M.H. Richer and W.J. Clancey, "Guidon-Watch: A Graphic Interface for Viewing a Knowledge-Based System," *IEEE Computer Graphics and Applications*, Nov. 1985, pp. 51 – 64.

21. O. Balci and R.G. Sargent, "Validation of Multivariate-Response Trace-Driven Simulation Models," in *Performance '83*, A.K. Agrawala and S.K. Tripathi, eds., North-Holland, New York, N.Y., 1983, pp. 309–323.
22. O. Balci and R.G. Sargent, "Validation of Simulation Models Via Simultaneous Confidence Intervals," *Am. J. Math. and Management Sciences*, Vol. 4, Nos. 3 and 4, 1984, pp. 375–406.
23. J. Cohen, "Weighted Kappa: Nominal Scale Agreement with Provision for Scaled Disagreement or Partial Credit," *Psychological Bulletin*, Vol. 70, No. 4, 1968, pp. 213–220.
24. G.W. Williams, "Comparing the Joint Agreement of Several Raters With Another Rater," *Biometrics*, Vol. 32, No. 2, 1976, pp. 619–627.
25. J.L. Fleiss, *Statistical Methods for Rates and Proportions*, John Wiley and Sons, New York, N.Y., 1981.

Part II

Tools and techniques

Part II of the book provides additional depth to the discussions of technology in Part I. The purpose of the six papers in Part II is to begin to transfer expertise from the field to the reader. While AI is complex and multidisciplinary, it is by no means incomprehensible. The tools and techniques of AI are now quite developed (though by no means omnipotent, as some would have us believe).

Part II attempts to explain the mainstay of AI: knowledge engineering. The elicitation of knowledge from domain experts, or codified doctrine, policies, and procedures can be time-consuming, tedious, and cost-ineffective. If done improperly the knowledge base that drives an expert system, for example, will be shallow and brittle, and provide nowhere near the expertise necessary to solve the problem at hand. However, when done well, a truly useful expert system can emerge.

There are many ways to represent knowledge. Some of the tools include production rules, frames, semantic networks, inference networks, and scripts, as well as the myriad hybrids. Most of us are very familiar with "if-then" production rules: *if gold falls below $250 per ounce, then invest 50% of the portfolio in gold* is a rule that an investment counselor might apply.

Other issues are addressed in Part II, such as how to deal with incomplete and ambiguous information, and how to program knowledge-based applications in languages other than the famous list processing (LISP) language.

Forsythe and Buchanan introduce Part II with a look at the process by which knowledge is acquired and represented from domain experts. The paper is prescriptive, offering suggestions for how to enhance the process by which we extract, model and represent heuristic problem-solving processes.

Rook and Croghan relate knowledge acquisition and engineering to some well understood concepts drawn from "conventional" systems engineering. In and of itself this contribution is important because it addresses the synergism between systems analysis, design, engineering and testing, and the design and development of knowledge-based systems.

Steven Salzberg looks at knowledge representation in the real world. Like many of the papers in this sourcebook, Salzberg's looks at the knowledge engineering process from the trenches. He offers some insights from the perspective of someone who has had to acquire and represent knowledge from imperfect domain experts in organizations that do not always adequately support the knowledge engineering process.

Butler, Hodil, Richardson, Coffee and Strauss all deal with the conversion of rules, frames, scripts, and inference networks into working computer programs. Not so many years ago, if you failed to program in LISP, SAIL or FUZZY you were disenfranchised from the AI community; more recently, practitioners have learned that many high-level languages can be used to implement knowledge-based systems. C, Ada and others have been used successfully to field and maintain expert and other knowledge-based systems. (We also now appreciate alternative platforms to the so-called "LISP machines" of the late 1970s and early 1980s. Today, knowledge-based systems can be developed even on personal computers, certainly on workstations, and—of course—on a variety of minicomputers and mainframes.)

Part II is intended to provide additional technical details about intelligent systems technology. It is comprised of papers that address the mainstay of AI—knowledge engineering, but also papers that address some of the important knowledge processing issues, such as uncertainty management and (conventional) software engineering.

Part II deals with the essential difference between conventional systems engineering and the engineering of intelligent systems. The emphasis is on knowledge and knowledge processing, not on data and data processing.

Parts I and II together constitute an AI primer. The papers selected for publication in these first two parts of the sourcebook should well prepare you to tackle the essence of the book, the applications in Part III.

5

Knowledge acquisition for expert systems
Some pitfalls and suggestions

Diana E. Forsythe
Bruce G. Buchanan

Editors' note *This paper deals with a problem that few analysts have tackled. The focus here is on the communication process between knowledge engineers and domain experts, between those who elicit knowledge and those who provide it. It is widely believed that unless the relationship between the knowledge engineer(s) and the domain expert(s) is productive, then development of the knowledge base will suffer. The paper presents some new ideas for enhancing communication. It is reprinted here because it deals with an extremely important aspect of the knowledge-based systems design process in a practical manner. (Reprinted with permission from the May/June 1989 issue of* IEEE Transactions on Systems, Man and Cybernetics. *©1989, IEEE. All rights reserved.)*

I. Introduction

Although the technology of representing and using knowledge in expert systems has been a major focus of artificial intelligence (AI) research for three decades, the practical problems of building such systems have only recently become a topic of research. In this paper we address the problem of identifying and mitigating difficulties of communication in the process of eliciting information from one or more human experts for the purpose of building a knowledge base.[1]

Knowledge acquisition (KA) has come to be seen as a bottleneck in the process of building expert systems [1]. This task, sometimes called "extracting knowledge from

[1] In this paper we distinguish between "knowledge acquisition" and "knowledge elicitation." Knowledge acquisition typically involves gathering information from one or more human experts and/or from documentary sources, ordering that information in some way, and then translating it into machine-readable form. Sometimes knowledge acquisition includes face-to-face interviewing of the expert(s) by the knowledge engineer(s). We refer to this interview process as "knowledge elicitation."

human experts," can be slow, inefficient, and frustrating for expert and knowledge engineer alike. As Stefik and Conway [2] noted,

> ". . . knowledge acquisition is sometimes considered a necessary burden, carried out under protest so that one can get on with the study of cognitive processes in problem solving."

Several years later [3], the same problem persists:

> "Collecting and encoding the knowledge needed to build an ITS [intelligent tutoring system] is still a long and difficult task and substantial project resources must still be allocated to this stage. Of course, the lack of good high-level tools for knowledge acquisition is a serious problem . . ."

There have been numerous attempts to solve the knowledge acquisition bottleneck. One approach has involved the development of automated or semi-automated methods of knowledge acquisition. These include intelligent editors, such as Teiresias [4], Roget [5], Mole [6], More [7], and ETS [8]. Another approach has been the creation of tools for aiding in the conceptualization of a knowledge base. Such tools include protocol analysis [9] and personal construct theory [10]. A third approach involves the development of heuristics for knowledge engineering [1], [11].

Characteristic of all such proposed solutions from within the AI community is a tendency to focus on higher-level issues such as classifying information collected from the expert or ensuring that this information is complete, while glossing over detailed questions of how to gather the material in the first place. Although KA typically requires a lengthy interview process, it would be impossible to learn how to carry out an interview from the AI literature alone. When actual problems of face-to-face data collection are addressed, reference to such notions as "chemistry" and "rapport" implies a certain sense of helplessness among practitioners about how to approach the task [12]. While recent publications have come closer to addressing some of the practicalities of interviewing for KA [13]–[18], they still suffer from the general tendency to name methods without providing much information on how to apply them.[2] To date

---

[2] To illustrate this point, we take an example from one of the better recent books on the subject of KA methodology. On "The elicitation of data on domain knowledge," Breuker and Wielinga [46] provide the following advice: "Because written sources hardly ever contain information on how knowledge is used, other data have to be elicited from experts by interview techniques, and in particular by thinking-aloud procedures." They then name six "elicitation techniques" and list the types of data each is intended to elicit. Although this passage appears in a volume intended as a practical handbook, however, and Breuker and Wielinga are clearly aware that knowledge elicitation is not just a matter of common sense, they do not in fact provide practical information on how to carry out the procedures they name. Reading the passages mentioned here, for example, the reader is left with such questions as the following. What sort of "focused interview," "thinking-aloud procedures," and so forth do the authors have in mind here, and how should a knowledge engineer go about learning and applying them? What do "factual knowledge," "support knowledge," etc. mean, and how can a knowledge engineer recognize them?

there is nothing in the AI literature that could serve as a useful "how to" guide for the novice knowledge engineer.[3]

In short, we know a good deal about how to represent and manipulate knowledge in expert systems, but have very little systematic understanding of how best to gather that knowledge in the first place. Attention to this problem is a priority for speeding up and teaching knowledge acquisition. Recognition of this state of affairs prompted us to approach the knowledge acquisition problem from a new perspective. Reasoning that the design of heuristics for knowledge acquisition should begin with a detailed understanding of the knowledge elicitation process itself, we decided to undertake research on that topic.

This paper presents our initial report on this research. The first section introduces the interdisciplinary anthropological study of knowledge elicitation (ASKE) project. Next, we discuss the choice of anthropological methodology for the project, pointing out the relevance of anthropology to knowledge engineering in general. In the third section we give examples of pitfalls that we have observed in the knowledge elicitation process, including problems related to both interviewing technique and conceptual approach. And finally, we draw some preliminary conclusions based on our work to date.

II. An empirical study of knowledge elicitation

In 1986 we inaugurated a research initiative on knowledge acquisition. One of the projects begun under that initiative is the ASKE project, which uses anthropological methods to analyze knowledge elicitation as a process of face-to-face communication. ASKE is a qualitative empirical study: we are observing and analyzing the processes by which knowledge engineers acquire and order the domain knowledge to be encoded in their systems. The outcome of this research will be an improved understanding of the KA process itself—including some of its pitfalls—and the development of heuristics for coping with or (better yet) avoiding such difficulties.

We recognize that many factors determine the success or failure of a knowledge engineering effort. For example, knowledge engineers must be technically competent. Communication skills on the part of both knowledge engineers and experts are clearly important, as are many other social and technical factors involved in building a computer program for human use. In this study, we have chosen to focus primarily on the communication skills of the knowledge engineer as one important determinant of success.

ASKE is an interdisciplinary project primarily involving anthropology and AI. The central component of the project is observation of face-to-face knowledge elicitation in a range of scientific and engineering projects, including both academic and commercial

[3] Several companies, including Digital Equipment Corporation, Texas Instruments, and Teknowledge, have created training courses in knowledge engineering methodology. However, since the written materials that accompany these courses are not in the public domain, we are unable to evaluate their contents.

settings. These observational data are supplemented with material drawn from interviews with AI professionals and from extended participant observation in a Silicon Valley AI lab. In addition, we draw upon data taken from our own videotapes of novice knowledge engineers engaged in practice interviews with real experts.

Anthropology is involved in two ways. First, we are using anthropological field methods to gather information about communication during the knowledge acquisition process. Second, we believe that some of the same methods (in particular, participant observation and interviewing methods) are appropriate approaches to include in the repertoire of knowledge engineering.

This study has been underway for a year and a half, and is still in progress. To date Forsythe has completed eighteen months of participant observation in the AI lab, over 200 h of formal meeting observations involving 12 projects, and about 80 h of formal observation of KA sessions. Of the latter, ten hours were recorded on videotape.

III. The appropriateness of anthropological methodology

While artificial intelligence has drawn heavily on linguistics and psychology, it has paid much less attention to the neighboring disciplines of anthropology and qualitative sociology.[4] In the areas of both problem definition and methodology, however, there is a great deal of overlap between the concerns of AI and those of these other social science disciplines. With respect to the definition of problems for research, all three are concerned with investigating how human beings understand, organize, process and make use of symbolic information. With respect to methodology, anthropologists and qualitative sociologists rely on the same primary data-gathering methods as knowledge engineers—face-to-face interviewing of one or more specialist individuals, supplemented by the use of documentary evidence and observational data. From the standpoint of a social scientist this disciplinary overlap is striking,[5] a fact reflected in a growing literature in which the methods of anthropology and sociology have been applied to the analysis of AI-related problems [19]–[28].

There are also some noteworthy differences between these disciplines, two of which deserve mention here because of their potential utility for AI. First, whereas AI is a relatively new discipline with a newly-emerging body of theory, the social sciences have built up an extensive literature on the nature and functioning of human intelligence in a range of naturally occurring cultural, social and material contexts. This liter-

[4] The lack of discussion about possible connections between sociology and AI has been noted by Woolgar, [47] who comments: "Although the associations between AI, on the one hand, and disciplines like psychology and philosophy, on the other, have been widely recognized and lengthily debated in terms of the implications of one for the other, the important possibility of an association between AI and *sociology* has hardly been noticed. On the few occasions it is alluded to, sociology is assigned the role of dealing with matters left over by other disciplines" [original emphasis].

[5] In fact, from a methodological standpoint knowledge engineering would seem to have more in common with the fieldwork orientation of anthropology and qualitative sociology than with the experimental orientation of many in the cognitive sciences.

ature can offer AI some relevant theory and vocabulary. It can also serve as a useful counterbalance to the psychological data derived from contrived experimental settings on which many AI researchers rely for information about the nature of human thought. Second, while (as we have noted) the AI literature contains little discussion of data-gathering methodology for knowledge acquisition, the conduct of face-to-face research has been a major topic in anthropology and qualitative sociology, again resulting in a large body of literature.

Two sections of that literature are of particular interest for knowledge engineers. First, the discussion on qualitative methodology [29], especially interview methodology [30]–[32], offers numerous pointers for increasing the success of knowledge elicitation and analysis. Second, the literature on the ethnographic method of research used by anthropologists discusses ways of combining directive and nondirective interviewing with observation and the use of documentary material. Ethnographic methodology has been developed to facilitate data-gathering in the informal, unstructured, and sometimes unpredictable situations typically encountered by anthropologists in the course of field research [33]–[35]. It is particularly relevant to knowledge engineers for two reasons. First, knowledge elicitation involves data-gathering under conditions that are in many ways comparable to those in which anthropologists are accustomed to work. For example, the ethnographic approach explicitly recognizes the fact that in the early stages of research, knowledge engineers/fieldworkers not only do not know the answers they are seeking, they do not even know the right questions to ask. Becoming familiar with a particular domain implies learning to understand the types of questions and answers that have meaning in that domain. And second, the method promotes the collection of uncodified "common sense" knowledge as well as knowledge that is formally ordered. As AI researchers have noted, both kinds of knowledge may be necessary if expert systems are to function in anything but very narrowly specified domains [36], [37].

Recognition of the common ground between anthropology and artificial intelligence is just beginning to emerge in the AI community:

> "Anthropologists, it could be argued, are also in the ontology and inventory business. They visit foreign cultures and as part of their field work, attempt to compile an explicit ontology. We believe that KA for systems development is fundamentally an anthropological activity."[38]

The ASKE project grew out of the insight that this overlap can be of considerable benefit to knowledge engineers. Not only do the theory and methodology of the social sciences constitute a valuable resource for AI, but the ethnographic method itself can be applied to contribute to the analysis and solution of the knowledge acquisition problem.

IV. Some pitfalls of knowledge elicitation

There is a great deal more to understanding what an expert says and does than what one can obtain from interview material alone, or from interview material supplemented by textbooks. Such material is not self-evident: it must be interpreted [20], [39]. This job requires, for example, that one sift through the experts' reports about their own thoughts and actions, and add in information that was not reported but that is necessary for understanding the nature of their expertise. This may include tacit knowledge [40], contextual information, and unreported actions that experts may or may not be aware of, but which nevertheless constitute part of the process being modeled. For instance, in a project modeling the expertise of a scientist skilled at assessing the credibility of statistical studies, the expert produced a detailed list of formal statistical criteria that he used to judge methodological quality. After hours of watching him engaged in this task, however, we realized that he consistently paid attention to other information that he had not reported. This included social factors (e.g., the reputation of the statisticians involved in the studies, and whether or not he knew them personally).

To an anthropologist it appears obvious that the best approach to knowledge elicitation would be to apply ethnographic methodology. In this case, knowledge engineers would attach themselves to an expert or group of experts as participant observers for a period of weeks or months. This would enable them to learn as much as possible about a particular sort of expertise by observing, questioning, and attempting to apply the skills themselves, while simultaneously learning about the social and material context in which the expertise is normally constituted and practiced. Such participant observation would provide knowledge engineers with the opportunity to notice and collect informal, uncodified information, some of which may not be directly accessible to the experts themselves.

At the present time, however, few knowledge engineers have received any training in ethnographic methods and few seem open to trying this approach. On the contrary, under pressure of time and money, most appear to want to spend less rather than more time with their experts [23]. Recognizing this state of affairs, we focus here on proposing change of a more modest kind. Since knowledge elicitation generally involves face-to-face interviews with one or more experts, the discussion below aims at encouraging knowledge engineers to undertake these interviews in a more informed and self-conscious way.

Knowledge engineers—particularly novices—can encounter various difficulties in connection with the communication aspects of knowledge acquisition. In this section we list examples of two of the types of pitfalls that we have observed during interview sessions.[6] Errors of the first type reflect problems in interview technique, in which the knowledge engineer mis-applies or fails to apply appropriate interview strategies. Errors of the second type involve inappropriate assumptions that knowledge engineers may bring to the job of face-to-face data-gathering.

Maxims for knowledge engineering have been formulated before. They tend to be extremely general, not to be based upon systematic observation of knowledge acquisition, and not for the most part to concern themselves with problems of communication

---

[6] These are only two out of several possible types of pitfalls. Our data also demonstrate that knowledge engineers encounter difficulties that relate to such factors as nonverbal communication and the spatial organization of the interview setting. In latter publications we will present further material on pitfalls in knowledge elicitation. We will also take up related questions such as the problem of knowledge engineering configuration (e.g., the effects on knowledge elicitation of the size, structure, and composition of the knowledge engineering team and the expert team).

between knowledge engineer and expert. For example, of the 43 maxims offered by Buchanan *et al.* [1], only three relate to knowledge elicitation.[7] In contrast, the communicative processes of knowledge elicitation are our major concern. We are particularly interested in alerting knowledge engineers to the importance of communication on the nonverbal as well as the verbal level. Although few knowledge engineers seem to be aware of this fact, the way in which they ask questions of the expert may influence the success of their enterprise as much as the content of those questions.

A. Interviewing problems

Because interviewing takes place through the medium of conversation, and because the latter is an everyday activity, knowledge engineers sometimes assume that KA is just a matter of chatting with the expert. As Gorden [41] comments, "To the uninitiated, interviewing is 'just talking to people!' " The influence of this attitude among knowledge engineers can be seen in two examples from the literature. First, in an article on "methods for knowledge acquisition," Olson and Rueter [42] describe interviewing in the following terms:

> "Interviews are the most common method for eliciting knowledge from the expert. In conversation, the expert reveals the objects he/she thinks about, how they are related or organized, and the process he/she goes through in making a judgment, solving a problem, or designing a solution. There are simple guidelines that can be followed to make interviewing efficient."

Second, one of Gammack's "rules of thumb" is, "If interviewing comes naturally to both parties, then interview methods may be fruitful."[43]

These statements sound naive. Interviewing does not just happen: the knowledge engineer must make it happen. Far from coming naturally, interviewing is a difficult task that requires planning, stage-management, technique, and a lot of self-control. It also demands skills very different from—indeed, in some cases opposite to—those usually required of graduate students, corporate employees, or programmers. Unfortunately, it is very easy to interview badly, with the result that one may learn little and/or alienate the expert. Below we outline some of the shoals that knowledge engineers must navigate during the interview process. No simple solutions are presented here; indeed, interviewing is such a particularistic process that no general solutions could be presented to many of these problems. Rather, our goal is to increase awareness of the problems themselves, since that is the first step toward finding appropriate solutions.

1) Obtaining data versus relating to the expert as a person Experts are people with personalities and agendas of their own, and they frequently have the authority to refuse further interviews. Successful interviewing requires negotiating and maintaining a balance between obtaining data and acknowledging the expert as a person and a professional. To some extent, these two goals are in conflict: our data include examples of interviewers who were highly personable but didn't learn much about their

---

[7] Buchanan et al. urge the knowledge engineer to "record a detailed protocol of the expert solving at least one prototypical case" [1, p. 161], to "use the terms and methods that the experts use" [1, p. 164], and to "watch (the expert) doing examples" as well as talking with him/her [1, p. 164].

topic, and others who were so topic-oriented that the expert felt irritated and even abused. Concerning a knowledge engineer in the first category, the expert commented, "He wasted my time." Concerning one in the second, the expert said, "He treated me like a dog!"

2) Twin dangers of over- and under-directedness Interviewing also requires maintaining a balance between being directive and being responsive. This principle applies in several senses, including both decisions concerning the subject-matter of particular interviews and the degree of intrusiveness used by the interviewer in steering the expert. Knowledge engineers must find a middle ground between deciding upon an approach and a list of questions beforehand, and being completely open to changing approach on the basis of what the interviewee says and does. Similarly, they must consciously weigh the cost in time and efficiency of letting a loquacious expert carry on at will, versus the possible cost in good-will (and possibly data) of interrupting repeatedly to keep the expert on course. Again, our data include a range of examples. Some interviewers were so preplanned that they ignored the expert when he/she showed irritation or suggested that their approach was inappropriate. For example, some stuck stubbornly to a case-based approach when the interviewee was trying to tell them rules. On the other hand, some interviewers were so nondirective and so unplanned that they simply floundered without appearing to have any approach in mind. Surprisingly, perhaps, some interviewers managed during the same session to be both under- and overdirective, veering between the two extremes. Once again, the goal is balance: steering the interviewee gently while remaining open to the possibility of having to change course.

3) Fear of silence and failing to listen Some interviewers don't allow the expert sufficient time to speak. This may be the result of nervousness and/or a rapid interactional rhythm on the part of the interviewer. Novice knowledge engineers may confuse an interview with an examination, and waste time unnecessarily trying to demonstrate their own competence to the expert. Simple as it sounds, it is imperative to learn to listen; for many interviewers this requires considerable self-control. Silence is an ally in this task. Knowledge engineers should not be afraid to sit silently for a while in case the expert has more to add, or in order to gather their own thoughts. We observed knowledge engineers who were so afraid to let the conversation lag that they fired questions at the expert without really listening to the responses. In such cases no one's goals were met: the experts were offended because they didn't feel they had been heard, while the knowledge engineers gathered information that was less accurate than it could have been.

4) Difficulty asking questions Asking good questions well is an art. Knowledge engineers may encounter several problems in this area. First, for some knowledge engineers, questioning the expert at all is clearly difficult. The age, gender, status, and cultural background of both interviewer and expert are likely to affect this situation. After all, an interview is a social encounter as well as a professional one. It is impossible usefully to prescribe a particular strategy or style: our observations illustrate that the tactics appropriate in any particular situation depend on the individual knowledge engineer and expert involved. For example, of two female experts we have observed so far, one preferred to be treated deferentially; she responded best to female interviewers and to a young male knowledge engineer of Chinese background. In contrast, the other expert responded well to a less deferential approach, apparently pleased that a rather brash male interviewer found her approachable. Clearly, face-to-face knowledge acquisition demands considerable sensitivity and flexibility on the part of the knowledge engineer (and the expert) to be able to assess and adjust to the social constraints posed by the interview. Whatever the tone of the interaction, the interviewer must actively question the expert. The worst pitfall of all is to fail to ask for information.

Second, since the questions one asks influence the answers one gets, knowledge engineers need to pay attention to question formulation. Almost everyone finds it challenging to formulate carefully worded questions that are appropriate to a particular domain, interactional situation, and stage of research. This is especially difficult when the domain is unfamiliar. Payne [44] provides a useful discussion of some of the issues involved in question formulation. Our own observations suggest that novice knowledge engineers in particular should beware of the following.

- Asking long, complicated, repetitious questions. Ask one short, clear question at a time and then stop talking. Resist the temptation to repeat and elaborate questions.
- Using AI vocabulary not necessarily known to the respondent. Try to speak the expert's language.

Third, a lack of awareness of different types of questions makes it difficult to conduct an interview. Knowledge engineers must have at their command a repertoire of questions that perform such tasks as:

- probing for further information ("Tell me more about that") and checking for completeness ("Is there anything else?");
- asking for clarification ("I don't understand; could you explain?", "How does that relate to our topic?");
- following up points mentioned by the expert ("How/why/when do you do that?", "What do you do next?");
- prompting to keep the expert talking ("I see", "Um hmm');
- feeding back information to check on its accuracy ("Let me try to summarize—please correct me if I'm wrong").

5) Interviewing without a record Interviewing is difficult in part because it requires the knowledge engineer to pay attention on many levels at once. In addition to asking questions and monitoring progress on the substantive level, knowledge engineers must maintain awareness of time, personality, interactional and sometimes political factors, as well as hardware and software requirements of the proposed expert system. Given these demands, it is inevitable that the interviewer will miss—or fail to grasp the significance of—some of what the expert says. Therefore, it is necessary that some sort of objective record of each interview be maintained. The easiest and least obtrusive recording device is a small tape recorder. Like many of our points in this section, this may appear obvious; but only a minority of the knowledge engineers we have observed have actually recorded their sessions on tape. Too often, knowledge engineers seem to trust their memories and their handwritten notes.

To sum up these comments on interview technique, no single approach or method will work all the time; rather, an interviewer must be able to draw upon a repertoire of approaches. It pays to prepare carefully ahead of time, planning what seems like a sensible way of focusing the interview, but remaining flexible in case this turns out not to be the best way of doing things. An interview is a social occasion during which social convention and personalities enter in significant ways. It is necessary to analyze the expert's personality, interactional style, and tolerances, and adapt oneself to them. This requires flexibility. Knowledge engineers also need to be aware of their own personality, interactional style, etc., and to try to keep them under control while interviewing.

B. Conceptual problems

A second category of pitfalls in knowledge acquisition is conceptual errors that have methodological implications. Three such assumptions will be mentioned here.

1) Treating interview methodology as unproblematic Some knowledge engineers seem to perceive the question of interview methodology as trivial or "just a matter of common sense" [23]. One AI professional we interviewed likened explicit discussion of how to interview to telling grown-ups how to tie their shoes. In response, we would like to point out that common sense is anything but common: as Minsky [45] notes, "what people vaguely call common sense is actually far more intricate than most of the technical expertise we admire." The KA bottleneck is a matter of clear concern to knowledge engineers themselves. We suggest that there is a connection between this bottleneck and the apparent reluctance to take seriously the question of interview methodology. This point has major implications for expert systems development, because interview technique may affect the quality of the data gathered as well as the time it takes to collect them. If the information that goes into a knowledge base is poorly understood or incomplete, the most sophisticated representation or inference schemes will not produce a good system. As Gorden [41, p. 4] points out:

> "It is clear that no amount of refinement in data analysis can counteract the effects of faulty data-collection methods that provide raw information which is false, distorted, or incomplete. Nevertheless, there is still a tendency for the advances in data-gathering methodology to lag behind those in data analysis."

Gorden [41, pp. 4 – 5] identifies several causes of this attitude, two of which are relevant here:

> "First, there is an unfortunate tendency to consider data gathering as a lower status activity than data analysis or theorizing about the data . . .. Another barrier to the actual application of the best data-gathering methods is the fact that it often costs more in time or money to collect valid data than it does to collect invalid data. Of course, this is a false economy if any real decisions are to be based on the data."

2) Blaming the expert Knowledge engineers often blame the expert for difficulties encountered in the elicitation process. This attitude was expressed in interviews; for example, one experienced knowledge engineer asserted that "experts are a cantankerous lot." It is also reflected in the literature (e.g., [12]). However, where AI scientists resort to speculation about the psychological difficulties of experts in dealing with knowledge engineers or computers, the experienced ethnographic fieldworker suspects a lack of interviewing expertise on the part of the knowledge engineers involved and/or an inappropriate pairing between interviewer and expert.

3) Reifying knowledge Knowledge engineers appear to think of knowledge as a material entity, a thing that lends itself to extraction like a diseased tooth [23]. As Kidd also pointed out, the language used to talk about knowledge acquisition serves to obscure the nature of the process.

> "A popular view of KA has been to consider experts' heads as being filled with bits of knowledge and the problem of KA as being one of 'mining those jewels of knowledge out of their heads one by one' [Feigenbaum and McCorduck, 1983] . . .. The analogy is misleading; there is no *truth* in that sense. Rather, it is the case that KA involves the following:
>
> 1. Employing a technique to elicit data (usually verbal) from the expert.
> 2. Interpreting these verbal data (more or less skillfully) in order to infer what might be the expert's underlying knowledge and reasoning process.
> 3. Using this interpretation to guide the construction of some model or language that describes (more or less accurately) the expert's knowledge and performance.
>
> . . . Knowledge engineers need to recognize that this is the basic process in which they are engaging . . ." [48].[8]

Rather than conceptualizing knowledge as a material entity, we suggest that it is more useful to view it as shared understanding produced through the collaborative efforts of interviewers and respondents [49], [50]. Knowledge that may be needed by knowledge engineers is "stored" not only in the experts' conscious models but also in their unarticulated understanding of the world and the task at hand, and in the social and physical milieux that form the normal context of the experts' work [20], [22], [28].

V. The nontechnical nature of these pitfalls

Accustomed to thinking in terms of technical problems with technical solutions, knowledge engineers may be unimpressed by the fact that the KA pitfalls identified here are nontechnical in nature. However, we believe that this is one reason they are pitfalls for knowledge engineers, since the training and biases of the latter may lead them to overlook such difficulties. Since the ASKE project began, we have been asked about "the latest knowledge acquisition techniques" by colleagues who clearly did not want to hear about other disciplines or about ideas that could be categorized as "just common

[8] Kidd's reference is to E. Feigenbaum and P. McCorduck *The Fifth Generation*. New York: Addison-Wesley, 1983.

sense." However, many important insights seem obvious once they have been articulated; the trick is to notice and articulate them. Furthermore, people do not always do what is obvious. Therefore, we repeat that every factor just discussed has been observed repeatedly to interfere with the knowledge acquisition process.

VI. Conclusion

In this paper, we have pointed out that discussion of knowledge acquisition methodology in the AI literature has neglected consideration of the methodology involved in gathering data in a face-to-face context. Both this fact and the spontaneous comments of knowledge engineers suggest that this topic is widely viewed in the field as trivial and/or self-evident. However, observations of actual knowledge acquisition sessions reveal that knowledge engineers not infrequently commit errors in interview technique that are severe enough to alienate the expert and/or to jeopardize the amount or quality of data gathered during the interview. To an anthropologist this is not surprising, since social scientists do not view interview technique as self-evident. On the contrary, anthropological common sense suggests that there is a link between the knowledge acquisition problem, and the naive approach apparently taken by many knowledge engineers to both the theory and the practice of acquiring knowledge from experts through the medium of face-to-face interaction.

The job of the present-day knowledge engineer is not exclusively technical; it requires communication skills in several areas, one of which is knowledge elicitation. It follows that the education of knowledge engineers should not be exclusively technical either. At best, it should include formal training in the social sciences. At the least, it should include training in interview methodology (which is aided by the use of videotaped practice interviews to give specific feedback on interview style and content), in interview theory (covering such topics as question formulation, interactional rhythm, and nonverbal communication), and in the sociology of knowledge.

References

1. B.G. Buchanan, D. Barstow, R. Bechtel, J. Bennet, W. Clancey, C. Kulikowski, T. Mitchell, and D.A. Waterman, "Constructing an expert system," in *Building Expert Systems*, F. Hayes-Roth, D.A. Waterman, and D.B. Lenat, Eds. Reading, MA: Addison-Wesley, 1983.
2. M. Stefik and L. Conway, "Toward the principled engineering of knowledge," *AI Magazine*, Summer 1982, p. 4.
3. J.R. Miller, "Human-computer interaction and intelligent tutoring systems," MCC Tech. Rep. No. HI-294-86, *Handbook of Intelligent Tutoring Systems* in M.C. Polson and J.J. Richardson, Eds. Hillsdale, NJ: Lawrence Erlbaum Associates, 1987, p. 27.
4. R. Davis, *Applications of Meta Level Knowledge to the Construction, Maintenance and Use of Large Knowledge Bases*. Stanford, CA: Computer Science Dept., Stanford Univ., 1976.
5. J.S. Bennett, "ROGET: A knowledge-based system for acquiring the conceptual structure of a diagnostic expert system," *J. Automated Reasoning*, vol. 1, no. 1, 1985.
6. L. Eshelman and J. McDermott, "MOLE: A knowledge acquisition tool that uses its head," in *Proc. Fifth Nat. Conf. Artific. Intell.*, Philadelphia, PA, 1986.
7. G. Kahn, S. Nowlan, and J. McDermott, "MORE: An intelligent knowledge acquisition tool," in *Proc. Ninth Int. Joint Conf. Artificial Intell.*, Los Angeles, CA, 1985.

8. J.H. Boose, *Expertise Transfer for Expert System Design*. New York: Elsevier, 1986.
9. D.A. Waterman and A. Newell, "Protocol analysis as a task for artificial intelligence," *Artificial Intell.*, vol. 2, no. 3 – 4, 1971.
10. J.H. Boose, *Expertise Transfer for Expert System Design*. New York: Elsevier, 1986, pp. 33 – 50.
11. W.J. Clancey, "The knowledge engineer as student: Metacognitive bases for asking good questions," *Learning Issues for Intelligent Tutoring Systems*, H. Mandl and A. Lesgold, Eds. New York: Springer Verlag, 1988.
12. R.H. Hill, Automating knowledge acquisition from experts. MCC Tech. Rep. Number AI-082-86, Microelectronics and Computer Technology Corp., Austin, TX, 1986.
13. A. Hart, *Knowledge Acquisition for Expert Systems*. New York: McGraw-Hill, 1986.
14. R.R. Hoffman, "The problem of extracting the knowledge of experts from the perspective of experimental psychology," *AI Magazine*, Summer 1987.
15. A.L. Kidd, Ed., *Knowledge Acquisition for Expert Systems—A Practical Handbook*. New York: Plenum, 1987.
16. M. LaFrance, "The knowledge acquisition grid: A method for training knowledge engineers," in *Proc. Knowledge Acquisition for Knowledge-Based Systems Workshop*. Banff, AB, Canada, 1986.
17. J.R. Olson and H.H. Rueter, "Extracting expertise from experts: Methods for knowledge acquisition," *Expert Systems*, vol. 4, no. 3, 1987.
18. D.S. Prerau, "Knowledge acquisition in the development of a large expert system," in *AI Magazine*, Summer 1987.
19. J. Blomberg, "Social interaction and office communications: Effects on user evaluation of new technologies," *Technology and the Transformation of White Collar Work*, R. Kraut, Ed. Hillsdale, NJ: Erlbaum Press, 1986.
20. H.M. Collins, "Expert systems and the science of knowledge," *The Social Construction of Technological Systems: New Directions in the Sociology and History of Technology*. W.E. Bijker, T.P. Hughes, and T.J. Pinch, Eds. Cambridge, MA: MIT Press, 1987.
21. ______, "Expert systems, artificial intelligence, and the behavioural co-ordinates of skill," *The Question of Artificial Intelligence: Philosophical and Sociological Perspectives*, B. Bloomfield, Ed. London: Croom Helm Ltd., 1987.
22. H.M. Collins, R.H. Green, and R.C. Draper, "Where's the expertise? Expert systems as a medium of knowledge transfer," *Expert Systems 85*, M. Merry, Ed. Cambridge: Cambridge Univ. Press, 1985.
23. D.E. Forsythe, "Engineering knowledge: An anthropological study of an artificial intelligence laboratory," presented to meeting of the Society for Social Studies of Science, Worcester, MA, Nov. 19 – 22, 1987.
24. L. Grasser, "The integration of computing and routine work," *ACM Trans. Office Inform. Syst.*, vol. 4, no. 3, 1986.
25. ______, *The Social Dynamics of Routine Computer Use in Complex Organizations*. Los Angeles, CA: Computer Science Dept., Univ. of Southern California, 1984.
26. J.E. Orr, "Narratives at work: Story telling as cooperative diagnostic activity," *Field Service Manager: The Journal of the Association of Field Service Managers International*, vol. 11, no. 6, 1987.
27. ______, "Talking about machines: Social aspects of expertise." In The ARI Project: Section III: Research in Modeling, Reasoning, and Expertise: Four Papers from Research into the Semantics of Procedures, a final report to the Army Research Institute, Contract MDA 903-83-C-0189, Xerox Palo Alto Research Center, Palo Alto, CA, July 1987.
28. L. Suchman, *Plans and Situated Actions: The Problem of Human-Machine Communication*. New York: Cambridge Univ. Press, 1987.
29. A.L. Strauss, *Qualitative Analysis for Social Scientists*. New York: Cambridge Univ. Press, 1987.
30. R.L. Gorden, *Interviewing—Strategy, Techniques, and Tactics*, 4th ed. Chicago, IL: The Dorsey Press, 1987.
31. R.L. Kahn and C.F. Cannell, *The Dynamics of Interviewing—Theory, Technique, and Cases*. London: Wiley, 1961.
32. E.G. Mischler, *Research Interviewing*. Cambridge, MA: Harvard Univ. Press, 1986.
33. R.F. Ellen, Ed., *Ethnographic Research*. London: Academic Press, 1984.

34. O. Werner and G.M. Schoepfle, *Systematic Fieldwork*. Newbury Park, CA: Sage Publications, 1987.
35. R.H. Wax, *Doing Fieldwork: Warnings and Advice*. Chicago, IL: Univ. Chicago Press, 1971.
36. D.B. Lenat and E.A. Feigenbaum, "On the thresholds of knowledge," in *Proc. Tenth Int. Joint Conf. Artific. Intell.*, Milan, Aug. 23 – 28, 1987.
37. D. Lenat, M. Parkash, and M. Shepherd, "CYC: Using common sense knowledge to overcome brittleness and knowledge acquisition bottlenecks," *AI Magazine*, vol. 6, no. 4, 1986.
38. S. Regoczei and E.P.O. Plantinga, "Ontology and inventory: A foundation for a knowledge acquisition methodology," in *Proc. Knowledge Acquisition for Knowledge-Based Syst. Workshop*, Banff, AB, Canada, 1986, p. 8.
39. J. Breuker and B. Wielinga, "Use of models in the interpretation of verbal data," *Knowledge Acquisition for Expert Systems—A Practical Handbook*, A.L. Kidd, Ed. New York: Plenum Press, 1987, p. 19.
40. M. Polanyi, *The Tacit Dimension*. New York: Doubleday, 1965.
41. R.L. Gorden, *Interviewing—Strategy, Techniques, and Tactics*. Homewood, IL: The Dorsey Press, 1975, p. 32.
42. J.R. Olson and H.H. Rueter, "Extracting expertise from experts: Methods for knowledge acquisition," *Expert Systems*, vol. 4, no. 3, p. 153, 1987.
43. J.G. Gammack, "Different techniques and different aspects on declarative knowledge," *Knowledge Acquisition for Expert Systems—A Practical Handbook*, A.L. Kidd, Ed. New York: Plenum Press, 1987, p. 160.
44. S.L. Payne, *The Art of Asking Questions*. Princeton: Princeton Univ. Press, 1963.
45. M. Minsky, *The Society of Mind*. New York: Simon and Schuster, 1988, p. 72.
46. J. Breuker and B. Wielinga, "Use of models in the interpretation of verbal data," *Knowledge Acquisition for Expert Systems—A Practical Handbook*, A.L. Kidd, Ed. New York: Plenum Press, 1987, pp. 21 – 22.
47. S. Woolgar, "Why not a sociology of machines? The case of sociology and artificial intelligence," *Sociology*, vol. 19, no. 4, 1985, p. 558.
48. A.L. Kidd, "Knowledge acquisition; An introductory framework," in *Knowledge Acquisition for Expert Systems—A Practical Handbook*. New York: Plenum, 1987, pp. 2 – 3.
49. C.L. Briggs, *Learning How to Ask: A Sociolinguistic Appraisal of the Role of the Interview in Social Science Research*. Cambridge: Cambridge University Press, 1986.
50. E.G. Mischler, *Research Interviewing*. Cambridge, MA: Harvard University Press, 1986.

6

The knowledge acquisition activity matrix
A systems engineering conceptual framework

Frederick W. Rook
Joseph W. Croghan

Editors' note *Rook and Croghan perform a great service to the applied AI community here, as they link knowledge engineering to systems engineering—and thereby dispel some of the (unnecessary) mystique of AI. Systems engineering is a generic systems design and development methodology; the design and development of knowledge-based systems is a unique case of systems engineering. The authors place the knowledge acquisition and representation process in the larger systems engineering context. They inadvertently answer the often-asked question: "How is all this stuff different from good ol' fashioned systems analysis?" For many, the answer is: "Not all that much." This paper helps to relate knowledge engineering to older, more familiar requirements analysis concepts. (Reprinted with permission, from the May/June 1989 issue of* IEEE Transactions on Systems, Man and Cybernetics *©1989, IEEE. All rights reserved.*

I. Introduction

Parallel to the increasing transition of knowledge-based systems from the research laboratory to operational settings, there exist increased challenges for knowledge acquisition and knowledge specification methods. The ultimate success of knowledge-based system (KBS) functioning day-to-day in a critical operational environment is determined, to a large extent, by the depth, robustness, and flexibility of the knowledge embedded within the AI system. While there exist numerous methods and techniques for knowledge acquisition, there is a distinct lack of knowledge acquisition frameworks that specify the goals, constraints, and results of knowledge acquisition activities as they relate to a systems engineering development process. By viewing a KBS as a component of a larger decision-making system organization, we view the development methodology of knowledge-based subsystems as amenable to systems engineering principles and requirements. This paper presents a systems engineering conceptual framework that provides a structure for the specification of knowledge acquisition activities throughout the system development lifecycle.

Objectives

The objectives of this paper are threefold.

1. Review general knowledge acquisition requirements for the development of applied knowledge-based systems.
2. Present a systems engineering conceptual framework, in the form of the knowledge acquisition activity matrix (KAAM), for structuring knowledge acquisition activities.
3. Discuss the specific goals, constraints, and results of knowledge acquisition steps in the context of the system development lifecycle.

The focus of this paper is the knowledge acquisition conceptual framework (contained in Section III), which includes a review of systems engineering methodologies, presents the KAAM and discusses knowledge acquisition activities in terms of system development phases, knowledge acquisition steps, and the system environment continuum.

II. Knowledge acquisition requirements

The knowledge acquisition bottleneck

Knowledge acquisition has often been described as the bottleneck in KBS development. As ample documentation for this claim exists (see Hoffman [1] for a review of topic), we will not review the supporting evidence for this assertion. We do believe, however, that this bottleneck is exacerbated when the KBS is being developed as an operational system in a real-world environment. Most responses to countering this bottleneck phenomenon focus on specific knowledge elicitation methods and techniques. In a thorough discussion of knowledge extraction methods, Hoffman [1] addresses such questions as the following.

- How can one find good tasks for extracting the knowledge of an expert?
- How can various tasks be compared?
- Can tasks be tailored to extract specific subdomains of knowledge within the expert's broader domains of knowledge?

These, and related questions, are of critical relevance to addressing the knowledge acquisition bottleneck. However, we feel that a repertoire of knowledge extraction methods (e.g., structured and unstructured interviews or constrained processing tasks) is insufficient to comprehensively alleviate the bottleneck problem. What we feel is critical to overcoming the difficulties of knowledge acquisition is a knowledge acquisition framework that structures knowledge acquisition steps within the context of KBS development phases.

We propose a conceptual framework for knowledge acquisition that seeks to address such questions as the following.

- What are the goals of knowledge acquisition activities in the requirements analysis phase of KBS development?
- What are constraints to knowledge acquisition activities during the KBS development phase?
- Are specific knowledge acquisition steps inappropriate for certain KBS development phases?
- How does one know what the differing role of knowledge acquisition is throughout the system development lifecycle?

Our proposed conceptual framework may be viewed as complimentary to knowledge acquisition method descriptions such as Hoffman's [1] in terms of providing a framework in which specific knowledge extraction techniques may be embedded. We believe that this conceptual framework facilitates the integration of knowledge acquisition techniques into a structured framework, specifying the goals and constraints of knowledge acquisition steps and system development phases, that we feel will substantially contribute to alleviating the knowledge acquisition bottleneck problem. The following section discusses operational KBS development challenges.

Operational knowledge base system development challenges

We view the environment that a KBS is developed for, will be installed in, and will reside in, as falling along a continuum ranging from a basic research setting to a field installation setting. This environment continuum may be described in terms of its three primary regions: the laboratory environment, the simulated operational environment, and the operational environment.

The laboratory environment is typically the setting for both basic research and exploratory development KBS prototyping. Typically the result of KBS development for the laboratory environment centers on a proof of concept technology demonstration usually enhanced by an advanced user interface. The ultimate goal of a KBS developed for a laboratory environment is to demonstrate a KBS technology application to a domain of interest in order to advance the KBS technology as well as provide the foundation for additional technology development work.

The simulated operational environment is the setting for more applied KBS technology applications incorporating advanced technology or advanced systems efforts. The output of a KBS project for this environment is usually a KBS installed in the customer's or end user's analysis or training facility. The ultimate goal of a KBS developed for this simulated operational environment is to act as an evaluation test bed for the KBS technology by users representative of future real-world KBS users. At this point in the environment continuum, however, the KBS is not operating in a day-to-day functional capacity.

The operational environment represents the setting of the fielded or deployed KBS. The results of engineering or operational systems development types of efforts, this class of KBSs must function in the real-world field setting for which it was initially conceived. The primary goal of this type of KBS is to function as a powerful, problem solving system whose interface inspires confidence and acceptance. The KBS at this end of the continuum must operate day-to-day over a prolonged period of time with minimal system maintenance.

The following three premises summarize our view of the knowledge acquisition challenges associated with the development of KBSs for an operational environment.

1. KBSs are increasingly being developed to function in real-world operational environments.
2. The transition from a laboratory KBS prototype to an operational KBS is a difficult one.
3. Knowledge acquisition methodologies appropriate for laboratory prototyping are often inadequate for operational KBS development.

Most KBSs developed to date, fall at the laboratory environment end of the environment continuum. This implies that most existing KBSs reside in either university, industry, or government laboratories, as opposed to field settings. We strongly believe, however, that for KBS technology to have an impact on real-world, important problems, KBS development efforts must increasingly focus on the operational environment end of the environment continuum. This raises an important question, namely, "Can we effectively transfer a laboratory-based KBS prototype into a field-deployable one through additional KBS design and development?" We believe the answer is a complex one; that is some aspects of the prototype (e.g., KBS architectures, inferences mechanisms, or search strategies) have good potential to be expanded to meet the requirements of an operational setting, while other aspects (most notably knowledge representation languages and the knowledge bases themselves) have only minimal potential.

There are three primary issues in KBS development that account for the difficulty in transitioning knowledge bases from laboratory-based KBS prototypes to operational KBSs.

1. Problem sampling and scoping. Laboratory systems typically scope the problem domain in both size and complexity to establish as manageable a problem as possible in order to apply KBS technology. Laboratory KBS projects often scope a real-world problem to such an extent that the resulting laboratory problem is no longer representative of the real-world. Reversing this process is difficult because the knowledge bases resulting from the laboratory KBS may not be robust enough to incorporate the size and complexity needed for operational problem solving.
2. Knowledge fidelity. Laboratory systems typically incorporate domain knowledge acquired from a single (or a small number of) knowledge source(s), often several steps removed from an operational environment. Knowledge acquired from these sources may be outdated or have a low correlation to knowledge of the current real-world problem.

3. The role of knowledge. Because they typically focus on advancing KBS technologies as opposed to building powerful and robust knowledge bases, laboratory KBS projects often direct a comparatively minimal percentage of the project time/effort to knowledge base development. On the other hand, operational KBSs must ensure that their knowledge bases are comprehensive enough to address all information processing requirements. We believe domain knowledge (i.e., the knowledge bases) plays an increasingly important role in KBSs as they progress along the environment continuum.

In the context of an increasing number of KBSs aimed at deployment in operational settings and the apparent difficulty of transitioning laboratory-based KBSs (and particularly knowledge bases) to operational settings, structured approaches to facilitate efficient and productive knowledge acquisition and knowledge base construction will be of significant value to a KBS development effort. There currently exist numerous knowledge acquisition methods or techniques that may be used to elicit or extract expertise from human domain experts. However, there are few knowledge acquisition frameworks that structure these knowledge acquisition activities. The knowledge acquisition methodologies prevalent in laboratory prototyping are often inadequate for operational KBS development. Many laboratory-based KBS knowledge acquisition methodologies are very *ad hoc*, i.e., they vary from system to system, project stage to project stage, and demonstrate little correlation to general system development stages or phases. Operational KBS development, however, is subject to a stricter adherence to standard system development methodologies. Although there exist numerous software engineering methodologies to subscribe to, the extensive laboratory-based KBS development efforts completed to date have provided the operational KBS developer with few tools or methods for structuring knowledge acquisition.

Structuring the knowledge acquisition process

It is within the context of the knowledge acquisition bottleneck and knowledge acquisition challenges posed by operational KBS development that requirements for structuring the knowledge acquisition process are increasing. Specifically, the knowledge acquisition process should be structured in order to:

1. Specify the goals of knowledge acquisition as they relate to phases in the KBS development cycle;
2. Identify the specific steps or tasks involved in each phase of the KBS development project;
3. Specify the specific goals of each knowledge acquisition step;
4. Identify constraints or barriers to successful knowledge acquisition activities;
5. Provide a knowledge acquisition task structure that will facilitate the selection of appropriate knowledge acquisition methods or tools.

A framework that aids the knowledge engineer in structuring the numerous and complex knowledge acquisition activities will be a valuable and useful tool in building KBSs. The following two sections present what we believe is such a framework.

III. A systems engineering conceptual framework

Review of systems engineering frameworks

Throughout the design and development of many knowledge-based systems, we have incrementally designed a framework for knowledge acquisition focusing on the relationships between knowledge acquisition activities and generic knowledge acquisition steps as they relate to the system development lifecycle. Our systems engineering conceptual framework for knowledge acquisition is structurally similar to frameworks reviewed by Sage [2] that focus on a variety of systems engineering domains, including such diverse problems as policymaking, urban transport systems, health care planning, and so forth. Specifically, our systems engineering framework is a modification of the three-dimensional (3D) framework presented by A.D. Hall [3] and overviewed by Sage [2]. Hall's systems engineering framework encompasses a time dimension (the sequences or phases that comprise a system development project), a logic dimension (the subphases or steps embedded within each phase), and the knowledge dimension (diverse, disciplinary knowledge). Hall's activity matrix specifies the relations between the project phases and project steps in the context of the knowledge dimension.

In addition to Hall's systems engineering framework, two frameworks particularly relevant to the development of our knowledge acquisition framework are those of Miles [4] and Kline and Lifson [5]. Like Hall's, both the Miles and the Kline-Lifson frameworks consist of the specification of phases and steps within each phase. Miles' five phases consist of system concept, system design, system implementation, system operation, and system completion, while his steps include problem statement, objectives and criteria development, systems synthesis, systems analysis, systems selection, and systems implementation. In similar fashion, the Kline-Lifson framework consists of ten phases, namely concept formulation, system definition, preliminary design, engineering development, detail design, test and evaluation, production design, production and installation, operations and support, and modification and retirement. Within each phase there exists the following eight steps: gather available information, formulate value model, synthesize alternate solutions, analyze and/or test, evaluate, decide, optimize, and communicate.

While there exist other systems engineering frameworks (see Sage [2] for a review and comparison), the Hall, Miles, and Kline-Lifson frameworks provided the structural foundation for the development of our systems engineering framework for knowledge acquisition. The intent of our framework is to outline a methodology for the specification of knowledge acquisition activities throughout the system development cycle.

The knowledge acquisition activity matrix

In order to structure knowledge acquisition activities throughout a knowledge-based system design and development process, we propose a systems engineering framework represented by a 3-D activity matrix. Structurally, similar to Hall's [3] 3-D morphology as described by Sage [2] the KAAM is a representation of three major dimensions of knowledge acquisition from a systems engineering perspective. Depicted in FIG. 6-1, the KAAM consists of the following three dimensions.

1. Time dimension—the phases or sequences that are characteristic of systems engineering and extend from the initial definition and specification of a problem and its environment to the postinstallation maintenance and refinement.
2. Logic dimension—the knowledge acquisition steps that are conducted throughout the system engineering phases.
3. Environment dimension—the setting or environment that the completed system will be developed for and reside in.

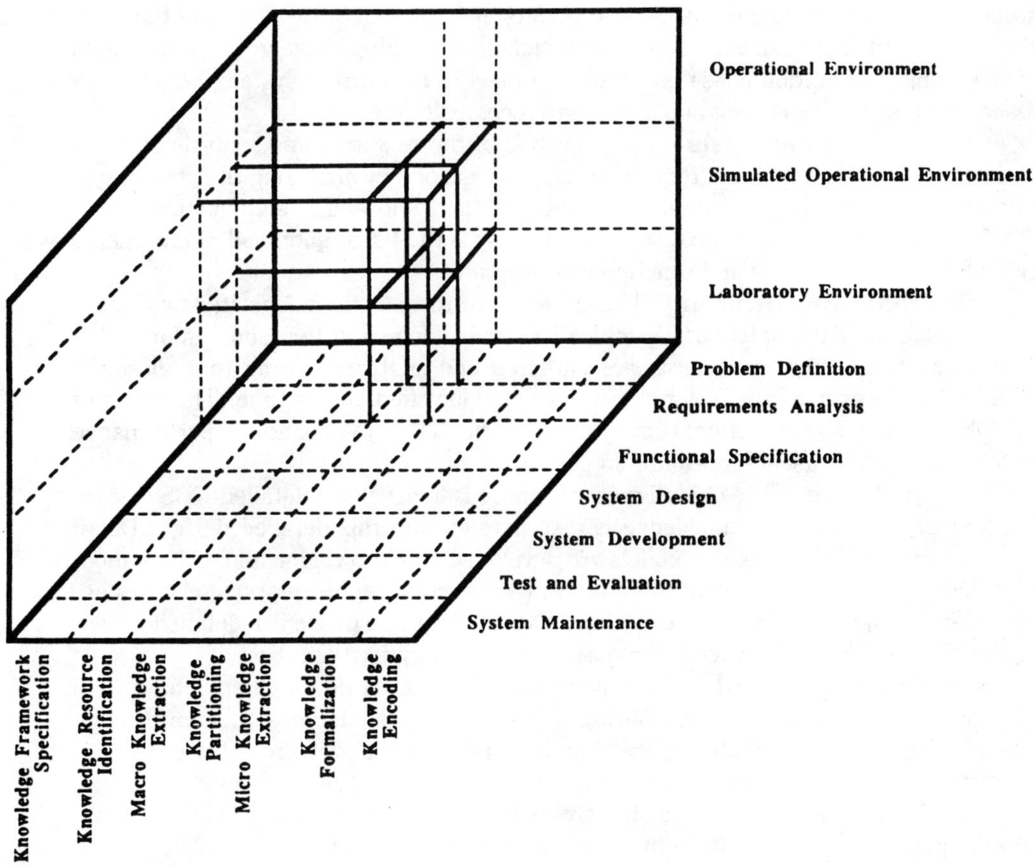

Fig. 6-1. Knowledge acquisition activity matrix: System engineering conceptual framework.

The time dimension, or system development phases, consist of problem definition, requirements analysis, functional specification, system design, system development, test and evaluation, and system maintenance. The logic dimension, or knowledge acquisition, steps consist of knowledge framework specification, knowledge resource identification, macroknowledge extraction, knowledge partitioning, microknowledge extraction, knowledge formalization, and knowledge encoding. The environment dimension, and the system development continuum components consist of laboratory environment, simulated operational environment, and operational environment. Descriptions of the components of these three dimensions are presented in the following three sections.

System development phases

Problem definition The objective of the problem definition phase is to develop a detailed understanding of the current system's operations and the knowledge associated with those operations. A clear understanding must be developed of the functional goals of the system and current approaches to reaching those goals. The results of the problem definition phase is a detailed model of the current system including an assessment of the critical relationships and processes.

Requirements analysis The objective of the requirements analysis phase is to develop the KBS functional requirements. This is done by analyzing the critical system requirements and partitioning the processes and knowledge subdomains within the detailed system model. The result of this phase is the KBS functional requirements categorized by knowledge and functional subdomains.

Functional specification The objective of the functional specification phase is to develop the KBS functional specification. Knowledge and functional information concerning the KBS requirements are gathered and analyzed during this phase. In addition, performance criteria for the system are identified at this time. The result of this phase is a detailed functional specification of the KBS system and the performance criteria that will be used to measure its effectiveness.

System design The objective of this phase is to develop a detailed KBS design. Contextual and metalevel knowledge is incorporated into this detailed design. Detail information processing module models are developed and knowledge about these modules gathered. KBS inferencing methods and knowledge representation schemes are specified through the use of these models. The result of this phase is a detailed design of the inferencing and knowledge representation strategy for the KBS.

System development The objective of the system development phase is to develop and implement the KBS. During this phase the detailed design from the previous phase is implemented and the detailed knowledge about the KBS domain is extracted and encoded. The output is a functioning knowledge-based system.

Test and evaluation The objective of the test and evaluation phase is to quantify the performance of the KBS based on the performance criteria established in the functional specification phase. This is done by executing test procedures that are defined in this phase and based on knowledge about system performance criteria and evaluation methodologies. The output of the test and evaluation phase is a quantified evaluation of the KBS performance.

System maintenance The objective of the system maintenance phase is to evaluate and enhance the KBS as necessary to improve system performance. This involves collecting knowledge about KBS performance and deficiencies, as well as defining changes that need to be made to the KBS inferencing mechanisms of knowledge bases. The output of this phase is an improved KBS and knowledge bases.

Knowledge acquisition steps

The knowledge acquisition steps of the Activity Matrix may be viewed as global stages or groups of activities in knowledge acquisition. It is important to note that these steps are not necessarily sequential or, in fact, even applicable to each of the system development phases. Our knowledge acquisition steps may be best viewed in terms of their relationship to the systems engineering phases in the activity matrix, as opposed to comprising a knowledge acquisition methodology alone. There have been several presentations of knowledge acquisition stages or steps. For example, Buchanan *et al.* [6] describes the stages of knowledge acquisition as consisting of 1) the identification stage, consisting of participant identification and roles, problem identification, resource identification, and goal identification; 2) the conceptualization stage, consisting of making explicit the key concepts and relations; 3) the formalization stage, consisting of the mapping of key concepts, subproblems, and information flow into formal representations; 4) the implementation stage, consisting of mapping the formalized knowledge into the knowledge-based system's representational framework; and 5) the testing stage, consisting of evaluating the prototype system and the representational forms used to implement it.

The specification of knowledge acquisition stages such as that of Buchanan *et al.* provides useful descriptions of knowledge acquisition stages. However, what is generally lacking is a specification of how specific knowledge acquisition stages map into a systems engineering development process. For example, one can assume that the Buchanan *et al.* knowledge acquisition stages are directly applicable to the general system development phase of system development, which would incorporate knowledge base development. This leaves unanswered questions, however, about the role, objectives, and methods of the knowledge acquisition stages in other system development phases. Our knowledge acquisition framework is designed to extend previous descriptions of knowledge acquisition stages a step further into the realm of the entire system development lifecycle. The seven knowledge acquisition steps that comprise the logic dimension of our activity matrix are discussed below.

Knowledge framework specification The specification of the knowledge domain or the subject of knowledge. Examples of knowledge frameworks are:

- knowledge about the configuration of a computer system;
- knowledge about a C^2 decision-making environment;
- knowledge about diagnosing a specific medical illness;
- knowledge about evaluating battlefield courses of action.

Knowledge framework specification involves the identification of a specific knowledge class, subdomain, or subset of the larger problem domain under study. Typically, the knowledge framework represents the starting point for knowledge resources and subsequent macroknowledge extraction.

Knowledge resource identification The specification of the knowledge resources or sources of expertise related to the specified knowledge framework. Knowledge sources include specific human experts, documentation, doctrine, or other sources of procedures, methodologies, or guidelines relevant to the knowledge framework. It is important to note that the knowledge resource identification is not simply a list of sources; rather it is a list of sources within the context of a specific type of knowledge. For example, seldom are several human experts identical in their areas of expertise. Three intelligence analysts may have similar analysis tasks and responsibilities, although it is unlikely that their subdomains of expertise are identical. Each may, for example, be a specialist in a specific aspect of the analysis process. It is important during the knowledge resource identification step to explicitly identify subdomains of individual expertise.

Macroknowledge extraction The extraction, analysis, and integration of knowledge about the previously identified knowledge framework. The macroknowledge resulting from this step consists of general domain descriptions, identification of major information processing modes, and high-level descriptions of object/entity classes relating to the knowledge framework. Macroknowledge extraction is not the acquisition of specific object descriptions, problem-solving heuristics, or lowest-level detailed knowledge about how to represent the expertise related to the knowledge framework.

Knowledge partitioning The examination, analysis, and partitioning of the high-level conceptual macroknowledge into knowledge modules. These packets of knowledge provide the structure for flushing out the specific, detailed knowledge that will evidentially comprise the KBS's knowledge bases.

Microknowledge extraction The identification, acquisition, and specification of detailed knowledge formalisms that comprise the knowledge bases. The results of this step are detailed descriptions of all knowledge base objects/entities, problem-solving heuristics (e.g., rules), algorithm designs, and evidential reasoning schemes that will form the basis for knowledge base construction. It is important to note that the microknowledge resulting from this step is still not formalized in terms of specific knowledge representation schemes or software implementation.

Knowledge formalization The translation of the microknowledge into specific knowledge representation schemes (e.g., rules, frames, object-oriented representations) ready for software encoding. Knowledge formalization results in specific knowledge data structures that incorporate all microknowledge into the KBS's knowledge representation language.

Knowledge encoding The software implementation of the knowledge base data structures resulting from the knowledge formalization step. For example, the pseudolanguage rules are encoded in the KBS-specific rule representation language. The results of this step are complete, software-implemented knowledge bases.

System environment continuum

The system environment continuum of the Activity Matrix may be viewed as representing the environment that the KBS is developed for, will be installed in, and will function in. As described in Section II, the three primary regions of the system environment continuum consist of the laboratory environment, the simulated operational environment, and the operational environment.

The laboratory environment focuses on the goals and constraints involved in the development of a first-pass, KBS prototype. Due to the relatively small (compared to full-scale operational KBS development) level-of-effort [associated with laboratory-based KBS], as well as the necessary problem-scoping, the knowledge acquisition structuring requirements are only moderate at this end of the environment continuum.

The simulated operational environment involves the development of KBS for real-world end user evaluation. As such, issues such as a problem sampling and scoping, knowledge fidelity, and the role of knowledge itself are made more critical to successful KBS development in the simulated operational environment term in the laboratory environment. There are increased challenges in terms of expanded knowledge acquisition goals and constraints in this region of the continuum.

The operational environment houses KBSs designed and developed for day-to-day operational use. Knowledge acquisition constraints are the greatest in this region of the continuum. Additionally, the scope of the real problem dictates significant attention to the knowledge acquisition activities undertaken to both problem understanding and knowledge extraction. Whereas *ad hoc* knowledge acquisition structuring may have sufficed until this point, the lack of a systematic methodology to structure operational KBS's numerous and complex knowledge acquisition activities may contribute to incomplete, inflexible, and nonrobust knowledge bases, thereby constraining ultimate KBS success.

As depicted in FIG. 6-1, the intersection of the three dimensions results in a cube of knowledge acquisition activities. For example, FIG. 6-1 identifies a knowledge acquisition concept for the knowledge partitioning step in the requirements analysis phase of a KBS developed for a simulated operational environment. Each of the 147 knowledge acquisition cubes of the KAAM may be described in terms of goals, constraints, and results of knowledge acquisition activities. The following section discusses these cubes by focusing on the system development phases.

IV. Goals, constraints, and outputs of knowledge acquisition steps

The previous section presented our proposed systems engineering conceptual framework by discussing the KAAM. The utility of this matrix is to systematically structure knowledge acquisition activities in terms of system development phases, knowledge acquisition steps, and the operational environment. In the course of a knowledge base system development project, the knowledge engineer should be able to use the systems engineering conceptual framework to specify the applicability and appropriateness of knowledge acquisition methods/techniques in system development phases. The systematic structuring of these methods/techniques based upon the knowledge acquisition goals, constraints, and results embedded within the activity matrix, will facilitate efficient and successful knowledge acquisition efforts.

The KAAM provides a knowledge acquisition framework consisting of the specific knowledge acquisition activity requirements associated with system phase/knowledge acquisition steps. In order to discuss this framework, we have examined the activity matrix in terms of the seven system development phases. Our framework discussion focuses on seven planes of the activity matrix, with each plane representing the knowledge acquisition steps relevant to a specific phase over the continuum of the environment dimension. The following sections discuss our knowledge acquisition activity requirements by discussing the system development phases, starting with problem definition and continuing through system maintenance.

Problem definition

Knowledge framework specification The goals of this step are to identify and specify the organizational system (e.g., information processing) or decision-making environment. This specification will include a description of the knowledge domains resident in the organizational environment. The constraints within this step consist of a lack of general knowledge about the environment, a lack of information sources, and the lack of an explicit model of the environment as a dynamic, functional system. The outputs of this step are a high-level conceptual model of the environment as a dynamic system and a general description of the knowledge domains and subdomains that exist within the system.

Knowledge resource identification The goals of this step are to identify and describe the diverse sources of knowledge about the operation of the organizational system. The constraints within this step consist of the availability and accessibility of knowledge sources (e.g., both human experts and critical documentation). The outputs of this step are a list of knowledge sources and a description of their knowledge domains, a quantification of the value of each specific knowledge source, and the identification of existing gaps of expertise as relevant to the organizational system.

Macroknowledge extraction The goals of this step are to extract and integrate from the knowledge sources knowledge of the system's (e.g., the decision-making environment) functional operations. The constraints within this step are defined by any lack of depth or thoroughness of the knowledge resources' expertise level. The output of this step is an analysis of the organizational system in terms of system components (e.g., subsystems), system primary functions, and subsystem interrelationships.

Knowledge partitioning The goals of this step are to synthesize and refine the system analysis by integrating system functional (e.g., information processing) components into a detailed system model. The constraints within this step consist of deficiencies in the accuracy and detail of the system macroknowledge. The output of this step is a detailed functional model of the organizational environment specifying critical relationships and processes of system (and subsystem) components. An additional output is a criticality assessment of each knowledge module.

Microknowledge extraction Because the focus of problem definition is on the development of a general model of the organizational environment, microknowledge extraction is inappropriate during this phase. Extensive microknowledge extraction activities will, in fact, be counterproductive at this time. Because of the inability to intelligently focus on appropriate components of the organizational system, description of specific system objects/attributes, reasoning heuristics, and detailed information aggregation strategies interfere with the development of a general system model.

By definition, the lack of microknowledge precludes the applicability of knowledge formalization and knowledge encoding during this phase.

Environment continuum As KBSs transition to the operational environment, there are several issues that need to be addressed during this phase. In operational KBS development, there is a much greater need for accurate and detailed knowledge of the problem. A focus on a simplistic subproblem isolated from the real-world context will yield knowledge acquisition technology solutions inadequate for real-world constraints. In order to fully define the problem environment, it is necessary to investigate multiple problem viewpoints (e.g., from multiple human sources) of a complex problem that is often embedded within a larger context.

Requirements analysis

Knowledge framework specification The goals of this step are to identify the classes of knowledge relevant to the critical system functions as defined in the system model resulting from the problem definition phase. The primary constraint within this step is the level of detail of the system model, particularly details of functions deemed critical to overall system performance. The outputs of this step are descriptions of knowledge categories or classes for each of the system model's primary functions.

Knowledge resource identification The goals of this step are to identify sources of knowledge about the critical system functions. The constraints within this step consist of the availability and accessibility of knowledge sources. The outputs of this step are a list of knowledge sources and a description of their knowledge domains, a quantification of the value of each specific knowledge source, and the identification of existing gaps of expertise as relevant to system functions.

Macroknowledge extraction The goals of this step are to extract and analyze knowledge about both global system functions (from an organizational perspective) and critical subsystem functions in the context of defining the role, requirements, and functions of a new, undesigned system component. The constraints within this step focus on the depth of knowledge about the organizational system, its current functions and performance, and its potential capability expansion areas. The output of this step is a high-level description of KBS functional requirements that will either improve or enhance current system operations or provide additional, currently nonexistent, system functions.

Knowledge partitioning The goals of this step are to organize and synthesize the identified KBS requirements (e.g., the macroknowledge) into categories of KBS functional requirements. The constraints within this step consist of lack of detailed knowledge about current or predicted system functions (i.e., KBS requirements). The outputs of this step are descriptions of system requirements aggregated by function, knowledge domain, and application within the detailed system model. These requirements will provide the basis for the functional specification of the yet to be determined KBS.

Microknowledge extraction Because the focus of requirements analysis is on the WHAT (i.e., specification) of system functional requirements as opposed to HOW specific requirements will be addressed (e.g., through KBS functions), microknowledge extraction is inappropriate during this phase. By definition, the lack of microknowledge precludes the applicability of knowledge formalization and knowledge encoding during this phase.

Environment continuum KBSs transitioned from the laboratory environment or simulated operational environment often either minimize or bypass altogether the critical requirements analysis phase. The development of operational KBSs requires a detailed requirements analysis that focuses on well-defined, specific requirements critical to addressing the needs of the operational environment. Laboratory-based KBSs require less focus on the requirements analysis phase, as one goal of the prevalent prototype and iterate process is to elicit requirements.

Functional specification

Knowledge framework specification The goals of this step are to identify and describe the knowledge subdomains that contain knowledge relevant to each functional requirement. An additional goal is to specify knowledge of the constraints imposed by environmental requirements (e.g., real-time processing, user/system interaction needs). The constraints within this step consist of a scarcity of knowledge about requirements previously unaddressed by the system. The outputs of this step are a specification and description of knowledge categories relevant to each functional requirement resulting from the requirements analysis phase.

Knowledge resource identification The goals of this step are identify and describe the diverse sources of knowledge about the functional requirement knowledge categories. The constraints within this step consist of the availability and accessibility of knowledge sources. The outputs of this step are a list of knowledge sources and a description of their knowledge domains, a quantification of the value of each specific knowledge source, and the identification of existing gaps of expertise as relevant to system requirements.

Macroknowledge extraction The goals of this step are to extract and analyze knowledge about both global KBS requirements (from an organizational perspective) and critical KBS subsystem requirements in the context of defining the specifications a new system must address. The constraints within this step focus on the depth of knowledge about the organizational system and the identified KBS requirements. The output of this step is a high-level description of KBS functions that will either improve or enhance current system operations or provide additional, currently nonexistent, system functions.

Knowledge partitioning The goals of this step are to organize and synthesize the identified system functions (e.g., the macroknowledge) into categories of KBS functional specifications. Functions and subfunctions are decomposed into KBS processing tasks. The primary constraint within this step consists of a lack of detailed knowledge about what functions are required to meet specific requirements. The output of this step is a detailed functional specification describing KBS functional modules which consist of subfunctions that map directly to the requirements. This KBS functional specification describes how specific requirements will be met in the context of what functions will be performed. In addition, performance criteria will be identified for each KBS processing task.

Microknowledge extraction Because the functional specification details KBS functional capabilities and does not address HOW processing tasks are implemented in terms of reasoning strategies, detailed domain reasoning knowledge is not needed. Therefore microknowledge extraction is inappropriate during this phase. By definition, the lack of microknowledge precludes the applicability of knowledge formalization and knowledge encoding during this phase.

Environment continuum There are several differences in the functional specification phase depending upon where the KBS falls in the environment continuum. Laboratory-based KBS functions tend to be confined exclusively to functions amenable to AI technology. Typically these KBSs focus on a single (or few) human decision makers while addressing only a subset of required system functions. Additionally, these KBSs often involve a single level of automation, e.g., the KBS is either always autonomous, or either always requires user interaction, but does not incorporate a wide spectrum of user/KBS cooperative problem-solving allocations. In contrast, because many operational KBSs must be embedded within a larger system, the functional specification must address the integration/cooperation with other processing modules or subsystems. Operational KBSs often focus on the expert functions of multiple human experts involving a dynamic aiding/automation level.

System design

Knowledge framework specification The goals of this step are to identify and describe the knowledge subdomains relevant to each KBS function, the functional interrelationships (e.g., modules of task-related functions), contextual knowledge, and metalevel knowledge concerned with the control of KBS functions. The constraints within this step consist of a lack of an information processing model for each KBS function in addition to domain experts' difficulty in expressing human reasoning frameworks. The outputs of this step are knowledge categories or subdomains relevant to reasoning structures of each KBS function.

Knowledge resource identification The goals of this step are to identify and describe the diverse sources of knowledge about the knowledge subdomains for each KBS functional reasoning structure. In addition, sources of knowledge pertaining to contextual and metalevel knowledge must be identified. It is important to note that contextual and metalevel knowledge sources are often different than KBS function-specific domain knowledge sources. The constraints within this step consist of the availability and accessibility of knowledge sources. The outputs of this step are a list of knowledge sources and a description of their knowledge domains, a quantification of the value of each specific knowledge source, and the identification of existing gaps of expertise.

Macroknowledge extraction The goals of this step are to extract and analyze knowledge about the reasoning framework of each functional knowledge module within the KBS, each contextual knowledge module, and each metalevel knowledge module. The constraints within this step focus on the depth of knowledge about possible reasoning structures or frameworks for each of these three knowledge classes. The output of this step is a specification of the high-level inference strategy (e.g., goal-driven, depth-first search of a hierarchical hypothesis structure) for each knowledge module.

Knowledge partitioning The goal of this step is to identify the structures (e.g., object classes, hypotheses, and conclusions) that are necessary to implement the inference strategy framework for each knowledge module. The primary constraint within this step is a lack of expertise about how the domain knowledge may be described in terms of object classes, hypotheses, or conclusions. The outputs of this step are information processing models of each knowledge module that, when integrated, represent a top level design of the KBS.

Microknowledge extraction It is important to note that system design is the first phase to include microknowledge extraction. The goals of this step are to identify, acquire, and specify detailed knowledge concepts in the context of the information processing models defined in knowledge partitioning. The primary constraints to this task are the difficulties human experts have in articulating their reasoning process. The output of this step consists of knowledge about the various aggregation or assimilation processes that integrate the information processing models' components (e.g., specific object classes, objects and entities, multiple top-level, mid-level, and low-level hypotheses, intermediate and final conclusions).

Knowledge formalization The goal of this step is to specify the knowledge representation schemes and detailed inference mechanisms that will be used to implement all knowledge modules within the KBS. The constraints within this step consist of KBS technology constraints in the areas of knowledge representation and inference technology. The outputs of this step comprise the detailed design of the KBS's knowledge bases. This design includes not only specific knowledge of subdomains and their components (e.g., objects, hypotheses, or conclusions) but also the KBS technology to represent them in the development of the KBS (e.g., frames, production rules, object-oriented representations, evidential reasoning methods, etc.). The detailed design resulting from this step acts as the KBS development specification.

Knowledge encoding There are no knowledge encoding activities during this phase.

Environment continuum Due to the increased scope and complexity of operational KBSs, the design phase must be more systematic and structured than in laboratory-based system development. The partitioning of design specifications will typically involve multiple knowledge engineers/designers and multiple KBS modules. Unstructured activities in this phase may provide adequate design (often very informal) for a laboratory-based KBS, but are certainly inappropriate for simulated operational or operational systems.

System development

Knowledge framework specification The goals of this step are to review and analyze the knowledge subdomains and their components relevant to each knowledge base. The constraints within this step consist of ill-defined development specifications for the KBS's knowledge bases. The outputs of this step are high-level knowledge base development requirements.

Knowledge resource identification The goals of this step are to identify and describe the diverse sources of knowledge to be examined in the development of all the KBS's knowledge bases. The constraints within this step consist of the availability and accessibility of the knowledge sources. The outputs of this step are a list of knowledge sources and a description of their knowledge domains, a quantification of the value of each specific knowledge source, and the identification of existing gaps of expertise.

Macroknowledge extraction The goals of this step are to extract, formulate, and document in a pseudocode representation language the KBS's knowledge bases. The constraints within this step focus on the depth and breadth of domain knowledge within each knowledge base. The output of this step is a high-level representation of the KBS's knowledge bases incorporating specific reasoning processes (e.g., heuristics, logic, or algorithms).

Knowledge partitioning The goal of this step is to partition the macroknowledge (i.e., knowledge about the knowledge base subdomains and their reasoning processes) into appropriate, predefined knowledge representation classes (e.g., rulesets grouping function-related heuristics). The primary constraint to this step is the lack of adequately specified knowledge bases. The results of this step are knowledge base classes (i.e., a defined partitioning of the knowledge classes within their associated knowledge bases) to be implemented in knowledge encoding. An example output of this phase is a description of several rulesets that comprise a specific knowledge base.

Microknowledge extraction The goals of this step are to identify, acquire, and specify detailed knowledge formalisms (e.g., rules) that make up all the declarative and procedural reasoning knowledge throughout the KBS's knowledge bases. The primary constraints to this task are the difficulties human experts have in articulating their reasoning processes. The output of this step consists of full and complete domain knowledge ready for formalization into KBS representation structures.

Knowledge formalization The goal of this step is to formalize the domain knowledge into the KBS representation schemes provided by the KBS representation language (e.g., a rule-based language, object-oriented language). The primary constraint is the power, flexibility, and robustness of the KBS representation language. The results of this step are knowledge representation language data structures to be encoded in the KBS.

Knowledge encoding The goal of this step is to implement the knowledge base data structures in the KBS. The primary constraint to this step is the lack of domain knowledge often held by the knowledge base development software engineer. The results of this step are the completed, functional knowledge bases.

Environment continuum The application of a structured methodology is most valuable in the system development phase, and specifically when developing an operational KBS. An operational KBS usually contains very large, complex knowledge bases, as opposed to the laboratory-based KBS's relatively small, manageable knowledge bases. In order to develop the KBS knowledge bases, operational KBS development involves a relatively large knowledge engineering team interacting with a large number of knowledge sources. For example, the efforts of eight knowledge engineers acquiring knowledge from 14 different domain experts in approximately nine knowledge subdomains must be systematically structured from both a technical and a management perspective in order to address the numerous knowledge acquisition goals.

Test and evaluation

Knowledge framework specification The goals of this step are to identify and describe knowledge about the KBS performance criteria and evaluation methodologies. The constraints to this step focus on a lack of knowledge base evaluation benchmarks. The output of this step is a list of knowledge categories relevant to the design of sound KBS test and evaluation procedures.

Knowledge resource identification The goals of this step are to identify and describe the diverse sources of knowledge to be examined in the development of the KBS's knowledge base test and evaluation plan. The constraints within this step consist of the availability and accessibility of the knowledge sources. The outputs of this step are a list of knowledge sources and a description of their knowledge domains, a quantification of the value of each specific knowledge source, and the identification of existing gaps of expertise in knowledge base evaluation.

Macroknowledge extraction The goals of this step are to review, analyze, and refine the knowledge base evaluation criteria and benchmarks identified in the functional specification phase. The constraints to this step are the lack of KBS performance evaluation methodologies. The output of this step is a refined list of knowledge criteria and methods.

Knowledge partitioning The goal of this step is to evaluate the knowledge base performance criteria resulting from macroknowledge extraction and formulate a comprehensive knowledge base evaluation methodology described in the KBS test and evaluation plan. The primary constraint to this step is the lack of domain expertise in KBS evaluation methodologies. The output of this step is the knowledge base evaluation section of the KBS test and evaluation plan.

Microknowledge extraction, knowledge formalization, and knowledge encoding are not applicable to this phase.

Environment continuum The test and evaluation of laboratory-based KBSs usually involves evaluation criteria and performance metrics that focus on AI technology, as opposed to functional capabilities, and often a rather nebulous evaluation process. In contrast, the evaluation criteria of operational KBSs are often prescribed by the organizational system the KBS resides in. To test and evaluate an operational KBS, knowledge acquisition must focus on the refinement of existing evaluation criteria and the development of new ones. Criteria will tend to be solution-based, as opposed to the technology-based criteria prevalent in laboratory-based KBSs.

System maintenance

Knowledge framework specification The goals of this step are to review and analyze the knowledge subdomains and their components relevant to each knowledge base with respect to the results (i.e., identified knowledge base deficiencies) of the test and evaluation phase. The constraints within this step consist of ill-defined development specifications and evaluation results for the KBS's knowledge bases. The outputs of this step are high-level knowledge base development requirements necessary to improve or enhance KBS capabilities.

Knowledge resource identification The goals of this step are to identify and describe the diverse sources of knowledge to be examined in the development of all KBS's knowledge base modifications. The constraints within this step consist of the availability and accessibility of the knowledge sources. The outputs of this step are a list of knowledge sources and a description of their knowledge domains, a quantification of the value of each knowledge source, and the identification of existing gaps of expertise pertaining to the knowledge base modification requirements.

Macroknowledge extraction The goals of this step are to extract, formulate, and document in a pseudocode representation language the KBS's knowledge base modifications. The constraints within this step focus on the depth and breadth of domain knowledge within each knowledge base. The output of this step is a high-level representation of the KBS's knowledge base modifications incorporating specific reasoning processes (e.g., heuristics, logic, or algorithms).

Knowledge partitioning The goal of this step is to partition the macro knowledge (i.e., knowledge about the knowledge base subdomains and their reasoning processes) into appropriate, predefined knowledge representation classes (e.g., rulesets grouping function-related heuristics). The primary constraint to this step is the lack of adequately specified knowledge base enhancements. The results of this step are knowledge base classes (i.e., a defined partitioning of the knowledge classes within their associated knowledge bases) to be implemented in knowledge encoding. An example output of this phase is a modification of several rulesets that comprise a specific knowledge base identified as requiring modification.

Microknowledge extraction The goals of this step are to identify, acquire, and specify detailed knowledge formalisms (e.g., rules) that make up all the declarative and procedural reasoning knowledge throughout the KBS's knowledge bases. The primary constraints to this task are the difficulties human experts have in articulating their reasoning processes. The output of this step consists of full and complete domain knowledge ready for formalization into KBS representation structures.

Knowledge formalization The goal of this step is to formalize the domain knowledge into the KBS representation schemes provided by the KBS representation language. The primary constraint is the power, flexibility, and robustness of the KBS representation language. The results of this step are knowledge representation language data structures to be encoded in the KBS.

Knowledge encoding The goal of this step is to implement the knowledge base data structures in the KBS. The primary constraint to this step is the lack of domain knowledge often held by the knowledge base development software engineer. The results of this step are the completed, functional knowledge bases.

Environment continuum The position of a KBS in the environment continuum directly affects the system maintenance phase. Laboratory-based KBSs are maintained only minimally, and on these occasions solely by the KBS developer. Maintenance is important for a KBS in a simulated operational environment, as KBS users will identify both maintenance and enhancement issues. However, because the KBS is not relied on for day-to-day operational functioning, maintenance is not a critical requirement. It is the operational KBS that requires structured methodologies to maintain operational performance while minimizing downtime. Knowledge acquisition must focus on knowledge base refinement, correction, and enhancement. These tasks are difficult due to the size and complexity of the knowledge bases, and therefore require systematic structuring in order to ensure their success.

The above discussion comprises one methodological viewpoint on the goals, constraints, and results of knowledge acquisition activities within system development phases. The intention of the conceptual framework is to stimulate a knowledge engineer to define a methodology applicable to the current KBS effort.

V. Conclusion

This paper has reviewed the knowledge acquisition challenges posed by operational KBS development, presented a systems engineering conceptual framework for specifying knowledge acquisition activities, and described the goals, constraints, and outputs of knowledge acquisition steps as they relate to the system development lifecycle. Our primary premise for the need of a knowledge acquisition framework is that a repertoire of knowledge extraction and knowledge representation methods is insufficient to comprehensively alleviate the knowledge acquisition bottleneck problem.

The heart of this paper is our systems engineering conceptual framework, represented by the KAAM. We believe our framework provides the knowledge engineer with a systems engineering tool that structures the knowledge acquisition process in terms of:

- specifying the goals of knowledge acquisition as they relate to phases in the system development cycle;
- identifying the specific steps or tasks involved in each phase of a KBS development project;
- specifying the specific goals of each knowledge acquisition step.
- identifying constraints or barriers to successful knowledge acquisition activities;
- providing a knowledge acquisition task structure that facilitates the intelligent selection of knowledge acquisition methods, techniques, or tools.

A knowledge engineer may view the KAAM as a design/management tool to be used throughout a KBS development effort. The cost of using the tool is an increased amount of time used in "planning" as opposed to "conducting" knowledge acquisition activities. For small, laboratory-based KBSs, the labor cost of using the tool may be excessive when compared to the net gain in knowledge acquisition productivity. However, in large KBS development efforts faced with multiple and diverse knowledge bases, we feel the tool provides a cost-effective approach for structuring knowledge acquisition activities.

We view our framework as applicable to the design and development of a variety of KBSs, although it is in the development of KBSs for operational environments that it is most valuable. We are currently in the process of refining the framework and expanding it to include the prescription of knowledge acquisition methods and techniques as related to knowledge acquisition activities. In addition, we are applying the framework to several operational KBS development efforts. We are confident that the application of this framework will facilitate a successful and cost-effective knowledge acquisition process.

References

1. R.R. Hoffman, "The problem of extracting the knowledge of experts from the perspective of experimental psychology," *AI Magazine*, vol. 8, no. 2, Summer 1987.
2. A.P. Sage, "A case for a standard for systems engineering methodology," *IEEE Trans. Syst. Man. Cybern.*, vol. SMC-7, no. 7, pp. 156–160, July 1977.

3. A.D. Hall, III, "Three-dimensional morphology of systems engineering," *IEEE Trans. Syst. Man. Cybern.*, vol. SMC-5, no. 2, pp. 156 – 160, April 1969.
4. R.F. Miles, Jr., *Introduction to Systems Concepts*, R.F. Miles, Jr., Ed. New York: Wiley, 1973.
5. M.B. Kline and M.W. Lifson, "Systems engineering and its application to the design of an engineering curriculum," *J. Syst. Eng.*, vol. 2, no. 1, pp. 3 – 22, Summer 1971.
6. B.G. Buchanan, D. Barstow, R. Betchal, J. Bennet, W. Clancey, C. Kulikowski, T. Mitchell, D. Waterman, "Constructing an expert system," *Building Expert Systems*, F. Hayes-Roth, D. Waterman, and D. Lenat, Eds. Reading, MA: Addison-Wesley, 1983.

7

Knowledge representation in the real world

Steven Salzberg

Editors' note *Salzberg has said it all. "Certain aspects of real-world applications make demands research labs didn't always anticipate." As many of us have learned, perhaps the hard way, there is often a disconnection between what is believed to be true in the lab and what turns out to be true in the trenches. This paper addresses that and related issues with regard to knowledge representation. Project demands, defined in terms of day-to-day versus prototypical use, can alter even the best development plans. Salzberg offers some criteria for assessing the kind of technology you may need. (Reprinted, with permission, from the July 1987 issue of* AI Expert. *© 1987,* AI Expert. *All rights reserved.)*

Inheritance hierarchies, also called semantic networks, are the fundamental representation tools used in developing expert systems today. Every commercial expert system shell has its own representation scheme; most are based on academic work done in the 1970s at various AI research centers.

These representation schemes go by names like KRL, SRL, and KL-ONE, (short for Knowledge Representation Language, Schema Representation Language, and Knowledge Language One, respectively). For example, the shells ART (Inference) and Knowledge Craft (Carnegie Group) use languages based on SRL; KEE (IntelliCorp) is based on a language called Units.

Despite many similar features, these languages are not identical. In fact, as AI moves into the marketplace, certain classes of applications require distinctions to be drawn between some of these languages.

This article will discuss some of these distinctions and explain why some applications need them while others do not. Emphasis will be placed on case-based systems—those that use a generic knowledge base to process large numbers of different but similar cases, where each case might represent one customer. The distinction between subkind and instance links is more important in case-based systems than in others.

Two other distinctions, cross-indexing mechanisms and slot attachment, will also be discussed. Different languages handle these distinctions more or less aptly, and some do not handle them at all.

Subkind links

A semantic network or net defines and describes the terms used in an application. These terms are represented as structured objects (often called schemata or frames) in most knowledge representation languages and are connected to one another by links. Some applications contain hundreds or even thousands of schemata. Much of the power of semantic nets derives from the power of links. In a network diagram, subkind links are drawn between two of the same kind of objects, from a more general object to a more specific one. For example, if *BankAccount* is one kind of object and *CheckingAccount* is another, we could draw a subkind link from *BankAccount* to *CheckingAccount*.

Links always have a direction: a subkind link points toward a more specific kind of object. We can also draw links pointing in the opposite direction; these are called superkind links. Most representation languages allow you to specify either kind of link and the inverse one will be created automatically.

In some languages subkind links are called *is_a* links—when they're pointing in the opposite direction—but I think "subkind" is preferable to *is_a* because it is much easier to remember that superkind is the inverse of subkind. The inverse of *is_a* is sometimes called "kinds" (for example, ART uses this name), which gives no indication of its direction.

Furthermore, *is_a* can be confusing because of its English interpretation. The use of the phrase "is a" in English is much less restrictive than its use in semantic nets. We can say "a checking account is a bank account," but we can also say "my home computer is a computer." The latter use, we will see, should be represented with an instance link, not an *is_a* link.

Usually a subkind link means that the more specific objects will share properties (or slots, as they're called in frame-based representation schemes) with more general objects. For example, on *BankAccount* we can store information such as balance, interest rate, and account number. Once we say that *BankAccount* has this information, all subkinds of *BankAccount* inherit the information automatically. We don't need to say anything about *CheckingAccount* once we have drawn the subkind link pointing to it. We can, however, add more specific information to *CheckingAccount* that will not be shared by *BankAccount*, such as a minimum balance requirement.

Subkind links provide a pathway for shared information to flow through a network. In other words, a schema passes all information about itself to all of its subkinds. The subkinds can accept this information, augment it, or reject it.

Instance links

Semantic networks can contain many kinds of links besides subkind and superkind links, but the most important is the instance link. An instance link points from a schema to an individual object, which is an instance of that schema. For example, the checking account you have at your local bank is an instance of the schema *CheckingAccount*. In general, instances are unique objects that cannot have any subkind links of their own. All they have is a parent link—the inverse of instance link—and it points in the opposite direction.

If a schema is an instance of another schema, we call it an instance schema (or just an instance). Schemata connected by subkind and superkind links are called classes since they represent groups of objects rather than individuals. As a simple example, suppose I wanted to reason about my home stereo system. I might create one class called *StereoEquipment* and another class called *CDPlayer*, which would be a subkind of *StereoEquipment*. I could then create an instance schema called *MyCDPlayer*, which would be an instance of *CDPlayer*.

Now that we know about the basic machinery, we can reexamine the features of slots already mentioned. In general, you can store any information you want in a schema by putting it in a slot. In the banking example, we had slots for balance, interest rate, and account number on *BankAccount*. *CheckingAccount* had an additional slot, which we called "minimum balance." When we put these slots on classes, we were actually describing instances of those classes.

One of the powerful features of semantic net representations is that we don't have to know about any instances before we describe them. Because we want this descriptive information to be passed on, we define the instance link similarly to a subkind: a schema passes all information about itself to all of its instances.

When we look at your checking account, we know it should have all the slots we defined on *CheckingAccount*. So far, so good. Some representation languages stop at this point; that is, the distinctions we just made are all the distinctions the languages make. Note that we defined instance and subkind links almost identically—at this point, the real distinctions are in the knowledge engineer's head.

Some languages, like ART and Knowledge Craft, blur the distinction further by allowing instances to have their own instances. Instances of instances might occur if you added a metalevel to your system. For example, if you had "the set of all classes of animate objects" as a class, then "animal" would be an instance of that class, and "Fido" would be an instance of animal.

Metaobjects are rarely necessary in real-world applications, though. In the research community, this blurring of distinctions is sometimes considered advantageous since it allows a looser style of programming. A researcher running experiments may try out many bizarre knowledge representations, so a language that allows trying anything is preferable to a restrictive one. For case-based applications, languages that maintain a strict distinction are more powerful.

Case-based applications

Case-based applications require the processing of many cases, where each case shares many features with other cases. The most common kind of case is a collection of all the relevant data about one individual. Other cases are more heterogeneous collections of data; for example, a case could include all the financial data about several individuals who had formed a business partnership.

Many standard data processing applications fit this description, and it's not surprising that a number of AI applications do too. A tax planning system is a case-based application: each case might consist of a particular person and all the relevant data about his or her taxes (and maybe data about the family finances). The kinds (or classes) of data are the same from one person to the next, although the data itself differs. In other words, the data that goes into each case is a collection of instances. We might store instances of bank accounts, dependents, stock investments, and real estate holdings for every person.

Looking at our knowledge representation machinery, we start to see where the distinction between classes and instances (and between subkind and instance links) makes a difference. When we build a tax planning expert system, we can build a semantic network that contains every kind of schema we might expect to need to do our reasoning. The network will not contain any instances, because those don't appear until we get some real clients to process. The rules we write will mention objects such as stocks and IRAs, but they will not refer to any particular stocks or IRAs since each case will include different instances of these schemata.

If a knowledge representation language maintains a strict distinction between instances and classes, it can be augmented with a case management facility. The language itself should provide a way to save the network of classes by themselves without any instances. The case management facility does the same thing for instances: it stores a set of instances in a file of its own. If needed, the instances can be read (through a preprocessor) from standard database files. The semantic net can then be loaded separately from the instances.

The research environment in which most knowledge representation languages were developed was not sensitive to this need; as a result, most frame languages do not have case management facilities. This is not to say such facilities can't be built within any commercial shell; however, they will be more difficult to build in languages that do not maintain the instance/class distinction.

Let's suppose we built a system in two ways, for the sake of comparison. In System 1, we used a knowledge representation language that made only a very loose distinction between instances and classes. In System 2, we used a language that maintained a very strict distinction and also provided a case management facility.

In System 1, case management works in an ad hoc fashion. The knowledge case is a big collection of schemata, including both generic and case-specific information, and new instances are loaded to define each new client.

The obvious way to load a new case is simply to delete all the instances in the knowledge base. But because the knowledge base may contain instances, simply deleting all instances may wipe out permanent parts of the knowledge base, so these deletion routines may have to be complex. In System 2, a case management facility automatically loads and unloads cases. Furthermore, this facility allows someone to change a case (for what-if analysis) and save the new version of the case on a file.

In System 2 the notion of a knowledge base has been separated from that of a case. A knowledge base contains general terms and objects used to reason about a domain, whereas a case contains no new objects, only instances of objects defined in the knowledge base. The set of cases the system processes corresponds in conventional terms to a database, and the knowledge base corresponds to a data dictionary. The seeming inflexibility of enforcing a strict distinction between instances and classes has been transformed into greater flexibility via a powerful case management mechanism.

A caveat to keep in mind is that not all applications are case based—the distinctions I am making are not as critical for other kinds of applications. In particular, simulation systems are not usually case-based applications.

Suppose your system simulates the flow of work through a set of machines in a factory. Since the machines themselves remain constant from one run of the system to the next, and each machine is an instance of some class of machines, it might be desirable to have a knowledge representation language that treats instances and classes similarly.

The need for cross indexing

Another powerful feature of knowledge representation languages—one that few languages provide—is the ability to view a case from a variety of different perspectives. In many domains of expertise, an expert looks at the data in many different ways, grouping it differently depending on the answers desired. Normally, semantic nets provide classes for all the data in a case and we can examine these classes by looking at all the instances of one class.

Suppose our expert system manages stock portfolios. This knowledge base allows us to examine all of the energy, high-tech, or retail stock in a portfolio. However, portfolio management is a complicated problem, and most expert systems in this area would need to take different views of the data. A system might want to look at all stocks with a high price/earnings (P/E) ratio. What we need is an efficient cross-indexing mechanism that will get what we want at a low cost.

Most knowledge representation languages (including all those in the largest expert system shells) provide a way to cross index using slots that works as follows. We can put a slot called *P/E ratio* on the most general class, which means that every subkind and instance would inherit this slot. Now we could say something like "get me all the schemata with a P/E ratio > 15." This request would look through every instance in the case and return the ones with high P/E ratios.

Unfortunately, this is inefficient. Getting all instances of *Stock* is fast because *Stock* has links directly to all its instances. However, searching every instance in a case for those that pass a certain test is much slower. In general, a slot can appear on any schema in the knowledge base, including, in this example, schemata that are not subkinds of *Stock*.

Certain knowledge representation languages provide more efficient alternatives to this approach. The most common is to allow multiple parents; just as a class can have many instances, an instance can belong to many classes. With this approach, an instance of *Stock* could also be an instance of high-P/E stock.

Although this approach is efficient, it has one drawback that can be serious: if an instance has many parents, it inherits information from all of them. If that information is inconsistent, a convention for resolving the inconsistency must be followed. For example, both high-tech stock and high-P/E stock may have a slot called *buy__factors*. The value of this slot may be a list of factors to consider before deciding to buy the stock. For different classes, the slot will typically have different values, yet it is possible for something to be an instance of both of these classes.

The simplest convention for deciding which value to inherit is to ask the user, although it is possible to specify in some languages (such as KEE) that one slot will override another. In a large knowledge base, keeping track of overlapping slots can become a significant problem.

Another less common approach is to provide alternative semantic networks. This is more complicated than the previous approach, but it doesn't have the same drawbacks. An expert system would be allowed to reason about instances as if they belonged to either hierarchy by switching contexts from one knowledge base to another. If context switching is fast, this approach is very powerful.

All the larger shells (ART, KEE, and Knowledge Craft) provide a form of context switching. A note of caution: most knowledge bases cannot be completely restructured in a useful way. The most useful knowledge representation capability will allow an expert system to consider a small piece of a knowledge base from many different vantage points.

Again, it is important to remain sensitive to the kinds of applications that need the powerful capability provided by the previously mentioned cross-indexing mechanisms. A small prototype probably does not need this capability, nor does a larger one-shot system. On the other hand, a system with a large knowledge base, especially one that will grow and evolve over time, cannot afford to be without it. As a system evolves, reorganization of its knowledge is inevitable, and the knowledge engineers maintaining it need powerful tools to manage this task.

Slot attachment

Slots store information on schemata. For instance, a schema for *John* might have slots such as age, height, and weight. Since at least two distinct meanings can be attributed to slots, it's vital to keep them straight. First, a slot stores information about the schema to which it is attached (direct attachment). Therefore, the age slot of *John* stores John's age. Second, a slot stores information about all the instances of the schema to which it is attached. The slot is attached only indirectly to these instances.

This use of slots is similar to type declarations in conventional programming languages. For example, the age slot on a schema called *person* might store the information that the age of an instance of person must be a number. The owner slot on a schema called *personal auto* can indicate that the owner must be a person.

If you want to get fancy, some languages allow you to say even more, such as that the age slot must contain a number between 0 and 120 or that the owner of a car can be either a person or a corporation. This kind of information is especially useful to ensure the integrity of data coming into a system.

What's surprising to some non-LISP programmers is that knowledge representation languages tend to be very lax about enforcing such type restrictions. This is because LISP, unlike most programming languages, does not restrict the types of objects that can be stored in a variable. You can store a string in a variable that's supposed to contain a number, and your program will continue to run happily until—possibly much later—it tries to multiply the contents of that variable by a number. Then it will crash. Since no one wants an expert system to crash while it's running, one solution is to add some features to the data entry system to do type checking.

However, it's much nicer to keep declarations about slots in the knowledge base where they belong. If a knowledge representation language explicitly provides both kinds of slots described here (KEE, for example, has both), it is probably not necessary to modify the data entry system. The expert system can, in this case, take care of its own knowledge.

Certain aspects of real-world applications make demands that research labs didn't always anticipate. In particular, research systems are often one-shot systems—they're not built to process thousands of cases, but rather to do something interesting with a small number of examples. It's not surprising that commercial applications require case management systems and type checking, but it's interesting to observe that some of the commercial expert system shells are still heavily oriented toward prototype development. Prototypes correspond most closely to the kind of systems built in research labs. For anyone looking to build a prototype to test some ideas, these shells are definitely the best thing going. Building a product or a production quality system puts many more demands on a system.

Some questions to ask when deciding which tools to use to build a system are:

- Will the system be a prototype requiring maximum flexibility or will it be used in a production environment, where data integrity is critical?
- Will it need to maintain a client database?
- Will it process thousands of cases?
- Will the knowledge grow and change over time?

Depending on the answers to these questions, the features described here may turn out to be critical requirements of the knowledge representation language at the core of your expert system.

Thanks to Lou Odette, Russell Siegelman, and Jim Stansfield for their helpful comments.

References

R. Brachman, "What IS___A Is and Isn't: An Analysis of Taxonomic Links in Semantic Networks." *IEEE Computer* 16(10): 30–36 (1983).

R. Brachman and J. Schmolze, "An Overview of the KL-ONE Knowledge Representation System." *Cognitive Science* 9(2), 1985.

D. Bobrow and T. Winograd, "An Overview of KRL, a Knowledge Representation Language." *Cognitive Science* 1(1): 3–46 (1977).

R. Roberts and I. Goldstein, *The FRL Manual.* Cambridge, Mass.: MIT AI Laboratory Memo 409, 1977.

M. Stefik, D. Bobrow, S. Mittal, and L. Conway, "Knowledge Programming in LOOPS." *AI Magazine* 4(3): 3–13 (1983).

W. Woods, "What's in a Link?" In *Representation and Understanding,* edited by D. Bobrow and A. Collins. New York, N.Y.: Academic Press, 1975.

8

Building knowledge-based systems with procedural languages

C. W. Butler
E.D. Hodil and G.L. Richardson

Editors' note *This paper appears because it bridges the gaps among several persistent ideas, namely, that all knowledge-based systems should be programmed in interpretive LISP, that older symbolic languages are preferable to newer procedural or "conventional" high-level languages, and that AI systems should stand pretty much by themselves. The authors challenge all of these assumptions. (Reprinted, with permission, from the Summer 1988 issue of* IEEE Expert. **

Expert or knowledge-based (KB) systems represent the first wave of AI technology to move from academic laboratories into productive operational environments. Developers wrote early versions of KB systems using Lisp or Prolog as a development language, and they implemented the systems on special-purpose processors. Phase two of the implementation stressed the use of "shell" systems that allowed users to input rule bases in a high-level-language format, thereby avoiding the vagaries of new language constructs.

Now, at the threshold of phase three, large organizations are debating how to integrate KB systems technology and implement successful KB systems prototypes into operational environments. Initial thinking placed the technology in a special systems domain with unique development requirements. More recent evidence raises serious questions about the benefits of this approach. A growing understanding of technology and techniques argues for implementing KB systems with traditional hardware and software products.

One might ask, "Why should traditional languages and hardware be used to implement this class of software?" The answer is multifaceted. First, the training investment for data processing professionals makes such a strategy highly desirable economically. Second, the ability to provide access to a broad community of users connected to computer resources through established telecommunications networks is a further economic argument. Third, the cost of special-purpose equipment is not justified for many applications—and it may never be. Fourth, KB systems may need access to production databases, which can be accomplished more readily through existing hardware and software architecture.

The literature supports using traditional languages to implement KB systems technology; for example, Intellect, [1] ESE, [2] Expert, [3] and KES [4] are all written in traditional procedural languages. The above factors provide reasonable justification and motivation for the arguments presented here.

We will demonstrate some techniques that need to be added to the programmer's tool kit for successful construction of KB systems using procedural languages. These techniques, kept simple enough to show elementary mechanics, are not intended to be comprehensive. Basically, we seek to provide an orderly expansion of the traditional environment into an operational KB realm while not completely scrapping techniques developed during the early years of systems development. Our material represents an orderly evolution of programming techniques that is accomplished by introducing certain logical KB building blocks within traditional software engineering methodologies. Looking critically at the development requirements for an operational KB system, one finds many similarities to traditional systems architecture. On the other hand, some notable differences exist that will represent new conceptual hurdles for KB system builders. Our goal is to focus on the techniques that can be implemented with procedural languages and that support the construction of KB system components.

As with all systems, the selection of an implementation language is controversial. PL/I was chosen to demonstrate concepts. However, the techniques will work with Ada, Fortran, and Pascal. Access to production databases through DBMS software, existence of a preprocessor, and the ability to handle recursive procedures were the primary reasons for selecting PL/I.

Reasoning and inferencing

KB systems come in many forms. The particular form depends largely on the characteristics of the problem to be addressed as well as target hardware and software environments. One of the most commonly used paradigms (at least for pedagogical purposes) is the backward-chaining, depth-first-search KB system. Backward chaining can be logically represented as a tree structure, with each node in the tree representing a goal to be resolved.

Figure 8-1 shows an example KB for a phone feature selection system. At the top of the hierarchy is the master goal, Phone Feature. The subgoals—Job Level, Outside Contacts, and Call Load—are factors that, if known, will allow the determination of values for Phone Feature. The subgoal Outside Contacts in turn has subgoals—Group and Job level. Notice that the logic tree represents inferential relationships, *not* flow of control as in the typical module design chart. In particular, the decision tree can be "entered" from any point; that is, the user can inquire on Job Level or Outside Contact and completely bypass the Phone Feature goal. Also, the tree shows the complete set of subgoals for any goal. A particular value for a goal can be determined from a subset of these subgoals.

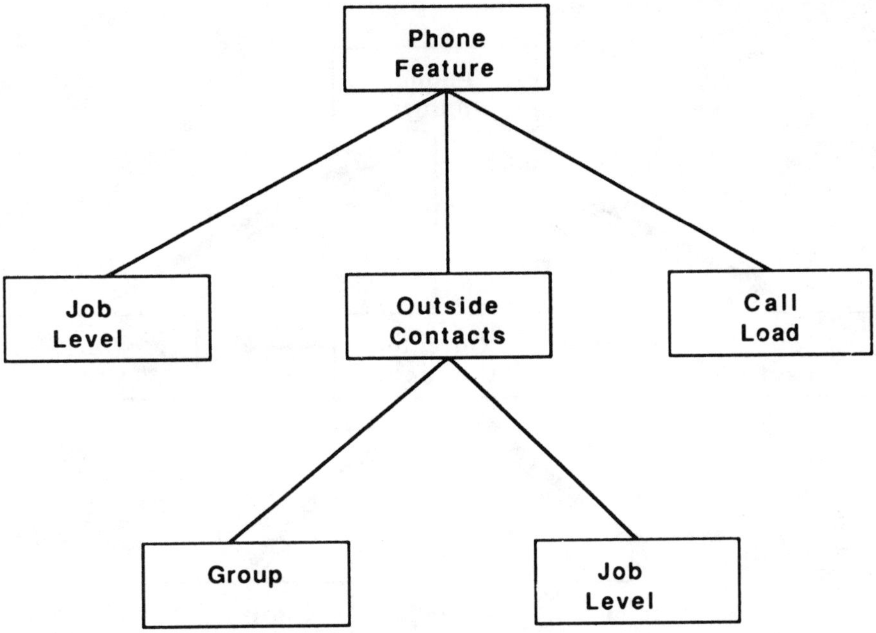

Fig. 8-1. The Phone Feature knowledge base.

Rules determine the actual combination of subgoals mapping to a particular goal value. A rule that maps the Auto Answer feature to Outside Contacts and Call Load is given by

```
If      Outside Contacts is Many        And
        Call Load is High
Then
        Phone Feature is Auto Answer
```

Other rules can map still other phone features to one or more subgoals. In the terminology of KB systems, the If part of the rule is called the antecedent and the Then part is called the conclusion or consequent. In nearly all rule-based KB systems, allowances are made for conjoined (Anded) or disjoined (Ored) antecedent clauses. Moreover, consequents may have more than one clause, some that are assertions of values and some that may actually be invocations of procedural code.

One very popular subgoal resolution strategy is top to bottom, left to right—commonly called depth-first search. In the phone feature example, if a particular query's main goal is Phone Feature, the nodes would be traversed as illustrated in FIG. 8-2. Other search strategies are possible—breadth first, for instance—but few are as prevalent in KB systems as depth-first search.

Nodes in the KB system goal hierarchy are typically called attributes. As seen in the phone feature example, not all attributes are alike. The values for some attributes

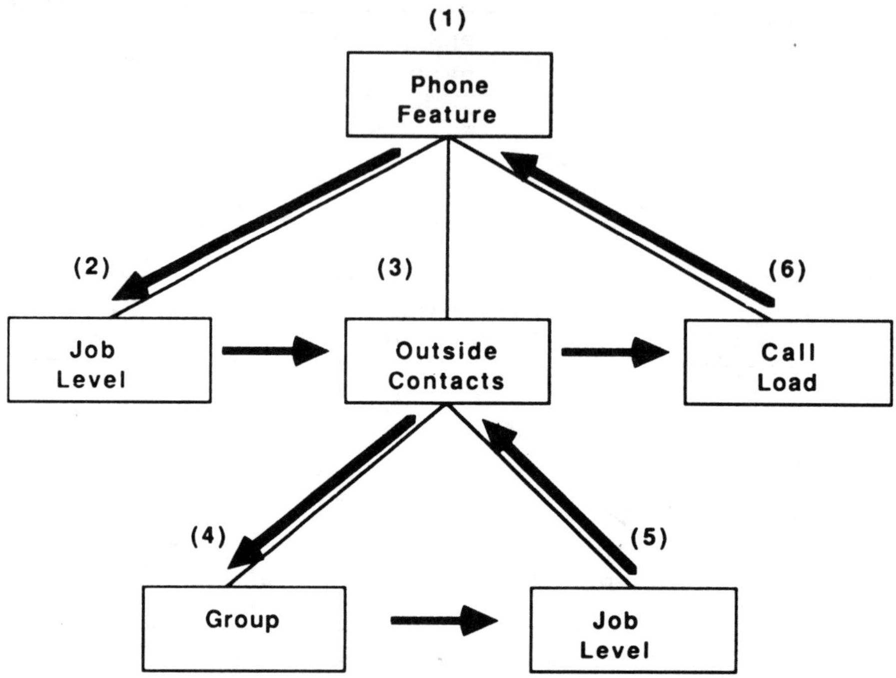

Fig. 8-2. Depth-first search.

can be determined from the value of other attributes. These are inferred attributes, so called because the rules of a KB are used to infer their values. The collection of rules whose consequents assert values for an attribute is sometimes called a *procedure*. As we will see shortly, we can translate rule procedures directly into procedures or functions in traditional programming languages. Other attributes require outside sources of information (user input, databases, and sensing mechanisms) and are called noninferred attributes. Additionally, the cardinality of attributes may be different. In most schemes an attribute may take only one value (single valued) or many values (multivalued). The inferencing structure is used to model the basic problem structure. From this basic design component, other portions of the system are attached.

Procedural flow of control

To illustrate the reasoning process, consider the hypothetical problem of deciding what type of tie to wear. This example is taken from documentation for the KES shell system from Software Architecture & Engineering. [4] However, the rules appear here in English format, as opposed to a shell system's rule specification language. In FIG. 8-3 the rules are intentionally grouped into attribute procedures. Thus, the first group represents a procedure for determining values for Tie, the second for determining Lifestyle, and so on. A further amplification of this example is presented in the sections that follow.

Tie rules

Rule1:	If	the person is laidback	and
		the person lives in the west	
	Then	that person should not wear a tie.	
Rule2:	If	the person is a professor	and
		that person is socially active	or
		that person is laidback	
	Then	that person should wear a bow tie.	
Rule3:	If	the person lives in the west	and
		the person is a professor	
	Then	that person should wear a string tie.	
Rule4:	If	the person is a businessman	and
		the person is socially active	
	Then	that person should wear a necktie.	

Geographical location rules

Rule5:	If	the person lives west of the Mississippi River	
	Then	that person lives in the west.	

Lifestyle rules

Rule6:	If	the person is a businessman	and
		the person is married	
	Then	that person is socially active.	
Rule7:	If	the person is a professor	and
		the person is married	
	Then	that person is laidback.	

Profession rules

Rule8:	If	the person's job is teaching	and
		he teaches graduate students	
	Then	that person is a professor.	
Rule9:	If	the person's job is accounting	or
		the person's job is programming	or
		the person's job is managing	
	Then	that person is a businessman.	

Fig. 8-3. The Tie rule base.

Inferred attributes If values have not been established, the rules are tried sequentially.

The ordering of rules can be arbitrary or based on some heuristic organization. For example, one might want to order rules by the strength of their assertions (that is, some rule antecedents may contain evidence that results in more certain conclusions than others). Alternatively, rules can be ordered in such a way that the rules with shorter paths to conclusions are tried first.

Procedures for single-valued inferred attributes return control once a value has been established. Most KB systems save the value so that subsequent invocations of the procedure within a session will not attempt to reestablish a value. However, this is not a cut-and-dried rule, and there may be circumstances (such as process control applications) where procedures are implemented that overwrite previously established values. In contrast, multivalued inferred attributes will try all rules and will therefore assign many values.

Both flowcharts show a query to the user as the source of last resort. Sometimes it makes more sense to place the user query before the rules, thereby allowing a shortcut if users know the answer already (don't ask if the vehicle has wheels, a motor, and a windshield if you suspect the user can identify a car!). Lastly, the most reliable or best source may not be human at all. It may be better to first try queries to a database or a remote sensing device.

Noninferred attributes Rules of the inferred attributes contain references to other attributes. For a rule to fire, these other attributes must have values assigned to them. In some sense, rules can be thought of as "calling" the procedures for other attributes to determine values for them. Some subgoal attributes may in fact have procedures containing rules. These rules will in turn invoke other attribute procedures until the more primitive attributes, noninferred, are reached. Noninferred attributes contain no rules. As before, the first test is to determine whether values have already been established. If not, then external sources such as users, databases, or remote sensors are tried. When the external sources have been exhausted, control is returned to the calling procedure.

Both Tie and Job are subroutines of a larger program (called Ties) that constitutes the KB for Tie. Of particular interest is the mechanism by which Ties invokes the attribute procedures. The Ties program accepts a character-string argument indicating the attribute to be resolved. As stated earlier, one of the hallmarks of KB systems is that their knowledge may serve many different queries. Thus, while Tie is logically at the top of the Ties hierarchy, the user may wish to bypass Tie and query on a value for Job. Consequently, a table lookup is performed matching the attribute name parameter with a table of attribute function names and entry-point addresses. When a match is found, a subscripted function call is made to start the backward-chaining inference process. At the end of the inferencing process, a value (possibly null) is returned to the main procedure, where it is formatted and subsequently passed along to the calling program.

Basic data structures

At a bare minimum, some facility must be provided for the storage of attribute values. This storage can be in main memory or in secondary storage. KB builders pondering this design issue should consider the usual storage-versus-speed trade-offs.

The primary data structure for rules is program code (that is, If statements). In addition to code, we need to store English-like text rules. This can be accomplished using an array. This auxiliary structure is not essential to the basic data structure, but it exists primarily to help explain reasoning and inference.

Explanation facilities

While the receding example is sufficient for illustrating the backward-chaining flow-of-control mechanism, it ignores several facilities considered to be integral parts of KB systems. One such facility is explanation. On demand, KB systems can explain end results and reasoning direction. Three explanation facilities are included in most KB systems: the Rule query, where the text of a rule is shown; the Why query, which inspects the path of reasoning the system is currently exploring; and the Explain (sometimes called How) query, which presents all paths that have led to a particular state. The Why is usually offered at the AskUser prompt. Explain is typically offered at the end of a session, after an attribute value query has been satisfied. However, Rule may appear in both locations.

The Rule query The Rule query is the simplest logic to implement. The English text of rules can be stored in an array, as done in the Ties KB system, or in secondary storage. When the user requests a particular rule (by name), the text for the rule is retrieved and written to the screen. Another approach is to use a screen management facility such as IBM's ISPF or DEC's FMS to store and display the rule text.

The Why query The Why query requires program logic to "remember" the path taken to get to the point from which the Why query was issued. The most logical way to maintain the path is with a stack. The design data structure for a stack can be a linked list or an array. Processing logic is equally simple. Before a rule is tried, its name is pushed onto the stack; after the rule has been tried, its name is popped off the stack. Thus, at the AskUser prompt it is easy to service the Why query by listing the stack's contents. A more verbose Why might also use the function of the Rule to print the text of each rule listed in the stack.

The Explain query The Explain query is the most difficult of the three queries to handle. It requires an expansion of the Rule array to contain "pointers" to attributers. Likewise, subscript pointers to rules must be added to the attribute arrays. Most significantly, the processing of the rules must be modified to assign values to new pointers at appropriate places. This first occurs when an antecedent clause of a rule succeeds (for example, is shown to be true). When this happens, the rule's attribute pointer array must be filled in with the subscript number (from either the SGL__ATR or MTL__ATR arrays) of the antecedent clause's attribute.

If, at the end of a consultation, the user issues an "Explain" query, an Explain utility is called to service the request. Explain recursively follows the trail of pointers contained in the rule and attribute arrays. An attribute points to a rule, which in turn points to other attributes, as indicated. Each line of the "explanation" contains the name of a rule with an appropriate amount of indentation (as shown earlier) to illuminate the dependencies. Explain, as described here, "explains" rule-to-rule relationships. It also "knows" actual values for attributes that caused rules to fire. Hence, without too much programming, these values can also be displayed.

Certainty factors

Often a KB designer will want to consider as a factor user intuition regarding the relative strengths of conclusion-supporting evidence. An example taken from the Ties KB is the rule that states

```
If      Lifestyle is laidback           And
        Geographical location is west
Then
        A tie is inappropriate (certainty = 50%)
```

This means that if the antecedents are 100-percent true, we are 50-percent sure of the conclusion. Of course, the determination of lifestyle and geographical location is also rule based, which makes it very likely that we will not be 100-percent certain of their values.

Certainty factors (CF) can be propagated from earlier inferences. The methodology from the early MYCIN project [5] is commonly used. Simply stated, if the antecedents in a clause are conjoined (Anded), then their minimum certainty factor is multiplied to obtain the CF in the conclusion. If they are disjoined (Ored), the maximum CF is used. From the previous example, if the CF for life-style is 50 percent and the CF for geographical location is 80 percent, the certainty factor for Tie is calculated as follows:

0.5 (CF for Lifestyle, the minimum of Anded clauses)
Times
0.5 (CF for Tie conclusion)
Equals
0.25 (actual CF for Tie)

Another design consideration when handling certainty factors is the threshold for firing rules. Since the rule propagation for certainty factors involves the multiplication of fractions, it is easy to see that trivial depths of backward chaining will result in extremely low certainty for final conclusions. In some cases all conclusions may be desired, regardless of the certainty level. Diagnostic systems are often this way. In other cases only those conclusions asserted with high certainty are viewed. To handle both situations, a variable filtering mechanism must be built that will disallow conclusions not meeting a dynamically specified level of certainty. The usual method for accomplishing this is to compare the resultant CF of the antecedent with some threshold value and fire the rule if that value is exceeded.

Implementation of CFs requires considerable modification of the previously described architecture, since calculations are needed while the antecedent clauses of rules are being considered. To produce these dynamic calculations, one can no longer rely on the built-in Anding and Oring of If statement expressions (this can be done, but only at the expense of And and Or optimization, which can add considerable overhead in lengthy chains of inference). In fact, a number of utility functions must be introduced to handle the addition of certainty factors in the model.

Procedural certainty factor components All rules begin with the True function, which takes three arguments. The first is a character string indicating subgoals to be tried. The keywords And and Enda indicate the conjunction of the subgoals they bracket. Similarly, Or and Endo indicate disjunction. The Is and Isa keywords are comparison operators for single-valued and multivalued attributes, respectively. The Rulen argument identifies the rule for explanation processing (see previous section). The third and final argument, CUMCF, is the storage location where the True function places the cumulative certainty factor upon return. The certainty factor can then be used (provided the rule fires) to associate a level of certainty with the asserted attribute's value.

The True function selects the major clause type of a rule and invokes a support function to handle the type of clause it finds. A subroutine called GetWord is used to extract words from the string. Since the rule "language" used in this example is in prefix notation, we can determine from the first word of a clause what type it is (for example, conjunction or disjunction). The support functions invoked by True are named for the type of antecedent clause they process. The And procedure handles conjunction processing, and the Or procedure handles disjunction processing. Both return a value between 0 and 1.0 that is the cumulative certainty factor.

Since rules may contain composite structures of conjuncts within disjuncts within conjuncts and so on, the support functions And and Or must be recursive. After the string is processed, True checks to determine whether the CF threshold has been satisfied. If it has, True returns a Boolean "true" value (thereby firing a rule). Otherwise, it returns the value "false."

The And function loops until a matching Enda is found. Inside the loop a selection identical to the one in True is made to handle the lower level antecedent clauses. If the lower level clause is an "and," the procedure And will invoke itself recursively. After each clause of the conjunct is processed, a test determines whether the certainty factor is zero. If it is, processing is halted (since zero is the absolute minimum CF). If no zero CF clause is encountered, And returns the minimum CF. The Or function works similarly, except that the first nonzero clause causes Or to return to its parent routine. These in-loop tests for early termination of both And and Or are optimizations of the technique and are not logically necessary. However, their inclusion will greatly reduce unnecessary searching.

Subgoal subroutines are actually invoked within Is, the next-to-lowest-level function. Among other items passed to Is are attribute names and values to be compared. The Is function uses the name received to do a table lookup (similar to the main processing described above) and a subscripted function call to the target attribute's procedure. If the attribute function returns a value equal to the target value passed to Is, then the CF associated with the returned value is returned to the Is caller. Multivalued attribute processing is slightly more complicated in that Is must check all values returned from an attribute function. Note that while only equality comparisons are shown here, other operators could easily be implemented within this architecture.

Another pair of utilities useful in rule processing is Asserts (for single-valued attributes) and Assertm (for multivalued attributes). These utilities perform several functions:

1. They assign a value to the attribute.
2. They compute the CF for the value by computing the CUMCF from antecedent processing with the rule's a priori certainty factor.
3. They record the rule's subscript (in the rule array) for explanation processing.

These tasks could be performed in line, but the resulting attribute functions would become somewhat bloated with redundant code.

Procedural logic differences

From the preceding discussion, it is apparent that commercial data processing programmers and systems analysts will need to adjust their thinking to accommodate the integration of KB systems techniques into their development tool box. At least three features of KB systems represent potential stumbling blocks. First, programming problems requiring KB system techniques are not usually solved in a serial and algorithmic manner. More often they appear as a random walk through the logic with very complex path tracing. Programmers accustomed to building logic hierarchies using relatively simple flow of control will have trouble with this approach in the beginning. Second, many KB system logical constructs are best viewed as pop-up stacks, which may not be a common view for programmers accustomed to writing commercial code. Finally, data in a KB system can come from multiple sources during execution—user, database, default—or it can be allowed to remain missing. Furthermore, the data may be probabilistic or estimated. A "fuzzy" view of data has implications in the logic construction process that are quite different from those encountered by the traditional systems developer.

Conclusions and future evolution

Collectively, the above sections provide insight into the logical techniques used in building KB systems using procedural languages. Traditional systems development requires a significant amount of time for such activities as screen management, data management, and variable definition. Each of these activities is essentially unchanged in the KB system environment. From a maintenance viewpoint, the tool-kit approach and traditional language development strategy should be considered positive support for the strategy described here. Also, training of future KB system developers is made easier, since they would be starting from a more familiar base point.

Space does not permit further discussion of the various implementation issues one might encounter in attempting to use the tool-kit approach described. However, in practice these additional issues appear to be more in the domain of the application and are less likely to be concepts of KB systems design. We must keep in mind that KB system problems are in fact conceptually different and may require a new examination of the way systems are constructed.

Denning [6] and others have recognized that expert systems traditionally use one of three methods to represent knowledge: rule based, logic programming, or frame (object) based. The discussion in this article aligns best with the rule-based school of thought. The logic-programming method is often viewed as the Prolog notational-rule-design approach of predicate and consequence. The third system's view is the frame-based perspective, which provides a technique to concretely and modularly conceptualize a system and its interrelationships. Each of these schools of thought is attempting to assert its view of the problem domain as the expert system field matures.

At present, system programming practices are passing beyond a single system view to combine ideas from other schools of thought. No longer does the issue hinge primarily on a language's view of the problem set. As an example, we have had the personal experience of attaching a limited Prolog notational inference utility to a rule-based problem design set. In another case, the modularity and object orientation from the frame-based school provided great insight into the design of a specific system. For both of these cases, the utilities developed were not judged to be of truly reusable toolkit quality. However, the key point is that a tool kit should continue to evolve, and we have every reason to believe that improved specification notation will emerge from Prolog proponents and that new development methodologies will be contributed by the frame-based school. The various schools of thought all bring new insights to this problem domain, as well as to the computing field in general. Certainly, these new trends are healthier than arguments over which language is best for implementing a system.

Quite possibly the most noticeable trend in expert system technology will be the embedding of KB systems directly into the traditional systems architecture as an adjunct to existing systems. If successful integration is to occur, a tighter coupling with the procedural language environment is expected. One likely evolutionary strategy would favor attaching new logical constructs to older views of languages. Yet to be determined is whether a traditional language approach or a specially designed syntax based on Lisp and/or Prolog will be the prevalent strategy.

References

1. *Intellect, General Information Manual*, G320-9199, IBM Corp., available through IBM branch offices.
2. *IBM Expert System Consultation Environment VM and Expert System Development Environment/VM, General Information Manual*, GH20-9597, IBM Corp., available through IBM branch offices.
3. S.M. Weiss and C.A. Kulikowski, *A Practical Guide to Building Expert Systems*, Rowman and Allanheld, Totowa, N.J., 1984.
4. *KES Knowledge Base Author's Manual*, Software A&E, Arlington, Va., 1983, pp. 7–14.
5. F. Hayes-Roth, D. Waterman, and D. Lenat, eds., *Building Expert Systems*, Addison-Wesley, New York, N.Y., 1983, pp. 93–94.
6. P.J. Denning, "Towards a Science of Expert Systems," *IEEE Expert*, Summer 1986, pp. 80–83.

9

Conventional languages and AI

Peter C. Coffee
Daryll J. Strauss

Editors' note *Not too many years ago, people were stoned to death for disparaging LISP. Early AI zealots believed that conventional programming languages could not handle knowledge processing. In recent years we have come to see the error of these early ways; today, many high-level languages—especially C and Ada—perform knowledge processing tasks quite well. Coffee and Strauss are reprinted here because they make sense, and because applied AI demands cost-effective practical implementation strategies. (Reprinted, with permission, from the May, 1988 issue of* AI Expert. *© 1988,* AI Expert. *All rights reserved.)*

One often sees references to the "commercialization of AI," as if it has been a simple transition from laboratory to marketplace. The commercialization process has actually gone through three intermediate phases: from a research discipline to a market and, only recently, to a marketable technology. This distinction is crucial; it is one of the keys to understanding the current movement toward AI development and delivery in conventional languages.

The latter phrase itself begs the question: "What makes a programming language conventional?" As noted by B.J. MacLennan, citing 1978 conference remarks by FORTRAN pioneer John Backus, "the preliminary specification of FORTRAN was met with 'indifference and skepticism.' " [1] The notion of generating acceptably efficient programs from a higher-level, easily readable notation promised such a breakthrough for programmer productivity that it was termed "automatic programming." [2]

This label has persisted as an AI subdiscipline, [3] though it must be the canonical example of shooting at a moving target. However easy the programmer's job becomes, some portion of the task will always be thought sufficiently tedious to justify automation—whether by compilers in the fifties or fourth generation languages in the eighties.

Early in the evolution of AI as a discipline, however, a basic difference in priorities existed in the design of AI's programming languages and tools. "We did not regard language design as a difficult problem," Backus recalls, "merely as a simple prelude to the real problem: designing a FORTRAN compiler which could produce efficient programs." [2] Contrast this with the motivations for the design of LISP, as described by

John McCarthy's original paper in 1960. [4] LISP was meant, first and foremost, to provide a basis for understanding the theory of computation.

E. Charniak and D.V. McDermott recount the peculiar transition of LISP from a mathematical concept to a working tool: "McCarthy showed that one could write a universal function in LISP that could interpret any LISP function. This was necessary if he wanted to convince mathematicians since . . . a universal Turing machine . . . can simulate any other Turing machine. McCarthy called his universal LISP function *eval* . . .. One of McCarthy's students, Steve Russell, pointed out that if he hand-coded *eval*, they could run the language. McCarthy's first reaction was to tell Russell that he had theory and practice mixed up. But *eval* was written, and LISP was born." [5]

Brains and brawn?

In terms of both software (optimizing compilers) and hardware (floating-point processors), there is little question that mainstream techniques have been superior for solving mainstream problems. That sounds suspiciously like a tautology, but by "mainstream" we mean the execution of well-understood algorithms in environments where a finished program is used for many years with only incremental modification. (The adoption of the euphemism "maintenance," as if software were wearing out rather than being found buggy or inadequate, is just a little white lie that protects the egos of both the developer and the client.)

By contrast, AI research was attacking problems whose algorithms—if any—were yet to be discerned, under research conditions where the production of working code marked the beginning of problem redefinition rather than delivery of a final product. Under the circumstances, it is hardly surprising that the AI community became the world's most demanding users of software development tools. "In order to pursue the barely possible," observes John Seely Brown of Xerox, "the Artificial Intelligentsia have been forced to develop a powerful arsenal of programming tools that manage the complexity of writing and experimenting with gigantic programs, programs constantly undergoing radical change . . ." [6]

A Symbolics representative summed it up in remarks delivered at AI Expo, Long Beach, Calif., in April 1987. He said, "Debugging in conventional software environments is like being an arson inspector: 'Where's the match? It must be in here somewhere!' " His point, of course, was that true software engineering requires the ability to construct prototypes and observe their behavior—including failure—under controlled and reproducible conditions. By contrast, in conventional development environments, a failure often destroys vital clues to its cause.

The costs catch up

But a funny thing happened on the way to the 1990s: the world of production software took on many of the characteristics of AI research environments of the 1960s. Programs became larger and more complex, especially as the systems hosting them became highly distributed. Programs had to exhibit more judgment in the evaluation of their input, especially as they were required to support more interaction with users who were not computer professionals. Development cycles and software lifetimes became shorter, especially as hardware evolution accelerated and software became a component of competitive strategy—both commercial and military—rather than a piece of the overhead.

Compare and contrast the following two quotations:

- "Programs are judged not only by whether they faithfully carry out the intended processing but also by whether they are understandable and easily changed." [7]
- "A programming language shapes the way we think about the solutions to our problems. We need a language that leads to systems that map directly to their problem space." [8]

The first quotation sounds as if it might come from some bastion of structured programming. In fact, it's from D.G. Bobrow and M.J. Stefik's *Perspectives on Artificial Intelligence Programming*. [7] The second quotation sounds like a characteristically AI point of view; it comes from one of the leading authorities on Ada. [8] Many might consider the ultimate goal of a machine intelligence to be nearly antithetical to that of reliable performance in embedded software systems, the latter being Ada's design milieu. It may surprise them to realize how complementary the resulting perspectives are proving to be.

But another faction—and a large one—may be crying, "a plague on both your houses." Some feel that LISP (particularly the extensive Common LISP dialect) and Ada (also a large language) merely represent two equally undesirable extremes: the former bearing the burden of programmers' demands to do things any way they like, and the latter going to great pains to make sure things are done in the one true way.

This large body of capable talent prefers to work instead with a tool that is efficient, small, and semantically close to the hardware (these adjectives are drawn, in case you haven't already recognized them, from S.P. Harbison and G.L. Steele Jr.'s reference manual for C [9]). Despite these genuine differences in language design philosophy, however, C also has an important role to play in the development and delivery of marketable AI. But we are getting ahead of ourselves.

No code is an island

At this point, we must catch ourselves before we fall into one of the most dangerous traps in programming: the illusion that it is possible to compare the merits of languages without regard for the task to be performed. We should instead be asking ourselves some rather simple questions like: "What makes a program an AI program?"

Today the dominant form of deliverable AI is the production system, colloquially known as the rule-based software architecture—the heart of most of today's knowledge-based systems. When such a system's rules represent expert-level knowledge of facts and associated problem-solving heuristics, we call such a program an expert system. In practice, this label is often applied without such discriminating regard for the quality of the knowledge base: this is regrettable, but it is an issue for another time and place.

Production systems rely on two internal databases: one of facts and derived conclusions, often called working memory, and the other containing the rules whose application is used to modify the working memory's contents. The numbers of facts and rules required to provide nontrivial capability often prove startling to those new to this field. For example, XCON, a Digital Equipment Corp. system for configuring computers, contains 6,200 rules and a database of more than 20,000 components. [10]

The task of keeping such systems' knowledge bases current is of comparable magnitude. As reported by E. Soloway, J. Bachant, and K. Jensen, "50% of the rules in XCON are changed each year . . . there is no end in sight . . . Unfortunately, the problems of . . . updating such a large system *do not grow linearly* . . ." [10]

Searching and matching

The process of searching the collection of facts—a collection subject to constant and substantial revision—for those that satisfy the conditional tests (left-hand sides) of one or more rules is therefore a critical bottleneck for the performance of the active component (inference engine) of such a system. When the subject of search arises, it is de rigueur to nod wisely and cite some authority such as P.H. Winston, who assures us that "search problems are ubiquitous, popping up everywhere artificial intelligence researchers and students go." [11]

The fact that much of AI is search, however, does not mean search is necessarily AI. For example, the use of hashing techniques (to speed search and permit explicit speed/space trade-offs) is an undergraduate computer science topic that arises in many of the least-glamorous domains. It even appears as a tutorial example in B.W. Kernighan and D.M. Ritchie's *The C Programming Language*. [12] More complex searches (for example, those performed by database managers) have been discussed extensively elsewhere. [13] Suffice it to say that the vast majority of these were implemented in mainstream languages.

Beyond a certain level of complexity, we cease to think of search per se as the primary difficulty; rather, we start to describe the task as one of pattern matching. Though likewise essential to any semblance of intelligence, pattern recognition is not the private preserve of the relatively specialized languages, such as PROLOG, [14] that provide pattern recognition as an intrinsic feature. An excellent example is the LFIND algorithm described by E.J. Smith, [15] which finds multiple words in strings with a run time independent of the number of words in the search list. A state machine design, exploiting the XLAT instruction of the much-maligned 8086 microprocessor, is the key: the published code is in Pascal.

The paragon of pattern matching is the Rete algorithm, discussed extensively elsewhere [16] and best known for its public-domain LISP implementation as the heart of the OPS5 production system language. Rete also appears in the public domain in C, however, as part of the NASA-developed CLIPS (C Language Production System). [17]

For large but essentially simple structures, the performance advantages of C—at least, with present compiler technology—become even more pronounced. Much of today's neural-like network research, for example, is done in C, despite C's status as one of the most speculative and research-oriented subtopics of AI. What's wrong with these people? Don't they know C is for well-understood problems? The question is rhetorical, as we shall see.

Unnatural selection

A clue to the resolution is provided by a recent comment from Roberto Shironoshita at the University of Pennsylvania in Philadelphia. Responding to a criticism of FORTRAN interactive input/output facilities, Shironoshita observed: "Interactive programs are not an impossibility in FORTRAN . . . . The answer is good standard libraries. That's where C's main power resides . . . ." We may extend this to a more general principle: a language is good for doing things people have already figured out how to do with that language!

In this sense, few of us pick a language entirely on its intrinsic merits—indeed, such "merits" may be a myth. We select a language for what it allows us to adapt from existing code, as much as for any other reason.

This brings us back to our opening observation: the early years of commercial AI have been warped by the fact that the market consisted of AI developers building and selling tools largely for and to each other. In this environment, doing "AI things" was considered the top priority. Most of the existing code to do such things was written in AI languages such as LISP, so tools were developed to facilitate refinement of this code in LISP and in other specialized environments.

As AI moves into the wider world of production, however, where the expensive and difficult-to-replace code components are already written in mainstream languages, the cost to convert our essential ideas—such as search and matching—into other languages now looks (relatively) much smaller than before. This is especially true when one considers the relative cost and availability of programming skills for various language environments.

Prospects for performance

Many argue that we should discount the true importance of the existing pool of conventional language skills. After all, a frequent claim for the AI languages is that higher productivity will arise from their higher levels of data and procedural abstraction. [18]

This benefit is illustrated by the Common LISP *sort* function, which accepts as its argument either a list or a vector (a one-dimensional array) with no need to declare the argument's type. This and other LISP functions can simply call the function *type-of* to determine at run time the kind of value they have received as an argument. This is characteristic of an overall LISP philosophy that often allows the programmer to change the physical representation of a data structure with minimal impact on another code.

Similarly, the Smalltalk-80 and other object languages, the type (or class) of an object receiving a message (such as *sort*) must recognize that message as a selector for a method defined for either that object's class or for some more general superclass. For example, *number* is a superclass of *integer*, and the notion of sorting objects by comparing their numeric magnitude is common to all numbers. The sender of the message, however, need not be concerned with the class of the receiving object. [19] Again, the impact of representation changes is confined to the immediate neighborhood of the change.

By contrast, C function definitions require that parameter types be explicitly declared. Type errors in C, such as passing a floating-point value to a C expression that expects an integer, may simply produce incorrect results. This is not necessarily regarded as a flaw in the language; as one reference observes, "the lack of checking gives programmers some freedom in violating conventions on certain rare occasions . . . ." [8] Programmer attention to details of representation is therefore required, a burden only partially alleviated by tools such as the *lint* utility and the introduction of innovations such as function prototypes.

But the choice between abstraction during design and efficiency during execution is not necessarily mutually exclusive: conceptually, Ada combines the benefits of both approaches. Ada allows the same kind of flexibility as many object languages in letting a single concept, such as sorting, apply to many types of data. One might define a *sort* procedure for each of many different data types, even for programmer-defined abstract types such as *DegreesF*, producing a set of so-called "overloaded" subprograms.

When the programmer calls *sort*, it need not be specified which one of these identically named procedures is meant. Rather, "the compiler may take the types and order of the actual parameters, the name of the formal parameters (if named parameter association is used), and the result type (for functions) to resolve an overloaded subprogram call." [8] Figuratively speaking, if one tells the compiler to sort eggs, it will sort them by weight, not by zip code.

Unlike conventional object languages, however, Ada performs this "disambiguation" at compile time. The result is to preserve a high level of procedural abstraction in the source code without incurring the performance penalties of looking up methods at run time. When combined with Ada's other advantages, such as inherent semantics for multitasking, this synthesis of strengths for both design and execution makes Ada an interesting option for real-world AI.

Conventional wisdom dismisses Ada as a language no one would use without the pressure of defense contract requirements, but one should first ponder this finding: "In Europe, more than 80% of Ada use is commercial. In Japan, it's all commercial. Only in the United States is Ada associated with the military." [20] Furthermore, the original specifications for what eventually became Ada were drafted to describe a proposed new commercial language "designed for use in large applications with continuously changing structural requirements, rigorous reliability requirements . . . [and] parallel-processing requirements." [20] These are not uniquely military criteria.

This is not to say Ada is ready to take the place of LISP for exploratory development. Its stringent declaration and interface definition requirements are bound to impede the process of incremental development to some extent, though this impediment will diminish with experience. Nor is Ada ready to take the place of C as a universal systems language. For one thing, C's compactness would seem to guarantee that a C compiler will be available for any radically new hardware architecture well before a competent Ada can be produced practically.

Indeed, this relative timing would seem to have been recognized by those who currently produce both LISP and Ada compilers that compile their respective source code to C rather than directly to native code. By using C as a universal assembler, these developers can piggyback their expertise in the higher-level languages on top of the intense commercial competition in machine-specific C compiler development.

Decisions, decisions

What we may ultimately derive from this discussion, however, is nothing less than the key to language choice. That key is the identification of the single greatest obstacle to a particular project's "success" (the latter being recognized as a context-sensitive term).

If your main concern is figuring out what you want to do (for example, in areas such as planning and natural-language recognition), the exploratory facilities of LISP may be of prime importance. If your primary concern is that you make the most of available hardware (for example, in the simulation of massive neural-like networks), C may be the most effective vehicle. If the sheer complexity of the proposed system is its most daunting aspect, as in highly distributed financial services or manufacturing applications, then the intrinsic software engineering disciplines built into Ada may be a compelling feature (Pascal and Modula-2 may also be candidates, [21] especially in view of their broader availability).

When integration of AI techniques into existing systems is the criterion, almost any AI concept can be implemented in the dominant language of the target environment. AI is a perspective for understanding problems as well as a technology for solving them. One can find successful AI tools implemented in almost any language, and most mainstream languages are evolving in ways that encourage this trend.

Debugging facilities, for example, long held to be a benefit of AI development environments, are also becoming an important point of product differentiation among mainstream language compilers. The development and debugging environments of Microsoft's QuickC and QuickBASIC and the Turbo products from Borland International are setting new standards for this area in both technology and price. As this trend continues and the increasing adoption of object semantics narrows the conceptual differences between various languages, today's pronounced divisions between language camps will become much less important.

Those who think best in LISP will continue to use it as their coding notation, especially for writing programs that do things never before done well by software. To them, C may always be "that glorified PDP-11 assembler." Others will continue to expostulate: "You just wrote a line of code with three open parens in the first six characters!" These people will probably be FORTRAN users for many years to come.

And the mathematicians who like to write x for the time derivative of x will probably always consider dx/dt an ugly kluge. Like this and other issues of notation, language choice is essentially a matter of preference and convenience. It is a decision that should be made on the grounds of what it will do to make the real job easier. It should reflect design goals and priorities rather than being an independent subject of intense but sterile debate.

References

1. B.J. MacLennan, *Principles of Programming Languages: Design, Evaluation, and Implementation.* New York, N.Y.: CBS College Publishing, Holt, Rhinehart & Winston, 1983.

2. J.W. Backus and H. Herrik, "IBM 701 Speedcoding and Other Automatic Programming Systems," in *Proceedings of the Symposium on Automatic Programming for Digital Computers*. Washington, D.C.: Office of Naval Research, 1954.
3. A. Barr and E.A. Feigenbaum, *The Handbook of Artificial Intelligence, Vol. II*. Los Altos, Calif.: William Kaufmann Inc., 1982.
4. J. McCarthy, "Recursive Functions of Symbolic Expressions and their Computation by Machine," *Communications of the ACM* 7: 184 – 195, 1960.
5. E. Charniak and D.V. McDermott, *Introduction to Artificial Intelligence*, Reading, Mass.: Addison-Wesley Publishing Co. Inc., 1985.
6. J.S. Brown, "The Low Road, the Middle Road, and the High Road," in P.H. Winston and K.A. Prendergast (eds.), *The AI Business*. Cambridge, Mass.: MIT Press, 1984.
7. D.J. Bobrow and M.J. Stefik, "Perspectives on Artificial Intelligence Programming, *Science*, Feb. 28, 1986.
8. G. Booch, *Software Engineering with Ada*, 2nd ed. Menlo Park, Calif.: Benjamin Cummings Publishing Co., 1987.
9. S.P. Harbison and G.L. Steele Jr., *C: A Reference Manual*. Englewood Cliffs, N.J.: Prentice-Hall Inc., 1984.
10. F. Soloway, J. Bachant, and K. Jensen, "Assessing the Maintainability of XCON-in-RIME: Coping with the Problems of a VERY Large Rule Base," presented at AAAI-87, Seattle, Wash., 1987.
11. P.H. Winston, *Artificial Intelligence*, 2nd ed. Reading, Mass.: Addison-Wesley Publishing Co. Inc., 1984.
12. B.W. Kernighan and D.M. Ritchie. *The C Programming Language*. Englewood Cliffs, N.J.: Prentice-Hall Inc., 1978.
13. J.D. Ullman, *Principles of Database Systems*, 2nd ed. Rockville, Md.: Computer Science Press Inc., 1982.
14. J. Malpas, "Programming in Logic," *Dr. Dobb's Journal*, Mar. 1985.
15. E.J. Smith, "Multiple Word Searches with LFIND," *COMPUTER LANGUAGE* 4(11): 47 – 53, Nov. 1987.
16. C.L. Forgy and S.J. Shepard, "Rete: A Fast Match Algorithm," *AI EXPERT* 2(1): 34 – 40, Jan. 1987.
17. C.J. Culbert, *CLIPS Reference Manual*, 87-FM-9, JSC-22552. Houston, Texas: NASA/Lyndon B. Johnson Space Center, Mar. 1987.
18. A.H. Slocum, "LISP from a FORTRAN Programmer's Perspective," *Lucid Moments*, Spring 1987.
19. A. Goldberg and D. Robson, *Smalltalk-80: The Language and its Implementation*. Reading, Mass.: Addison-Wesley Publishing Co. Inc., 1983.
20. D. ben-Aaron, "Ada Goes to Work," *InfoWEEK*, Sept. 8, 1986.
21. D. Coar, "Pascal, Ada, and Modula-2," *BYTE*, Aug. 1984.

10

How to choose natural language software

Marc Rettig
Madeleine Bates

Editors' note *The ability to interact with computers in free-form English (and other languages) has eluded the R&D community. It is still quite difficult to implement syntactic and (especially) semantic understanding programs. Rettig and Bates offer some insight into the technical problems and some prescriptions about how to implement natural language processors into your system concept. (Reprinted, with permission, from the July 1988 issue of* AI Expert. *© 1988,* AI Expert. *All rights reserved.)*

Why can't you pick up this magazine, flip through the advertisements, and order software that would let your application understand English? After all, research in natural language processing has been going on for 30 years. Suppose you manage to find one or more products that claim to meet your needs for natural language processing. How can you evaluate them? What capabilities should natural language software have? Can a nonlinguist hope to produce useful natural language applications using off-the-shelf software?

This article addresses several important issues that must be considered by anyone preparing to process natural languages with a computer. We'll discuss topics that affect your choice of software and the scope of your application. We'll discuss others that may help you decide whether your idea is workable or not. Viable systems in computational linguistics are just beginning to appear. This article takes the point of view of the systems integrator, not the linguistic researcher, and attempts to provide some insight into how you can apply available tools to the application at hand.

But first, a bit of theoretical background to prepare you for what might seem to be a skeptical tone. There is, as is often the case, both bad news and good news.

This is harder than you think

No computer program yet constructed can understand language as well as the average young child. People have managed to learn enough about the structure of language to write successful parsing programs that break sentences into their constituent parts and show how those parts are related to each other. But understanding language—knowing what it is trying to communicate—requires a substantial common-sense knowledge of the world; deeper knowledge than current techniques can provide.

For example, when I first moved to New York City, several people said to me, "You bad?" Puzzling out the syntax and partial semantics was no problem—I could tell I was being asked about some character trait. But I had no idea what was being asked of me or what response was expected. This meant, I found out, that I was not "bad."

This unsettling experience made me want to buy plane tickets for my new friends, and take them to work for my uncle Bun on his cattle ranch in Texas. Then I could watch them squirm when he told them to "Tahten that booma, wiya, er this heifer'll wand up in the bawr-deeich. Wussamata? Jevver heah uv a booma afoah?"

You see, world knowledge is essential to language understanding.

What exactly does it mean to say that we "understand" a sentence? In the context of computer systems, we usually judge a system's understanding by the appropriateness of its responses. If I ask a database front end, "Are any students failing AI-101?" a "yes" or "no" is probably not the best response. I'd like to see a list. And what if no such class exists? Can we say the system really understood the question if it just answers, "none"? A human would probably tell me that there was no AI-101, and ask if I meant AI-201—the AI class currently offered.

Understanding involves much more than simply finding the subject, verb, and object of a sentence. It involves even more than classifying agents, actions, and recipients. Somehow, when people hear a sentence, they are able to instantly relate it to the context of the conversation, call up a wealth of information about the subject at hand, resolve ambiguities, and infer the probable meaning of words and constructions they've never heard before. No computer program can come close to this, and the problems involved are relevant to current research in most branches of AI.

So this is the bad news. If you want to build a system that will understand free speech over a large subset of English, you'll have to wait. Probably for years. AI is still waiting for its Einstein or Mendel.

Practical systems are possible

Most real-world applications don't need to deal with speech or unrestricted English. Either the user is expected to use a subset of English (it's often very easy for the user to adapt) or the subject matter (domain) of the application is predictable enough that the system doesn't need to know an overwhelming amount of semantic information.

For example, a medical system developed at New York University's Linguistic String Project (LSP) takes patient histories as input. The design process included careful investigation of the language used in sample histories, with the goal of discovering what categories of words take part in special grammatical relationships. Instead of just *NOUN* and *PROPER-NOUN*, word categories include *PATIENT, BODY-PART*, and *SYMPTOM*. This careful definition of the medical sublanguage contained in the input yielded tremendous benefits in the robustness of the system.

The sentence, "Patient had pain in chest and stomach" would be ambiguous to many systems (compare "Patient had pain in chest and fever"). But the LSP system understands the medical sublanguage and knows that body parts can't play the role of symptoms. So it is able to eliminate the nonsensical interpretation, "Patient had pain in chest and patient had stomach."

In many cases, you can carry the sublanguage idea even further since you know in advance that the user is restricted to a particular set of commands or that only the contents of a particular database will be discussed. A good natural language system designer will take advantage of any such domain restrictions inherent in the application and avoid the theoretical barriers to handling unrestricted English.

(The term "system designer" is not quite appropriate. We need to distinguish the basic system designer from the person who adapts it to a particular application. A few people designed and built Intellect, but hundreds of people have adapted it to particular databases. We will use the words "builder" and "adapter" to distinguish these roles, and "designer" to refer to them together.)

When considering a particular application, an adapter must ask several questions. What will the user expect of this system? How big should the system's vocabulary be? How wide a range of sentence constructs should the system handle? The answers to these questions will influence the choice of software.

Levels of sophistication

There are many ways to make use of language. Some of them don't require the sophistication of a jumbo-size English interface. Before evaluating natural language software, carefully evaluate the demands of your application. If you can get by with a restricted subset of English, you stand a much better chance of building successful software.

In fact, it is possible to do much more with a relatively unsophisticated interface than you would judge by the products on the market. Nicholas Negroponte, director of the MIT Media Lab, has pointed out two advantages of speech: its long reach (you can talk to somebody 20 feet away and around corners and up stairs) and the fact that it is an extra channel (you can talk and still have both hands free). A volt-ohm meter with speech input and output could get a lot of use out of a very small vocabulary. You could stand across the table from it, leads in hand, and shout "OHMS!" or "VOLTS!"

Such command systems are relatively easy to deal with. In fact, this really doesn't qualify as natural language processing since no understanding of language is required to convert the spoken text into application commands. While most of this article relates to larger problems, consider this a challenge to make creative use of the speech technology already available.

For most natural language applications, it is not desirable to restrict the user to a small set of simple commands. One of the motivations for using natural language input is to free the user from the restrictions of a command language—to allow use of full sentences. However, if an application deals with a very restricted domain, the set of sentences in actual use may turn out to be fairly small.

For example, if you are building a query language for a database filled with information about traffic violations, it is unlikely that the grammar will have to handle many of the kinds of sentences found in *Moby Dick* or *Science* magazine. Rather, it will only need to cover English questions, including implied questions such as "Tell me how many . . ." or "List the. . . ." It will also need to be able to resolve the referents of pronouns, so it can answer questions like "How many drivers were arrested for DWI in

March, and how old were *they?*" To add to the simplicity, the vocabulary will be quite small compared to unrestricted English—you're not likely to need the word "pajamas" in the traffic violation system.

This is not to give the impression that building an English database query language is a simple problem. On the contrary, it has been the focus of a great deal of study for many years, with varying degrees of success. The subset of language required is nontrivial and requires a robust parsing mechanism and semantic representation (as we will discuss later). However, the problem is well enough understood that useful commercial software products are available. Other applications that might get by with a very restricted subset of English are voice control of a robot or manufacturing tool, or a natural language interface to a CAD system.

If a study of your application fails to reveal a small subset of language that will meet the user's requirements, you are not likely to build a successful product with today's technology. Leave this work for the research labs.

Of course, "large" and "small" are relative terms, and it may be difficult for a nonlinguist to evaluate the linguistic requirements of an application with enough precision to predict a project's success. We hope the rest of this article will help. We've tried to describe language characteristics that the best commercial products today can handle.

Choosing software

Now we approach the tough problem of choosing software suited to your application. You really need to ask two sets of questions, one that concerns your application and another the software packages you are evaluating.

For the reasons just mentioned, it is imperative that the application requirements are carefully defined before choosing software tools. This may sound like nothing more than good design practice, but natural language introduces a few new areas to consider.

If you are dealing with a keyword application like the voltmeter, you may not require specialized natural language software. It may be cheaper and more efficient to write your own pseudo-language processor. Good sources of public domain programs can be adapted to such purposes (for example, the *AI EXPERT* Bulletin Board Service and CompuServe forum). YANLI and ATN/LISP are two products that might be helpful since they supply complete source code in LISP.

Applications of great syntactic and semantic complexity usually require the ability to convert natural language into a formal representation; here, a commercial natural language product is in order. Unless you have considerable training in both computer science and computational linguistics, you are unlikely to build a successful system yourself.

Some advertisements for AI tools (such as PROLOG or LISP) would have you believe otherwise. Many PROLOG implementations include a way to write grammars in something very close to the Backus-Naur format familiar to computer scientists, creating an instant parser without writing additional code. Since PROLOG contains a built-in backtracking control structure, you might think this would be just the thing. But you soon run into the complexities of natural language and the inefficiencies of uncontrolled backtracking, and anything but a very trivial application will require some degree of linguistic sophistication. Researchers have been working on these problems for several decades. Only now are we beginning to see viable commercial systems. We are not yet at the point where the uninitiated can write robust, useful natural language software.

Your choice of natural language software may be limited by the kind of computer equipment you plan to use. Or perhaps it will be the other way around—you'll be forced to choose hardware based on the demands of the natural language program. Many natural language products require large amounts of RAM and disk space and run only on minicomputers or well-fed workstations. You might be able to handle the speech input on a PC but need a Symbolics or VAX to run the software of choice. However, this situation is changing rapidly due to market pressures and the ever-increasing power of desktop computers.

If your application is to be embedded in some device rather than running on a free-standing computer, your choices will be even more limited. Most packages assume the presence of a keyboard and display and want to be the boss of the hardware and the flow of control. It may be difficult to get them to do otherwise; check with the developers of the package.

If this is your situation, look for natural language software that can be buried in your own programs—communicating not with a human user but with other software. This can be accomplished in several ways. Carnegie Group's LanguageCraft is made up of several modules. The parser and interpretation software is a separate, embeddable program. Other products (such as Texas Instruments' Speech Applications Toolkit) supply hooks to LISP, C, or Pascal programs at strategic points in their processing. These can be used for connection to nonstandard user interfaces or to other products.

Finally, it is sometimes possible to acquire the source code for a natural language system or contract with the vendor to modify the software for your own purposes. At least one company, Cognitive Systems Inc., specializes in contracting for natural language applications.

Evaluation criteria

How can you find natural language software to fit your application? How do you measure the performance of parsers, the adequacy of dictionaries, and the performance of a language processor? These are not easy questions to answer, but we can at least set some guidelines and mention a few critical points to consider; in particular, vocabulary, syntactic, and semantic coverage, as well as matters of discourse and domain coverage.

The vocabulary of natural language software is stored in a lexicon or dictionary. (We'll use the two words interchangeably.) People who are not familiar with this technology are likely to picture this as little more than a list of words, but it is so much more. A spelling checker can get away with such a dictionary, but as soon as you try to assign meanings to words, you bump into all of the difficulties that make even paper dictionaries very complicated in both structure and content. The lexicon can be scepter and crown or ball and chain to natural language software.

How can you evaluate the worth of a vendor's dictionary? By counting the number of entries? Reading its contents? Listening to the marketing representative? There's no simple answer. But here are a few points to keep in mind while you are reviewing the lexical capabilities of a piece of natural language software.

It is often difficult to distinguish between semantics and vocabulary. Semantics, simply put, refers to the meaning of words. The meaning of words in this context is their connection to concepts and processes in the application domain. For example, the entry for "person" in the lexicon may somehow be related to the *LNAME* and *FNAME* fields in the *EMPLOYEE* table of a database.

So what's really important to your application is not the number of words in the lexicon but how well the subject matter of the application is covered. Do you have a way to talk about employee, department, and client names? Can you use the word "name" to refer to any of those concepts? Does this require one entry in the lexicon or three?

Don't be impressed just because a product claims to have 10,000 entries in its lexicon. There is a good chance it will have better coverage than a product with 2,000 entries, but not necessarily. Maybe the former has 8,000 city names, and you don't plan to ask about cities very often. Or maybe it knows the part of speech of 8,000 words but has no knowledge of their meaning. When evaluating products, be sure to devise ways to measure vocabulary coverage, not just the number of lexical entries.

Vocabulary should not be used as a quick-and-dirty way around semantic problems. Consider the term, "last year." By itself, "last" usually means "final." When it modifies "year" or "night," it means "previous." A good natural language system will be able to deal with time constructs as part of its semantic processing. It may seem easier at first to simply add an entry into the lexicon for "last year" with the meaning "1987," but this is a very short-term solution. It is impossible to cover all of these kinds of special meanings in the lexicon.

Also, if you define "life insurance" and "health insurance" as separate lexical entries, the system won't understand a question like "Who has life and health insurance?" because "life" won't be understood. Often a commercial system gives users the ability to add simple dictionary entries. Be warned—be careful.

What's the relationship between items in the underlying system (field names and values in the database) and the vocabulary? As you construct your application, you'll need to link words in the lexicon to objects in the rest of your program. Some natural language products provide a convenient way of doing so. Many packages were designed to be front ends for database systems—if your application is different, make sure you'll be able to tie lexical entries to something other than database definitions. Remember also that you'll be spending a large part of your maintenance effort taking care of the lexicon. Make sure it will be convenient to add and update entries.

Check for special entities in input (part numbers, social security numbers, etc.) that should be recognized without additional words. You might want to say "Schedule 555-12-3456 for audit" rather than "Schedule the person with social security number 555-12-3456. . .." If you have many such items, you should consider how the software handles such things.

What kind of regularities does the morphology component know? Do you have to add separate entries for every form of a word or can the software automatically recognize plurals, possessives, past and future tenses, etc.? Typical parsers recognize word forms that follow the rules and allow you to enter exceptions separately. For example, a single entry for "follow" would cover "follows" and "followed," but "eat," "ate," and "eaten" would each require separate entries. The more the morphological software recognizes, the less work you have to do to build the lexicon.

It must be possible for words to have multiple meanings. For example, "In" may be a preposition or a state abbreviation, "Jan" may be a month or a person, "To" or "The" may be someone's last name. Even a word with a single part of speech may have multiple meanings. "Who is the oldest employee?" may refer to the person with the greatest age or the person who has worked for the company the longest.

Vocabulary size is a slippery concept. Words are hard to count, and the marketing brochure's method of counting may be very different from the technician's. This is true for a number of reasons:

- Counting dictionary entries may overcount some classes (such as abbreviations) and under-count others (such as regularly inflected words). If one dictionary entry can represent several word forms, a simple entry count will be deceiving. Furthermore, a verb root will cover more forms (tense, person, number) than a noun (usually only singular and plural).

  Here is a rough formula for calculating "effective vocabulary":

  ```
  number of nouns (excluding proper nouns) * 2
      + number of adjectives * 3
      + number of verbs * 4
      + number of other dictionary entries
  ```

- Some forms of words may never be used in actual practice. For example, you may want to ask "When was so-and-so born?" but never use the present tense "bear."
- Consider whether proper nouns should be included or counted separately. This depends somewhat on your application. If you are working with geographical information, it's handy if the product you buy already contains a large number of place names. If you're working with medical terminology, place names won't be very important. In any case, it should be easy to add large numbers of proper nouns yourself.
- Should multiword items ("the University of California") be counted as more than one word?
- Should words with more than one part of speech be counted more than once? For example, the word "list" can be used as both a verb and a noun. Should this be counted as two words?
- Should multisense words be counted more than once? The word "run" can refer to animals moving their legs quickly or to fluids moving downstream. Is this worth counting twice? If both senses are in the lexicon, the coverage is certainly greater than if only one was present.
- What happens to system performance when the number of particular kinds of words is increased? Suppose you add 5,000 city names to the lexicon. Will it suddenly take too long for the system to understand a question?

The moral here is this: it probably isn't worthwhile to try to measure vocabulary size precisely. Instead, find out what is behind specific claims. Consider what is really represented by the dictionary entries and their value to your particular application.

Also, take note of the facilities for managing the lexicon. Is there software to help you add and change entries? Can you easily find duplicate or conflicting entries? When you give a new definition to an old word, what happens to the old definition? Can you define new word categories or are you forced to live with those supplied by the vendor? How valuable are these things in your situation?

Syntactic coverage

"Syntax" is what most people call the grammar of a language. The syntax of a language is the set of rules that describes how words can be combined into phrases, clauses, and sentences. In this short space, it's impossible to describe all the matters of syntax that need to be covered by a general-purpose natural language system.

Native English speakers take the syntax of language for granted. We understand everything so effortlessly that we are surprised when someone points out the complexities of English grammar. These complexities become painfully obvious when you try to process language with a computer. So the grammatical component of a natural language product is of central importance. You can have the most carefully tailored lexicon imaginable, but without adequate syntactic coverage your software will be useless. Look at these pairs of sentences:

1A. List the employees of the department that was moved to Connecticut.
1B. List the employees of the department that were moved to Connecticut.
2A. The man who knew him went left.
2B. The man who knew he went left.

The natural language software must figure out the relationships between the nouns and verbs in these sentences. Who moved, and who went where? Solving this puzzle doesn't require an elaborate lexicon or a deep understanding of the world. For examples 1A and 1B, it is enough to know that the subject and object of a sentence must agree in number. For examples 2A and 2B, knowing that "him" is in the objective case would prevent the program from analyzing the sentence as Tonto might: "Him went left."

Troublesome constructs

This isn't the place for an exhaustive description of English syntax. But we can at least mention some constructs that could be important to your application and may or may not be covered by the grammar supplied with a piece of commercial software. Use these to help make up test sentences when evaluating a package. Remember that if you can't come up with a query in your domain with one of these features, you probably don't need it.

- Quantifiers: "all," "some," "two," "few," "most"
- Subcategorization (verb complements): "I believed that he left." "I waited for him to leave." "He promised to go." "I believed him to be hurt." "When did it begin to rain?"
- Indirect objects (some take "to," some "for"): "They made him a cake." "They made a cake for him." "They gave him a book." "They gave a book to him."

- Bitransitive verbs (don't allow "to" or "for" with the direct object); "We envy you your wealth."
- Verb particles: "Look the address up." "Look up the address." "Look up the street."
- Possessives: "the smallest department's average salary"; "flight A57's arrival time"
- Negation (noun phrase and verb phrase): "Who has no phone number?" "Who doesn't have a phone number?"
- Determiners: "Did all six of the programmers quit?" "Which departments have seven or more managers?"
- Sentential noun phrases: "That John exists is a fact."
- Infinitival noun phrases: "To strive is better than to give up."
- Pre- and postnominal modifiers: "a bigger ship than the Stark"; "a ship bigger than the Stark"
- Partitives (partitives divide something into parts): "three of the ships"
- Complex tenses and modals: "He could not have been seeing her then."
- Verb phrase deletion: "John is leaving and Mary is too" (Will the system figure out that Mary is leaving?)
- Wh-movement ("wh" refers to words and phrases starting with "who," "what," "where," etc.): relative clauses—"the book he gave her" ("which" is missing; will the system know which book you're referring to?); Pied Piping—"a book the author of which . . ." (will the system think you're referring to a book or the author?); unbounded dependencies—"Which banks do they appear to be willing to consider allowing us to remove gold from?"
- Conjunction: "and," "or," "but," "except," "not only," "both . . ."
- Comparatives: "John is more than three inches taller than Bill." "Who makes more, John or Bill?" "Who earns more than the average salary?" "Which rich men earn more than the richest woman?"
- Extraposition: "Of all the departments, which is the biggest?"
- Ellipsis: "Count the ships in the Mediterranean." "the submarines" "with nuclear capability" (Will the system know the last fragment is a request for a count of ships in the Mediterranean with nuclear capability? Or did you mean submarines? In the Mediterranean? With nuclear capability?)
- Adverbials: "quickly," "recently"

This could go on and on. If it seems a little overwhelming, you're just getting a realistic idea of the complexity of human language. The bad news is that many problems in language understanding are still very hard research problems. Any commercial system you evaluate is bound to choke on some of your test sentences. The good news is that many of the hard problems in computational linguistics are not relevant to the practical use of language in computer systems.

Your evaluation of natural language software should not focus on whether the system can handle any English grammar you can think of but whether it can handle the English grammar you need for your application. There are probably more syntactic problems than you anticipated. But if you've chosen your application domain wisely, you will still be able to build something useful.

Sometimes you'll have the luxury of choosing a level of sophistication to fit the available technology. For example, imagine you are designing the Hear It and Say It Voltmeter. You have some alternatives: have the software pick out keywords or understand full sentences. In the simpler case, the software is just looking for keywords and responding with current readings (voltage? ohms?) You could build such a meter with current off-the-shelf technology.

Now suppose you want to make your meter seem smarter. You might want to make the language software recognize sentence constructions and handle ellipses ("What were the last three voltages? Ohms?") Now instead of responding with the current resistance measurement, the meter takes the last request in the context and lists the previous three ohm values. This approach is tougher and far more expensive. You will make a design choice to fit the available technology.

Semantic coverage

How intelligent or powerful do you want your application to appear? The user's perception of your system will depend primarily on the depth of the system's knowledge of the application domain. Of course, this knowledge is really the application itself: the contents of a database, the state of a machine, whatever the user is ultimately working with. Typically, natural language software converts sentences into an internal representation—a formal description of the sentence that can be converted into the terms of the application.

There is no standard way to represent the meaning of a sentence. This is an active research topic, the subject of more debate and more filled with difficulties than the topic of syntax. As with vocabulary and syntactic coverage, the semantic coverage you need will vary with the complexity of the application. For a command system, the commands are the semantic representation. Once the software recognizes the command, it can execute it without further analysis.

But what about more complicated systems? Consider a database query language, for example. Several semantic issues are important—problems of sentence understanding that cannot be solved with a large vocabulary or syntactic sophistication. One is quantifier scope, the problem of deciding which words in a sentence are modified by quantitative statements. For the sentence "List the trains that go to every city in Wisconsin," two interpretations are possible: "Consider, one at a time, each city in Wisconsin and list the trains that go there" and "List the trains whose route passes through every city in Wisconsin." Probably the latter is more desirable, but how should a system know this?

Another example is this pair of phrases: "the directive of every manager" and "the secretary of every manager." In its most natural reading, the first phrase assumes a single directive applies to all managers. The second refers to a different secretary for every manager.

Many other issues exist:

- Multiple nouns: "computer hardware documentation specifications," "aluminum soup pot cover," "clearance sale" (Will the system know what database entity these refer to?)

- Comparatives: "Who earns as much as Smith?" "Who is 30 years old?" (really means "Whose age is at least 30 and less than 31?")
- Tense and time: "Where will the meeting be Monday?" "Where is the Monday meeting?" "Where was the meeting Monday?" "Where was the Monday meeting?" (Does the system know that the first pair of sentences refers to the next Monday on the calendar and the second pair to the previous Monday?)

If a system performs strong semantic analysis, it should be able to eliminate some nonsensical sentence interpretations. It will seem more intelligent about recognizing the speaker's intent. The preceding sentences are within the reach of current technology, so if your application needs to handle such questions, don't despair.

If you are buying commercial natural language software, you won't have much control over the semantic representation. The important thing for the success of a natural language system is the connection between the application's subject matter and the analyses produced by the sentence parser. If you are asking questions about a database, you'd like sentences to be converted into the database query language. If you're talking to a machine, you'll want some formal representation of the sentence that can be examined by the machine's controlling software.

Products such as LanguageCraft let the user specify mapping rules by which the internal semantic representation is converted into application-specific data structures, function calls, or commands. If you require the sophisticated linguistic capabilities of something like LanguageCraft or BBN's Parlance, be sure you have some such mechanism for connecting to your own programs.

Practical issues

Natural language software can be extremely sophisticated in its linguistic analysis but still frustrating to use. A piece of software has a spirit or personality that reflects the designer's attitude toward the user. When you design a product with language capabilities, you are setting the course of perhaps thousands of future conversations. What personality will you project to your users, and how does the natural language software help you build a likable system? What if your user misspells a word or uses bad grammar? What if a sentence can legitimately be interpreted in several ways? Does the system recover gracefully from errors? Does it always provide helpful answers? Can you teach it new words easily?

Many natural language systems correct spelling errors automatically and only complain if they are unable to make the correction. An error may have been a true misspelling or a word that wasn't in the system's dictionary. Find out how the software reacts in those cases. If you are building an embedded speech application, will you be able to customize the error-handling procedure?

Your users will certainly make mistakes. Or the speech-processing hardware may handle some things differently than you expected. How will your natural language system deal with these surprises? It should be graceful and robust in such situations, never crashing or confusing the user with technical messages.

If your application involves answering questions, think about providing helpful answers at all times. Some questions contain implicit expectations that should be recognized by the software. For example, "Can you count the employees?" should result in more than a "yes" or "no" answer. There are many examples of this kind of thing, and some systems are more complete than others in this respect.

Some questions and statements contain assumptions on the part of the user that the system understands conventions of conversation of facts about the world. These assumptions can be very domain-specific. How flexible is the software in handling such assumptions? Can one build domain-knowledge into the system?

Of particular importance to question-answering systems is the notion of ambiguity. Many sentences have more than one valid interpretation, and the software may need help from the user before giving a proper response. At least three kinds of ambiguity exist:

- Lexical: Is "New York" a city or a state? "Run" can be a noun or a verb.
- Syntactic: "the Boston train" (To or from Boston? From or to where?), "Count the minority men and women" (minority women or all women?), "Remove the nut from the tie-down bolt and lubricate it" (lubricate the nut or the bolt? It can often be difficult to decide what a pronoun is referring to.)
- Semantic: "How many men and women work here?" (Do you want one total or two?), "List the salary of scientists and engineers" (aggregate or enumerate?)

Text-based question-answering systems usually handle ambiguity by paraphrasing the different interpretations and asking the user to choose one. This works fine, but it might be inconvenient for a voice system to carry on such a conversation. In some (rare) cases, it may be enough to respond with a simple, "That was an ambiguous sentence. Please rephrase the question."

If that sounds wishy-washy, it's because the appropriate response depends very much on the individual application and user community. Keep in mind the user's convenience, and look for natural language software that gives you control over multiple interpretations.

Extensibility

Most commercial natural language software was originally intended for use as a database query language. The vendor provides all of the linguistic support and the user adds terms to the dictionary that describe the target database. There is no question of modifying the product for other kinds of applications.

However, some products provide exits for calling programs written in a language like LISP or C. One or two are provided as source code. For speech applications, the more chances you have to supply your own code, the better.

Unless you purchase both the speech- and language-processing software from the same vendor, chances are you'll have the job of integrating several components with software of your own to make the final package. Of course, this situation will change as more companies announce speech-related products. But for the time being, the state of the art in natural language software says "customize."

Tread carefully . . .

So where does this leave you? If you are considering an English language interface to a database, you probably have the best hope of finding good commercial software to meet your needs. If you're building some kind of custom natural language interface, you should evaluate your needs very carefully and evaluate the available software even more carefully.

Lest we end this article with too cautious a mood, we should say that this work is well worth the effort and is sure to get easier. Natural language understanding systems are here today, here to stay, and will undoubtedly have an increasing impact on our ability to communicate with computers in the future.

References

J. Allen, *Natural Language Understanding.* Menlo Park, Calif: Benjamin-Cummings Publishing Co., 1987.

M. Bates and R. Bobrow. "Natural Language Interfaces: What's Here, What's Coming, and Who Needs It," in *Artificial Intelligence Applications for Business.* Ablex Publishing Co., 1984.

M. Bates, D. Meltzer, and S. Shea, "Designing a Practical Interface," *AI EXPERT* 2(5):60 – 66, May 1987.

S. Brittain, "Understanding Natural Language," *AI EXPERT* 2(5):31 – 38, May 1987.

F.J. Damerau, "Problems and Some Solutions in Customization of Natural Language Database Front Ends," *ACM Transactions on Office Information Systems* 3(2):165 – 184, Apr. 1985.

M.D. Harris, *Introduction to Natural Language Processing.* Reston, Va.: Reston Publishing, 1985.

R.C. Moore, "Natural Language Access to Databases—Theoretical/Technical Issues," in *Proceedings of the 20th Annual Meeting of the Association for Computational Linguistics,* 1982.

T. Winograd, *Language as a Cognitive Process.* Reading, Mass.: Addison-Wesley, 1983.

Part III

Application areas

Part III is subdivided into nine sections. Each section presents some application of artificial intelligence. The purpose of Part III is to provide you with a sense of how far the applications have gone and, by implication, how far they may yet go. When we hear about applications in AI, they are often described as one-shot applications in exotic domains, like strategic forecasting. The fact of the matter is that most of the most successful applications have been in relatively simple and very routine domains, such as diagnostics, quality control, and forms processing. Many of these problem areas are often deductive, suggesting "backchaining" as the preferred knowledge processing methodology.

Many of the most successful expert systems use production rules to represent knowledge and work in more or less bounded domains, where uncertainty is not an enormous problem. As you read through the papers you will notice that some of the "best" applications are in very simple domains, domains that might benefit from consistent inference-making procedures ready to go at a moment's notice. When we move into domains that are unbounded, heavily inductive, and plagued by uncertainty and ambiguity, then all kinds of problems arise.

The applications discussed in Part III range all the way from applications in manufacturing and design to how AI has been applied in our legal system. The papers together suggest where and how to apply AI; if you are interested in determining just how far intelligent systems technology might take you, Part III will suggest many possibilities.

In many respects, Part III represents the fruits of the labors of those in academia that pioneered knowledge engineering and processing technology. Many in academia are much less interested in specific applications of this technology than they are in the validation of old tools and techniques and the development of new ones. In other words, there may well be more in Part III for those in the applied trenches than those still in academia, though there may well be many academics quite interested in how their tools and techniques have been applied in practice.

Section A of Part III contains some papers that describe applications in manufacturing and design. Rowan looks at expert systems in process industries; Johnson,

Woodhead and O'Brien describe Ford's attempt to develop a labor management system; Jansen and Puttgen present a system that assists in electric power plant design; and Gabbert and Don Brown describe a knowledge-based system that aids the design of materials handling systems. These are all good applications, and while some of the systems are working prototypes, they all match nicely with the requirements of their respective domains.

Section B describes work in the area of computer-assisted instruction (CAI) and its more recent subfield of intelligent computer-assisted instruction (ICAI). Rickel surveys the field. Merrill describes an expert system for instructional design, while Clancey focuses on intelligent tutoring systems.

Section C looks at the application of AI to national defense. It is no secret that several Department of Defense (DOD) agencies (particularly the Defense Advanced Research Projects Agency, or DARPA) have generously supported basic and applied AI research over the past two decades. Some have argued that without this support, the field itself would not exist today in its present form. Section C contains a paper by Hopple that explores the application of AI to logistics, a paper by Anderson and Oritz that describes a knowledge-based system for aircraft loading, while Franklin and his colleagues describe basic and applied research in military AI. Andriole completes the section with a prognosis for future applications of AI to national defense.

Section D looks at how the financial community has applied AI. Sobkowski and Tischler describe an intelligent financial quote system. Keyes describes CITIBANK's pension expert system. Heuer, Koch and Cryer present INVEST, an expert system that helps with financial investment planning. It is interesting that the financial community, which came somewhat late to the technology, has recently found many applications for knowledge processing. The papers in Section D present but a snapshot of such applications.

Section E describes some applications in robotics, a field that has exploited progress in AI for years. McTamaney presents some control systems for mobile robots that must process data, information and knowledge in real-time. Bares and his colleagues describe Ambler, a planetary explorer. Applied (intelligent) robotics is a field that synthesizes a great deal of intelligent systems technology, ranging from intelligent sensor technology, to obstacle avoidance, reasoning and route planning. The two papers in Section E suggest how robotics systems engineers apply intelligent systems technology to all phases of the autonomous behavior process.

Section F focuses on natural language, or the ability to interact with computer programs in (near) free-form English (or other languages). Many argue that when true syntactic and semantic natural language understanding arrives, that the distribution of computing power will grow by several orders of magnitude. We do not currently have intelligent systems capable of understanding the nuances of language and the subtleties of discourse—but we are making progress. Jakobson, Nyberg and Piatetsky-Shapiro describe an intelligent database assistant; Sedlock details the natural language-database connection; while Ishikawa, Izumida, Hoshiai and Makinouchi describe KID, a knowledge-based natural language interface. Hendrix and Walter complete section F with a description of their intelligent assistant.

Section G describes how AI has solved some problems in the airline industry, like flight itinerary planning (Bose, Biswas and Padala), and gate assignment and tracking (Brazile and Swigger).

Section H presents a look at how AI has helped solve some of the problems in our legal system. Warner looks at the general issues connected with expert systems and the law. Ashley and Rissland describe a case-based approach to modeling legal expertise. Berman and Hafner squarely assess how AI might help solve some of our legal system's most pressing problems.

Section I suggests that AI can help with the design of interactive systems by enhancing the requirements engineering and prototyping processes. Czuchy and Harris focus on knowledge-based requirements engineering, while Luqi focuses on knowledge-based prototyping. Schoen, Smith and Buchanan suggest that knowledge-based expert systems can be designed with the aid of knowledge-based expert systems!

Part III of this Sourcebook should leave little doubt about the applied potential of AI; at the same time, it should also—hopefully—help develop a realistic appreciation for the kinds of problems best suited to the technology (and those that lie beyond its reach).

Section A

Applications in manufacturing and design

11

On-line expert systems in process industries

Duncan A. Rowan

Editors' note *Du Pont believes in AI, argues Rowan, in this paper about the application of sensor-based, on-line knowledge-based systems in process-manufacturing. The paper appears in the Sourcebook because, like so many others, it describes progress made in the real world, progress that can be traced to laboratory success in the 1970s. This paper is the first that reports on applied AI in this book; the paper is representative of the kinds of applications that have occurred over the past five to ten years, and the kinds of applications we can expect in the future. (Reprinted with permission, from the August 1989 issue of* AI Expert.

The manufacturing sector of the economy can be divided broadly into two operation types: discrete parts (automobiles, airplanes, appliances, electronics, and computer hardware) and continuous or batch-process manufacturing (petroleum, chemicals, paper, pharmaceuticals, food, and utilities). These industries employ different manufacturing technologies and equipment that influence their application of automation technology, including AI and expert systems.

Within E.I. du Pont de Nemours & Co. Inc. (Du Pont) and the process industry in general, AI and expert systems are receiving much attention. Du Pont has an extensive program of expert-system applications, including advisory, scheduling, and process-control systems. Advisory systems encompass troubleshooting and product-selection applications that use off-line information from databases or data provided by question-and-answer keyboard input. Scheduling systems require information on the market forecast, customer orders, and plant equipment status. They establish practical constraints that narrow the search space and then search for an acceptable schedule. Scheduling systems run once a day to once every several days. Process-control systems include on-line expert systems that receive data primarily from sensor-based process monitoring and control systems and respond in real time to process problems.

This article focuses on applications of sensor-based, on-line, expert-system applications in the process-manufacturing environment. It describes various types of on-line applications, examining the potential benefits, application experience, and tool requirements for implementing these applications. Du Pont views these expert-system applications as extensions to rather than replacements of process-control technology.

Motivation for applying AI

The general demand for higher-quality domestic products is induced by worldwide competition. Improving quality requires us to have better data and analyze it to make appropriate decisions.

As discussed by Laffey *et al.*, real-time, on-line expert systems can benefit problem-solving situations in which humans suffer from cognitive overload, fail to monitor all available information or resolve conflicting constraints, are expensive or scarce, make high-cost mistakes, miss high-revenue opportunities, or cannot simultaneously manipulate all the relevant information to obtain optimal solutions or provide a solution quickly enough. [1] High-revenue opportunities certainly exist in the chemical and paper industries because many products are over-sold; hence the economic incentive to improve plant utility. Automation in general and expert systems in particular do this by helping to prevent costly, unscheduled shutdowns due to equipment failure. Expert systems can also improve the percentage of time the process produces top-grade products by interpreting errant process behavior and advising corrective action. Companies understand that much of their competitive advantage results from knowledge about how to operate the process and process equipment most effectively. Because human expertise is perishable, interest in capturing this knowledge in expert systems is growing.

Much of the motivation for building on-line expert systems in the process industry is consistent with the published benefits for knowledge-based systems in general; that is, expertise is scarce, vague, and dispersed and should be preserved, made precise, focused, and applied continuously. Also, once captured, knowledge can be distributed among similar applications. Another motivating factor for applying on-line expert systems is reducing plant staffing. However, this is not a primary justification since operating labor typically represents a very small percentage of the total production cost. But reducing the routine technical assistance to manufacturing required of process engineers is of great interest. If expertise is leveraged in expert systems, engineers could move to more productive, creative, and valuable tasks. Domestic companies are also motivated by the fact that the Japanese are moving aggressively into the application of on-line expert systems. [2]

Process control

Improvements in process-control technology have been evolutionary. Before the 1940s, process parameters—flows, temperatures, and pressures—were controlled by human operators who adjusted valves manually while watching local instrument indicators, such as sight glasses and pressure gauges. In the 1940s and 1950s, pneumatic instrumentation was developed for sensing process parameters and providing feedback control. This gave operators hands-off control and allowed signal transmission to a remote control room, thus improving operator safety and comfort. With the advent of the transistor in the 1960s, analog electronic instrumentation became available on the market. Electronic instrumentation became more stable and precise than its pneumatic counterparts, and signals could be transmitted instantaneously over long distances. This allowed control areas to consolidate further, requiring less labor to operate the plant.

Beginning in the 1960s, digital computers were applied for process control. Computer inputs from process-measurement instrumentation and computer output signals to control valves were directly connected to the computer, providing direct digital control. Most process industries rejected this technique because having many control variables concentrated in a single computer was risky. This concern was alleviated in the 1970s when microprocessor technology allowed acceptable distribution of computing, control activity, and cost-effective redundancy, where required. Microprocessor-based, programmable logic controllers replaced discrete relays and other electronic logic systems for performing safety/process interlocks and sequencing operations for batch control. Distributed control systems consisting of CRT-based consoles and microprocessor-based controllers replaced panel boards of individual analog feedback controllers.

Today, digital-control systems dominate the industry. On larger processes, these systems typically feed data to a higher-level host computer for data archival, further data manipulation, and more sophisticated control manipulation. Sophisticated control strategies—linear and nonlinear optimizations, times-series analysis, control strategies based on process models, and statistical process-control techniques—reside at this level. These host computer systems are usually networked in a hierarchy of technical and business computing systems to make process information available to the appropriate technical and managerial personnel. Thus, many processes contain the necessary information networks to permit on-line, expert-system applications.

Even so, expert-system technology's entrance into process-control applications has been gradual and continues to evolve slowly. On the whole, this industry is rather conservative when it comes to using novel technology. Any misapplication can have severe consequences in terms of capital equipment and product loss, human safety, or possible environmental contamination. Despite this operating philosophy, the motivation for applying expert-systems technology is too compelling to disregard, and tools and techniques have evolved until beginning system implementation is cost-effective. Application areas that have benefited include sensor validation, data reconciliation, on-line equipment diagnosis, and model-based knowledge systems. We routinely find applications with a 10:1 rate of return.

In the past, computer-based applications have approached what we call artificial intelligence today. In many cases, these systems were designed for one-of-a-kind applications related to a critical process problem. Generally, they take multiple-process sensor inputs, analyze the data, make nonroutine decisions about process operation conditions, and adjust process target values. In most cases, these applications have been written in procedural computer languages.

In one example, a water-cooled process reactor for an exothermic chemical reaction is operated at maximum cooling to gain the greatest product-to-ingredient yield. Increased cooling promotes a fouling problem that reduces heat transfer from the process fluid to the cooling water and eventually causes a severe loss of cooling and subsequent shutdown (with the potential for a runaway reaction). A supervisory computer monitors the differential temperatures of the process fluid and the cooling water to calculate a heat-transfer coefficient. When the supervisory computer determines that heat transfer is inadequate, it ramps the process temperature upward until the fouling clears and then gradually ramps the temperature back down to approach optimum yield once again. This system definitely embodies process expertise, though not designed as an expert system.

In the case of this computer program, the sensor data exists and changes fairly slowly with time; that is, the heat-transfer coefficient will change over tens of minutes. Such long time constants are typical for many petrochemical processes. However, much smaller time constants, on the order of tens of milliseconds, are involved in diagnosing electromechanical interlock systems. In one case, phantom shutdowns of a $3 million, 20,000 horse-power compressor result in down time costing $15,000 per hour. Capturing and quickly analyzing data for one of 40 possible interlock conditions capable of shutting down the compressor is absolutely necessary. A high-speed event recorder has been developed to log data such as vibration, stator temperature, over-voltage or over-current conditions, and high process temperature or pressure every millisecond.

This data collection rate is required to obtain sufficient resolution since the dropout time for the interlock relays is about 20 milliseconds. After an interlock event, experts determine the trip's cause. In this case, data analysis has not been reduced to an expert system, although such an operation is possible. The key to this application is having the available data with sufficient resolution to diagnose the problem. In this example, responding with any kind of corrective action during the tripping process is impossible; however, by aiding the postmortem analysis, the system reduces the mean time to repair, thereby increasing compressor availability.

In terms of process dynamics, we find some extremely long time constants in chemical processes with large residence times. These time constants can be several hours, meaning the process response to adjustments made by one operator may not be fully developed until hours later or perhaps until the next operating shift has taken over. (The new operator may not be aware of the previous action.) In these cases, great expertise and patience are required to control the process. The long time constants and large inertial loads of these processes make operating them much like navigating a supertanker: any need for corrective action must be anticipated and patience is required to allow process response to develop. Because these are not natural human tendencies, automatic process control and expert systems can benefit the operation of these processes.

These examples emphasize a point regarding real-time process-control systems, including expert systems: real time depends completely on the time constants of the process. A real-time system must collect and analyze data and issue a response within a time acceptable for resolving a problem.

AI applications

Du Pont has explored many application areas: sensor validation, data reconciliation, process and equipment diagnosis, and model-based expert systems. Individual measurements generated by on-line process sensors are fundamental to on-line expert systems. These sensors range from basic physical measurement devices such as thermocouples to extremely complex devices such as on-stream process analyzers (complex chemical or electrical processes). The sensor's characteristic behavior reflects its design, specific installation, and process behavior. Many sensors are critical to process operation because they supply feedback and closed-loop control. In typical wet-chemical processes, about one-third of all process measurements serve as interlock sensors or are used in closed-loop control systems. These systems operate on the principle that the incoming measurement signal accurately reflects the process condition. Typically, these control systems only recognize a sensor fault for extreme conditions (open circuit, short circuit, and so on).

The objective of using expert systems for sensor validation is to improve the measurement system's overall reliability. This may simply mean recognizing that the sensor is suspect and an alternate measurement or control strategy should be instituted. A further objective is to improve the overall availability of the process measurement by providing troubleshooting assistance to the maintenance technician, thus reducing the mean time to repair. In general, systems that perform sensor validation can be used in multiple applications, generating more compelling economic incentives for their development.

Process engineers and plant operators develop experience in distinguishing normal from abnormal behavior of specific sensors. As an elementary example, consider the reactor temperature. Due to the large thermal inertia of the process, this signal is not expected to make an abrupt shift in value but will exhibit smooth, highly damped behavior. Therefore, any sudden shifts indicate a faulty signal (probably an electronic failure).

Other common physical-process measurements are pressure and flow detection. These signals exhibit a certain level of high frequency noise. A change in the noise band such as an increase or decrease in the noise level may indicate a faulty signal. A typical low noise level may indicate that the sensor has become detached from the process; for example, by a closed block valve. While the average pressure remains unchanged, the noise level will drop to zero. An increase in noise may indicate instability in the measurement. Engineers and operators recognize the typical signal patterns on strip-chart recorders or equivalent CRT displays. This process has been automated by developing algorithms to detect suspicious sensor behavior. With a short-term history of process data, these algorithms compute the rate of change, moving average and standard deviation, and other variables.

Du Pont also has an expert system that performs sensor validation on complex process analyzers. This system diagnoses mechanical and electronic failures in the analyzer, abnormal sample presentation to the analyzer, and adverse ambient conditions relative to the process or analyzer. The expert system is segmented into a monitoring component that continuously scans and processes on-line data and a rule-base component that analyzes a snapshot of information and manually entered data. The expert system monitors on-line data for suspicious behavior, including the signal stability of the measurement and reference signal, and the characteristics of internal signals, such as the automatic gain control.

If the expert system determines that a fault has occurred, it alerts the operator. The maintenance technician can then activate the diagnostic expert system, which reads a snapshot of information from the on-line scanner, processes the data, and collects the additional information necessary to diagnose the problem from the technician.

As in most other applications, human observation enhances on-line data. In most cases, a complete data set does not exist on line because some measurements or observations cannot be performed on line cost-effectively.

In a well-instrumented chemical process, redundant process data exists because of the process's inherent physical interaction. Consider the process by which inflow, outflow, and tank level are measured. These measurements are related by the mass-balance equation, which states that any difference between in-flow and out-flow results in a level change; the rate of level change is proportional to the difference in the two flows.

Any of the three measured variables could be calculated from the other two using the mass-balance equation; however, all three are usually measured. This creates redundant data, allowing cross-checks on all signals. Knowledge in the form of these governing equations is deep and provides additional information about the health of individual sensors and the process in general.

Drift in individual sensors may occur over a long period. Although it may not be detectable by sensor-validation techniques, it can often be detected by data-reconciliation techniques. Much work has been done in this area using both traditional data-reconciliation techniques [3] and expert-system methodology. In both approaches, noisy, imprecise measurements impede data reconciliation; however, sensor repeatability may be sufficient to allow data reconciliation even though sensor precision may be poor. [4] Relationships other than mass-balance and reaction-rate equations, can reconcile process data. In addition, data-reconciliation techniques can be applied to process measurements and control-system outputs associated by feedback control. Since feedback-controller outputs often control variables such as pump speed or the automatic valve position, they provide a crude indication of process flow.

The reconciliation scheme can also include laboratory data. Since lab analysis is considered the ultimate proof that product properties meet specifications, lab data are of major importance. In addition, laboratory methods are sometimes required because techniques for on-line measurement of specific product composition may not be practical. In reconciling laboratory data with on-line process data, care must be taken that the data is adjusted in time. Because it may take several hours for the sample to be taken and processed in the lab and results returned, the lab data must be compared to the corresponding historical data taken on-line. Laboratory data can provide the final validation of on-line sensors and process operation.

Sensor validation and data-reconciliation techniques allow process measurements to be validated wherever measurement methods may fail or drift from the necessary accuracy. If measurement data are considered highly reliable, these steps may not be necessary. In any case, once process data have been judged reliable, individual data values may be combined into patterns, providing a higher information level. As a simple example, consider a liquid-flow process that normally operates under pressure. If the process flow increases and the pressure decreases rapidly, the process equipment or piping may have ruptured.

In another example, an exothermic batch reactor may be charged with ingredients and catalysts and then heated with steam to initiate the reaction. As the reaction begins, the process temperature increases rapidly. The expert system monitoring this process watches for the characteristic temperature profile when activation conditions have been met (the ingredients have been charged and the steam has been on long enough). Insufficient temperature rise indicates that not enough catalyst has been charged or that the catalyst's activity level is too low to initiate the reaction. These pattern-matching techniques are implemented in production-rule-based expert systems.

In addition to sensor data, these process-diagnostic applications often require observation by a human operator. This applies less to highly automated wet-chemical processes and more to sparsely instrumented mechanical operations, such as paper-manufacturing processes and film- or sheet-drying operations. In film- or sheet-processing applications, about 50% of the information required for a process diagnostic system must be entered manually. Expert systems for these applications must have a well-designed operator interface. Applications in the utility [5] and paper manufacturing industries [6] use manually entered data.

In addition to diagnosing process malfunctions that affect product quality, diagnosing supporting equipment, such as refrigeration machines, boilers, compressors, and instrumentation systems, is frequently desirable. The analyzer diagnostic system previously described is also an example of an equipment diagnostic application. Another example of this type of expert system is a diagnostic package for refrigeration equipment, which uses pressure and temperature data from both the process and refrigerant sides of the machine to detect degrading performance. Problems may occur in the compressor, condenser, evaporator, or purge unit and consist of abnormal conditions, such as compressor surging, loss of heat transfer, lubricating oil problems, and bearing failure. The system is being prototyped in an off-line system. Both of these examples represent systems that can be applied in many similar (though not all identical) applications because the supporting equipment is common to many processes and plants.

Model-based expert systems involve deep knowledge about the process. Models are derived from first-principle relationships of physics and chemical engineering and from empirical models based on statistical regression of process data. Incorporating this type of deep knowledge into an expert system allows for a very compact, precise system design. This has been proven true in diagnosing electronic circuits [7] and detecting chemical plant faults. [4] On-line models have been used for process-control strategies relying on the model to make process measurements unattainable on line with physical methods. Product properties or chemical compositions may be computed indirectly using available sensors to supply data for the model.

A simple example is using a model to calculate polymer viscosity from pressure, temperature, and flow measurements on a transfer pipeline. The biotechnology industry applies models to determine cell growth in bioreactors from the measurements of bulk properties, such as oxygen feed, ammonia evolution in the off-gas, and biomass temperature. Du Pont has developed expert systems that interact with process models and use the model-generated results as input information to the inference engine. On-line dynamic models can reason about the projection of process variables into the future. Modern AI tools allow model parameters to be included as object attributes (in an object-oriented tool). Combining the power of object-oriented modeling with an object-oriented expert system can be very powerful yet easy to understand and maintain.

Knowledge-base development

Much has been written about knowledge extraction and knowledge-base development. Du Pont's experience has not been unique in these areas. We have found the accuracy and validity of the resulting expert systems to correlate directly with the quality of the domain expert's knowledge and ability to communicate this knowledge. Applying expert system technology demands the same understanding of the industrial process required when applying conventional control strategy and modeling techniques. In many cases, knowledge extraction has elucidated valuable information and produced new insights into the expert's reasoning. Therefore, performing initial problem analysis can be valuable even before the expert system is constructed. Du Pont has succeeded in staffing these projects by providing AI education to engineers experienced in process control. Using so-called knowledge engineers unfamiliar with this domain has proven impractical. In process-control AI application, domain experience outweighs AI experience. Other companies have come to similar conclusions. [8]

In many applications, existing domain expertise is adequate. In may exist in many forms: heuristics and empirical understanding from operating experience, fundamental understanding of first principles, existing models, and so forth. In our applications, most knowledge comes from engineers who have practical experience with the process or technical specialists who have studied it from a fundamental point of view. Senior operators' experience has also been included in some applications.

For applications in which cause-and-effect relationships are vague, we have run statistically designed experiments or less formal step tests to obtain better knowledge of these relationships and map cause and effect. Though these techniques are not novel AI technology, they clarify knowledge another way.

Du Pont has applied various tools and knowledge-representation techniques, including induction and rule-based, object-oriented, and frame-based systems. We have found that object-oriented knowledge powerfully represents the physical entities (such as sensors, pumps, valves, and pipes) and conceptual entities (such as mass and energy balances). The object structure affords much more efficient development of large applications. Logic has generally been represented in the form of production rules; however, we have seen the need for other pattern-matching techniques such as truth tables.

Du Pont has employed straightforward inferencing techniques for on-line expert systems. These systems are usually data-driven; they use forward chaining but employ some backward chaining for gathering data with respect to specific goals. Using tools that allow the knowledge base to be partitioned into compact modules that can be activated at the appropriate time has been very advantageous. Our expert systems run in several modes. Some systems run in a continuously scanning mode, monitoring for certain events to occur. Others are executed by periodic scanning when fresh data is available, usually once a minute (but perhaps more often). Some are activated by external events such as the input of lab data, while others are activated manually as needed. The inference engine must be able to continue processing real-time data while it seeks manually entered data; the system must not freeze under any conditions.

Several approaches to system validation have proven acceptable. For simple systems designed to detect process phenomena, some applications have been built simply and put on line. The performance of these systems is monitored as the particular process condition recurs. In most cases, however, capturing data related to process phenomena is desirable so the system can be tested off line. The sets provide case studies for alterations and refinements to the knowledge base. These data sets may be derived from archived plant data or captured during designed experiments. Validation of a system around very rare events, such as detection of catastrophic failure, requires process simulation as the only source of test data.

To validate the Falcon fault detection system, we used a benchmark data set of 11 sets of actual process data and 10 sets of simulated data. [4] Many interactions existed in this knowledge base and subtle changes were thoroughly tested using the benchmark data set. In general, we prefer testing the system in fast-forward mode (that is, faster than real time) to speed up the validation process.

Human-machine interface

The ideal human-machine interface for plant operators would integrate directly with any existing control console. To date, this has not been achievable because control system vendors have not yet offered expert-system tools or capability. Many Du Pont process-control systems also include company-proprietary, host computer systems with additional consoles that display information generated by expert systems. Several plants use Digital Equipment Corp. (DEC) workstations (VAXstations) as expert-system operator interfaces.

Operators desire a very intuitive interface with basic functionality. Whereas system developers may function efficiently using a graphic interface with multiple overlaying windows, operators prefer an interface with hard boundaries and simple pushbuttons to call up other information on the screen. Display areas on the screen include scrollable, time-tagged, text-alarm messages; areas that will call up trend recordings, enter comments, and indicate the value of critical process variables; and facilities for activating these features. In addition, the engineers and production supervisors can call up an area of logged messages, including alarms and operator comments. In some instances, process graphics are also useful; however, these may appear on other control consoles and may not be duplicated in the expert system.

Since Du Pont regards the operator as the customer for these expert systems, we request assistance from operators when designing the human-machine interface for an application. Including operator suggestions in the design results in a more acceptable product and generates ownership by user contribution, which facilitates the technology transfer process.

The expert system explains its reasoning and conclusions. This explanation capability enhances the credibility of the expert system and is very valuable to operators. The value of explanation facilities has been recognized by the RESCU developers in the U.K. [9]

On-line, real-time system applications provide a genuine challenge for software designers building expert-system tools. Capabilities essential to these applications include data scanning over networks, temporal reasoning (collecting and analyzing time-varying data), calculation, logic solving in rule form, and other pattern-matching facilities. To handle time-varying data, the tool should have an internal historian for buffering data used to establish trends, rates of change, and other signal characteristics (like noise level). A library of common signal-processing functions is also useful. Highly desirable characteristics include an object-oriented structure allowing for multiple levels of classes, subclasses, and instances. Class (generic) rules are essential for efficiency when reasoning about common objects in the process; for example, a single rule should be able to check all temperature sensors against a high limit.

Though text editors may be a plausible development environment for small applications, graphic editors are decidedly more efficient and desirable. The editor should make as many syntactic and semantic checks as possible and provide on-line assistance for developing the proper rule grammar. Validation capability using canned data files and run-time debugging facilities such as break points, watch points, and single-step mode should be included. Facilities for constructing an operator interface as previously described are necessary; this interface should allow operator data entry.

Because these applications are critical, the on-line system and its tool must include facilities for error handling when communication errors occur, data supply systems go down, or bad data is returned from the process. Because these events are inevitable, the tool and application must be designed to cope with them, adding yet another level of complexity to the on-line application.

For more complex applications, Du Pont uses the commercial tool G2 from Gensym Corp. G2 offers most of the required functionality and runs on many platforms, including standard DEC VAX computer hardware platforms that prevail in our plants. Du Pont and Gensym have formed a working partnership to provide enhanced solutions to real-time AI applications. For smaller applications, we apply hybrid approaches by processing temporal data in an external program and calling an off-line tool such as Level5.

Vision of the future

Du Pont applies a broad range of on-line expert systems. These initial successes create more interest and generate additional applications; therefore, we predict AI will become widespread in the company and the process industries in the future. Though we view AI and expert systems as extensions to conventional automation and process-control technology, new tools and improved application skills will allow further improvement in the rate of accomplishment.

This article reflects the experience and efforts of J.T. Cardinal, R.K. Cox, K.A. Kosanovich, R.R. Lott, S.R. McBride, L.I. Morganstein, S. Padilla, P.D. Schnelle, R.J. Taylor, and B.D. Tyreus.

References

1. T.J. Laffey, P.A. Cox, J.L. Schmidt, S.M. Kao, and J.Y. Read. "Real-Time Knowledge-Based Systems," *AI Magazine*, Spring 1988, pp. 27–45.
2. R. Funakoshi, "Operation Instruction System: On-Line Process Monitoring and Fault Diagnosis," *Proceedings of AIChe Annual Meeting*, Paper 88G, Nov. 1987.

3. A.C. Tamhane and R.S.H. Mah. "Data Reconciliation and Gross Error Detection in Chemical Process Networks," *Technometrics*, 27(4): 409 – 422, Nov. 1985.
4. D.A. Rowan, "Applying On-Line Expert Systems: Technical Issues and Business Concerns," *Making Change Work* (Chemical Manufacturers Assoc. Sixth Process Control Users Forum), New Orleans, La., Apr. 1988.
5. R.L. Osborne, A.J. Gonzalez, J.C. Bellows, and J.D. Chess. "On-Line Diagnosis of Instrumentation through Artificial Intelligence," *Proceedings of the ISA Meeting*, Paper #85-0985, 1985.
6. D.R. Myers, J.F. Davis, and C.E. Hurley, "Application of Artificial Intelligence to Malfunction Diagnosis of Sequential Operations which Involve Programmable Logic Controllers," *Extended Abstracts of AICHe Annual Meeting*, Abstract 37B, Apr. 1989.
7. R. Davis, H. Shrobe, W. Hamscher, K. Weickert, M. Shirley, and S. Polit. "Diagnosis Based on Description of Structure and Function," *Proceedings of the National Conference on AI*, pp. 137 – 142, 1982.
8. G.V. Ricketts, "How to Do More in Less Time," *AI EXPERT*, Jan. 1988, pp. 46 – 52.
9. R. Shaw, "RESCU—On-Line Real-Time Artificial Intelligence," *Computer-Aided Engineering Journal*, 7(3): 29 – 30, 1987.

12

ASDEP
An expert system for electric power plant design

John J. Jansen
Hans B. Püttgen

Editors' note *This paper describes the application of AI to the design of a power plant's electrical auxiliary system. It is described by the authors as a feasibility study to determine the applied potential of AI. But it is important to note that "feasibility" means different things to different people. In the lab it means "proof of concept": can I demonstrate that something is there!? In the field, feasibility tries to answer the only important questions: "If I build this thing, will it work, and will it save me money?" Jansen and Püttgen describe the domain and the process by which they designed and developed the expert system known as ASDEP. (Reprinted with permission, from the Spring 1987 issue of* IEEE Expert. *©1987, IEEE. All rights reserved.)*

This article presents ASDEP, an expert system for designing a power plant's electrical auxiliary system, implemented to demonstrate the feasibility of AI techniques for solving specific power system design problems. Overall, ASDEP received positive comments during its evaluation. Specifically, AI techniques proved feasible to address the particular design problem discussed.

Most design problems encountered in the electrical utility industry are complex and time consuming. Designers must deal with interactions between alternatives, uncertainties, and important nonfinancial parameters in most design phases. Typically, designers face the following issues:

- Multiple objective functions;
- Multiple (and often conflicting) constraints;
- Complex system interactions;
- The need for accuracy;
- The need for trade-off, optimization, and "what-if" analyses;
- Coordination of the decision-making process.

Presently, human experts solve design problems based on experience, specialized knowledge, and engineering judgment, using the computer only for analysis. Conventional CAD programs build on the basic assumption that feasible solutions do indeed exist to solve design problems; however, this premise does not always apply in real-world design. Human experts frequently deal with designs not meeting all constraints and objectives imposed upon them.

Developers have successfully applied AI techniques to some difficult engineering design problems, but little has been applied to electrical power system design. In this field, the major design problem areas are generation planning, transmission planning, substation design, and auxiliary-system design.

Generation planning Generation planning determines the appropriate generation mix (such as nuclear, fossil, hydro, or solar) required to satisfy future customer needs at minimum cost while providing adequate returns on stockholder investments. Customer needs encompass concerns from reliability and quality of electrical supply to environmental, political, and geographical impacts. These concerns often conflict, and are further complicated by numerous constraints, uncertainties, and trends imposed on the design.

Electric utility generation planning is a multiobjective problem; generally, no single strategy exists to optimize all objectives involved. Furthermore, many objectives are inherently difficult to quantify and are, therefore, not suitable for combination into a single analytical function [1].

Transmission planning Transmission planning determines how many additional power system transmission facilities are required to meet the design criteria at acceptable capital costs. Design criteria cover such issues as reliability, security, dynamic stability, and environmental impact. This problem is amplified by its size (that is, the combinatorial explosion of possible choices), the uncertainty of predicting the future, and how far in the future to plan.

Substation design Substations supply electrical energy from high-voltage transmission systems to users at lower voltage levels. Electric loads fed by substations are fundamentally random in nature; therefore, we need probabilistic measures to ascertain design quality. During design, many initial skeletal configurations can potentially be used that somehow must be ranked before selections can be made.

Auxiliary-system design Power plant electrical auxiliary systems supply electrical energy, either from the plant or from the transmission system, to electric loads (such as circulation coolant pumps or measurement and security monitoring systems) required to operate the plant. An electric power generating plant can produce full power only if its auxiliaries are fully operational. When power is lost to the auxiliaries, a generating unit may have to reduce power or shut down completely. Typically, auxiliary electric systems cost five to 10 percent of total plant cost [2]. During a large plant's long-term outage, due to the repair of major auxiliary subsystem components, corresponding replacement energy costs can exceed the total auxiliary system's capital costs; hence, the need to carefully design such auxiliary systems.

Of the four major design problems described above, auxiliary-system design offers the least formidable challenge insofar as AI techniques are concerned. Auxiliary-system design does not present as great a dimensionality curse as the other problems do; moreover, verification is fairly straightforward to implement.

This article will address various AI techniques proposed and implemented to design auxiliary systems, discuss ASDEP's features, and present an evaluation of ASDEP carried out by an independent engineering design group. While our research has established the feasibility of AI techniques for solving specific power system design problems, additional work is clearly required to lift ASDEP to industrial design levels.

ASDEP

Present design methodology related to electrical auxiliary systems evolves from engineers and technicians who, after examining a plant's load requirements, propose possible configurations. They analyze each configuration, performing economic short-circuit, load-flow, and motor-start studies. Then, subjective evaluations are usually performed based on each design's reliability, flexibility, maintainability, and expandability. The designers select the design scheme best meeting design goals. After selecting the design scheme, they produce equipment specifications and obtain bids. Following equipment selection, they reexamine the final design.

Figure 12-1 (excerpted from a preliminary draft of the IEEE P666 Standard) provides a task organization flowchart of the design process, indicating approximate times required to complete each step. No provisions are made for feedback, or to answer various "what-if" questions, until the end of the process.

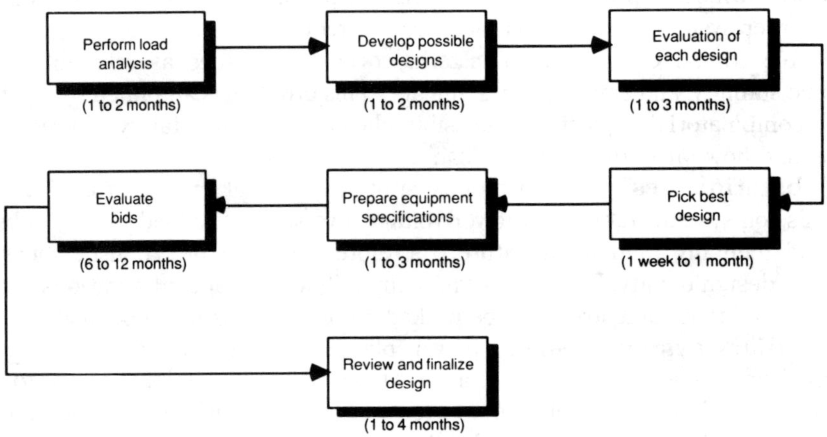

Fig. 12-1. Flowchart of design process.

Past experience reflects the adequacy of utility industry auxiliary-system designs. However, the following areas need improvement:

- Clearly stated design and system performance criteria are often not properly formulated, in writing, before the design.
- Typically, individuals with little formal training perform power system analysis.
- Few analysis programs supporting auxiliary-system design are available.

- Most "what-if" questions are not explored because they would delay the design process (note the lack of feedback loops in FIG. 12-1's flowchart).
- Due to the large staffs involved, overall system objectives can become unclear and conflicting.
- Insufficient reference material exists to support systematic auxiliary-system design.

Can knowledge-based systems alleviate some of these deficiencies?

The goal ASDEP seeks to design *good* (as opposed to *optimal*, since optimality is awkward to define related to electric power designs) electrical auxiliary systems meeting operational requirements. We measure design quality against operational performance, reliability, maintainability, flexibility, expandability, and cost. Consequently, we conceive ASDEP to be truly design-oriented.

Objectives and limitations ASDEP evaluates how state-of-the-art AI techniques can be applied to power system design, using practical and physical examples. Primary issues are to (1) evaluate AI potential, and (2) implement existing AI techniques. This research does not attempt to produce a problem-free expert system, but rather seeks to evaluate the feasibility of using general AI frameworks for such designs.

Since our research focused on demonstrating feasibility, we imposed the following additional limitations on ASDEP to highlight major concerns during its construction:

- Functional boundaries of the auxiliary system to be designed (for example, the switchyard) must be clearly defined beforehand.
- Low-voltage systems are not explicitly considered (that is, less than 1000 volts); however, low-voltage loads are implicitly considered as lumped loads at intermediate voltage levels.
- We designed ASDEP to handle only single-unit power plants.
- ASDEP's final output, not intended as a detailed engineering drawing, describes the auxiliary system's fundamental topology.

We based our research on existing AI techniques; therefore, ASDEP's evaluation phase was very important as it might have been determined that AI techniques cannot adequately address problems related to power system design. We will specifically address evaluation in due course.

Observations incorporated in ASDEP Transcribing problem-solving expertise from human experts to computer programs is at the heart of expert system development [3]. Design engineers rely on the following observations when designing auxiliary systems:

- Using little or no backtracking, they follow an orderly progression from initial designs (containing little detailed information) to detailed designs.
- They use general problem-solving techniques in conjunction with analytical methods during design development.
- They generally use analytical methods that are relatively simple mathematical formulations relating key design parameters to targeted constraints.

- They cannot satisfy all constraints initially imposed on the design.
- They primarily seek satisfactory (as opposed to optimal) solutions.
- They articulate preferences during the entire design process, called for by intermediate design results.

ASDEP embeds these six observations.

ASDEP's main components

Let's consider ASDEP's general methodology, concentrating on AI issues faced during its implementation. Later sections will briefly discuss an actual design and review an evaluation of an auxiliary-system design generated by ASDEP.

Figure 12-2 illustrates ASDEP's organizational flowchart. Major features of the flowchart's basic blocks follow.

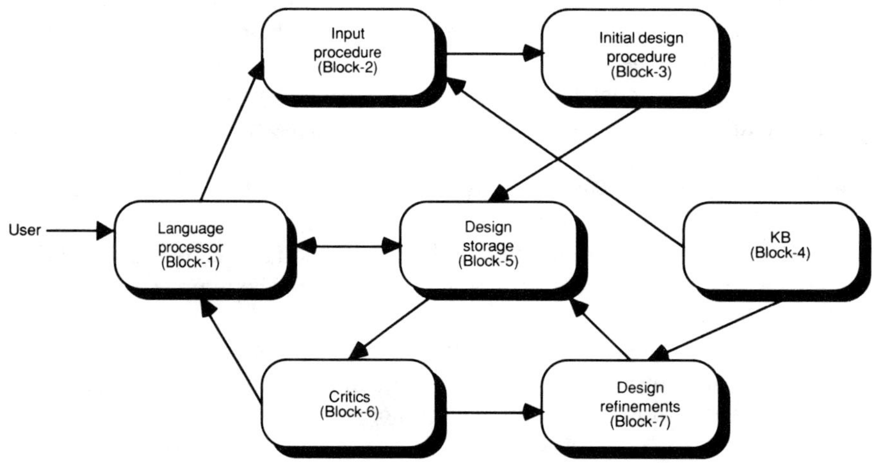

Fig. 12-2. An organizational flowchart of ASDEP.

Block 1: Language processor Designers use a problem-oriented language, relying on a user-oriented and fixed vocabulary, to (1) conveniently input and display data and (2) select and apply the appropriate rule group when prompted by the program to do so.

Block 2: Input procedure We must provide ASDEP with specific design information before design can begin. We sort this information into three parts: (1) load and system data, (2) equipment inventory, and (3) goal and constraint data. A major problem frequently encountered is the lack of accurate information regarding load and equipment components. We use default rules in the knowledge base to reasonably approximate missing load and equipment information, and can later modify this information as desired during design.

Block 3: Initial design procedure The initial design proposal is an inherent part of most design processes. Fortunately, due to the nature of many power system design problems, a simple initial design can be proposed meeting some (but usually not all) design goals and constraints. We can use two extreme methodologies to automatically propose an initial auxiliary-system design, a highly reliable but high-cost design, or a less reliable but low-cost design.

Using the first approach, ASDEP would modify the initial design by tearing it down to achieve lower cost while still meeting stated constraints. Using the second approach, ASDEP would modify the initial design by building it up, or by changing the proposed design's structure, to produce a higher cost design meeting stated constraints. Human experts take an approach resembling the second method. ASDEP generates an initial design based on the second approach as well, intending to use top-down refinements to produce a satisfactory design.

Figure 12-3 presents ASDEP's initial design procedure flowchart. The following additional comments are appropriate. The system

- Divides all loads into two broad groups, emergency (or vital) loads, and non-emergency (or nonvital loads), based on information obtained in Block 2;
- Creates the load buses simply based on load goals and electrical conductors enabling electrical loads and supply feeders to be connected);
- Distributes the loads on the buses, balancing the kVA loading on similar buses;
- Selects load bus voltage ratings based on rules contained in the system's knowledge base;
- Determines the kVA load on each load bus by adding all loads connected to each bus;
- Automatically proposes a radial distribution system connecting *most* load buses to the main generator and the switchyard.

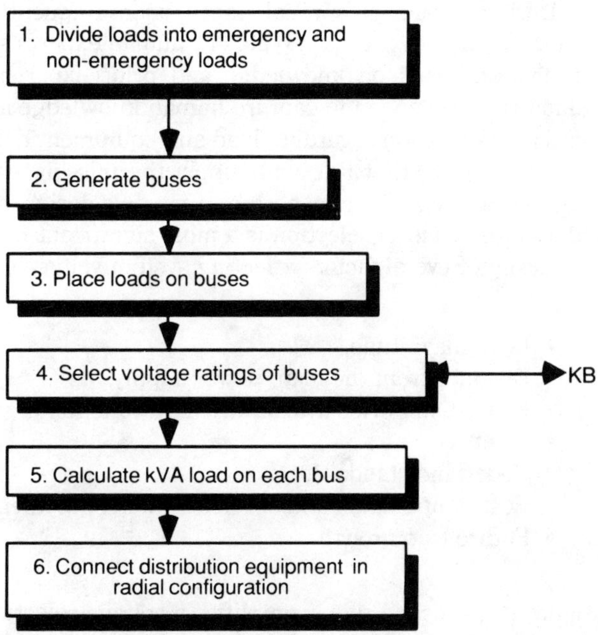

Fig. 12-3. The initial design procedure.

In an effort to remain at a preliminary stage, the initial design may not be fully connected. As will be seen, the design will be fully connected progressively as provided for in Block 6 (dealing with "critics") and in Block 7 (dealing with design refinements). We use this approach, resembling NOAH's underconstrained method [4], to avoid backtracking.

Block 4: Knowledge base The knowledge base is an expert system's heart. Knowledge acquisition is most difficult, frequently constituting a bottle-neck during expert system construction [3]. How knowledge is acquired, represented, and organized represents a central issue for all expert systems.

Most of ASDEP's application-specific knowledge is represented using production rules. ASDEP employs the following rule language structure based on the Backus-Naur form:

<RULE>::=(IF<ANTECEDENT>THEN<ACTION>)

where ANTECEDENT is a Boolean expression composed of preconditions that must be satisfied before a rule can be activated, and where ACTION is a Boolean expression that will either change a design, select another rule group, or change a design parameter.

We use a rule-based formalism to capture human expert knowledge and experience, and to store that expertise in the knowledge base. Knowledge base rules diverge into two major groups: equipment default rules, and design change rules. Whenever ASDEP calls the knowledge base, the system selects the appropriate rule group by using metarules [5]. Next, ASDEP checks each rule's preconditions and (if valid) performs the appropriate binding between rule variables and the specific design. Due to the subjectivity inherently attached to knowledge base rules, users must have the option to add, delete, or modify all knowledge base rules. Figures 12-4 and 12-5 exemplify rules found in each major group, using Lisp computer language code.

During any design's initial stages, users frequently lack some information needed to start the design process. Typically, human experts supply their estimates of missing information based on knowledge and prior experience. Likewise, knowledge base default rules (intended to capture human knowledge and experience) will supply most missing information regarding load and equipment data.

Figure 12-4's first rule will supply the missing kVA motor rating, if required. In addition, a decision must be made for any design as to appropriate voltage levels; indeed, voltage level selection is a most significant factor in power plant auxiliary-system design. Several factors affecting system voltage selections [6] are

- Load magnitude,
- Distance from the main power supply,
- Utilization device availability (as a function of voltage ratings and limitations),
- Safety,
- Codes and standards,
- Cost of utilization and service system equipment,
- Future load growth.

Figure 12-4's second rule exemplifies a voltage selection rule.

```
(RULE09 % kVA-SELECTION RULE %
        (IF (EQ? kVA UNKNOWN))
        (THEN (SETQ kVA (* HP (DIV 0.746 (* EFF RPF)))))
)
(RULE12 % VOLTAGE-SELECTION RULE %
        (IF (EQ? VOLT UNKNOWN)
                (LT? HP 2000)
                (GT? HP 1000))
        THEN (SETQ VOLT 4160))
)
```

Fig. 12-4. An example of default rules.

Figure 12-5 gives a design change rule related to a switchgear's continuous current limit violations. Design change rules typically will not undo the effects of previously triggered design change rules, an approach often called "conchronological backtracking [3]."

```
(RULE26 % DESIGN-CHANGE RULE %
        (IF (EQ? CONTINUOUS-CURRENT 'VIOLATED))
        (THEN (SETQ ADVICE'INCREASE-MVA-RATING-20%))
)
```

Fig. 12-5. An example of a design change rule.

Since auxiliary-system design progressively articulates preferences, metarules play an important part in selecting appropriate design change rules. Each rule group selection will depend on a particular condition and the particular design stage.

Block 5: Design storage Intermediate design specifications are stored in three major sections: load data, branch data, and bus data. The load data section lists all loads with their associated specifications. The branch data section lists the buses connected to each branch, in addition to each branch's associated kVA rating. The bus data section lists the loads connected to each bus, in addition to each bus's associated kV rating.

Block 6: Critics Realizing designs from the goals and constraints imposed upon them is difficult. Not surprisingly, many initial designs don't satisfy all goals and constraints. We must evaluate designs to verify adequate performance levels, and to determine appropriate corrections.

ASDEP uses two critics to evaluate designs. The first critic (PCritic) ascertains whether physical constraints imposed on designs are satisfied. The second critic (RCritic) evaluates overall design reliability.

Using critics to evaluate designs resembles the Hacker program philosophy [7]. To a large extent, Hacker's critics help correct plans containing conflicts among their subgoals. Both PCritic and RCritic are written in Pascal, in view of Lisp's limited numerical handling capabilities.

PCritic PCritic examines a design's physical constraints to determine (1) which are violated and (2) optimal equipment selection for switchgear and transformer impedances. The violated constraints will vary depending on equipment selection, making the problem difficult even for simple cases. For example, the continuous current limit of a 4.16-kV switchgear can vary from 1.2 to 3.0 kA; its short-circuit current can vary from 49 to 88 kA, while its closing-latching current can vary from 19 to 78 kA.

In addition, it is usually impossible to satisfy all physical constraints, bringing on a new problem: How to determine which constraints must be satisfied, and which can be somewhat violated. The set of constraint violations will be used later to modify the design during the design change phase.

PCritic contains three stages. Stage 1 minimizes the number of constraints violated. Stage 2 optimizes design parameters subject to the set of satisfied constraints determined in Stage 1. Stage 3 classifies all constraints into three sets: satisfied constraints, almost-satisfied constraints, and violated constraints.

During Stage 1, PCritic addresses the following five constraints:

- The continuous current limit,
- The interrupting current limit,
- The momentary current limit,
- The steady-state voltage limit,
- The starting voltage limit.

PCritic applies each constraint to every load bus, consecutively. These five physical constraints are applied not only to each bus, but also to each mode of plant operation (start up, and normal running mode, for example). Based on the number of constraints violated, PCritic selects the worst-case mode for evaluation.

Since designers are normally not interested in finding optimal solutions, precise analytical results aren't necessary. Designers are usually interested in finding satisfactory solutions or a "satisfactum [8]." A satisfactum is an acceptable design: that is, any design within acceptable parameters. This concept is fortuitous when designing auxiliary systems because conventional analytical methods [9] such as load-flow and short-circuit programs cannot be applied to partial designs that are not fully connected, as may be the case for the initial design. However, using simplified mathematical formulations, PCritic can break the problem into noninteracting subproblems for each load bus.

RCritic RCritic evaluates design reliability. Electrical auxiliary systems supply energy to motors, such as those driving circulating water pumps for coolant systems and circulating fans for combustion systems. Power plants require other auxiliaries providing noninterruptible power for computers, instruments, and vital loads that must always function, even when main generator and switchyard supplies are not available. The reliability of these systems must be evaluated to quantitatively understand tradeoffs between supply reliability and cost.

RCritic's basic reliability techniques rely on the minimal-path approach to determine minimal-cut sets [10]. For auxiliary systems, RCritic applies conventional reliability indices to each load bus. Basic load bus indices are (1) expected failure rates, (2) average repair times, and (3) expected annual outage times.

Block 7: Design refinements Using knowledge base design change rules and critic evaluations, users can correct the current design. In addition, they may change some constraints previously imposed on the design (an option called "articulation of preference") [8].

ASDEP's basic design change strategy partitions design changes into the following four subproblems:

(SP1) Physical constraint satisfaction,
(SP2) Load bus connection to satisfactory supply buses,
(SP3) Reliability satisfaction,
(SP4) Determination of the appropriate grounding system.

ASDEP addresses these subproblems sequentially, SP1 through SP4. It solves subproblems SP2, SP3, and SP4 using knowledge stored in the knowledge base. It solves subproblem SP1 in the same way; however, a progressive ordering triggers the rules. Initially, rules yielding only minor design changes (least expensive modifications) are triggered. Next, rules yielding more drastic design changes (expensive modifications) are triggered progressively in the hope that all physical constraint violations can be alleviated.

ASDEP's design change strategy contains four categories of rules.

1. Bus-PC1, Bus-PC2, and Bus-PC3 rules generate design change proposals to alleviate any physical constraint violation (subproblem SP1).
2. Sort rules generate design change proposals to ensure the auxiliary system's full connectivity (subproblem SP2).
3. Reliab-rule01, Reliab-rule02, and Reliab-rule03 generate design change proposals to improve the auxiliary system's reliability characteristics (subproblem SP3).
4. Grounding rules generate design change proposals to size the auxiliary system's appropriate grounding system (subproblem SP4).

Based on observations by human experts who design electrical auxiliary systems and who generally carry out an entire design process before seeking critical evaluation, we decided not to incorporate backtracking methods in ASDEP and designed the knowledge base accordingly. The validation procedure, to be discussed next, proved this basic assumption valid.

Evaluation of ASDEP

This section will clarify the function of each of the seven blocks and the role the user plays in the design process.

Evaluation criteria ASDEP is prototypical. Evaluation at this stage will demonstrate that AI techniques are applicable for designing a power plant's electrical auxiliary system. We will not demonstrate full expert level performance or implement a production grade program. Furthermore, evaluation at this stage is informal. A more structured approach will be taken when appropriate at a later stage of development.

We solicited and obtained the assistance of recognized human experts from Southern Company Services, Incorporated. It was agreed that Southern Company Services would select a particular power plant auxiliary system, for which a design had already been completed, and provide the data required for ASDEP to generate its version of the same auxiliary system. An evaluation of the ASDEP design was then to take place. That evaluation was to address the following issues:

- Load groupings,
- Bus voltage selections,
- Equipment selections,
- System topology.

Additional comments from Southern Company Services design engineers were also encouraged.

Problem statement Southern Company Services engineers selected a single-unit, 990-MVA fossil power plant. They considered only medium voltage loads. Furthermore, they allowed no generator circuit breakers or generator power switches in the design. Our references provide all relevant design data and criteria provided by Southern Company Services [11].

ASDEP's results Rather than stepping through a detailed computer trace of dialogue between the user and ASDEP, we will provide the design evolution and major reasons for design changes. ASDEP completed the design in four steps.

Fossil plants employ two basic modes of plant operation: start-up, and running. Running, the more severe mode, was the mode considered for evaluation; however, ASDEP can model both modes.

Mainly, the load data provided by Southern Company Services contained categories and quantities of each load type plus related horsepower and kVA. We relied upon default rules to provide the considerable missing data, in this case intentionally omitted, to exercise the default rules.

ASDEP first generated a primitive initial design (Design D0). The system then triggered design change rules in the knowledge base to alleviate the current and voltage violations. This action split the loads on buses.

All constraint violations have been updated to Good with the exception of the Voltage-start constraint (now at the Poor level). The system triggered design change rules in the knowledge base to alleviate the Voltage-start constraint. ASDEP then selected a lower motor start voltage level of 85 percent, changing the Poor status to Good.

Next, RCritic evaluated the design. Since this concerns a fossil plant, reliability was not as vital as it would have been for a nuclear plant. However, RCritic did supervise the user in combining two-two winding transformers into one-three winding transformers.

Finally, ASDEP triggered the grounding rules and selected a resistive grounding system for both the main generator and the unit auxiliary transformers.

Evaluation The Southern Company Services engineers delivered an overall evaluation of "positive." Our references give their comments and recommendations [11]. In part, they reported that

> The basic system developed by the expert system [ASDEP] was one of the arrangements originally evaluated for the subject plant. This scheme was rejected as a result of an economic evaluation. This fact does not discount the validity of the expert system designs, but points out the need for an economic evaluator in the

expert system. Presently, ASDEP does not evaluate design economy explicitly, nor does it evaluate the comparative economy of design decisions.

The following summarizes Southern Company Services comments for each of the four points in the evaluation criteria and lists the necessary corrective actions to be taken:

- Load groupings were "good overall." However, two loads "need to have redundant supplies, but this factor was not specified by us [Southern Company Services] in the original data package . . ." RCritic can readily handle this point. No action need be taken.
- Bus voltage levels were identical to "one of the original systems we [Southern Company Services] evaluated." However, Southern Company Services engineers selected a dual operating voltage level of 4.16 kV to better handle small motors. By expanding the knowledge base's voltage selection rules and incorporating an economic evaluator, ASDEP should arrive at similar decisions.
- Equipment selection had mixed reviews. However, the only major difference was in switchgear selection. ASDEP properly selected switchgear selections for two of the four load buses. The other two were improperly selected due to a misinterpretation of switchgear data provided by Southern Company Services. Using correct input data, ASDEP correctly calculated the generator neutral resistor and correctly selected all four switchgears.
- Circuit topology for the running system was good. However, reliability of the starting system was considered poor. Swapping buses 20 and 22 would remedy most reliability deficiencies. Presently, ASDEP doesn't examine starting-system reliability in the same detail as it does the running system. Expanding knowledge base reliability rules to better handle the starting system should correct this problem.

Most of this commentary can be readily integrated into ASDEP's next version. The major addition needed to enhance ASDEP's performance is an economic critic with appropriate economic rules in the knowledge base.

ASDEP incorporates the following AI techniques and concepts:

- Default knowledge,
- Underconstrained initial design,
- A knowledge base,
- Plan refinement,
- Critics,
- Metarules,
- Skeletal plans.

The methodology used to implement ASDEP is not limited to auxiliary system design. Indeed, both substation design and distribution design resemble auxiliary system design. In all three cases, we must deal with strictly radial structures where simplified analysis techniques can be successfully applied to subsets of the entire system.

However, while auxiliary system design application is limited to relatively few new power plant constructions, substation and distribution designs have broad and frequent applications. In this latter direction, ASDEP methodology will demonstrate its full applicability. The fact remains that the methodology used in ASDEP will probably not be readily extendible to transmission system planning because piecewise and local analysis techniques, used in the ASDEP critics, are invalid for the highly meshed structures found in all modern transmission networks.

Acknowledgment

The authors wish to sincerely thank William E. Underwood for his time and valuable commentary. In addition, we thank Lowell Brothers, Tom Higgens, and Bippen Patel of Southern Company Services for their effort in providing a test case and for their professional commentary.

References

1. D. Geraghty et al., "Strategic Planning: Why Do We Need It?", *IEEE Trans. Power Apparatus and Systems*, WM064-2, IEEE Service Center, 445 Hoes La., Piscataway, N.J., 1984.
2. R.N. Allan, R. Billinton, and M.F. DeOliveira, "Reliability Evaluation of the Auxiliary Electrical Systems of Power Stations," *IEEE Trans. Power Apparatus and Systems*, IEEE Service Center, 445 Hoes La., Piscataway, N.J., Sept./Oct. 1971.
3. D.B. Lenat, D.A. Waterman, and F. Hayes-Roth, *Building Expert Systems*, Addison-Wesley, Reading, Mass., 1983.
4. E.D. Sacerdoti, "A Structure for Plans and Behavior," Tech. Report 109, AI Center, SRI Int'l., Menlo Park, Calif., 1975.
5. W. Gevarter, "Expert Systems: Limited but Powerful," *IEEE Spectrum*, Aug. 1983.
6. D. Beeman, *Industrial Power Systems Handbook*, McGraw-Hill, Hightstown, N.Y., 1955.
7. P.R. Cohen and E.A. Feigenbaum, *Handbook of Artificial Intelligence*, Vol. 3, Addison-Wesley, Reading, Mass., 1986.
8. A. Goicoechea, D.R. Hansen, and L. Duckstein, *Multiobjective Decision Analysis with Engineering and Business Application*, John Wiley and Sons, New York, N.Y., 1982.
9. J.R. Neuenswander, *Modern Power Systems*, International Textbook, Scranton, Penn., 1971.
10. R. Billinton and R.N. Allan, *Reliability Evaluation of Power Systems*, Plenum Press, New York, N.Y., 1984.
11. J.F. Jansen, *Application of Artificial Intelligence Techniques to Power System Design*, doctoral dissertation, School of Electrical Engineering, Georgia Inst. of Technology, Atlanta, Ga., 1985.

13

Knowledge-based computer-aided design of materials handling systems

Paula Gabbert
Donald E. Brown

Editors' note *Gabbert and Brown describe a knowledge-based system that assists facility designers in the selection and configuration of materials handling equipment. The project was supported by the Electronics Automation Application Center at General Electric. It is another example of a field prototype that yielded positive results. (Reprinted with permission, from the March/April 1989 issue of* IEEE Transactions on Systems, Man and Cybernetics. *)*

I. Introduction

The materials handling system in a manufacturing facility consists of the equipment used to store and transport components and end products within the facility. Material with its associated overhead accounts for approximately 55 percent of product costs. Hence the design of a materials handling system represents a significant part of the total facility design.

A facility is divided into many cost centers where common tasks are performed. Each cost center can have various work stations where one or more tasks are performed on the material. For example, an assembly cost center might contain two work stations, one to insert a chip into a board and another to put solder on the board to hold the chip in place. It is the function of the materials handling system to transport the materials to the cost centers, move the materials through the work stations, and store the materials in the facility.

A materials handling system design must be both feasible and meet additional requirements imposed by the designer. Feasibility means the materials handling system can physically transport and store the materials in the facility. Acceptability is a stronger criterion and implies that the materials handling system satisfies all design specifications. According to these definitions, all acceptable designs must be feasible.

This paper describes a prototype knowledge-based system called MAHDE (materials handling design) that generated acceptable materials handling system designs.

MAHDE was developed in a joint project with the Electronics Automation Application Center (EAAC) of General Electric to assist facility designers with the design of materials handling systems. Because of the complexity of the materials handling design domain, techniques from both artificial intelligence and the decision sciences were integrated in MAHDE to provide an effective approach. The remainder of this paper describes the design process in MAHDE, the current approaches to this design problem, the representation and use of knowledge by MAHDE, the results from the application of MAHDE to an example design, and future direction for research.

II. The design process

The design of a materials handling system includes selecting and configuring the equipment which stores and transports materials in the facility. In simplified form, the process of facility design involves

1. obtaining specifications,
2. producing a design,
3. evaluating the design for feasibility,
4. if the design fails the evaluations or further improvement is sought then generating a new design (step 2),
5. if no improvements are possible and the design is unacceptable then modifying the specifications (step 1),
6. recommending a design.

Despite the algorithmic character of this description, materials handling system design in particular, and most large-scale design in general, is not amenable to a strictly algorithmic approach. There are a number of reasons for this, and several of the most important are 1) design is unstructured problem-solving requiring trade-offs between multiple conflicting, noncommensurate and imprecisely stated objectives; 2) the goals of the client are dynamic; 3) the future performance of the design components is uncertain; and 4) generating acceptable designs is the result of experiential knowledge. Each of these four points is described below as they relate to materials handling system design.

In most instances the facility designer must trade off performance on different design objectives using modifications to the design components. For example, productivity gains are frequently in conflict with minimizing the cost of the materials handling system or improving the security for materials. The assessment of the preferences of these multiple, conflicting, and noncommensurate objectives is based on imprecisely stated objectives in the design specifications of a facility.

The materials handling system design process is also complicated by the changing goals of the client. For example, as more information is acquired, a high priority goal such as low cost might be tempered by a lower priority goal such as high reliability of equipment. Therefore, design involves updating the current preferential knowledge about the objectives that might result in a design change reflecting the new information.

The process of materials handling system design is also confounded by the growing number of materials handling equipment types and vendors. Not only do facility designers have more equipment to choose from, but they must also subjectively evaluate the performance of this equipment in an as yet unrealized environment. Hence there is uncertainty in the design process regarding both the performance of new equipment and the proposed operating environment of the equipment.

Finally, the currently practiced materials handling system design process incorporates generally accepted procedures for selecting and configuring equipment. These general procedures, or heuristics, are learned from on-the-job experience through trial and error. Experts in the field of facility design are able to describe the procedures that they have refined over their years of experience. Consistent use of the heuristics results in the effective design of materials handling systems because inferior designs are rejected early in the design process.

A. Current techniques

This section describes the current techniques available for facility design including facility layout and materials handling system design. Many computer-based design aids are used to generate facility layouts [1], [3], [7], [16], [17], [22], [23], [26], [29], but few of these aids incorporate the materials handling system design process.

Knowledge-based technology has recently been applied to facility design. Facility design expert system (FADES) [13], [14] is a prototype computer-based design aid to assist facility designers in selecting appropriate quantitative tools, generating relationship charts and flow/distance matrices, and acquiring appropriate data.

Because facility layout aids do not explicitly consider materials handling system design, numerous special characteristics of materials handling systems are not specifically addressed by these aids. The designer must resort to trial and error testing of various alternatives for design. However, methods currently exist for evaluation of materials handling system designs and are loosely categorized into management techniques [2], [15], [22], [35] and analytical techniques [8], [16], [20], [25].

As with facility design, research into the use of knowledge-based systems for materials handling system design is just beginning. An example of this work is MATHES (materials handling equipment selection), which is an expert system representing over 170 rules to aid in the selection of 16 different materials handling devices [9]. This system is limited, however, by the lack of an uncertainty management scheme and the use of only five parameters for design selection. If more parameters are needed, extensive changes to the rule base are required.

Outside of the materials handling and facility design domain, knowledge-based systems exist to aid in the solution of other configuration and design problems. The most well-known of these, XCON [24], configures VAX 11/780 computer components by reasoning with a set of production rules, or set of heuristics that represent knowledge previously used for the configuration task. Knowledge-based systems have also been used for mechanical design [4], digital system design [33], boiler design [5], and telecommunications network design [34]. These systems use heuristics to prune the design problem into a manageable size.

While all of these domains have similarities with the materials handling systems design problem, none of them effectively treat all of the important process issues described in Section II. MAHDE represents a new approach to design aiding for large-scale systems with demonstrated effectiveness in materials handling system design.

B. An integrated approach

MAHDE is a hybrid system employing both decision theoretic and knowledge-based system techniques. A hybrid approach benefits from the coherence provided by a normative methodology, and it accrues distinct advantages from a knowledge-based approach. Some of these advantages include:

1. heuristic rules that guide the design process can be easily changed without modifying the control structure;
2. the changing characteristics of the design environment are incorporated within the knowledge-based system;
3. designs are generated based on the empirical knowledge of designers which is incorporated in the system;
4. knowledge is represented in a domain where expertise is diminishing.

Integrating decision theoretic techniques with knowledge-based systems in and of itself is not new [6], [12], [32]. The contributions in MAHDE are the unique manner in which techniques from both areas are combined, the specific techniques themselves, and the organization of knowledge within the system to accommodate effective application of the hybrid approach. With regard to the last point, knowledge in the materials handling domain can be classified into two areas: preferential knowledge and operational knowledge. Preferential knowledge reflects the changing acceptability measures for designs, while operational knowledge reflects the process of generating the actual designs. The following sections describe the operational and preferential knowledge used in MAHDE.

III. Operational knowledge

The operational knowledge of a designer consists of the heuristics used to generate a feasible materials handling system design that is acceptable to the client. EAAC uses three criteria to determine the set of feasible designs: weight of the carriers while holding the materials, size of the carriers, and transaction rates. The feasibility of a materials handling system also involves the configuration of the devices to guarantee that all materials are capable of reaching their destinations. Design acceptability is measured by attributes, such as cost, and by environmental characteristics, such as the incline grade of the floor. The attribute values of a design might be uncertain or might change as the design environment changes. MAHDE represents the uncertainty in the attribute values and the heuristics used to modify these attributes in the operational knowledge.

Operational knowledge was acquired through interviews with the facility designers at EAAC. Much of the interviewing process involved determining the important attributes of materials handling systems, methods for evaluating the attributes, and models for describing the uncertainty in attribute values.

Although a materials handling system consists of devices for storing and transporting materials, MAHDE considers only those devices that transport materials. EAAC felt that the storage devices were not as significant to the materials handling system design process because the designers can generally agree on the storage devices for a facility easily. The operational knowledge of MAHDE, therefore, describes the important characteristics of the transport devices available for use in a design. However, the knowledge about storage devices is very similar to transport devices, and so MAHDE can easily accommodate this additional information.

A. Transporters

A transport device is a mechanism used to move materials from one location to another. As noted before, several physical capacities (weight, size, and transaction rate) of the transport devices determine the feasibility of the design. Although the values for these capacities vary between vendors, maximum values for each type of transporter can be defined. It is assumed that all vendors can provide a transporter satisfying the maximum value, given a large enough investment level.

Other characteristics that are important in evaluating transport devices measure how well the device satisfies the objectives of the client and are more difficult to measure. Nonetheless, expert designers have heuristic value functions which they use to compare design performance. For example, the value function for flexibility scores each type of transport device on its relative flexibility with respect to competing transport devices. The range for this function is [0, 1]. These value functions are modifiable through an interactive procedure.

B. Representation

The main knowledge representation scheme used in MAHDE is the frame. A frame is a data structure which holds all pertinent knowledge about a single concept. Frames are nested with a hierarchical network to indicate relations between concepts. Each piece of knowledge about a concept is called a slot, and the control structure of the frame system reasons with rules associated with the slots to assign values to the slots. The value in a slot can be a single item, another frame, or a set of frames.

MAHDE uses two hierarchical frame structures to represent knowledge about the materials handling equipment and the materials handling system design. Frames are organized in the hierarchy in increasing levels of detail. Slots that are lower in the hierarchy (i.e., detailed concepts) can inherit values from or place constraints on slots higher in the hierarchy (i.e., generalized concepts).

The hierarchy of frames used to represent the materials handling equipment is shown in FIG. 13-1. The second level of the hierarchy represents the distinction between storage devices and transport devices as previously defined. The various types of each class of equipment are listed on level 3 of the hierarchy. Each of these types of devices can be refined until the bottom level of the hierarchy represents particular instances or definitions of actual pieces of equipment. The hierarchical structure allows the values of the slots for these instances to inherit values from any higher level, depending upon how much detail is desired by the designer.

The materials handling system design is represented in a similar hierarchical structure as shown in FIG. 13-2. Level 2 distinguishes between the two types of materials handling equipment used in the facility: storage devices in the stockrooms and transport devices in the process areas. Level 3 defines the particular instances of the storage and transport devices located in a facility, level 4 represents the carriers that hold the materials while on the device, and level 5 represents the materials either stored or transported in each carrier.

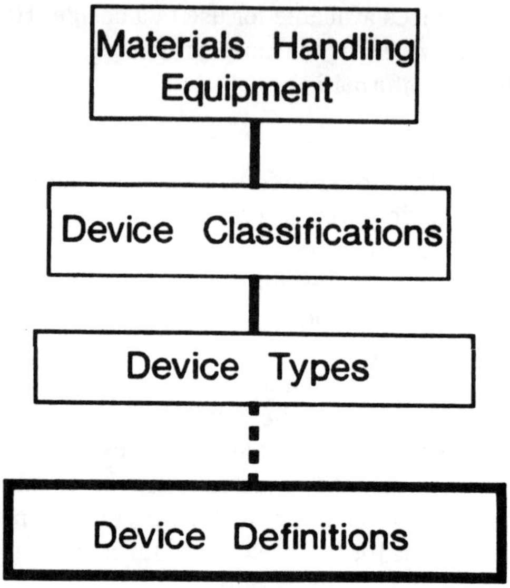

Fig. 13-1. Materials handling equipment hierarchy.

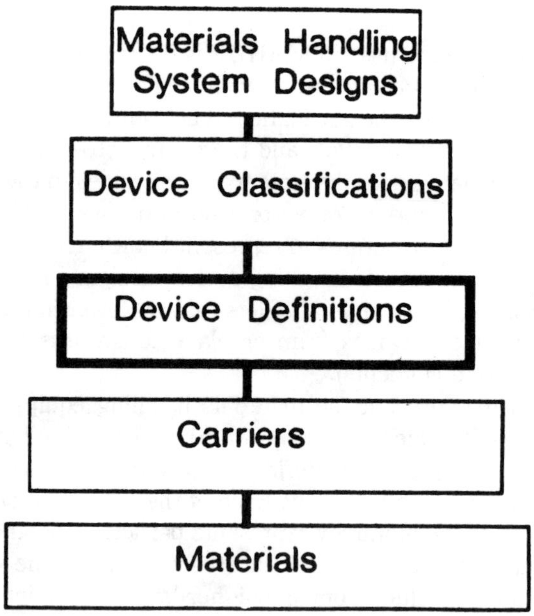

Fig. 13-2. Materials handling system hierarchy.

C. Designer heuristics

The control mechanism in MAHDE uses forward chaining to combine the two hierarchical frame structures by assigning instances of devices from the bottom level of the equipment hierarchy to device definitions on level 3 in the system design hierarchy. To accomplish this, experts at EAAC provided rules that are used to generate the instances of feasible devices in the equipment hierarchy and also to modify the values in the frames defining these devices. With this information, preference-directed search (described in Section IV) assigns items of equipment from the equipment hierarchy to requirements in the design hierarchy. Examples of the heuristics are given below in condensed format:

IF device instance *I* is feasible for device definition *D*
D is located in area *A*
A's incline grade is greater than 0 percent and less than five percent
THEN decrease *I*'s up-time

IF device instance *I* is feasible for device definition *D*
I is a conveyer
D requires more than two turns
THEN decrease *I*'s up-time

D. Uncertainty in operational knowledge

In materials handling systems design the designers must anticipate and predict equipment performance in a manufacturing facility that is not yet constructed. Because of this need for prediction in an imprecisely specified environment, the representation of operational knowledge must account for designer uncertainty.

MAHDE represents uncertainty in operational knowledge using beta distributions on the attribute values for each piece of equipment. The beta distribution is used because it effectively models the uncertainty expressed by the experts at EAAC. Additionally, this distribution is easily parameterized with three point estimates (minimum, mode, and maximum). If no information is known about the design environment, then the beta distribution for an attribute value defaults to a distribution previously defined for each piece of equipment in the equipment hierarchy. As the designer acquires more information about the environment, MAHDE uses heuristics to modify this distribution by altering one or more of the three point estimates. The distributional information is used to obtain expected values and other moments required in the performance analysis of the designs.

IV. Preferential knowledge

In addition to operational knowledge described in the previous section, preferential knowledge is also represented within MAHDE. This knowledge forms the basis for differentiating among competing feasible designs to find the most acceptable design. In this manner preferential knowledge is used to generate improvements to the current design. Hence the representation of preferential knowledge is critical to the performance of MAHDE, and its explicit inclusion in MAHDE is the feature that most dramatically differentiates it from earlier design and configuration systems (e.g., XCON).

Note that two related functions are performed by this preferential component of the system: evaluation and guidance. The evaluation function allows designs to be compared on more than feasibility which is the province of operational knowledge as discussed in the previous section. Guidance means providing the knowledge to search for an improved design. The preferential knowledge of the designer must be acquired and represented in a form that facilitates both evaluation and search activities. The remainder of this section describes the representation and acquisition of preferential knowledge within MAHDE and its use in generating improved designs. While the discussion is specific to MAHDE, care is taken to orient the presentation to general principles that could be used in other design domains.

A. Representation

The representation of preferential knowledge within MAHDE is based on an extension of multiattribute utility theory [21]. Thus this is a numerical representation. While this form of representation is inherently shallow, important advantages accrue from its use in the materials handling system design problem. First, it allows for rapid knowledge acquisition in a situation-dependent domain. Second, the system adapts to the preferences of the user and is, therefore, capable of aiding a variety of designers. Both of these features contribute to the overall flexibility of the system and encourage its use.

The specific representation of preferential knowledge used by MAHDE is an additive decomposition of a joint utility function under uncertainty. This decomposition assumes mutual preferential independence among attributes (see [21] for a definition). This assumption was tested and verified during knowledge acquisition.

Under this representation, the value of a design δ in the set of all feasible designs D is given by

$$V(\delta) = \sum_{i=1}^{\alpha} v_i(\delta) w_i$$

where $v_i(\delta)$ is the value of attribute i for feasible design δ, $0 \leq v_i(\delta) \leq 1$; w_i is the weight of attribute i; and $\Sigma_i w_i = 1$. As previously noted, MAHDE may use a variable number of attributes.

The $v_i(\delta)$ are mappings from the space of design variables onto [0, 1] and are the sums of the expected values of attribute i for each piece of equipment in δ. The attributes are scored and scaled (to [0, 1]) in accordance with expert evaluations. This process provides a score of zero to the worst alternative, a score of one to the best, and either of these equipment alternatives can be used in a design. Any remaining equipment alternatives receive intermediate values. Hence, given precisely specified weights w_i for $i = 1,\cdots,\alpha$, two designs can be compared using (1). In particular, δ_1 is at least as preferred as δ_2 if $V(\delta_1) \geqq V(\delta_2)$ where $V(\cdot)$ is given by (1). Unfortunately, for materials handling system design, these weights are *not* precisely known. The next section describes the procedure in MAHDE for dynamically acquiring this knowledge.

B. MITA: minimal information trade-off assessment

Minimal information trade-off assessment (MITA) is the procedure developed for MAHDE for assessing the weights in an evaluation function such as (1). The techniques used in this procedure find the amount of information gained by a distribution of weights where relative entropy is the measure of information. The use of relative entropy in this fashion is new, although it can be justified by results from information theory found in [27], [28], [30].

MITA begins with alternatives and a representation of the preference structure of the facility designer defined as $W = (w_1, w_2, \cdots, w_\alpha)$. The goal of MITA is to produce a unique set of weights W, given only the currently available information about the designer's preference structure. This information is represented by defining a subspace of the possible values of W.

Suppose the designer wants to consider a specific number of attributes, say α, for evaluation of designs, and let Λ be the subspace of $[0, 1]^\alpha$ (the Cartesian product of [0, 1] with itself α times) formed by linear inequality constraints placed on W. MITA takes the information represented by the subspace Λ and the normalizing constraint $\Sigma_i w_i = 1$ and generates a unique W using only this information (in Λ) and no more.

To understand how W is generated, suppose that no information is provided by the designer. Hence $\Lambda = [0, 1]^\alpha$ and the only constraint on W is the normalizing constraint. In this case, the experts at EAAC give equal weight to each attribute, so W is given by $W_i = 1/\alpha$ for $i = 1, \cdots, \alpha$. If a constraint is added, for example $w_1 \geqq 2w_i$ for $i \neq 1$, then the experts use $w_1 = 2/(\alpha + 1)$ and $w_i = 1/(\alpha + 1)$ for $i = 2, \cdots, \alpha$. In these two examples the choice of any other W is equivalent to imposing additional and unstated information constraints on the problem.

To solve for W, a measure of the information represented by any specific W is needed. A convenient measure that satisfies the aforementioned properties and other relevant inferential properties [31] is relative entropy. The use of entropy to measure attribute importance was proposed in a different context by [36]. However, the MITA technique, which uses relative entropy, is a new approach to acquiring trade-off weight information and provides an effective means of modeling expert problem solving in materials handling system design.

MITA finds a specific value for W as the solution to the mathematical programming problem to minimize:

$$H(W) = \sum_{i=1}^{\alpha} w_i \log w_i/w_i' \qquad \text{subject to } W \in \Lambda \sum_{i=1}^{\alpha} w_i = 1$$

where $W' = (w_1', \cdots, w_\alpha')$ is a prior preference structure or a uniform preference structure if no prior exists. A sufficient condition for the uniqueness of the solution for W is that Λ be described by linear equality and/or inequality constraints. Hence the MITA procedure used by MAHDE guarantees a unique W given the current information regarding the designer's preference structure. In this manner a recommended design is produced because W is then used in (1) to order the available designs and produce a recommendation.

H in (2) measures the amount of information given by the preference structure W relative to W'. H is a continuous function over all W. Another important property of H is that refinements on the attribute space also indicate information content and are measured by H. Let $B = \{b_1, b_2, \cdots, b_\beta\}$ be a refinement of attribute space $A = \{a_1, a_2, \cdots, a_\alpha\}$ such that, for some $b_i, b_j \in B$ and $a_k \in A$, $b_i \cup b_j = a_k$ (Fig. 3). H dictates that $H(A) \leqq H(B)$ or that less information is known about refined spaces of attributes (given the same set of constraints on the weights). For example, assume that COST is an attribute of A and OPERATING COST and INITIAL COST are attributes B such that COST = OPERATING COST ∪ INITIAL COST. Given a specific Λ, more information cannot be known about OPERATING COST and INITIAL COST since they are refinements of COST.

MITA relies on the information represented by the weight constraints defining Λ. Once the space Λ can be acquired and refined, a search process can use this information to find the most acceptable design. The next two sections discuss these two processes of MITA.

C. Weight constraints

When subjectively assessing probability distributions, humans often exhibit biases [19] that result in distributions that violate the laws of probability. Hence techniques were developed to reduce the impact of these biases [10]. Set inclusion has been shown to be a useful technique for describing the bounds of a probability distribution [11], and these bounds are then used to assess the distribution subjectively.

Decisionmakers have similar difficulties expressing the importance of an attribute numerically. Fortunately, in the presence of alternatives, they can usually "describe" the relative importance of these attributes using the following kinds of statements:

1. COST is the most important attribute;
2. it is better for the OPERATING COST to remain low at the expense of a higher INITIAL COST;
3. COST is twice as important as FLEXIBILITY;
4. high FLEXIBILITY and low COST are equally important;
5. COST is at least as important as FLEXIBILITY.

Although most of these statements are vague, MITA uses set inclusion to define the information represented in these statements.

The preference statements provide the necessary information to form linear inequality constraints on the weights. This process is based on the assumption that the statement $A_i \varrho A_j$ for attributes A_i, A_j, and preference relation ϱ holds if and only if $c_1 w_i \Delta c_2 w_j$ for some real numbers c_1 and c_2 and $\Delta \epsilon \{>, =, \leq, \geq\}$. Under this assumption, the "more important than" relation for attributes is a "greater than" relation on the weights, the "equivalence" relation for attributes is an "equality" relation on the weights, and the "at least as important" relation for attributes is a "greater than or equal" relation on the weights. The "c times more important than" relation for attributes is a "greater than" relation on the weights where c is multiplied by the weight of the less important attribute. The process provides a generalized set of mappings from preference statements into weight constraints which define the subspace Λ in which W must lie.

D. Preference directed search

The precision of the weights generated by MITA is intricately related to the precision of the preference information defined in Λ. Because this preference information is acquired from statements which are usually imprecise, the resulting weights may not accurately reflect the importance of the attributes, and therefore more information about the attributes is necessary.

A second component of MITA uses the relative entropy measure of the information in W to determine new sets of weights given the prior preference structure. Given new preference information about the importance of the attributes, (2) is minimized to generate a new set of weights based on this new information.

The decision process can now be cast as a search through the set of alternatives, where the decisionmaker selects the direction of the search by indicating the importance of the attributes. MITA requires that 1) the decisionmaker be capable of formulating new preference relations among the attributes based on either new environmental conditions or an assessment of the current best decision and 2) these new relations are consistent with any previously stated preference relations. If this second condition does not hold, then the inconsistent statements are examined and appropriately altered.

At any point in the decision process, a set of alternatives will be denoted as the "best" because they maximize (1) given the current information about the attributes. Call this set l^*. New information about the preferences is obtained from the decisionmaker and captured in Λ. The operator O for generating the next nodes in the search space l'^* is based on solving (2) given the prior preference structure and the new preferences of the decisionmaker (i.e., W' and Λ). This process is repeated until the minimal information set has been defined to generate a solution acceptable to the decisionmaker.

V. Application

In this section a simplified example taken from an actual design problem is given. The MAHDE system is used to select three transport devices for a facility. Clearly, a realistic facility has many more devices and materials than used in this example. However, the process shown here is exemplary of that used by MAHDE in more complex design domains for which it was developed.

The three transport devices defined for this example facility are the Kit-Mover, Assembly, and Testing-Transport. The carriers and materials assigned to these transporters define the constraints on the feasible devices possible for each transporter. This example also illustrates the impact of environmental characteristics. The two important characteristics considered in this example are the incline grade of the cost center and the Number of turns required by the device. The Kit-Mover is located in a cost center with incline grade that is greater than zero percent and Assembly requires three turns to move the materials through the process.

MAHDE's first task is to determine which devices are feasible based on the weight and size of the carrier holding the material and the required transaction rate. for this example, the number of feasible devices for the Kit-Mover, Assembly, and Testing-Transport devices are 8, 5, and 5, respectively. Therefore, there are 200 feasible designs for the facility. The preferential knowledge manipulation techniques described in Section IV are used to acquire preferential information dynamically from the designer and find the optimal feasible design based on these preferences.

The preferential information acquired centers around important attributes which are defined to measure specific objectives of the facility. For this example, six attributes are considered important: INVESTMENT, LEAD-TIME, UP-TIME, FLEXIBILITY, MEAN-TIME-TO-REPAIR, and PRODUCT-PROTECTION. Given the initial specifications of the facility, the following preferences were determined:

1. INVESTMENT is somewhat more important than FLEXIBILITY because new product lines will probably not be manufactured in the facility in the future;
2. UP-TIME is very important and the client is willing to pay for a reliable system.

These preferences are entered into MAHDE through an interface mechanism that allows comparisons between two attributes. Imprecise terms such as "somewhat" and "very" are captured using a bar graph that can be raised or lowered for relative comparisons of attributes.

This type of search process continues until the designer is satisfied that all the preferences on the attributes have been satisfied, and the designer is certain that these preferences are not going to change. As mentioned earlier, MAHDE does allow for the generation of multiple designs since, in many instances, the client may want to have several options to choose from. However, MAHDE provides important trade-off information about these designs so that informed decisions can be made based on the relative importance of attributes.

VI. Conclusion

The objective of this project with EAAC was to develop a prototype knowledge-based system to determine the feasibility of the approach and direct research further into this application. The feasibility of the approach has been demonstrated through evaluations by EAAC. Based on the evaluation of the MAHDE system, it appears that the approach used for selection and improvement of design develops the most acceptable solutions for a materials handling system given the preference structure of the designer. The system shows how a powerful design tool can be developed by integrating knowledge engineering and decision science techniques. This integration, although a relatively new area of research, has applications to many design problems.

The incorporation of the preferential component with the knowledge base is a powerful addition necessary for unstructured problem solving. The MITA approach for acquiring this preferential knowledge provides easy and efficient methods for updating based on new environmental information. The MITA approach is a general preference updating scheme extendible to other domains. The use of a knowledge-based approach for representing and manipulating operational knowledge provides an effective means of incorporating designer heuristics to generate feasible designs.

Knowledge-based technology has many advantages to offer the manufacturing industry, and research has just recently begun in this area. Further investigations will continue to enhance the productivity of the facility designers by providing powerful design aids.

Future research in related areas include examining the theoretical impacts of the relative entropy approach for assessing weights in utility functions, exploring the uncertainty management techniques within design domains, and expanding MAHDE into other design applications. The first of these is important, because while the relative entropy approach employed by MITA had descriptive merit in the materials handling design domain, it is not clear that it possesses normative merit over a broader class of design problems.

As this research is expanded into other design applications, the MAHDE frame structure will evolve into an expert system shell. As such, it will provide the framework for the integration of decision theoretic techniques and knowledge-based systems necessary for design applications. This extension of MAHDE is a current research project, and it is anticipated that an integrative shell of this sort will have widespread application in other large-scale design domains.

References

1. J.M. Apple, *Plant Layout and Materials Handling*, New York: Ronald Press, 1950.
2. ______, "Designing material handling system with management issues in mind," *Ind. Eng.* vol. 16, no. 3, pp. 56 – 59, 1984.
3. G.C. Armour and E.S. Buffa, "A heuristic algorithm and simulation approach to relative location of facilities," *Management Sci.*, vol. 9, no. 2, pp. 294 – 309, 1963.
4. D. Brown and B. Chandrasekaran, "Knowledge and control for a mechanical design expert system" *IEEE Computer*, pp. 92 – 100, July 1986.
5. D.E. Brown and C.C. White, "An expert system approach to boiler design," *IEEE Trans. Syst. Man Cybern.*, vol. SMC-17, no. 2, 1987.
6. G. Bruno, A. Elia, and P. Laface, "A rule-based system to schedule production," *Computer*, vol. 19, no. 7, pp. 32 – 40, 1986.
7. T.E. El-Rayah and R.H. Hollier, "A review of plant design techniques," *Int. J. Production Res.*, vol. 8, no. 3, pp. 263 – 279, 1970.
8. E.A. Elsayed, "Algorithms for optimal material handling in automatic warehousing systems," *Int. J. Production Res.*, vol. 19, no. 5, pp. 525 – 535, 1981.
9. J.B. Farber and E.L. Fisher, "MATHES: Material handling equipment selection expert system," NCSU-IE Tech. Rep. 85 – 16, Dept. Ind. Eng., North Carolina State Univ., 1985.
10. B. Fischhoff, "Debiasing," in *Judgement Under Uncertainty: Heuristics and Biases*, D. Kahneman, P. Slovic, and A. Tversky Eds. New York: Cambridge Univ. Press, 1982.
11. P. Fishburn, "Analysis of decision with incomplete knowledge of probabilities," *Oper. Res.*, vol. 13, pp. 217 – 237, 1965.
12. E.L. Fisher, "Expert systems can lay groundwork for intelligent CIM decision making," *Ind. Eng.*, vol. 17, no. 3, pp. 78 – 83, 1985.
13. E.L. Fisher and S.Y. Nof, "FADES: Knowledge-based facility design," in *Proc. 1984 Annu. Int. Industrial Engineering Conf.*, Atlanta, GA: Inst. Ind. Eng., 1984, pp. 74 – 82.
14. ______, "An AI-based methodology for factory design," *AI Mag.*, vol. VII, no. 4, pp. 72 – 85, Fall 1986.
15. N. Glenney, "Modular integrated material handling system facilitates automation process," *Ind. Eng.*, no. 11, pp. 118 – 124, 1981.
16. D.R. Herzog, *Industrial Engineering Methods and Controls*. Reston, VA: Reston, 1985.
17. G.G. Hitching and M. Cottam, "An efficient heuristic procedure for solving the layout design problem," *OMEGA, Int. J. Management Sci.*, vol. 4, no. 2, pp. 205 – 214, 1976.
18. E. Jaynes, "Prior probabilities," *IEEE Trans. Syst. Sci. Cybern.* vol. SSC-4, no. 3, Sept. 1968.
19. D. Kahneman and A. Tversky, "Subjective probability: A judgement of representativeness," in *Judgement Under Uncertainty: Heuristics and Biases*, D. Kahneman, P. Slovic, and A. Tversky, Eds. New York: Cambridge Univ. Press, 1982.
20. E. Kay, *A Mathematical Model for Handling in a Warehouse*, New York: Pergamon, 1968.

21. R. Keeney and H. Raiffa, *Decisions with Multiple Objectives: Preferences and Value Tradeoffs*, New York: Wiley, 1985.
22. S. Konz, *Facility Design*, New York: Wiley, 1985.
23. R.C. Lee and J. Moore, "Corelap-computerized relationship layout planning," *J. Ind. Eng.*, vol. 18, no. 3, 1967.
24. J. McDermott, "R1: A rule-based configurer of computer systems," *Artificial Intelligence*, vol. 19, pp. 39 – 88, 1982.
25. W.T. Morris, *Analysis for Materials Handling Management*, Homewood, IL: Richard D. Irwin, 1962.
26. M.C. Nutt, *Functional Plant Planning, Layout and Materials Handling*, New York: Exposition Press, 1970.
27. A. Papoulis, *Probability, Random Variables, and Stochastic Processes*, New York: McGraw-Hill, 1984.
28. F. Reza, *An Introduction To Information Theory*, New York: McGraw-Hill, 1961.
29. J.M. Seehof and W.O. Evans, "Automated layout design program," *J. Ind. Eng.*, vol. 18, no. 12, 1967.
30. C. Shannon, "A mathematical theory of communication," *Bell Syst. Tech. J.*, vol. 27, pp. 379 – 423, 623 – 656, 1948.
31. J.E. Shore and R.W. Johnson, "Axiomatic derivation of the principle of maximum entropy and the principle of minimum cross-entropy," *IEEE Trans. Inform. Theory*, vol. IT-26, pp. 26 – 37, 1980.
32. G. Stoebel, R. Baxter, and M. Denney, "A capacity planning expert system for IBM system/38," *Computer*, vol. 19, no. 7, pp. 42 – 50, 1986.
33. G. Sussman, "Electrical design—A problem for AI research," in *Proc. Int. J. Conf. Artificial Intell.*, Aug. 1977, pp. 894 – 900.
34. E. Sykes, "Multiobjective intelligent computer-aided design," Ph.D. dissertation, Syst. Eng. Dep., Univ. Virginia, Jan. 1987.
35. J.A. Tompkins and J.D. Smith. "Keys to developing material handling systems for automated factories," *Ind. Eng.*, vol. 15, no. 9, pp. 48 – 54, 1983.
36. M. Zeleny, *Multiple Criteria Decision Making*, New York: McGraw-Hill, 1982.

Section B

Intelligent computer-assisted instructional systems

14

Intelligent computer-aided instruction

A survey organized around system components

Jeff W. Rickel

Editors' note *Rickel provides a superb survey of the field of intelligent computer-aided instruction (ICAI). If you are unfamiliar with ICAI (or CAI), this paper will prove extremely useful. It describes how AI tools and techniques have been used to design and develop intelligent instructional systems of all kinds, and how AI research has contributed to the evolution of ICAI. (Reprinted, with permission, from the January/February 1989 issue of* IEEE Transactions on Systems, Man and Cybernetics. *© 1989, IEEE. All rights reserved.)*

I. Introduction

Although computer-aided instruction (CAI)[1] has been around for some time now, there has been much discontent with the current state of educational software. Traditional "frame-oriented CAI" requires teachers to fully specify presentation text, all questions and their associated answers, and a strict flow of control through the course, allowing at best different branches to be taken based on the student's preenumerated possible responses. This style of teaching has often been referred to as "electronic page turning."

Manuscript received April 23, 1988; revised September 26, 1988. This work was supported in part by Texas Instruments Incorporated, Dallas, TX.

J. Rickel is with the Artificial Intelligence Laboratory, Department of Computer Science, University of Texas, Taylor Hall 2.124, Austin, TX 78712-1188. He is on educational leave of absence from Texas Instruments Incorporated.

IEEE Log Number 8825070.

[1] Because this paper concentrates on ICAI, a CAI straw man is used for comparison. In fairness to CAI researchers, it should be noted that the problems with CAI were well known, and many practitioners developed ingenious solutions for them. Nevertheless, our characterization of CAI is adequate for the purpose of this paper.

A step in the right direction was made with generative CAI. In these systems, techniques such as textual templates, problem-generation grammars, and random numbers were used to generate problems for the student. Still, the systems lacked the ability to adapt to the student or relate his incorrect answers to the correct ones, and the problems were usually limited to simple drill-and-practice questions [40].

Educators and computer scientists alike saw the need for "intelligence" in these systems. Dubbed ICAI for "intelligent" CAI, these systems would have a rich representation of their domain that would allow them to use their knowledge in ways unspecified by the course designer. Also, by modeling the student himself, these systems could individualize their instruction, tailoring their presentation to the level of the student's knowledge and his rate of learning.

Although there has been much research in ICAI, few if any commercial systems exist due to the current cost of building such systems and the lack of experienced people in the area. As noted by Psotka *et al.* [43], "When one considers the ICAI systems that have been built to date, one is impressed with the fact that each is somewhat like the work of a craftsman, a combination of technical skill and artistic creativity." ICAI is still very much a research topic, with today's systems suffering the same basic limitations as more general AI systems (i.e., lack of common-sense reasoning). Yet ICAI is a natural test bed for AI techniques since it requires reasoning from a rich knowledge representation, modeling the user, and communication of information structures. While today's ICAI systems are carefully crafted, one of the primary motivations for further research is the potential for educational systems that generate their pedagogical abilities automatically given only a base of domain knowledge. As AI and ICAI research continue to advance, computer-based tutors should become both more effective and more economical.

The remainder of this paper will survey the important contributions of past ICAI research efforts. Most previous surveys have been organized around the seminal systems. While this gives an important historical perspective, it leaves to the ICAI system designer the task of drawing together the contributions of each effort to our understanding of the various components of a typical ICAI system. Having been through this process, the author will present in this paper this latter perspective so that the designers of future ICAI systems can readily leverage the lessons learned by their predecessors. The interested reader is referred to Fletcher [19], Feigenbaum and Barr [18], and Park *et al.* [40] for good surveys of past ICAI systems, and to Park *et al.* [40] for an extensive comparison of CAI and ICAI.

II. Learning scenarios

A learning scenario is the situation in which the student's learning is to take place. The most important criterion with which to view a learning scenario is the balance of control between student and tutor. Along this dimension, learning scenarios range from the simple "rule-example-practice" paradigm used in traditional frame-oriented CAI programs to controllable simulation to mixed-initiative dialogue to discovery learning [20]. This dimension forms a continuous spectrum from frame-based CAI, in which the student cannot explore things of interest, to open-ended discovery environments, such as Logo [39], in which the student may get stuck or waste a lot of time. The knowledge required by the tutoring system is minimal on either end of this spectrum, but increases towards the middle [7].

Evidence suggests that learned information is retained longer if the student is an active participant in the learning process (rather than a passive "absorber") and if the presentation involves several of the student's senses. One study reports that people retain about 25 percent of what they hear, 45 percent of what they see and hear, and 70 percent of what they see, hear, and do [17]. Experts in diverse fields suggest that true understanding of knowledge gained from formal training comes when the student later combines that knowledge with actual experience and application [38], [53]. Indeed, the backlash against traditional CAI has focused on the passive role of the student and has prompted educators and instructional designers to seek more effective uses of computers for education. This explains the more ambitious computer learning scenarios that will be described in this section.

One particularly popular form of instructional philosophy is that of the computer coach [22]. Brown and Moskowitz sum up the coaching scenario as follows: "At your request, the intelligent coach "looks over your shoulder" while you attempt to carry out tasks, offering timely but unobtrusive advice" [8]. One advantage of computer coaches is that training becomes more cost-effective since the coach is available at the convenience of the student and thus off-site learning is minimized. The coach is available not just for formal training, but also to help out during normal work activities, saving the user time that might otherwise "be spent thumbing through a manual or waiting for help from a colleague" [8]. In this sense, we can see that tutorial ICAI and job aiding need not be mutually exclusive [38], [49]. Coaching is most effective in tasks where the student's performance tends to reach plateaus [25]; the exposition of key knowledge often opens up a whole new area for exploration by the student.

Gaming environments can combine the characteristics of both coaching and informal discovery learning [10]. In such a scenario, a game is designed to teach more general skills. The student learns these skills by applying them in the context of the game and may even discover them through their positive influence on his game position. A coach can point out when the student is consistently employing a suboptimal strategy and can demonstrate the use of the desired skills in winning the game. This learning scenario has the advantages of discovery (the student often discovers the skills himself), application (the student learns the skills by using them), coaching (the computer coach can lift the student off plateaus and guide him when he seems misdirected), and, most importantly, the student's attention is heightened by his interest in the game itself.

The prototypical example of a game-based learning scenario is the West system of Burton and Brown [10]. West is a computer tutoring system which coaches students through the game "How the West was Won." The game requires students to combine numbers, using arithmetic operators and parentheses, into expressions that evaluate to the number of board positions they would like to move. Proficiency in the game thus requires mathematical as well as tactical skills, and it is the job of the West coach to determine whether or not the student is employing the right skills and when he needs guidance. Their paper [10] is an excellent treatise on the issues involved in computer coaching, especially in gaming environments.

Many educators have lamented the one-sided nature of CAI. They claim that the student should be allowed to ask questions of the tutor and in general affect the directions of the tutoring session. In 1970, Jaime Carbonell launched the field of ICAI by using AI techniques to build a mixed-initiative tutoring system. His seminal tutor, Scholar [13], tutors students in geography by carrying on a natural language dialogue with the student in which the student can respond to computer questions or initiate a line of questioning that Scholar must answer. Carbonell emphasizes the benefits of mixed-initiative tutorial dialogue, pointing out that it results in a more reactive tutoring system and that allowance for student initiative is crucial to effective education [13].

Closely related to mixed-initiative dialogue is the use of the Socratic teaching method [42]. The Greek philosopher Socrates believed that education could not be attained through passive exercises such as reading or listening, but instead came from actual problem solving. His technique involved posing problems to the student, each one carefully crafted to require the student to use new knowledge, to point out gaps in the student's knowledge, or to entrap the student into discovering his own misconceptions. Stevens and Collins have explored the use of a Socratic method in their Why tutor [55], [58], which tutors students on the causal relationships and factors affecting rainfall.

Gaming environments and mixed-initiative dialogue scenarios differ in the demands they put on the tutoring system. In a dialogue system, the tutor must be able to articulate its knowledge in response to queries, whereas a game-based tutor need only recognize that a student's answer/action is not optimal and provide guidance. On the other hand, a computer coach must infer student shortcomings from the context of the game, whereas mixed-initiative dialogue systems allow the computer tutor to test hypotheses by asking new questions [10]. Woolf and McDonald [63] draw an important distinction between "context-dependent" tutoring systems, in which the tutoring system adapts its strategy based on the state of the student, and "retrieval-oriented" systems like West that place their emphasis on retrieving the correct answer, and suggest that the former provide more reactive tutoring. Both learning scenarios offer unique advantages and disadvantages, however, and each introduces its own architectural requirements.

Another popular instructional paradigm is that of the articulate expert exemplified by the famous Sophie systems [6]. Sophie[2] is designed to teach students about troubleshooting electronic circuits by allowing them to view the tutor solving problems before they are given their own problems. The student is allowed to insert faults in an electronic circuit, and Sophie then troubleshoots the circuit, explaining along the way not only the justifications for its decisions, measurements, and conclusions, but also its high-level troubleshooting tactics. The student, after watching several expert performances, is then given some problems to solve while Sophie watches and occasionally provides guidance and advice. In particular, Sophie would not let students make measurements unless that particular measurement can actually distinguish between several candidate faults.

Many researchers have pointed out the importance of rationalizing each action

[2] There are actually three distinct Sophie systems, known as Sophic I, II, and III. This paper categorizes them under the general name Sophie.

when teaching procedural skills. Beyond learning *when* actions are appropriate, a student must know *why* those actions are appropriate. A tutoring system must therefore present procedural skills at varying levels of abstraction and should explain actions in terms of their causal effects in the domain. For instance, in the fault isolation procedure (FIP) tutor [38], [37], the current goal hierarchy is maintained. Tracing up this goal hierarchy answers the question "Why am I doing this action?" This goal-oriented perspective, along with qualitative, causal knowledge of how a system works, enables students to fully understand why and when certain actions are appropriate [38], [53].

Another way to give students a feel for the causal relationships in a domain is to provide them a simulation of that domain with which they can explore the consequences of their actions without fear of real-life consequences. Also, by thrusting the student into the ultimate performance environment, and coaching him into the right actions, the student will be more likely to carry his training into real-life situations.

Steamer [29] is the archetypal example of an interactive, inspectable simulation. Although Steamer grew into more generic tools, its original purpose was to provide simulation-based instruction on the workings of a basic steam propulsion system. It is interactive in that students can manipulate controls and see their effect. It is inspectable in that Steamer includes an extensive graphics interface that allows students to view the workings of the steam system in a much more animated form than would otherwise be possible. Its authors coined the expression "dynamic graphical explanations" to describe Steamer's style of instruction, noting that "relationships that are difficult to describe unambiguously in words are often easily depicted graphically" [29].

In a more recent attempt at simulation-based training, Woolf built a tutoring system for the Kraft recovery boiler whose goal "is to challenge an operator to solve boiler problems and to maintain his incentive to play with the tutor" [65]. In the recovery boiler tutor (RBT), students are presented with a graphical window into the process and given problems to correct. Based on their actions, RBT offers coaching and advice. Although RBT is a real-time simulation, updating its process variables every one or two seconds, operators who have used it seem to like the ability to stop the process to ask questions or explore boiler characteristics [65]. An actual RBT tutorial dialogue[3] extracted from [65] follows.

(Note: a partial blackout is in progress and it will lead to deterioration of the combustion process if no action is taken. Meters indicate that CO, SO_2, and O_2 readings are abnormally high.)

Tutor: What action are you going to take?

Student: Check smelt spout cooling water. (Student's action does not result in a change in the boiler.)

Tutor: It looks as though the liquor isn't burning . . .

Student: Help. What is going on? (Student requests help.)

Tutor: A partial blackout is occurring and this causes TRS, CO, SO_2, and O_2 to increase. Steam flow and steam temperature are dropping. I think part of the bed is not burning.

[3] Student input in RBT is done through menus and tutor output is canned text extracted from emergency-specific text files.

Student:	Rod the primary air ports. (A small improvement in the boiler readings can be observed.)
Tutor:	Your action is correct; however, at this time rodding alone is not effective . . .
Student:	Raise the liquor temperature. (Student's action does not reverse the emergency and a new alarm buzzer sounds.)
Tutor:	Rodding the air port apparently was not enough to undo the blackout.
Student:	Increase the oil fuel supply. (Student's action reverses the emergency.)
Tutor:	That solved the problem alright. Good thinking.

The authors of Steamer raise an important point about simulation-based training. It is not enough to simply present the simulation as a black box with which the student can play. The training tool must provide "conceptual fidelity" [29]; that is, the information must be presented to the student in a way that helps him build the correct cognitive constructs for thinking about the domain. These cognitive constructs need not accurately model the internal behavior of the domain, but should instead reflect the way experts think about it. For instance, if electronics experts think about electricity as discrete electrons flowing through the circuit, the student should be presented with this graphical model rather than the more accurate quantum mechanical model or just the voltage and current readings at various points. Give the student a useful mental model of the domain that is at the appropriate level of abstraction.

As a final note on simulation-based training, it should be noted that simulations can be time consuming to construct and are challenging from an educational standpoint because it becomes harder to detect student misconceptions (compared to mixed-initiative dialogue, for instance). Most successful simulation-based instructional programs have combined a simulator with more traditional ICAI methods to produce a more versatile tutoring system.

Discovery learning is at the opposite end of the spectrum from frame-based CAI. This learning scenario can take many forms, but the basic philosophy is to present the student with some sort of microworld in which to explore and discover general rules and concepts. The idea is that the student, being in full control, can let his own curiosity and interest drive the session, and that those principles that he discovers on his own will be more likely to stay with him. Obviously, this sort of learning also prepares the student for future scientific inquiry and real-life problems since it forces him to develop his own problem-solving skills and learn to think creatively. We will have little more to say about this learning scenario since it is very different in character from the other basic approaches and in fact deserves a survey of its own.

Having explored the various forms of ICAI learning scenarios, it is now relevant to ask what knowledge is needed to support their respective requirements and what form this knowledge should take. This is the topic of the next section.

III. Domain knowledge representation

The biggest problem with traditional CAI systems is that they have a poor knowledge of their domain. This knowledge typically consists of a canned presentation of the information to the student, canned problems with which to test his knowledge, canned answers, and prespecified branches in the presentation based on a preenumerated set of possible responses. It is hardly surprising when these systems are criticized for their lack of adaptation to the student. Their canned text prevents them from adapting the presentation to the needs of the student. Their prespecified branches prevent them from handling unanticipated answers. They have no facilities with which to ferret out the student's true misconceptions. They cannot construct problems which specifically address the student's needs. And their prespecified answers leave them with no criteria for judging student responses other than as right or wrong. A human teacher with the same level of knowledge of his subject could not do much better. We expect more domain competence on the part of our human teachers; we should strive for no less in computer tutors.

In a nutshell, the goal of ICAI is to plug the necessary knowledge into computer-based tutors to correct the above limitations. However, the knowledge needed to correct all the above shortcomings is tremendous, and no tutoring system to date has encompassed all the requisite knowledge even for the most limited domain; this indeed would exceed the current state of the art in AI. On the other hand, all the previous shortcomings have been solved at some level in one system or another. The challenge for each new ICAI system is to provide a domain knowledge representation rich enough to support the desired level of understanding and therefore flexibility in teaching.

If there is one lesson that thirty years of AI research has taught us, it is that knowledge, rather than general thought mechanisms, is the key to intelligent behavior. Furthermore, the form in which we store this knowledge is crucial to our abilities to use it. Finally, no general form seems suitable for all knowledge. Instead, different types of reasoning and types of knowledge require different representations for efficient and effective use. The bottom line, then, is that intelligent behavior (and thus tutorial capabilities) requires extensive knowledge structured in such a way as to facilitate the desired types of reasoning and cognitive capabilities. Our challenge in ICAI is to determine the types of knowledge required, and suitable representations for that knowledge, to support teaching particular subjects. To quote several of the most influential ICAI researchers, "By far the most important issue we have been forced to confront is the overwhelmingly central role of detailed, domain-specific knowledge in governing almost every aspect of the tutorial process" [58].

The structure and interrelationships of knowledge needed for tutoring are much greater than for typical problem-solving expert systems. This important lesson was clearly demonstrated by research at Stanford University in which they tried to use the famous Mycin expert system [9] as a tutor for medical students. The resulting system, Guidon [14], was shown to be inadequate in many ways, all resulting from Mycin's uniform rule-based knowledge representation. Woolf and McDonald summarize: "Guidon helped demonstrate the need for a cognitive base to the expert module and defined the importance of placing logical and relational abstractions, both of which are important in learning and tutoring, into the expert knowledge base . . . . The suggestion has been made that the original rules of the Mycin system represent 'compiled' knowledge devoid of the low-level detail and relations necessary for learning and tutoring" [63]. Bill Clancey, the prime architect of Guidon, concurs: "Teaching and explanation, we came to recognize, place different demands on an expert than simply solving problems. A teacher can provide analogies, multiple views, and levels of explanation which are unknown to Mycin. In building Mycin, we did not make explicit how an expert organizes his knowledge, how he remembers it, and strategies he uses for approaching problems. We need to be able to articulate how the rules fit together, how they are constructed" [16]. A tutoring system, then, needs not only knowledge of its domain, but also the perspective on this knowledge that allows it to convey it to the student.

The complexity of an ICAI system far exceeds the more typical frame-based CAI techniques. Building a knowledge-based CAI system requires investigation of such questions as "What is an effective taxonomy of question types, from both a semantic and syntactic point of view?", "What classification of errors should be utilized, if it is to apply regardless of the specific subject matter?", and "What different efficient techniques can possibly be defined and used for diagnostic and remedial purposes?" [13]. Although the expert module or domain knowledge of the system does not necessarily have to have the ability to solve problems it poses to the student, it must at least recognize an incorrect answer [63]. Goldstein and Papert [23] suggest the use of a "glass-box" expert that can both solve domain problems and explain its reasoning to the student. Burton and Brown [10], on the other hand, state that a black-box expert that solves domain problems in the most efficient (albeit possibly obscure) way may be more efficient than a more complex glass-box, articulate expert. They suggest the combination of a black-box expert, which solves domain problems and compares its answers with the student's to detect errors, with a possibly incomplete glass-box expert, which cannot solve all domain problems, but can solve enough to be able to explain to the student how his solution differs from the ideal. Many such trade-offs exist, and it would be foolish to think that one best answer applies to all domains.

The choice of knowledge representation in a tutoring system depends on both the type of knowledge to be stored and its intended tutorial use. Why [55], [58], for instance, is a Socratic tutoring system that teaches the causal relationships and factors affecting rainfall. Stevens *et al.* [58] list the sorts of knowledge that are represented in Why along with sentences that illustrate each type; these are as follows:

- Factors: "Do you think the amount of moisture in the air affects the amount of rainfall?"
- Results of processes: "Condensation is the process by which moisture in the air becomes liquid water again."
- Functional relations: "What happens to the temperature of the air as it rises?"

The intended use of this knowledge is to test the student's understanding of the major causal factors involved in rainfall. When the student has a misconception with a particular causal factor, they would like to shift their discussion down one level to discuss the more intricate causal relationships at work in that factor. Therefore, their knowledge dictates a representation that emphasizes causality, while their intended teaching strategy necessitates different levels of abstraction from high-level factors to lower-order ones.

The representation that they chose was the "script" [51]; their use of scripts is described in detail in [58]. Their version of the script representation has nodes, which represent processes and events, and links between these nodes that express such relations as "*X* enables *Y*" or "*X* causes *Y*" (where *X* and *Y* are processes or events such as evaporation or condensation). Thus, each script depicts a partially ordered sequence of processes and events linked by temporal or causal connections. Furthermore, each node can have a hierarchically embedded subscript that describes the causal relationships at work within it. Finally, these scripts have roles (e.g., air-mass or body-of-water) that will be bound to particular geographic or meteorological entities when the script is applied to a particular case (e.g., Ireland). The scripts therefore capture the causalities involved in rainfall.

Their representation not only expresses the causalities of rainfall, but also provides the necessary organization to support their desired teaching strategy. They test the student over the relationships in the top-level script. Missing or erroneous steps cause the tutor to shift down to the appropriate subscript in order to determine why the student does not understand the process which that appropriate subscript describes. If a student masters steps at one level in the script, the tutor has the choice of moving down to the subscript level for a more detailed examination or proposing a specific case, such as a particular geographic location, and asking the student to apply his general knowledge to this specific case. Why provides a perfect example of how the domain knowledge and teaching strategies together drive the choice of knowledge representation.

Scholar, on the other hand, demonstrates the needs of a mixed-initiative, fact-oriented tutoring system. Scholar stores its knowledge in a semantic network [44], which is essentially a highly interconnected network of nodes and links representing objects and their properties. Carbonell sees the semantic network representation being used in the following ways: "answering questions not specifically anticipated, constructing questions on given topics, and generally carrying on a mixed-initiative contextual dialogue with a human in a rather free and comfortable subset of English" [13]. Obviously, this requires a highly structured database in which concepts and facts are connected along many dimensions and in which linguistic information can be embedded. The semantic network knowledge representation fills this need.

Rather than store any specific pieces of text, questions, predicted answers, errors, or branching information, Scholar's contribution was that it generated all this from its semantic network of geographic knowledge [13]. Each unit of the semantic net is organized as an object with properties. Each property consists of the property name (attribute), a set of tags, and the property value. Values themselves can either be properties or pointers into other units. The tags tell the executive program how to interpret the properties and values and thus lend "semantics" to the structure. Furthermore, procedures may be embedded into the network that can use the semantic network to make inferences; an example is a procedure that infers climate from local conditions like latitude and altitude [13]. By organizing the information in such an interconnected way, Scholar avoids storing information redundantly in the database, and it can index into the information in a variety of ways, thus supporting a very flexible method of query and reasoning.

Wexler [61] independently developed a system very similar to Scholar. In Wexler's domain-independent system, knowledge is encoded in an information network and is used to generate questions, statements, and answers. Net objects are grouped into classes and each object includes a value/character string and unlabeled links to other objects. More complex relationships can be built by creating new classes, such as "family" (that could be used to link mother, father, and children) [61]. Questions, statements, and answers are constructed from the network using prespecified "skeleton patterns," which are textual templates annotated with information net paths and constraints. Thus, Wexler's information net is similar to Scholar's semantic net, and is used for similar purposes, albeit through different mechanisms.

Reasoning in a semantic net involves a lot of pointer following. In Wexler's system [61], the net is searched (using backtracking) for nodes that satisfy the question skeletons. The search is begun at class nodes and proceeds to the various instances. Carbonell [13] notes that Rockart, who uses a semantic network to represent accounting information [48], "makes an interesting use of the semantic representation to find relations via intersections between two concepts in the database." Scholar uses a similar intersection search to answer questions like "Is Buenos Aires in Brazil?" Scholar can determine what two things have in common by searching both their SUPERP (superpart) or SUPERC (superconcept) links for an intersection [18]. This allows Scholar to relate a student's answer to the correct one and thus realize that if a city with certain characteristics was asked for, the student is not as far off if his answer is an incorrect city as if he answered with some country [13]. There are many other techniques for information retrieval in a semantic net, but the point is that, by endowing the executive program with knowledge of the semantics of the various links, most of the facilities needed for effective tutoring are reduced to graph search procedures.

Besides representing geographic knowledge, Scholar's semantic net represents other world knowledge and even "metaknowledge" (knowledge about knowledge). Representing commonsense knowledge such as reasonable temperatures enables the system to recognize ridiculous answers, such as 200 degrees in response to "What is the average temperature in Minnesota?" [13]. In order to reason about the extent of its knowledge, properties are tagged as to whether Scholar has complete or incomplete knowledge of them. For instance, I have complete knowledge of my family members, but incomplete knowledge of all AI researchers. Since Carbonell places great emphasis on determining the contextual relevancy of properties, all properties are tagged with their relevancy to their attached object. For example, the author of a book may be more important than its Library of Congress number. Carbonell notes that it would be nice if the relevancy of one node to another was simply the distance between them in a graphtheoretic sense, but it turned out that solution was not refined enough [13]. Although not included in Scholar, Goldstein [25] suggests that an estimate of cognitive complexity for different tasks should be maintained so the presentation and necessary remediation for that topic can reflect the expected difficulty the student will have; the tutor should know if it is teaching a hard task or an easy one. The goal to which each of these commonsense and meta knowledge annotations aspires is to provide the tutoring system with the same commonsense world knowledge as its students, but obviously such a rich knowledge base is beyond the state of the art in AI.

The semantic network has a rich history of use in intelligent tutoring and continues in popularity today. Brown *et al.* [5] discuss the use of a semantic net to store factual knowledge and an augmented finite automata structure for describing causal process relationships. Recently, Woolf [64] used KL-ONE, which is a semantic net representation tool, annotated with pedagogical information about the relative importance of domain topics, for her Ph.D. work on tutorial dialogues. The attraction of semantic networks is that they have been used in many branches of artificial intelligence, including natural language understanding, question answering, problem solving, and learning, and many general-purpose techniques have been developed for their use in knowledge-based reasoning.

Simulation-based training has quite a different set of representational requirements. Obviously, one component of such a system is a simulation, so the challenge is the integration of this simulation with the rest of the tutoring system. The Sophie systems teach electronic troubleshooting and hence include circuit simulator. Brown *et al.* [6] report that the simulator used in Sophie II requires careful use since violation of the assumptions on which it depends could yield unexpected and inaccurate results. To deal with this problem, Sophie II uses pieces of code termed "procedural experts" that know how to run the simulator, how to use the results, and what the limitations are [6].

Steamer [29], the interactive, inspectable, simulation-based tutor described earlier, is connected to a detailed mathematical simulation of a steam propulsion system. The Steamer graphical editor allows graphics objects to be tied to the underlying simulation. They allow icons to reflect the value or state of various simulation variables and also permit the user to change variables by clicking on these icons. Hollan *et al.* [29] discuss the difficult problems of this so-called "tapping." In an effort to achieve the conceptual fidelity mentioned in Section II, Steamer also represents operating procedures in a form that allows explanation at different hierarchical levels, and it associates operating procedures with their underlying engineering principles. They report the development of "a frame-based representation system[4] that supports multiple perspectives and permits an integration of the vast amount of structural, functional, topological, and graphical information contained within Steamer" [29].

Sophie III [6], the successor to Sophie II referenced above, takes a different approach to simulation than its predecessor. While Sophie II used a black-box circuit simulator with procedural experts as the glue between the simulator and tutoring system, Sophie III includes specially-designed circuit simulation techniques that are more articulate. Based on propagation of constraints, their circuit reasoning component can not only predict circuit behavior, but it can explain why it predicted this behavior. Connections between circuit wires (i.e., a transistor, resistor, or even physical connection) are modeled as constraints on those wires (which are the terminals of the constraint box). By propagating values from known measurements (i.e., current or voltage) through the many constraints in the circuit, Sophie III can predict measurements at other points. Furthermore, these inferences can be recorded as they are made so that Sophie can justify the predictions to the student [6]. Such an articulate simulation has pedagogical benefits that far exceed a simple black-box simulator.

Besides its use of scripts, Why [55], [58] also makes use of constraint-based reasoning, in this case to describe functional relationships at work in processes. For instance, a process such as evaporation can be modeled by a constraint prototype with "actors" (the instance variables or terminals that are being constrained). The constraint can be instantiated and connected to real actors, such as a body of water and a land mass.

[4] Frames [36] are really very similar to semantic nets, although the two have different conceptualizations. While a semantic net is a graph of nodes and links, a frame encodes the same information in structure with slots. However, since these slots are usually links to other frames (nodes), semantic nets and frames have evolved into largely equivalent data structures, with the difference lying mainly in the mental picture they evoke.

"Factors" used by the constraints are attributes of the actors, such as temperature and size. Problems can be generated that provide all necessary inputs but one. The constraint can infer the remaining one and compare this with the student's answer. The constraint knows how to describe itself in the abstract and can give examples using its instantiated actors. This provides an articulate inference procedure for causal, factor-oriented concepts.

The paper of Stevens *et al.* [58], an excellent treatise on the knowledge representation issues in tutoring and one that has greatly influenced this author's understanding, emphasizes the need for "multiple representational viewpoints." Using their Why system as an example, they point out that scripts serve well to guide the sequencing of topics, but are particularly weak in diagnosing student misconceptions. To overcome this problem, they added a second viewpoint, the previously described functional perspective, which exposes the functional relationships between rainfall parameters (e.g., evaporation is a function of a body of water and an air mass, and increases proportionally with increases in the water temperature, the air temperature, and their relative proximity). While scripts are "ordered and sequential," the functional perspective is "nonlinear and interactive" [58]. This functional perspective embodies the viewpoint that was lacking with scripts; while the scripts convey the causal sequencing of events, the functional perspective describes the "interaction microstructure" [58]. They note that the availability of multiple viewpoints allows a tutoring system to view student errors as a reflection of some perspective missing in the student's knowledge. With such a multiple-perspective view of knowledge representation, we see the enterprise of knowledge-based CAI in a new light, in terms of the partitioning of knowledge between different viewpoints and the determination of when and how to invoke a particular viewpoint.

Condition/action rules, also known as production rules, have enjoyed a widespread popularity in AI, and this has spread into ICAI. Such rules, which model behavior as "recognize a condition, initiate an action," have long been considered as a possible model of human intelligence and thus serve as the domain knowledge for many different tutoring systems. One example is Goldstein's Wumpus tutor [25]. This tutor serves as a coach for students playing "Hunt the Wumpus," a game requiring mathematical and logical skills whose goal is to find and kill the deadly Wumpus in a dark cave filled with many perils. The requisite skills are modeled by condition/action rules that choose moves based on probabilistic and logical evidence. When the student makes suboptimal moves, he is postulated to be missing the appropriate rule. More recently, Anderson and Reiser used rules in their respective Geometry [1] and Lisp [46] tutors. The attractiveness of rules is their modular nature, since each rule is, ideally, independent of all others and thus rules can be added and deleted with only an incremental effect on system performance. The criticism of rule-based approaches has been that their uniformity masks the underlying abstractions and cognitive models of the domain necessary for teaching [16].

While most ICAI systems revolve around their knowledge representation, some attempts have been made to combine heterogeneous knowledge in a more modular architecture. Bonar *et al.* [4] describe an object-oriented tutoring architecture in which domain knowledge classes, called "bites," are organized into a hierarchical inheritance lattice to take advantage of shared structure. Generic classes of bites include abstraction hierarchy bites, which represent an ordering of concepts in the curriculum; definition bites, which are relatively standalone; input/output (I/O) bites, which represent black-box (functional) behaviors; and discovery bites, which include skills such as scientific inquiry which allow the student to explore an environment with minimal coaching [4]. Abstraction hierarchy bites are especially critical in student diagnosis since only they have connection to other related bites and so can test for understanding of concepts that span several bites. In contrast with other efforts that separate "explainer," "diagnoser," "tutor," "user modeler," etc. components, an object-oriented architecture provides these facilities as "mix-ins" that can be inherited by domain knowledge classes. There can be several different diagnoser mix-ins, representing different strategies, and different knowledge bites can include different diagnoser classes. In this way, multiple forms of knowledge can coexist in the same knowledge base, each with its own preferred techniques for presentation, student diagnosis, and problem solving.

This section has emphasized the importance of domain knowledge and its representation in tutoring systems, but the important point is that this knowledge representation is driven by both the domain knowledge to be modeled and, equally important, by the intended use of this knowledge in the tutor. Since the differentiator in an intelligent tutoring system is the flexibility with which it handles student misconceptions, the choice of knowledge representation is driven largely by the needs of the student diagnosis module. This module is the topic of the next two sections.

IV. Student modeling

The student model is simply a model, maintained and used by the computer tutor, of the student's knowledge and capabilities. Its purpose is to evaluate and account for the student's actions and responses. Human tutors do an excellent job of judging the student's answers in the context of his assumed level of understanding and past learning behavior, thus effectively adapting their instruction to the student's competence and abilities. Yet traditional CAI has done a poor job in this area.

The most common technique for student modeling in CAI has been a tally of the student's correct and incorrect answers. Adaptation to the student was limited to branching to different points in the instruction based on the student's answer, his tally exceeding some threshold, or his tally as a percentage exceeding some threshold. Thus, these programs did not keep track of the student's current knowledge except at some coarse level, and what little they did maintain about the student was insufficient for anything beyond grading the student's performance over the session.

Ideally, a tutor should know what the student knows, his level of competence, his past learning behavior (i.e., slow, fast), the presentation methods to which he responds best, and even his areas of expertise and interest beyond the current subject matter. Armed with this information, the tutor can choose a suitable level and method of presentation, it can relate new topics to things with which he is familiar, and it can evaluate his responses in terms of the areas he knows well and those in which he is more likely to have misunderstandings. Although ICAI still has a long way to go in this area, it has made much progress over earlier CAI attempts.

Ira Goldstein of MIT introduced the now widely used method of "overlay modeling", in that the student's knowledge is viewed in terms of the tutor's domain knowledge; that is, the student model is embedded (conceptually anyway) in the tutor's knowledge [24]. This permits an easy comparison between that which the student knows and that which he should know. Of course, annotating the tutor's knowledge base with student model information implies that there is a knowledge base to annotate, which explains the simpler models used in CAI.

In later papers, Goldstein showed that it may not be sufficient to model the student's knowledge in terms of the coach's mature, general knowledge. He suggested the explicit representation of intermediate forms of knowledge such as specialized rules that the student may discover before he recognizes the general form. Goldstein uses a genetic graph exposing relationships between intermediate and mature pieces of knowledge such as analogy links, specialization links, etc. [25], [26].

Different approaches have been taken to the construction of the student model. In Wexler's system [61], the student model is constructed as a semantic net, with nodes and links added as they are taught. Carbonell [13] states that building a student model from scratch is too inaccurate and that the system should instead start with what it thinks the student knows (perhaps an ideal student) and tweak this model as is necessary. This opinion is reflected in Scholar, which, in contrast to Wexler's approach, starts with the expert knowledge base as the student model and annotates deviations that are subsequently discovered [13]. Burton and Brown's West tutor [10] typifies a skill modeler, that is an overlay modeler in which expert knowledge is represented as skills, and the student is modeled by the set of skills he has mastered (used successfully). They also introduce the notion of "differential modeling" [10], which is similar to Carbonell's method of modeling explicitly the differences between expert and student knowledge. As mentioned earlier, Goldstein's Wumpus tutor [25] includes intermediate forms of knowledge linked with the expert knowledge in a genetic graph [26] and therefore can model the student not only on his mastery of the expert knowledge but also on his progress toward this mastery. All these methods are variants of the basic overlay modeling paradigm.

Other domains, however, have been shown to defy simple overlay modeling techniques. The research described by Burton [11] clearly indicates that the bizarre nature of children's arithmetic bugs suggests that no subset of the expert's knowledge could explain the incorrect procedures used by novices. Instead, Burton's "Buggy model" employs both correct and "buggy" rules that the student may be following [11]. Understanding a student's error then becomes a task of finding a suitable combination of these correct and buggy rules that together would produce the same incorrect answer as was produced by the student. This approach is different from Goldstein's work on genetic graphs in that buggy rules may be in no special way related to correct rules, but instead may be empirically determined typical errors.

While ICAI student modeling techniques are designed to overcome the limitations with CAI tallies of right and wrong answers, such tallies are often still embedded within richer student models. Burton and Brown [10] have pointed out the difficulties with keeping such tallies, pointing out that even after a student has mastered an area, this model would continue to reflect his past weaknesses. Pieces of the model should really decay with time, yet the computational costs involved would then be prohibitive.

In their West tutor, they dealt with this by allowing successful immediate behavior (the last three moves) to clear out past problems.

Student models more complicated than those presented in this section have been developed and tested, although they are beyond the scope of this paper. The interested reader is referred for instance to Sleeman [54]. It should be pointed out that the student model is potentially very open-ended, and its design should therefore be driven by the domain knowledge representation [38], [41] and, more importantly, by the needs of the student diagnosis module, which will be discussed in the next section. In order to diagnose student misconceptions and explain student errors, it is necessary to understand his current state of knowledge and past history. The design of the student model is driven foremost by the level of abstraction needed to make sense of his errors.

V. Student diagnosis

As Schank and Slade have noted, the opportunity to fail is an important part of learning and one that the computer can readily provide without the fear of peer or teacher judgment [52]. But the computer must capitalize on each student failure as an opportunity to correct a misconception. If it merely tells the student that he is wrong, it has done no teaching at all, but has rather pushed the problem off on the student, who must somehow determine why he was wrong. As Brown and Moskowitz note, ". . . good teachers don't just mark off points. Rather, they try to determine the student's misunderstandings as the best basis for correcting those misunderstandings" [8].

The techniques for student diagnosis are intertwined with student modeling methods; the reader will notice the close connection between topics in Section IV and this section. The way to view this connection is that the types of domain knowledge and the desired level of student diagnosis drive the domain knowledge representation, which in turn largely determines the actual student diagnosis techniques, which then determines the student modeling needs and methods.

Student diagnosis is similar to other diagnostic tasks such as equipment or disease diagnosis. Carbonell views student errors as symptoms of diseases (misconceptions) and notes that our diagnostic reasoning should operate on an open set of alternatives [13]. Koffman and Blount [31] similarly suggest that an intelligent tutoring system should make and test hypotheses concerning the source of student errors, considering his past problems. We in fact have a rich base on which to make such hypotheses, including the student model, typical mistakes with the topic we are teaching, the constraints of the current problem, and, hopefully, additional knowledge about the student's answer. The rest of this section will outline several different techniques that have been used.

The experience of Stevens *et al.* with Why led them to state perhaps the most important maxim of student diagnosis: "The types of misconceptions in a student's knowledge that a system can diagnose are heavily dependent on the knowledge represented in the system" [58]. For instance, student shortcomings in discovery learning environments can only be detected through comparison with a computer-based expert, because you need some way of determining when particular knowledge is applicable [10]. In their West tutor, Burton and Brown use an "issue recognizer" to detect student shortcomings and an "issue evaluator" that uses the student model to decide if the student is really lacking the skill or is using an equally valid strategy. This is based on a differential model of the student's behavior (as compared with the expert's behavior). Such a differential model is effective only when there is a relatively ". . . unique and well-defined closed set of correct answers . . ." [13].

An alternative to differential modeling is direct interpretation of the student's answer in terms of semantic memory, considering the compatibility and relevancy of the answer in relation to the question [13]. Wexler's system [61], for instance, which stores its domain knowledge in a semantic net, evaluates the student's response by searching the net for nodes that satisfy the conditions of the question. If no such node matches the student's answer, it then tries to fit the answer into the question skeleton by successively removing the constraints on the answer. If the resulting skeleton matches anything in the network, it relates this to the student. For instance, if the question was "What is the capital of Texas?" and the student replied "Madison," I would imagine Wexler's system replying "Madison is the capital of Wisconsin." The issue here is giving extra information about the student's incorrect answer and making sure that this information is relevant.

Student diagnosis is not as easy as the aforementioned example would suggest, however. Sometimes the student has the correct answer but expresses it in a fundamentally different way [63]. Similarly, in gaming environments, the student may appear to be missing certain skills when instead he is employing a totally different strategy from the expert [10]. Finally, Stevens *et al.* [58] note that sometimes bugs interact, so we must always consider the possibility that an error resulted from a combination of student misconceptions.

One of the few techniques that handles multiple bugs is Burton's Buggy model [11]. In this model, the system has rules corresponding to both correct domain skills and typical buggy techniques. Applying this model to subtraction, Burton built "procedural networks" [50] of the techniques (both correct and incorrect) needed to perform subtraction. These procedural networks are partially ordered sequences of arithmetic operations, noting not only when certain skills such as borrowing are needed but also when particular buggy techniques are likely to be used (such as erroneous forms of borrowing). The student's answer is evaluated by searching for a path through this network of skills that yields the student's answer. If the path contains only correct skills, we know which skills he has successfully used. If the path contains buggy skills, we know exactly which misconceptions he has. The problem with this approach is that the number of possible paths through the network grows exponentially with the number of correct and buggy techniques, so that even for a simple domain such as subtraction we must resort to some heuristic search. Also, this method requires an explicit enumeration of possible bugs, which certainly runs counter to Carbonell's opinions.

Similar in spirit to the Buggy model, Genesereth suggests evaluation of student actions through "plan recognition" [21]. Plan recognition is the inverse of planning; while in planning we search for a sequence of operators that will accomplish our goals, building such a plan through top-down refinement of those goals, in plan recognition we search for the goals that might underlay the apparent plan corresponding to the student's actions. This is similar to language parsing; domain actions serve as terminals, goals and subgoals serve as nonterminals, and we want to find a parse of the student's actions that will tell us the goals he is following. Genesereth's system uses a combination of top-down and bottom-up parsing and considers both correct and buggy actions. The difference between plan recognition and the buggy model is that the former considers more levels of abstraction.

While not everyone subscribes to the Buggy method, most see the need for some sort of error taxonomy. As Stevens *et al.* [58] so aptly point out, "A good teacher must possess knowledge of the types of misconceptions that arise in the domain being taught." Carbonell [13] suggests a taxonomy of errors, which would allow the tutor to determine the significance of various errors, choose appropriate remediation strategies, and notice patterns of related errors in the student's answers/actions. Misconceptions that can arise in a particular domain should be represented, and their commonalities should be abstracted into more general misconceptions ranging from basic misconceptions that people experience, such as misusing a metaphor, down to the ways in which these misconceptions manifest themselves in particular domain concepts [58].

There have been various approaches to such an error taxonomy, each being somewhat tied to a particular type of knowledge. Many people have distinguished between problems local to the immediate topic, problems involving relationships between various topics or pieces of knowledge, and problems that indicate downright confusion on the part of the student. Carbonell [13] suggests the following generic error types (which, not surprisingly, have strong ties to semantic net representations): 1) missing information, 2) misfiled fact, 3) wrong entry, 4) lack of a concept, 5) wrong superordinate (superpart or superconcept), 6) overgeneralization, 7) failure to draw some superordinate inference, 8) failure to draw some negative inference (i.e., that some information contradicts the rest). Stevens *et al.* [58] identified 16 common bugs that accounted for 58 percent of the errors of students in the area of rainfall (72 percent ignoring omissions). They discuss the more abstract error types that underlay these sixteen bugs, including application of an incorrect metaphor and missing generalizations. The idea of a taxonomy, then, is a useful one; at some level of abstraction, human errors are domain independent, but teachers must also recognize instances of these abstract errors that occur in the domain to be taught.

While most systems treat diagnosis as a separate module, the object-oriented approach of Bonar *et al.* [4] allows different classes of knowledge to use different diagnosis techniques. Each knowledge class inherits diagnostic capabilities from a particular Diagnoser class. Using these inherited capabilities, a knowledge bite sends messages to each component bite asking if that component bite has knowledge relevant to the student's response, the current tutoring goals, and the current mode. If some component does, the Diagnoser routines then check to see if the student has misused the knowledge contained in this component bite. Misuse is defined by that component bite's own Diagnoser class. The Diagnoser then updates the student model, which of course is local to each knowledge Bite, and invokes the task selector to choose the next action [4].

It is important not to become so wrapped up in diagnosing the student's misconceptions that we lose sight of our goal. Carbonell [13] reminds us that student diagnosis is a means rather than an end and that the real objective is for the student to overcome his misunderstandings, not for the teacher to magically infer them. If we can narrow down the set of possible misconceptions, it is usually easy to determine through further interaction where the student is confused. Often we can use the Socratic method of posing carefully selected problems to the student in order to allow him to see his own misconceptions. Finally, a little meaningful feedback in the style of Wexler [16] discussed above can go a long way towards helping the student find his error.

VI. Pedagogical knowledge

A good teacher is more than just knowledgeable. The communication of a body of knowledge to a person does not simply follow a protocol of information transfer as between two computers. It is guided by strategies and techniques which are selected and combined dynamically in reaction to the student. Therefore, teaching itself can be considered a knowledge-based skill that we can model computationally. In the words of Brown and Moskowitz [8], ". . . we must formalize the intuitive knowledge that guides good teachers."

Instructional strategies deal with choosing an effective presentation method, determining the balance of student and tutor control, governing the amount and timing of feedback, and choosing evaluation criteria with which to judge student competence [20]. Perhaps the two most important pedagogical decisions are when to interrupt and what to say [10]. There is a distinction between determination of what to say (the content) and the actual choice of words and I/O behavior of the machine. The scope of the tutoring knowledge ends with choosing the content, just as it ends with the choice of a presentation method or an evaluation strategy [63]. Thus the pedagogical knowledge guides the overall goals and strategies of the tutor, but the other modules carry out these intentions.

Although, as outlined above, the pedagogical knowledge is tasked with many responsibilities, the most important is the determination of a strategy to deal with student errors. Since students are seldom consistent, and since diagnosis of one's own misconceptions is often more effective than too much guidance, a tutor cannot just provide remediation whenever the student errs. Woolf and McDonald [63] suggest that the pedagogical component be applied "after the expert and student modules have been accessed and some assessment [has been] made about the level of the student's knowledge." At this point, the tutor must select between ignoring the error, pointing it out, correcting it, or somehow guiding the student towards recognizing and correcting it himself. Obviously this choice must be made based on instructional heuristics.

Most intelligent tutoring systems have represented pedagogical knowledge in the form of production rules. These rules trigger on such things as student errors, recognized situations in the tutorial session, the history of the tutorial session, significant student actions, the nature of the knowledge being taught, and comparisons between student and tutor knowledge. Probably no two systems have adopted the same tutorial philosophy or set of rules, thus pointing out another recognized advantage of using production rules for pedagogical knowledge: the rules can easily be added, deleted, or modified independent of one another (ideally), thus allowing the course author to experiment with various strategies.

In a seminal paper with respect to the development of a theory of teaching, Stevens and Collins [57] discuss their analysis of a number of human tutorial dialogues and present a detailed theory in the form of condition/action rules of the goals, strategies, and priorities that guide an effective teacher. In a less detailed way, Burton and Brown [10] list twelve general guidelines that tutoring systems should follow. The following list of some example pedagogical rules gives a general feel for the content of various systems' instructional strategies.

- "If the student is about to lose interrupt and tutor him only with moves that will keep him from losing" [10].
- "If 1) a student proposes a rule or makes a prediction based on one or more factors that are insufficient, or 2) is entrapped by a rule (ENS 1 or ENS 9) based on one or more factors that are insufficient, then 3) pick a case that has the values specified on the insufficient factors, but not the value specified on the dependent variable" [57].
- If "the present topic is complete, but the tutor has little confidence in its assessment of the student's knowledge," then generate ". . . an expository shift from detailed examination of a single topic, to a shallow examination of a number of topics" [64].
- IF: The recent context of the dialogue mentioned either a 'deeper subgoal' or a factor relevant to the current goal THEN: Define the focus rule to be the *d*-rule that mentions this focus topic" [14].

As a further perspective on instructional strategies, we can survey some of the conclusions reached through other research efforts. Often these conclusions depend heavily on the particular learning scenario used; for instance, instructional strategies for discovery learning differ markedly from mixed-initiative tutoring on geography. However, it is interesting to note the similarities across domains and learning scenarios.

Many researchers have investigated the trade-offs between correcting a student explicitly, trying to entrap him into discovering the error himself, and simply letting him make mistakes and view the consequences. Burton and Brown [10] discuss this point at length, pointing out that "every time the Coach tells the student something, it is robbing him of the opportunity to discover it for himself." Their paper points out the importance of allowing students to observe the results of incorrect decisions. The coach's role, in their view, is to intervene when the student is likely to miss the evidence of his error or misconception. Woolf [65] contrasts her philosophy of letting students explore possible wrong paths with Anderson *et al.* [1] and Reiser *et al.* [46], whose geometry and Lisp tutors immediately correct student errors. This immediate feedback is justified by its authors because errors in geometry and Lisp are so ambiguous and delayed that much fruitless effort could be wasted on erroneous solution paths. Thus, although immediate feedback is not always desired, it may be chosen for domain or technical reasons.

Besides deciding when to interrupt, pedagogical rules must decide what to say (the content). For instance, tutor responses in the recovery boiler tutor (RBT) [65] fall into three categories: redirect the student, synthesize data (point out relationships), and confirm correct actions. In RBT, instructional condition/action rules based on specific emergencies and student responses are "designed to verify that the student has asked the right questions and has made the correct inferences about the saliency of his data" [65]. Pedagogical rules in Why fire on the type of knowledge being taught and the type of misconception the student is having and suggest a strategy for exposing this misconception to the student [57]. Rules in Meno-tutor [63], [64] take the tutor off some default dialogue path and suggest a different tutorial strategy or tactic. Woolf's thesis work [64] in particular is an attempt at a domain-independent set of pedagogical rules to guide tutorial discourse; this work will be described further in Section VII.

Finally, the course author should be able to specify high-level strategies for ordering topics. For instance, a teacher should be able to tell the tutor to teach about a phylum, then its classes, then the class species, and finally the characteristics of each species [61]. Other teachers may prefer a different ordering, and so the tutoring system should give each teacher access to these ordering heuristics.

As has been stated, the general purpose of pedagogical rules is to indicate discourse directions, strategies, and tactics. In the next section, the more global problem of discourse management, of which pedagogical rules are a component, will be considered.

VII. Discourse management

As Carbonell [13] so elegantly put it, "Man-computer interaction is basically a communication between two information structures, including their computational abilities." Without a formal protocol, this communication must be driven by the goals and needs of both parties. Each side must not only communicate its knowledge, but must reactively structure its dialogue to meet the needs and goals of the other. Effective communication lies not in the words, but rather in the determination of what the tutor and student need to communicate [63].

Stevens and Collins [56] argue further that a good human tutor does not follow a prespecified syllabus, but instead lets the responses and misconceptions of the student drive the dialogue. The tutor should "opportunistically adapt material to the needs of the dialogue" [18]. While traditional CAI efforts notoriously hardcoded the syllabus (allowing prespecified branches based on predicted student responses), this problem of discourse management and topic selection has been addressed at some level by most ICAI efforts. Flexibility in the tutorial discourse is a hallmark of ICAI.

In Scholar, the executive program that uses the semantic network to generate teaching material and questions is almost independent of the subject matter in the semantic net [13]. Carbonell [13] discusses the issue of "contextual continuity" and topic coverage, noting that traditional "*ad hoc* frame-oriented" (AFO) systems have a large degree of anticipation (they know what they are going to do next), while Scholar has almost none (it is very reactive). He describes Scholar's use of a simple push-down list (stack) of contexts, which it builds and maintains dynamically, to maintain contextual continuity, but admits that more anticipation may be desirable and could be implemented by a straightforward use of deterministic strategies for material presentation and question generation, although he prefers the more reactive system.

As ICAI research developed, more sophisticated discourse control schemes were utilized. Koffman and Blount [31] briefly describe a control scheme based around a student model and a concept tree of prerequisites. The system, based on the student model, determines whether the student prefers to advance quickly to new material or build a solid foundation on current material. Based on the student model, the system "decides at which plateau of the concept tree the student should be working" [31]. The concepts on this plateau are evaluated with respect to recency of use, the student's progression, his current knowledge, the impact of the concept on his current knowledge, and relevance to other concepts. The concept that scores the highest by this criteria is selected, a problem is generated based on his experience level, and the solution is evaluated.

A similar idea was developed further by researchers at Stanford University and resulted in the notion of a curriculum information network, used in the Stanford Bip system [3], in which skills to be taught are related to tasks that exercise those skills. The curriculum net is organized as a large set of problems (in their case, Basic programming problems) indexed in terms of the generic skills they require. Thus the curriculum net also serves as a student model; when the student successfully solves a problem, they know which skills he has used and can therefore choose a new problem with an appropriate set of requisite skills. In this way, although the problems are canned, they are selected and sequenced reactively based on student successes and difficulties. In a second-generation Bip system, known as Bip-II, the curriculum net was generalized into a semantic network of skills, each interconnected to other skills via relational links that denote prerequisites, relative difficulty, and analogies, as well as taxonomic links such as component and kind [60]. They also developed a sophisticated task selection procedure that uses the various links to guide the sequencing and selection of problems for the student. Note the similarities between this new curriculum net and Goldstein's genetic graph.

In [55], Stevens and Collins present a theory of the goal structure of a Socratic tutor based on an analysis of human tutorial dialogues. This tutorial control structure has four parts: 1) an agenda of goals and subgoals, 2) priority rules for adding goals and subgoals to the agenda, 3) strategies for selecting cases that satisfy the goals, and 4) the student model. They argue that human tutors have a few initial goals for the tutorial session and that further pedagogical goals and subgoals are added to the agenda dynamically in reaction to the student. Although they acknowledge the possibility of inserting goals at arbitrary places in the agenda, they note that most tutorial discourse can be seen as a pushing and popping of goals and subgoals onto a pushdown stack. Their priority rules determine the order in which to add new goals to the agenda when several are uncovered simultaneously, and their strategies are used to select examples with which to teach certain goals. Their work is significant because of the experimental data (human tutorial design) on which it is based.

The control structure used in the object-oriented architecture of Bonar *et al.* [4] uses a similar scheme. They have a stack on which TutoringMode objects are stored. Each TutoringMode object includes a satisfaction criteria and a floundering threshold. The satisfaction criteria determines when the TutoringMode object can be popped, while the floundering threshold determines when a remedial object should be pushed onto the stack. They currently have six modes, including exploration, experimentation, elaboration, didactic, demonstration, and coaching [4].

Task-oriented dialogue understanding system (TDUS) [47] is a natural language understanding system built at SRI International as part of research into the knowledge structures and reasoning mechanisms needed to guide a human apprentice through a task. Their thesis was that knowledge of the human's current progress through the task would allow them to disambiguate and therefore understand his questions and comments. Their basic task representation is the procedural network [50], which models the task as a partial order of actions organized into a hierarchy of goals. They also represent the objects that are associated with actions, such as tools or the target of the action. With this representation, they not only have a way of guiding the advisory discourse (through the task), but they also have a way of recording the apprentice's progress through the task, inferring actions not explicitly mentioned, and understanding his natural language utterances in terms of the current context.

The most recent work in tutorial discourse management was performed by Woolf as her Ph.D. thesis [64]. She uses a "discourse management network" (DMN) to guide the tutorial session, plan pedagogical strategies and tactics, and determine natural language utterances. The discourse management network has three successive levels: the tutoring approach, the strategy, and the tactics. These are organized into states of an "augmented transition network" (ATN) [62], with additional metarules that can affect the transitions [63].

In a nutshell, an ATN is a finite state machine in which nodes and arcs can store information in global registers for later use, and arcs are dynamically activated or deactivated based on these register values and other input. ATN's were popularized by work in natural language understanding in that the transition network is used to parse natural language sentences and semantic information can be incrementally added to the registers during the parse to further constrain later transitions. ATN's are also hierarchical in that a particular node may itself consist of another ATN that must be traversed before continuing the higher-level ATN. Besides natural language parsing, ATN's have been used in many other contexts including natural language generation [34] and plan recognition in a programming tutor [33].

Woolf's DMN is isomorphic to an ATN but is conceptually a top-down refinement of tutorial goals through the strategies and tactics that implement them. At the top level, states represent the basic tutoring approach such as "introduce" or "tutor." These states lead to refinement states that specify the strategy, such as "explore competency" or "repair misconception." Strategy states are further refined through tactical states such as "teach specific knowledge," "evaluate input," or "suggest new topic." The current tutoring mode is a state in this DMN and determines the next action of the tutor. Transitions through the states follow a default path, but pedagogical rules fire off the student model, current mode, and student responses to lift the tutor off its default path and onto some other state in the network, thus creating a discourse transition [63]. These transitions could be between states at the same level, such as two tactical states, or they could lift the tutor from its current level up to a higher level, effecting a more radical shift in the tutorial directions. Woolf points out the absence of any need for a goal agenda, as used by Stevens and Collins [55], and suggests that her approach more closely mirrors the behavior of human tutors [64]. She also claims that her DMN is relatively domain independent, although she acknowledges that it may need some further refinement.

Work in discourse management for tutorial purposes has thus followed several distinct transitions. In a backlash against the very deterministic branching structure of early CAI systems, Carbonell's Scholar [13] included a very loose organization of tutorial goals and basically just reacted to the student. Work by Stevens and Collins [55] showed that human tutors maintain an agenda of goals and that the challenge is to add and remove goals from this agenda in a last-in-first-out (LIFO) manner. Other work, exemplified by Bip [3], showed the utility of a richly structured knowledge of the course curriculum that can be used to dynamically sequence the domain topics. Finally, Woolf's work [64] returns us to a prespecified network of tutorial states, but now the network is a domain-independent model of discourse knowledge rather than the earlier-used sequences of domain topics. This trend indicates continuing realization that more and more knowledge is necessary for tutoring, ranging from the pedagogical strategies of teachers, through their rich knowledge of the course topics and their interrelationships, right down to commonsense knowledge about discourse.

VIII. Problem generation

Early CAI efforts included canned problems with canned answers. There are several difficulties with this approach. First, it places a large burden on the course author to develop a broad set of problems on which the tutoring system can draw. Second, it is very difficult to match canned problems to student needs and abilities and impossible to customize the problems to fit the situation. Finally, canned answers do not allow meaningful feedback on student errors unless the error can be anticipated, and justifications for the answer and explanations must also be canned. Thus, canned problems and answers reduce the flexibility of the system to exactly those interactions that were anticipated and prespecified by the course author.

Early attempts to correct these problems were called "generative" CAI due to the programs' abilities to generate new problems. Although the ideas developed in this period have been of further use, the techniques were usually limited to simple drill and practice in arithmetic and language vocabulary and were rarely adapted to the student's learning needs [40]. While early attempts at problem generation substituted values for variables in canned question templates, later efforts generated problems from deeper structures, yielding a richer mix of problems that were potentially better suited to the student's needs [32]. As work progressed, people noticed the applicability of AI techniques and the suitability of rich knowledge representations as a base from which to both generate and solve problems.

Problem generation can be viewed as a tree-structured decision process in that each level represents another decision on what to include in the problem, each branch represents one alternative, and the branches can be augmented with probabilities based on the student's competence and prior experience [31]. Koffman and Blount [31] go into some detail on such a generative scheme, pointing out the need to avoid regenerating problems the student has solved. They discuss adaptation to the student as a process of determining at which plateau of the concept tree the student should be working and the effect of this decision on problem generation. They also make the interesting observation that the tutoring system should solve subproblems for the student that he has already solved before, thus allowing him to concentrate on those aspects of the problem from which he can derive the greatest benefit.

Ramani and Newell [45] provide a more thorough treatment of problem generation. They suggest that one must first identify and analyze the various sets of problems in the domain and then develop suitable structures from which to generate these sets. Like Koffman, they view the basic control structure of problem generation as a tree-structured decision process and, like Koffman, they show how a context-free grammar can be used to implement this technique. In essence, each choice shifts control to the part of the grammar that includes alternatives for lower-level choices. The limitations of this approach, they note, are that the representation is not rich enough to generate broad but meaningful classes of problems and that even simple holding variables that record choices in order to constrain later choices are not possible. Too much information must be specified in the grammar itself, which is not the right level of abstraction [45].

They sum up the problems with generative grammars by explaining that problem generation needs semantic information, while grammars bundle syntax and semantics all into syntactic structures. They then shift their analysis of the problem to view it as a design procedure, in which decisions must be made, with some decisions independent and some dependent on other decisions. While this view still has a basic tree-like decision process, it can operate on a richer knowledge base such as a semantic net, it allows some decisions to refer to earlier decisions, and it generalizes the criteria for decisions to include the rich knowledge base and the student model. While generative grammars are driven by top-down refinement of choices, this new view on problem generation is more constraint based, a paradigm that was later to have profound influence on planning and design research in AI.

The basic techniques of Ramani and Newell's [45] problem generation theory are relatively simple. The underlying data structure is a semantic net that encodes the types of manipulable objects (i.e., numbers, symbols, sets, and sequences) and relevant attributes of these objects. For each class of problems, there is a generative procedure whose job is to fill in the particulars of the problem (i.e., the slots). Slots can be filled through various means; a slot could be a random or probabilistic selection from a list of alternatives or class of objects, it could be a function of other slot values (to implement relationship constraints among slots), it could be a function of external data such as the student model, or there could be hierarchical relationships between candidate values that allow increasing difficulty with time. By suitably structuring the semantic net of candidate objects and classes, much of the above functionality becomes simple retrieval; for instance, we could define many classes of objects organized into a taxonomy, and this semantic net of objects can include annotations of previously used values as well as embedded functions that reference the student model or other objects. Text generation routines can be associated with problem classes and can "know" how to word a problem given the slot values. Thus, a richly structured knowledge base again gives us the desired flexibility (if the reader is noticing that this is a recurrent theme of this paper, he is correct).

Of course, if new problems can be generated, they must also be solved, since answers cannot be canned if the problems are not. This is where the domain knowledge comes into play and serves as a sort of expert system operating on the representation of the problem. Basically, some executive module must take the problem data structure as input and reason from the domain knowledge to produce the corresponding answer. The techniques mentioned in section III are all relevant.

As one last observation linking problem generation, expert problem solving, and student diagnosis, consider that problems can be viewed as a set of constraints on their solution. If the generated problems in an ICAI system are expressed directly in terms of such constraints, we can easily evaluate student answers by checking that all constraints are satisfied. In this manner, we need not even have the ability to solve the problems ourselves, because we not only have an easy way of validating the student's response, but we can also give him meaningful feedback on wrong answers by telling him which constraints he failed to satisfy.

IX. User interface

Although most of an intelligent tutoring system can be considered as user interface, it is useful to distinguish those aspects that are explicitly concerned with communication with the student. This includes the actual presentation of text and graphics as well as acceptance of user input. Because this topic is so broad, I would not even attempt to provide a survey, but instead will present a few representative examples.

As was stated earlier, one study reports that people retain about 25 percent of what they hear, 45 percent of what they see and hear, and 70 percent of what they see, hear, and do [17]. This is a strong argument for user interfaces that include not only text but also visually exciting graphics and the ability for the user to interact with the graphical environment as though he were a part of it. The authors of the Steamer paper [29] feel that graphical depiction of causal relationships and topology are very important and that some concepts can be elucidated through graphical animation that defy textual explanation. They also give the student the ability to control the steam propulsion plant by touching icons on the screen. RBT [65] similarly uses graphical animation of its process, a recovery boiler, including visual clues such as a darkened smelt bed, acoustic clues such as ringing alarm buzzers, and textual help and explanations. The user of RBT responds to process alarms by selecting actions from menus and watching their real-time effect on the screen. Although the process simulation runs in real time, students are allowed to stop the simulation in order to ask questions, a feature that many users mentioned that they like [65]. The more a student feels connected to his learning environment, the richer his experience will be, and interactive graphics help with this connection.

Since communication with the student is primarily through English, the system must have the abilities to both understand the student's response and generate text of its own. Many different approaches have been taken for text generation in tutoring systems, most of which avoid true natural language mechanism. In Woolf's RBT, tutor output is created by extracting text from emergency-specific text files that are loaded when the emergency is invoked [65]. In West, textual explanations are attached to each issue (skill); each issue is responsible for presenting a few lines of text explaining itself [10]. West therefore distributes prestored text to the actual knowledge structures and combines the text dynamically to fit the situation. In Woolf's Meno-tutor, a description of the content of the textual output is constructed and sent to a surface language generator, although she dummied up the surface language generator for her thesis work [64]. In Sophie, each concept has an associated grammar rule that provides alternate ways of expressing the concept in terms of other concepts [18]. Thus, none of these systems generates English from deep linguistic knowledge.

One of the few tutoring systems to incorporate rich natural language generation mechanisms is Scholar. Carbonell separated question generation into two distinct levels: semantic and syntactic. Semantic information comes from the semantic net and determines what is being asked. For syntax, Carbonell identified classes of questions, such as what, which, where, who, and how many questions, fill-in questions, multiple-choice questions, and true-false questions. Each class contains relevant syntactical information. For statements, Carbonell's strategy was to make use of short sentences with simple syntax and a limited repertoire of verbs, mostly variant forms of the verb "to be." All knowledge in the semantic net contained linguistic annotations such as its part of speech. Thus, no text is canned in Scholar, and all sentences and questions are processed completely from the semantic internal representation into English [13].

Another approach to text generation, intended for use in explanation and tutoring, was recently developed by Perry Miller [34]. His Prosenet is an ATN-based approach to text generation. Each arc in the ATN has three components. The action component can be push, pop, jump, a prose fragment to output, a function call that may generate text, an option, a sequence of arcs, or an end sequence, which terminates a sequence. The other two components are a destination state and an action routine that is invoked whenever this arc is traversed. The system places the information to be conveyed into global registers, and the appropriate Prosenet network is activated. To maintain coherency in the text, sentence-level, paragraph-level, and global constraints may be introduced as the text is generated [34].

Natural language parsing is another difficult area; even a survey of this area is beyond the scope of this paper. Few systems, however, have allowed true natural language input. Scholar included rich natural language facilities that allowed it to understand most student questions and answers. Sophie used a technique called semantic grammars, in which the basic idea is to look for understandable fragments in the input rather than parse the entire sentence [6]. Most other systems have bypassed the natural language problem by using graphical or menu-based input.

It is worthy to note that experts in the field of intelligent tutoring have labeled natural language the "Achilles' heel" of potential tutoring systems [2], [28], and warn against its use because of its potential to consume project resources. However, it is often difficult to provide adequately flexible interactions with the student without some level of natural language.

The bottom line on user interface in intelligent tutoring systems is that input should be robust, allowing flexibility on the part of the student, and output should be rich, appealing to as many of the student's senses as possible. Future interfaces will likely be superior to today's due to technological advances. The use of varied media (i.e., Mixing speech, graphics, text, sound, video disk, etc.) will someday be the norm.

X. Conclusion

As we have seen, the design of an intelligent tutoring system is complex, with many issues to consider and still more that remain topics for research. It all begins with the choice of a good learning scenario that is appropriate to the domain knowledge. This learning scenario, along with the nature of the domain knowledge and the types of misconceptions we must detect, determines the necessary functionality and hence structure of the knowledge representation. The knowledge representation has a profound influence on the explanatory capabilities of the tutor as well as its competence in student diagnosis. In order to customize instruction to the student's abilities and determine the cause of his errors, we must maintain a student model. Finally, both pedagogical knowledge and knowledge of discourse patterns are needed, and we must wrap it all up in a sensory-stimulating user interface to achieve maximum tutorial efficacy.

This survey has provided a springboard for those interested in understanding or designing ICAI systems. Much research has been done and many important lessons have been learned, but much remains. While this paper has provided a tutorial survey, it also acts as an index into the literature for more detailed studies of particular techniques. ICAI has produced some exciting results, but the real excitement lies in the future.

Acknowledgment

I would like to thank the following people for their help: Rick Herrod and Don Candy for making this research possible; Ellen Rickel and Mike Smith for their proofreading; William Pervin, Fillia Makedon, and Ivor Page for reading an earlier version and suggesting that I publish it; Dan Russell and Allan Collins for improving the accuracy of my references; the anonymous referees for their excellent comments; and my wife Rickie.

References

1. J.R. Anderson, C.F. Boyle, and G. Yost, "The geometry tutor," in *Proc. IJCAI-85*, Los Angeles, CA, August 1985, pp. 1 – 7.
2. J.R. Anderson, "The expert module," *AFHRL Research Planning Forum for Intelligent Tutoring Systems*, San Antonio, TX, Sept. 1986.
3. A. Barr, M. Beard, and R.C. Atkinson, "The computer as a tutorial laboratory: The Stanford BIP project," *Int. J. Man-Machine Stud.*, vol. 8, pp. 567 – 596, 1976.
4. J. Bonar, R. Cunningham, and J. Schultz, "An object-oriented architecture for intelligent tutoring systems," in *Proc. OOPSLA-86*, Portland, OR, pp. 269 – 276, Sept. 1986.
5. J.S. Brown, R.R. Burton, and F. Zydbel, "A model-driven question-answering system for mixed-initiative computer-assisted instruction," *IEEE Trans. Syst. Man Cybern.*, vol. SMC-3, no. 3, pp. 248 – 257, 1973.
6. J.S. Brown, R.R. Burton, and J. deKleer, "Pedagogical, natural language and knowledge engineering techniques in SOPHIE I, II and III," in *Intelligent Tutoring Systems*, D. Sleeman and J.S. Brown, Eds. Cambridge, MA: Academic Press, 1982, pp. 227 – 282.

7. J.S. Brown, R.R. Burton, and W.J. Clancey, "Applications of AI to training and education," AAAI-84 Tutorial No. 2, Austin, TX, 1984.
8. J.S. Brown and G. Moskowitz, "AI: Windows of opportunity in office automation," Xerox Corp., July 1985.
9. B.G. Buchanan and E.H. Shortliffe, Eds., *Rule-Based Expert Systems: The MYCIN Experiments of the Stanford Heuristic Programming Project.* Reading, MA: Addison-Wesley, 1984.
10. R.R. Burton and J.S. Brown, "An investigation of computer coaching for informal learning activities," in *Intelligent Tutoring Systems*, Sleeman and Brown, Eds. Cambridge, MA: Academic Press, 1982, pp. 79 – 98.
11. R.R. Burton, "Diagnosing bugs in a simple procedural skill," in *Intelligent Tutoring Systems*, Sleeman and Brown, Eds. Cambridge, MA: Academic Press, 1982, pp. 157 – 183.
12. ———, "The environment module of intelligent tutoring systems," presented at the AFHRL Research Planning Forum for Intelligent Tutoring Systems Conference, San Antonio, TX, Sept. 1986.
13. J.R. Carbonell, "AI in CAI: An artificial intelligence approach to computer-assisted instruction," *IEEE Trans. Man-Machine Syst.*, vol. 11, no. 4, pp. 190 – 202, Dec. 1970.
14. W.J. Clancey, "Tutoring," in *Rule-Based Expert Systems*, B.G. Buchanan and E.H. Shortliffe, Eds. Reading, MA: Addison-Wesley, 1984, Part 8.
15. ———, "From guidon to neomycin and heracles in twenty short lessons," *AI Mag.*, vol. VII, no. 3, pp. 40 – 60, Conference Issue 1986.
16. ———, "Methodology for building an intelligent tutoring system," in *Artificial Intelligence and Instruction*, G.P. Kearsley, Ed. Reading, MA: Addison-Wesley, 1987.
17. M. Edwards, "The Mercedes Benz of interactive video," *Hardcopy*, vol. 14, no. 5, pp. 74 – 80, May 1985.
18. E.A. Feigenbaum and A. Barr, Eds., *The Handbook of Artificial Intelligence*, vol. 2, Los Altos, CA: William Kaufmann, 1982, ch. 9.
19. J.D. Fletcher, "Intelligent instructional systems in training," in *Applications in Artificial Intelligence*, S.A. Andriole, Ed. Princeton, NJ: Petrocelli, 1984.
20. R.S. Freedman and J.P. Rosenking, "Designing computer-based training systems: OBIE1:KNOBE," *IEEE Expert*, pp. 31 – 38, Summer 1986.
21. M.R. Genesereth, "The role of plans in intelligent teaching systems," in *Intelligent Tutoring Systems*, Sleeman and Brown, Eds. Cambridge, MA: Academic Press, 1982, pp. 137 – 155.
22. I.P. Goldstein, "The computer as coach: An athletic paradigm for intellectual education," AI Memo 389, MIT, Cambridge, MA, 1976.
23. I.P. Goldstein and S. Papert, "Artificial intelligence, language, and the study of knowledge," *Cognitive Sci.*, vol. 1, no. 1, pp. 84 – 123, 1977. Also in AI Memo 337, MIT, Cambridge, MA, Mar. 1976.
24. I.P. Goldstein, "Overlays: A theory of modelling for computer-aided instruction," AI Memo 406, MIT, Cambridge, MA, Feb. 1977.
25. ———, "Developing a computational representation for problem-solving skills," AI Memo 495, MIT, Cambridge, MA, Oct. 1978.
26. ———, "The genetic graph: A representation for the evolution of procedural knowledge," in *Intelligent Tutoring Systems*, Sleeman and Brown, Eds. Cambridge, MA: Academic Press, 1982, pp. 51 – 77.
27. R. Guindon and P. Sladky, "Analysis of user-expert dialogues: Task networks, subdialogue boundary markers and antecendent distribution," MCC Tech. Rep. No. HI-084-85, Microelectronics and Computer Technology Corp., Austin, TX, Dec. 1985.
28. H.M. Halff, "Curriculum and instruction in automated tutors," presented at the AFHRL Research Planning Forum for Intelligent Tutoring Systems Conference, San Antonio, TX, Sept. 1986.
29. J.D. Hollan, E.L. Hutchins, and L. Weitzman, "STEAMER: An interactive inspectable simulation-based training system," *AI Mag.*, vol. 5, no. 2, pp. 15 – 27, Summer 1984.
30. W.B. Johnson, "Pragmatic considerations in development and implementation of intelligent tutoring systems," presented at the AFHRL Research Planning Forum for Intelligent Tutoring Systems Conference, San Antonio, TX, Sept. 1986.
31. E.B. Koffman and S.E. Blount, "Artificial intelligence and automatic programming in CAI," *Artificial Intell.*, vol. 6, pp. 215 – 234, 1975.

32. E.B. Koffman and J.M. Perry, "A model for generative CAI and concept selection," *Int. J. Man-Machine Stud.*, vol. 8, pp. 397 – 410.
33. M.L. Miller and I.P. Goldstein, "PAZATN: A linguistic approach to automatic analysis of elementary programming protocols," AI Memo 388, MIT, Cambridge, MA, Dec. 1976.
34. P.L. Miller, *A Critiquing Approach to Expert Computer Advise: Attending.* Boston, MA: Pitman Advanced Publishing Program, 1984.
35. J.R. Miller, "Human-computer interaction and intelligent tutoring systems," presented at the AFHRL Research Planning Forum for Intelligent Tutoring Systems Conference, San Antonio, TX, Sept. 1986. Also MCC Tech. Rep. HI-284-86, Microelectronics and Computer Technology Corporation, Austin, TX, Sept. 1986.
36. M. Minsky, "A framework for representing knowledge," in *The Psychology of Computer Vision*, P. Winston, Ed. New York: McGraw-Hill, 1975. Also in *Readings in Knowledge Representation*, R.J. Brachman and H.J. Levesque, Eds. Los Altos, CA: Morgan Kaufmann, 1985.
37. T. Moran, D.M. Russell, D.S. Jordan, F. Halasz, J. Orr, and J. Shrager, "ARI project phase 1 report: Problems in training and procedure-oriented job performance aids," Xerox PARC Internal Rep., Intelligent Systems Lab, Palo Alto, CA, Oct. 1984.
38. L.H. Nawrocki, "Artificial intelligence applications to maintenance training," in *Artificial Intelligence and Instruction*, Kearsley, Ed. Reading, MA: Addison-Wesley, 1987.
39. S. Papert, *Mindstorms*. New York: Basic Books, 1980.
40. O.C. Park, R.S. Perez, and R.J. Seidel, "Intelligent CAI: Old wine in new bottles, or a new vintage?," in *Artificial Intelligence and Instruction*, Kearsley, Ed. Reading, MA: Addison-Wesley, 1987.
41. P.L. Pirolli and J.G. Greeno, "The problem space of instructional design," in *Intelligent Tutoring Systems: Lessons Learned*, Psotka, Massey, and Mutter, Eds. Hillsdale, NJ: Lawrence Erlbaum Assoc., 1988.
42. Plato, *Laches, Protagoras, Meno, and Euthydemus* (trans. by W.R.M. Lamb). Cambridge, MA: Harvard Univ. Press, 1924.
43. J. Psotka, D.B. Pliske, and W.D. Gray, "Intelligent design environments and assistant systems," in *Proc. Expert Systems in Government*, Oct. 1985.
44. M.R. Quillian, "Semantic memory," Rep. AFCRL-66-189, Bolt Beranek and Newman Inc., Cambridge, MA, 1966.
45. S. Ramani and A. Newell, "On the generation of problems," SDL 348, Carnegie Mellon University, Pittsburgh, PA, Nov. 1973.
46. B.J. Reiser, J.R. Anderson, and R.G. Farrell, "Dynamic student modelling in an intelligent tutor for LISP programming," *Proc. IJCAI-85*, Los Angeles, CA, Aug. 1985, pp. 8 – 14.
47. A.E. Robinson, D.E. Appelt, B.J. Grosz, G.G. Hendrix, and J.J. Robinson, "Interpreting natural-language utterances in dialogs about tasks," SRI Memo 210, SRI International, Menlo Park, CA, Mar. 1980.
48. J.F. Rockart, M.S. Morton, and Z.S. Zannetos, "Associative learning project—phase-1 system," working paper, Sloan School of Management, MIT, Cambridge, MA, Jan. 1970.
49. D.M. Russell, T.P. Moran, and D.S. Jordan, "The instructional design environment," in *Intelligent Tutoring Systems: Lessons Learned*, J. Psotka, L.D. Massey, and S. Mutter, Eds. Hillsdale, NJ: Lawrence Erlbaum Assoc., 1988.
50. E. Sacerdoti, *A Structure for Plans and Behavior*. New York: Elsevier North-Holland, 1977. Also SRI Memo 109, SRI International, Aug. 1975.
51. R.C. Schank and R. Abelson, *Scripts, Plans, Goals, and Understanding*. Hillsdale, NJ: Lawrence Erlbaum Assoc., 1977.
52. R.C. Schank and S. Slade, "Education and computers: An AI perspective," *Report 431*, Yale Univ., Oct. 1985.
53. J. Shrager, D. Jordan, T. Moran, G. Kizcales, and D.M. Russell, "Pragmatic issues in qualitative modelling: Lessons learned from modelling xerography," *Commun. ACM*, vol. 30, no. 12, Dec. 1987.
54. D.H. Sleeman, "Assessing aspects of competence in basic algebra," in *Intelligent Tutoring Systems*, Sleeman and Brown, Eds. Cambridge, MA: Academic Press, 1982, pp. 185 – 199.
55. A. Stevens and A. Collins, "The goal structure of a socratic tutor," BBN Report 3518, Bolt Beranek and Newman Inc., Cambridge, MA, 1977.

56. A. Stevens and A. Collins, "Diagnosing student's misconceptions in causal models," BBN Report 3786, Bolt Beranek and Newman Inc., Cambridge, MA, 1978.
57. A. Collins and A.L. Stevens, "Goals and strategies of inquiry teachers," in *Advances in Instructional Psychology II*, R. Glaser, Ed. Hillsdale, NJ: Lawrence Erlbaum Assoc., 1982, pp. 65 – 119.
58. A. Stevens, A. Collins, and S. Goldin, "Misconceptions in students' understanding," in *Intelligent Tutoring Systems*, Sleeman and Brown, Eds. Cambridge, MA: Academic Press, 1982, pp. 13 – 24.
59. K. VanLehn, "Student modelling in intelligent teaching systems," presented at the AFHRL Research Planning Forum for Intelligent Tutoring Systems Conference, San Antonio, TX, Sept. 1986.
60. K.T. Wescourt, M. Beard, and L. Gould, "Knowledge-based adaptive curriculum sequencing for CAI: Application of a network representation," in *Proc. ACM-77*, Seattle, WA, 1977, pp. 234 – 240.
61. J.D. Wexler, "Information networks in generative computer-assisted instruction," *IEEE Trans. Man-Machine Syst.*, vol. 11, no. 4, pp. 181 – 190, Dec. 1970.
62. W.A. Woods, "An experimental parsing system for transition network grammars," in *Natural Language Processing*, R. Rustin, Ed. New York: Algorithmics Press, 1972, pp. 113 – 154.
63. B. Woolf and D.D. McDonald, "Building a computer tutor: Design issues," *IEEE Computer*, pp. 61 – 73, Sept. 1984.
64. B. Woolf, "Context-dependent planning in a machine tutor," Ph.D. dissertation, Dept. Comput. and Inform. Sci., Univ. Massachusetts, Amherst, MA, 1984.
65. B. Woolf, D. Blegan, J.H. Jansen, and A. Verloop, "Teaching a complex industrial process," in *Proc. AAAI-86*, Philadelphia, PA, Aug. 1986, pp. 722 – 728.

15

An expert system for instructional design

M. David Merrill

Editors' note *Merrill describes research and development connected with the design of a knowledge-based system that will help with the process of instructional systems design. The focus here is on the process by which instructional systems are conceived and implemented. ISD Expert is intended to assist instructional designers. (Reprinted, with permission, from the Summer 1987 issue of* IEEE Expert. *© 1987 by IEEE. All rights reserved.)*

Significant progress has been made in developing advanced programming techniques enabling computer-based instructional systems to demonstrate considerable intelligence. But instructional models involved in this development have often been based on expediency or the project investigator's previous educational experience, rather than on careful analyses of learning and instructional literature. Many system developers are now seeking information about instruction and learning that can be incorporated into these advanced computer-based tools.

Unfortunately, much available information on learning and instruction is rather nonspecific—requiring considerable interpretation to translate these general educational principles into the precise rules needed to implement an intelligent instructional system. Many key investigators of intelligent instructional systems have computer science backgrounds, but lack extensive instructional design experience. While many areas exist where available information is insufficient, a considerable amount of instructional theory and practice exists that has been demonstrated as effective for other delivery systems and educational environments. This information needs to be synthesized into a systematically organized body of prescriptions that can be coded into rules appropriate for various intelligent instructional systems under development or to be developed.

Sponsored by the Army Research Institute, Human Technology Incorporated, and Teknowledge Incorporated, we are developing an ISD (instructional system design) expert system incorporating much of what is known about instructional design. Our system prototype will be implemented using the Teknowledge S.1 expert system shell. We expect the prototype to be operational by mid 1987. This article overviews the proposed system and discusses types of expert knowledge that must be represented.

ISD Expert aims at instructional designers—designers with only minimal training in instruction, learning, and related disciplines. Its purpose is to guide instructional design decisions so that resulting products can more adequately implement what is known about learning and instructional design.

We have limited ISD Expert to instructional design decisions commencing after front-end task analysis has been completed, and resulting in specifications useful for system implementation. ISD Expert focuses on specifications for computer-based learning materials. While many principles and practices on which the system is based are equally appropriate for other delivery systems, the specifications resulting from system interaction focus on computer-based instruction.

ISD Expert does not include many specifications necessary for system implementation such as screen design, answer processing, error checking, program structure, data structures, and programming. Since it is not an authoring system, ISD Expert does not include screen editors, graphics editors, or other tools for developing computer-based learning materials. We expect the system to contain explanation capability so that designer/users can query regarding the reasoning behind given recommendations. The system's final version will also include cross references to instructional design and learning literature.

Functional components of computer-based instruction

One can conceptualize computer-based instruction in many ways. We will identify and define components of computer-based instruction for which ISD Expert provides design guidance—components chosen to represent various computer-based learning materials. We chose these components to implement different learning experiences including such often-identified computer-aided instruction (CAI) categories as tutorial, simulation, drill and practice, and games.

The proposed functional components are also appropriate for limited forms of so-called "intelligent CAI," including experiential environments and expert advisors. However, initial system versions do not guide knowledge acquisition for designing resident specific-domain experts or for designing strong student models (strong student models are programs simulating students and what students know).

Three major instructional design activities are involved in preparing specifications for computer-based instruction: The first is to *identify* modules to be included. The second is to *design*—that is, describe primary components for each module. The third is to *organize*—that is, arrange and sequence these modules for presentation to students. Key terms used in describing computer-based instructional systems follow.

Modules Modules are instruction units composed of standard components. For computer-based instruction, modules consist of three components: (1) a content representation, (2) a transaction set enabling students to interact with the content representation, and (3) a set of strategy rules determining the "next" transaction.

Instructional goals Instructional goals—that is, instructional objectives or outcomes—are statements about what students will be able to do (their learned performance) following instruction. To determine the appropriate category of learned performance, ISD Expert contains an instructional-goal taxonomy and rules for helping instructional designers analyze tasks to be learned. Classifying instructional goals is an intermediate decision; it facilitates content structure determination that, in turn, facilitates instructional module identification and course organization selection and specification.

Content structure Content structure diagrams important content components and their interrelationships. ISD Expert contains a content structure taxonomy and rules to help instructional designers select, specify, and instantiate content structures appropriate for instructional goals. Content structure serves two purposes in the design effort: (1) as content to be taught, and (2) as a means for determining which modules to include and their appropriate organization.

Content representation Also called knowledge representation, content representation is the content material with which students interact. There are two major categories of content representation: (1) *experiential* representations simulating events or processes and enabling students to interact directly with those simulations, and (2) *structural* representations consisting of specific-domain segments that can be selected and presented to students. ISD Expert includes a content representation taxonomy and rules necessary to help instructional designers select and specify appropriate content representations for given modules.

Transactions Defined in Webster's as "a communicative action or activity involving two parties or two things reciprocally affecting or influencing each other," a transaction is a mutual, dynamic, real-time give-and-take between program and student in which they exchange information. Many CAI programs are described in terms of frames and questions, but frames and questions are too narrow and often lead to static presentations. A transaction is the complete sequence of presentations and reactions. ISD Expert includes a transaction taxonomy and rules necessary to help instructional designers select and specify appropriate transactions for given modules.

Strategy rules Rules for selecting the next transaction and determining when students should shift to the next transaction, strategy rules also indicate whether the learner or the system should make these decisions. ISD Expert contains a strategy component taxonomy and rules necessary to help instructional designers select and specify appropriate strategy components for given modules.

Course organization Course organization represents the module network and possible paths that students may take in traversing that network. ISD Expert consists of a content organization taxonomy. It also consists of a content structure taxonomy from which various content organizations can be derived. The system contains rules for selecting, specifying, and instantiating content structures appropriate for given instructional goals. The system also contains rules for selecting and specifying appropriate modules and a course organization for those modules.

Sequence rules Rules for selecting the next module and determining when students should shift to the next module, sequence rules also indicate whether the learner or the system should make these decisions. ISD Expert contains a sequence component taxonomy and rules necessary to help instructional designers select and specify appropriate sequence components for the content structure and instructional goal involved.

Instructional design—processes, decisions, and outputs

ISD Expert requires instructional designers to engage in three distinct activities: selecting, specifying, and instantiating. Each decision category contains a taxonomy of possible values. The first part of decision making is to select the appropriate category. The system helps instructional designers make appropriate selections.

Second, designers must specify parameter values, enabling the system to recommend more refined versions of selected categories. The system helps instructional designers verify or provide necessary parameter values.

Finally, instructional designers must provide data necessary to instantiate the system. ISD Expert requires and guides instructional goal and content structure instantiation, but the system's remaining parts result only in a not-yet-instantiated specification. A later ISD Expert version will contain guidance for specification instantiations currently beyond the scope of the present project.

Fundamental instructional design activities involved in preparing a specification for computer-based instruction require the following eight major instructional design decisions:

- Identify each module to be included—
  a. Select, specify, and instantiate categorized objectives.
  b. Select, specify, and instantiate content structure.
  c. Select and specify course modules.
- Organize, arrange, and sequence modules—
  d. Select and specify course organization.
  e. Select and specify sequence components.
- Design and describe each module—
  f. Select and specify each module's content representation.
  g. Select and specify each module's transaction set.
  h. Select and specify each module's strategy components.

Module identification

We based ISD Expert's instructional design on the Gagne assumption that different instructional outcomes require different conditions for learning. [1], [2]

Categorized objectives—selection, specification, and instantiation The first instructional design decision requires determining the appropriate learning-outcome category for each task or training objective from the front-end analysis. In addition to training objectives or tasks, this consultation with ISD Expert requires instructional designers to clarify actions and objects involved—thereby determining the appropriate instructional-outcome category. This activity outputs a standardized, categorized statement of objectives—an intermediate document and not necessarily the objectives as they will be presented to students.

This article lacks the space to illustrate a complete consultation with an instructional designer/user for each instructional design decision involved. Portions of a sample dialogue will follow for the next three steps—content structure, course modules, and course organization. We have omitted a consultation for selecting, specifying, and instantiating categorized objectives. That step would output the following information:

Objective type: concept classification
Objective: Given new examples of < written passages containing writing errors > the student will be able to < identify and correct each error > with < 90 percent ≧ correct for each type of error.

Content structure—selection, specification, and instantiation Traditional ISD procedures have not always included these design tasks. Most ISD models include only a single step here, based on Gagne's prerequisite objectives hierarchies, which involve arranging objectives to show prerequisite relationships. [2] Component display theory is based on the premise that there are different relationships between content ideas, and that selecting an appropriate content structure and its instantiation provides the basis for more appropriately selecting instructional modules and their organization. [3]–[7] Such activity provides a formal content structure diagram or description indicating relationships between content elements to be included. This content structure guides module selection and organization, but the instruction may also include the structure as content to be learned by students.

An example The system knows that the most appropriate content structure for concept classification objectives is a kinds-of taxonomy. The following dialogue guides designers in specifying and instantiating a kinds-of taxonomy content structure. Items shown in brackets (such as [Writing__Errors]) indicate information the system gathered and displayed to students. The dialogue follows a specific hypothetical consultation and does not reflect all the available alternatives. Numbers in curly brackets (such as {3.1}) indicate values on various parameters that enter into later rules. This information is not shown to users. Designer/user response is shown in italics. The dialogue is hypothetical and based on preliminary system specifications. Since S.1 programming is underway as this article is being written, actual interactions with the system are not yet available.

SYS2 Fill in the blank: The student will be able to identify kinds of □_____[a]_____

Writing__Errors

SYS3 Do you want to specify kinds of [Writing__Errors]? Y/N

Y

Choose one of the following alternatives:

a. Kinds of [Writing__Errors] can be classed into distinct categories. {3.1 or 3.2 or 3.3}

b. Kinds of [Writing__Errors] can be classed into categories but the categories overlap. {3.4}

c. Kinds of [Writing__Errors] lie on some continuum without distinct categories of [Writing__Errors]. {3.5}

a

Type in the major kinds of [Writing__Errors]. Press Enter twice to indicate list is complete.

☐____[a_1]____

Noun__Errors
Pronoun__Errors
RTN RTN

Choose one of the following alternatives:

a. It is not likely that the student will confuse instances of [Noun__Errors] with instances of [Pronoun__Errors]. {3.1}

b. [Noun__Errors] and [Pronoun__Errors] are coordinate concepts where instances of [Noun__Errors] may be confused with instances of [Pronoun__Errors]. {3.2}

c. [Noun__Errors] and [Pronoun__Errors] are coordinate concepts where instances of [Noun__Errors] may be confused with instances of [Pronoun__Errors] and where [Noun__Errors] and [Pronoun__Errors] are ordered with respect to each other. {3.3}

a

{SYS4 and SYS5 gather information relative to continuous and overlapping categories. They are not relevant to the current case and are not included here.}

SYS6 There are distinct ways to focus a student's attention in learning kinds of content. Please identify the focus of the instruction.

{The first two questions would not be asked in this situation but are included to show a more complete set of questions for focus.}

»IF 3.2 or 3.3
Is the primary focus to learn to differentiate [a1] from [a2]? Y/N {6.3a}

»IF 3.4 or 3.5
Is the primary focus to learn to rank instances of [Writing__Errors] along [C]? Y/N {6.3b}

»IF 3.1 OR IF N then ask
Is the primary focus to learn to identify instances of [Noun__Errors]? Y/N {6.2}

N

Is the primary focus to learn to identify instances of [Pronoun__Errors]? Y/N {6.2}

N

»IF N then ask
Is the primary focus to learn that [Noun__Errors] and [Pronoun__Errors] are all instances of the more general concept [Writing__Errors]? Y/N {6.1}

N

»IF N then ask
Is the primary focus to learn that [Noun__Errors] and [Pronoun__Errors] are all kinds of [Writing__Errors]? Y/N {6.4}

N

»IF N then ask

Are [Noun__Errors] and [Pronoun__Errors] primarily Place Holders to organize the content? This means that it is unnecessary for the student to learn to identify instances of these concepts or to discriminate instances of these concepts from one another. It may be unnecessary because the student has already learned [Noun__Errors] and [Pronoun__Errors]. Y/N {6.5}

Y

SYS7 Concepts in a kinds-of taxonomy often have prerequisite relationships with one another. Please indicate the prerequisite relationships involved by answering the following questions.

»IF below second level in taxonomy then ask {Would not be asked in this instance}
Must students be able to discriminate instances of [Writing__Errors] from instances of [2] before they can identify or discriminate instances of [Noun__Errors] and [Pronoun__Errors]? Y/N {7.3}

»IF N then ask
Must students be able to identify instances of [Writing__Errors] before they can identify or discriminate instances of [Noun__Errors] and [Pronoun__Errors]? Y/N {7.2}

N

{The following two questions would not be asked in this situation. They are included here to show other options}.

»IF N and IF 6.1 then ask
Must students be able to discriminate instances of [Noun__Errors] from [Pronoun__Errors] before they can identify instances of [Noun__Errors] and [Pronoun__Errors] as instances of [Writing__Errors]? Y/N {7.5}

»IF N and IF 6.1 then ask
Must students be able to identify instances of [Noun__Errors] and instances of [Pronoun__Errors] before they can identify instances of [Noun__Errors] and [Pronoun__Errors] as instances of [Writing__Errors]? Y/N {7.4}

IF N then ask
Are we correct to conclude that there are no prerequisites to learning to identify or discriminate instances of [Noun__Errors] and [Pronoun__Errors]? Y/N {7.1}

Y

»repeat SYS3, SYS6 and SYS7 until the entire taxonomy has been specified.

SYS3 Do you want to specify kinds of [Noun__Errors]? Y/N

Y

Choose one of the following alternatives:

a. Kinds of [Noun__Errors] can be classed into distinct categories. {3.1 or 3.2 or 3.3}

b. Kinds of [Noun__Errors] can be classed into categories but the categories overlap. {3.4}

c. Kinds of [Noun__Errors] lie on some continuum without distinct categories of [Noun__Errors]. {3.5}

a

Type in the major kinds of [Noun__Errors]. Press Enter twice to indicate list is complete.

☐____ [a_1]____

Noun__*Possessives*

Noun__Plurals

RTN RTN

Choose one of the following alternatives:

a. It is not likely that the student will confuse instances of [Noun__Possessives] with instances of [Noun__Plurals]. {3.1}

b. [Noun__Possessives] and [Noun__Plurals] are coordinate concepts where instances of [Noun__Possessives] may be confused with instances of [Noun__Plurals]. {3.2}

c. [Noun__Possessives] and [Noun__Plurals] are coordinate concepts where instances of [Noun__Possessives] may be confused with instances of [Noun__Plurals] and where [Noun__Possessives] and [Noun__Plurals] are ordered with respect to each other. {3.3}

b

SYS6 There are distinct ways to focus a student's attention in learning kinds of content. Please identify the focus of the instruction.

»IF 3.2 or 3.3

Is the primary focus to learn to differentiate [Noun__Possessives] from [Noun __Plurals]? Y/N {6.3}

Y

SYS7 Concepts in a kinds-of taxonomy often have prerequisite relationships with one another. Please indicate the prerequisite relationships involved by answering the following questions.

Must students be able to discriminate instances of [Noun__Errors] from instances of [Pronoun__Errors] before they can identify or discriminate instances of [Noun__Possessives] and [Noun__Plurals]? Y/N {7.3}

N

»IF N then ask

Must students be able to identify instances of [Noun__Errors] before they can identify or discriminate instances of [Noun__Possessives] and [Noun__Plurals]? Y/N {7.2}

N

Are we correct to conclude that there are no prerequisites to learning to identify or discriminate instances of [Noun__Possessives] and [Noun__Plurals]? This could mean that the student has already learned the necessary prerequisite information. Y/N {7.1}

Y

»repeat SYS3, SYS6 and SYS7 until the entire taxonomy has been specified.

SYS3 Do you want to specify kinds of [Noun__Possessives]? Y/N

Y

Choose one of the following alternatives:

a. Kinds of [Noun__Possessives] can be classed into distinct categories. {3.1 or 3.2 or 3.3}

b. Kinds of [Noun__Possessives] can be classed into categories but the categories overlap. {3.4}

c. Kinds of [Noun__Possessives] lie on some continuum without distinct categories of [Noun__Possessives]. {3.5}

a

Type in the major kinds of [Noun__Possessives]. Press Enter twice to indicate list is complete.

□____[a_1]____

-'s__Noun__Possessives

-s'__Noun__Possessives

RTN RTN

Choose one of the following alternatives:

a. It is not likely that the student will confuse instances of [-'s__Noun__Possessives] with instances of [-s'__Noun__Possessives]. {3.1}

b. [-'s__Noun__Possessives] and [-s'__Noun__Possessives] are coordinate concepts where instances of [-'s__Noun__Possessives] may be confused with instances of [-s'__Noun__Possessives]. {3.2}

c. [-'s__Noun__Possessives] and [-s'__Noun__Possessives] are coordinate concepts where instances of [-'s__Noun__Possessives] may be confused with instances of [-s'__Noun__Possessives] and where [-'s__Noun__Possessives] and [s'__Noun__Possessives] are ordered with respect to each other. {3.3}

b

SYS6 There are distinct ways to focus a student's attention in learning kinds of content. Please identify the focus of the instruction.

»IF 3.2 or 3.3

Is the primary focus to learn to differentiate [-'s__Noun__Possessives] from [-s'__Noun__Possessives]? Y/N {6.3}

Y

SYS7 Concepts in a kinds-of taxonomy often have prerequisite relationships with one another. Please indicate the prerequisite relationships involved by answering the following questions.

Must students be able to discriminate instances of [Noun__Possessives] from instances of [Noun__Plurals] before they can identify or discriminate instances of [-'s__Noun__Possessives] and [-s'__Noun__Possessives]? Y/N {7.3}

Y

»repeat SYS3, SYS6 and SYS7 until the entire taxonomy has been specified.

SYS3 Do you want to specify kinds of [-'s__Noun__Possessives]? Y/N

N

»repeat SYS3, SYS6 and SYS7 until the entire taxonomy has been specified.

SYS3 Do you want to specify kinds of [-s'__Noun__Possessives]? Y/N

N

»repeat SYS3, SYS6 and SYS7 until the entire taxonomy has been specified.

SYS3 Do you want to specify kinds of [Noun__Plurals]? Y/N

Y

Choose one of the following alternatives:

a. Kinds of [Noun__Plurals] can be classed into distinct categories. {3.1 or 3.2 or 3.3}

b. Kinds of [Noun__Plurals] can be classed into categories but the categories overlap. {3.4}

c. Kinds of [Noun__Plurals] lie on some continuum without distinct categories of [Noun__Plurals]. {3.5}

a

Type in the major kinds of [Noun__Plurals]. Press Enter twice to indicate list is complete.

□____[a_1]____

-s__Noun__Plurals
-es__Noun__Plurals
-ies__Noun__Plurals
RTN RTN

Choose one of the following alternatives:

a. It is not likely that the student will confuse instances of [-s__Noun__Plural] with instances of [-es__Noun__Plural] with instances of [-ies__Noun__Plural]. {3.1}

b. [-s__Noun__Plural], [-es__Noun__Plural] and [-ies__Noun__Plural] are coordinate concepts where instances of [-s__Noun__Plural], [-es__Noun__Plural] and [-ies __Noun__Plural] may be confused with each other. {3.2}

c. [-s__Noun__Plural], [-es__Noun__Plural] and [-ies__Noun__Plural] are coordinate concepts where instances of [-s__Noun__Plural], [-es__Noun__Plural] and [-ies __Noun__Plural] may be confused with each other and where [-s__Noun__Plural], [-es__Noun__Plural] and [-ies__Noun__Plural] are ordered with respect to each other. {3.3}

b

SYS6 There are distinct ways to focus a student's attention in earning kinds of content. Please identify the focus of the instruction.

»IF 3.2 or 3.3

Is the primary focus to learn to differentiate [-s__Noun__Plurals] from [-es__Noun __Plurals] from [-ies__Noun__Plurals]? Y/N {6.3}

Y

SYS7 Concepts in a kinds-of taxonomy often have prerequisite relationships with one another. Please indicate the prerequisite relationships involved by answering the following questions.

Must students be able to discriminate instances of [Noun__Possessives] from instances of [Noun__Plurals] before they can identify or discriminate instances of

[-s__Noun__Plurals] from [-es__Noun__Plurals] from [-ies__Noun__Plurals]? Y/N {7.3}

Y

»repeat SYS3, SYS6 and SYS7 until the entire taxonomy has been specified.

SYS3 Do you want to specify kinds of [-s__Noun__Plurals]? Y/N

N

»repeat SYS3, SYS6 and SYS7 until the entire taxonomy has been specified.

SYS3 Do you want to specify kinds of [-es__Noun__Plurals]? Y/N

N

»repeat SYS3, SYS6 and SYS7 until the entire taxonomy has been specified.

SYS3 Do you want to specify kinds of [-ies__Noun__Plurals]? Y/N

N

»repeat SYS3, SYS6 and SYS7 until the entire taxonomy has been specified.

SYS3 Do you want to specify kinds of [Pronoun__Errors]? Y/N

Y

Choose one of the following alternatives:

a. Kinds of [Pronoun-Errors] can be classed into distinct categories. {3.1 or 3.2 or 3.3}

b. Kinds of [Pronoun__Errors] can be classed into categories but the categories overlap. {3.4}

c. Kinds of [Pronoun__Errors] lie on some continuum without distinct categories of [Pronoun__Errors]. {3.5}

a

Type in the major kinds of [Pronoun__Errors]. Press Enter twice to indicate list is complete.

☐____[a_1]____

Pronoun__Possessives
Pronoun__Contractions
RTN RTN

Choose one of the following alternatives:

a. It is not likely that the student will confuse instances of [Pronoun__Possessive] with instances of [Pronoun__Contraction]. {3.1}

b. [Pronoun__Possessive] and [Pronoun__Contraction] are coordinate concepts where instances of [Pronoun__Possessive] may be confused with instances of [Pronoun __Contraction]. {3.2}

c. [Pronoun__Possessive] and [Pronoun__Contraction] are coordinate concepts where instances of [Pronoun__Possessive] may be confused with instances of [Pronoun __Contraction] and where [Pronoun__Possessive] and [Pronoun__Contraction] are ordered with respect to each other. {3.3}

b

SYS6 There are distinct ways to focus a student's attention in learning kinds of content. Please identify the focus of the instruction.

»IF 3.2 or 3.3

Is the primary focus to learn to differentiate [Pronoun__Possessive] from [Pronoun __Contraction]? Y/N {6.3}

Y

SYS7 Concepts in a kinds-of taxonomy often have prerequisite relationships with one another. Please indicate the prerequisite relationships involved by answering the following questions.

Must students be able to discriminate instances of [Noun__Errors] from instances of [Pronoun__Errors] before they can identify or discriminate instances of [Pronoun__Possessives] and [Pronoun__Contractions]? Y/N {7.3}

N

»IF N then ask

Must students be able to identify instances of [Noun__Errors] before they can identify or discriminate instances of [Pronoun__Possessives] and [Pronoun__Contractions]? Y/N {7.2}

N

»IF N then ask

Are we correct to conclude that there are no prerequisites to learning to identify or discriminate instances of [Pronoun__Possessives] and [Pronoun__Contractions]? This could mean that the student has already learned the necessary prerequisite information. Y/N {7.1}

Y

»repeat SYS3, SYS6 and SYS7 until the entire taxonomy has been specified.

SYS3 Do you want to specify kinds of [Pronoun__Possessives]? Y/N

N

»repeat SYS3, SYS6 and SYS7 until the entire taxonomy has been specified.

SYS3 Do you want to specify kinds of [Pronoun__Contractions]? Y/N

N

SYS The kinds-of-taxonomy content structure you have specified is represented by the accompanying diagram.

Course modules—selection and specification We can select course modules in two ways: First, we can provide a module for each major objective in some prerequisite hierarchy. Second, we can identify a module set that systematically elaborates the selected and instantiated content structure. The system will guide these procedures, and will guide instructional designers as to when each procedure may be most appropriate. Modules are selected and organized by a set of system rules—rules illustrated in the next section.

Module organization

Content organization is the module network to be learned and the paths that students can take from one module to another. Content organization must also contain the control mechanisms, menus, advice, and other components necessary to organize the course.

Course organization—selection and specification Instructional designers must select the most appropriate sequence options based on the students involved, the constraints of the instructional situation, and the organization most appropriate to elaborate the content structure involved. For example, having gathered information about content structure, the system knows how to analyze that content structure to recommend a preliminary module set and a course organization (that is, an instruction sequence). Using these rules, the system recommends instructional modules and instructional objectives for each module.

Values for the category (3.0), focus (6.0), and prerequisite variables (7.0) are associated with each set of coordinate concepts. A coordinate concept set is the next level of nodes under a single node in the kinds-of taxonomy tree structure. The nature of the kinds-of taxonomy tree structure and rules considering values on these variables determine the recommended modules. The following rules are not as they appear in the actual S.1 system, but are conceptual to facilitate reader understanding. These rules do not constitute the complete set—they are merely illustrative.

The integrative module rule Any node with two or more levels below defines a potential integrative module. All sequences include a preintegrative module and a postintegrative module with instructional modules between. The transactions in integrative modules may include overviews, summaries, syntheses, and pre- and post-testing.

For the writing-errors kinds-of taxonomy content structure, two integrative modules exist—one for writing errors and one for noun errors. Instructional modules are determined by considering each set of coordinate concepts and the parameter values associated with that set as determined by consultation with designer/users.

Branching rule If there are separate modules in each branch then there is a menu option for each branch.

Map rule If there is more than one module in a branch then a map symbol is indicated on the course sequence diagram. If there is only one module in a branch then an instructional module symbol is indicated on the course organization diagram.

For the writing-skills case, the first branch has more than one module. But branch two has only one module. The integrative module, branching, and map rules are applied to each map symbol on the first-level course organization.

The prerequisite rule If prerequisite = 7.3 (discrimination of superordinate) then the superordinate module appears before the subordinate modules.

The prerequisite option rule Single prerequisite modules appear with a menu option in the course organization.

For the writing-skills case, the main course sequence map is further analyzed by applying the above rules to yield second-level course organization. Many course sequences can be obtained from various configurations of content structures. The system provides users with an efficient way to analyze complex structures and to obtain a recommended set of modules and a recommended course organization.

Sequence components—selection and specification Sequence components are various on-line decision structures controlling access to course modules. They include menus, decision rules, information to the student, and other components controlling the sequence. Instructional designers must select sequence control components to include and provide criteria needed to operate these on-line sequence control processes. Content organization decisions produce specifications for course organization, usually consisting of flow charts or structure diagrams together with criteria, decision points, menu items, and other components necessary for implementation.

To implement menus and decision points in the above content organization, for example, consultation at this point would gather more information from designer/users. Our system prototype will not implement this decision.

Design modules

Much traditional CAI is based on the frame (display) concept, in which course organization is seen as a file of screens to be presented to students. ISD Expert takes a more dynamic approach, seeing a module not as a series of screens but rather as a knowledge database together with a transaction series for using that database. Different types of knowledge representation enable different kinds of transactions. Certain representation/transaction sets are appropriate for different outcomes. Selecting the content representation most appropriate for the objective being taught by a module represents an important instructional design decision.

For example, associated with each module in the content structure are various content representations that are then used by transactions associated with the module. Consultation here would gather additional information to provide the selection and specification for this content representation. Eventually, the system will help instantiate this content representation.

Transactions—selection and specification Rather than construct screens consisting of text and questions, ISD Expert designs interactive sequences consisting of numerous transactions with a given content representation. Furthermore, the system assumes that different transaction sets are appropriate for different outcomes. The instructional design decision selects that set of transactions to accompany a given content representation, and selects from that set those most appropriate to the specific module being designed. This produces a specification for each transaction.

For example, each module has associated with it at least two transactions. Consultation would continue here to gather additional information about which of the possible transactions might be appropriate to include for each module. Transactions are defined by a series of attributes determining the nature of interaction with students. System rules constrain transactions depending on content organization, content structure, and certain parameters about instructional situations and students involved.

Ultimately, this specification should include screen design, error checking, answer processing, and other considerations not part of the initial ISD Expert version.

Strategy components—selection and specification Just as course organization sequences exist with on-line decisions about which module is "next," module organization strategies exist with on-line decisions about which transaction is "next." Instructional designers must select those menus, decision rules, criteria, and other strategy components necessary and appropriate for a given module. Student characteristics and instructional situation constraints, as well as the instructional outcome category, help determine these decisions.

This produces a specification for each module's organization, usually consisting of a flow chart or structure diagram showing the decisions, criteria, menus, and other strategy components needed to implement the module. Additional consultation helps determine the transaction sequence within each module. This decision will not be implemented in our system prototype.

Since we are developing the ISD Expert prototype as this article is being written, our initial work seeks primarily to illustrate the feasibility of such an expert system and to codify some of the knowledge involved. We plan to demonstrate our prototype in the summer of 1987. Following development of the prototype, we will undertake a much larger effort to more fully implement the system.

Acknowledgment

The Army Research Institute funded the work reported in this article. The views expressed herein are the author's and do not necessarily reflect the views of the sponsoring organization.

References

1. R.M. Gagne, *The Conditions of Learning*, First ed., Holt, Rinehart, and Winston, New York, N.Y., 1965.
2. R.M. Gagne, *The Conditions of Learning*, Fourth ed., Holt, Rinehart, and Winston, New York, N.Y., 1985.
3. M.D. Merrill and R.D. Tennyson, *Teaching Concepts: An Instructional Design Guide*, Educational Technology Publications, Englewood Cliffs, N.J., 1977.
4. C.M. Reigeluth, M.D. Merrill, and C.V. Bunderson, "The Structure of Subject Matter Content and its Instructional Design Implications," *Instructional Science*, Vol. 7, 1978, pp. 107 – 126.
5. M.D. Merrill, "Component Display Theory," in *Instructional Design Theories and Models*, C.M. Reigeluth, ed., Lawrence Earlbaum Associates, Hillsdale, N.J., 1983.
6. M.D. Merrill, "An Illustration of Component Display Theory," to appear in *Instructional Design Theories in Action: Lessons Illustrating Selected Theories*, C.M. Reigeluth, ed., Lawrence Earlbaum Associates, Hillsdale, N.J., 1987.
7. M.D. Merrill, "Applying Component Display Theory to the Design of Courseware," to appear in *Instructional Designs for Microcomputer Courseware*, D.H. Jonassen, ed., Lawrence Earlbaum Associates, Hillsdale, N.J., 1987.

The author can be reached at Utah State University, Department of Instructional Design, L-122, Logan, UT 84322-3025.

16

Intelligent tutoring systems

A tutorial survey

William J. Clancey

Editors' note *Bill Clancey's excellent tutorial survey describes the elements of tutoring systems, the range of teaching scenarios, and their relation to "a theory of instruction." The paper chronicles decades of research and development and assesses the field in terms of its impact on traditional instruction, learning, and human performance. This paper first appeared as an Office of Naval Research technical report in 1989.*

1. Introduction

What are intelligent tutoring systems? Why is it necessary to call them "intelligent"? Shouldn't every tutoring system be intelligent? This name in part reflects the history of the research (Sleeman and Brown, 1982, Wenger, 1986). The people who began this work—in particular John Seely Brown, Alan Collins, and Ira Goldstein—wanted to contrast their work with traditional, computer-aided instruction, so they called their programs, based on Artificial Intelligence programming techniques, Intelligent CAI (ICAI) programs. The name Intelligent Tutoring System (ITS) means the same thing.

Perhaps the best reason for attributing intelligence to these programs is their ability to solve the same problems that they present to students. This capability greatly enhances student modeling and explanation. It provides an efficient foundation for explaining all of the details of solving a problem, not just what a teacher decided ahead of time might be useful. It also allows us to build a student modelling program that can solve problems in alternative ways. Obviously, to do this the modelling program first has to be able to solve the problem in at least one way.

Explaining how a problem is solved is by no means easy, and the idea of what constitutes an explanation has changed very much in the last ten years. In MYCIN, just saying what rules were used and printing them was an innovative accomplishment. We now call this an *audit-trail explanation*, similar to an inspectable record of financial transactions. The audit-trail explanation program can tell you every step, but doesn't necessarily know the rationale behind the steps. There is a difference between saying what happened and explaining why it was the right thing to do.

Another major characteristic of an ITS is the degree of individualized instruction it provides. Early CAI programs were contrasted with classroom teaching in terms of the individualized instruction they allow. An ITS provides improved individualized instruction by building a distinct model of what the student knows, as an interpretation of how he behaves (Clancey, 1986). Thus, an ITS relates instruction to an understanding of the individual student's goals and beliefs.

Earlier CAI programs are sometimes described as branching programs. At each point, the program makes an evaluation as to whether the student's answer at some place in solving a problem is correct or wrong. The teacher builds in the program: If the student gives answer A go to this section, if the student gives answer B, go to this section. The program can only recognize these built-in answers. No coherent model of patterns in the student's behavior is recorded. Of course, it is possible using conventional programming to build student models. For example, you could keep a history of all of the branches that a program made and have each new decision about where to branch based on the history of what branches have occurred before. This could be very complex because you would have to anticipate all of the possible histories. The methodology of artificial intelligence provides an easier way.

Intelligent tutoring systems dynamically analyze the solution history and use principles to decide what to do next, rather than requiring situations to be anticipated by the author of the program. Also, the person who writes the traditional CAI Program is not expressing his strategies of why the branching is occurring at any point. At each time, when he designs a new step in his program, he may be redundantly using the same ideas of how to teach. In intelligent tutoring systems we want to extract these principles so they can be applied automatically, as well as expressing them explicitly, so we know what they are.

A final point is that we shouldn't think of intelligent tutoring systems as being one kind of program with one kind of interaction with the student. There are really many different types of programs that have different capabilities. Some are completely reactive or passive in their behavior, they wait for the student to do something and then respond. Others, like GUIDON, make an attempt to present new information in what is called *opportunistic tutoring* (Clancey, 1982). There is also a distinction between "coaching" and "tutoring." This was a point that Goldstein made in his early work (Goldstein, 1977). A coach is of course someone who watches and doesn't constantly interfere, but stays on the sidelines and lets you play the game. Then, perhaps when you ask for help or in a crucial moment of play, the coach interrupts and states an important lesson. This is a non-intrusive pedagogical strategy, based on the idea that people should just solve the problem and act on their own. If you interrupt, you won't be giving them the opportunity to develop skills to monitor their own problem solving, such as the capability to detect and back out of false starts.

1.1. Components of an ITS

Figure 16-1 is a diagram that I adapted from (Goldstein, 1978). I will go over it in some detail because these components occur in most intelligent tutoring systems.

The central idea is that there is a knowledge base, some formal model, of how the problem is to be solved, which is in the kernel of the program. For example, suppose that the student's problem is to diagnose a patient, to see if the patient has a disease and to prescribe therapy. The problem might be, as we'll see in some other examples, a game that the student is playing. It might be a child's game, intended to teach mathematics. As the student is solving this problem, he might be receiving new information, and he's making certain solution steps that we'll call "moves" in general.

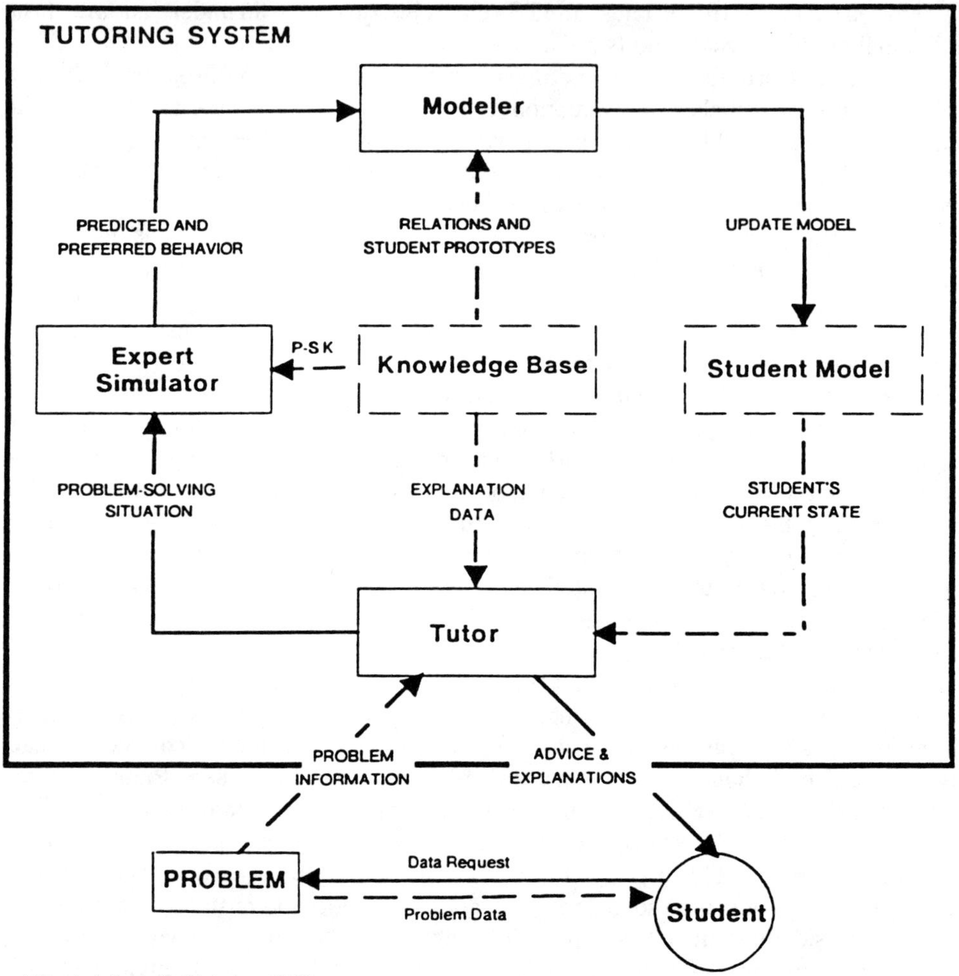

(Adapted from Goldstein, 1978)

Fig. 16-1. Components of an ITS.

Suppose now that the student requests some patient data. The tutor is watching and passes on to a problem-solving simulator program (often called an *expert system*) all of the information that the student has received about the problem. If this were a game, such as a board game like chess or checkers, the tutor would tell the expert where all of the pieces are, the current configuration. The expert simulation program examines its knowledge base. This could include procedures, facts, plus maybe the rules of the game. The expert then generates the preferred behavior of what to do next, possibly as a set of plausible alternatives. For medical diagnosis, this would be a set of good questions to ask about the patient, and maybe an indication of the expert's preferred next question. In a game, this would be the next move to make.

This idealized information is given to the modelling program, which combines it with some additional information, perhaps about different types of students and what students know depending on their background, maybe very complex patterns. (I'm describing an idealized architecture which is more complicated than any existing ITS.) In addition to these prototypes or patterns of different types of students and student behavior, there may be descriptions of typical misconceptions or incorrect knowledge. The modeling program may also be given knowledge about prerequisite ordering of facts and procedures—what does it make sense to know given what you already know, what would it be difficult to understand given what you know? (Wescourt, et al., 1977, Goldstein, 1982).

The modelling program combines these patterns with the student's and expert's recent moves and rationalization for them, and updates the model of the student's goals, what he believes about the current problem, and what he knows in general. Thus, the core of the student model, the result of relating student behavior to the expert rationalization, is a description of what the student knows, expressed as a subset of the expert knowledge base, with degrees of belief attached to each item. For example, GUIDON's model states what the student is believed to know about the current problem, his goal structure in requesting new data, and for each rule in MYCIN's knowledge base a certainty measurement indicating whether the student knows the rule. This *differential* or *overlay* model then is fed back to the tutor, which has to decide, given principles of teaching, what to say next. Should it make an interruption and give some advice, or just let the student continue to solve the problem on his own?

Note that the separate boxes in the figure correspond to separate parts of the tutoring system. This is our programming methodology: Rather than writing one program that arbitrarily combines the knowledge, we abstract the components. This enables the expert simulator, modeling, and tutoring modules to operate upon different knowledge bases, as in GUIDON.

Are there any questions?

Question: "What is saved between sessions?" There is also a cumulative record from one problem to the next of what the student knows. Maybe some future tutoring program will save certain things that it couldn't understand about a student's behavior that, later on, it would be able to disambiguate. In fact, this confirms fairly well to the Schank model of memory that the exceptions are saved, and they help you generalize concepts later on (Schank, 1981). Part of the problem of course is how much are we going to save; there is a space problem. This is why we need a combination of abstraction and good indexing.

Question: "Can you say more about Schank's method for remembering exceptions?" The basic idea was called MOPS (memory organization packets). Janet Kolodner did the most relevant follow-on project in her dissertation research, involving memory organization for efficient retrieval and storage (Kolodner, 1983). She models how knowledge, as a memory of many specific facts, is organized. The program is thus able to answer questions about what happened in the past and what typically happens. The idea is that generalizations form a hierarchy of concepts.

The name of Kolodner's program was CYRUS. This was a model of Cyrus Vance who was the U.S. Secretary of State at the time. She would feed the program stories of the travels of Vance and what he did on his various trips. Then you could ask the question: "When Cyrus goes to Egypt, will he visit the pyramids?" The program knows that this is a sightseeing event and looks at its memory to see where there were other sightseeing events. Is it common? Are there any times when Cyrus made a visit to a country but didn't do any sightseeing? The program would then say: "Well, yes, Cyrus will probably visit the pyramids, because every time he has been in the Middle East, he has gone sightseeing." But if you asked about Asia, Cyrus might be uninterested in sightseeing in Asia, and the memory of exceptions would indicate that visits to Asia involve no sightseeing.

The basic idea is that a discrimination net organizes and filters events in memory. The program will notice that, up to a certain point, there have been several similar events, and an exception, a different specific event, is saved. If there are two exceptions, the program looks for similarities. The network, as a pattern of generalizations, provides an efficient way of saving exceptions: An exception is defined with respect to some pattern. This is related to other discrimination models of memory, such as (Carbonell and Collins, 1973).

I found this model to be very stimulating for thinking about teaching and learning. The most intriguing thing is that this is not how knowledge bases are typically organized. In fact, Janet Kolodner is now building an expert system using her model of memory and having the program record and consider exceptions as times when its heuristic generalizations might not apply. If the program has a record of all of the cases it has solved, and if generalizations constitute its rules for classifying each new experience, the program might notice that a new case is more similar to the exceptions than to the generalizations. It will now have an ability to say that it should be careful, that this case is something different than what it can understand, and maybe it should make an attempt to generalize the exception. Of course, it's a very difficult problem to start extracting medical knowledge in this way and it requires knowledge of the mechanisms of disease; Kolodner hasn't considered causal representations. She is working in an area of psychiatry with a superficial theory of causal mechanisms, and this makes the simple classification approach tractable.

1.2. Teaching scenarios

John Seely Brown makes the point that teaching programs differ along a spectrum of learner control. Who is in charge of the interaction? In the case of a traditional program, what we call frame-based CAI, the branching type mentioned earlier, the program is constantly deciding what to do next. Again, this is a generalization and by no means describes every non-AI system. On the opposite side, a good example is the LOGO work of Papert and DiSessa at M.I.T., inspired by the Piaget exploratory school of discovery learning (Papert, 1980). The idea is to give the student a good environment to explore in which he can use his own innate curiosity, combining things in new ways to learn the underlying principles. If the environment is very rich, as in LOGO, with the concepts of recursion, iteration, modularity, hierarchy—which can be discovered as part of designing programs—the student may learn very general principles that can be of value to him.

When we have extremes there are often disadvantages on each side. For example, if we don't allow the student the ability to move around as he wants, he cannot use his curiosity to explore new areas. The other extreme is that, if there is no initiative by a coach or the program, the student may get stuck or unable to progress. This may also be viewed as an inefficient use of the student's time. If someone would just say; "Here is what I expect you to learn," then the student can say, "I understand that already" or, "Explain to me how this is different from something else." We can efficiently bring the student's conception of the world closer to what we think he should understand.

As you might imagine with these two alternatives, we want a combination. We want to give the student an ability to explore, but we also want some kind of an active agent, some kind of a coach perhaps that watches the student and guides him, redirecting him at various times. John Brown points out here that in some ways this is the most difficult system to build because it requires the most knowledge. If the program is always in control, we needn't understand what the student is saying to us when he wants to do something different, and we needn't do something intelligent when he asks us for something different. In the case of a program which is not attempting to present something in some logical order, there are no large and complex student modelling, tutoring, system and explanation programs to build. We just design a good language, like LOGO, and a good set of problems. It's an interesting fact about LOGO that you observe the teacher going around and helping the students, or the students helping each other. Pedagogical control can be subtle to detect and describe.

Different forms of computer-based learning can be contrasted in another way. Early programs individualized instruction by *drill and practice*. I give you a problem and you solve it; I give you another problem and you solve it; and I keep selecting problems so that they get more difficult or they follow some logical sequence. This is a good idea, and it is something that we will always want to do; sometimes you can select five good problems and if the student follows them, he will learn something. In the SOPHIE program John Brown and Richard Burton used a traditional CAI front-end to get the student familiar with the electronic circuit that they were going to learn how to diagnose. There can be a place for drill and practice.

Another perspective on computer-based learning might be called *intelligent machines*. GUIDON is a classic example, and there are maybe six or seven similar systems from the 1970s. These programs exploit the idea of a mixed-initiative discourse to replicate many aspects of teaching. Through the use of general teaching procedures, the program can respond flexibly to the student's initiative. Whenever the student says "help" to GUIDON, it uses its general procedures to provide help in any context. This was begun by Carbonell in the SCHOLAR program (Carbonell, 1970), which parsed natural language using a keyword parser, allowing the student to type in questions and respond.

It's an interesting historical point that from about 1979 to 1984 people stopped building these programs. The experience of building programs like GUIDON made us realize we were trying to do everything at once. We didn't have a good knowledge representation, and we didn't really understand what kind of misconceptions the students have. The idea of modelling the student became the central idea. Almost every project from the late 1970s until today has started with this one problem: How do we write a program that can understand what the student is doing? There is no need to consider strategies for teaching if we don't understand what the student is doing. It was a logical step in the research to ignore the teaching problem and emphasize the problem of understanding.

The third form of computer-based learning involves the use of *simulation*. By the late 1970s with LISP workstations and fancy graphics, it became possible to design new kinds of interaction in a teaching system. A good example is the STEAMER project. Here the idea is to use the program to give the student a realistic situation. STEAMER uses graphics and color to show dials and process change which is very similar conceptually to what happens in the world.

These three types of approaches—drill and practice, intelligent instructor, and simulation—can be combined, but they are useful extremes to consider.

1.3. Learning scenarios for an intelligent tutor

Focusing now on the intelligent tutoring form of computer-based learning, we can further categorize learning scenarios by how the knowledge in the program is used. Here we have different pedagogical philosophies.

First, we have the *Socratic* approach, in which the teacher keeps asking questions and giving new cases to force the student to realize gaps and inconsistencies in his understanding. In GUIDON, using this pedagogical approach we wouldn't spend two hours talking about one patient. Instead we would contrast cases, asking hypothetical questions and leading the student to see similarities and differences. This is the idea in the WHY program (Collins and Stevens, 1980). For problem solving that is strongly based on precedent and particular experiences, such as law and medicine, this is obviously a good way to proceed.

In contrast, a *reactive environment* is used in SOPHIE. The student solves a problem, but the program does not interrupt. It reacts to the student and gives feedback. In *learning by doing*, the apprenticeship alternative, the teacher actively contributes. The teacher watches to see whether the student is making progress and checks his understanding. After classroom learning, medical students follow the physicians around the hospital and help them solve problems. The student takes a patient's history, and then the physician will ask, "What do you think the problem is?" He will quiz the student to test his understanding and encourage him to consider alternatives. This is essentially the approach in GUIDON.

Learning while doing differs in a subtle way. Consider a job performance aid, a tutor built into the machinery of the normal working environment. An example would be a copying machine that could watch what you're doing when you make copies. Copying machines are complicated. If you want to make reverse double-sided copies with collating, there might be more than one way to solve the problem. If we build a coach into the copying machine, the coach would observe what you do. Perhaps you never use a certain combination of options. The tutor might know that people who know what they are doing use these options. Unless there is something special about your task, you might not know how to use the machine effectively, and the program will interrupt to offer assistance. Thus, a job performance aid would help you learn while you're in your normal course of business.

These examples illustrate how the research is proceeding: We are still discovering different ways in which instruction occurs and devising new opportunities for applying computers. Brown summarizes what we have learned by the aphorism that "teaching involves using knowledge, rather than just presenting it." Thus, in GUIDON we give the student a problem to solve, rather than converting the knowledge base into a multiple-choice exam. In some sense, knowledge is inherently active. What it enables you to do is important, and this is what "learning while (or by) doing" seeks to exploit.

1.4. A naive theory of coaching

Brown points out that our theory of coaching involves a computer-based coach with many different kinds of knowledge. He indicates the lesson that we learned in GUIDON, that it is more than an expert system, to say the very least. Yes, the tutor has expert problem-solving strategies, but it needs knowledge about explanation, how to model the student and tutoring or kibitzing strategies (an interruptive strategy for probing the student's understanding and presenting information). From all of this, we construct the model of the user, a differential model, in which difference in behavior is explained in terms of a difference in knowledge.

One thing we haven't considered here is *metacognitive knowledge*, such as knowledge about the mind, memory, and learning. Schank's model of memory organization is one example: It describes how new experience is stored and generalized. When a problem solver uses such knowledge to improve his problem solving or learning, we call such reasoning metacognition (Collins and Brown, ress). Researchers take for granted that we also need a strong theory of how people learn in order to design an ideal tutoring program. Our study of misconceptions and student models in general is just the first step in this direction. Goldstein drew a box in his early diagrams that he called the *learning model*, corresponding to this idea. Nothing in our programs corresponds to it. However, Anderson has recently incorporated a learning theory in the design of his tutors for Lisp programming and geometry (Anderson, et al., 1984a).

1.5. Making latent knowledge manifest

An important theme behind ITS research is the attempt to make *latent knowledge* manifest. Latent knowledge hasn't been expressed or stated, but is implicit in the behavior of a person or some physical process. By manifest, we mean articulating it in words or making it visible in pictures. A simulation shows this in a simple way. We can simulate how a device works by using graphics and show the student step by step the mechanism and the interactions. The design and the process might be very hard to see if you look at the real device; graphically it can be simplified and idealized. This is the central idea in STEAMER. Another example is modelling the knowledge of an expert; we are taking the expert's knowledge and making it manifest. An expert might not be able to state what he does, but we look for patterns in his problem solving. We say, "You have a procedure that you use. There is something you do that is regular." We make the procedure explicit.

John Brown also speaks of *reifying*—to make concrete or to make visible (Brown, 1983). For example, we can reify the space of possible ways of solving a problem. One strategy we might use for teaching is to show a student a graphic history of his various steps and compare alternative ways of solving the problem. Here is a simple example: We show the student a tree of rules and goals and show the student that if he had done things in a different order, it would not have been necessary to do as much work. This is one idea that we are pursuing in NEOMYCIN. Specifically, if the student asked a general question first, let's say about infection, rather than considering specific infections, he might save ten questions about specific infections by determining categorically that there is no infection. One way to show that is to lay out a kind of visible history and say, "You went all of the way down here in all of these details, but if you had done it this way, you could have pruned the search earlier." This is what John Brown means by reifying the problem space.

Another example of latent knowledge is the idea of a *plan* behind a procedure. Several examples occur in the programming tutor. There is the superficial behavior: What is it that the expert does? Behind that is a plan: Why is that a good procedure? To give the example of medicine again, I might ask, "Does the patient have a fever, has he lost weight, has he had a trauma, has he fallen?" This is my superficial behavior, what you see me doing when I solve the problem. More abstractly described, my procedure is to reason categorically. I'm asking very general high-level questions before going down any path. We can now state the procedure separately, as an abstraction of the original questions. Obviously, the idea of reasoning categorically has nothing specifically to do with medicine. We could also ask why it makes sense to reason categorically. If the search space is organized hierarchically, it can be more efficient to work from the top and work down rather than to work from the bottom, because you can eliminate possible paths. We call this description the plan behind the procedure.

Finally, the Socratic method is another way of making latent knowledge manifest. Asking the student questions makes him realize that there are things that are incomplete or contradictory in his knowledge. The Socratic teacher chooses examples that will force the students to realize a paradox in his behavior and in his understanding, and leads him to express a question that will resolve that misunderstanding.

In building a teaching system, we're making different kinds of knowledge explicit: the domain knowledge, the method for explaining and the tutoring rules about interrupting and making presentations. We also make meta-cognitive knowledge explicit, knowledge about learning. To "teach" all of this to a computer involves theorizing, not just writing down what we all know for granted, but an abstraction process.

In building an expert system to be used for teaching, we learned that it is advantageous to work with good teachers. A good teacher has theories of knowledge organization and inference and learning. That is, he has knowledge about his reasoning, metacognitive knowledge, which he can impart to students to help them learn.

Similarly, because of our interest in making latent knowledge manifest, not every expert system makes a good tutoring system. In fact, we might ask whether any expert system makes a good tutoring system today. We need certain kinds of knowledge to be explicit and separate, which is the point of NEOMYCIN (Clancey and Letsinger, 1984), in which the diagnosis procedure is separated from the facts about diseases. We may need alternative ways of solving problems, including the ability to understand misconceptions. We may need to justify the knowledge base to help the student understand why it's correct. In particular, to understand misconceptions, we need to understand why the preferred rules are correct.

2. Survey of specific systems

2.1. SCHOLAR

The SCHOLAR Program is the first attempt to use an AI representation as the basis of a teaching program (Carbonell, 1970). Carbonell saw the possibility of stating the teaching knowledge separately from the domain knowledge which was to be taught. So we have a semantic network for stating geographical facts, and we have a program for carrying out the interaction with the student. One of the later developments of SCHOLAR, work done by Collins, enabled answering questions that were not stored in the knowledge base. The program performs what is called "plausible reasoning" to infer what might be true, given certain assumptions about the world (Collins, 1978). It is a very interesting development, because people now understand this form of meta-cognition to be an important part of expertise. SCHOLAR is the first attempt to use AI for building a general system, allowing multiple use of the same knowledge, rather than encoding it as part of the teaching program.

Figure 16-2 shows part of an interaction with SCHOLAR, illustrating a mixed-initiative form that Carbonell and Collins sought to develop. The program asks a question, "What is the language of Argentina?" The student answers, "Probably Spanish." The program says, "Very Good," and then asks another question. A transition-network parser is used here.

You also see the student taking initiative, rather than answering the question that the program has asked. This clearly inspired Carbonell a great deal. In comparison with earlier AI programs, SCHOLAR allows the student to do whatever he wants at any point. The dialogue also illustrates retrieval of information from the semantic network. There is a hierarchy of countries and geographical areas, so it knows that Peru is located in South America. It has superconcepts and instantiations of them. Carbonell also used a clever kind of response, "Now answer the question you didn't answer before." This reminds me of how people were so excited about automatic spelling correction in early Lisp programs, reminiscent of the joke about the dancing dog—it is superficial, but intriguing that it can be done at all. Carbonell also used a timer to see how long the student takes to solve the problem. The program interrupts after a while, and says: "You are taking a long time."

When the student asks, "Is Asuncion hot?", the program says, "Since it is part of Paraguay, yes." This is an example of a fact that is not stored explicitly. The program knows that if a city is located inside of a country, and country has a climatic property like temperature or rainfall, then we can infer plausibly (with uncertainty) that the city has the same property. This does not always work, and it is not too hard to think of counterexamples where there is a country with coastal and mountain cities.

More complex examples are given by Collins. The student asks whether a particular country engages in a certain type of manufacturing or trade. The program has associated with it a number indicating how important each fact is, in this case importance of various trade facts related to each country. Let's say the question was, "Does Brazil have oil wells?" The program would look at other countries and see that oil wells were mentioned, but not for Brazil, and that these wells were very highly ranked. So if a

What is the language of Argentina?

** Probably Spanish

Very good. Approximately what is the area of Argentina?

** Tell me something about Peru

Peru is a country.
It is located in South America.
The capital of peru is Lima.
Now answer the question you didn't answer before.

** The area of Argentina is 1,100,000 square miles

Approximately true, but a more exact value is 1,200,000.
The eastern bordering country of Peru is ---.

** Catholicism

Wrong. Catholicism is not a country but a religion.
The correct answer is: Brazil.
Where is Peru?

** Is Asuncion hot?

Since Asuncion is part of Paraguay, yes.

** What is the most important difference between Peru and Paraguay?

The primary difference is: The population of Peru is larger by a factor of 7.8.

Fig. 16-2. Excerpt from a dialogue with SCHOLAR.

country has oil wells, it was rated at number 9, out of 10. So the program could infer that if Brazil had oil wells, and it were important for Brazil, it would be rated high, and would therefore be in the knowledge base. Assuming that you know everything about the world to a certain point, a certain degree of importance, the lack of knowledge allows you to make an assumption about what is true. This is another form of meta-cognitive ability. We can say with some degree of belief that certain things are true or false, even if we have not learned them explicitly. We can infer them from general patterns of what we know. The idea was developed further to explain how we can answer so quickly that we don't know certain things. Collins also did some psychological studies with Quillian, measuring how long it takes people to answer certain questions, and used the results to support a model of memory.

2.2. WHY

WHY is the follow-on work to SCHOLAR, developed by Collins and Stevens after Carbonell passed away (Collins and Stevens, 1980). They changed the domain from purely factual reasoning of geography to casual reasoning of meteorology, opening up many new problems.

Figure 16-3 shows the program generating certain questions for the student: "Do you think the Amazon jungle has heavy or light rainfall?" Collins has made explicit the teaching rules for generating these questions. They are stated abstractly, referring to predictions, particular cases, prior causes, general rules, insufficient causes. This kind of terminology is a major advance. It inspired me in GUIDON to express teaching knowledge abstractly, separate from the medical knowledge.

Ask for a prediction about a particular case.

Do you think the Amazon jungle has heavy or light rainfall?
** Heavy rainfall

Ask for prior causes

Why does the Amazon jungle have heavy rainfall?
** Because it has mountains nearby.

Form a general rule for an insufficient cause.

Do you think that any place with mountains has heavy rainfall?
** Yes

Pick a counter example for an insufficient cause and
Ask for prior causes.

Southern California has mountains.
Why doesn't Southern California have heavy rainfall?

Fig. 16-3. Excerpt from a dialogue with WHY.

Collins attempted to mimic the Socratic dialogues that we find in the writings of PLATO. He also analyzed teachers teaching law by the case method and looked at physicians teaching medicine. Notice the systematic logic behind these questions: "Why does the Amazon jungle have heavy rainfall?" The student has just said that he thinks it has heavy rainfall. The student replies, "Because it has mountains nearby." This suggests that the student has a rule, "if there are mountains, then there is heavy rainfall." The program can look in the knowledge base to see if it is always true that mountains are correlated with heavy rainfall. The program observes that's an insufficient cause in its model of rainfall. So it asks, "Do you think any place with mountains has heavy rainfall?" This forces the student to realize that he has stated something that is not a necessary factor. Here the student says: "Yes, of course." Now the program looks in the knowledge base and picks a counterexample. We have gone far beyond just retrieving facts, which occurs in SCHOLAR, to analyzing the student's responses to see if he understands the particular model that we want to teach. Again, the idea of formalizing the questioning methods is a major accomplishment.

Collins and Stevens built in a tutoring plan that detects the facts that the student doesn't seem to understand. A teaching strategy then selects one of these misconceptions to work with. It says something like: "Deal with misconceptions before unnecessary factors." In this way, the program maintains a plan for its dialogue.

It's not clear how well WHY could understand the student's misconceptions. In their follow-on program, Collins and Stevens enumerate possible misconceptions to be recognized. After working with many students, they found patterns in what students tended to believe. The tutor checks to see if a student has these particular misconceptions. When I said, "The program now sees that the student knows the rule," I don't know how explicitly this was modelled. In particular, it does not appear that WHY followed the student during long dialogues, characterizing model changes and consistency.

2.3. WEST

WEST is an example of a coach system. It is built on top of the game "How the West was Won." It is a child's game, a variation of a game also called "Chutes and Ladders." There are sets of spinners or dials, and the student spins these to get three numbers, which he can combine using subtraction, addition, and multiplication, or group the numbers using parentheses. The objective of the game is to get to the end first. You have the advantage of various ladders, which are shortcuts. So you want to choose the mathematical operators that will allow you to take the shortcuts. If you land on a place where your opponent is located, that bumps the opponent back. Therefore, it might be an advantage not to maximize your own forward progress, but to land where your opponent is to make him go back.

The game was originally available on the PLATO system. PLATO is the tutoring environment that was developed by Computer Development Corporation, CDC, in the 1960s. Given that this program was intended to teach mathematics, Brown and Burton decided that it would be good to add a coach to observe and critique the student's use of the various operators.

They developed a paradigm that they call *Issues and Examples*. They enumerated in the program all of the various kinds of operator combinations that a student should be able to use, called *issues*. For example, a student should be able to know that multiplication can be applied next to a parenthesis for example; this is legitimate syntax. Obviously the first thing that the student should know is that he can use any of these operators. To give a simple example, the program watches the student as he plays the game, maybe over several sessions, and after a while notices that there is a pattern, say, the student never uses parentheses. If the student used parentheses at various times, then he might be able to play better. So, the program finds an opportunity to interrupt and says: "You never use parentheses and if you used parentheses, as in this example, you would be able to land here and you would be way down here . . ." The student would see that using parentheses was to his advantage. This was the idea: The interruption should be well-motivated by something that the student will understand. You shouldn't just say at some random time "You never use parentheses." Rather, pick a moment when the student will appreciate what parentheses are all about; this will help him remember. This is one of WEST's kibitzing strategies concerning when to interrupt: Pick a time when there is a good example of an issue that you want to bring to the student's attention.

The study of WEST was very complex and I strongly recommend to you the paper by Burton that appears in *Intelligent Tutoring Systems*. Their analysis of strategies is impressive. They found that there were students who were using the PLATO system with these color graphics who enjoyed the game so much, they would keep trying to go back in order to make the game last longer. This raises a problem: The student modelling program that is looking at parentheses may be missing a more general plan. So Brown and Burton invented the idea of what they called "a tear" in the model: Can you detect a time when you think you don't understand what the student is doing? For example, suppose that the student seems to be using parentheses some times, but not always, and you can't understand the pattern. One way of understanding tear is that there are constant breaks in known patterns. It raises the larger issues of how do we detect strategies, and how do we detect if a model is good or bad, and what does it mean to recognize new strategies that were not built into the program?

The issues and examples paradigm is very useful for understanding how to build a tutoring or teaching system. The idea is very simple. You build into the program concepts or rules (the issues) that you want to teach the student, in this case the use of mathematical operators. Then you build in recognizers (procedures) for detecting whether or not the student knows each issue. In GUIDON the issues are the EMYCIN rules, and the recognizers are replaced by a single, general modelling program, which attempts to determine whether the student knows the rules used by the EMYCIN expert program. In contrast, in WEST each issue has a program for recognizing it, called a *specialist*.

Today in the US there is increasing interest in applying some of these early ideas, especially programs like SCHOLAR and WEST. At San Francisco State University, and in several other universities in California, they are trying to teach high school teachers how to use this paradigm in their own areas of expertise. They are receiving computers from Hewlett Packard, new Lisp machines and networks. This is encouraging because it is something that researchers don't have the time to do—setting up projects to teach high school teachers what we did ten years ago and trying to make the ideas practical.

To summarize the research paradigm, we are stating teaching rules in an attempt to formalize principles. We've considered three examples: The WHY system illustrates the principle of constructing a counterexample for an insufficient factor. In GUIDON (in an earlier lecture) we considered part of the procedure for completing a topic; GUIDON simply states a domain rule rather than belaboring the discussion. In WEST, we considered the principle of illustrating an issue by an example that is dramatically superior to the move made by the student. I think this shows a science in a very early stage of writing down what is intuitively, in common sense terms, believed by the researchers to be reasonable.

After this, we must represent this knowledge explicitly so it can be reasoned about by the programs and can be explained. Every complex system like GUIDON will have hundreds of teaching rules. They form another knowledge base, that we want to be easy to change. The program has to be able to explain its behavior, easy to modify, and so on. Next, we must study this formalized knowledge and understand why these are good things to do. What is the underlying model of learning and of human reasoning that makes these good teaching rules? For example, if we look at fifty GUIDON rules, we might find that they are inconsistent. Maybe we want to build different versions of GUIDON that systematically test alternative ways of teaching. For example, Collins studies Socratic tutoring in many different domains.

This is a good place to mention the work of Beverly Woolf. She went back to GUIDON, studied it in some detail, and restated the tutoring discourse according to natural language conceptions of patterns in a dialogue. She essentially tried to extract the strategies that were implicit in the alternative ways of tutoring that I had compiled together in GUIDON's rules. Her program, the MENO-TUTOR, reasons in more layers of abstraction about what to do (Woolf and McDonald, 1984).

2.4. The WUMPUS ADVISOR

Goldstein and his colleagues developed a coach for the WUMPUS game, adapting it for teaching probabilistic reasoning to a student (Goldstein, 1982). In a manner similar to SCHOLAR, WEST, and GUIDON, Goldstein used production rules for stating teaching principles. Various rules produce explanations and select examples. In the game, there are many caves, bats and pits. You move through the caves to find your way out or to find some treasure. When you arrive in a particular cave, you receive information about what might be nearby. You are told that it's cold or that you can hear certain sounds. You know that pits will have cold air coming from them, and so on. As you go through this network of caves, you can collect evidence of what is nearby.

At one point the coach might interrupt and say, "Mary, it isn't necessary to take such large risks with pits. We have seen that multiple evidence is more dangerous than single evidence for bats . . ." We want to teach the student the general rule preferring single dangers over multiple dangers, and this becomes instantiated or specialized for three different types of dangers. Thus, here a previous explanation about how the rule applies to bats is referred to when explaining its application to pits. Goldstein points out that the program needs to keep records of what it has explained already so it has an opportunity to draw an analogy. Notice that in this formal domain, unlike medicine or meteorology, there is no underlying causal model, just axioms describing how the world works. This greatly simplifies the modeling problem.

2.5. TURTLE

The next three programs are concerned with teaching computer programming. We see a student's program and want to understand its design. What is the student's plan? Why is he using these steps in this way?

"Turtle" was one of Papert and DiSessa's constructions for teaching using LOGO (Papert, 1980). The instructions in the language are very simple, you can simply turn the turtle or you can move in a certain direction or you can have it lower its pen and draw as it moves. They actually have a mechanical device that draws on paper in the room; the student types in the program and the little robot turtle moves around. In this way the students can watch what their programs do, another example of reification. This was part of Papert's idea of an environment that would give students feedback.

The TURTLE system is extremely simple; it has the capability to only write four programs, and the solutions are canned (built into the program). The program is able to detect certain types of errors. It has prespecified hints that it prints out, which are intended to help the student (FIG. 16-4).

Here is how the program proceeds. The problem is to draw a well with a roof on it. We have a box, a square and then a pole. It's like a triangle on top of a box. Miller analyzed in detail the various ways that people solve this problem. In the interaction the student says that his first step is to draw the top using another procedure. Then he wants to have the pen go 200 steps forward, draw a box, and then stop. This is his program for drawing a well with a roof. The program has to relate the terminology of the student's names for his programs to the internal names that the programmer has defined. This is a very interesting problem in programming tutors. The modelling program has to understand what the variables stand for. The program infers here that "Top" is the roof of the well and "Draw 200" is the pole and "Box" is the student's name for the base. This was done by building into the program various synonyms that people are likely to use.

Figure 16-4 shows a mapping between the student behavior and the internal model of the task. It shows in a simple way the importance of being able to recognize alternative solutions, in this case by using something as trivial as different terminology. Next, the student defines these functions for Top and Box, and the program analyzes where the pen moves around.

Next the TURTLE program points out that there is some basic step that has been left out. It says, you have provided no "Set-up" for the Well task. "Set-up" is a general programming concept. Before you call another procedure you have to get the turtle in the right position to do the next procedure. It's a kind of initialization that makes the next procedure perform correctly. If you look at the picture, the roof might have been sideways, or maybe the pole might have the wrong angle. The program analyzes what the drawing looks like and relates it to what the correct step should be. It points out that two steps were left out as part of this interface.

This is a very simple example of conveying to the student that programming has certain plans behind it and there are certain recurrent operations in programming, in particular, performing a set-up as part of calling a subprocedure. The program has

```
First step? TOP
Next step? DRAW 200
Next step? BOX
Next step? QUIT
OK, WELL is defined!

Let me see if I understand your program:
The function TOP draws the ROOF of the WELL-TASK.
The code: DRAW 200 draws the POLE of the WELL-TASK.
The function BOX draws the BASE of the WELL-TASK.

Does that seem correct? YES
```

After the student defines functions TOP and BOX

```
Did you intend to interface the function TOP to the step DRAW
200 by following the path C D? YES

Here is the interface you defined between the mainsteps in the
function TOP and the step DRAW 200 in WELL:

        TURN 180


Analysis:

Correct code        Commentary

TURN 180            Correct interface to turn through angle BCD
MOVE 50             Missing interface to move over segment CD
TURN 90             Missing interface to turn through angle CDE

. . .

You provided no setup for the WELL-TASK.
```

Fig. 16-4. Excerpt from a dialog with TURTLE.

related the student's behavior to the underlying model, isolated an error, told the student what the error is, and indicated what he should do differently. Notice that there is no attempt to understand the student's error, why he did this, just what he did wrong and the correction that should be performed.

2.6. MENO

MENO (Soloway, et al., 1981) is the work of Elliot Soloway, who is now at Yale and did his thesis work at the University of Massachusetts in the late 1970s. MENO attempts to understand a student's programming bug, to articulate the misconception. It not only fixes the plan as in TURTLE, it helps the student resolve his misconception. To summarize these levels: There is the surface behavior of the program; there is the plan, which is the design; and there is the underlying misconception that generates the design that generates the program.

Figure 16-5 shows the input to the MENO program; it is a very difficult task to understand a program like this. It requires knowledge of the problem that is to be solved and knowledge about alternative solutions. The purpose of this program is to compute an average. It initializes the sum and then counts how many numbers have been input. While the input is not equal to 999 (a *sentinel*, a strange number that would not be part of the input) we add the input to the sum and increment the count. Notice that the student adds 1 to the input and then continues. This obviously takes a long time, but eventually we get to 999, exit the loop, and divide the number of times we've gone around into the sum.

A student's program...

```
PROGRAM AVERAGE1(INPUT, OUTPUT);
VAR
    SUM, POSIDEN, COUNT: INTEGER;
      AVE: REAL;
  BEGIN
      SUM: = 0;
      COUNT: = 0;
      READ(POSIDEN);
      WHILE POSIDEN<>9999 DO
        BEGIN
          SUM : = SUM + POSIDEN;
          COUNT : = COUNT + 1;
          POSIDEN : = POSIDEN + 1;
        END;
      AVE : = SUM / COUNT;
      WRITELN('THE AVERAGE IS ', AVE)
  END.
```

Fig. 16-5. Program interpreted by MENO.

The student has made a mistake of putting the READ statement outside of his loop. Why did he do that? Soloway and his collaborators have performed a very interesting analysis to get at the misconceptions.

Consider what MENO says to the student (FIG. 16-6). First, like TURTLE it finds a mapping between the student's names and the internal names of the program. It says,

MENO's analysis...

POSIDEN is the New Value Variable
COUNT is the Counter Variable
SUM is the Running Total Variable

You modified POSIDEN by adding POSIDEN to 1
where as...
you should modify the New Value Variable by calling the READ procedure: READ(POSIDEN).

Two misconceptions can be associated with this bug:

1. You might be thinking that the single call to the READ procedure at the top of your program is enough to define a variable which will always be read in from the terminal....

2. You might be thinking that POSIDEN is like COUNT... The computer does not know to reinterpret + 1 in the former case to be like a READ.

Fig. 16-6. Excerpt from a dialogue with MENO.

"Positive identifier is the new value variable and count is the counter variable." There is a general plan that MENO has for doing averages. It doesn't have variable names like X, W, A, B, but it has general names that correspond to the meaning of the variable: to get the new value, the counter, the running total, etc. And so again, we're relating the student's behavior to the plan that's in the program. MENO has many plans for the problems that it solves. The program points out the bug, "You modified the new value variable by adding 1 to it whereas you should modify it by calling the READ-procedure."

MENO then goes further than TURTLE. It has a library of misconceptions, not generated by the program, but built-in by Soloway. One possibility is that the student thinks that READ is like a declaration and so, every time he mentions X, its value should be read. It is like saying that X is an integer, describing a property that should persist through the entire program.

MENO builds a semantic net, a parse of the program, and then relates each of the variables and the operations to an internal model of the problem. Then it associates certain bugs with various plans. The analysis is not generative; the program cannot take an arbitrary program and understand it. It has to be an "Average program" or another one in the library. Explaining bugs requires a lot of creativity. The explanation of the bug as an alternative model is often as complicated and difficult as what you are trying to teach. People probably rely a great deal on experience and receiving information from students. It's uncertain how many teachers could understand what the students are doing. We are certainly far from being able to write a program that could generate similar explanations for misconceptions, especially in domains like medicine or programming.

MENO was re-implemented by Lewis Johnson in his dissertation research as the PROUST program (Johnson and Soloway, 1984). Rather than matching bugs as specific segments of code, it constructs a complete parse of the code on different levels of abstraction. This provides a more robust, generative capability for understanding student programs and is the first step beyond the template approach of TURTLE and MENO. The misconceptions are still built-in, but the program bugs are stated abstractly, rather than as specific lines of code to be matched.

2.7. The MACSYMA Advisor

The MACSYMA Advisor (Genesereth, 1982) is very similar in style to the MENO system. We have the same problem of understanding a sequence of student behavior. We want to extract the user's plan. MACSYMA, developed at MIT by Joel Moses, is a mathematical manipulation system for simplifying and combining the equations. The problem is to take a user's sequence of interactions with MACSYMA and to provide help or consultation.

Figure 16-7 shows an example in which the user is surprised by an answer of zero. The user asks for help, indicating that there is a problem. The point is, when we type in commands to a program like MACSYMA, we have some kind of plan in mind, that is, a method or approach for solving a problem. In this case the user was trying to solve an equation (to determine values of X for which the formula evaluates to zero). The MACSYMA Advisor has to examine the sequence of user actions, and given the user's goal, infer his plan for using the MACSYMA program. The Advisor has a built-in library of different ways of using MACSYMA, somewhat similar to MENO's library of program patterns. The Advisor provides a remediation in terms of correct set of steps of what to do, plus an explanation of the student's behavior in terms of a misconception.

The user says, "I was trying to solve equation that was stated in D6 for X and I got 0." At this point, the program determines that, if this is the user's goal and this is what he did, he must believe that the COEFF command or operator has a certain effect. The user has a misconception. He believes that COEFF returns the coefficient of a particular formula, but it returns the coefficient of X to the first power. The program goes on to say that, "If this is what you are trying to do, it's important that the expression be expanded with respect to the variable, and you should use RATCOEFF to get the right result."

The important point is how the MACSYMA Advisor constructs this interpretation. Unlike the other programs we've seen, where the misconceptions were pre-enumerated, the MACSYMA advisor has the capability of generating the misconception by an analysis of the student's plan.

To make the user's actions fit together in a coherent explanation, the program makes certain assumptions about the user's beliefs. The Advisor indicates the actual input and output for each operator and general constraints that the input and output

```
(C7) (A:COEFF(D6, X, 2), B:COEFF(D6, X, 1),
      C:COEFF(D6, X, 0))$

(C8) (- B + SQRT(B**2 - 4*A*C)) / (2*A);

(D8)          0

(C9) HELP()$

------------------------------------------------------------
```

USER: I was trying to solve D6 for X and I got 0.

ADVISOR: Did you expect COEFF to return the coefficient of D6?

USER: Yes, doesn't it?

ADVISOR: COEFF(exp, var, pow) returns the correct coefficient of var^{pow} in exp only if exp is expanded with respect to var. Perhaps you should use RATCOEFF.

USER: Okay, thanks. Bye.

Fig. 16-7. Excerpt from a dialogue with the MACSYMA Adviser.

must satisfy. Thus, the interpretation of the user's misconception, as a model of his beliefs, is stated as both specific computation results and general facts about MACSYMA's operators.

In particular, the analysis shown here is made complete by assuming that the user believes that this particular operator, COEFF, returns a particular value that has a certain input and output. This assertion about COEFF is technically incorrect, but it makes the plan coherent; the user's sequence of behavior is now understandable. Constructing such a plan is a complex search problem. The program generates multiple parses in both a bottom-up and top-down way. Having the behavior constrains possible interpretations, and knowing the goal constrains the possible operations that are performed. Different template (canned) plans are used by the program to generate and to recognize the sequence of behavior.

We see here the power of a logic formalism in which Genesereth expresses the various constraints on each of the operators and what the operators accomplish. Again, an appropriate language enables writing a program that can reason about the knowledge involved. If these operators were in LISP, the plan recognizer wouldn't be able to reason about them. Notice how far this is from the SCHOLAR system, which has only an idea of right and wrong answers. Here we generate a structural analysis of what the user believes, given his behavior. I think this is one of the best examples of student modelling. It shows us how to generate misconceptions, rather than building them into the program. Contrast this with the work of Stevens and Collins where the misconceptions about meteorology and heavy rainfall are pre-enumerated, so the program has only a fixed library of possible misconceptions. It helps of course to be working in a mathematical, closed domain. Genesereth has gone on to develop the ideas of the representation system that was used here, MRS, and to examine in more detail architectures for problem solving (Genesereth, 1983).

2.8. DEBUGGY

DEBUGGY is a program for modelling a student's knowledge of the subtraction procedure. It models incorrect procedures, to be contrasted with modelling (factual) misconceptions. DEBUGGY builds a procedure that describes how a student does subtraction, based on a set of example problems solved by the student.

The idea of DEBUGGY is that there are systematic errors that people make and we can analyze the problems to detect these errors. You should realize that there is significant computational problem in generating this description from all of the possible alternative procedures DEBUGGY can construct. On the order of a hundred bugs were found to occur in students. There were thousands of students whose problems were examined.

2.9. Repair theory

Recalling the distinction between describing student behavior and the rationale behind this behavior, Kurt VanLehn's project was to understand where subtraction bugs come from. We start with the surface behavior: The student can't subtract from 0 or doesn't subtract from 0. We describe the procedure, and now we ask, "Why does he do that?" Where did this bug come from? It is a model based on how people learn. In repair theory, rather than just recognizing the bugs, we try to understand the cause of the misconception. This is like taking the MACSYMA Advisor one more step. Suppose you have isolated a misconception, what is the reason for it? It's an attempt to understand learning problems. Recalling the MENO example, why does the student believe that READ is a kind of declaration. How can we explain why students have certain bugs and not others? We want a theory of where the bugs come from that allows us to generate the bugs and explain the systematic errors in more primitive terms.

The central idea in repair theory is that an incomplete correct procedure causes an impasse during problem solving, which is repaired by a general problem solver and critics. This is an interesting first-order theory which seems to have a lot of power. In one sense, this is the idea of an *overlay model* again: The students know a subset of the correct procedure. But the next part is different. Suppose a student doesn't know what to do when there is a zero on top or when it's necessary to borrow (in a subtraction problem), but they do everything else correctly. Without a complete procedure, the student gets stuck. This is called an *impasse*.

For example, if you don't know what to do when the top number is smaller, you have to do something. You're supposed to write down some number when you're doing a subtraction, you can't just leave it blank. Students know that and so they need some kind of alternative way of acting. When they reach this impasse, they repair their procedure in some way. This is the origin of the name "repair theory." VanLehn assumes that people have general problem-solving methods that they will follow when they get stuck. They don't sit there paralyzed, they do something. He wanted to study how a repaired impasse might generate bugs.

Figure 16-8 gives an example. Suppose we take the bug of not being able to borrow when the top digit is smaller than the bottom digit (not being able to subtract 6 from 3 here). This is modelled by deleting part of the procedure that allows us to behave when we reach that situation. It's a simple production rule view of subtraction. There are situations and operations you can perform. If you see a large number on top of a small number, you just look it up in your table. So if you see 8 over 2, you can look it up: $8-2=6$.

```
1. Delete rule of procedure:
        "borrow when top digit is too small"


2. Problem solving ends with an impasse:

             638
           - 462
           -----
              ?6       => impasse occurs in second column


3. Different repair methods produce different procedural bugs:

        REPAIR                          BUG

        Skip                            blank-instead-of-borrow
        Quit                            doesn't-borrow
        Swap vertically                 smaller-from-larger
        Dememoize                       zero-instead-of-borrow
```

Fig. 16-8. Analysis of a bug provided by Repair Theory.

But now you get to $3-6$, and let's say that there is no table for that. You can't write down -3. It's not permitted to write down a negative number here, but you have to write something down. So it is time to borrow. But if we delete the knowledge about borrowing, there is an impasse.

VanLehn gives the general problem-solving strategies that he believes are sufficient to generate the observed bugs. First is to skip the column, write down nothing. Some students do that. Second is to quit, stop the problem right there. Don't write down any more numbers, go on to the next problem. Third, (this is very creative) just turn the numbers around and subtract. Fourth, called *dememoize*, just look up the answer in an idiosyncratic table of arithmetic facts.

These repair strategies will generate different bugs. We have the opportunity now of systematically deleting rules in the correct subtraction procedure, applying the problem-solving strategies and generating the bugs. We can go backwards from actual problems and determine how the people applied the strategies and so on. DEBUGGY discovered 89 different bugs in several thousand problem sets. Repair theory explains (generates) 21 bugs that have been observed. Also interesting, it generates 10 bugs that have not been observed but are at least plausible or possible. VanLehn uses the term *star bug* (from language theory) for a bug that we, for many reasons, believe could never occur. (This is from the idea of a sentence in a language that we would never expect anyone to utter.) Obviously we want the fewest number of star bugs; VanLehn takes this as a measure of quality of his theory that there is only one star bug. As for the ten originally unobserved bugs, he want back and found some of these in the problem sets. There are many detailed parts of this theory; it has recently been extended to explain the origin of impasses in what is called *Step Theory* (VanLehn, 1983).

Finally, *bug migration* concerns changes in bugs over time. Using Repair Theory, VanLehn and Brown were able to make certain predictions, based on the idea if the student has one bug, he might replace it by another one because his impasse says the same. He still doesn't know how to borrow, but he might apply a different problem-solving strategy. One time he might leave it blank, and the next time he reverses the numbers. Thus, the bugs are related to one another, and VanLehn and Brown found a systematic change from, say, Friday to Monday when retesting the student. This also turns out to be an interesting concept because, originally, we might have said the behavior was random because the bugs seem to be changing. But a deeper analysis shows that there is some systematic pattern. VanLehn has written extensively about the problem of developing a principled theory (VanLehn, 1984). I've gone into some detail with his work because even though DEBUGGY and Repair Theory are not tutoring programs, they provide a good example of how AI methods are used to develop detailed models of human problem solving.

2.10. SOPHIE

SOPHIE is a very large, complex program of three different versions developed by Brown and Burton from about 1974 through 1978. Most of this work was done at Bolt, Beranek and Newman. SOPHIE stands for "Sophisticated Instructor for Electronics," but it was also the name of Richard Burton's dog. SOPHIE versions 1 and 2 did not contain an expert system in the sense that we define it today. At their core is a mathematical FORTRAN program that simulates how a particular circuit behaves under different loads. The simulator is used by the tutoring program to evaluate a student's diagnostic hypotheses. SOPHIE 3 is an attempt to formulate a procedure for doing diagnosis, an expert system, that the student can watch and emulate.

Recall that SOPHIE provides a reactive environment; it does not attempt to teach anything to the student in a systematic way. The student is given a version of the circuit with a bug in it, or a *fault*, as it is called in this context. He is to determine which component is faulty. The student makes measurements and then poses a hypothesis. He can ask questions about what could possibly be wrong, given the information is received.

The program starts with a fault in the circuit. The student is told various readings, such as voltage. Burton developed a "semantic grammar" for parsing the student's input. This parser consists of a set of procedures corresponding to various phrases and expressions. The parser is capable of disambiguating pronouns and filling in omitted references (anaphora). The program has a fact table in which it looks up circuit information.

The student makes a measurement, "What is the voltage between R8 and Q1?" Later he poses a hypothesis, "Is it possible that Q6 is open?" The program has to disambiguate this description, and then, using the simulator, determine if the hypothesis is consistent with the current setup of the circuit. It turns out that this is not the fault. The program points out that, if it were the fault, the measurements would have been different. To do this, it sets up the circuit again, using the student's fault and runs the FORTRAN simulation to determine how the circuit would behave given the fault that the student has stated. Using the FORTRAN simulation program in this way requires considerable intermediate knowledge structures and reasoning to set up meaningful boundary conditions for the hypothesized situation. This integration of multiple knowledge representations is a major contribution of SOPHIE research: the FORTRAN program simulates the circuit; a semantic network describes the components of the circuit; and semantic parsing procedures disambiguate student input.

The program comments that even though the student's hypothesized fault is incorrect, it is consistent with two of the values that the student received. We've seen this tight logical analysis of consistent, necessary, and sufficient factors in several programs (WHY, GUIDON, WUMPUS ADVISOR).

The student could also ask, "What are all of the things that could be wrong?" This has to be answered with respect to the current known measurements. The program has to run multiple simulations, setting up the circuit in different ways to determine all possible faults that could account for the behavior that's been observed so far. This is also a very complicated type of analysis.

While SOPHIE has no teaching knowledge in it, it provides a laboratory work bench, a kind of smart tool. In any lab, we could take a faulty circuit and have the student try a diagnosis. But here using the computer with a simulation, the student can pose hypotheses and ask for alternative analyses.

We can summarize the type of inference that SOPHIE can perform as follows:

1. Hypothetical question answering: What happens when the circuit is changed in a certain way?
2. Hypothesis evaluation: Could the circuit be faulty in some way?
3. Hypothesis generation: What could be wrong, given the information known so far?
4. Redundancy checking: Does a particular measurement add any new information, given the set of possible faults and what's been observed so far? (Is the student testing a useful hypothesis or is he just randomly making measurements?)

It is possible to apply these ideas to a tutor built upon NEOMYCIN. But imagine the difficulty of answering the question, "What if the patient didn't have a fever? What if the patient's fever were 110?" Imagine the complexity of the model of the body and the kind of computations that would be necessary to deal with any question of this form. The power of SOPHIE comes from the complete simulation model, which makes certain assumptions, of course, about how the circuit works and what the current environment is. In medicine we can't perform this hypothetical generation and question answering. We can't say everything that could be wrong. We have a model, but we don't have a basis for performing experiments for determining how the patient would behave under different environmental loads.

This is a subtle point. The problem arises not just because we have represented a small part of the space of possible diseases in NEOMYCIN. Diseases in medicine are different from faults in a circuit. Diseases in medicine are not faulty components, they are interactions that the "device" has with the world that cause the components to fail. You cannot possibly enumerate all of the world knowledge that could cause all the possible diseases that are or could be observed.

To give an example: Consider a disease like tennis elbow. Suppose someone plays tennis and gets a sore arm and he comes to you and says, "Something is wrong with my arm." You need to know to tell him to stop playing tennis. Just having a model of the body says nothing about tennis. You need to know all of the ways that people interact with the world. SOPHIE's form of electronic diagnosis has nothing to do with how the circuit interacts with the world. If the fault is caused by a room that is too warm or because somebody dropped the power regulator before they installed it, SOPHIE will fail. To restate, a disease in medicine is not a component fault, but what caused the fault in the world. [This might remind you of the difference between a procedural bug (DEBUGGY) and the problem-solving and learning process that generated this bug (Repair and Step Theory).]

There is a lot more to say about SOPHIE; read the paper in the *Intelligent Tutoring Systems* book. It explains in detail the work of deKleer which came later, involving an expert system that could perform and describe the diagnostic process.

2.11. STEAMER

STEAMER teaches how to operate a steam plant in a ship (Hollan, et al., 1984). The use of graphics coupled to a mathematical simulation program and semantic network descriptions allows the program to provide a high-fidelity conceptual model of how the steam plant works. STEAMER is the work of Stevens, Forbus, and several people of the Naval Personnel and Research Development Center, including Jim Hollan and Mike Hutchins. The project was originated by a psychologist, Mike Williams, who had experience on a ship teaching and learning steam-propulsion plant operation.

The project was designed to be put into the field as a prototype within a few years; today they are using STEAMER to train new recruits. In general, the military is excited about automating teaching because of their high turnover and the great deal of technical expertise to be learned in many different areas.

The major difficulty here is to understand the rationale for why the procedures for running the steam plant are correct, particularly to facilitate remembering and modifying them. Valves, pipes, and wires are arranged in a complicated jumble inside the ship.

When a student is brought on board, it's very hard for him to understand how things are connected to one another. Graphics provide an easy way of retrieving the information. You can look at the lubricating system and you can look at the steam system. This graphics system is connected to the underlying simulation program, using the idea of active images or "active values" in the LOOPS programming system, developed at Xerox-Parc. The program sends a message to a particular concept or a unit, say one that corresponds to a valve. The valve instance is then responsible for setting itself on the screen to reflect its value.

The procedure says, "Step 5, align the drain valves D1 and D2." Much later, it says, "Open valve I17." This is what you are supposed to do. The rationale for this procedure is not explicit—why should you do step 5 at all? Why should you do it before step 12? We want to teach the rationale as well as the procedure: Whenever steam is admitted to a chamber, you must align the drains first. If you don't, the water that is left in the chamber will mix with the steam, and high-energy water pellets will get thrown downstream.

STEAMER research included new work in explanation. Using the description of the current state of the plant, the program generates explanations of what is happening. For example, it can describe a feedback process. They've studied to some extent the problem of packaging the text and presenting overviews, as well as going through causal detail. There is some natural language work, but the research has emphasized causal modelling.

3. Conclusion

How well do these programs perform? Is anybody using them? Some of them have been tested, but there is no system that has in any significant way replaced the traditional methods of teaching. These are mainly pilot studies that demonstrate plausibility. STEAMER might be the closest to a system that has replaced some traditional teaching and maybe greatly augmented what can be taught. DEBUGGY has been used for thousands of students, but as data collection to verify the model, not interactively. MENO is being used at Yale, for teaching introductory programming. The WEST system was used as an exploratory system for a couple of months in an elementary school. SOPHIE was used experimentally for a few years over a computer network within the U.S. Recent programs by Anderson and Reiser are effectively teaching Lisp and Geometry (Anderson, et al., 1984b, Anderson, et al., 1985).

In short, education has not been turned upside down. The process of developing these ideas and getting the programs to be used is very slow. I believe that professional educators in the schools today, not the researchers who developed the programs, will be the people who eventually take these ideas and apply them.

So what is all this worth? How would we compare the state of CAI and ICAI today? There is a mixture of goals and accomplishments. I think if we did a very simple analysis of the best traditional programs today, we would say that they are much better than almost any of the ICAI tutoring systems. They are better when viewed in terms of being operating, portable programs that students can actually learn from. Many hours of work were put into designing CAI programs, with a lot of handcrafting of the design to make them useful. I know a physician at Stanford who has been cranking out CAI programs for probably 20 years. He felt embarrassed when he saw what we were doing. He felt that we were coming from another planet and believed that now all of his work was obsolete. I told him that was not true at all. He is teaching students today with his programs, and it might be ten years before we have anything to give him. That was in 1977. His programs still work, and they are teaching many students every year. ICAI is mainly a lot of promises still.

On the other hand, these promises are profound and changing not just how we think about teaching, but our understanding of what needs to be taught. We should remember that CAI systems don't have a systematic conceptual representation of what is being taught. The person who designs the traditional system is not provided with a language that allows him to write down what he knows in a structured, reusable way. Very little cumulative science or engineering is occurring. Each CAI author is building in his knowledge and not effectively sharing it with other teachers except to say, "Here is my program, you can learn from my example." The field will advance much more quickly if people could share their knowledge of learning and pedagogy, and develop formal theories. While WEST, WHY, GUIDON, and other ICAI programs take many years to develop, ICAI researchers can now say, "Here is my set of rules: Use them in your system." The idea of shared knowledge bases is something that excites me a great deal when I consider where we might be in ten or twenty years, after collecting and abstracting knowledge in tutoring and expert systems.

Acknowledgments

This paper is an edited version of a presentation given in Namur, Belgium in May, 1985, as part of the program for the International Professorship in Computer Science (Expert Systems), Universite de L'Etat, sponsored by the Belgian National Foundation for Scientific Research and IBM. I sincerely thank my friend Axel van Lamsweerde for his hospitality during my stay and for his arduous efforts to produce a transcript of this presentation. While the original transcript has been edited a great deal, this paper is intended to reflect the extemporaneous nature of an oral presentation, rather than a scholarly work. I have however added citations to bring the material up-to-date. As indicated in the text, much of the material was prepared by John Seely Brown and Richard R. Burton, or in collaboration with them. Much of what I know about Intelligent Tutoring Systems comes from working with John and Richard.

My research was sponsored in part by ONR (contract N00014-85-K-0305) and by a grant from the Josiah Macy, Jr. Foundation. Computational resources have been provided by the Sumex-Aim National Resource (NIH grant RR00785).

References

J.R. Anderson, C.F. Boyle, R. Farrell, and B. Reiser, *Cognitive principles in the design of computer tutors*, in *Proceedings of the Sixth Annual Conference of the Cognitive Science Society*, pages 2 – 10, Boulder, June, 1984.

J.R. Anderson, R. Farrell, and R. Sauers, Learning to program in LISP. *Cognitive Science*, April – June 1984, *8(2)*, 87 – 129.

J.R. Anderson, C.F. Boyle, and G. Yost, *The geometry tutor*, in *Proceedings of the Ninth International Joint Conference on Artificial Intelligence*, pages 1 – 7, Los Angeles, August, 1985. Volume 1.

J.S. Brown and R.B. Burton, Diagnostic Models for Procedural Bugs in Basic Mathematical Skills. *Cognitive Science*, April – June 1978, *2(2)*, 155 – 192.

J.S. Brown, *Process versus product—a perspective on tools for communal and informal electronic learning*, in *Education in the Electronic Age, proceedings of a conference sponsored by the Educational Broadcasting Corporation, WNET/Thirteen*, July, 1983.

J.R. Carbonell, *Mixed-initiative man-computer instructional dialogues*. Technical Report 1971, Bolt Beranek and Newman, 1970.

J.R. Carbonell and A.M. Collins, *Natural semantics in artificial intelligence*, in *Proc. 3rd IJCAI, Stanford, CA*, pages 344 – 351, IJCAI, August, 1973.

W.J. Clancey, GUIDON. In Barr and Feigenbaum (editors), *The Handbook of Artificial Intelligence*, chapter Applications-oriented AI research: Education pages 267 – 278. William Kaufmann, Inc., Los Altos, 1982.

W.J. Clancey, Qualitative student models. (To appear in the first *Annual Review of Computer Science*, Palo Alto: Annual Reviews, Inc., 1986.).

W.J. Clancey and R. Letsinger, NEOMYCIN: Reconfiguring a rule-based expert system for application to teaching. In Clancey, W.J. and Shortliffe, E.H. (Editors), *Readings in Medical Artificial Intelligence: The First Decade*, pages 361 – 381. Addison-Wesley, Reading, 1984.

A. Collins, *Fragments of a theory of human plausible reasoning*, in *Proc. 2nd Conference on Theoretical Issues in Natural Language Processing*, pages 194 – 201, TINLAP, July, 1978.

A. Collins and J.S. Brown, The computer as a tool for learning through reflection. In H. Mandl and A. Lesgold (editors), *Learning Issues for Intelligent Tutoring Systems*, Springer, New York, In press.

A. Collins and A.L. Stevens, *Goals and strategies of interactive teachers*. BBN Technical Report 4345, Bolt, Beranek, and Newman, 1980.

M.R. Genesereth, The role of plans in intelligent teaching systems. In D. Sleeman and J.S. Brown (editors), *Intelligent Tutoring Systems*, pages 137 – 155. Academic Press, New York, 1982.

M.R. Genesereth, *An overview of meta-level architecture*, in *Proceedings of The National Conference on Artificial Intelligence*, pages 119 – 124, August, 1983.

I.P. Goldstein, *The Computer as Coach: An Athletic Paradigm for Intellectual Education*. AI Memo 389, AI Laboratory, Massachusetts Institute of Technology, 1977.

I. Goldstein, *Developing a computational representation for problem solving skills*, in *Proc. Carnegie-Mellon Conference on Problem Solving and Education: Issues in Teaching and Research*, October 9 – 10, 1978.

I.P. Goldstein, The genetic graph: a representation for the evolution of procedural knowledge. In D. Sleeman and J.S. Brown (editors), *Intelligent Tutoring Systems*, pages 51 – 77. Academic Press, London, 1982.

J.D. Hollan, E.L. Hutchins, and L. Weitzman, STEAMER: An interactive inspectable simulation-based training system. *The AI Magazine*, 1984, *5(2)*, 15 – 27.

W. Lewis Johnson and Elliot Soloway. *Intention-Based Diagnosis of Programming Errors*, in *Proceedings of the National Conference on Artificial Intelligence*, pages 162 – 168, Austin, TX, August, 1984.

J.L. Kolodner, Maintaining organization in a dynamic long-term memory. *Cognitive Science*, 1983, *7*, 243 – 280.

S. Papert, *Mindstorms: Children, Computers, and Powerful Ideas*. New York: Basic Books, Inc. 1980.

R.C. Schank, Failure-driven memory. *Cognition and Brain Theory*, 1981, *4(1)*, 41 – 60.

D. Sleeman and J.S. Brown, (editors), *Intelligent Tutoring Systems*. New York: Academic Press 1982.

E.M. Soloway, B. Woolf, E. Rubin, and P. Barth, *Meno-II: An intelligent tutoring system for novice programmers*, in *Proceedings of the Seventh International Joint Conference on Artificial Intelligence*, pages 975 – 977, Vancouver, August, 1981.

E.M. Soloway, E. Rubin, B. Woolf, J. Bonar, and W. L. Johnson, *Meno-II: An AI-based programming tutor*. Technical Report CSD/RR No. 258, Yale University, December 1982.

K. VanLehn, *Human procedural skill acquisition: Theory, model, and psychological validation*, in *Proceedings of the National Conference on AI*, pages 420 – 423, Washington, D.C., August, 1983.

K. VanLehn, J.S. Brown, and J. Greeno, Competitive argumentation in computational theories of cognition. In Kintsch, Miller, and Polson (editors), *Method and Tactics in Cognitive Science*, pages 235 – 262. Lawrence Erlbaum Associates, Hillsdale, NJ, 1984.

E. Wenger, AI and the communication of knowledge: an overview of intelligent teaching systems. To be published by Morgan-Kaufmann, Los Altos, CA.

K.T. Westcourt, M. Beard, and M. Gould, *Knowledge-based adaptive curriculum sequences for CAI: Application of a network representation.* Tech Report 288, Stanford University, Institute for Mathematical Studies in the Social Sciences, 1977.

B. Woolf and D.D. McDonald, *Context-dependent transitions in tutoring discourse*, in *Proceedings of the National Conference on Artificial Intelligence*, pages 355 – 361, Austin, August, 1984.

Section C

Defense applications of artificial intelligence

17

Artificial intelligence and simulation

An application to logistics modeling

Gerald W. Hopple

Editors' note *This paper looks at the extent to which advanced knowledge-based concepts, tools and techniques can be applied to military logistics. The specific focus is the Logistics Composite (LCOM) modeling and decision support system of the future. The paper suggests where and under what circumstances AI might best be applied.*

This chapter provides an overview of artificial intelligence (AI) technology as a potential approach to the Logistics Composite (LCOM) modeling and decision support system of the future. LCOM 2000 is designed to advance LCOM simulation well beyond today's baseline system, and AI can be expected to appear as an item on the agenda to be considered as a central element in the overall design and development blueprint.

After a brief review of AI and an elucidation of several AI families relevant to LCOM 2000—especially expert system (ES) technology as well as natural language and intelligent training systems—the linkage between ESs and simulation methodology will be explored. Both the concept of statistical expert systems (SESs), an increasingly important facet of the nexus between AI and operations research tools and techniques, and a taxonomy of the potential role of ES approaches to simulation will be illuminated. A perspective on LCOM 2000 based on the idea of *knowledge-based simulation* or *expert simulation systems* will be advanced.

Then, the specific options regarding ES-based strategies for the modules of LCOM 2000 will be identified. Knowledge-based or expert system approaches are potentially useful for all of the stages of LCOM modeling and analysis, but are particularly valuable for four functions:

- A standalone expert system for network generation;
- An expert system that interfaces with the audit process;

- A statistical expert system focusing on:
  a. The LCOM simulation process per se (including a knowledge-based error response interpretation aid);
  b. The post-processor module;
- An intelligent, standalone, and probably microcomputer-based training system.

Especially as intelligent front ends, expert system tools can provide genuine enhancements to LCOM.

LCOM is a large and complex system which simulates interaction between aircraft operations and maintenance, producing data on the demand for personnel and material resources. The model, initially developed in the middle 1960s by Rand and currently written in CACI's SIMSCRIPT II.5 simulation software, uses data on maintenance, supply data, and operations data (the flying schedule). Parameters which can vary in the model are sortie rates, manpower, spare parts, and ground support equipment. The model generates and recovers aircraft by mission through a simulation period. The cycle features scheduled mission take-off times, the number of aircraft involved, preflight tasks, the mission, and the operation of failure clocks for components. At the end of a mission, routine post flight tasks are performed; if resources are unavailable, the aircraft must wait. Maintenance actions involve series of networks and the accompanying flow of maintenance activities and tasks; a typical database consists of several thousand tasks and hundreds of networks.

LCOM is a very comprehensive and quite useful simulation system, but it is decidedly not "state-of-the-art." Consequently, two contractors—Synergy, Inc. and BITE (Built in Test Engineering)—were tasked to review the model, interview the large user community, and develop a preliminary portrait of and architecture for LCOM 2000, a new version of LCOM designed to incorporate sophisticated graphics and animation facilities, database management system (DBMS) capabilities, and the entire panoply of current and emerging decision support system and fifth and sixth generation software tools and techniques. Integral to this, of course, is AI, which was investigated in detail as a technology base for the LCOM of the future.

AI: An overview

Definitions of AI abound. One of the simplest and most useful defines AI as the attempt to incorporate human intelligence in computer-based problem solving systems. AI systems thus simulate or mirror (at least some of) the consensual characteristics of human thought—including the ability to learn, reason, solve problems, and understand ordinary human language. Particularly central to AI tools and systems are non-numeric or symbolic and non-algorithmic or heuristic paradigms for thinking and problem solving, a distinction associated with the fact that AI tools and techniques exploit the subtleties and power that accrue from *knowledge-based* (rather than conventional computer science's databased) problem solving strategies.

Several trends characterize AI now—and these trends will accelerate throughout the 1980s and into the 1990s. First, commercial AI systems, already on the market, credibly simulate aspects of human thinking—albeit in primarily crude ways; the prime example is expert systems (ESs), although restricted and domain-specific natural language interface systems (particularly as front ends to database management systems) have proliferated as well.

Second, it is becoming increasingly apparent to problem-solving methodologists and system engineers and designers in a variety of defense arenas and in the commercial sector as well that AI is only one of many useful tools—and that AI will be only one component of computer-based problem-solving systems. Already, decision support systems are emerging which blend AI with a number of statistical/operations research, DBMS, decision analytic, computer graphics, and other families of analytical methods and methodologies (Andriole and Hopple, 1987a; Hopple, 1986b, 1986c). AI is of special utility (and perhaps maximally useful) when coupled with other tools; only rarely can it be the sole technological base of a decision support system.

The future will witness more intelligence in aiding and decision support systems. Today's off-the-shelf expert systems, which are restricted to thin knowledge bases, will evolve into ESs characterized by increasingly deep knowledge; hardware and software developments will advance that state-of-the-art on multiple frontiers. AI on the microcomputer, a reality now, will experience continued growth—in volume and scope—as the micro technology base undergoes advances into the 1990s.

For LCOM 2000, the most pertinent subfield of AI is, as noted, expert systems (ESs). Vis-a-vis traditional programs, ESs show clear differences. Traditional computer programs put an emphasis on procedural instructions to the machine. ESs, in contrast, are oriented around the acquisition and organization of knowledge bases.

A second AI research arena with potential utility to LCOM 2000 is natural language. Open-ended natural language understanding and processing systems are restricted to the AI laboratory, but there are some commercially available, functionally delimited natural language systems—especially as interfaces or front ends to databases.

A good example of such an *intelligent database assistant* is FRED (an acronym for Front-end for Databases), which synthesizes database expertise with an intelligent user interface, providing the user with extensive help in query formulation, database selection, and data interpretation (see Jakobson et al., 1986). Functional differences between an intelligent data assistant and a traditional database system include:

- Querying in a cooperative natural language dialogue mode vs. querying in an isolated command mode;
- Querying on a conceptual level vs. querying on a factual level;
- Automatic database selection (based on embedded database knowledge and deductive reasoning capabilities) vs. explicit database specification.

Finally, intelligent training systems are changing the landscape of computer-based learning; Fletcher (1985) provides an overview of intelligent instructional system technology from the DoD viewpoint. Intelligent training merges mixed initiative dialogue routines with a system comprised of a knowledge base, a student model (for example, to track and rectify the learner's knowledge gaps and misconceptions), and a tutor module (a component designed to reflect one or more pedagogical templates, such as the Socratic approach). Also key to such systems is the method of knowledge representation (rule-based, semantic network-based, others).

There has been a stream of research in the past few years on AI applications to logistics and maintenance (for example, the collection of theoretical essays and applications summarized in Richardson [1985]) in such areas as troubleshooting and diagnosis, automatic test equipment, and robotics as applied to combat service support. LCOM 2000 represents another application environment where AI can make contributions; the link between ESs and simulation per se is a particularly fertile candidate marriage.

Expert systems and simulation

An ES simulates or reproduces the behavior (judgments and conclusions) of a human expert in a domain of expertise. The task of designing an ES is anchored in the premise that expert human performance is generally not a simple or straightforward application of a specifiable, rigorous algorithmic analytical process—but can nevertheless be made susceptible to embodiment in a computer program. The knowledge is assumed to be representational in nature, that is, it involves the representation in symbolic form of facts about the world.

Architecturally, an ES is comprised of a knowledge base, the inference engine, and the user interface. The knowledge base (KB) contains the knowledge (facts, data, rules) acquired from the domain expert—perhaps via a knowledge acquisition subsystem—in a representation suitable for symbolic processing. The inference engine houses the methods employed for manipulating the knowledge to reach conclusions. The user interface consists of tools designed to aid the interaction sequences between system and user.

The heart of an ES is the KB; AI features an array of schemes for encoding knowledge within the program (that is, alternative formats for knowledge representation). Logic, frames, and semantic networks are among the most popular, along with objects, object-attribute-value triplets, and if-then rule-based systems. Frame-based and other salient approaches to the representation of knowledge in ES/simulation models are discussed and compared in Ruiz-Mier et al. (1985); the pros and cons of the major options are surveyed from a military planning vantage point in Hopple (1986a).

The control or inference structure governs the system's problem-solving approach, the set of procedures used to control the process of knowledge utilization and enable the ES to derive conclusions by drawing a series of inferences from the knowledge in the KB; the strategies used may be irrevocable or tentative in nature, with the latter permitting backtracking when and if necessary to reach a solution path. The knowledge representation scheme(s) are the static module of the ES; the inference engine is the active component, the agent which operates on the KB and its associated knowledge representation latticework.

If the inference-making task is viewed as a search in some state space, the inference engine shapes the search pattern and applies AI heuristics to avoid the combinatorial explosion danger and prevent blind search. Two well known control strategies are backward chaining and forward chaining (others include problem reduction and constraint propagation). Backward chaining starts with a goal and attempts to reason back from the goal to evidence or data in support of the top level hypothesis at the beginning of the chain. Forward chaining or data-driven search proceeds from facts or data to conclusions or goals, reversing the sequence of backward chaining. Backward chaining yields a more directed (and smaller) sequence of questions.

User-system interaction is the province of the ES's interface module. An important aspect of this is the system's questioning strategy, which must be compatible with the user's understanding of the domain. Most ESs also contain a feature for explaining and justifying their conclusions (for example, in rule-based systems, this would involve a listing of the rules and facts which make up the inference chain which culminated in the conclusion offered). The user interface must be well human engineered, and natural language dialogue capability is being built into some interfaces.

Expert system and operations research/statistics hybrids

Among many others, Assad and Golden (1986) and Hahn (1986) discuss the nature of, prospects for, and existing applications of ES approaches to operations research (OR) methodologies and statistics. Gale (1986) brings together the seminal works in the emerging area which joins expert systems and statistical techniques: what could be referred to as statistical expert systems (SESs)—in contrast with today's off-the-shelf mainframe and micro statistical packages, which offer limited on-line guidance to the user (at best) and are unintelligent systems. The ES/OR interface, which seeks to combine the expertise of a statistician (at least in a rudimentary sense) with prepackaged OR tools such as linear programming, modeling of various genres, and forecasting techniques, subsumes ES/simulation systems.

How could ESs and OR be fused to create hybrid problem solving systems? Assad and Golden (1986) and Hahn (1985) envision a number of ways in which ES/OR partnerships could be promoted:

1. *Selection of Models.* An ES could help the user identify appropriate models for his/her problem—via a series of questions to isolate and refine the central problem characteristics.
2. *Model Generation.* By injecting intelligence into interactive model generation (for example, prompts to the user to add side constraints to an optimization model), an ES could facilitate model building.
3. *Search for Solutions.* ESs could be used to elicit criteria and interact with the model to build in procedures for their satisfaction.
4. *Interpretation of Data.* Data analysis results are not always straightforward or obvious, and the user could benefit from an ES to explain and point out limits to and other caveats about results.
5. *Open Simulations.* A simulation tool can be endowed with an intelligent superstructure to facilitate a user's familiarization with a complex system. By using an ES for navigational purposes to change the system's parameters and inputs, the user is enabled to develop a mental model of the operation of a complex system.
6. Training Systems. Intelligent training systems have, as noted earlier, the potential for instruction in simulation and other OR application realms.
7. Introspective Models. AI systems often strive for the capability to reason about their own problem-solving strategies and modify the latter when necessary. For example, an ES could aid in the process of fine tuning results by performing extensive empirical tests of various options or parameter settings.

Most of these questions also pertain to the specific area of ES/simulation, where knowledge-based or intelligent systems could be of inestimable value for building and refining specific LCOM models, automatically searching for solutions and conducting sensitivity tests, interpreting the results, and training new users. The concept of *statistical expert systems* (SESs) reflects this emphasis.

Hahn (1985) and Hand (1986) provide useful portrayals of the SES terrain. A high level distinction between embedded guidance as opposed to automated statistical analysis systems is crucial at the outset; the former ES development strategy entails the building of expertise (or perhaps "research assistant" level guidance) into a statistical package whereas the automation route attempts to turn the ES into a full blown statistical consultant and data analyzer. AT&T Bell Laboratory's Regression Expert ES (REX) exemplifies the embedded expert guidance approach; STATPATH (Statistical Pathfinder), designed to help the user identify analytical pathways appropriate for the data in hand, illustrates the second type. Embedded guidance is of course more feasible; automated analysis systems are distant goals (especially beyond the realm of a functionally specific technique) and pose some clear dangers as well.

A second noteworthy distinction separates front end processors (designed to aid in the selection of a tool to solve a problem) from back end systems (used to guide the user in the application of a previously selected tool). Both add intelligence to statistical software, but the former is targeted at problem identification and structuring at the outset of a problem-solving process, while the back end system strategy—like REX, which checks variables for regression analysis, estimates the linearity of a model, and reviews the residuals for problems—assumes the existence of a templated problem. The second approach is potentially quite applicable to the LCOM problem-solving environment, where an SES could function very effectively as an *intelligent front end* to model structuring, constraining, post-processing, and the interpretation of output.

The concept of an SES for LCOM analysis, however, does not exhaust the potential for applying ES technology to LCOM 2000; in addition to an intelligent front end for statistical/simulation methodology expertise (across the phases of design of a specific study, selection of an analytical strategy and research design, the conduct of actual analysis and numerical processing, and interpretation), it is also conceivable to build AI tools into the simulation model via a knowledge base, solution strategies, and AI language application. This is a much broader potential R&D pathway, and warrants a discussion of AI and simulation compatibilities and a typing scheme which indexes the full range of ES-simulation relationships.

A taxonomy of expert system-simulation linkages

Phrases such as *knowledge-based simulation* or *expert simulation systems* are beginning to saturate the literature on simulation. Few devotees of this hybrid, however, anchor this projected marriage in a comprehensive typology of alternative ways to engineer the union. O'Keefe (1986), in a notable and laudable exception, specifies such a taxonomy, underlining the discrete points that confront the designers of the LCOM 2000 blueprint—from an ES as a smart front end to the option of ES-based (and other AI offspring) as part of a larger simulation network to a full blown, AI-based, new LCOM written in Lisp or Prolog.

Initially, however, the feasibility of ES-based simulation should be demonstrated. Shannon et al. (1985) point out that, in the light of standard ES development feasibility criteria (which reflect the stock of experience across a large number of successes, near hits and misses, and egregious failures), simulation seems to be an ideal contender. As with successful past ES domains, simulation requires the existence of real experts, operates on a reasonably bounded domain, involves the explicit consideration of various alternatives (where *the* optimal solution is elusive or nonexistent), injects uncertainty into the problem statement, and embraces a bounded set of entities and attributes.

In a more general sense, simulation and ESs share some core ideas. For example, entities or processes have the ability to carry along (and change dynamically) attributes which describe their characteristics, thus illustrating the use of frames, a prominent ES knowledge representation scheme, in simulation. Simulations involve the dynamic modification of the flow of entities through a system via production rules and conditional probabilities, two standard concepts in AI. Typically, knowledge about a simulated system is represented in the form of a network. Furthermore, it is trivial to represent simulation in an object-oriented mode, and list processing—so central to AI-based programming (Lisp stands for *Lis*t *P*rocessing)—is at the heart of discrete event simulation.

There are also some salient differences: simulation models are constructed and run in an iterative fashion, while an ES could generate a model based on initial user inputs of knowledge (especially objects) about the system and avowed goals; AI separates the database, knowledge base, and control structure, whereas simulation, at least until recently (with the new trend toward decoupled models, experimentation, and output analysis), features integrated information and control; simulations tend to be numeric and algorithmic, but ESs specialize in symbolic processes, model-based expertise, and pattern invoked search rather than the explicit identification of the requisite solution steps.

None of these differences if fatal to the prospects for ES-based simulation, and it can be argued that the separation of the knowledge base and inference engine is desirable in any case and that simulation is by its nature a process involving knowledge as well as data. The user declaration of knowledge and goals activating an automated computerized search for the appropriate model and the solution, it should be emphasized, represents the full blown AI option on the continuum—and is not realizable now and may not be achievable—or desirable—in the LCOM 2000 time frame. But this certainly does not preclude an SES to accompany the LCOM system or a more ambitious ES-within-LCOM.

This SES (a statistical [simulation methodology] expert system) design option vis-a-vis the concept of an expert system module with LCOM per se raises a very central LCOM blueprint distinction, a point of departure for introducing the taxonomy featured in O'Keefe's (1986) review of ESs and simulation.

First, there is the embedded model, in which the ES is contained within (and part of) a simulation system (or the latter is embedded within the former, also a logical possibility). It has been maintained, in fact, that ESs and simulation are *mutually dependent* because simulation handles the dimension of time very efficiently and effectively, and ES technology is notoriously inadept at incorporating time into its inferencing and reasoning; facilities for dealing with time-based processes are an area of weakness in AI generally.

Second is the parallel model, in which simulations and ESs, designed and implemented as separate software (but in a parallel mode), may interact. A simulation model could conceivably query an ES (for example, if a simulation is developed for a complex system, and an ES already exists to model the system's decision making); in many such contexts, it would be easier (and more veridical) to access the ES than for the simulation software to mimic or encode the decision rules. (Alternately, as the figure suggests, ESs may use the results of simulations rather than test an ES on a user or a real environment, in, for instance, such domains as real-time process control.)

The cooperative model assumes the combined use of an ES and a simulation in the performance of a task; note that the user interacts with both directly (and the two problem solving systems cooperate at least in part) or with the two in a larger context—that is, an extended decision support system environment (again, the two are cooperating modules of the DSS).

Each may share data, requiring cooperation in the task; the integration of LCOM databases (failure rates, and so forth) with knowledge bases (objects and their attributes within the system, repair procedures, and other symbolic logistics knowledge) would necessitate the overlap depicted in 1e. A knowledge-based LCOM married to a numeric processor module—in a larger DSS context—is the architecture reflected by 1f.

Finally, the fourth ES/simulation integrated research design model is the use of the ES as an "intelligent front end," a pattern that, as was noted at the outset of this discussion, is a current trend in state-of-the-art DBMS packages—and also provides a model for the SES or embedded statistics assistant paradigm. In addition, intelligent front ends can also be viewed in a training context (for example, an intelligent training system to link a new user to LCOM—or embedded training at several levels of sophistication for novices, simulation experts who are otherwise unfamiliar with the LCOM model environment, *and* LCOM experts who need a review or extended help session).

Intelligent interface architecture per se has emerged as an increasingly important subject in its own right, attracting sustained attention in military planning and decision aiding (Andriole and Hopple, 1987a, 1987b) and specifically in the study of how people naturally view reality and how computer-based systems should exploit this (Hopple, 1985, 1987). Intelligent interface technology will be incarnated in intelligent and knowledge-based front ends of the 1g type to serve as system navigation aids, graphic process monitoring devices, and robust and sophisticated explanation subsystems for a variety of problem-solving systems; the approach is being applied to several military planning support systems (Andriole and Hopple, 1987b; Andriole, 1986), and has obvious relevance as well to simulation modeling of the LCOM type, where the overall process can be graphically portrayed via flow charts and network models and system features such as graphic displays and animation can be expected to be prominent.

Examples of expert simulation systems

To illustrate the potential for an expert simulation system or knowledge-based simulation approach to LCOM 2000, this section presents several AI-oriented simulation modeling systems. Background information on expert simulation systems and examples of various prototype and more advanced projects are provided in Birtwistle (1985), Coelho and Tavares (1986), Haddock (1987), Moser (1986), Murray-Smith (1984), Shannon et al. (1986), and a number of other recent publications.

An excellent example of knowledge-based simulation is Rand's work on ROSS (= Rule-Oriented Simulation System), profiled in Klahr (1984) and elsewhere. ROSS provides a new simulation language and environment which integrates ES technology and recent advances in object-oriented languages. ROSS seeks to overcome the well known limitations of large-scale, conventional simulation systems, including difficulties in understanding, obstacles to easy modification (except for preselected input parameters), and the fact that they are very slow to run; in addition, typically, domain knowledge is buried in unreadable computer code and available simulators rarely provide adequate browsing and explanation facilities. All of these shortcomings surfaced repeatedly in interviews of LCOM users.

The goal of the developers of Ross was to make the system understandable by and responsive to the needs of users. Domain knowledge exists in an accessible and readable English-like format. Assumptions are explicit and modifiable. Knowledge is structured efficiently and logically. Users are provided with powerful browsing, explanation, and graphics facilities. This list of system characteristics sounds like a credible portrait of many of the desiderata for LCOM 2000.

Klahr (1984) reports that the AI/knowledge engineering approach employed for ES development was applied with domain experts who were military analysts responsible for combat simulations. Their organization of domain knowledge clearly clusters around three conceptual nodes:

1. Knowledge relative to various *classes of objects*.
2. These objects are involved with *extensive communications* with each other during the simulation.
3. These *communications trigger certain actions* on the part of the objects receiving the messages.

The following exemplifies how the experts typically express behavioral rules:

Object: Command-center
Message: Radar-x tracking aircraft at position-xyz
Actions: Determine if aircraft is hostile
If aircraft is hostile, send message to nearest air base to scramble fighter to intercept.

In the ROSS language, a set of domain objects (such as, radars, aircraft, missiles, etc.) is specified, along with their attributes and behaviors. Objects are organized in a hierarchy of class-subclass links; this hierarchy allows an object to inherit the attributes and behaviors of the classes to which the object belongs.

To execute simulations, ROSS also has the necessary primitives for running simulations (a clock, an event scheduler, and so forth). ROSS has been employed to develop two battle simulations. SWIRL, a strategic example, simulates an offensive air attack of invading bombers; TWIRL implements a tactical scenario, a land battle with about

140 objects and 200 behaviors. Both contain extensive color graphics capabilities which visually depict simulations as they execute.

ROSS is operations-oriented, but could be applied to logistics and the logistics-operations interface. The research of Ruiz-Mier and colleagues (1985) on a knowledge-based network simulation environment offers an even more directly relevant example; their prototype is of a hybrid AI programming system for the simulation of network concepts based on the idea of using object-oriented programming as a unifying principle for procedure-oriented (for example, Lisp), access-oriented (demons and attached procedures), and rule-based programming. As in Smalltalk, each object (class or instance) is associated with a unique database which contains its properties and knowledge about the object's behavior. The system's databases, a generalization of relational databases, are regarded as logic programming environments in which properties are expressed as assertions, protocols are coded as production rules, and control is exercised through four unified programming paradigms (goal directed inference based on a powerful pattern matcher; object-oriented, message-passing; access-oriented procedures; and procedure-oriented programming via Lisp expressions).

To define a model, the user simply describes the network by initializing system objects such as activities, branches, and so forth. Ruiz-Mier et al. illustrate the system's functioning with the classic teller problem:

```
(model TELLER
    (Arrival CREATE)
    (Wait__for__service WAIT)
    (Service ACTIVITY)
    (Departure TERMINATE))
```

When the system evaluates this expression, it creates instances of the objects CREATE, WAIT, ACTIVITY, and TERMINATE. The model is completed by specifying

```
(simulate TELLER)
```

which prompts the start of the simulation as soon as the value of a message is input:

```
What is the value of property
<prop> for object <obj>?
```

Mention should also be made of several discrete simulation systems written in Prolog. Futo and Szeredi (1982) describe T-PROLOG, which combines the simulation language-based time-handling concept with AI problem-solving techniques of pattern matching and backtracking. In such a logic-based discrete simulation language, models are defined using logical formulas. Also written in Prolog is a prototype knowledge-based system discussed in Rodrigues (1986) and called SIMLOG.

The existing stockpile of expert simulation systems—conceived as intelligent front ends and knowledge-based simulation tools—augurs well for the application of AI to LCOM 2000. The following and final section of this chapter addresses this issue in more detail and focuses on the modules of the system in relation to the prospects for considering AI solutions.

Expert simulation systems and LCOM 2000

LCOM could be converted into a fully AI-based modeling system, which represents one pole of the continuum. The other pole could denote "no AI" in LCOM 2000. There are of course a variety of discrete points along the way from full AI to no AI.

Projecting LCOM into the 1990s should suffice to demonstrate that AI should play a role in the system. The critical question, of course, is what kind of a role and how extensive the involvement of AI should be. It makes the assessment task more tractable analytically if we look at the modules of LCOM.

The AI potential is rated (none, low, medium, high) for the six modules in FIG. 17-1. For none of the six is the AI potential nonexistent, but the assessed relevance varies from low to high across the six stages of LCOM modeling.

For database development, user responses clearly supported the idea of adding a DBMS capability to the system. AI could enhance such a feature in two ways. First, a natural language query capability would make sense as an option to explore; FRED (the DBMS front end described earlier) and a variety of other DBMS/natural language hybrids (for example, R:base 5000 has a natural language interface) are available or under development. Second, it has been noted earlier in this chapter that AI knowledge representation techniques provide a flexible, efficient, and—from the LCOM conceptual framework vantage point—very natural way to encode and manipulate information in the form of knowledge; a knowledge representation structure which integrates database and knowledge base characteristics offers a very useful and effective mechanism for capturing and dynamically activating the elements, relationships, and logistics processes required.

Overall, however, AI-based approaches to LCOM database development are not primary. State-of-the-art and emerging DBMS systems offer the user a panoply of advanced and flexible features, and developments such as database machines should also be noted. AI should play a role (and will become more prominent in the future as intelligent data assistant perspectives permeate DBMSs), but is less pertinent to this phase of the LCOM problem-solving process than to several later stages.

For the audit and network generation aspects of LCOM modeling, consensus emerged from the user community about the desirability of using portable computers for field audits and the viability of the idea of using system-built networks (or embedded procedures and templates to guide and automate portions of the network building process and the inclusion of a mechanism for automating network debugging). Both—and particularly the latter task—could exploit AI tools and techniques. A standalone expert system—coupled with advanced graphics and computer-assisted design facilities—could considerably ease and structure the network construction/debugging task.

For scenario development and coordination, AI has relatively little to offer, although an intelligent front end—knowledgeable about the nature and elements of LCOM scenarios—would provide a valuable adjunct to the scenario construction process and could serve to guide the user. In addition to the idea of an intelligent scenario templating device, specific "scripts" (a popular AI knowledge representation scheme) could be stored, and the script knowledge base could be updated whenever a new scenario is input. This would enable users to access an increasingly deep and extensive scenario knowledge base, thereby simplifying (and even automating) portions of the LCOM scenario development process.

AI's potential is high for the actual simulation process stage. For building the LCOM simulation modeling structure, the strategy of embedding an ES within the simulation makes sense because, as was previously noted, the two offer distinct and vital but decidedly complementary functions and strengths: simulation is ideal for predicting the values (and stochastic parameters) of complex sets of variables over time (an analytical endeavor for which ESs are poorly equipped) and ESs are strong on their reasoning ability and the ease, transparency, and validity with which they analyze output, draw inferences, and reconstruct the line of thought which led to a conclusion. In addition, the advisability of recasting much of the simulation "knowledge" (defining entities as objects with attributes and attached behaviors, specifying processes in logic-based terms, expressing simulation parameters and processes as rules in, for example, the form of a queue priority rule) as an explicit knowledge base reinforces the appeal of this argument.

The actual running of a simulation model also introduces the notion of an ES-simulation linkage. In this case, the process could be enacted in a cooperative ES-simulation paradigm, where the user interacts with both (in the overall context of a larger LCOM DSS or decision support system). The joint operation of the two distinct methodologies would be transparent (and irrelevant) to the user, but its specification is important from a system architectural and development viewpoint. (Alternatively, an ES approach and simulation could conceivably be employed in a parallel fashion, in which the first handles reasoning and inference-making and the second assumes responsibility for the time dimension.)

For setting up the model, initialization, and constraining, a variety of condition-action pairs or if-then rules could be embedded to advise the user and even automate aspects of these tasks. Automation of the constraining process, along with real interactivity between the user and the system, emerged as a high priority enhancement in user interviews.

More generally, the concept of a statistical expert system (SES) focused on simulation methodology—reflecting the principles of embedded guidance and the back end system philosophy discussed in the earlier overview of types of SESs—should rank very highly as a candidate for inclusion on the LCOM 2000 agenda. An intelligent front end LCOM SES would subsume the manifold simulation process-related tasks outlined briefly here, serving to guide the user from design through the actual conduct of analysis. Especially desirable would be the inclusion of an ES-based error response interpreter to translate error messages for the user and provide detailed diagnostics and recommended steps to rectify the problem.

Similarly, an intelligent front end to the post processor is also an attractive option. Again, an output-oriented SES knowledgeable about LCOM reporting contexts and interpretation-related functions would facilitate the user's interaction with the post processor module. Default parameters could be provided based on the user's responses to a series of menu-driven queries; manual overrides would of course be essential. The intelligent front end would intervene between the user and the system. This model assumes that a variety of specialized and user friendly report generation capabilities will be built into LCOM 2000 along with the intelligence.

Finally, FIG. 17-1 assigns a high rank to AI-based training. A microcomputer-based, scaled down version of LCOM would provide a mechanism for incorporating a powerful suite of intelligent, computer-assisted training paradigms and tools.

	AI Potential			
Stage of LCOM	None	Low	Medium	High
(1) Data base development		X		
(2) Audit/Network				X
(3) Scenario		X		
(4) Sim process				X
(5) Postprocessor			X	
(6) Training				X

Fig. 17-1. AI and LCOM 2000.

The matrix in FIG. 17-1 can be summarized in relation to O'Keefe's (1986) taxonomy of ES-simulation linkages as follows:

- For database development: an ES embedded in an LCOM simulation system
- For the audit/network generation functions: a parallel (1d) approach or stand-alone ES;
- For scenario development/coordination: an intelligent front end (1g) to LCOM modeling;
- For the simulation process per se:
  a. An ES within simulation (1a);
  b. A cooperative paradigm for the actual modeling (types 1e/1f);
  c. An LCOM SES as an intelligent front end (1g);
- For the post processor: an SES (also 1g);
- For training: an intelligent instructional system interfaced with the system (type 1g).

Shannon et al. (1985) present an optimistic scenario regarding expert simulation systems or knowledge-based simulation; given a user's request parameters, the ES's control structure will do the necessary interpreting, decide on the requisite data input, determine automatically how to process the information, and generate the output. In the logic programming paradigm, knowledge declaration and goal definition will enable the computer to take over and find the solution to the problem. Available to the user in this scenario will be very powerful—and machine-driven—shells for developing and running simulation systems.

This is, as noted, the optimistic version of the story. This machine-dominated model puts the user in the loop only in a very minimal way, and poses problems (and dangers) because of this. However, it is hardly necessary to embrace this optimistic scenario on the grounds of practicability (or desirability) to recognize that any decision support system for simulation can be expected to feature AI components in the very near future. The specifics of the blueprint, however, must be worked out, and a variety of technical and practical issues confronted and resolved in future work on the design and development of LCOM 2000.

References

S.J. Andriole, (1986) "Graphic Equivalence, Graphic Explanations, and Embedded Process Modeling for Enhanced User-System Interaction." *IEEE Transactions on Systems, Man, and Cybernetics*, SMC-16 (November/December): 919 – 26.

S.J. Andriole and G.W. Hopple (eds.) (1987a) *Defense Applications of Artificial Intelligence: Progress and Prospects*. Lexington, MA: Lexington/DC Health.

S.J. Andriole and G.W. Hopple (1987b) "Inference-Making and Option Selection in Army Corps-Level Tactical Planning: Some Hybrid Models and a Systems Concept Storyboard." Marshall, VA: International Information Systems.

A.A. Assad and B.L. Golden (1986) "Expert Systems, Microcomputers, and Operations Research." *Computers and Operations Research*, 13, 2/3: 301 – 321.

G. Birthwistle, (ed.) (1985) *Artificial Intelligence, Graphics, and Simulation*. San Diego, CA: Society for Computer Simulation.

J.D. Coelho and L.V. Tavares (eds.) (1986) *Operations Research Models on Microcomputers*. Amsterdam: North Holland.

J.D. Fletcher, (1985) "Intelligent Instructional Systems in Training," pp. 427 – 51 in S.J. Andriole (ed.), *Applications in Artificial Intelligence*. Princeton, NJ: Petrocelli.

I. Futo and J. Szeredi (1982) "A Discrete Simulation System Based on Artificial Intelligence Methods," pp. 135 – 50 in A. Javor (ed.), *Discrete Simulation and Related Fields*. Amsterdam: North Holland.

W.A. Gale, (ed.) (1986) *Artficial Intelligence and Statistics*. Reading, MA: Addison Wesley.

J. Haddock, (1987) "An Expert System Framework Based on a Simulation Generator." *Simulation*, 48, 2 (February): 45 – 53.

G.J. Hahn, (1985) "More Intelligent Statistical Software and Statistical Expert Systems: Future Directions." *The American Statistician*, 39, 1 (February): 1 – 8.

D.J. Hand, (1986) "Patterns in Statistical Strategy," pp. 355 – 387 in W.A. Gale (ed.), *Artificial Intelligence and Statistics*. Reading, MA: Addison-Wesley.

G.W. Hopple, (1987) "Knowledge Structures and Intelligent Interfaces: Cognitive Modeling for the Sixth Generation." Marshall, VA: International Information Systems.

G.W. Hopple, (1986a) "Alternative Defensive Plan Generation and Evaluation: Object-Attribute-Value Knowledge Base." Marshall, VA: International Information Systems.

G.W. Hopple, (1986b) "Assessment of the State-of-the-Art of Commercial and Military Decision Aids and Support Systems: Steps Toward a Coherent Acquisition and Investment Strategy." Presented at the Applied Military Decision Aids and Support Systems Conference, Magnavox Decision Support System Applied Center of Excellence (DACE), Fort Wayne, Indiana, September.

G.W. Hopple, (1986c) "The Law of the Hammer and Other Maxims." *IEEE Transactions on Systems, Man, and Cybernetics*, SMC-16, 6 (November – December): 948 – 964.

G.W. Hopple, (1985) "Intelligent Support Systems for Command, Control, Communications, and Intelligence (C3I): A Prototype Causal Schema Knowledge-Based System." Presented at the Human Factors in Manned Systems Integration Meeting, Kansas City, MO, July.

G. Jakobson, C. Lafond, E. Nyberg, and G. Piatetsky-Shapiro (1986) "An Intelligent Database Assistant." *IEEE Expert*, 1, 2 (Summer): 65 – 79.

E.J.H. Kerckhoffs and G.C. Vansteenkiste (1986) "The Impact of Advanced Information Processing on Simulation—An Illustrative Review." *Simulation*, 46, 1 (January): 17 – 26.

P. Klahr, (1984) "Artificial Intelligence Approaches to Simulation," pp. 87 – 92 in D.J. Murray-Smith (ed.), *Proceedings of the 1984 UKSC [United Kingdom Simulation Council] Conference on Computer Simulation*. London: Butterworths.

J.G. Moser, (1986) "Integration of Artificial Intelligence and Simulation in a Comprehensive Decision-Support System." *Simulation*, 47, 6 (December): 223 – 29.

D.J. Murray-Smith, (ed.) (1984) *Proceedings of the 1984 UKSC Conference on Computer Simulation*. London: Butterworths.

R.O. O'Keefe, (1986) "Simulation and Expert Systems—A Taxonomy and Some Examples." *Simulation*, 46, 1 (January): 10 – 16.

J.J. Richardson, (ed.) (1985) *Artificial Intelligence in Maintenance*. Noyes Publishers.

A.J.L. Rodrigues, (1986) "Knowledge-Based Modelling and Simulation," pp. 161 – 9 in J.D. Coelho and L.V. Tavares (eds.), *Operations Research Models on Microcomputers*. Amsterdam: North Holland.

S. Ruiz-Mier, J. Talvage, and D. Ben-Arieh (1985) "Towards A Knowledge-Based Network Simulation Environment," pp. 232 – 236 in D. Gantz et al., (eds.), *Proceedings of the 1985 Winter Simulation Conference*.

R.E. Shannon, R. Mayer, and H.H. Adelsberger (1985) "Expert Systems and Simulation." *Simulation*, 44, 6 (June): 275 – 84.

18

AALPS
A knowledge-based system for aircraft loading

Debra Anderson
Charles Ortiz

Editors' note *The automated air load planning system, or "AALPS," is a knowledge-based expert system that assists in the planning for loading military cargo planes. AALPS is an example of an expert system application in a relatively well-bounded problem area. It was developed with support from DARPA and the US Army. Note that the system concept can be generalized beyond military cargo planes. In fact, optimizing cargo space is a goal that extends well into the commercial aviation industry as well as the family sedan. (Reprinted, with permission, from the Winter 1987 issue of* IEEE Expert. *©1987, IEEE. All rights reserved.)*

The automated air load planning system (AALPS)—a knowledge-based expert system using the expertise of highly trained loadmasters—helps users perform the complex task of loading military cargo planes. SRI developed the system through close interaction with users and domain experts; the Army now employs it daily. In this article, we (1) describe the complex set of constraints driving the AALPS planning function, (2) outline the steps in the system's development, (3) review the problem representation and reasoning methods used, and (4) discuss the system's success as shown by its widespread use.

AALPS grew out of the US Army's data distribution system testbed (ADDS), established by the Army and DARPA at Fort Bragg, North Carolina in 1979 [1]. During this period, Army users at Fort Bragg identified the need to develop an automated tool for planning and executing aircraft loads in real time. Previous approaches for developing such a tool had been unsuccessful because they relied on computationally intensive optimization techniques, and because they lacked the flexibility for modifying either the loading strategy or the many constraints restricting sets of allowable cargo arrangements. By employing AI techniques and a sufficiently flexible spatial representation, however, we were able to model the heuristic techniques commonly used by experts to load aircraft.

Automatically generating valid cargo loads (that is, ones satisfying all constraints while making good use of available space), AALPS assists transportation officers in their day-to-day planning for mission contingencies as well as for real-time load planning at the airfield. Typically, users specify a list of equipment to be loaded and the types of aircraft to be used. For each aircraft type, the system then outputs an arrangement of equipment satisfying equipment, aircraft, and mission requirements. Once at the airfield, preplanned missions can be brought up by the system, and planning parameters can be replaced with actual information obtained at the marshaling area. In this way, the system revalidates generated loads as required by run-time mission requirements.

The system also evaluates the consequences of particular loading strategies—a key factor in long-range planning and feasibility studies comparing current Army policies and equipment with proposed replacements to see how changes will affect deployment. For example, a new and slightly larger truck model might replace two of an older model—thereby affecting the number or type of aircraft needed to carry them.

Finally, AALPS verifies that user-derived loads satisfy all problem-specific constraints. AALPS' inherent flexibility enables users to repeat load planning by changing certain parameters slightly, executing the program with new parameters, and comparing results with prior executions. For example, a typical aircraft load planning mission involving 1000 aircraft normally takes a loadmaster about a week to perform—whereas AALPS can do the same work in a matter of hours.

The problem description

AALPS creates cargo manifests when given a list of cargo to be transported, the aircraft types to use, and the specific type of mission. A *manifest* lists valid arrangements of cargo for each aircraft. Figure 18-1 shows a sample AALPS-generated manifest. Prior to the development of AALPS, expert loadmasters produced such manifests by shuffling templates of items on graph paper and manually calculating constraint values—a tedious and time-consuming process.

The Army uses three standard types of aircraft to transport equipment and personnel: the C130, the C141, and the C5 (in order of increasing capacity). We can load each aircraft with cargo including any or all of the following items:

- Wheeled vehicles,
- Palletized cargo,
- Tracked vehicles,
- Helicopters,
- Miscellaneous equipment,
- Personnel.

Usually, we classify each mission by both aircraft type and delivery method. Missions may contain an aircraft mix, depending upon availability and need. We then consider the following loading methods:

- Strategic air/land: This delivery method stresses maximum utilization of aircraft space, ignoring tactical considerations such as offloading.

- Tactical air/land: In this method, the ease with which items can be loaded and offloaded must be taken into consideration when preparing a load. For example, palletized cargo is loaded aft of wheeled cargo to make loading and offloading easier. Trailers are loaded hitched to trucks to speed offloading.
- Airdrop: In this delivery method, personnel and equipment are offloaded by parachute. Items that cannot be airdropped are loaded by one of the other methods. Items to be airdropped are mounted on special platforms. Aircraft balance throughout the airdrop process is a prime consideration.
- The low-altitude parachute extraction system (LAPES): This method allows for the aerial delivery of items that cannot be airdropped. It is executed by flying the aircraft very close to the ground over a flat, cleared area. An extraction parachute is deployed from the rear of the aircraft, and the aircraft "flies away" from the item. The item is mounted on a special platform enabling it to skid to a stop.

AALPS MANIFEST

unit being airlifted:	unit identification code:
type movement plan:	movement date:
unit chalk number:	acft serial number(last 5):
mission number:	departure airfield:
configuration:	destination airfield:
load planned by:	system chalk number:

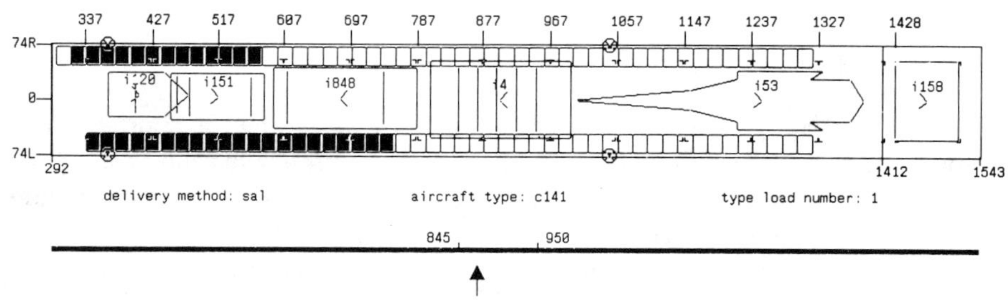

item#	bmpr#	nomenclature	l	w	h	wt	cb	from	to	shrg	vnt	2reqd	fuel	data
i120	none	tlr cgo 1/4 ton m416	109	62	53	1080	410	368	477	n	n	n		p
i151	none	trk util 1/4 ton 4x4 m15	132	64	52	2950	517	451	583	n	n	y	1/2	p
i848	none	trk util 1 1/4 ton hmmwv	195	85	69	7500	682	593	788	n	n	y	1/2	p
i4	none	carrier,command post lt	192	106	104	21700	899	804	996	y	n	y	1/2	p
i53	none	helicopter observation:	392	82	104	2110	1251	997	1389	n	n	y	1/2	p
i158	none	4631 pallet (7,500 lb)	88	108	72	7500	1472	1428	1516	n	n	n		p

total # of pax:	34			load planned by:
weight/pax:	240	total pax weight:	8160	
total cargo weight:	42840			
total load weight:	51000	ACL: 60000	%ACL: 0.850000	load approved by:
load cb:	871	cb range: 845 950		

Fig. 18-1. A sample AALPS manifest.

In addition to general spatial considerations related to fitting the maximum cargo into a given space, four constraint classes restrict an item's location on an aircraft. These classes relate to

1. Aircraft type: A load's center of gravity must fall within a center-of-balance window for each aircraft and for all loading methods, although that window's loca-

tion and extent differs from plane to plane. Aircraft floor limitations restrict the gross weight of items, the axle weight of items, the PSI values of tires, and the like; such constraints frequently involve more than one item and relationships to surrounding items. For example, a weight limitation may be imposed on a given region and, within that region, individual items may be limited to a certain fraction of the overall limit.

2. Delivery method: Strategic air/land missions stress maximum use of aircraft space. In a tactical air/land mission, however, speed and the ease with which cargo can be on-loaded and off-loaded takes precedence. Airdrop and LAPES missions must maintain aircraft balance while dropping cargo and must also provide space between items for parachute cables.
3. Equipment type: Numerous considerations are associated with each item's classification as well as with the particular item itself. Classes of items such as trucks and trailers require special consideration; these are best loaded in pairs so that the truck can unload the trailer. On the other hand, certain restricted articles (or items containing hazardous cargo) cannot be loaded with other hazardous items on the same aircraft. Finally, some items must be loaded at particular locations within the aircraft (for venting or refrigeration).
4. Particular mission requirements: When loading cargo for several planes, we must take into account the mission's tactical and logistical considerations. For instance, some types of cargo must be distributed among different planes in a mission to ensure that critical assets are available in case some aircraft are lost—a tactic called "cross-loading."

This is by no means an exhaustive list of constraints that the system must consider. Anderson et al. discuss the subject further [2].

The AALPS functional architecture

The design of AALPS' functional architecture enables the system to interact with users when automatically considering and fulfilling the above constraints. This architecture serves three basic functions: the automatic generation of valid loads by the system, user generation of new loads, and user modification of existing loads. Figure 18-2 illustrates the architecture supporting these functions.

The *user interface* is composed of two modules—the *command interpreter* and the *typeload editor*. The command interpreter provides a friendly interface between the user and AALPS, incorporating a dynamic user model and several other congenial and adaptive interface features that vary the presentation and that support the remaining AALPS application software [3]. The typeload editor maintains a graphical image of aircraft and equipment as items are loaded. It treats these items as active objects, enabling users to select them with a mouse and graphically manipulate them on the aircraft. The system can later revalidate loads altered in this way. This tool is useful at deployment, when we know with certainty actual cargo characteristics (such as axle weights and center of gravity).

The *equipment database* contains both dimensional information and special characteristics of cargo items.

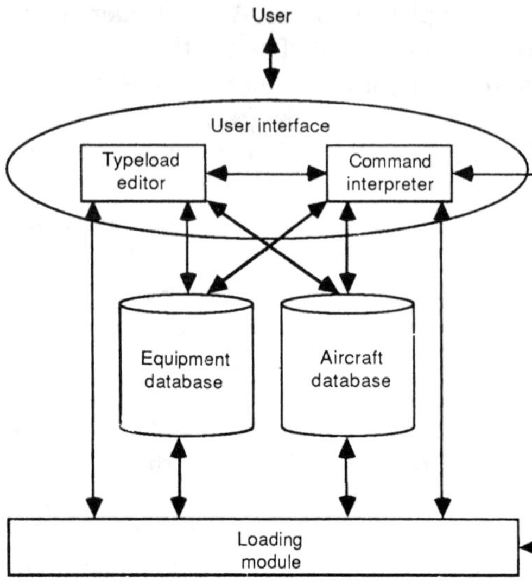

Fig. 18-2. The AALPS functional architecture.

The *aircraft database* contains detailed aircraft characteristics including dimensions, constraint regions, and special requirements for each aircraft.

The *dynamic loading requirements database* contains the user's dynamically updated preferences regarding loading strategies.

The *loading module* contains procedural knowledge used to generate valid aircraft loads. It is a collection of representations, each delineating sequential actions associated with a particular loading strategy. These actions are represented by Prolog procedures that can specify conditional, recursive, or iterative actions associated with the loading strategies employed. AALPS uses this knowledge to determine individual aircraft load configurations as well as total mission aircraft requirements.

System development

To understand both problem process and content when developing AALPS, SRI worked closely with Military Airlift Command (MAC) loadmasters at Fort Bragg. These users became involved in the development process itself. Initial contact with experts and users, beginning during the last quarter of 1979, has continued throughout the system's evolution.

To sustain expert/user involvement at a level sufficient to achieve project goals, AALPS developers generated a system prototype in about two months. Experts and users tested the system, providing almost daily feedback. As a result, system developers could better understand the overall problem, and could improve and enhance existing versions. The rapid prototyping approach became a standard cycle for AALPS' development, ensuring its evolution according to user requirements.

During the development cycle, AALPS developers met with sponsors and users to provide in-process reviews approximately every four to six months. These reviews gave developers the opportunity to discuss achievements and advances made during the previous development period, and gave users the chance to express their views. Beginning in 1980 and for about two years, AALPS served as a Corps planning tool for military exercises, providing the opportunity for additional evaluation. The initial version of AALPS, written in Pascal, was executed on a DEC20. In 1984, the system was redeveloped in Prolog because it could provide the same underlying representation for both declarative database knowledge and procedural loading knowledge. We felt that Prolog would result in a more modular system, permitting a straightforward modification of program heuristics—thereby accommodating various loading strategies for test and use. That the AALPS Prolog version meets these objectives proves the correctness of our choice.

We developed the current version of AALPS in Quintus Prolog on Sun workstations, each having approximately 2M bytes of memory and access to approximately 50M bytes of disk space from a central file server. We wrote the databases and loading module, as well as portions of the user interface, in Prolog. The typeload editor was written in C and accessed from within Prolog. The runtime environment is a compiled version for both the Sun workstation and a VAX 11/780. Both the Sun and the VAX run 4.2 BSD Unix.

Throughout AALPS development and knowledge acquisition, the typeload editor served as a debugging and development tool—enabling developers to graphically view the consequences of adding new procedural knowledge or changing aircraft database specifics. By watching the program work as it loads, developers and expert consultants can observe loading order. Graphic aircraft database representation helps us to check for database inconsistencies and to evaluate where changes or corrections are needed.

Problem representation

The related bin-packing problem is known to be NP-hard in the strong sense, suggesting it unlikely that a polynomial solution exists [4]. However, as has been pointed out in other NP problems—the traveling salesman problem, for example—if the requirement of finding the *best* solution is relaxed to finding a *good* solution, then heuristic techniques can be applied successfully [5]. This motivated us to adopt a heuristic approach modeling the procedural knowledge commonly used by loadmasters.

To accomplish this, we have adopted a production system formalism consisting of a database of facts, a set of operators, and a control strategy that iteratively transforms the initial state of the cargo into a final arrangement. In this way, we can represent an action sequence as a chain of operators. We find the appropriate chain of operators by searching through a space of possible arrangements. Adopting this sort of formalism lends itself to a modular problem-solving approach [6]. AALPS expresses a set of actions as a Prolog goal in which the antecedents of the goal statement represent the sequence of actions. Tests are associated with the application of an operator—such as two- and three-dimensional spatial checks, as well as aircraft-, equipment-, and mission-specific constraint checks. The type of operator used depends on the particular loading strategy; some of the more important operators are described below.

The *make-pile* operator creates piles of items—conceptual collections of items with common characteristics. For example, a pile of similar-weight items might be constructed, or a pile might specify that its items be loaded in a certain order. As described in the next section, piles are useful in the reasoning process.

Slide, swap, and *reorder* operators rearrange items in the aircraft. For example, the slide operator—usually invoked if a piece's placement violates some constraint—slides items to new locations. If necessary, it can slide other pieces in the general neighborhood or even slide the entire load.

The *pick-item* operator chooses the most promising item for placement from the piles of available items; that is, the one most likely to satisfy constraints under consideration.

The *position-item* operator chooses a location on the aircraft for an item. Balancing longitudinally (from front to back) is implicitly considered when positioning items in the aircraft; one strategy frequently employed by loadmasters in the field and adopted by the system here is to load heavier items in the center of the aircraft, because the center can bear more stress, and to position lighter items toward the ends. After invoking position-item, the system conducts various tests. For example, if the plane is full, the system will proceed to balance the plane; if an item's location violates constraints, the system will pick another item or slide the item to a different position.

The spatial representation we chose was Cartesian coordinate, rather than topological (such as quad trees) [7]. We evaluated and rejected a quad-tree approach because it (1) complicated the maintenance of variable granularities in the representation, and (2) made it difficult to represent complex topological boundaries that resulted when spacing between items was varied.

The AALPS 3D spatial representation presents all items as blocks—cubes at various levels of resolution; that is, as a collection of rectangular prisms with their edges parallel to the axis of a reference coordinate frame. For example, while it may be appropriate to consider a truck as a single block at one level, at another level of resolution it may be appropriate to consider the truck as a cube with smaller cubes underneath representing the wheels. And at an even more detailed level, it may be appropriate to consider a truck as three blocks—the hood, the driver's cabin, and the cargo bed.

We encoded the system in horn-clause logic [8] using the Prolog programming language [9]. Prolog represents database facts as unit clauses. Along with a large assortment of facts regarding equipment and aircraft characteristics (such as length, width, height, and weight) is a series of facts representing constraint regions described earlier. AALPS represents these constraint regions with "checkerboards." The system divides aircraft interiors into regions of uniform constraint values. If an item rests on more than one weight checkerboard, for example, that item can weigh no more than allowed by the weight checkerboard with the lowest limit.

The reasoning approach

Loading cargo resembles the assembly of jigsaw puzzles. When loading aircraft with AALPS, however, the final arrangement can only be judged in terms of how well one has modeled a loadmaster's procedural knowledge. The system must reason about how items are loaded, and not just what the final arrangement looks like—an important consideration for tactical loading methods.

The search space is the set of all possible arrangements of items to be loaded. At any step during problem-solving, an item can be located somewhere on a plane or in a set of piles constructed according to predefined rules. Piles effectively partition a load into manageable groups of items, precluding a search through an entire list of items at each load-planning step. For example, the system can place cross-loaded items in a separate pile containing items that must be loaded on different planes. Items of similar size and weight can be kept in a pile; if a particular arrangement of items from that pile results in a *good fit* on one side of the plane, the same arrangement can be duplicated fairly easily on the other side. A similar strategy is often used when solving jigsaw puzzles to avoid sorting through all the pieces—a good jigsaw heuristic might involve separating blue pieces (perhaps representing the sky) from border pieces, and so on.

In general, we have adopted a hill-climbing approach with a limited number of backtracking points in which heuristics direct the search in the most profitable direction [6]. We believe this approach approximates typical loadmaster techniques and also significantly reduces system search. In effect, this typifies expert system methodology by supplanting excessive search with more and more domain knowledge.

Domain knowledge, in this case, includes standard loading methodologies that were developed as a result of many meetings with experienced Air Force loadmasters. When differences of opinion were observed, this knowledge was coded into the dynamic loading rules database whenever possible. This loading rules database allowed the expert user to modify those rules to suit personal requirements. For example, many of the loadmasters interviewed insisted that loading oversized cargo first was the best way to structure the loading process and we encoded this knowledge in the system's control structure. In other cases, we noted that the order in which experts selected items to load on the aircraft varied with the loadmaster interviewed, and this difference of opinion resulted in an entry to the Prolog loading rules database that dictates cargo selection choices.

The majority of loading strategies share the following common order of necessary actions:

1. Sorting the cargo: Prior to loading, cargo is sorted into appropriate piles. Initially, users input loading parameters and list the cargo to be loaded. Using this information, the system sorts equipment into piles, enabling effective cargo selection when filling each aircraft.
2. Filling the aircraft: Based upon several criteria, the system selects items from the cargo list—considering cross-loading, aircraft balance, aircraft cargo area, and proper use of cargo weight capacity. The system checks for a three-dimensional fit by reasoning at the appropriate level of resolution. A single block representation of an item might suffice—or a more complex one might be appropriate—depending on the shape of available space. As each item is positioned in the plane, the system also checks constraints. In air/land missions, we load from aircraft center out toward the ends. In airdrop and LAPES missions, we load from nose to tail. Our strategy in all cases seeks a good first try—one requiring the fewest alterations to achieve a valid load.

3. Aircraft balance: Once it fills the aircraft, the system checks the load's center of balance against acceptable limits for the aircraft. If the load is out of balance, the system balances it by applying appropriate operators to the configuration. It first attempts to slide the load, then tries to rearrange items, and finally considers swapping items in the load for others on the cargo list.
4. Validating constraints: Since balancing the aircraft may entail repositioning items, the system conducts a final check of constraints. This includes checking individual items in the load as well as groups of items. Once the load has been validated, the system rechecks center of balance and (if necessary) repeats Steps 3 and 4 until all constraints are satisfied.
5. Generating typeloads: To increase efficiency, once the system generates a valid load, it replicates as many copies of that load as possible (depending on the number of items remaining to be loaded).

The system contains about 300 rules so far, and roughly 4M bytes of declarative knowledge in its database. This includes the aircraft database, the equipment database (consisting of approximately 1500 items), and miscellaneous other databases. Because of its tightly coupled development and user environments, and the capabilities it provided for aircraft load planning, AALPS demonstrated marked success with the XVIII Airborne Corps. Sound development methodology combined with the system's successful user support caused MAC to request early initiation of tests and evaluations.

Representatives of MAC, the Air Force, and the Army viewed a live AALPS demonstration early in 1982. One result of this demonstration was an agreement that, within certain constraints, the AALPS manifest could be used for actual aircraft load plans. A statement from MAC HQ presented guidelines for using the AALPS manifest and auxiliary documentation. This event, representing a major milestone in the program's development, was the first major hurdle in transferring AALPS technology to the Army.

Following MAC approval, the Army officially used AALPS for planning and execution (AALPS produced actual manifests), and deployed it in support of the Corps during numerous field exercises. In addition, AALPS supported the deployment of the XVIII Airborne to Granada. The success of AALPS, coupled with user enthusiasm, caused the US Army deputy chief of staff for logistics to recommend that AALPS be enhanced and adopted as the Army's single aircraft load planning and execution system, and that it be included in the Joint Transportation Coordinator-Automated Command and Control Information Coordinator program—a recommendation endorsed by the US Army chief of staff.

AALPS represents a significant improvement over traditional, manual methods. Because of this, and because of the Army's strong commitment, AALPS should soon become the Army's standard air cargo planning system.

Acknowledgments

We would like to acknowledge the early work of Greg Stachnick and Richard Grise, who were responsible for initial system versions. We would also like to thank the rest of the AALPS team for their dedicated contributions: Reggie Hutcherson, Eric Negaard,

Bill Park, and Julie Wong. And finally, we wish to acknowledge the useful comments that Mike Frankel, Len Karpf, Bell Baeck, and Jeff Peck provided as we prepared this article.

AALPS research was supported by the Defense Advanced Research Projects Agency and the Department of the Army under contract MDA903-84-C-0261.

References

1. M.S. Frankel et al., "Army Data Distribution System/Packet Radio Testbed," Quarterly Report 2, SRI Int'l, Menlo Park, Calif., July 1980.
2. D. Anderson et al., "AALPS: Automated Air Load Planning System—Final Report," tech. report, Information Sciences and Technology Center, SRI Int'l, Menlo Park, Calif., 1986.
3. R.F. Grise, "Considerations in the Evolution of a Congenial and Adaptive Human Computer Interface," tech. report, Information Sciences and Technology Center, SRI Int'l, Menlo Park, Calif., 1985.
4. M.R. Garey and D.S. Johnson, *Computers and Intractability: A Guide to the Theory of NP-Completeness*, W.H. Freeman, San Francisco, Calif., 1979.
5. J. Pearl, *Heuristics: Intelligent Search Strategies for Computer Problem Solving*, Addison-Wesley, Reading, Mass., 1984.
6. N.J. Nilsson, *Principles of Artificial Intelligence*, Tioga Publishing, Palo Alto, Calif., 1980.
7. D.H. Ballard and C.M. Brown, *Computer Vision*, Prentics-Hall, Englewood Cliffs, N.J., 1982.
8. Kowalski, *Logic for Problem Solving*, Elsevier, New York, N.Y., 1979.
9. W.F. Clocksin and C.S. Mellish, *Programming in Prolog*, Springer-Verlag, New York, N.Y., 1981.

19

Expert system technology for the military

Selected samples

Jude E. Franklin
Cora Lackey Carmody,
Karl Keller, Tod S. Levitt
and Brandon L. Buteau

Editors' note *Jude Franklin and his associates provide an in-depth description and analysis of the range of AI in national defense, as well as insights about several of the key challenges in knowledge processing, including inference-making under conditions of uncertainty. It is the kind of paper that should be read by all those interested in what the military has done—and plans to do—with intelligent systems technology. (Reprinted, with permission, from the October 1988 issue of* Proceedings of the IEEE. *©1988. All rights reserved.)*

This paper is concerned with the applications of expert systems to complex military problems. A brief description of needs for expert systems in the military arena is given. A short tutorial on some of the elements of an expert system is found in Appendix I. An important aspect of expert systems concerns using uncertain information and ill-defined procedures. Many of the general techniques of dealing with uncertainty are described in Appendix II. These techniques include Bayesian certainty factors, Dempster-Shafer theory of uncertainty, and Zadeh's fuzzy set theory. The major portion of the paper addresses specific expert system examples such as resource allocation, identification of radar images, maintenance and troubleshooting of electronic equipment, and the interpretation and understanding of radar images. Extensions of expert systems to incorporate learning are examined in the context of military intelligence to determine the disposition, location, and intention of the adversary. The final application involves the use of distributed communicating cooperating expert systems for battle management. Finally, the future of expert systems and their evolving capabilities are discussed.

I. Introduction

The increasing complexity of weapon systems and the growing volume of complex information creates numerous problems for the military [1]–[5]. Commanders must make decisions faster than ever before and maintain operational readiness in spite of limitations on manpower and training. Artificial Intelligence (AI) technology can potentially solve many of these problems for the military, with some AI applications already demonstrating their utility. The military and industry have made major investments in the area of AI. This paper will concentrate on the potential of expert systems, a subordinate category of AI, to the military arena.

Within the last few years the military has witnessed an almost explosive expansion of the field of expert systems within various agencies of the Department of Defense (DOD). This has been sparked by the rapid growth in computer technology, by the development and better understanding of expert systems concepts, by the progress that has been made in sensors and control devices, and by the growing need caused by an information explosion. For example, typical military command and control centers handle thousands of messages in a single day and commanders must decide promptly on correct actions. Commercial applications in the fields of financial investment, manufacturing, and business planning have similar high information volume and time constraint problems. Although this paper concentrates on military applications of AI, there are analogies in the commercial arena.

While the field of expert systems is still a long way from solving the military's most persistent problems, this research activity for creating intelligent machines has demonstrated certain machine properties that offer great help and promise, particularly in the area of manpower reduction. There are reasonable expectations of future computers that can learn; reason; understand text and speech; perform complex problem-solving operations; recognize anomalous behaviors and warn the decisionmaker; understand drawings and photographs; and process signals such as speech, sonar, radar, and imagery.

Early DOD investments [3] have helped to establish the scientific foundations upon which the present U.S. capabilities and thrusts in AI and robotics are based. For example, the Office of Naval Research (ONR) and the Defense Advanced Research Project Agency (DARPA) have been supporting research in AI for over 20 years through the support of "Centers of Excellence" at several prominent universities. These centers have published extensively, hosted symposia for government and industry, and spawned technological innovations such as the DARPA-sponsored Strategic Computing Program (SCP) that has applications including the Air Force Pilot's Associate, the Army Autonomous Land Vehicle and the Naval Battle Management programs. The Navy has created a Center for Applied Research in AI at the Naval Research Laboratory (NRL) and has major programs in maintenance and troubleshooting of complex electronic equipment, target identification from radar or acoustic sensors, machine learning, and fusion of data from multiple sensors. More recently, the Army Research Office (ARO) has invested in a long-term AI research, development, and training effort with two major universities (the University of Texas and the University of Pennsylvania). The Army has started an AI center in the Pentagon with a concentration on information management for logistics. One of the Army's first problems is the correct distribution of critical equipment such as cellular radios for the signal corps. The Army has major programs in planning and threat analysis from multiple sensors. The Air Force has just started a consortium of universities oriented toward AI in the region around Rome Air Development Center (RADC) and has ongoing programs in software automation, indications and warning systems, and decision systems for military commanders. The Air Force Office of Scientific Research (OSR) has sponsored research in manufacturing science, spacecraft image understanding, systems automation through AI, and software automation. The Strategic Defense Initiative (SDI) is considering the use of AI techniques to accomplish accurate, time critical decisions and to provide robust adaptive communications for battle management applications.

The remainder of this paper discusses the use of expert systems in the military. Section II gives an overview of expert systems technology and what expert systems do; what the components are; and what some of the interesting problems have been. Section III presents several examples of military applications using expert systems; Section IV discusses a learning system applied to the military; Section V considers the next step of distributed problem solving; and Section VI provides a summary and conclusion with a glimpse at realistic expectations for how expert systems can help solve future military problems and what research areas need to be addressed.

II. Background on expert systems and uncertainty

A. Expert system overview

Expert systems are computer programs that attempt to duplicate results obtained by *actual* experts in a particular field or domain. Recent results have demonstrated that this technology can be used by the military. This section provides a short introduction to expert systems terminology. The real power of an expert system is found in the knowledge base, which contains the fundamental facts and assertions necessary to solve a specific problem. The knowledge can be stored in at least three structures. The first is to represent statements about the problem domain as predicate calculus (logic). The second is to represent the knowledge as if-then rules, and the third representation is a collection of attribute-value pairs known as frames. The best representation schemes use a combination of several of these strategies.

The *inference engine* accepts the input data and the information in the knowledge base to develop a means of solving the problem. The inference engine may use a goal-directed scheme that examines various potential hypotheses and determines which one is true. This technique works backwards from the goals toward the input data. Another approach is to start with the input data and infer conclusions in a forward direction. The final approach is to combine both techniques. The inference engine will usually contain various search strategies that take advantage of how best to examine alternatives and what search paths will provide the fastest solutions.

The knowledge engineer attempts to work with the actual domain expert and represent his problem-solving techniques on the computer. The knowledge engineer is the key to the total knowledge acquisition process. Frequently, the domain expert becomes the knowledge engineer, and optimum results are achieved with fewer errors and misunderstandings.

B. Uncertainty representations and approaches

A popular maxim pertinent to the study of expert systems is "In the knowledge lies the power." By design, expert systems augment human reasoning; it is a natural extension to basic reasoning approaches within expert systems to include the ability to form reasonable conclusions from uncertain and incomplete knowledge. Associating a representation of our degree of belief with the knowledge constrained in a knowledge base is one of the most common approaches to reasoning with uncertainty. Unfortunately, most of the representations bear little resemblance to human cognitive processes—their primary virtue is that they can be implemented within an expert system and can help to solve the problem. References [11]–[32] and the additional readings section also provide background for this research area.

The problem of reasoning with uncertainty takes on greater importance when the application area concerns the fusion of information from many knowledge sources, e.g., the command, control, communication and intelligence (C^3I) sensor environment. In particular, when the independent knowledge sources are sensors producing low-level perceptual outputs, it is essential to have a methodology for assigning uncertainty values to evidence from different knowledge sources, and for combining these values when evidence from these knowledge sources supports (or contradicts) the same basic conclusion.

Generally, sensor systems do not report results with 100-percent accuracy and certainty. This is a particular problem when multiple sensors must be combined. For example, when output from Sensor *A* support the conclusion "The target is a type X relocatable weapon" with certainty 0.42, and outputs from Sensor *B* support the same conclusion with certainty 0.87, a mechanism should exist for combining these figures in a coherent manner. Furthermore, the method must deal with the situation when a similar conclusion from Sensor *C* is incorporated at a later time, or when even later Sensor *B* retracts its conclusion or updates the certainty factor associated with its conclusion.

Approaches to dealing with uncertainty often take some variation of numeric characterization. Numeric representations usually take the form of the assignment of a point value (as the application of Bayes' Theorem or maximum entropy), intervals on a range (as in Dempster-Shafer Theory) or points within an evidence space. A variant on a numerical approach with foundations in set theory is Zadeh's Fuzzy Logic, or Fuzzy Set Theory.

C. Methods of dealing with uncertainty

One of the first problems with numeric methods of uncertainty lies in allocating initial numbers. Where do the numbers come from? Are the numbers intended to capture truth (i.e., in terms of frequency data), or are they representing a consensus of belief from one or more experts? These two interpretations lead to different sets of problems. In most military applications, existing frequency data is not available, so a foundation for further calculations must be defined in another manner. There are at present no standard methods for laying this foundation.

If the numbers are to represent confidence or belief, the initial assignment of certainties must come from the expert whose assertions form the knowledge base. Different experts may well assign different certainty numbers, and may have different reasons for the assignments. The reasons for assignment are left behind, once the numbers are assigned to assertions or rules. Apart from the loss of reasons, there is some question as to the quality or precision of the initial numbers.

Another basic problem is in the interpretation of the numbers. Just what does it mean to say that "The target under observation is an SS-25 missile" with certainty 0.87. Does this mean that "I'm 87% sure that it's an SS-25," "The probability is 87% that it's an SS-25," "The odds are 87 in 100 that it's an SS-25," or "87 out of 100 targets that we've tracked with these kinds of characteristics turned out to be SS-25s?" Interpretations of certainty values vary between degrees of belief, probabilities, betting, and frequency of occurrence. A number is only a measure of how uncertain we are about a proposition and does not convey our reasons for doubt.

Within specific numeric methods, there are problems with single point implementations, such as Bayes' Theorem, since the degrees of belief and degrees of disbelief in a proposition must always sum to one; any doubt must be represented as an unknown hypothesis. Another problem with the Bayes approach is that in order to update certainty values effectively, a large amount of information is needed. Two of the applications, BATTLE and the ship identification expert system, described in Section III-A and Section III-B, use a variation and extension of the Bayesian techniques.

In contrast, the Dempster-Shafer method provides a representation which separates values for belief and disbelief (they need not always sum to one), and a propagation algorithm which will accept initial ignorance in a proposition, so that reasoning can proceed without a large amount of initial information. The Dempster-Shafer method provides a model for the gradual accrual of new knowledge into an expert system, and its inverse may be computed in order to retract evidential contributions. There are, however, significant implementation difficulties in the full-scale theory as discussed in Shafer [17]. The original theory calls for creating supersets of all possible propositions and deals with independent knowledge sources. Obviously, this full approach will cause serious difficulties when the problem area exceeds a very simple problem space, or when the knowledge sources are interdependent. Ginsberg [29] and Barnett [30] have recommended ways to solve the potential difficulties, and Lowrance and Garvey [31], [32] have successfully implemented a slightly more advanced subset of Dempster-Shafer theory and applied it to the military problem of sensor fusion in support of electronic warfare. An additional flaw in the Dempster-Shafer rule of combination is discussed by Zadeh [13]. The Dempster-Shafer technique is used in the distributed expert system example that depicts an indications and warning problem involving terrorist activities and is discussed in Section V.

III. Applications

This section discusses several applications of expert systems that are in varying stages of development for military applications. The choice of the applications was driven by the authors' personal experiences and by no means represents an exhaustive discussion. The samples that were selected represent work at the Naval Research Laboratory (NRL), Defense Advanced Research Project Agency (DARPA), the U.S. Army, Planning Research Corporation (PRC), Mitre, and Advanced Decision Systems (ADS).

A. Combat management for the Marine Corps

The Naval Research Laboratory, under the direction of Slagle, developed an expert consultant system for weapon allocation. The present status of the system is a working prototype tool. This system, called BATTLE [33], [34], generates weapon allocation plans for a system with requirements similar to the Marine Integrated Fire and Air Support System (MIFASS).

The BATTLE expert system evaluates the effectiveness of individual weapons to targets and then it produces complete evaluation plans that consider the possible allocation of all weapons to all targets. Normally, this would involve exhaustive search techniques. The goal of the system is to maximize the destruction (total value *D*) for all targets. In an allocation plan, the destruction value for a target is the product of the target's strategic value and the expected percentage of the target that will be destroyed in the plan. When the destruction value is maximized, the plan is considered optimal. Unfortunately, achieving this optimal plan in real conditions using exhaustive search techniques can consume too much time. For example, if we have W weapons and T targets, there are $(T + 1)^W$ different options. For an optimal plan that considered 8 weapons and 17 targets, the computer run time, using exhaustive search, was 11 minutes and 43 seconds. The BATTLE expert system took 6.75 seconds for the same problem and achieved 98 percent of optimality. Reduction in processing time was due to the heuristic search mechanism that eliminated investigating unlikely weapon-target allocations.

A few of the 55 factors used by BATTLE to arrive at its weapons allocation are:

- Range and position
- Personnel readiness
- Counterfire ability
- Resupply
- Ammunition status
- Number of tubes per group
- Experience of enemy group
- Maintenance status
- Replacement crew status
- Physical condition

The first step of the problem computes the effectiveness of a single weapon to a single target, and the second step assesses the complete matchup of all weapons to all targets. BATTLE uses rules specified by a military expert to accomplish this matchup. The single weapon target allocation network is a generalization of the inference networks of PROSPECTOR. PROSPECTOR was an early expert system that was developed to assist in mineral exploration.

The artillery allocation network uses many different quantitative and qualitative parameters. Quantitative parameters include reliable range estimates for weapons or target counterfire capabilities. The qualitative parameters include readiness of personnel or maintenance status of equipment. The computational network uses several different techniques to combine information prior to allocating weapons to targets. Classic Boolean operators of *and* and *or* are used to combine information such as resupply alternatives and counterfire capability. The Bayesian evidence functions indicated by the triangular symbols are used to combine information such as friendly versus target readiness, friendly and target supply status, or target appropriateness. In this case, there is a degree of uncertainty in the information that is used as well as uncertainty in how this information should be combined. As discussed earlier, the Bayesian technique provides a means to combine these various forms of uncertainty. Expert defined heuristics are indicated by the filled-in symbols. These heuristics usually represent empirical results that aid in reliable weapon to target allocations.

Frequently, there are situations in which all of the information is not available for the expert system to perform the required allocation. For this case, the expert system must ask questions of the user. The BATTLE system uses a new technique, merit, to ask the highest payoff questions first, and to minimize the user's time and cost to provide answers. The merit system performs this function by considering how easy it is for the user to provide the information and how useful the answer will be for the weapon-to-target allocation.

The merit system starts with the concept of the self merit. The self merit is defined as the expected variability in the answer to a question divided by the cost to acquire the answer. The potential variability in the answer to a question would be very high, for example, with matters associated with weather since it is expected to change frequently. The cost is associated with the difficulty in providing the answer. One measure of cost could be the time it takes to find an answer to a question. Therefore, the self merit of a node involving weather would be relatively high because of the large expected variability of the response divided by the relatively low cost of acquiring weather information.

The self merit associated with the node G_1 is the absolute value of the change in the response parameter (ΔP_1), divided by the cost (ΔC_1). The next important consideration is the effect of this answer at node G_1 and the impact it will have on the next higher node G. This is referred to as the edge merit. It is the absolute value of the change in node $G(\Delta P)$ divided by the change at node $G_1(\Delta P_1)$. The total merit at node G associated with G_1 is the product of the self merit and the edge merit.

The other two strategies are the random selection of questions and the fixed order strategy. The fixed order strategy is calculated prior to the availability of answers to any questions and it is not updated as answers become available. This reduces the need for online computation but it results in a fixed order in the set of questions and frequently takes more time. The error on the Y axis refers to the difference between the optimal plan that maximizes the destruction value and the actual destruction value for the three strategies. The merit strategy arrived at a solution that is within five percent of an optimal plan and required less than a dozen questions. The other two strategies used in the comparison would require 18 to 25 questions to achieve this same level of performance as the merit strategy. The expert system must minimize the questions asked of a Marine artillery officer when he is in a stressful combat environment, and the merit strategy helps reduce unnecessary questions.

The description of this project has been used as the initial example to show the application of AI to a real military problem, in this case one of resource allocation. Several points should be mentioned. First, the implementation of expert systems is at best an empirical problem. There is no sure tried and true technique that is universally applicable. In this case the PROSPECTOR paradigm was useful, but it needed additions and alternatives such as the merit questioning strategy and a pruning technique that was customized to the problem. This project demonstrated that the resource allocation problem was one that could be useful for the military. The next project to be discussed used many of the tools developed by BATTLE and applied them to a ship identification effort. In fact, one of the things being studied at the time was the question of whether the BATTLE expert system could be used in other domains. This is a very real problem in the extensibility of expert systems. Frequently they can work fine in one problem domain but are utterly useless in an apparently similar problem domain.

B. Applications of AI for ship identification

Another project at the Navy Center for Applied Research in Artificial Intelligence concerns the correct identification of ships from images. The methodologies used in this expert system are spin-offs of the BATTLE system discussed above. A prototype decision aid has been developed that demonstrates the feasibility of using AI techniques to help human interpreters recognize images of ships. The heuristic reasoning processes used by an expert analyst were modeled to perform this task. The prototype system uses heuristic rules provided by a human expert to determine the most likely classification, given the available feature data. The system has been tested on over 100 images of 10 similar classes of ships, and it provides the correct identification 84 percent of the time [35].

Accurate identification of ships in real time can be a very difficult task. It is desirable to identify these ships within minutes of detection. The images are hard to interpret for numerous reasons such as weather, turbulence, lighting, interference, and viewing angle. When these difficulties are coupled with the hundreds of classes of ships that sail the oceans and the time constraints to make accurate decisions, we can understand the need to help operators as much as possible. Experience has shown that even expert operators will have bad days or be so burdened with numerous target detections that they will become less accurate and on occasion even miss obvious clues. The average operator is frequently inconsistent and uncertain. He also has a difficult time determining what should be the next clue to be pursued to reduce the target class ambiguity and finally to narrow his decisions to a specific selection. The thrust of the NRL research headed by Booker [35] was to allow for the use of automatic equipment that performs signal processing and pattern recognition and combine this equipment with AI techniques to aid the operator. It was very important to have the expert system capture the operator's judgment, pattern recognition capabilities, the knowledge and the reasoning that he uses for his expert analysis.

The system guides the operator to investigate specific clues or parameters and then suggests an identification for a specific unknown ship. The Explanation System uses the logic provided by the expert and can show the user why the expert system made a specific decision regarding the identification of an image as a specific ship class. The Questioning System decides what question should be asked next. It uses the merit strategy, which is also used in BATTLE, to optimize the order of the questions. The Volunteer System allows the operator to provide as much initial data as he deems fit. It also allows the operator to volunteer additional information during the questioning period. The Propagator calculates the effect of the uncertainty of the data and the operator's observations as the initial information travels throughout the computational network toward the goal of ship identification. The techniques used here are a variation of the Bayesian techniques described earlier. The Inference Network Combines the initial observations and clues into intermediate hypotheses that are combined further towards a final conclusion.

The order of the questions is changed dynamically by the merit strategy developed at NRL and used for the first time in BATTLE. This technique that was described previously has been shown to reduce the required number of questions needed to identify a ship. Excerpts of an actual session using this expert system are shown below.

Expert system question 1: To what degree do you believe that the profile-has-isolated-directors-fwd-of-bridge-with-a-linear-taper?

Human response to question 1: (–3)
Note that the operator does not believe that this condition is present.
Expert system comment: I neither suspect nor doubt the possibility of ForestSherman, Bainbridge, Sverdlov, Coontz, Leahy, Belknap, Truxtun, California or Virginia.
I doubt that image84 could be LongBeach

Note at this point that the machine already doubts the Long Beach ship class is likely and is neutral about the rest.

Expert system question 2: To what degree do you believe that the profile-has-a-gap-between-aft-mast-and-aft-superstructure-block?

Human response to question 2: (+5)
Note that the operator strongly believes that this clue is present.
Expert system comment: I strongly suspect that image84 is Coontz
I doubt that image84 could be ForestSherman, Sverdlov, Leahy, Belknap, Truxtun, California or Virginia
I strongly doubt that image84 is Bainbridge or LongBeach

Note at this point the machine has asked a question using the merit strategy to determine the most useful question to answer. Indeed, with the response from the user, it is already focusing on the Coontz class.

These questions continue, and at the end the machine responds with its list of potential classifications (identifications) in a priority order. In addition, the machine gives its confidence of these classifications as shown below.

Class	Confidence	Class	Confidence
Coontz	4.9	Virginia	−5.0
California	−4.8	Sverdlov	−5.0
Bainbridge	−5.0	Leahy	−5.0
Truxtun	−5.0	ForestSherman	−5.0
Belknap	−5.0	LongBeach	−5.0

Expert system comment: I strongly suspect that image84 is Coontz
I strongly doubt that the image84 is ForestSherman, Bainbridge, Sverdlov, LongBeach, Leahy, Belknap, Truxtun, California or Virginia

Note that the expert system has listed the Coontz first with a confidence factor of positive 4.9. The California class was listed second, but the expert system was not very confident of this because it has a confidence factor of −4.8. Clearly it did not believe it was the California class or any of the others that are on the list. This is an extremely useful feature since it can help the operator decide if he is satisfied with the expert system's conclusions. In this case, the expert system was very confident that it was the Coontz and none of the others.

There were 119 images investigated. This included 101 total images that were from the chosen ship classes that were represented in the expert system. The other 18 were for ships not contained in the chosen category and the expert system did not know of their existence. The success rate was 84 percent. In 85 of the 101 trials, the ship class ranked first by the expert system was the correct identification. In 94 of the 101 trials, the correct target class was listed as a plausible identification. The expert system provided consistently useful discrimination between the top ranked class and the second rated class. The summary of this discrimination is shown below.

Correct trials:
- Average confidence in top ranked class was 1.7.
- Average confidence in second ranked class was −2.4.
- This means that the system usually comes up with only one plausible classification.

Incorrect trials:
- Average confidence in top ranked class was −0.16.
- Average confidence in second ranked class was −0.99.

Note that in 84 percent of the cases where the machine correctly identified the ship, the expert system average confidence was 1.7 and this indicates a relatively high positive belief that the chosen top ranked identification is correct. Further, the expert system had a confidence of −2.4 in the second ranked class and this indicates a fairly strong belief that this is not the correct class. This helps the user believe in the expert system's results because of the large separation of +1.7 and −2.4. In the cases where the machine incorrectly identified the image, its confidence in the first choice was −0.16. Clearly, the machine was not "sure" of its choice, and the user can see this and would probably want to acquire a new image and add more results prior to a final selection. More detailed results can be found in a publication by NRL's Booker [35].

C. Maintenance and troubleshooting

Since the early 1960s military equipment has steadily increased in complexity and variety, while at the same time the pool of trained technicians has been decreasing. A major cost of operations is in fault diagnosis and repair, the procurement of maintenance equipment, and the training of technicians and operators. Each of the armed services has problems which are unique to its mission, but all share problems of space, difficulty in providing logistics support, and limited technical manpower. These factors coupled with the demands of operations place heavy emphasis on speedy and accurate diagnosis and repair in the field. These difficulties have created prime opportunities for the application of AI, and a number of efforts are underway.

All three services are investigating alternatives using AI in the area of maintaining and troubleshooting electronic equipment. The Air Force has two major programs. The first is the Integrated Maintenance Information System (IMIS) project that is designed to give flightline personnel access to all onboard diagnostic data as well as maintenance and scheduling records. The second program is the Generic Integrated Maintenance Diagnostics (GIMADS) effort that proposes to use AI and conventional techniques to address the diagnostics problem for an integrated system. The Navy has two major programs, Integrated Automatic Test Generation (IATG) and the Integrated Diagnostic Support System (IDSS). The IDSS will use expert systems to assist the equipment technician to troubleshoot by providing optimal test trees that are adaptive to the changing conditions. The following examples of AI being applied to the field of maintenance and troubleshooting will draw heavily on the efforts of DeJong, Pipitone, Shumaker, and Cantone [36], [38]–[41] at the Navy Center for Applied Research in Artificial Intelligence. Other relevant work includes Duda *et al.* [37], DeKleer [42], and Davis *et al.* [43].

There are some basic technical issues that should be addressed when AI is applied to maintenance and troubleshooting. It is not a straightforward transition from an application of medical diagnostic successes such as MYCIN to electronic troubleshooting, because too many unexpected causes of equipment malfunctions cannot be anticipated in a traditional if-then rule-based backward-chaining paradigm. For example, solder splashes that short out several components on a printed circuit board, a cable that is crushed because someone rolled a heavy piece of equipment onto it, or a piece of equipment that was doused with a pot of hot coffee are typical unfortunate circumstances that sometimes approach the routine. All of these conditions cannot be anticipated with appropriate rules, and thus a more general methodology must be used.

As an insight to the reader, the following description of an actual expert system at NRL will be used. The system design was evolutionary and several distinct systems were developed and tested. The initial rule base consists of the heuristics, ad hoc rules, and information about the specific design and the operating environment. In this way the knowledge of the designer, the operator, and the technician can all be tapped, and the results of their experience and understanding of the problem can be exploited and put into the initial knowledge base. This initial rule base will not be adequate to resolve all of the troubleshooting problems that will be encountered in the field. As an augmentation to the system, a more general source of information will be used. This portion of the knowledge base must use other sources of information that can be used to generate rules by the expert system. These rules should be in the same form as those that come from the initial rule base. Some sources of this information are block diagrams of the actual equipment indicating the interconnection and the functionality of the system components. The basic information about the circuit can be combined with generalized circuit analysis techniques and fault diagnosis techniques. In this way, new rules can be generated by the expert system from an understanding of the circuit and the problem. Reliability and maintainability analysis should also be used. This would include statistical data associated with past failures as well as failure prediction algorithms.

One of the new features of the approach by Pipitone [41] is that he has included relationships of how the module will react functionally to various faults. An example for a voltage controlled oscillator (VCO) would be that an input voltage that is outside of the desired range will cause the output to be outside of the desired frequency range, in the same direction and with the same relative magnitude. Another causal relation could specify that if the output load is reduced below a certain value the signal will decrease. Another example associated with a high pass filter would be that if the output of a high pass filter is a high dc voltage, the high pass filter is very likely to have failed. More examples can be found in recent publications [38]–[43]. One of the desirable features of an approach using a causal functional description of each module is that it can be used with slight modifications when describing a similar module in another system. Recent results indicate that the addition of this causal functional knowledge requires fewer tests than an approach that uses no functional information.

The next best test should consider what test will cost the least and will result in the most information gain. Initial attempts at calculating the next test used game theory derived from earlier AI research. This technique would consider the machine as the opponent, similar to an opponent in a chess match, and the strategy would be to maximize your gains and minimize the anticipated losses caused by your opponent's move. This proved to be computationally infeasible [36]. Next, a Gamma Miniaverage [38] technique by Slagle was used. In this case, average losses were calculated, since the equipment was not actively plotted against the technician (although some technicians have argued to the contrary). The miniaverage approach was still computationally too costly. Pipitone [36], [39]–[41] introduced heuristic screening at first and then used a one level miniaverage computation. The results in the Pipitone work have shown that functional knowledge is a necessary component of the troubleshooting process and that the total number of necessary tests can be reduced. In addition, the functional knowledge can be used to show the technician how the test can be done and what results should be anticipated.

The progress to date has shown that expert systems can help in the area of diagnostics and troubleshooting. The first expert systems will be used as decision support systems to aid the technician. As progress is made, the state of the art will allow the use of expert systems to be used in an autonomous mode in applications such as generating automatic test equipment code or space-based maintenance and troubleshooting.

D. Advanced digital radar imagery exploitation system (ADRIES)

The Advanced Digital Radar Imagery Exploitation System (ADRIES) is a software prototype testbed for research on extraction of information from radar imagery. Its objectives are to provide a system for enhancing and automating various aspects of digital radar image interpretation, for applications including tactical intelligence missions, military situation assessment, and target recognition. ADRIES is capable of producing interpretations of the possible military situations with a set of radar imagery, collection parameters, *a priori* terrain data, such as maps or digital terrain databases, and other tactical data. ADRIES is currently under development. Key work on terrain, detection, and non-radar intelligence source reasoning will be presented in future publications. Here we emphasize intermediate results in knowledge and model-based military unit inference.

ADRIES is founded on a theory of model-based, Bayesian probabilistic inference. Models represent knowledge of the organization and formations of military units, and they also specify how knowledge of terrain provides evidence in support or denial of the presence of types of forces at given locations. A probabilistic certainty calculus [44] specifies how evidence extracted from SAR imagery and terrain databases is matched against the models and combined to infer the presence or absence of military forces. In particular, radar data, forces, terrain or other entities that have been modeled in the certainty calculus can be used as evidence for inferences output by the system. This is the basis for a clean split between inference and control in ADRIES.

The model database of ADRIES implicitly contains all possible chains of inference that the system can use to draw any conclusion. However, any information whatsoever can be used for control in the system. As an extreme example, if a human intelligence report was available that indicated the presence of a force in a region, ADRIES could use that to direct processing of imagery and terrain of that region without danger of circular reasoning in its conclusions. This is because any output hypotheses about forces in the region must be supported by image and terrain evidence as specified in the model database, and that inference is necessarily from the certainty calculus.

As another example, other source (other than SAR imagery) intelligence data can be used to direct search, make predictions, or act as a trigger to activate agents or other processing, but it cannot be fused to provide evidential support for system outputs unless it is modeled in the model database and in the certainty calculus. It follows that to extend ADRIES to a full fusion system, it will be necessary to do the research on the knowledge representation of other source information, and the probabilistic relationships between other source intelligence and the entities already accounted for in models and the calculus.

In the model-based Bayesian inference in ADRIES, evidence, such as clusters of detections, are matched against the geometry of formations that are explicitly represented in the model database. Matches lead to generation of alternative hypotheses of the presence of forces, such as battalions and companies, that are dynamically created (as imagery is processed, for example) and instantiated in a data structure called a Bayesian network. Terrain rules are applied to the terrain extracted from terrain databases of the area corresponding to the imagery, and the certainty calculus combines that evidence with the model match in computing the probabilities associated to the hypothesized forces in the Bayesian network. In practice it does not matter in what order the terrain evidence probabilities or goodness of formation match probabilities are calculated, as the certainty calculus will obtain the same values regardless of the processing order. The calculations used for computing prior and runtime probabilities in the calculus are presented in [45], [46], [44]. See also [47].

In the course of the ADRIES program, theoretical work has also been performed on detection algorithms [48], [49], clustering algorithms, and elicitation of terrain rules and probabilities [45], [46]. All of this work is incorporated in functionality of the relevant distributed processing agents.

ADRIES is built as a distributed set of software agents communicating by message passing. There is also a set of databases used by multiple agents in their processing. All agents have access, either directly or indirectly, to all databases. Individual agents may have additional databases. In the following, we briefly summarize the functionality of each agent.

Control/inference agent The Control/Inference agent plans system processing to fulfill the exploitation requests (ER) received from the user interface. Basically, an ER specifies what forces to look for in which geographic locations. It posts its processing as messages sent to the Agenda agent. The Control/Inference agent maintains the Bayesian network and decides when to generate a new hypothesis in the Bayesian network based on the available evidence. It also decides when to terminate processing on an ER.

Agenda agent The Agenda agent receives process plan messages from the Control/Inference agent and sends them on to the Exec agent. It provides a loose coupling between the planning in the Control/Inference agent and the resource allocation in the Exec agent.

Exec agent The Exec agent picks up the current processing plans from the Agenda agent, and performs resource allocation to distribute processing on the distributed system. It sends back a summary of its process messages to the Control/Inference agent.

Imagery location agent The Imagery Location agent is a spatially indexed database of imagery in ground coordinates. It keeps track of virtual sub-images cut from larger images, and maintains message-level records of the processing done to imagery. The imagery files are not resident with this agent; in particular, the Imagery Location agent does not send or receive actual imagery.

Registration agent It performs coarse registration to compute the ground coordinates of an image based on its platform parameters and flat world assumptions. The Registration agent also computes a refined registration of the image to the ground. For a given image, it computes a function that takes the elevation at a point in the terrain and outputs the corresponding point in the image.

Lo-res detection agent This agent detects potential vehicles in low-resolution imagery. It also computes the likelihoods corresponding to the hypotheses vehicle versus non-vehicle.

Clustering agent The Clustering agent takes detections and their probabilities as inputs, and outputs clusters of detections and the probability that the cluster contains a military unit of "array" size (e.g., 8 – 15 vehicles). It accounts for inter-vehicle spacings, likelihood of false alarm detections, and dispersion of the cluster on the ground versus the expected extent of the array-sized formation.

Spot mode detection agent This agent performs vehicle detection on high-resolution imagery. It also computes probabilities of vehicle versus non-vehicle.

Vehicle classification agent This agent performs vehicle recognition on high-resolution imagery, and also computes probabilities over the set of hypotheses of the vehicle type.

Other source agent This agent provides signals intelligence and other source intelligence summaries indexed by geographic location and force type.

Focus agent Focus takes as input a geographic region and a force type and outputs a prioritized list of sub-regions for search for forces of that type in the region. Focus uses inputs from the Terrain agents and the Other Source agent.

Matching/prediction agent Matching/Prediction takes as input the locations of hypothesized forces and matches them against doctrinal formations. It also interacts with the Terrain agent to adjust military formation models to fit the underlying terrain according to military doctrine of deployment. Predictions are provided by reasoning about the forces missing from partial matches. Matching/Prediction also provides the probabilities for goodness of fit to formation used as evidence by the Control/Inference agent.

Terrain analysis agent Terrain Analysis is currently performed over three different terrain rule bases. Local Terrain Analysis takes as input a force type and a geographic region and uses terrain rules to compute sub-regions of constant probability indicating the likelihood that a force of that type will be located in the sub-region. The terrain rules used are those that take as pre-conditions terrain attributes that can be gotten from direct access to the terrain database. The reason for separating these rules from "structural" terrain rules is that we have created a probability model for local terrain rules. Thus, these probabilities can be combined as evidence by the Control/Inference agent as part of the probability of output hypotheses.

The Mobility Corridors sub-agent takes as input a force type and geographic region and outputs sub-regions through which a force of a given type can move across the entire region. This sub-agent is intended to be upward compatible with a future Avenues of Approach agent that does more global reasoning over the tactical situation.

The Structural Terrain Analysis sub-agent takes as input a force type and a geographic region and uses terrain rules to compute sub-regions that are acceptable for a force of the given type to occupy. These rules are relational in nature; that is, they use as pre-conditions terrain attributes that cannot be gotten by direct access from the terrain database. No probability model currently exists for these rules. Instead, they interact with formation matching to adjust expected force formations based on terrain and military constraints.

User interface agent User Interface allows the user to interactively input an exploitation request. It also displays all system results, including imagery, terrain overlays, and multi-level force hypotheses. The user can interact with the outputs to obtain explanations for the system's conclusions.

Inference in ADRIES is performed over a space of hierarchically linked hypotheses. The hypotheses typically (although not solely) represent statements of the form "There is a military force of type *F* in deployment *D* at world location *L* at time *T*." The hierarchy in the hypothesis space corresponds to the hierarchy inherent in military doctrine of force structuring. Thus, "array-level" hypotheses of military units such as companies, artillery batteries, and missile sites are linked to their component unit hypotheses of vehicles, artillery pieces, and missile launchers. Similarly, moving upward in the force hierarchy, companies are grouped to form battalion hypotheses, battalions to form regiments, etc.

The hypotheses are generated by hierarchical and partial matching of military force models to evidence available in radar imagery. Thus, ADRIES is a model-based radar vision system. Evidence of the truth (or denial) of a hypothesis is accrued numerically from probabilistic estimates about the sub-hypotheses that comprise their parent hypothesis.

Although control of processing in ADRIES can be complex, the structure of inference follows a pattern based on the models of military forces. These models consist of force types (i.e., names) and spatial-geometric deployment data relating force types. Models are also represented along "is-a" or type relationships by appropriately weakening model constraints. For example, a "tank company in defensive deployment" is-a "tank company" which is-a "company" which is-a "array-level force."

The models are represented as constraints in semantic nets. A constraint consists of a relation name, parameters associated with that relation, and additional model attributes. Figure 19-1 illustrates the internal representation of the constraints in the force-deployment models as semantic nets. At the top of each constraint is a parent model item that is represented by a rectangular box. A box with rounded corners represents the relation and its associated parameters. Both parent and subordinate model items can be forces or formations.

ADRIES has a utility and model-based approach to control of force-deployment pattern matching. Algorithms are employed opportunistically, as determined by the utility of tasks in light of the currently available data, rather than necessarily being checked or applied in a fixed order. (The inference chain pictured uses more models and rules than are shown in the figure.) The utility theory is derived from decision analytic methods on top of the Bayesian inference. For details of the approach, see [57], [58].

The concept of conflict resolution and numerical accrual of evidence is that, while it is often the case that automated matching can be locally incorrect, the weight of the global evidence will override local mismatches and result in an unambiguous interpretation of the tactical situation. The global picture is presented in ADRIES as a set of goals about what it expects to see in the SAR imagery. For example, a command to verify the presence of a division sets up a goal to find a division. The Control/Inference agent then looks up the structures according to the local terrain and military situation. The model is used to set up subgoals recursively to find the component military units of

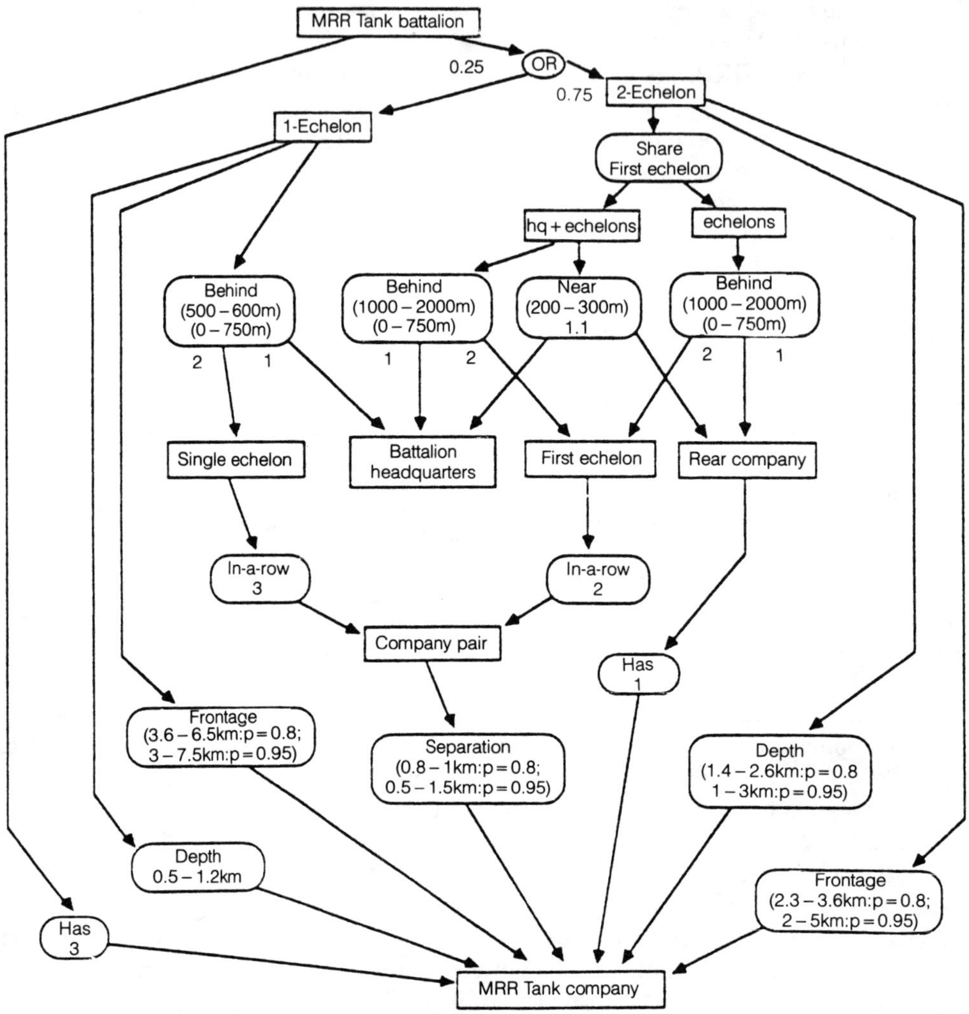

Fig. 19-1. Battalion semantic net.

the division. The existing force-deployment hypotheses are stored as nodes in a Bayes net. These represent the goals and subgoals that have already been pursued or have been satisfied.

Thus, the goal structures and the force-deployment hypothesis space are dual to each other. In the course of processing, control moves back and forth between them. Goal structures help predict where to look for forces in the imagery and the force deployment hypothesis space. Having localized a search area, data is retrieved from the Bayes net and matched against the models associated to the goals. Matches may trigger bottom up actions to infer other forces hypotheses, which may in turn trigger the generation of new goals.

A fundamental concept here is that, while vision system processing may be complex, with numerous feedback loops, multiple levels of resolution, recursion, etc., in the end we should be able to associate a deductive chain of evidence to a system output, along with an associated probability that supports that result.

We selected probability theory as the underlying technology for this numerical accrual of evidence. One of the major motivations for this choice is that Bayesian inference, a well-developed scientific theory, already exists for probabilistic evidential reasoning; see, for example [50]. This approach requires us to lay out, *a priori*, the links between evidence and hypotheses in the models over which the system will reason. Having laid out these links, we then need a numerical interpretation of the conditional belief, i.e., probability, in a hypothesis, given chains of evidence that support it through links. This is similar in spirit to propagation networks [51], to influence diagrams [52], and other probabilistic accrual models. Hierarchical Bayesian inference was introduced by Gettys and Willke [53], Schum and Ducharme [54], Kelly and Barclay [55] and has been carried forward by others, e.g., [44], [56], [57].

The evidential accrual for the generated hypothesis is performed by using a Bayesian network. This paradigm supports the propagation of evidential probabilities through a hierarchical tree of hypotheses in a coherent, stable, and efficient manner [51]. The result of the evidential accrual is a posterior belief value for each hypothesis indicating its relative likelihood. Mutually exclusive conflicting hypotheses are collected in a single Bayes net node. Each node then consists of a belief vector indicating the current relative belief that each of the conflicting hypotheses is true. For example, a node can group the beliefs for a cluster being a battalion or being a false alarm (i.e., not a battalion). The links connecting the nodes consist of conditional probability matrices indicating the relationship of the hypotheses. These probabilities are derived from terrain constraints and locality of the hypothesized forces. For example, for a Bayes link connecting a battalion node (X) with a company node (Y) these probabilities specify:

P(particular image clusters are companies|particular region is battalion)
P(particular image clusters are companies|particular region is false alarm)
P(particular image clusters are false alarms|particular region is battalion)
P(particular image clusters are false alarms|particular region is false alarm).

These conditional probabilities form the elements of a matrix, $M(Y|X)$, where the (i,j)th entry specifies $P(Yj|xi)$.

Messages passed between Bayes nodes consist of probability vectors providing evidential support (child to parent) or model-driven support (parent to child). Evidence coming into a node will normally be in the form: P(image features are due to $Y|Y$).

Evidence for a Bayes company node, for example, would therefore consist of the message: [P(image features are due to a company|company), P(image features are due to false alarms|false alarm)].

A model-driven support message from a node X to its child Y consists of a vector derived by dividing (component-wise) the current belief vector by the current evidential message from Y to X.

Upon receiving a new message from a parent or child, a Bayes node, *X*, (for single parent trees) computes its overall evidential support vector, *Dx*, by multiplying (component-wise) all evidential vectors, *Dx*, from all its children *Yi*. The new resulting belief vector is the result of: *Dx* * [(transpose *Mwx*) *o* *Cw*], where * indicates component-wise multiplication, o indicates matrix multiplication, *Cw* is the model-driven support message from the node's parent *W*, and *Mwx* is the conditional probability matrix from *W* to *X*. New messages are then generated for each of the node's children *Yi*, by dividing (component-wise) the belief vector by the current evidential message from *Yi* to *X*. A new message is generated for the node's parent *W*, by computing: *Mwx o Dx*, where *Mwx* is the conditional probability matrix from *W* to *X* and o indicates matrix multiplication.

The advantage of using Pearl's algorithm for belief propagation is that it can be implemented as an active network of primitive, identical, and autonomous processors. The primitive processors are simple and repetitive and thus can be implemented in a distributed environment. Each node in the Bayes net can be assigned a virtual processor that sends messages in the form of probabilistic belief vectors to parent or children nodes. When a virtual processor receives a new message, it updates its belief vector and propagates the change to its other relatives. Therefore, equilibrium is guaranteed to be reached in time proportional to the network diameter.

Pearl specified his propagation algorithm for static hypothesis spaces. His results have been extended for dynamic hypotheses in order to apply to the ADRIES application. The Bayes net evolves dynamically during processing. New hypotheses get generated for aggregation of lower level hypotheses into higher level hypotheses, while refinement stages generate more possibilities for a hypothesis. Conflicting hypotheses are then merged into single Bayes nodes. The structure of the Bayes net parallels the structure of the Force Models Database. As larger force hypotheses are generated, Bayes nodes corresponding to force models further up the part-of hierarchy will be generated. As the force type and deployment type of the hypotheses are refined, Bayes nodes corresponding to force models further down the is-a hierarchy will be generated.

At the current state of system development, ADRIES successfully infers the presence and locations of military units through the regimental level in high false alarm data, demonstrating the feasibility of the approach. Knowledge is being added in ADRIES to accomplish reasoning about situation deployment of forces in terrain. This will enable ADRIES to predict deployment variation to accommodate terrain constraints. Capability for software simulation of input data is being developed to make statistically significant testing of ADRIES possible.

The research for ADRIES was originally supported by the Defense Advanced Research Projects Agency (DARPA), by the U.S. Army Intelligence Center and School (USAICS) under U.S. Government Contract DAEA 18-83-C-0026, and by Air Force Wright Aeronautical Laboratories (AFWAL) under U.S. Government Contract F33615-83-C-1070. It is currently supported by DARPA and the U.S. Army Engineer Topographic Laboratories (USAETL) under U.S. Government Contract DACA76-86-C-0010. ADRIES is the joint work of many researchers at Advanced Decision System (ADS) in Mountain View, CA, Science Applications International Corporation (SAIC) in Tucson, AZ, and the MRJ Corporation in Oakton, VA. The project supervisors and principal investigators are Bob Drazovich and Tod Levitt at ADS, Dick Kruger and Larry Winter at SAIC, and Bob Ready and Chris McKee at MRJ.

IV. A learning system for intelligence analysis

A. The need for learning

The previous sections have demonstrated the expert systems approach to computer-based problem solving. This approach is applicable to a wide variety of problems and provides a convenient mechanism for expressing knowledge. Unfortunately, there are difficulties associated with the approach that limit its intrinsic usefulness. The inability of expert systems to adapt to new situations outside of a particular sphere of knowledge (frequently termed *brittleness* or *falling off the knowledge cliff* [59], [60]) unacceptably limits performance. Machine learning is an emerging technology that can potentially solve a significant portion of this problem by making systems self-modifying, which will improve performance. In expert systems, the improvement of rules in the system can lead to an improvement in system performance.

B. The machine learning approach

Given that the objective of learning is to improve performance, several design constraints can be placed on any system that claims to learn. First, for a system to improve its future performance in a nonrandom fashion it must, at some level, evaluate its current and past performance. The evaluation or critique must consist of comparing observable behavior with some desired behavior. The problem of evaluation is referred to as apportionment of credit [61], or credit assignment [62]. The apportionment of credit is to those elements of the system responsible for good performance. In the context of an expert system, the apportionment of credit problem boils down to rewarding good rules and (possibly) punishing bad rules. Secondly, the evaluation should lead to or support some lasting modification of the system so that the system avoids the same mistakes next time. Again, for expert systems, this requires that a system be able to alter its rules on the basis of the evaluation.

The rest of the section on learning describes research at the MITRE Corporation, an attempt to apply production system technology to problems in military intelligence. The difficulties associated with knowledge engineering of a large-scale expert system (e.g., extended knowledge acquisition, preference-biased expert knowledge, static knowledge in the face of adaptive adversaries) led to the consideration of incorporating learning capabilities.

Learning systems are usually characterized by three basic elements: domain of application, knowledge representation, and learning strategy. Sections D, E, and F discuss these elements in the context of an existing implemented system called M2. The discussion concludes with issues and further research topics. This brief overview of the basic approaches to machine learning is not intended to be a tutorial on learning; rather, it serves to place M2's approach in the context of previous research.

C. Machine learning paradigms

A number of approaches to incorporating learning into computer systems have been developed since the 1950s. Michalski [63] has identified three basic paradigms in the machine learning field that include the learning of concepts (with an extensive domain model and without one), and learning by self-organization.

Acquiring concepts Symbolic concept acquisition, SCA, attempts to formulate general concepts from specific examples. These systems have a teacher that provides explicit positive and negative instances of a target concept. In this case the feedback mechanism is simplified by the description of the example as a positive or negative instance of the concept. An example system which makes use of this approach is Quinlan's ID3 program [64]. One application of ID3 produces classifications of chess end games using King-Rook versus King-Knight positions. The approach shows significant speed improvement over more traditional search procedures like minimax and discovered winning strategies overlooked by expert human players.

Using domain models A second paradigm, referred to as knowledge-intensive domain-dependent learning, KDL, uses large amounts of domain-specific knowledge to build a model of the domain from which modifications can proceed. The primary difference between this and the SCA approach is in the amount of knowledge used by the system to formulate useful concepts and their frequent use of symbolic logic and theorem-proving approaches to develop consistent concepts. A well-known system which discovered interesting mathematical concepts using this approach was Lenat's AM system [65]. In AM, the search through the space of possible concepts is guided by a utility function with multiple objectives defining the *interestingness* of the concept being explored. In general, the DKL approach has an applications orientation.

Building from the ground up The last paradigm, termed self-organizing systems, often exploits sampling-based learning algorithms rather than symbolic logic approaches to improve performance [66], [67]. These systems use a series of evaluation functions and a direct feedback mechanism to the rules, nodes, or networks which determine the behavior of the system. An example of this approach is the work done in classifier systems and genetic algorithms by Goldberg [68]. This system was given a random set of rules and tasked to perform a gas pipelining problem. The system developed rules to efficiently route and control gas flow in the network. The genetic approach is discussed in more detail in Section F. As a matter of perspective, it should be noted that these paradigms are not mutually exclusive and that opportunities exist for cooperative learning efforts.

D. The military intelligence problem

The problem associated with intelligence analysis is characteristic of a broad class of problems associated with substantiating hypotheses given a model and some data. Consider a set of sensors which provide the intelligence analyst with a data stream of reports of enemy activity at varying time intervals. The task of the analyst is to generate a description of the enemy units that are generating the activities detected by the sensors. This description consists of identities (e.g., UNIT 1), locations (.g., RIVER1 at TIME *t*), and goals (e.g., to have UNIT 1 MOVE UNIT 2 to RIVER 1 at TIME *t*). The description leads to expectations of further reports and suggests experiments (sensor tasks) which the analyst should execute. An example of expectations would be:

> If I believe that the goal of UNIT 1 is to move UNIT 2 to RIVER 1 at TIME *t*, then I expect UNIT 1 to move his lead elements to RIVER 1 at TIME *t* − 2. Further, if I put a sensor there, I expect a report at TIME *t* − 2 or TIME *t* − 1.

In general, no information is received which directly corroborates the hypotheses made by the analyst. The only feedback available is in the substantiation of (hypothesis generated) expectations by the continuing stream of reports emanating from the sensors. The analyst generates the hypotheses by applying an underlying model of the enemy's behavior to the data. There are four basic sources of errors in the analyst's description that require more than the traditional expert systems approach to solve: 1) noisy and incomplete data, 2) incorrect models of enemy behavior, 3) deceptive enemy behavior, and 4) adaptive enemy behavior. Arguably, problems 2 and 3 could be solved with enough knowledge engineering, if deception is considered to be another set of rules to be captured.

These domain considerations lead to some projections about the capabilities of a learning system performing the analyst's task. First, it must generate its description without access to ground truth. This requirement is representative of the self-organizing class of learning systems; however, the strategy employed is one of inductive learning in general. See Section F for more on learning strategies. The analyst never knows absolutely whether his analysis is correct even when his hypotheses are substantiated. Second, the system will operate in noisy and possibly discontinuous search spaces in which behaviors are incompletely or improperly executed. In general, this requirement most closely reflects the capabilities demonstrated by research in the self-organizing approach. Finally, the system should take advantage of the existing organization and models of the domain, rather than learning from the ground up (an argument for the KDL approach). The existence of a model is a good reason for not starting the search (for good rules) from scratch. Any reliable search strategy will do better given a starting point closer to the objective, and it is assumed that existing models are fairly accurate to begin with. The existence of a domain model points up a need for being able to construct and manipulate high-level data structures like production rules. The structures with which M2 stores and manipulates the model are the topic of the next section.

E. Knowledge representation

The knowledge in M2 is represented in two forms: the "declarative" knowledge and vocabulary of the system, in our case an object description and datatype language, expressed as a taxonomy of the terms of interest; and the "assertional" dynamic knowledge of the system expressed by pattern-matching production rules.

Fact bases In M2, objects in the domain are stored in a frame representation language. The classes of other related objects help organize the description by characterizing the object in terms of its class membership as well as its properties and their values [69].

Rule bases The behaviors associated with objects, and the relationships between object behaviors and attributes, and object goals are stored and manipulated in production rules. The clauses, frequently called relations, have the same internal structure as their object counterparts. Thus, the datatypes associated with the fields of each relation are restricted in the same way that attributes of the objects are restricted. The details of these datatype restrictions become important when the learning mechanism begins creating rules of its own. We want the learner to explore the space of *legal* rules rather than the greater set of all possible combinations of syntactic elements. The production rules that can be generated by combining relations define the space of possible rules to be searched by the learning strategy. Obviously, a simple enumeration of all the legal rules is impractical since the number of rules varies exponentially with the number of relations. The next section describes a procedure for searching the space of legal rules efficiently, focusing on areas that need improvement.

F. Strategies for learning

A strategy is a plan or series of plans whose actions accomplish a goal. A learning strategy then, is that set of actions or the methodology that will be invoked to improve performance. The general types of strategies available are: 1) learning by rote, 2) learning by instruction, 3) learning by deduction, 4) learning by analogy, and 5) learning by induction [63]. Although a full description of these learning strategies is beyond the scope of this paper, it is useful to notice that the learning strategy defines the search mechanism employed in the space of rules. The strategy of learning by induction is used because it closely models what the human analyst must do. (A strategy is inductive when it performs the inference by generating plausible hypotheses and selecting among them.)

M2 architecture Previous sections have attempted to describe the constraints under which a learning system in the intelligence domain must act. The system receives input from the user in the form of a goal for the planner to achieve. The planner, without access to the analyst's knowledge bases, generates a plan to achieve the goal and sends the plan to the simulation. The simulation carries out the actions of the plan and generates activity assertions that are available to the analyst's sensor rules. Sensor rules generate reports based on their own coverage (in time and space) of the activities. The reports are used by rules to generate a description of the planner (as described above), and predictions of future reports are made. The degree of correlation between these reports and incoming reports prompts the learner to modify the analyst's knowledge base of the planner. The primary points of interest in the architecture are: 1) separation of planner and analyst knowledge bases, the ground truth restriction, 2) user input to planner in the form of some goal to be achieved, and 3) learning driven by the output of the analyst to modify the analyst model of the planner.

Learning module The learning module is divided into two distinct components oriented around the evaluation and modification of knowledge. Evaluation results drive the modification of knowledge. We begin by discussing M2's apportionment of credit mechanism, a variant of the bucket brigade algorithm [70], which was reimplemented in the context of our rule representation and in an OPS-like [71] inference mechanism.

Bucket brigade and apportionment of credit A complete description of the bucket brigade implementation in this system and results are presented in [72]; however, it will be useful to review the ideas presented there. As we indicated in Section E, M2's rule clauses contain either variable or literal values in their fields. Let f_i represent the total number of fields contained in the rule i's clauses, and v_i represent the number of fields which have variable values. A heuristic measure of specificity is computed, s_i, for each rule as:

$$s_i = 1.0 - v_i/f_i$$

Specificity, as computed, acts as a measure of match for a rule to a set of short-term memory items that are matched by the rule's conditions. Strength will be used as a record of a rule's performance. Strength and specificity traditionally play a part in the bucket brigade serving as objectives in a utility function known as the bid. Let $S_i(t)$ represent the current strength of rule i at time t. A constant c represents a moderator much less than 1. Let the bid, $B_i(t)$, of a rule at time t equal the product of c, s_i, and $S_i(t)$:

$$B_i(t) = c * s_i * S_i(t).$$

The bid is used to produce a linear ordering of rules in the conflict set during the conflict resolution cycle of operation. Rules which support rule i at time t will be represented by $supp_i(t)$. Finally, ENV will be used to denote the environment. It has an attribute, ENV_{payoff}, which represents the amount of reward the environment provides to rules (typically an order of magnitude greater than the average interrule payoffs described below) whose predictions of observables exactly match observables from ENV.

The somewhat lengthy definitions above help to present succinctly the operation of the bucket brigade algorithm adapted to the rule representation. Rules that match items in short-term memory are entered into the conflict set. Each rule in the set submits its (closed) bid, $B_i(t)$. All rules in the set are then ordered based upon their respective bids. The highest bidder is selected for firing, is fired, and the bid made by that rule is distributed equally to $supp_i(t)$ and added to their strengths $Sj(t)$, {for j an element of $supp_i(t)$}. Conversely, this bid is subtracted from $S_i(t)$ of the winning rule. This primitive rule economy leads to reinforcement of rules on the basis of their utility to the system.

At this point, the flow of strength in a chain of rules is from last to first. The last rule in a chain has no mechanism for regaining its bid, leading to a gradual weakening of all the rules in the chain. This problem can be alleviated by ensuring that the rule base is capable of generating assertions which can be matched against observables in the system. The only observables of the analyst module are the continuing reports from the simulation. Our implementation employs a set of meta-level rules with the general pattern:

```
IF
    (there is a report of some kind)
    and
    (there is a prediction of that report)
THEN
    (payoff the prediction rule with ENV_payoff),
```

The behavior of the bucket brigade is greatly influenced by the value of c. The constant acts as a moderator and restricts rules to risking only a small fraction of their wealth on any cycle. This acts as a mechanism for reducing the chances of overfitting the data. The form of strength revision in the bucket brigade is a form of learning because it has lasting effects on the performance of the system, i.e., rules that have done well have an increasing advantage for firing over rules that performed poorly. However, strength revision may not be adequate if the rules do not contain the right sets of relations and restrictions in the first place. This points out the need for structural modification of the rules.

Modification operators The performance of rules in the system is reflected by the rule strengths and the frequency with which the rules are used. (A rule that has never matched and never fired can hardly be evaluated beyond its general inapplicability.) The rule base in M2 is divided into rule sets whose member rules make the same class of inference. For example, rules that reason about equipment behaviors are separated from those that reason about battalion behaviors. If one considers the operation of the bucket brigade, it can be seen that a differential in strength from the beginning of the reasoning chain to the end develops. However, within a single class of inference any difference reflects more of the relative merits of the rules and less of their position in a chain of inference.

This research takes advantage of the strong attributes of inductive approaches to learning developed by Holland and the genetic algorithms community. This initial approach does not preclude the use of other learning techniques nor does it provide commentary on their efficacy in the domain; rather it is a starting point. The primary effort has been in the adaptation of genetic modification operators to the M2 representation language [73]. Although genetic algorithms have been implemented in *n*-ary languages, they have not been implemented in systems employing rigid datatyping and hierarchically organized object and behavior spaces.

When to modify The indications for modifications come in two significantly different forms. The first, cataclysmic failure on the part of the system, indicates a lack of the rule sets (or possibly the entire rule base) to lead to useful and correct predictions about the environment. Ordinarily, randomly generated rules would not exhibit such failures unless a drastic shift in the application domain of the system had just been undertaken. A second, less disheartening indicator is the gradual differentials which arise in the strengths of rules at the same reasoning level. An examination of the conditions under which this differential arises would suggest the appropriate *when* and *how* of modification. The M2 system assigns a threshold to the standard deviation of rule strengths in a rule set. Passing this threshold serves to direct the attention of the modification operators to the offending rule set. One of two things could be true in this situation: 1) some rules are winning a lot and collecting all the payoff, or 2) some rules are losing a lot and losing all of their strength. Whether the rules were winning or losing they must have been firing, which means they must have been matching situations in the system. The strength and frequency of firing depends in part on the types of rules extant in the rule set. The two different varieties of rules in rule sets are: 1) specialist rules matching specific sets of assertions, and 2) generalists, that can match a variety of assertions. The learning task is to discover the proper mix of generalists and specialists (notice the bias in the bidding functions toward specific rules) capable of producing good overall performance.

How should I modify? The M2 system contains three basic kinds of modification operators: specializers, generalizers, and recombiners. In terms of the pattern-matched rules discussed above, specialization amounts to either changing variable values to literals, or adding constraints on variable values. Generalization, on the other hand, is exactly the opposite. Generalization operators change literals to variables and remove constraints [73]. If the operators strictly modify the rules, then the orientation of these operators, as expressed, is completely different than that of the bucket brigade and the stated purpose of our modifications. Note that a strict replacement scheme tries to generate *the best rule* for performing in the environment, rather than generate an increasingly stratified (in terms of specificity and generality) population of rules to produce better performance. The incorporation of operator modified copies of these rules can produce the desired effect at the expense of an initially expanding rule base. The remaining requirement is that these operators have some conditions for use. The utilization of meta-rules in learning generalizations and specializations is one of M2's approaches to modification. An example of a (rabid) generalizer meta-rule in M2 is shown below:

```
IF
    (rule-is ?name ?rule-set ?strength ?frequency ?specificity)
    (rule-set-is ?rule-set ?ave-strength ?ave-specificity)
    (exceeds-threshold ?strength ?ave-strength)
    (specific-rule ?specificity ?ave-specificity)
THEN
    (associate ?new-rule (make-copy ?anem))
    (remove-predicate-constraints ?new-rule)
    (variablize-literals ?new-rule).
```

This meta-rule makes a copy of the rules that satisfy its conditions, removes the constraints in the new rule, and changes its literal values to variables.

Preservation of rules and parts of rules is a natural element of the recombination operators in M2. The recombination operators make use of notions from natural genetics and were first described in the context of machine problem solving by Holland [67]. The idea behind the recombination of rules is that through fitness proportionate replication of rules and the recombination of the replicants with the original population, the average performance of the rule population will improve. The parts of the good rule are extant in the population at a greater frequency and thus appear on average in more rules. For example, consider the river-crossing rule above. The constraints of the rule, WITHIN-DISTANCE and INCLUDES, may be applicable in a broad class of rules about crossing objects, and the fitness proportionate reproduction and recombination methods would promote the use of these constraints.

The experimentation into the behavior of the modification operators in M2 is continuing. Current work is centering on strengthening the theoretical foundations of the recombinant approach in the higher-level representations M2 employs. A series of experiments to determine relative measures of performance between the two approaches to modification is planned as of this writing.

G. Issues and future topics

A variety of technical issues with respect to the M2 system exist. In terms of evaluation, the rate of learning is limited by the number of rules in a chain of inference before an ENV_{payoff} is received. As implemented, the system requires, as a lower boundary, a number of iterations equal to the length of the chain before the stage-setting rules at the head of the chain receive a payoff. Holland has suggested [70] (and Riolo implemented) [74] a remedy for this problem; the implementation in M2's representation remains as a future topic. A second issue related to evaluation is the use of the utility measure as a strength revision mechanism. Notice that the system as described selects for useful rules rather than strictly correct rules.

Some of the most creative work in the field of machine learning is in the development of useful modification operators. A current debate in the field is the relative merits of the logic-based approach compared to the sampling-based approaches we have described. Future research will focus on this issue particularly in the context of the required knowledge representations for each approach and the constraints those representations impose.

This section deals with expert systems as primarily notational, problem-solving conventions rather than as models for the human cognitive process. The area of learning research concerned with modeling human learning [75] is not treated here. Cognitive psychologists have made significant advances toward building systems that model human learning phenomena [76]. Discoveries in these endeavors have led to formal theories of general learning mechanisms.

Machine learning is a field in its infancy. Many very difficult problems remain unsolved including issues related to the rate of learning, overfitting of data, and general problems related to efficient search and inference. A final issue related to knowledge representation is the use of the most efficient versus the most transparent representation. The performance of learning techniques in large-scale problems will determine the efficacy of approaches being developed.

V. The next step: distributed problem solving

The potential benefit of systems such as BATTLE, ADRIES, and M2 is extensive. It is unclear, however, how the potential utility of these and other expert systems will be transferred to real applications in operational environments. Test methodology, configuration management, reliability, maintainability, performance, and system security are just some of the practical issues that must be resolved.

A. Blackboards in DPSS

A blackboard is a global data structure used to communicate facts, inferences, and goals between multiple expert nodes in a DPSS. Its power results from the way it provides a common framework and interface for sharing useful information both within and among expert nodes. Its flexibility supports both data-driven and goal-driven operation.

Three major types of information are represented in the full blackboard paradigm. The first type is frequently referred to as "data," but it can be further divided into *facts* and *inferences*. A fact is some datum that has been inserted into the system from an external data stream or a human user. It may have a confidence factor assigned by (or because of) its source, but it is not generated by the system itself. By contrast, an inference is produced by the application of some sort of knowledge to the facts and inferences already available to the system. The confidence factor associated with a given inference is a function of the system's confidence in the knowledge that produced the inference and in the other facts and inferences used to support that inference.

The second type of information is "control" information. Again, this is further broken down into *knowledge sources* and *goals*. Knowledge sources are the procedures that define how inferences are to be drawn and actions are to be performed by the system during its normal mode of operation. In some implementations, knowledge sources are able to pre-identify both the data required for them to be effective and the types of inferences that they can produce. Goals represent more general activities that may be undertaken by an expert, such as the generation of an inference that matches a certain pattern (if possible). In some of the literature, a separate data structure known as an agenda is established for the maintenance of goals. Expert nodes will generally have numerous goals to choose from, and will use some criteria for selecting the most valuable goal at a particular time.

The final type of information associated with a DPSS blackboard is derived from its distributed nature. This information is required to control the flow of information from one expert's blackboard to those of other experts. In a single-node expert system using a blackboard architecture, one blackboard will be the central repository of all information about the problem. With a DPSS, however, each separate expert node requires access to blackboard information. This implies that expert nodes should use local blackboards that are actually individual partitions of an abstract global blackboard. One or more strategies can be employed by each expert to select the information that should be transmitted from or accepted into the local blackboard, the other experts that should participate in an information exchange, and the conditions under which such exchanges are desirable. The alternative is a single blackboard maintained as a service for all of the experts. However, this technique has severe drawbacks when the experts are physically distributed. Since the blackboard is a vital resource to the inference process, the communications load involved in supporting a centralized blackboard would be immense. In addition, a single global blackboard would provide a single point of failure in a physically distributed DPSS.

Thus, each expert node of a networked DPSS should have a local blackboard composed of information directly available to that expert. Some of this information may be irrelevant to that expert, and some of it may be required by other experts. During the course of problem solving this "misplaced" information will be communicated from one blackboard to another according to blackboard communications criteria. For instance, when a particular confidence threshold was reached in an inference generated by one expert, it might be "leaked" to a sibling or higher-level expert for further processing. In the case of information needed by the receiving expert, it will be used as an inference to drive further processing. In the case of information received by an expert node via this process and substantiated, a return flow would be used to bolster the confidence of that inference in the original node. In the case of conflicting information, a reverse return flow would lower the confidence and/or spot error recovery actively in one or both experts. In the case of goals propagated between blackboards, the receiving expert node would have to choose among externally-supplied goals and its own goals when evaluating which to execute [79]. This localized control ability is discussed in more detail later in this section.

The blackboard paradigm thus provides a method of loosely coupling various expert nodes supporting conflict resolution and individual activity. The paradigm is not centralized, so that there is a graceful degradation if one or more nodes are removed from the system (assuming that the loss of one node's expertise or information does not prohibit effective problem solving altogether). The system may be data-driven as information islands are propagated upward to higher-level or sibling nodes, or it may be goal-driven by placing goals on the local blackboards attached to various nodes. Communication load may be tuned by changing the rules controlling inter-blackboard information movement.

B. DPSS attributes

A number of different attributes may be used to compare and evaluate alternative DPSS architectures. Each of these attributes can have a profound impact on the performance or even the viability of a given DPSS architecture with respect to a particular problem domain:

- *Physical Distribution:* The individual expert nodes of a DPSS can be resident in the same processor (i.e., a *logical distribution*) [84], assigned to individual processors in a tightly-coupled parallel system [85], or distributed across multiple processors communicating through a LAN. A combination of physical and logical distribution is possible within a single DPSS. The degree and type of physical distribution for a given DPSS is largely a function of the overall goals of the system architects. For example, logical distribution provides a means for flexible experimentation with different network topologies while requiring a minimum amount of processing and communication hardware.
- *Data Distribution:* During normal operation, each expert node in a DPSS will receive a different set of facts about the world and inferences from other experts. (The utility of any architecture where all experts receive the same information is unclear, due to the implicitly redundant activity required at each node.) The set of facts available to each expert node can be influenced by many factors, including the spatial distribution of data, the network topology, and the distribution of knowledge sources throughout the DPSS. The inferences available to each expert node are a function of the facts it receives, the knowledge sources it has available, the control decisions it makes, and the communication policies that regulate the transfer of inferences between experts.
- *Knowledge Source Distribution:* In some DPSS architectures, all of the knowledge sources are directly available to all of the expert nodes [86], while in others, each expert has access to only some knowledge sources [85]. The determination of which knowledge sources will be available to each expert is usually made by the system architect, based on an evaluation of the difficulty of hosting different knowledge sources on different nodes. Knowledge sources that are initially

designed to be part of a given DPSS are likely to be easier to share among experts than knowledge sources that already exist when the DPSS is designed.

- *Task Distribution:* When considered as a monolithic operation, each knowledge source is capable of performing one or more units of work or *tasks*. The potential tasks that knowledge sources can perform are usually represented as goals, which define tasks in terms of the possible result produced by knowledge sources. During DPSS operation, the set of tasks under consideration at an expert node is a function of the inferences produced by its own knowledge sources, the communication policies that regulate the transfer of goals between experts, and the degree to which a given goal can be easily factored into local subgoals. Since any one node can actually work on only a limited number of tasks (usually one) at one time, the method by which it evaluates and activates potential tasks has a critical influence on the usefulness of its problem-solving activities (as discussed in the next section).
- *Communication Policy:* As already noted, each expert node in a DPSS must implement a communication policy, which need not be the same for all nodes. From the perspective of a sending node, this policy determines when the node will transmit information (either inferences or goals) to other nodes, what types of information will be transmitted, and which nodes are appropriate recipients of the information. From the perspective of a receiving node, this policy determines when the node will accept information, what types of information will be accepted, which nodes are appropriate originators of the information, and how the accepted information should be evaluated locally. The choice of a particular set of communication policies may be influenced by any predetermined organizational structure for a given DPSS. However, the possible subtle interactions of different aspects of communication policies make it difficult to establish an *optimal* set of policies without extensive experimentation in real or simulated environments [87].
- *Organizational Structure:* It is possible to bias the evaluation of tasks by each expert node so that it prefers certain activities over others, regardless of the current state of problem-solving. This type of bias, in conjunction with communication policies, implements an organizational structure across the DPSS. In a hierarchical structure, for example, each node accepts tasks from at most one other node, thereby permitting higher-level nodes to control and coordinate the activities of lower-level nodes to control and coordinate the activities of lower-level nodes. In a flat (committee) structure, each node can accept tasks from any other node, thereby maximizing the availability of a given node's services to the whole network. Of course, many other organizational structures are possible. The combination of an organizational structure and a set of communication policies establishes a distributed problem-solving strategy within a DPSS.
- *Organizational Development:* If the DPSS architect pre-establishes an organizational structure for the system, then no organizational development is required. Alternatively, the DPSS can develop an appropriate organizational structure as part of its initial problem-solving activity. This can be achieved by requiring nodes to negotiate (as in the "contract net" approach of Smith and Davis [88], [89], an appropriate task distribution prior to the start of problem solving.

Another option is to permit the DPSS to alter its organizational structure during the course of problem solving, by allowing nodes to detect and respond to strong mismatches between their knowledge of local task requirements and their knowledge of current organizational responsibilities [90]. The choice of an appropriate organizational development scheme for a given DPSS depends on whether an optimal organizational structure: 1) can be predetermined for every problem-solving situation, 2) can be determined once for each problem-solving situation, or 3) must change during the course of problem-solving activity.

The possible interplay among these attributes can yield complex system behavior that is not easy to anticipate. Consequently, it is important for DPSS developers to incorporate extensive internal auditing and measuring capabilities in their systems, so that they can sensibly test, understand, and modify problem-solving results and strategies. In fact, some DPSS environments [84] have been developed primarily for the purpose of measuring the effectiveness of different problem-solving strategies.

Regardless of the specific attributes of a given DPSS, its expert nodes must incorporate a method for determining when a potential task should actually be performed (i.e., for determining the *focus of attention*). Each expert may be attempting to satisfy multiple goals, and some of these goals may be generated locally, while others may be supplied by other experts. The mechanism for resolving these competing claims implements a local problem-solving strategy within each node.

C. The focus of attention mechanism

The DPSS techniques that have been developed at the University of Massachusetts [90], [91] include an elaborate focus of attention mechanism. The technique functions by giving each expert node the ability to decide which of its possible goals it should pursue (through the activation of its available knowledge sources). These goals include both those generated by the expert itself and those generated by others. The focus of attention is determined by first evaluating potential knowledge source activations against various criteria, and then by selecting the most highly rated task for execution. These criteria could include, but not be limited to, the following:

- *Validity:* If the information available for a task has a high confidence level, then that task should be performed before a task for which the information has a low confidence level, as the resulting information would be more valid.
- *Internal/External Control:* Tasks that are triggered by local activity may be preferred over tasks that are received from other experts (and vice versa).
- *Organizational Significance:* Tasks that are important to an expert because of its organizational bias should be performed before tasks that are less relevant to its known responsibilities.
- *Efficiency:* If it is possible to estimate effectively the cost of performing a task before it is executed, then less expensive tasks may be preferred over more expensive ones. This criterion may be especially useful when a given goal can be achieved by more than one local knowledge source.

- *Goal Satisfaction:* Tasks that are themselves subgoals or supergoals of several other tasks may be preferred over tasks that are less connected with other activities.
- *Task Age:* If a task has been awaiting activation for a long time or is approaching an age cutoff threshold, it may be preferred over tasks that were created more recently (or vice versa).

Thus a high priority request from another expert might take precedence over a local "business as usual" task, or a short, simple task might override a long task that is based on information of questionable validity.

These focus of attention criteria can be implemented as variable, weighted parameters of the DPSS. The operation of the system can be modified by altering these parameters for a single expert or a group of experts. Changing the balance between the criteria of validity and goal satisfaction, for example, can alter system behavior to become more data-directed or more goal-directed; modifying the internal/external control parameter can determine whether individual nodes are more locally directed or more externally directed.

The use of these criteria allows the focus of attention to vary with time. During normal operation, the focus would follow a logical "train of thought" with respect to a given expert. Anomalous situations, however, could be handled by shifting the focus to different types of tasks. Requests from a system user or another expert could be handled as interrupts to the train of thought, and critical warnings from input data or other experts could be dealt with in an effective manner. Thus, this approach permits DPSS nodes to function passively, actively, or interactively, depending on dynamically changing problem-solving requirements.

D. An example

As part of its ongoing research and development program, PRC has been exploring the potential military application of distributed problem-solving techniques by building a prototype DPSS. This system, called the Communicating, Cooperating Expert Systems (CCES) Framework, provides an evolving workbench for testing different DPSS concepts. A brief overview of this prototype and an example of its operation may help clarify some of these concepts.

The CCES Framework is implemented as a collection of physically and logically distributed nodes communicating via an Ethernet LAN. Each node has a similar internal structure consisting of three principal processing components: a blackboard-based expert system, a focusing tool, and a communications switcher. The expert system component exchanges information with the external world via a user interface and a message stream; its own knowledge sources use this information, in conjunction with what is received from other nodes, to produce new inferences and goals. The focusing tool uses a frame-based data structure describing goal rating factors to reevaluate items on the agenda; each node may use different criteria for agenda evaluation. The communication switcher exchanges locally generated inferences and goals with other nodes, and maintains records that allow it to broadcast local changes to previously transmitted information.

These three components run as asynchronous, concurrent processes in each CCES node (although a single communication switcher can service multiple nodes that are located in the same physical processor). This type of architectural decomposition should facilitate the replacement of local node expert systems with other "foreign" expert systems or perhaps more conventional ADP components. This potential adaptiveness is important to the overall goals of PRC's research in distributed problem solving, which include the need for a capability to coordinate heterogeneous nodes such as expert systems and conventional database systems.

In a current test scenario, the CCES Framework is configured to support four independent expert nodes, which collectively work on two problems at the same time. The four experts are: *Blue Intel*, which is assigned a current intelligence problem (monitoring the activities of *Terrorists*); *Blue Recon*, which primarily receives reports of visual contact with *Red Forces; Blue I&W*, which is assigned an I&W problem (monitoring the status and intentions of Red Forces); and *White Intel*, which is a source of allied intelligence. Each expert receives a different set of reports about the world, but they all have access to the same knowledge sources. Thus, each expert's name was chosen based on its data sources and assigned responsibilities, rather than on any unique local knowledge.

As reports and inferences (called hypotheses) are received or produced by an expert, they are added to the expert's local blackboard. Any knowledge source activations triggered by a new blackboard item are then added to the expert's agenda. Each expert maintains an interactive user interface to these data structures. Items are displayed on the blackboard from top to bottom in the order in which they were created. The visual representation of a blackboard item includes the name of the originating node, the type of information contained in the item, a brief textual description of the item (with times and grid locations for report items), and an indication of the expert's confidence in the item. The CCES Framework currently uses an adaptation of Dempster-Shafer technique for representing uncertainty (see Section II and Appendix II). The confidence is displayed graphically as a horizontal bar: the length of the solid left end indicates the degree of belief for the item, the length of the solid right end indicates the degree of disbelief for the item, and the length of the fuzzy middle part indicates the remaining, unaccounted-for belief (or uncertainty).

As part of each expert's blackboard display, the CCES Framework also maintains an agenda display window that describes the current status of that expert's agenda. Unsatisfied knowledge source activations are displayed in the order of their estimated value (also shown), along with the names of the knowledge sources from which they originate. Within the current test scenario, efficiency and task age are the only criteria used to evaluate the knowledge source activations.

The communication policies for this scenario generally allow one expert to transmit data to other experts only when it has first received a request for a pattern of information that matches that data. For example, the Blue Intel expert receives reports about various resources acquired by Terrorists (such as nuclear weapons expertise). These reports trigger the activation of knowledge sources capable of hypothesizing what can be manufactured from the newly acquired resources (such as a nuclear weapon trigger). However, since the Blue Intel expert's knowledge source is unable to determine locally whether or not Terrorists have acquired other resources required for manufacturing the same product (such as high explosives), it sends a pattern description of the missing information as a subgoal to the other experts. Until they receive this request, they will not transmit this type of information to Blue Intel.

A conservative communication policy of this type is appropriate when it is important to reduce the likelihood of experts flooding each other (and the scarce communication resources) with useless information. However, there are some circumstances where it may be desirable for one expert to transmit data to other experts, even when they have not expressed an interest in it. For example, when the Blue Intel expert hypothesizes that Terrorists are manufacturing a nuclear weapon trigger (and later, a nuclear device), its local knowledge source recognizes that these hypotheses are important enough to be treated as *warnings*. Warnings are displayed locally in a special window and are then transmitted to all known experts, where they are also displayed.

As additional assistance for human users and experts, each expert node maintains a situation map that presents a symbolized, geographic representation of items on the expert's blackboard. When two or more nodes share the same physical processor, they also share the same situation map. As the blackboard is updated, the situation map is modified to reflect the changes. Icons on the map and their corresponding entries on the blackboard can be selected by the user. Additional information is available for a selected item, including the tree of knowledge sources, hypotheses, and reports that were used to generate the item. This kind of dependency tracking not only explains how a given hypothesis is derived; it also supports a network-wide truth maintenance capability that allows warnings and hypotheses to be withdrawn if their supporting data is later retracted.

E. Cautions

The DPSS paradigm may eventually extend the applicability of expert systems technology to cover many intractable military problem domains, but it is not a panacea. In addition to spawning new problems (e.g., determining when a DPSS has actually finished solving a given problem), it may make existing problems, such as system security, more complicated. Nor is it likely that current focus of attention mechanisms or communication policies will be efficient enough to prevent a real-time DPSS from overloading itself with inter-expert communications (the DPSS equivalent of thrashing in a virtual memory architecture). Research at the University of Massachusetts [90], [92] suggests that DPSS performance may be improved by incorporating sophisticated nodes that can reason about their own plans (potential task sequences) and the plans of other nodes. Whether these advanced techniques will be sufficient to support fielded operational systems remains to be seen.

Nevertheless, the distributed problem-solving paradigm represents a promising direction of research in expert systems technology. Without it, some of the most critical, complex military problem domains will remain without the benefit of support from expert systems.

VI. Current and future research topics

This section summarizes selected expert system applications that have been used for the military. The remainder of the section addresses the key research issues that must be solved to enhance the use of expert system technology for future problems.

A. Summary applications

The expert system process was described briefly and then several key applications were presented. The first application was a resource allocation problem that was developed to help the Marine Corps match weapons or targets. New concepts were described that reduce the amount of questions that were asked and thus reduced the total amount of time to solve the problem.

A second expert system evolved from this first example that was used to help the operator identify complex images. This system will enhance the performance of existing military sensors by guiding the operator along a near-optimal solution to the identification of unknown targets. The third expert system example examined the area of troubleshooting electronic equipment. Prototypes have been developed that can reason about varying fault conditions and can guide the operator to identify the faulty component and to fix the equipment. The fourth expert system application was a digital radar imagery exploitation system. This system produced interpretations of military situations from radar imagery.

Next, an intelligence analysis system was described that had a learning component. Machine learning is crucial to avoid the brittleness of expert systems that is commonly encountered, and this learning system indicated encouraging progress. The final system description was a departure from conventional isolated expert systems. This distributed problem-solving approach used communicating, cooperating expert systems that work as a team to solve large complex problems.

B. Research issues

The examples of expert systems in the military presented in this paper illustrate that a great deal has been learned about knowledge, its representation, acquisition, and utilization since the beginnings of AI research. We believe that there are many reasons to be optimistic about the future applications of expert systems to real-world commercial and military problems but there are critical research issues to be solved. In a recent presentation Friedland [93] made several interesting observations on the future research issues in expert systems. He points out that the initial researchers in AI felt that the power of expert systems would be in complex, general-purpose inference engines able to emulate human beings. Friedland suggests that this led to a great deal of frustration and the growing realization that the power was in the knowledge. Feigenbaum refers to this as the Knowledge Principle. A very important point is that vast amounts of knowledge must be acquired and codified in the machine. Friedland shows that there are four major bottlenecks in the utilization of this knowledge. They are listed here and then discussed:

- knowledge acquisition
- knowledge consistency and completeness
- large knowledge base manipulation
- interface technology.

Knowledge acquisition This involves the process of getting the knowledge into the system. The standard use of a knowledge engineer is to act as an intermediary, which can cause delays and a loss of accuracy. Major research efforts directed at eliminating this intermediate step have developed two techniques. The automatic technique would use inductive and deductive means to acquire the knowledge without the knowledge engineer. This is clearly related to certain aspects of the learning projects such as Michalski [63]. The semi-automatic technique would use the domain expert as the knowledge engineer, which has become increasingly popular in the development of expert systems. The knowledge acquisition process, which can take from 50 to 90 percent of the time and effort in the development of an expert system, is not a single event process. The realistic view is that the knowledge must change throughout the life of the system.

Knowledge consistency and completeness This bottleneck involves the combination of knowledge in many different forms, from numerous, often disparate, sources with a second issue of whether there is enough knowledge for functional adequacy. As large expert systems are constructed, the sources of information will increase because no single human can possibly know more than a small percentage of the final system. Another complication is that much of the information will come from nonhuman resources. In the example in Section III on the expert system for maintenance and troubleshooting, much of the data comes from instruction manuals, design information, computer-aided design programs as well as data from the machine designers. The use of all of these different sources can lead to both apparent and real disagreements. The future research in this area involves the design of mechanisms to aid in the information entry in large systems. Knowledge source disparity can include contradictory heuristics (likely failure modes and design considerations), problems with the actual language of rules, frames, etc., and facts (tolerances, expected life-time and anticipated temperature and environmental conditions).

The second major issue in this knowledge acquisition bottleneck involves the completeness of the knowledge base. It is necessary to determine if this collection of knowledge is enough to solve the actual problem. The completeness issue can be solved for logic-based knowledge systems but no technique has been developed to solve the general problem. As systems evolve and the knowledge acquisition process continues through the life of the systems, as indicated in the first bottleneck, this problem will become even more difficult. The ultimate solution involves sufficient deep knowledge that can understand underlying principles in the realms of physics, chemistry, electronics, etc., to assess the completeness of its knowledge base.

Large knowledge base manipulation This bottleneck involves the problems of how data, procedures, and other problem-solving techniques must be manipulated in very large expert systems containing vast amounts of data. Traditional techniques of forward and backward chaining with rules, theorem proving, and object-oriented programming may not be adequate as the expert systems of today scale up to the large systems of tomorrow.

The present techniques in knowledge manipulation may be adequate if there are significant increases in the power and speed of computer hardware. Undoubtedly, hardware improvements will help solve this problem, but another generation of reasoning systems is needed to solve these large problems more efficiently.

Research in this area involves the direct solution to large knowledge base manipulation, or an attempt at distributed problem solving. One distributed problem-solving solution is to break the problem into many smaller communicating cooperating expert systems as discussed in Section V. Difficulties to be solved include the degree of independence in the individual expert systems, the required amount of communications among the individual problem solvers, the degree of autonomous behavior, and the use of robust learning techniques.

Interface technology This bottleneck involves the process of getting the information out of the machine and into a form that humans can understand and use effectively. Present systems do not use very much natural language to explain to the user what is happening and why. This problem will become increasingly difficult as the sizes of systems increase and the user requires more explicit explanations from the expert system.

1. *System Brittleness:* Today's systems cannot determine if the problem they are trying to solve is within their "area of expertise." For example, there is a definite possibility that a system designed to diagnose medical problems could easily be confused between measles and rust on a car. In addition, the systems expect their inputs in a fairly tightly defined environment and changes in language or syntax can often result in disarray.
2. *Common Sense Reasoning and Analogical Reasoning:* A human, stumped by a particular problem, will often try to use "common sense" to help in the solution. There is not consensus on what common sense means but Friedland [93] suggests that common sense means knowing a little about a lot and recognizing from a human's vast knowledge base what is relevant and can be linked to the particular problem at hand. Lenat [94] at Microelectronics and Computer Consortium (MCC) is attempting to codify the knowledge in a desk encyclopedia, which will be used as the basis for the knowledge contained in an expert system. An example that Lenat uses to show the difficulty of common sense reasoning is the problem of distinguishing the difference between the two phrases:

   - The pen is in the box.
   - The pen is in the corral.

   Lenat hopes that once he has entered the knowledge contained in his disk encyclopedia, the computer can determine the difference in the two uses of pen. Initially Lenat felt that learning would provide a solution but now he feels that hand crafted knowledge and hard work will be the solution for the next 10 years.

   The second mechanism is analogical reasoning. The process consists of two steps. The first step is to pick a potential analogous situation and the second step is to extract the common items. This sounds simple but is extremely difficult, and little progress has been made in this area of basic research. Progress made in the research on common sense reasoning may help to solve this problem too.
3. *Learning:* This area, discussed briefly in Section IV, needs additional development. Clearly there is a large gap between present-day expert systems and their human counterparts when it comes to learning. Friedland [93] points out that we would think a fellow human being hopelessly stupid if the same mistake were

repeated endlessly. This is exactly what happens to most expert systems when they do not have sufficient knowledge and reasoning components to solve a problem. Learning becomes mandatory when one considers that large systems, such as the NASA space station, are continuously evolving. Long-term mission projects will need learning to acquire new knowledge and to re-validate the system as knowledge is added. The addition of learning to future expert systems will probably provide the biggest change from today's expert systems to those of tomorrow. Potential aid for future learning lies in the fields of neural networks and causal modeling of physical systems.

4. *Synergism Among Intelligent Agents:* This area has great potential. The idea, related to communicating cooperating expert systems, or problem solvers, involves using them to provide synergism. This can only be accomplished when the problem solvers are organized as teams able to work effectively and cooperatively to solve a bigger problem. The organization of these problem solvers can be in many forms including hierarchical, committee, distributed in functional or geographic terms, etc. The final synergistic configuration is ultimately related to the actual problem. One major advantage of these cooperating problem solvers is that individual ones can be made relatively small. The state-of-the-art in small expert systems is far advanced to what can be done for very large expert systems, because it is easier to test them, there is increased confidence, and production costs are lower. The individual expert systems can then be hooked together as a team to solve a bigger problem. The existing examples of this at the University of Massachusetts, Stanford, and PRC are showing signs of promise for large synergistic systems.
5. *Generic Expert Systems:* It is hoped that domain independent expert systems can be used as financial advisers, medical diagnosticians, indications and warning analysts, target identifiers, and electronic troubleshooters. No single system can accomplish this. Indeed many medical diagnostic expert systems cannot be easily modified to work on apparently similar medical problems.

   Another issue with generic expert systems concerns a uniform approach to handling uncertainty. The present systems are ad hoc and usually not mathematically verifiable. When certain information is concatenated, the problem usually becomes more difficult because the propagation of uncertain information is not well understood. Knowledge representation is also not handled uniformly.
6. *Delivery Machines for Expert Systems:* There has been a big change in attitudes in the AI community. Originally everything was done on large high priced LISP machines with identical delivery machines. The user community is no longer willing to pay this price since conventional hardware has become increasingly powerful at lower cost. The new microprocessor-based workstations will be the delivery machine in many cases, and for some users the AI solutions will be provided on a mainframe. The development will still be on a mix of special AI machines and more general purpose microprocessors.
7. *The Degree of Expert in an Expert System:* It has become very clear that expert systems are nothing of the kind. The majority of expert systems are only slightly clever. This is not all bad. The trend in expert systems should be to

improve the user from an average grade of poor to mediocre, not mediocre to great. The reason is obvious. Most of the problems that we encounter are routine, time consuming, boring and mundane, and it is these irritating little problems that take from 50 to 80 percent of the human expert's time. The solution is to use our "clever" expert systems to solve the mundane and allow the human to free up his time, by as much as 40 to 50 percent, to solve the problems that the machine cannot solve.

These are genuine problems that must be addressed and solved before AI can be used successfully in the complex world of the present. In fact, the Defense Advanced Research Project Agency, the Army, the Air Force and the Navy are addressing all of the key issues listed above. The success of this research, by some of the best researchers in the United States, is expected to hasten the routine use of expert systems by the military and in the commercial marketplace.

Acknowledgment

The authors wish to thank Mrs. Ann Goddard for the tireless and careful preparation of this manuscript and Mrs. Bette Violette for her patient editing of this manuscript. We also thank Dr. Y.T. Chien and Ms. Michelle Younger for providing a great deal of guidance and direction. The IEEE reviewers' comments were thoughtful and well received in this revised paper, and we thank them for their useful inputs.

References

1. A.J. Baciocco, "Artificial intelligence," *Military Science Technology*, vol. 1, no. 5, pp. 38 – 40, 1981.
2. ______, "Artificial intelligence and C³I," *Signal Magazine*, AFCEA, Sept. 1981.
3. E.W. Martin, "Artificial intelligence and robotics for military systems," in *Proc. of The Army Conf. on Application of Artificial Intelligence to Battlefield Information Management*, Battelle Columbus Laboratories, (Washington, DC), Apr. 20 – 22, 1983.
4. A.B. Salisbury, "Opening remarks on artificial intelligence," in *Proc. of The Army Conf. on Application of Artificial Intelligence to Battlefield Information Management*, Battelle Columbus Laboratories, (Washington, DC), Apr. 20 – 22, 1983.
5. R. Shumaker and J.E. Franklin, "Artificial intelligence in military applications," *Signal Magazine*, vol. 40, p. 29, June 1986.
6. A. Barr and E.A. Feigenbaum, *The Handbook of Artificial Intelligence*. Los Altos, CA: William Kaufmann, Inc., 1981.
7. E. Charniak and D. McDermott, "Introduction to artificial intelligence." Reading, MA: Addison-Wesley, 1984.
8. P. Harmon and D. King, *Expert Systems*. New York, NY: Wiley, 1985.
9. P.H. Winston, *Artificial Intelligence*, Second Edition. Reading, MA: Addison-Wesley, 1984.
10. P. Jackson, *Introduction to Expert Systems*. Reading, MA: Addison-Wesley, 1986.
11. D.B. Lenat, A. Clarkson, and G. Kiremidjian, "An expert system for indications and warning analysis," *IJCAI Proceedings*, pp. 259 – 262, 1983.
12. R.O. Duda, P.E. Hart, and N.J. Nilsson, "Subjective Bayesian Methods for rule-based inference systems," Tech. Rep. 124, Stanford Research Institute, Palo Alto, CA, Jan. 1976.
13. L.A. Zadeh, "A simple view of the Dempster-Shafer theory of evidence and its implication for the role of combination," *AI Magazine*, vol. 7, no. 2, Summer 1986.
14. D. Heckerman, "Probabilistic interpretation for MYCIN's certainty factors," in *Uncertainty in Artificial Intelligence*, L.N. Kanal and J.F. Lemmer, Eds. New York, NY: North Holland, 1986.

15. B. Chandrasekaran and M.C. Tanner, "Uncertainty handling in expert systems: uniform vs. task-specific formalisms," in *Uncertainty in Artificial Intelligence*, L.N. Kanal and J.F. Lemmer, Eds. New York, NY: North Holland, 1986, pp. 35–46.
16. A.P. Dempster, "A generalization of Bayesian inference," *J. Roy. Statis. Soc. Ser.* B 30, 1968.
17. G. Shafer, *A Mathematical Theory of Evidence*. Princeton, NJ: Princeton University Press, 1976.
18. L.A. Zadeh, "Review of Shafer's book, a mathematical theory of evidence," *AI Magazine*, vol. 5, no. 3, Fall 1984.
19. ______, *A Computational Theory of Dispositions*. Berkeley, CA: University of California, 1984.
20. ______, "A theory of commonsense knowledge," in *Aspects of Vagueness*, Skala, Termini, and Trillas, Eds. Dordrecht, Holland: D. Reidel Publishing Co., 1984.
21. ______, "Syllogistic reasoning as a basis for combination of evidence in expert systems," in *Proceedings of the 9th International Joint Conf. on Artificial Intelligence*, (Los Angeles, CA), Aug. 1985.
22. R. Cohen and M.R. Grinbert, "A theory of heuristic reasoning about uncertainty," *AI Magazine*, vol. 4, no. 2, 1983.
23. ______, "A framework for heuristic reasoning about uncertainty," in *Proceedings of the 8th International Joint Conf. on Artificial Intelligence*, (Karlsruhe, West Germany), 1983.
24. R. Cohen and M.D. Lieberman, "A report on FOLIO: An expert assistant or portfolio managers," in *Proceedings of the 8th International Joint Conf. on Artificial Intelligence*, (Karlsruhe, West Germany), 1983.
25. Cohen *et al.*, "Representativeness and uncertainty in classification systems," *AI Magazine*, vol. 6, no. 3, 1985.
26. P.R. Cohen, "Heuristic reasoning about uncertainty: An Artificial Intelligence approach," Great Britain: Pitman Advanced Publishing Program, 1985.
27. J. Doyle, "Methodological simplicity in expert system construction: the case of judgments and reasoned assumptions," *AI Magazine*, vol. 4, no. 2, 1983.
28. ______, "A truth maintenance system," *Artificial Intelligence*, vol. 12, 1979.
29. M.L. Ginsberg, "Implementing probabilistic reasoning," Working Paper HPP 84-31, Stanford University, Stanford, CA, June 1984.
30. J.A. Barnett, "Computational methods for a mathematical theory of evidence," in *Proc. of the 7th Int. Joint Conf. on Artificial Intelligence*, (Vancouver, British Columbia, Canada), 1981.
31. T.D. Garvey, J.D. Lowrance, and M.A. Fischer, "An inference technique for integrating knowledge from disparate sources," in *Proceedings of the 7th International Joint Conf. on Artificial Intelligence* (Vancouver, British Columbia, Canada), 1981.
32. J.D. Lowrance and T.D. Garvey, "Evidential reasoning: and implementation for multisensor integration," SRI Technical Note 307, Dec. 1983.
33. J.R. Slagle and H. Hamburger, "An expert system for a resource allocation problem," *Communications of the ACM*, vol. 28, no. 9, pp. 994–1004, Sept. 1985.
34. J.R. Slagle, M.W. Gaynor, and E.J. Halpern, "An intelligent control strategy for computer consultation," *IEEE Trans. Pattern Anal. Machine Intell.*, vol. PAMI-6, Mar. 1984.
35. L.B. Booker, "An Artificial Intelligence (AI) approach to ship classification," in *20th Annual Technical Symp.*, Washington, D.C. Chapter of ACM (Gaithersburg, MD), 1985.
36. R.R. Cantone, F.J. Pipitone, W.B. Lander, and M.P. Marrone, "Model-based probabilistic reasoning for electronics troubleshooting," in *IJCAI-83*.
37. R.O. Duda *et al.*, "Development of a computer-based consultant for mineral exploration," Annual Report, SRI Projects 5821 and 6415, SRI International, Menlo Park, CA, Oct. 1977.
38. R.R. Cantone, W.B. Lander, M.P. Marrone, and M.W. Gaynor, "IN-ATE™: Fault diagnosis as expert system guided search," in *Computer Expert Systems*, L. Bolc, and M.J. Coombs, Eds. New York, NY: Springer-Verlag, 1986.
39. F.J. Pipitone, "An expert system for electronics troubleshooting based on function and connectivity," in *IEEE 1st Conf. on AI Applications*, (Denver, CO), 1984.
40. ______, "FIS, an electronics fault isolation system based on qualitative causal modeling," in *Aerospace Applications of AI Conf.*, 1985.
41. ______, "The FIS electronics troubleshooting system," in *Computer*, July 1986.
42. J. DeKleer, "Reasoning with uncertainty in physical systems," *AI Journal*, 1985.

43. R. Davis *et al.*, "Diagnosis based on description of structure and function," *AAAI Proceedings*, pp. 137–142, 1982.
44. T. Levitt *et al.*, "Design of a probabilistic certainty calculus for ADRIES," Contract DACA76-86-C-0010, Advanced Decision Systems, Mountain View, CA, Apr. 1986.
45. T. Levitt, L. Winter, T. Eppel, T. Irons, and C. Neveu, "Terrain knowledge elicitation for ADRIES: Part II," Contract DACA76-86-C-0010, Advanced Decision Systems, Mountain View, CA, Oct. 1987.
46. T. Levitt, W. Edwards, and L. Winter, "Elicitation of a priori terrain knowledge for ADRIES," Contract DACA76-86-C-0010, Advanced Decision Systems, Mountain View, CA, Nov. 1986.
47. DARPA, ETL, ADS, SAIC, MRJ, and TASC, "Advanced digital radar imagery exploitation system (ADRIES) program plan," Advanced Decision Systems (~ ~ADS), Mountain View, CA, Oct. 1986.
48. R. Drazovich *et al.*, "Advanced digital radar imagery exploitation system (ADRIES) annual technical report," Contract DAEA18-83-C-0026, Advanced Decision Systems, TR-1040-02, Apr. 1985.
49. D. Grantrath, "Estimation procedure for ROC curves," Science Applications International Corporation (SAIC) Internal Memo dated April 15, 1987, Tucson, AZ, Apr. 1987.
50. D. von Winterfeldt and W. Edwards, *Decision Analysis and Behavioral Research*. Cambridge, MA: Cambridge University Press, 1986.
51. J. Pearl, "Fusion, propagation, and structuring in belief networks," *Artificial Intelligence*, vol. 29, pp. 241–288, 1986.
52. R.A. Howard and J.E. Matheson, "Influence diagrams," SRI Technical Memo, Menlo Park, CA, 1980.
53. C.F. Gettys and T.A. Willke, "The application of Bayes' Theorem when the true data state is uncertain," *Organizational Behavior and Human Performance*, pp. 125–141, 1969.
54. D.A. Schum, "Current developments in research on cascaded inference," in *Cognitive Processes in Decision and Choice Behavior*, T.S. Wallsten, Ed. Hillsdale, NJ: Lawrence Erlbaum Press, 1980.
55. C.W. Kelly, III, and S. Barclay, "A general Bayesian model for hierarchical inference," *Organizational Behavior and Human Performance*, vol. 10, 1973.
56. J. Pearl, "On evidential reasoning in a hierarchy of hypotheses," *Artificial Intelligence*, vol. 28, no. 1, Feb. 1986.
57. T.O. Binford and T.S. Levitt, "Bayesian inference in model-based machine vision," in *Proc. AAAI Uncertainty in Artificial Intelligence Workshop*, (Seattle, WA), July 1987.
58. ______, "Utility-based control for computer vision," in *Proc. AAAI Uncertainty in Artificial Intelligence Workshop*. (Minneapolis, MN), Aug. 1988.
59. J.H. Holland *et al.*, *Induction: Processes of Inference, Learning, and Discovery*. Cambridge, MA: MIT Press, 1986, ch. 1, pp. 1–28.
60. A.E. Feigenbaum, "Lecture at the first U.S.-China joint seminar on automation and intelligent systems," Beijing, China, May 28–June 1, 1984.
61. A.L. Samuel, "Some studies in machine learning using the game of checkers," *IBM J. Res. Develop.*, vol. 3, pp. 211–232, 1959.
62. M. Minsky, "Steps toward artificial intelligence," in *Computers and Thought*, A.E. Feigenbaum and J. Feldman, Eds. New York, NY: McGraw-Hill, 1963, pp. 429–435.
63. R.S. Michalski, "Understanding the nature of learning: issues and research directions," in *Machine Learning*, vol. 2, R.S. Michalski, J.G. Carbonell, and T.G. Mitchell, Eds. Los Altos, CA: Morgan Kaufman, 1986, ch. 1, pp. 3–18.
64. J.R. Quinlan, "Learning efficient classification procedures and their application to chess end games," in *Machine Learning*, vol. 1, R.S. Michalski, J.G. Carbonell, and T.G. Mitchell, Eds. Palo Alto, CA: Tioga Publishing, 1983, ch. 15, pp. 463–482.
65. D.B. Lenat, "The role of heuristics in learning by discovery: three case studies," in *Machine Learning*, vol. 1, R.S. Michalski, J.G. Carbonell, and T.G. Mitchell, Eds. Palo Alto, CA: Tioga Publishing, 1983, ch. 15, pp. 249–263.
66. G.E. Hinton *et al.*, "Boltzmann machines: Constraint satisfaction networks that learn," Tech. Rep. CMU-CS-84-119, Carnegie-Mellon Univ., Department of Computer Science, 1984.

67. J.H. Holland, *Adaptation in Natural and Artificial Systems*. Ann Arbor, MI: Univ. of Michigan Press, 1975, ch. 6, pp. 89 – 120.
68. D.E. Goldberg, "Computer aided gas pipeline operation using genetic algorithms and rule learning," Ph.D. Dissertation, Ann Arbor, MI, Univ. of Michigan Press, 1983.
69. R.J. Brachman and J.G. Schmolze, "An overview of the KL-ONE knowledge representation system," *Cognitive Science*, vol. 9, pp. 171 – 216, 1985.
70. J.H. Holland, "Properties of the bucket brigade algorithm," in *Proc. of an Int'l. Conf. on Genetic Algorithms and Their Applications*, pp. 1 – 7, 1985.
71. C.L. Forgy, "Rete: A fast algorithm for the many pattern/many object pattern match problem," *Artificial Intelligence*, vol. 19, pp. 17 – 37, 1982.
72. K.S. Keller and H.J. Antonisse, "Prediction-based competitive learning in the M2 system," to appear in *Proc. Expert Systems in Gov't. Conf.*, 1987.
73. H.J. Antonisse and K.S. Keller, "Genetic operators for high-level knowledge representations," in *Proc. of 2nd Int'l. Conf. on Genetic Algorithms and Their Applications*, pp. 69 – 76, 1987.
74. R.L. Riolo, "Bucket brigade performance: I. Long sequences of classifiers," in *Proc. of 2nd Int'l. Conf. on Genetic Algorithms and their Applications*, pp. 184 – 195, 1987.
75. D. Klahr *et al.*, *Production System Models of Learning and Development*, D. Klahr, P. Langley, R. Neches, Eds. Cambridge, MA: MIT Press, 1987, ch. 1, pp. 1 – 53.
76. J.E. Laird *et al.*, "Chunking in Soar: The anatomy of a general learning mechanism," *Machine Learning*, vol. 1, pp. 11 – 46, 1986.
77. P. Nii, "Blackboard systems: Blackboard application systems," *AI Magazine*, vol. 7, no. 3, Conference, pp. 82 – 106, 1986.
78. J.R. Benoit *et al.*, "ALLIES: An experiment in cooperating expert systems for command and control," in *Proc. of the Expert Systems in Gov't Symp.*, pp. 372 – 380, 1986.
79. E. Durfee, V. Lesser, and D. Corkill, "Coherent cooperation among communicating problem solvers," Techn. Rep. 85-15, Department of Computer and Information Science, University of Massachusetts, Amherst, MA, pp. 2 – 8, 1985.
80. P. Nii, "Blackboard systems: The blackboard model of problem solving," *AI Magazine*, vol. 7, no. 2, pp. 38 – 53, Summer 1986.
81. D.R. Reddy, L.D. Erman, and R.B. Neely, "The HEARSAY speech understanding system: An example of the recognition process," in *Proc. of the 3rd IJCAI*, pp. 185 – 193, 1973.
82. L. Erman, F. Hayes-Roth, V. Lesser, and D. Reddy, "The Hearsay-II speech-understanding system integrating knowledge to resolve uncertainty," *Computing Surveys*, vol. 12, pp. 213 – 253, 1980.
83. R. Balzer, L. Erman, P. London, and C. Williams, "HEARSAY-III: A domain-independent framework for expert systems." in *Proc. of the 1st National Conf. on AI*, pp. 108 – 110, 1980.
84. V.R. Lesser and D.D. Corkill, "The distributed vehicle monitoring testbed: A tool for investigating distributed problem solving networks," *AI Magazine*, vol. 4, no. 3, pp. 15 – 33, Fall 1983.
85. L. Gasser, C. Braganza, and N. Herman, "Implementing distributed AI systems using MACE," in *Proc. 3rd Conf. on AI Applications*, pp. 315 – 320, 1987.
86. D.D. Corkill, "A framework for organizational self-design in distributed problem solving networks," Tech. Rep. 82-33, Department of Computer and Information Science, University of Massachusetts, Amherst, MA, pp. 17 – 20, 1982.
87. S. Cammarata, D. McArthur, and R. Steeb, "Strategies of cooperation in distributed problem solving," in *Proc. of the 8th IJCAI*, pp. 767 – 770, 1983.
88. R.G. Smith and R. Davis, "Frameworks for cooperation in distributed problem solving," *IEEE Trans. Syst., Man, Cybern.*, vol. SMC-11, no. 1, pp. 61 – 70, Jan. 1981.
89. R. Davis and R.G. Smith, "Negotiation as a metaphor for distributed problem solving," *Artificial Intelligence*, vol. 20, pp. 63 – 109, 1983.
90. D.D. Corkill and V.R. Lesser, "The use of meta-level control for coordination in a distributed problem solving network," in *Proc. of the 8th IJCAI*, pp. 748 – 756, 1983.
91. D.D. Corkill, V.R. Lesser, and E. Hudlicka, "Unifying data directed and goal directed control," in *Proc. of the National Conf. on AI*, pp. 143 – 147, 1982.

92. E.H. Durfee, V.R. Lesser, and D.D. Corkill, "Increasing coherence in a distributed problem solving network," in *Proc. of the 9th IJCAI*, pp. 1025 – 1030, 1985.
93. P. Friedland, "Knowledge servers—Applications of artificial intelligence to advanced space information systems," presentation at AIAA NASA Conf., Washington, DC, June 1987.
94. D.B. Lenat, "Overcoming the brittleness bottleneck," Keynote presentation to the IEEE Computer Science 3rd Conf. on Artificial Intelligence, Kissimmee, FL, Feb. 1987.
95. P. Harmon, Ed., *Expert System Strategies*, vol. 2, no. 8, San Francisco, CA, August 1986.
96. H.G.E. Kyburg, "Knowledge and certainty," in *Proceedings AAAI Uncertainty Workshop*, pp. 30 – 38, 1986.

20

Artificial intelligence and national defense

Real, imagined and likely applications

Stephen J. Andriole

Editors' note *This paper steps back a bit from the specific applications of AI and assesses how far intelligent military systems technology has gone and might go. But it also analyzes the funding backdrop and the interest the Department of Defense (DOD) has expressed in AI over the years. The paper suggests that the future may not be quite as bright as believed by many, that unless the impact of the technology can be measured quantitatively, AI may not receive the kind of backing that it has become accustomed to from DOD.*

Introduction

This book focuses on many aspects of applied artificial intelligence (AI). The articles themselves range all the way from brief tutorials to specific discussions of expert systems at work in real operational environments. The middle articles, of course, concentrate on the "stuff" of AI, describing a variety of projects that demonstrate the applied potential of AI. This article steps back a bit from the details described above and focuses on several issues that have enormous implications for the future of basic and applied AI—particularly as it applies to national defense.

The focus on defense is important for several reasons. First, if the truth be told, if it were not for the US Department of Defense there would be no basic or applied AI or a *Sourcebook of Applied Artificial Intelligence*. Secondly, expectations about the power of AI have nowhere been as high as in the Department of Defense. In many respects, defense domains have been a proving ground for applied AI. While there have been some great programs and projects—with measurable success—there have also been some expensive failures. This article discusses AI and national defense, though much of the issues raised here apply equally to non-Defense applications and expectations.

This final chapter thus deals with "context," the realities of systems design and development, some "ins" and "outs" of AI funding, and some of the "next generation" technology that will permit the AI community to expand their realm all the way to the design and development of truly intelligent systems.

AI in context

AI is on the tip of everyone's tongue these days, and for good reason. After years of struggling with complicated defense problems with methods and techniques that have been only partially successful, it should come as no surprise that a new problem-solving methodology—indeed *any* new problem-solving methodology—would be greeted with high hopes and great expectations. This backdrop is important to understanding the current enthusiasm for applications in AI. But it is also important to remember that with our methods, tool boxes are far from empty, that progress has been made elsewhere as well.

AI represents one class of methods among many. While there are various ways to identify analytical methods, it is reasonable to recognize operations research, decision analysis, and conventional (non-AI) computer science as some of the most applied methodologies. They all have their strengths and weaknesses—and their success and horror stories. The evolution of knowledge-based problem-solving represents a hybrid methodology that has only recently won its status as a bona fide problem-solving methodology.

The current rush to apply AI tools and techniques is occurring to some extent at least at the expense of the growing applied potential of other methods and techniques. Problems that were once unambiguously defined as optimization problems, for example, are often redefined to fit within diagnostic AI paradigms. Target value analysis, route planning, and many tactical maneuvers have been solved with linear programming techniques for years; today we see such problems retrofit with knowledge-based solutions that, while effective, tend to be much more difficult to develop and certainly more expensive to maintain.

The recommendation is thus simple. Our zeal to experiment with the formidable power of AI should be tempered with an appreciation for some old methodological friends, friends that have served us well in the past though perhaps without the "style" and flair of AI.

There are "problems" and there are *problems*

The power of AI is most formidable when it is focused—like a laser—at a specific, amenable target. Expert systems technology, for example, is best applied to well-bounded problems, that is, problems that have but a few widely understood analytical dimensions. The difference between finding the reasons why an M1 tank will not start and assessing Soviet intentions toward Poland in the 1990s illustrates the difference between bounded and unbounded problems.

There are of course countless bounded problems in national defense; there are therefore countless opportunities for knowledge-based problem-solving. Several of the articles in this book describe successful prototypes in bounded areas like tactical air targeting and information handling (see the Section on Defense Applications of Artificial Intelligence for additional details). The probability of success is of course inversely related to the complexity of the problem domain; applications in AI targeted at domains that are only partially understood or relatively complex are much less likely to succeed than those targeted at many of the same problems that for years have been approached by some of our old methodological friends. Recommendation: pick your problem carefully.

Systems are still systems, regardless of their intelligence

As FIG. 20-1 suggests, there are ways to structure the design and development of interactive and even fully automated problem-solving systems. Requirements must always be systematically described before functions can be modeled, and before the functions and their solutions can be programmed, a tasks/methods matching procedure must be implemented. Figure 20-1 suggests that there are at least three classes of methods to consider; you may well believe that there are four, five, or six. The point remains, however, that software engineering depends upon solid front-end work. The literature on systems analysis and design is clear on the need for structured requirements analysis and validation, just as the AI community stresses the need for structured knowledge engineering. But before one can scope a prospective knowledge engineering project, the other front-end tasks must be performed. In other words, regardless of whether one's system ends up with "knowledge" or just plain "data," it must be anchored in tested principles of systems design.

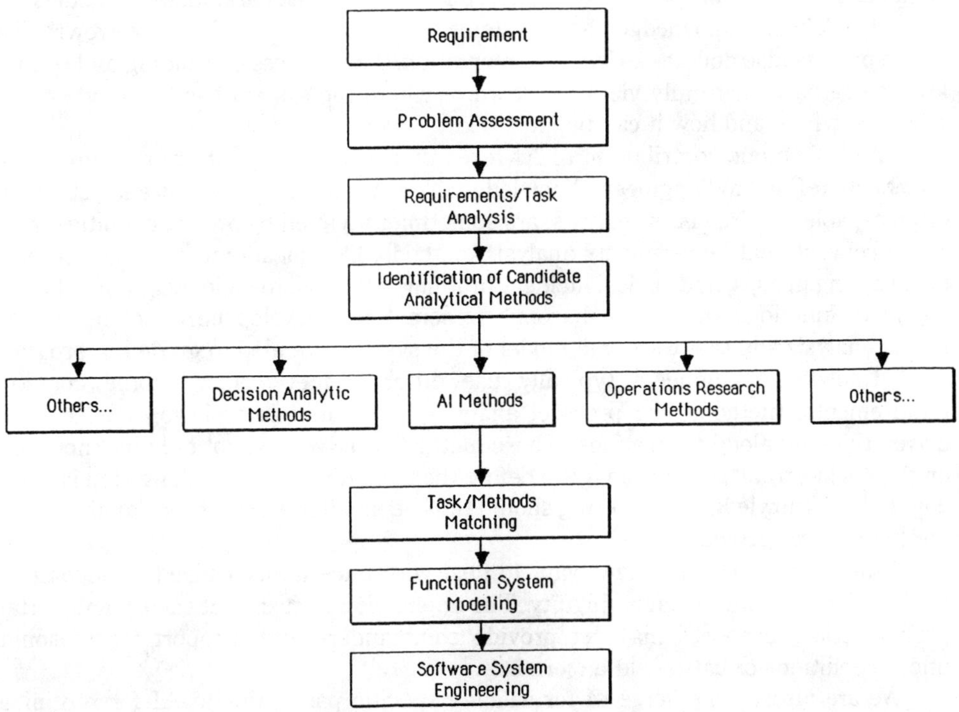

Fig. 20-1. Systems requirements/methods matching.

There is a tendency on the part of AI systems engineers to forego the tasks/methods matching process in favor of knowledge-based approaches that are sometimes predetermined. If a knowledge-based approach is called for, then the knowledge engineering process can begin; if it is not, then there will be some other ways to validate requirements and match them with optimal method(s).

Style, glitter, and real payoff

One of the criticisms most often heard about operations research and related mathematical-statistical methods is that they perform their magic within black boxes far removed from full view. Users of systems driven by these boxes cannot easily get inside to see how the solution was generated. As the articles above suggest, knowledge-based systems differ dramatically from closed systems in their explanation capability. Good intelligent systems permit users to "see" the analytical processes that lead to solutions. Users can query knowledge-based systems about perceived inconsistencies and ambiguities. They are also free to disagree with a system's inference-making procedures, just as you and I are free to disagree with colleagues and assistants.

This ability to query a system and inspect its problem-solving procedures is revolutionary in analytical computing. It widens the communications channel between users and systems and thereby contributes to enhanced problem-solving performance. It also permits revision. If some procedures are judged to be inadequate, they can be changed (again and again). While it is of course possible to change the parameters of models that live in black boxes, knowledge-based systems support interactive, iterative growth. The whole process also doubles as live documentation. The process of building and refining knowledge bases naturally yields a record of where the system has been, where it is now, and where and how it can be improved.

Another unique contribution of AI research and development are the procedures now being refined to "engineer" knowledge. Non-AI-schooled systems analysts, while often capable requirements analysts, are sometimes stymied by overtly cognitive tasks. Since conventional requirements analysis methods, like questionnaires, the use of ad hoc working groups, and critical incident profiling, often fail to yield insight into heavily cognitive functions and tasks, disconnects sometimes develop between the requirements analysis and the functional model of the system intended to guide the programmer. Knowledge engineers typically use different methods to profile cognitive requirements, methods like protocol analysis, structured interviews, and scenario-driven thinking aloud simulations. These methods can be used not only by knowledge engineers but by all systems analysts before the tasks/methods matching step is taken. The field of knowledge engineering should thus be monitored by systems analysts of all methodological persuasions.

AI also gives us some new ways to deal with uncertainty caused by incomplete information and situational ambiguity. The application of fuzzy set theory and certain probabilistic procedures may yet provide commanders with support for reasoning under conditions of battlefield uncertainty.

We are also on the verge of formalizing specific paradigms in AI for routinized problem-solving. There are whole classes of well-bounded deductive inference problems—like many diagnosis and rudimentary planning problems—that we now know are amenable to knowledge-based methods. Success in these areas is spreading, as is the expertise to recreate it in similar domains.

Perhaps as important as any of the above glitter and payoff is the exponential progress in analytical methodology that has been triggered by advances in AI. Hybrid methods are emerging at an incredible rate. Operations researchers, decision analysts, and database managers have taken new hard looks at their fields through the AI lens and have designed some methods that constitute wholes greater than the sum of their parts. The AI stimulus is at this point difficult to assess, though it is safe to say that it is fueling the development and testing of hybrid methods that without the stimulus would never have been conceived.

The locus of control: aiding vs. automation

Who should make battlefield decisions, human or software commanders? There are areas that are clearly black and white. Few of us would have any problems with computer-based assistants calculating the amount of fuel a convoy would consume crossing certain kinds of terrain over time; nor would we have any problem with the same computer program advising commanders about route planning opportunities and opportunity costs. At the other end of the continuum is the consensus that at this point in time we should not rely upon knowledge-based systems to induct about strategic threats or opportunities in the year 2025. As always, it is the grey problems that challenge us. In fact, there is rancorous debate about the range of the greyness itself. Some believe, for example, that strategic battle management is theoretically possible via intelligent systems, just as many others are not at all convinced about the possibility *or desirability* of machine control of tactical or strategic warfare. While this argument rages on, those who project tactical and strategic requirements regard the rhetoric as moot, since adversary technology will give us no choice but to field intelligent systems capable of responding in "ultra" real time to sophisticated threats. If we do not turn substantial amounts of decision-making power over to intelligent systems, they argue, we will lose all future conflicts.

The issues cannot be settled here. At the same time, it would benefit our community if a debate was launched to explore all "locus of power" questions. If this debate is not launched then the push of technology will ultimately define—and probably narrow—the proverbial grey area.

Good news, bad news

The bad news is that AI hype is outstripping the AI community's ability to produce reliable systems. It must be remembered that AI is an extremely young field of inquiry and a newcomer to the family of analytical methods. The AI research infrastructure is still under construction; we should refuse admission to those who want to move in and settle down before the concrete dries. Already there are fears that AI will smother itself again, like it did in the 1970s, under the weight of its own rhetoric. Just as serious consideration should be given to long-range basic research projects in AI, so too should there be an effort to restrain those who would promise too much too soon. Efforts should also be made to de-couple AI from certain major defense programs—like the Strategic Defense Initiative—until its role can be more clearly and realistically defined.

Defense-oriented AI systems are today also usually "prototypes" with enormous potential but with short track records. As such, they are expensive experiments. Only recently have tools emerged to control development costs somewhat, though we are still badly in need of standards in AI. Worse is the lack of AI system development metrics. We do not now have any reliable methods for determining how deep knowledge bases need to be, how fast they must be searched to be useful, or how to best represent them in software. It is possible today to ask two knowledge engineers to estimate the size and characteristics of a knowledge base in a specific domain and receive at least two completely different answers—all of which may in fact be "correct." Only time will help us "size" knowledge-based systems *before* they are built. For now, we gamble each time we try to determine just how much money to allocate to an AI system or how many man-days to bid to complete it. More than a few agencies and companies have felt the effect of the lack of metrics for AI systems design and development.

The good news is that due to its incalculable intuitive appeal (who can deny the appeal of intelligent assistants working away on the battlefield?), AI appears to have at least as many lives as a cat. Much more importantly, there is every reason to support continued experiments in AI: shortsightedness and high technology are incompatible.

It is essential that we take the high ground and the long view when it comes to AI. Note that we are not here asking for anything more than the fiberoptics, materials sciences, and propulsion sciences have already received. Years ago judgments were made about the eventual payoff from investments in these and other basic sciences, judgments that were based upon a relatively small number of successes. Once all the hype and rhetoric is stripped away, it is clear that there are at least as many successes in AI as there were in jet aircraft thirty years ago. Plans are now underway for the design and development of new generation hypersonic vehicles, just as plans for sixth and seventh generation computing should now be on the drawing boards.

There is more good news. In spite of the hype, a more balanced perspective about what AI can and cannot do seems to be emerging. It is now clear in the minds of even the most enthusiastic advocates that AI is simply not ready to take on some classes of problems—yet, and that hybrid intelligent systems may yet solve a variety of problems we have yet to encounter. There is a greening effect at work today within and beyond the AI community, an effect that has been stimulated by a bona fide "requirements pull." Five years ago, the AI community did not fully embrace the applied perspective so important to defense problem-solving. Criticisms were often heard about DOD's attempts to structure basic research in AI. More recently, however, the applied perspective has helped to define the applied potential of AI and has given us insight into where we need more ideas. DOD investments in AI have thus had a pruning effect on AI research and have focused attention to applications likely to yield near- and longer-term payoff. The overall result has been positive for the applied AI community, while at the same time has in no way threatened the viability of basic research interests. It should also be mentioned that the same pruning effect is at work in the applied industrial AI community where requirements in design, manufacturing, and production are focusing AI research and development in several high payoff directions, such as industrial robotics, computer-assisted design and engineering, and automated manufacturing. AI is, in short, coming of age throughout the industrial and defense economies.

From here to there

If AI is to achieve major success we must begin to treat it not as a problem-solving panacea, but as yet another powerful analytical methodology. While certainly precocious, we must remember that it is still very young. Just as there is enormous potential, there are also significant risks. A concerted effort must be made by the entire community—the R&D managers, the researchers themselves, and the decisionmakers that determine overall funding priorities—to develop research programs that are challenging and realistic, control the rhetoric, and search for just the right balance between technology push and requirements pull. This is surely the recipe for continued success. The articles in this book represent a snapshot of AI at a particular time in history. They also constitute a window into future opportunities. If all goes according to plan, five years from now another impressive snapshot can be taken and yet another window opened, and so on until the application of intelligent systems becomes cost-effective and commonplace.

Paying the bills

All of the above assumes that research and development funds will be available to support the maturation of the AI community. As suggested above, some members of the funding community are on to some members of the AI community: unrealistic expectations have come home to haunt more than a few AI labs.

By and large the AI community has over-relied on the Department of Defense for support. Countless millions have already been spent and some estimates suggest that DOD may well invest billions in AI before the end of the century. Will such funding continue?

Numerous corporations have also decided to invest in AI. Many labs, "institutes," "centers" and the like have been established with internal research and development (IR&D) funds, all anchored in the assumption that a little spent today will pay huge dividends in the future. Some corporate investments in AI have been stimulated by competition and the fear that rival companies may be developing an edge in a critical technology area. More than a few companies have thus blindly gone into the AI business without coherent strategic plans or even a rudimentary understanding of the technology.

Is all the money wisely spent? Certainly not. Much of the funding is undirected even in the corporate marketplace. Corporate investments in AI should be requirements- and problem-driven. If company X excels in the design and development of aircraft simulators then it should investigate the applied potential of intelligent simulation technology. If company Y produces cruise missiles then it should try to determine the role that AI might play in the design and development of smart weapons. Companies X and Y have no business focusing their IR&D dollars at extremely basic research issues.

Government and university labs specialize in basic research; corporations should specialize in surviving and prospering in a competitive marketplace.

The exception to this rule of thumb, of course, occurs when the government (or some other source of funding) decides to give company Y ten million dollars to study nonmonotonic reasoning, combinatorial explosions (no doubt the source of the confusion in this scenario), and fuzzy set theory—all within the context of the applied potential of catastrophe theory. In fact, many "applied" companies have actively sought basic research funds to educate their personnel.

Perhaps a rational investment strategy might consist of a set of goals and subgoals that track closely with larger corporate goals. Companies with genuine needs for knowledge-based systems should pursue research and development as closely related as possible, while companies with ill-defined needs should proceed cautiously.

It is not at all clear how long the current government frenzy in AI will last. Those who take the long view can remember when systems analysis, decision analysis, and operations research all enjoyed similar heydays. As suggested above, the community must get control of its rhetoric and begin to create realistic expectations in its client community.

A number of technical bills will come due soon; if the community cannot meet these obligations—at least via some installment payments—then the whole field could suffer. If government funding falls dramatically then corporate IR&D funds will shrink proportionately. The linkage between defense applications and AI and funding patterns is clear. If the Department of Defense softens its support of AI then DOD contractors will do exactly the same thing.

The promise of technology

Every technological revolution makes assumptions about the rate of new discovery. It is presumed that once a field develops an infrastructure and a few genuine breakthroughs occur, then it will begin to fuel itself via additional discoveries and breakthroughs. The AI community too makes presumptions about the future.

At the top of the list is the design and development of new intelligent systems based not on the old heuristic architectures but on more radical ones patterned after human neural models. Many in the AI community have begun to realize that (a) human beings do not think via rules or serially, and (b) if truly intelligent systems are to be designed we must adopt architectures that are more sequential and powerful. Currently there is yet another frenzy about the applied potential of neural network models which are by definition massively parallel. The goal is to create systems capable of solving complex problems via parallel processing and, through the same architecture, systems capable of learning. Neural network modeling—and the larger thrust in "biological emulation"—thus represents one promising avenue for the AI community to travel.

Very closely related is an essentially hardware emphasis upon the design and development of computers capable of handling more instructions, faster, and in parallel. It is widely believed that parallel and multi-processing systems will permit knowledge-based systems designers to crack the real-time computational barrier and deliver systems capable of solving problems in real and "future" time. If neural net modeling represents a conceptual breakthrough then the deployment of parallel and multi-processing computers represents an implementation breakthrough.

Still time-consuming is the process by which knowledge is extracted and represented. The "art" of knowledge engineering is not advancing rapidly toward becoming a science. There are a number of promising developments in the area, however. One involves the design and development of quasi- and fully-automated tools for extracting knowledge from experts (and codified expertise) and similar systems for selecting the "best" form of knowledge representation. The so-called "expert system shells" that permit designers of knowledge-based systems to develop rules, frames, nets, and inference networks are only the first small steps toward the development and application of genuinely useful knowledge engineering tools. There are several automated knowledge extraction tools on the market today; in time, they will mature to productive tools.

Another promising development is the evolving understanding of the kinds of problems for which knowledge-based systems technology is useful. In time we will develop a selection process that will permit the avoidance of intractable problems, the "sizing" of tractable ones, and criteria for deciding into which category problems should be located.

As suggested above, the real promise lies in the integration of many methods, tools, and techniques into problem-solving wholes greater than the sum of their parts. Multidisciplinary problem-solving methodologies will emerge that will call upon the knowledge-based sciences to play selected rather than dominant roles. As AI begins to share the spotlight with other methods and techniques it will in fact become a more influential problem-solving methodology than it is today.

Opportunities and challenges

The watchword is greening. AI tools and techniques have been center stage now for several years and have only very recently begun to find themselves within the larger context of computer-based problem-solving. It is time for AI to take its place among the family of methods already available to systems engineers. The application of AI tools and techniques should become requirements driven, particularly when the ultimate goal is to solve a specific defense problem. If the AI community fails to adopt a genuine problem-solving perspective it will remain an esoteric sub-field of computer and computational science. This, however, is not to suggest that the quest for basic research solutions should be abandoned but, rather, that divisions of responsibility within the field should be encouraged.

On the other hand, there are countless opportunities for the field to excel. There are many problems that require a knowledge-based approach; there are many problems that are quite amenable to existing AI tools and techniques.

It is time for the AI community to widen its perspective and begin the difficult task of transforming itself from inner- to outwardly-driven. The early years of AI research and development have been unfocused—as they should have been while the field was maturing. Now it is time to look beyond the nuances of selected technical issues first to the broadbrush applied potential of AI and then specific targets of opportunity. Once this transformation has occurred then AI will have arrived.

Section D

Financial applications of intelligent systems technology

21

The Citibank pension expert

Jessica Keyes

Editors' note *This paper by Jessica Keyes describes Citibank's pension expert system. This application is interesting because of how knowledge-based technology was integrated into an already large management information system. The inference engine was programmed in PL/I—not exactly a standard AI language. The modified system had to apply new tax laws so that accurate pension checks could be processed; it also had to interface with existing IBM hardware. (Reprinted, with permission, from the June 1989 issue of* AI Expert. *©* *1989,* AI Expert. *All rights reserved.)*

It's not the ides of March that scare us but the ides of April. The specter of taxes causes weak knees and fits of despair in the strongest of us. We spend the days before April 15 mired in a swamp of pencils, calculators, and self-help tax books. Fortunately, April 15 comes but once a year for mere mortals; the processors of giant pension funds are not so lucky. These banking institutions must calculate withholding taxes daily for hundreds of thousands of pensioners—taxes with a huge and complicated twist.

Citibank is one of the largest banks in the world. The size of its parent, Citicorp, boggles the mind: 90,000 employees, more than 3,000 offices, and $200 billion in assets. It has more data centers and more dollars invested in technology than a fair-to-middling-sized foreign country. Citibank is segmented into three major business lines: individual banking, investment banking, and institutional banking. A common thread among these three diverse areas is the corporate technology group. These gurus set the standards and make recommendations, but the hotshots in the line area really promote expert systems.

One such enthusiast is Abhik Dasgupta. When IBM and Citibank initiated a study in November 1987 to choose a flagship project for expert systems, Dasgupta jumped at the chance to get involved. IBM and Citibank considered three possibilities. The first was a statement system. The expert system in this case would process prior-period corrections of security transactions—a sort of transaction retrofitting. Another possible system was in stocks and bonds, where the system would identify dividends in stock splits and interest declarations. Third was the system ultimately chosen.

Pensions are big business for any bank. Hundreds of thousands of checks are processed and mailed to retirees every working day. What sounds like a simple process is complicated by the differing tax laws in our country. The federal government applies one tax formula nationally, but each state and local government has different taxing levels. Any pension system must be able to process a check with the correct deductions for where Joe resides and how many exemptions he claims. If Joe lives in New York with four dependents, his pension check will look different than had he moved to Kalamazoo, Michigan and had no dependents.

In 1986, Peter J. Coughlin found that he had a problem. Coughlin, a Citibank vice-president, learned that California had passed a tax law that was to have a profound effect on his then-COBOL-based pension-processing system. This COBOL system had only the capability of processing federal taxes. Adding the differing and complex state tax deductions would be difficult. The COBOL system was modified in early 1987, a 120-staff-day effort for the state of California alone. The estimation for adding the rest of the states to the system made Coughlin think there had to be a better way.

When IBM and Citibank began to consider the pension-processing system, Coughlin and Dasgupta pushed hard. Their efforts paid off when the Disbursement Online System (DOLS) was chosen—none too soon, because the bank demanded the final system be implemented no later than June 1988 and it was already January.

Lesser men and women would be horrified at having to learn a new tool and new techniques as well as implement a real system (not a prototype) in six months. The Citibank-IBM team was prepared for the challenge. Citibank had one constraint: the system must be developed on their IBM 3084 MVS/XA system, forcing the developers into the unexplored domain of mainframe expert system shells. Around this time, most expert systems were deployed on AI workstations or personal computers. Given the hundreds of thousands of transactions and the huge databases filled with tax and pensioner information, the mainframe platform was required. The IBM mainframe expert system shell, Knowledgetool, was selected because it exhibited the richness of toolset necessary for the system. Using a consulting paradigm, Knowledgetool employed forward and backward chaining as it processed each DOLS transaction by pensioner residence.

The Knowledgetool inference engine, written in PL/I, is a high-performance program that uses a very efficient but proprietary algorithm for pattern matching. Astute users of the tool employ the OS PL/I optimizing compiler on their applications, which increases throughput. Citibank found that this tool enhanced the system's performance over the more conventional COBOL approach. Remember, Citibank already had a good benchmark completed with the COBOL system, only recently redesigned for the state of California. In fact, the bank determined that it took 14.3% less time to run the expert system version for California.

How does Knowledgetool work? It processes a knowledge application in a *recognize-act* cycle (or for conventional programmers, loop). The inference engine matches rule conditions to existing class members and updates the conflict set with the instantiations recognized. This gives a set of rules ready to fire. Firing is the heart of the process, and Knowledgetool uses an IBM version of the OPS5 algorithm, one of the fastest available. During the second step of the cycle, the inference engine attempts to resolve the conflict set; that is, choose which rule, among many, to fire next. Citibank took the option of controlling or predetermining the order of rules, a Knowledgetool feature. In the last step of the cycle, the rule selected is fired. The rule fired is procedural and might add, change, or delete class members—it might even fire a nested *recognize-act* cycle for a nested block of rules.

Like most large MIS shops, Citibank's programming language of choice was COBOL. Only one staffer had ever used PL/I. Knowledgetool, written in PL/I, structured its development environment using a syntax similar to PL/I (Listing 1). When the project began, Citibank was unfamiliar with AI, Knowledgetool, and PL/I. Here's where IBM came in. Since this was a flagship project, IBM supplied technical help—everything from installation and knowledge engineering to training.

The project team consisted of three full-time staff members, one consultant and one intrepid IBMer. Since PL/I was virtually unknown at Citibank, the group spent a week learning the fundamentals. Another three days were spent in Knowledgetool training and two intensive weeks on the design. Developing the entire system took three months. The team averaged five to six complex rules per day to realize a staff usage reduction in the range of 12% – 13%, compared with the COBOL version. Since the original senior-level management goal was to find tools to increase productivity, Knowledgetool appeared to be a winner.

The goal of this expert system was to apply the tax law at the federal, state, and local levels uniformly and accurately to process pension checks. The stated user goal was to automate and integrate all tax processing. The unstated goal was to eliminate the system's department interference and let the business unit manage the processing. These goals could not have been achieved without an expert's knowledge. Walter Feldman, Vice President for Pension Disbursement at Citibank, provided the tax information. Feldman created the rules based on information from the tax department and was heavily involved in testing the accuracy of a system that would need to pass muster with the auditors. Since this system would disburse millions of dollars, the team tested and retested.

A case-history approach to system validation was used. This testing method for expert systems works because it permits a parallel test of the expert system vs. the current system or manual method, whichever applies. In this case, the team worked jointly on a representative sampling of test cases. Each case was run through the expert system and carefully compared with the manually derived results. When the testing was completed, the user department signed off.

The DOLS knowledge or rule base contains more than 100 rules. Since some of these rules are generic (they apply to all states), the total knowledge base can be estimated to contain more than 200 rules. The team learned from the much-publicized mistakes of forerunner expert systems such as DEC's XCON and organized the rules by state of residence. (XCON assisted in configuring DEC's one-of-a-kind computers. Its knowledge base contained more than 10,000 rules, which were entered randomly into the system, creating a nightmare when a rule needed to be modified or erased.) The DOLS design team combined their data processing experience, characterized by a love for the organized, with new theories of expert-system design to create a structured knowledge base. Organizing the rules by state of residence provides for easy maintenance.

The Knowledgetool shell is robust, containing a nice mix of expert-system features with the richness of traditional procedural languages. Knowledgetool permits rules, non-rule procedural code, and calls to external languages within a fairly easy-to-use syntax.

All the DOLS rules can be executed by any of the 50 states, but not all rules apply to all states. Using one of the many Knowledgetool features, Citibank could determine when these rules fired. To ensure maximum flexibility and permit easy rule maintenance, the Citibank team provided for a variety of options permitting the user to reorder the rules when and if desired. This capability is realized with Knowledgetool's runlist and its capacity to set the order of execution of blocks of rules and procedures written by knowledge engineers in other languages. The runlist permits rule ordering and external procedures, and it offers the flexibility of assigning a priority tag to a rule. Any rule can have a priority tag. The value of this tag is the inference engine's first consideration when deciding which rule to fire. Modification of this tag has the effect of reordering the knowledge base by idling rules with very low priorities and forcing the firing of rules with high priorities. Priority tags, alphanumeric field names such as "highest" or "lowest," are defined on a Knowledgetool runlist and acted upon during rule execution. Up to 100 priority tags can be defined on the runlist. In the following example, a runlist might contain this priority definition:

```
Priority(highest) = 99;
Priority(high) = 80;
Priority(low) = 10;
Priority(lowest) = 5;
```

Runlists are required for each application and include definitions used throughout the session. Listing 2 illuminates these features for a sample IBM application called *IMAGPLI* where the rule set named *IMAGIN* is executed before the *IMAGIM* rule set. Both precede the execution of an external procedure, *IMAGRF*, and a user-customized exit, *INPUTX*. The order of execution may be modified by simple editing of the runlist. The knowledge engineers could easily build a user interface to this editing procedure, permitting an interface with options for facile editing by users.

This feature was farsighted of the designers, since most deployed large expert systems require technical support to modify the knowledge bases. Although these users are not technically shy, Knowledgetool syntax precludes them from any real hands-on maintenance. This applies to all tools, save the smaller user-oriented PC shells; fortunately, tax laws change infrequently.

DOLS can be considered a two-tier system. The user interface permits operators to modify the ordering of the knowledge base. The second tier is the overnight processor. Issuing hundreds of thousands of checks is not a real-time application. In the dead of night, the conventional component of DOLS performs mundane processing routines. On ready standby is the DOLS expert system, embedded into the system architecture and able to calculate withholding amounts for complex check disbursements. Pension data is stored on a standard IBM VSAM file. One of Knowledgetool's strengths is the ability to integrate into the standard IBM VM or MVS batch or online environment. It can interface with the IMS/VS, DB2, and SQL/DS databases; there are hooks for the

PL/I, COBOL, FORTRAN, Pascal and Assembler languages. This variety permits Knowledgetool to integrate fluidly with any existing application through one of the interfaces or hooks, as was the case with Citibank. The expert system acts similarly to any other called application, except that its processing is more sophisticated.

Right on target, the first week of June 1988 saw the unveiling of the most sophisticated pension processor on the street—and the only one to use an expert system at its center.

22

INVEST

An expert system for financial investments

Stephan Heuer
Ulrich Koch, and Colin Cryer

Editors' note *INVEST is an expert system designed to help investment counselors advise clients about investment opportunities and strategies. In some respects it is a classic expert system, since it was designed in close consultation with investment experts. In operation, INVEST builds customer/client profiles, as well as hypotheses about investment strategies. INVEST was written using a special-purpose expert system shell known as Donald.*

INVEST is an expert system developed to help make financial decisions. In dialogues with bank officials, INVEST obtains information about a customer's wishes and attempts to make useful and well-founded investment proposals. Significantly, INVEST covers the entire spectrum of possible investments. We expect it to help investment experts advise customers. Another application could be in small branches of banks where the lack of adequately trained staff has made it impossible to provide investment advice.

We have worked over the last 18 months in close cooperation with the Volksbank Muenster and the Westdeutsche Genossenschafts-Zentralbank Muenster. The Volksbank belongs to a large group of banks, including many small banks in rural areas. Such banks could benefit from an expert system able to give investment advice. Even in its present state of development, the system can give very reasonable advice.

Investment advice has special features. INVEST is being written as an application of an expert system shell—Donald—specially developed for this purpose. Donald is a frame-based system using frame matching as its principal inference mechanism.

Caduceus is the best known expert system using a matching mechanism. [1], [2] Donald resembles the Caduceus system for internal medicine in several respects—for example, taxonomy, trigger mechanism, and hypothesizing of candidates. But, in contrast to medical diagnosis, one cannot expect a solution that accounts for all observed symptoms. Instead, the problem is to synthesize a solution (from probably inconsistent input data) that will best fit the customer's requirements.

To the best of our knowledge, the only operational expert systems in the field of investment advice are PlanPower and Customer Profiling, both marketed by Apex. Both PlanPower and invest are object-oriented expert systems that apply an overall strategy of "successive refinement." PlanPower is based on the multiasset allocation model. [3]

According to available information, PlanPower develops long-term investment plans for substantial assets such as real estate and precious metals. In contrast, Invest gives advice concerning specific securities that will meet a customer's immediate objectives—for example, short-term speculation or long-term capital growth.

We will describe the inference mechanism underlying INVEST and briefly outline a consultation scenario. Donald stores all knowledge as frames, so we will describe how INVEST uses frames to represent various objects such as stocks, hypotheses, and proposals. We will also outline frame matching and some other technical details about Donald. Finally, we will summarize results achieved so far and indicate future developments.

The inference mechanism

Choosing a suitable inference mechanism for an expert system is critical. We had lengthy discussions with our banking experts and experimented with various ideas before deciding to use the following model of a consultation between a customer and a human financial expert.

During consultation, a human expert gradually builds up a picture of the customer's financial situation and wishes. In the process, certain tentative ideas about suitable investments—we call them *current hypotheses*—will occur to the expert. A hypothesis can be quite general ("consider blue chips") or very specific ("buy General Motors Preferred"). Hypotheses that at first look reasonable are assigned one or more *trigger points*. A hypothesis with trigger points is checked more closely by comparing, or *matching*, the customer profile with the hypothesis prototype; that is, the profile of a customer for whom the hypothesis would fit exactly. The human expert will either accept or reject the hypothesis depending on whether the customer profile and the hypothesis prototype agree closely or disagree sharply. Otherwise, the hypothesis is ignored. Of course, before matching can take place, it may be necessary to obtain additional information about the customer. If a hypothesis is accepted or rejected, new hypotheses may automatically suggest themselves. When a hypothesis is accepted, it is incorporated into the investment proposal(s), which therefore becomes more specific.

The following simple example illustrates this consultation model: A financial adviser is consulted by an elderly widow. Immediately the hypotheses "consider blue chips" and "consider over-the-counter stock" suggest themselves. To check these hypotheses, the adviser asks, "How much stock do you own?" to which the widow replies, "$1 million." The expert considers blue-chip stock suitable up to a $250,000 limit and assigns a trigger point only to the second hypothesis, "consider over-the-counter stock." This hypothesis is now checked more thoroughly by comparing the widow's financial profile with that of a typical OTC investor.

We will describe briefly how this model is implemented in INVEST. A consultation with INVEST involves several cycles, each consisting of three steps. At the beginning of a new cycle, several hypotheses are current, and Invest tries to obtain all information needed to check them. In the beginning, when it knows relatively little about the customer, INVEST is forced to ask many questions. At a later stage of the consultation, the needed information can often be obtained with the help of production rules (backward chaining).

Certain answers or combinations of answers result in trigger points being given to certain hypotheses and rules. In steps 2 and 3, INVEST considers only hypotheses and rules with trigger points, thus avoiding a waste of computational resources by evaluating rules or matching hypotheses that are obviously irrelevant. The number of trigger points for a hypothesis does not serve as a measure of belief; rather, trigger points flag hypotheses that first appear most promising.

Once all necessary information has been obtained by inquiry or by logical deduction, and trigger points have been allocated, INVEST proceeds to the cycle's second step. This consists of two parts:

1. Hypotheses with trigger points are now considered more closely. The most interesting possibilities—those with the most trigger points—receive attention first. The customer profile contains all known facts about the customer. For each hypothesis under consideration, INVEST contains a prototype describing the ideal conditions under which the hypothesis is true. The matching procedure, described later, compares the prototypes and the customer profile. Depending on the degree of agreement between hypothesis prototypes and the customer profile, each hypothesis is determined to be true, false, or undecided.
2. In conclusion, rules with trigger points are evaluated in forward-chaining mode.

We now come to step 3. With each hypothesis, it is possible to associate actions that should be executed if the hypothesis is found to be either true or false. Thus, in this step, actions associated with hypotheses found to be either true or false in step 2 are executed. Typical actions with a true hypothesis are the construction of a new investment proposal or the more precise specification of a previous investment proposal.

Every hypothesis contains the names of successor hypotheses, that is, hypotheses that are more specific and should therefore be considered next. So, the system returns to step 1 and attempts to obtain information needed to check successors of confirmed hypotheses.

Cycling stops when no new successor hypotheses can be found. At this point, if not before, INVEST makes a specific investment proposal.

At the end of each cycle, it is possible to investigate the consultation's current status. One can inspect the (incomplete) list of investment proposals or the list of hypotheses currently of interest, or look at all stocks the system currently regards as possible investments.

Expert knowledge is incorporated in hypotheses, hypothesis prototypes, trigger mechanisms, and rules. So far, we have found it relatively easy to incorporate human experts' knowledge into INVEST, because the inference mechanism's operation resembles the way human experts think.

The representation of objects

All objects in Donald are represented as *frames*. Such objects are either concrete concepts from the real world (persons, specific stocks or bonds, economic conditions) or abstract concepts that form part of Donald's knowledge mechanism (rules, hypotheses, investment proposals). Below are examples of various types of objects and their representation as frames.

Frames As usual in expert systems, a frame contains several *slots*, used to describe features of the object the frame represents. If one wishes to use a frame to represent the stock of a particular company—John Deere, for example—one must store information of the following type:*

Name of company	John Deere
Selling price	76
Yield	3.3
P-E Ratio	45

To create the appropriate frame in Donald, we first create a frame called Stock to describe the class of all stocks. In this frame, we define various slots, and we specify the values that entries in a slot can assume. We then define a frame for John Deere stock as a particular instance of the frame for a stock. We will discuss this example in more detail later.

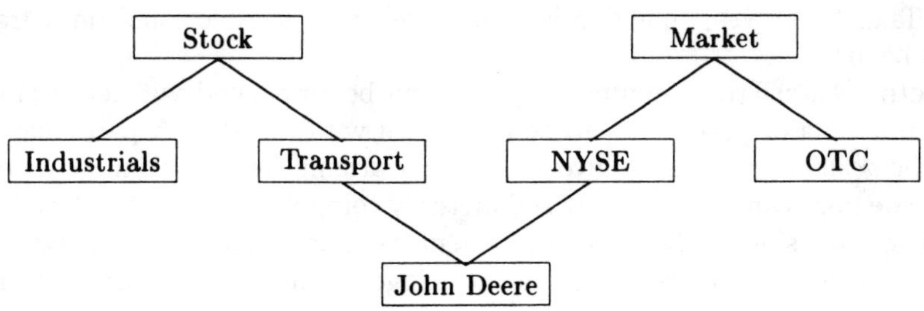

Fig. 22-1. A hierarchy of stocks.

Frame hierarchies The frame for John Deere stock is a specialization of the frame for stock. INVEST allows three types of frames: classes, subclasses, and instances. A frame of type class is used to represent an object that is not a special case of a more general object. A frame of type subclass has both predecessors and successors. A frame of type instance has no successors.

---

* INVEST currently holds only information about investments from the view point of German investors. U.S. investments are treated as foreign investments, which are subject to currency fluctuations. For reader convenience, we have tried to construct examples as they would be used in a U.S. version of INVEST.

Slots and views Within a hierarchy of frames, it is necessary to define slots and then specify the values in these slots. Slots can be defined in frames of type class or subclass. For each slot, the slot name and the range of possible entry values in the slot must be specified. The range of entry values in a slot must be of a predefined type. Most reasonable specifications are allowed: real (that is, decimal), integer, string, (OneOf 0 1 2), (OneOf yes no), (ListOf real), (SetOf integer), and so forth. At present, Donald does not allow mixed fractions such as $76^1/_8$, since these are not used in quoting German prices, but incorporating them would be trivial.

The values of slot entries are given in *views* contained in successor frames. Views, therefore, may only occur in frames of type subclass or instance. A view of a frame need not contain values for all slots in that frame.

Since a frame hierarchy is a net and not just a tree, a frame can contain views of several frames. For example, the frame for the customer profile may contain a view of the frame Investor and a view of the frame Tax Payer.

Inheritance All facts stored in views in a subclass are inherited by all successor frames. This applies not only to facts such as Yield: = 3.3 but also to *facets* (described below).

The principle of inheritance makes it possible to define general facts only once. Thus, since almost all US government securities are subject to tax, this fact can be given in the subclass Governments by setting the value in the slot Taxable to "yes," and successor frames will inherit it. However, if a frame explicitly contains a value in a slot, this value overwrites any inherited value. For example, the "flower" bonds were an exception to the rule that US government securities are taxable. The inherited value in the slot Taxable is "yes," but this is overwritten by "Taxable: = no" in a frame for "flower" bonds.

Facets An arbitrary number of *facets* can be associated with each slot. Such facets define data or procedures to be connected with the slot. A particular type of facet is the *demon*, a procedure invoked at every attempt to read from or write to the slot. Such demons can automatically and invisibly compute values to be placed in a slot and write to other slots. In INVEST, some demons react to a particular answer or combination of answers from the user, causing trigger points to be allocated to rules or hypotheses.

Some facets have standardized meanings in Donald:

- to ask — Text for use by Donald in generating questions to the user.
- to explain — Text for use in explaining questions.
- trigger — A list of hypotheses and rules that should be given a trigger point if certain specified conditions are satisfied.

The customer profile During a consultation, INVEST builds up information about the customer which is entered into an instance—Customer. We call this the *customer profile*. Information in the customer profile depends heavily on the course of the consultation. A customer who clearly should invest in bonds will be asked different questions than a customer who clearly should invest in shares.

Hypotheses and prototypes In contrast to the customer profile, built up during a consultation, hypotheses and prototypes are part of the knowledge base, and their construction requires the close cooperation of human experts.

Hypotheses are instances of the class Hypothesis. Hypothesis prototypes are instances of one or several classes designed to describe specific groups of investors. A hypothesis asserts that the customer profile is close to the corresponding hypothesis prototype. Thus the hypothesis Shareholder asserts that the customer profile is close to the shareholder prototype, which represents the human expert's concept of a typical shareholder.

Invest checks a hypothesis by using the function *match* to compare the customer profile with the hypothesis prototype. Match, briefly described later, returns a value, which is stored in the slot Confidence Factor and which is similar to confidence factors in other expert systems. A value close to – 1000 (+ 1000) implies that the hypothesis is rejected (accepted).

Hypothesis frames contain various pieces of information. If the hypothesis is accepted (rejected), the contents of the slot If Confirmed (If Disproved) are executed. Furthermore, hypothesis frames contain information about more specific hypotheses that should be put on the current hypothesis list if the hypothesis is accepted.

The purpose of hypothesis prototypes is to isolate aspects of a customer's profile that should be present—or absent—for the hypothesis to be true. To achieve greater flexibility, two previously unmentioned features are provided:

1. A weight w can be associated with any slot in a prototype frame. A larger value for w means greater significance for the slot when matching.
2. When matching the data types discussed so far, the match function returns + 1000 if the contents agree and – 1000 if they do not. In some cases this is too crude a measure. For example, the ideal investor in shares must be willing to accept high risk, but investors less willing to accept risk should also consider shares. The data type Heuristic List, or HList, can be used in heuristic prototypes to express this type of condition. An HList is a list of pairs in which the first element is a possible slot value and the second element is the corresponding value of the match function.

We illustrate the above-mentioned two features by an example. The class Investor contains slots for the length of the investment, the amount to be invested, and the customer's willingness to accept risk. In response to the question "How much risk are you prepared to accept?" the customer has answered that an average risk is acceptable.

```
(Instance Customer
  (View Investor with
        . . .
        (Acceptable Risk: = average)
        . . .))
```

The hypothesis prototype for the Shareholder hypothesis is

```
(Instance Shareholder
  (View Investor with
        . . .
        (Acceptable Risk :=
          (HList (low . -1000)
                 (average . 500)
                 (high . 1000))
          weight := 3)
        . . .))
```

When matching the Acceptable Risk slot, the value "average" in the customer profile corresponds to +500 in the Shareholder prototype's HList; so for this slot the value returned is +500 weighted with the weight 3. The numerical values used within the HLists are associated with a rough semantic. The nine multiples of 250 (−1000, 750, . . ., +1000) represent the spectrum from "doesn't fit at all" to "fits very well." The HLists in the prototypes were constructed from verbal statements of our investment experts and then tested on hypothetical examples. In only a few instances was it necessary to revise the values in the HLists.

Investment proposals All investment proposals are instances of the class Proposal. At the beginning of a consultation, the instance Proposal-1 is created:

```
(Instance Proposal-1
  (View Proposal)
  (View Securities))
```

This is the most general proposal possible and simply proposes that the customer buy securities.

As the consultation proceeds, Proposal-1 is refined by the addition of more views, and, if necessary, additional proposals are created. This is done by a special proposal-building mechanism, through actions associated with accepted hypotheses. Let's take a simple example.

Suppose that during the first cycle the hypothesis Stock, which asserts that the customer should consider buying stock, is accepted. Then the view Stock is added to Proposal-1. If during the next cycle the hypothesis Foreign Securities, which asserts that the customer should consider buying foreign securities, is accepted, then the corresponding view will be added to Proposal-1, which now has the form

```
(Instance Proposal-1
  (View Proposal)
  (View Securities)
  (View Stock)
  (View Foreign Securities))
```

and therefore proposes that the customer buy foreign stock.

To ensure that the proposals are feasible, INVEST makes a consistency check before adding a new view to an existing proposal. Continuing with the present example, let's suppose INVEST has only a small database not containing any foreign stock.

Then, instead of adding the view Foreign Securities to Proposal-1, INVEST will create a new proposal:

```
(Instance Proposal-2
   (View Proposal)
   (View Foreign Securities))
```

Meanwhile, Proposal-1 remains unaltered:

```
(Instance Proposal-1
   (View Proposal)
   (View Securities)
   (View Stock))
```

Two separate investment proposals now exist, and these will be refined as the consultation proceeds.

If the expert system currently believes a hypothesis but cannot accept any of its successors, then the proposal-building mechanism will not consider this hypothesis. Similarly, hypotheses lacking well-founded support—an unbroken chain of predecessors back to the most general proposal—will also be skipped. Thus, proposals can also be revised or even discarded. This nonmonotonicity produces a self-correcting effect as the consultation proceeds from cycle to cycle.

We note that the views in proposals may also contain slot values.

Rules All rules are instances of the class Rule, which contains the slots Premise and Action. The production rule

```
If <premise> then <action>
```

is created by storing the Lisp code for the premise and action in the corresponding slots.

The expert system shell Donald

We will provide some details about Donald; a complete description is available elsewhere. [4], [5] Donald is related to KRL, a knowledge representation language introduced by Bobrow and Winograd, [6] but it differs from KRL in several significant respects.

The internal representation of frames Externally—in communicating with a user—frames are represented as lists. For efficiency, Donald represents each frame internally as a vector. The first few elements of such a vector contain standard information: the frame's name, the type (class, subclass, or instance), the number of views, and the number of slots. Succeeding elements contain the definitions of the slots associated with the frame, and vectors for each view. Use of this internal representation has greatly increased Donald's efficiency.

Matching Matching is an essential mechanism in Donald. The function *match* can be applied to any two frames and returns a number m between -1000 and $+1000$ that provides a measure of similarity between the two frames. The larger m is, the greater the similarity between the two frames; the smaller m is, the greater the dissimilarity. If the two frames have no views in common, m is 0.

When two frames are compared, only views that occur in both frames are considered. If no such views are present, then $m = 0$. Otherwise, m is the arithmetic average of the results of match's application to the common views. Match's value when applied to two views is the weighted arithmetic average of the results of match's application to the common slots. Since slots may contain frames, recursion may occur. At the lowest level, the function match is explicitly defined by special functions for pairs of integers, pairs of lists, and so forth. The internal representation of frames was chosen so that match could be efficiently implemented.

In INVEST, matching is used principally to compare the current customer profile with a hypothesis prototype. Matching is ideally suited for this purpose. The human expert specifies the characteristics constituting an ideal customer profile for the hypothesis in question, and these are incorporated into the hypothesis prototype by the knowledge engineer. When matching occurs, these exact characteristics are considered.

Inheritance When a frame is created, its views are represented as vectors. In this process, the views inherited from preceding frames are taken into account; if the slot value occurs in two views, the value taken is the one occurring in the predecessor frame closest to the frame being created. Normally, then, the most recent value is used. When the value in a view's slot is changed, the values in slots in successor views are also changed if necessary.

So far we have been very satisfied with INVEST and increasingly confident that it can provide reasonable advice. As already mentioned, it has proved relatively easy to incorporate human expertise. In some instances, INVEST made unsatisfactory investment proposals; but by using the explanation facility (which we have not described), it has been possible to locate and correct faulty knowledge. Experts do not always agree; in some cases INVEST has been able to convince its creators that it has given the better advice.

Matching has proved successful as an inference mechanism. It makes it possible to compare similar (but not identical) objects and obtain a measure of their similarity. This is of great value in INVEST, since the ideal customer does not exist.

There is room for improvement in certain aspects. A customer may alter an opinion during the consultation after INVEST has made an investment proposal, perhaps because the proposed investment seems too risky. This can occur because certain concepts cannot be precisely defined. For example, a customer must indicate willingness to accept low, average, or high risk. However, a customer who has opted to accept high risk may well reconsider when confronted with a specific high-risk investment proposal.

Handling such situations requires revising "known" facts and all conclusions drawn from them (belief revision). In the long run, the use of a truth maintenance system, or TMS, seems unavoidable. A full TMS involves considerable additional complexity, [7] and the present implementation incorporates only a rudimentary mechanism.

At present, INVEST contains information about the classes stock, options, bonds, and so forth, together with information about numerous subclasses. This knowledge base of about 200 frames is being enlarged steadily. About 50 basic hypotheses exist which, when combined, represent almost all possibilities on the German securities market.

We have not yet considered in detail the practical question of implementing INVEST in a banking environment. However, INVEST's hardware requirements are relatively modest, and AI software is increasingly available on a wide range of computers, so we do not anticipate insuperable obstacles.

Acknowledgments

We gratefully acknowledge the assistance of E. Silkenbaeumer and B. Uhlmann, investment experts at the Volksbank Muenster and the Westdeutschen Genossenschafts-Zentralbank, Muenster, respectively.

The Cadmus computer on which INVEST is presently running was made available by Professor W.-M. Lippe.

In the early stages, financial support was provided by the Institut fuer Angewandte Informatik, Universitaet Muenster, and by the Ministerium fuer Wissenschaft und Forschung des Landes Nordrhein-Westfalen through project number 208 002 86.

References

1. P. Jackson, *Introduction to Expert Systems*, Addison-Wesley, Reading, Mass., 1986, pp. 115 – 125.
2. J.L. Alty and M.J. Coombs, *Expert Systems*, NCC Publications, The National Computing Centre Ltd., Manchester, England, 1984, pp. 120 – 128.
3. J.L. Joslin, G. Lorant, and R.E.C. Wegner, "The Multi-Asset Allocation Model: A Financial Planning Framework for Long-Term Investment Management," *Tax Management Financial Planning J.*, Oct. 1986, pp. 523 – 531.
4. S. Heuer, *Implementation of a Frame-Based Knowledge Representation for Expert Systems*, Diplomarbeit. Institut fuer Numerische und instrumentelle Mathematik der Westfaelischen Wilhelms-Universitaet zu Muenster, Mar. 1987 (in German).
5. U. Koch and S. Heuer, "Die Expertensystem-Shell Donald," in *Proc. Anwender-Forum Expertensysteme*, A.B. Cremers and K.-H. Becks, eds., Universitaet Dortmund, Lehrstuhl fuer Informations-systeme, 1987, pp. 115 – 125.
6. D.G. Bobrow and T. Winograd, "An Overview of KRL, a Knowledge Representation Language," in *Readings in Knowledge Representation*, R.J. Brachman and H.J. Levesque, eds., Morgan Kaufmann, Los Altos, Calif., 1985, pp. 263 – 285.
7. J. Doyle, "A Truth Maintenance System," AI Memo 521, Massachusetts Institute of Technology, Cambridge, Mass., 1979.

Section E

Applications in robotics

23

Mobile robots
Real-time intelligent control
Louis S. McTamaney

Editors' note *McTamaney describes research and development that led to the development of an autonomous vehicle "capable of real-time operation both on- and off-road." The paper is reprinted here because it constitutes a good example of multidisciplinary systems engineering that just happens to heavily feature AI. In fact, autonomous vehicle design and development require expertise that cross-cuts the behavioral, computer, mathematical and engineering sciences. The paper thus reports on a project that accords AI status equal to many other fields and disciplines. (Reprinted, with permission, from the Winter 1987 issue of* IEEE Expert. *© 1987, IEEE. All rights reserved.)*

Intelligent mobile robots can go where mortals cannot or do not want to go. Robots can mechanize repetitious, labor-intensive tasks and can safely operate in hazardous and contaminated environments. Applications include agricultural harvesting, factory floor material handling and transfer, combat and combat support systems, and planetary exploration vehicles. Such robots must be able to accept mission statements and constraints, plan their actions, execute those plans, perceive and adapt to their environment, and report successes and failures.

Substantial engineering challenges underlie the development of component technologies required for self-navigation—planning, perception, navigation, and control. A technology testbed facilitates the development and demonstration of emerging technologies necessary for intelligent mobile systems. At FMC, we have been developing such a testbed since 1982.

Our objective has been to develop an autonomous vehicle capable of real-time operation both on- and off-road. To date, our system has demonstrated mission planning, route planning with execution at 8 km/hr, obstacle detection and avoidance at 15 km/hr, and road following at 24 km/hr. In August of 1986, under the joint Army/DARPA advanced ground vehicle technology program, we integrated these autonomous capabilities with remote driving and mission package control to demonstrate a remotely managed route reconnaissance mission at vehicle speeds of up to 40 km/hr. Our current research efforts focus on multiple-vehicle control and advanced autonomous capabilities such as dynamic replanning, terrain typing, road attainment, road network navigation, local slope navigation, and landmark-based navigation.

We have extensively tested our system at the FMC facility in San Jose, California—at the Army National Guard facility at Camp Roberts, California—and at the Martin Marietta autonomous land vehicle (ALV) test facility in Denver, Colorado. Currently (August-September 1987), the system is undergoing an extensive concept evaluation by the US Army Armor Center at Ft. Knox, Kentucky.

System architecture and components

On-board versus off-board processing was a key system-level issue during the program's early stages. We selected off-board processing because the anticipated computer quantity, size, power requirement, and lack of robustness made on-board processing impractical if not impossible. Thus, as shown in FIG. 23-1, the system consists of a transportable command center and the robotic vehicle connected by a five-channel microwave link. Developing the command center and microwave link required a substantial engineering effort; however, this effort has paid off in system development ease, flexibility, and extensibility.

Going off-board relieved us of environmental, space, weight, and power constraints; consequently, we could focus a large percentage of program effort on developing system and hardware architecture, algorithms, and software.

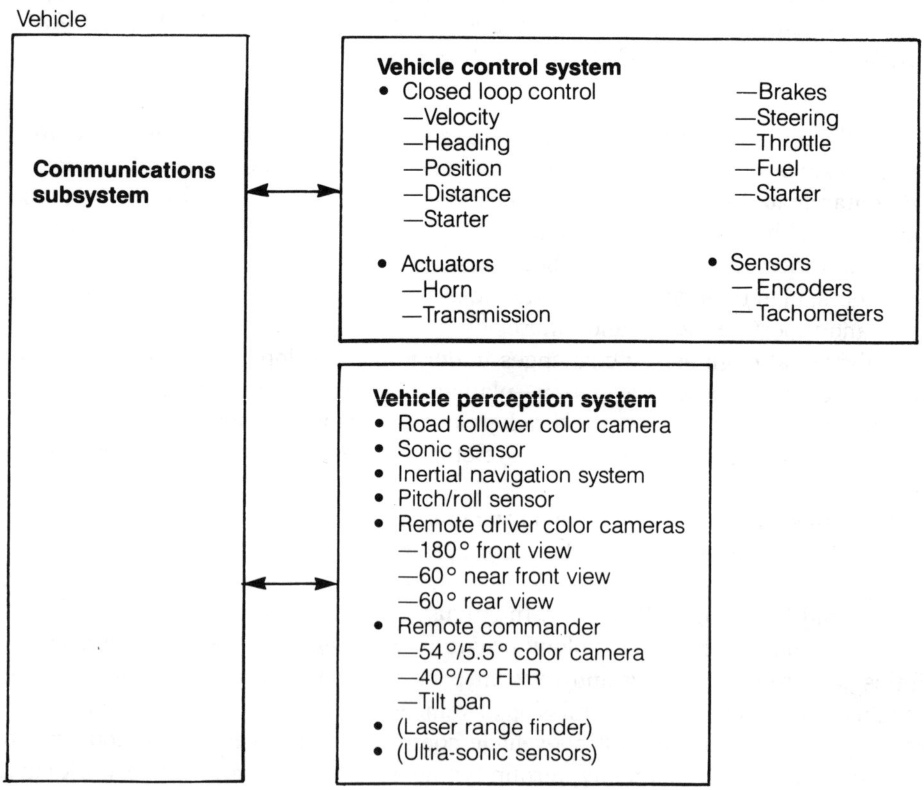

Fig. 23-1. The systems consist of a transportable command center and a mobile robot linked by a five-channel microwave link.

The command center We selected a transportable rather than fixed computing facility to permit test, evaluation, and demonstration at any test site. The command center, illustrated in FIG. 23-2, contains

- Communications and computer hardware needed to (1) receive and process robot mobility and sensor status data, and (2) transmit mobility and sensor control commands in real time to the robot;
- Two teleoperators, a remote driver and a remote reconnaissance sensor package operator; and
- A set of workstations (loosely coupled over an Ethernet) comprising the autonomous navigator, capable of mission- and route-planning and execution, obstacle detection and avoidance, and road following.

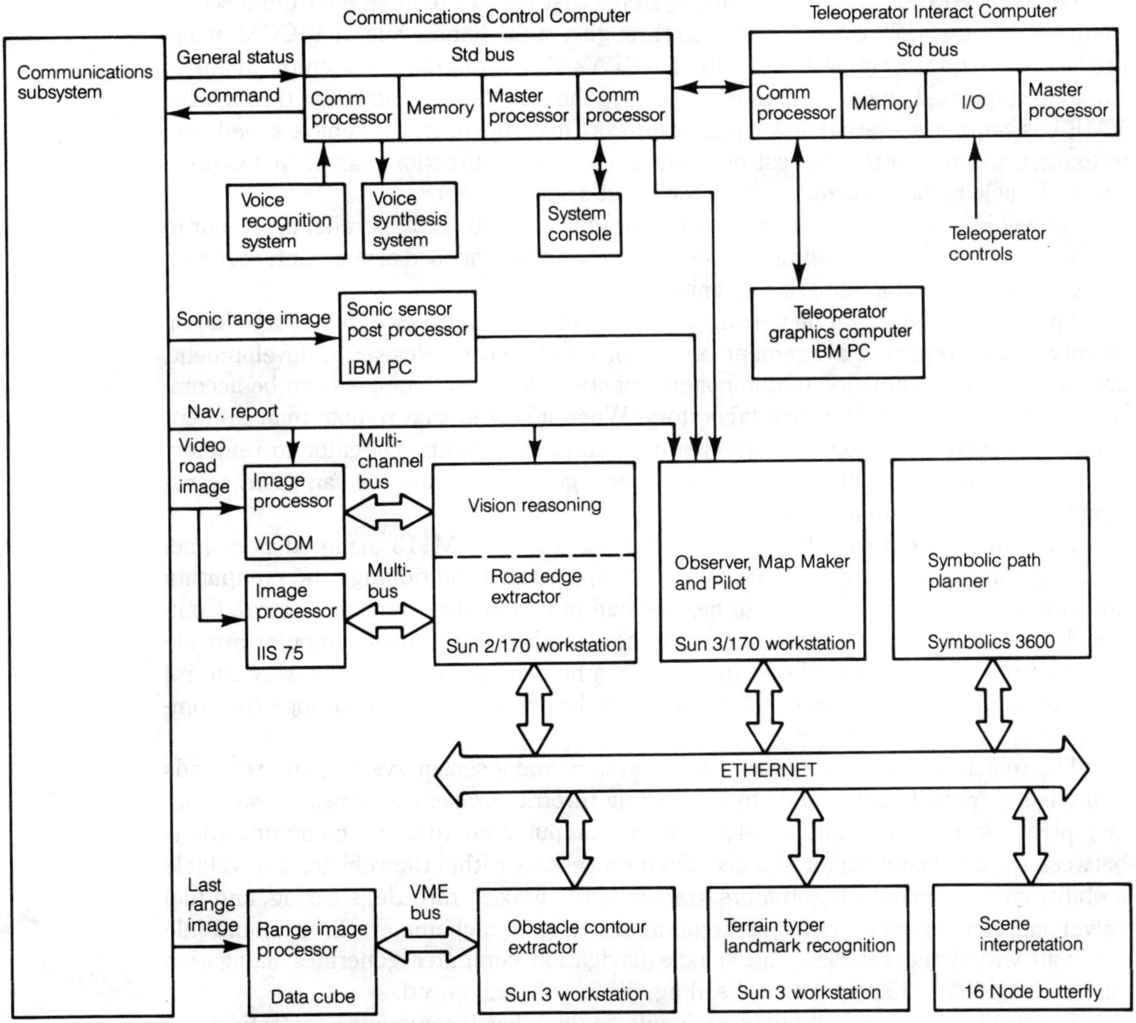

Fig. 23-2. The command center's hardware architecture.

Figure 23-2 illustrates how the communications control computer serves as a gateway to the robot and facilitates switchover between autonomous navigation and teleoperation. Our system routes all robot control commands generated by the teleoperators and the autonomous navigator through this computer. The autonomous navigator's mission-planning component resides on a Symbolics 3600. [1] Two route planners are available: a symbolic planner that also resides on the Symbolics 3600, [2] and a more conventional pixel path planner installed on a Sun 3 workstation. [3]

The autonomous navigator's three-part heart—the observer, mapmaker, and pilot modules—resides on a second Sun 3/170 Unix workstation. These modules interpret global plans, fusing them with locally sensed data to produce a map that the pilot analyzes to determine trajectories and concomitant mobility control commands for the robot.

We provided two image-processing systems that extract road edges from a scene. Coupled to a Sun 3/170 Unix workstation through a multichannel bus, A VICOM image processor provides compatibility with DARPA's ALV program; a memory-mapped Datacube pipelined image processor, coupled to the same Sun workstation through the VME bus, supports internal development efforts. To compensate for vehicle speed, and to extract distance to the nearest obstacle in each of 14 directions, an IBM PC processes obstacle maps transmitted from the robot's sonic sensor.

We will integrate additional Sun workstations and a Butterfly parallel processor to perform range image processing and scene interpretation for road attainment, road network navigation, and landmark recognition.

The system's organization permits use of the command center either as a field laboratory or as a remote management center for robot control. Research, development, and performance evaluation of component robotic vehicle technologies can be accomplished when it's used as a field laboratory. When it's used as a remote management center, the system employs the teleoperators and autonomous navigator to remotely manage the robotic vehicle and its mission package. Additionally, we can easily transport the complete system to test sites.

The mobile robot The mobile robot—a modified M113 armored personnel carrier equipped with self-contained power supplies, air conditioning, and computing and communications hardware, can be operated in two modes—remote or local. Commands routed through the command center communications control computer provide vehicle control in remote mode. In local mode, a human operator can manually control the vehicle but vehicle status is still returned to the command center through the communications control computer.

The vehicle includes a mobility control system and a sensor system, and responds to high-level mobility commands by controlling throttle, brake, transmission, steering, and pivot mechanisms. The master vehicle computer coordinates communications between the command center and dedicated processors within the vehicle. The vehicle mobility computer controls actuators (transmission, brakes, throttle, steering, and fuel valve) and monitors sensors (track tachometers, engine tachometer, throttle, and idle position) within the vehicle. The vehicle navigation computer generates navigation reports including vehicle position, heading, pitch, roll, and speed.

The vehicle sensor computer responds to high-level commands, selecting the reconnaissance sensor (a color camera or forward-looking infrared sensor), controlling an on-board video switcher, and controlling and monitoring sensor pan, tilt, zoom, and focus. All vehicle computers are Intel microprocessors in multiprocessor configuration. Initially, these computers were single processors. But as the system evolved and became more complex, processor-to-processor communications consumed most of the available processor power. We resolved this problem by converting to the current multiprocessor configuration where one (and in some cases, two) processors are dedicated solely to data communications—making the host processor fully available for control.

The sensor system includes seven color cameras, an inertial navigation system (INS), a dynamic pitch/roll sensor, a forward-looking infrared sensor, and a sonic-imaging sensor. Mounted on a stabilized pan/tilt base, the infrared sensor provides both day and night viewing.

The sonic-imaging sensor consists of a 9600-Hz sonic transmitter and 16 microphones spaced linearly to form an array. System requirements called for obstacle detection and avoidance by a 10-ton vehicle operating at 48-64 km/hr and capable of 0.2g deceleration. These requirements translated to a sensor system with a 120-degree field-of-view, an operating range of 32.7 meters, and an image frame rate of 5 Hz.

Because we could not satisfy these requirements with off-the-shelf sensors such as the Polaroid unit (10-meter range), we designed a sensor specifically for this application. A high-speed processor, operating at 5 MIPS, implements digital filtering and correlation algorithms to generate a 16×24 image every 200 milliseconds. The sensor and its associated processor performed well, detecting and avoiding obstacles in the range of 15-33 meters at vehicle speeds up to 15 km/hr.

However, the sensor had a blind spot (from 0-15 meters). And, at speeds greater than 15 km/hr, engine and track noise saturated the detector amplifiers. Sensor data processing filled in the blind spot by moving objects detected in the far-field array (15-33 meters) into the near-field array (0-15 meters) as a function of robot linear speed, thereby providing a complete obstacle map. Subsequently, detected obstacles were rotated out of the blind spot as they were passed or avoided. But this left the vehicle vulnerable to turning into deleted obstacles: When avoiding an obstacle, the vehicle could turn into a previously detected (cut currently deleted) obstacle within its blind spot.

To overcome our initial design's shortcomings, we developed a second-generation sensor operating in the ultrasonic spectrum (30 kHz) beyond the engine and track noise spectrum. It has a shorter range (21.3 meters) but a better depth of field (0.6-21.3 meters) and a wider field of view (180 degrees). Preliminary static tests indicate excellent detection of 30-gallon drums at ranges up to 21.3 meters.

The color cameras used for road following, teleoperation, and reconnaissance are standard solid-state CCD cameras with NTSC outputs. Video signals are routed through the video switcher to the microwave link. The INS provides vehicle heading and position data. The pitch/roll sensor provides vehicle pitch and roll attitude information. We selected a rugged and reliable military INS. But, because it was designed for use by a human operator (providing position to one meter at a one-second update rate) it proved inadequate for autonomous operations such as road following. We rectified this by reimplementing navigation equations on a dedicated coprocessor, thereby achieving a two-orders-of-magnitude improvement. Now, position to 0.1 meter is provided at 10 reports per second.

The communications system The five-channel microwave communications link operates line-of-sight over a range of 60 meters to 5.47 kilometers. We allocated four microwave frequencies for transmission of video and data from the vehicle to the command center; one frequency is used to transmit data to the vehicle. The video signals are modulated onto the main 4.5-MHz bandwidth carrier, and audio and data signals onto the audio subcarriers. We selected the microwave link based on availability of off-the-shelf equipment and ease of FCC licensing.

The communications system performs antenna tracking automatically through the use of a signal strength error correction amplifier associated with one of the carriers. This amplifier controls a two-axis servo system that positions antenna elevation and azimuth. As the vehicle moves with respect to the command center, the command center antenna automatically corrects its bore sight angles to optimize signal strength and transmits these angles to the vehicle. If communication is lost at any time, the vehicle maintains the last-calculated antenna elevation angle and constantly updates the azimuth angle according to available INS data and known command center coordinates.

Susceptibility to multipath reception is a significant problem with the microwave link. Signals bounce off hills, rock formations, and buildings. Future highly autonomous systems will obviate the need for wide bandwidth communications links. However, interim fielded systems require non-line-of-sight communication. Researchers must expend substantial effort to reduce bandwidth requirements and provide reliable non-line-of-sight communications links for remotely managed robotic vehicle systems.

Software architecture

The autonomous navigator software architecture shown comprises three major subsystems—planning, perception, and navigation/control. The planning subsystem uses knowledge about missions, terrain, and characteristics—plus capabilities of the autonomous system itself—to plan a sequence of tasks and routes that will accomplish stated goals. The plan-execution-monitoring module sends plan segments to the perception system. Each plan segment specifies only the desired behavior rather than the exact vehicle action because detailed world information is available only during plan execution. For example, the planning system may generate a plan segment requiring the vehicle to follow a road from point A to point B. Actual road boundaries will be available from the perception system only during plan execution.

The perception system directs sensors to acquire information and constructs descriptions of the local environment from sensory data. Currently, we have four functional modules that build local environment maps—road following, obstacle avoidance, terrain typing, and landmark recognition modules. The local map builder fuses these local maps with global constraints and goal direction to form a fused local map.

The navigation and control system's pilot module uses this fused local map and vehicle characteristics to plan a local path and to determine corresponding vehicle mobility commands. The plan-execution-monitoring module then uses INS data to update vehicle position and monitors plan execution.

The planning system The mission-planning process generates an action sequence to satisfy goals and constraints posed by a mission commander. Typically, such plans are constructed at varying levels of abstraction: high levels represent mission objectives; low levels represent more detailed tactical actions. As plans develop, the planner can make decisions refining high-level decisions or can make high-level decisions based on constraints and opportunities discovered during low-level planning. Thus, planning proceeds opportunistically—both top down and bottom up.

The mission planner uses an event-driven blackboard system that synthesizes an action sequence to achieve stated mission objectives. This system includes a globally accessible, multilevel solution blackboard (knowledge base); a flexible control structure that supervises planning space expansion; plus independent, problem-solving knowledge sources for synthesizing plan steps. The mission planner uses constraints such as concealment, visibility, and trafficability to choose the best task locations. Knowledge sources, interacting with the symbolic path planner, sequence locations together by computing routes among these locations.

To limit the number of potential plans, a three-tiered structure controls plan synthesis, varying control over the execution of knowledge sources. This structure establishes focus decisions, executes strategies, and ranks knowledge sources. Focus decisions represent heuristics against which the program rates knowledge sources. Strategies provide a rigid control structure that directly oversees the execution of knowledge sources; a strategy, consisting of a goal and a list of strategies and tactics, represents a procedure for achieving a particular goal. Ranking prioritizes knowledge sources grouped together due to similarities in function or strategy.

During problem solving, knowledge sources create decision elements in the plan hierarchy. As planning proceeds, the program activates more knowledge sources, making them available for execution. Using focus decisions, strategies, and rankings, a controller rates these knowledge sources. A scheduler selects a knowledge source for execution by choosing the source with the highest rating. The planner uses constraints based on terrain feature information, resource limitations, vehicle limitations, and military doctrine to limit the number of acceptable plans.

We organized knowledge bases using a structured approach—an approach that defines knowledge sources in a modular fashion employing principles of top-down refinement—so that knowledge sources can execute in sequences necessary for solving problems. Knowledge bases are partitioned into sets of knowledge sources with functional similarities. The mission-planning system has 105 domain knowledge sources collected into 18 knowledge source groups.

Two route planners compute routes between task locations. The symbolic path planner, using spatial reasoning, decomposes free space for efficient path planning. The route planner identifies critical-passage regions and corridors on a terrain map so the high-level planning module can take these into consideration for mission planning. The pixel path planner defines a cost function on a map grid that considers detection probability and fuel consumption, and uses dynamic programming to find the optimal pixel path on the grid.

The planning system represents plans as contiguous polygonal free space segments, each segment describing free space in which the robot is known to respect initial constraints. Each plan segment uses a path description language to describe constraints (for example, path borders, the global direction, and obstacles) as high-level composite functions acting on sensor data. Each segment also contains predicates specifying the conditions under which the description applies.

This approach offers great flexibility. Rather than simply outputting lists of values or simple orders, we can combine language primitives so that many sophisticated actions are possible without modifying the system. Our approach also eases elegant processing of fuzzy events, such as meeting a road whose exact location is unknown.

The perception system During plan execution, the intelligent robot perceives the world through its sensors. Data fusion from multiple sensors enables the perception system to construct descriptions of the robot's local environment. Based on these descriptions, the robot can (1) follow a road, (2) circumvent obstacles, hazardous terrain, and steep slopes, and (3) recognize objects and landmarks.

Developing a general perception system for autonomous vehicle navigation is an open-ended problem at nature's mercy. Changes due to time, weather, and shadow can easily fool sophisticated vision systems. A general vision system requires extensive world knowledge. Such a system is impossible to develop based on current technology.

We used the following requirements to guide our design and development: real-time operation, generality, adaptiveness, and robustness. Vision modules have been developed to perform road following, obstacle avoidance, terrain typing, and landmark recognition. The following subsections discuss these modules and examine the extent to which they satisfy our requirements:

- The road-following module Figure 23-3 diagrams the road-following module's operation. [4] During initialization, the vision system acquires a color image from a camera and uses an Ohlander-Price-style recursive-region-segmentation algorithm and a bounded-minimum-distance classifier to classify terrain types based on region properties such as color, texture, and shape. The system uses color statistics of road and nonroad regions to derive color transformation parameters that best discriminate the two classes. Red, green, and blue images combine into a single image during road following, according to these transformation parameters. Road segmentation uses a maximum-likelihood pixel classification technique to segment the image into road and nonroad regions, employing previous segmentation results to estimate the likelihood ratio between road and nonroad classes. This satisfies generality and adaptiveness to some extent. The road follower adapts to road changes in two ways: The program updates color transformation parameters infrequently to accommodate significant road color changes, and updates classifier parameters every processing cycle to deal with gradual color and intensity changes. To eliminate unnecessary computation, the program selects only the most likely road region in the segmented image, and transforms a polygonal representation of the detected road region boundary from the image coordinate system to the local vehicle coordinate system based on a flat-earth assumption. A geometric-reasoning module provides robustness, taking this input and using temporal and spatial constraints to perform model-based reasoning. [5] Cases involving incomplete sensor data (on curved roads, for example, where only one side of the road is visible) and incorrect segmentations (due to shadows, road patches, or unusual road conditions) can usually be detected and corrected.

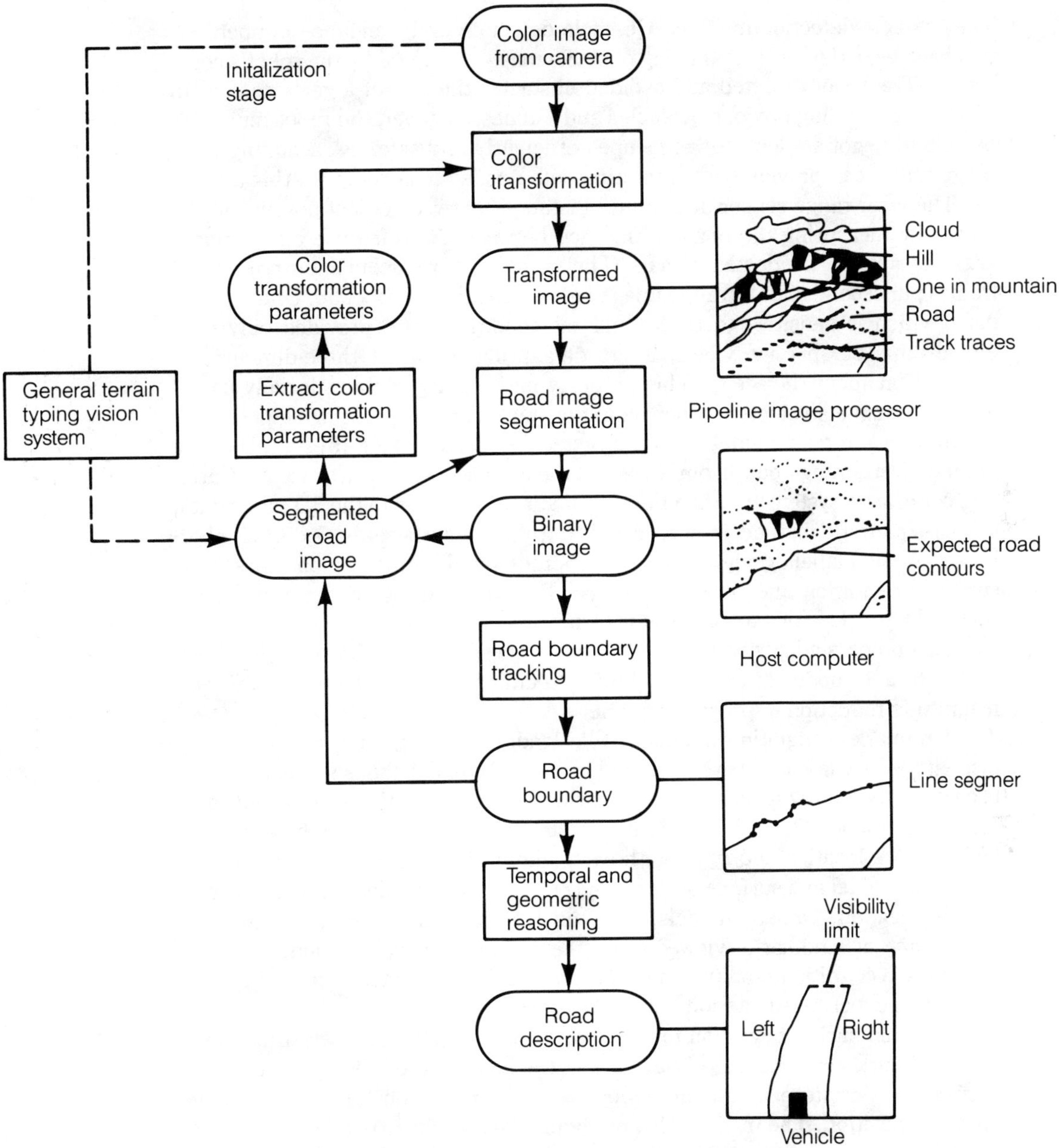

Fig. 23-3. The road-following module's operation.

With respect to real-time operation requirements, the road follower takes approximately one second to process each image. Using the color transformation derived from image statistics, this vision module can deal with paved, gravel, and dirt roads—encountering some difficulty on dirt roads due to poorly defined road boundaries.

- The obstacle detection module Obstacle detection and avoidance in open terrain have been demonstrated using obstacle maps generated by the robot's sonic sensor. The robot detected and avoided obstacles the size of a garbage can. In addition to avoiding obvious obstacles and ditches, however, the robot must also be able to negotiate local terrain slopes efficiently and safely. A scanning laser range finder can provide high-resolution data needed to accomplish this task.

  The laser range sensor determines distances between object points and the sensor by measuring the phase difference between the reference and a modulated laser beam's reflected signals. The range sensor's acquisition rate is two frames per second and the range image has a resolution of 64×256. Unlike video data, which is sensitive to environmental conditions and provides only two-dimensional perspective views, range data provides direct three-dimensional information about the scene. This property makes range data especially useful to an autonomous vehicle when avoiding obstacles and negotiating slopes.

  In a local terrain model being extracted from range data, [6] first, the program converts range data from a spherical coordinate system to an x-y-z Cartesian coordinate system and then fits planar surface patches to the 3D range data; a least-square-fit method is used for fitting planar surfaces to 5×5 neighborhoods. A blob-labeling algorithm then merges neighboring regions, based on surface orientation and normal distance. Regions with slopes greater than a threshold are classified as obstacle regions.

  This process adapts well to concurrent processing. The algorithm has been ported to a 16-node Butterfly machine. Preliminary results show an order-of-magnitude reduction in processing time.
- The landmark recognition module. The landmark recognition module recognizes stationary landmarks represented in a terrain map database. The robot can use triangulation to one or more landmarks to correct position errors caused by drift in the robot's INS. This module consists of (1) a landmark database indexed by landmark location and type, with each landmark represented in terms of its geometric model and surface properties; (2) a landmark prediction module using vehicle location, camera models, and the landmark database to predict the appearance of landmarks viewed from the current vehicle location; and (3) a landmark recognition module using the predicted appearance of a landmark to guide image feature extraction for landmark recognition.

  The landmark recognition process works as follows: After selecting a suitable landmark for vision-based navigation, the landmark prediction module calculates appropriate pan, tilt, and zoom parameters to control the camera for image acquisition. The module also predicts a landmark outline in the acquired image based on current camera parameters, vehicle and landmark locations, and the landmark's geometric model. The program then uses this outline to generate a landmark feature template that drives the generalized Hough transform algorithm for landmark recognition: A Sobel edge detector is used to extract edge points from images; a Hough vote image is generated based on the match between edge points and the landmark template; and peaks in the vote image are used to find the most likely landmark locations.

- The terrain-typing module. The terrain-typing module classifies terrain, using image region properties such as color, texture, and shape. It not only sets transformation parameters for the road follower (as described earlier) but it also determines trafficability maps and differentiates road from off-road positions. It consists of three stages—training, segmentation, and classification.

  Training. Applying a simple clustering scheme, the module uses sample images to train the terrain classifier. Feature statistics are calculated and a distance measure is evaluated among all existing class templates for each new terrain class, color, and texture. Each class can have a set of subclasses to further classify terrain; for example, the road class has paved, gravel, and dirt road subclasses.

  Segmentation. The module uses image features such as color and texture to segment the image into homogeneous regions, employing a region segmenter based on the Ohlander-Price style of recursive region segmentation. Once the image is segmented into homogeneous regions, properties such as statistical distribution of the region's color, texture, shape, and spatial relations are collected for classification against the reference templates created in the training process.

  Classification. A minimum-distance classifier assigns each region a class label. The module computes the distance measure between class templates and the region feature cluster, and selects the class with the minimum distance as the region's class label. If the minimum distance is greater than a preselected threshold, however, the region is classified as unknown. Final classification uses region shape and spatial relations as constraints.

Navigation and control The navigation-and-control system encompasses the pilot and the on-board control system. The pilot guides the robot along a dynamically feasible route, based on a unified representation of the local free space (provided by the perception system) that is a fusion of sensor visibility limits, global path segment boarders, road boundaries, and obstacle locations.

The real-time reflexive pilot analyzes this map and generates vehicle control commands in less than 20 milliseconds. [7] Our pilot operates in real time largely because it doesn't process a memory map of past subgoals and corridors. Many aspects of intelligent obstacle avoidance and local path planning can be based solely on current snapshots of local free space. We maintain sensor view of the subgoal we approach, and allow the localized optimal control problem to be solved, by restricting local path planning to a conical-shaped, usable subset of local free space.

The pilot processes the pilot map to generate possible subgoals that are then assigned weights. To avoid trap-like concavities, certain obstacle avoidance strategies may require temporary replacement of the global goal direction. At each cycle's end, the pilot generates and sends a command to the vehicle control computer. We designed the reflexive pilot to respond quickly in environments with wide passages separating obstacles. In reality, the vehicle may have to pass through forested regions where narrow passageways between trees is typical. Under such conditions, the reflexive pilot will stop the robot, turning control over to a more intelligent but slower copilot that uses a line model of the vehicle (rather than the point model used by the reflexive pilot) and operates as follows: [8] Detected obstacles are grown to form "walls" between which the vehicle must pass. If these enlarged obstacles block the path's opening, no feasible path exists; if all corners are reachable and there is no collision between the vehicle model's line and the obstacle wall, then the path is feasible. A feasible path may be seen through an opening or may be hidden behind a shadow line. Since there may be more than one opening and/or shadow, the copilot ranks them according to characteristics such as width and proximity to the desired direction.

The pilot considers all openings first because it is more desirable to traverse openings than to check for feasible paths behind shadows. Once the pilot has ranked all openings and shadows, the algorithm searches for a feasible path (beginning with the highest ranked opening) until it has exhausted all possibilities. When it finds the optimum path, the vehicle will move to a new position. The process continues until the vehicle reaches its goal position or until no feasible path exists in the local map.

We are directing current efforts toward extending the local map's representation and pilot to accommodate local slope data and to compute trajectories for road attainment.

The robot's on-board controller is a real-time system performing various motion control and data acquisition functions in response to high-level commands. Built-in usage rules that provide safe vehicle operation constrain these primary functions. The system can start and stop its engine, monitor its operation (stall, overspeed, and so forth), and can operate vehicle actuators directly in an open or closed loop fashion through rate and attainment control algorithms. Rate control provides closed loop controls on vehicle speed (a PID algorithm) and radius of turn (an incremental algorithm). Attainment control—based on rate control—provides control of heading, distance, and position. The system implements heading control as a PID algorithm, and implements distance control as a classic displacement control algorithm with acceleration, constant speed, and deceleration phases.

Position attainment, the most sophisticated controller function, is a dual feedback control algorithm that supervises vehicle position (expressed in UTM coordinates) and vehicle heading. This algorithm seeks to drive the vehicle to a goal position without crossing a pair of limit lines at the vehicle's right and left sides.

We have demonstrated a modular, extensible system that intelligently controls a mobile robot. Its architecture and associated Lisp-like plan generation language enable the system to perform global path planning from a digital terrain database and then to execute the planned path, avoiding unexpected obstacles along the way and following roads when directed to do so.

We have demonstrated the system in natural, outdoor environments such as Camp Roberts, California and Martin Marietta Aerospace's Denver ALV facility. The March, 1985 demonstration at Camp Roberts was the first and (so far) the only demonstration of autonomous navigation (path planning and execution from a map database with concurrent obstacle detection and avoidance over a 2-km open terrain route at 8 km/hr) by a full-sized vehicle in a natural, outdoor environment.

In July of 1986 at Camp Roberts, we demonstrated road following at a speed of 19 km/hr on a 0.8-km flat, S-shaped gravel road. We also demonstrated road following at

10 km/hr on the Denver facility's more difficult paved road (tighter curves, and a hill-and-dale effect).

On FMC's San Jose test track, we demonstrated recent improvements to the navigation and control subsystem. The robot—reliably following a virtual 6-meter wide oval road with a 49-meter radius of curvature—achieved speeds of 24 km/hr and 21 km/hr on the straight and curved sections, respectively.

Work in progress, when completed, will enable the system to accomplish the following operational scenario: Based on a plan generated by the mission planner, the robot vehicle will traverse open terrain from a starting point toward a paved road one kilometer away. It will use its laser range finder to detect and avoid obstacles and ditches. When the vehicle reaches a point 100 meters from the road, the road will appear in the image and—based on road location and orientation—the system will plan a path to get on the road. The vehicle will then follow the road at speeds up to 24 km/hr. At a specified location along the road, it will recognize an expected landmark and use the landmark's location to determine a road exit point. The vehicle will then continue to open terrain, avoiding obstacles until reaching a final goal.

Acknowledgments

This article is based on an earlier report, "Autonomous Land Vehicle Development" by Darwin Kuan and Louis McTamaney, that Gary Phipps presented at AI '87 in Long Beach, California.

Efforts described in this article were funded by FMC Ordnance Division's IR&D program, and by the joint Army/DARPA Advanced Ground Vehicle Technology program under contract DAAE07-85-C-R139. Significant scientific contributions were made by Bijan Abouzia, Farook Afsari, Mary Cole, Kamiar Fariba, Chin-Hu Feng, Remy Fourré, Mike Giusto, Minsui Huang, Darwin Kuan, Jorge Lastra, Jack Long, Jerry McComas, John Nitao, Alex Parodi, Glen Pearson, Gary Phipps, Steve Quen, Uma Kant Sharma, Babu Srinivasan, Jim Tucci, Jo-Lan Yao, Yue Min Wong, and Jim Zamiska.

References

1. G. Pearson, "Mission Planning for Autonomous Systems," *Proc. Workshop on Space Telerobotics*, Pasadena, Calif., Jan. 1987.
2. D.T. Kuan et al., "Automatic Path Planning for a Mobile Robot Using a Mixed Representation of Free Space," *Proc. IEEE First Conf. Artificial Intelligence Applications*, Computer Society Press, 10062 Los Vaqueros Circle, Los Alamitos, Calif. 90720, Dec. 1984.
3. A.M. Parodi, "A Route-Planning System for an Autonomous Vehicle," *Proc. IEEE First Conf. Artificial Intelligence Applications*, Computer Society Press, 10662 Los Vaqueros Circle, Los Alamitos, Calif. 90720, Dec. 1984.
4. D.T. Kuan et al., "A Real-Time Vision System for Road Following and Road Junction Detection," *Proc. Nat'l Conf. Artificial Intelligence*, AAAI, 445 Burgess Dr., Menlo Park, Calif., 94025, Aug. 1986.
5. D.T. Kuan and U.K. Sharma, "Model-Based Geometric Reasoning for Autonomous Road Following," *Proc. IEEE Int'l Conf. Robotics and Automation*, IEEE Service Center, 445 Hoes La., Piscataway, N.J. 08854, Mar. 1987.

6. U.K. Sharma and D.T. Kuan, "Obstacle Detection and Intelligent Navigation Using Range Data," *Proc. IEEE Workshop Computer Vision*, Computer Society Press, 10662 Los Vaqueros Circle, Los Alamitos, Calif. 90720, Nov. 1987.
7. J.J. Nitao and A.M. Parodi, "An Intelligent Pilot for an Autonomous Vehicle System," *Proc. IEEE Conf. Artificial Intelligence Applications*, Computer Society Press, 10662 Los Vaqueros Circle, Los Alamitos, Calif. 90720, Dec. 1985.
8. T.S. Chang et al., "A Real-Time Copilot for an Autonomous Land Vehicle," *Proc. 10th World Congress Int'l Federation Automotive Control*, IFAC Congress, VDI/VDE-Gesellschaft Mess-und Regelungstechnik GMR, Postfach 11 39D-4000, Dusseldorf 1, FRG, July 1987.

24

Ambler
An autonomous rover for planetary exploration

John Bares, Martial Hebert
Takeo Kanade, Eric Krotkov
Tom Mitchell, Reid Simmons
and William Whittaker

Editors' note *Ambler is a prototype legged rover that NASA is developing for a variety of applications. Ambler uses knowledge-based and other technologies to sense its environment, prioritize goals, and select among competing courses of action. The ultimate mission for a system like Ambler is planetary exploration. Knowledge-based tools and techniques—along with many others—will make such exploration possible. (Reprinted, with permission, from the June 1989 edition of* Computer. *© 1989, IEEE. All rights reserved.)*

For centuries people have been fascinated by Earth's planetary neighbors. There has been much speculation, in science and science fiction, about what lies on and under their surfaces. Despite considerable study, our knowledge remains very limited. Orbiting vehicles cannot examine internal features, and stationary vehicles, like the three Soviet and two US landers on Mars, miss what is over the horizon, atop mountains, and in ravines.

Active exploration of other planets could answer many questions about the nature and origins of our solar system. Sending astronauts or remotely controlled vehicles is a possibility, but a manned expedition is highly unlikely in the near future, and conventional teleoperation is impractical because of the long signal times (for example, up to 45 minutes for a round trip to Mars at the speed of light). A more promising approach is to launch an unmanned prospector and a vehicle to return collected samples to Earth—for instance, NASA's proposed Mars Rover and Sample Return mission. [1] The broad objectives of such a mission would be to observe and gather materials representative of the planet's geophysical, meteorological, and biological conditions and to return a varied selection of samples. Since the payload of the return vehicle is limited, the mission requires a sophisticated on-site system that can explore, assay, and select.

Recently we initiated a research program that addresses the central robotics challenges of designing a roving explorer capable of operating with minimal external guidance. The purposes of this research are to confront issues not faced by laboratory robots, to identify and formulate the difficult problems in autonomous exploration, and to generate insights, principles, and techniques for their solutions. We are not attempting to satisfy all the requirements of a system that would be flown to another planet (for example, space-qualified processors). Instead, we are building a prototype legged rover, called the Ambler (loosely an acronym for Autonomous MoBiLe Exploration Robot), and testing it on full-scale, rugged terrain of the sort that might be encountered on the Martian surface.

To undertake an extraterrestrial prospecting mission, we must extend existing robotic technology. Because the rover will be beyond the reach of timely aid from Earth, it must exhibit extreme self-reliance. It must be able to navigate, explore, and sample, and to know, moreover, what tasks do and do not lie within its capabilities. Particular issues critical to autonomous planetary exploration include locomotion, rough-terrain navigation, sample acquisition, perception, self-awareness, task autonomy, safeguarding, and system integration. Although semiautonomous and remotely assisted systems may be practical for some tasks, [2] our research strategy is to strive for full autonomy wherever possible, with the rover deciding when to ask for missing information.

In this article we present an overview of our research program, focusing on locomotion, perception, planning, and control. We summarize some of the most important goals and requirements of a rover design and describe how locomotion, perception, and planning systems can satisfy these requirements. Since the program is relatively young (one year old at the time of writing), this article aims to identify issues and approaches and to describe work in progress rather than to report results. Although our discussion concentrates on a Mars mission, we expect many of the technologies developed in our work to be applicable to other planetary bodies and to terrestrial concerns such as hazardous waste assessment and remediation, ocean floor exploration, and mining.

Locomotion

Our data on the Martian landscape indicates that an explorer would encounter a wide variety of terrain features, including a canyon 4,800 kilometers long by 7 kilometers deep, a mountain 27 kilometers high, and numerous sand dunes, rock fields, and craters.

Since the locomotion system must safely transport the vehicle over vast expanses of irregular terrain, perhaps the most important design criterion for the locomotion system is traversability: it must be able to navigate over extremely rugged terrain. Specifically, the rover should be capable of traversing a one-meter step, negotiating a 60 percent slope, and maintaining an average velocity of approximately one kilometer per day (these specifications, although somewhat arbitrary, reflect plausible assumptions [1] about the scale of objects on the Martian surface and about potential missions). Energy efficiency poses an additional design constraint because total on-board power generation is expected to be less than one kilowatt. As the dominant energy consumer, the locomotion mechanism must be extremely efficient. Another design consideration is that the locomotion mechanism must provide a stable platform for sensors and sample acquisition tools.

These design criteria admit a wide variety of possible locomotion candidates, including mechanisms that roll, walk, combine rolling and walking, or perform so-called hybrid locomotion. [3] Rolling machines have wheels or tracks in continuous contact with the terrain; they propel themselves by generating traction parallel to the terrain surface. Walkers suspend themselves over the terrain on discrete contact points and maintain principally vertical contact forces throughout propulsion; this allows more tractable models of terrain interaction than are possible for wheels. In addition, walking mechanisms isolate the robot's body from the underlying terrain and propel the body along a smooth trajectory independent of surface irregularities.

After comparing these candidates (see article by Bares and Whittaker [4] for a trade-off analysis of locomotion mechanisms with respect to these constraints), we selected legged locomotion because of its superior rough-terrain traversability characteristics, its theoretical efficiency, and its ability to keep sensors and sampling equipment steady and stable.

Our initial Ambler configuration consists of six legs stacked coaxially at their shoulder joints (FIG. 24-1). Each leg is mounted at a different elevation on the central axis of the body and can rotate fully around the body. Each leg (FIG. 24-2) consists of two revolute joints (shoulder and elbow) that move in a horizontal plane to position the leg, and a prismatic joint at the end of the elbow link that effects a vertical telescoping motion to extend or retract the foot. Thus, the locomotor has 18 degrees of freedom. The planar reach (combined length of shoulder and elbow links) of a leg is 2.5 meters and the vertical stroke (telescopic distance) is 1 to 2 meters, depending on the position of the leg on the stack. The average overall height of the Ambler is approximately 3.5 meters, and its nominal width is approximately 3 meters. With these dimensions, the Ambler can step over obstacles 1 meter high while maintaining a level body trajectory.

The Ambler body, a cylinder one meter in diameter situated below the leg stack, will contain equipment for power generation, computing, sample analysis, and scientific instrumentation. Sample acquisition tools can be mounted on legs or on the underside of the body. Communication equipment can be mounted either above the leg stack or in the body. Perception sensors will be mounted above the leg stack, where they will have large fields of view; other high-resolution sensors can be placed under the body or directly on legs.

This configuration has a number of benefits. First, decoupling the vertical and horizontal joints simplifies walk planning and motion control by reducing complex, six-dimensional problems to smaller ones. Second, the sampling tools under the body have a clear view of and close proximity to the terrain that they must access; body movements position and orient the tools, reducing the number of degrees of freedom they require. Third, during locomotion the legs isolate the body and sensors from terrain roughness.

In operation the Ambler will walk over rugged terrain much as one poles a raft floating over a rough lake bottom. The six vertical actuators in the Ambler's legs level the body over terrain, while the planar joints propel the body. As the body advances, one leg at a time moves ahead of the walker, much as the pole is placed ahead of the

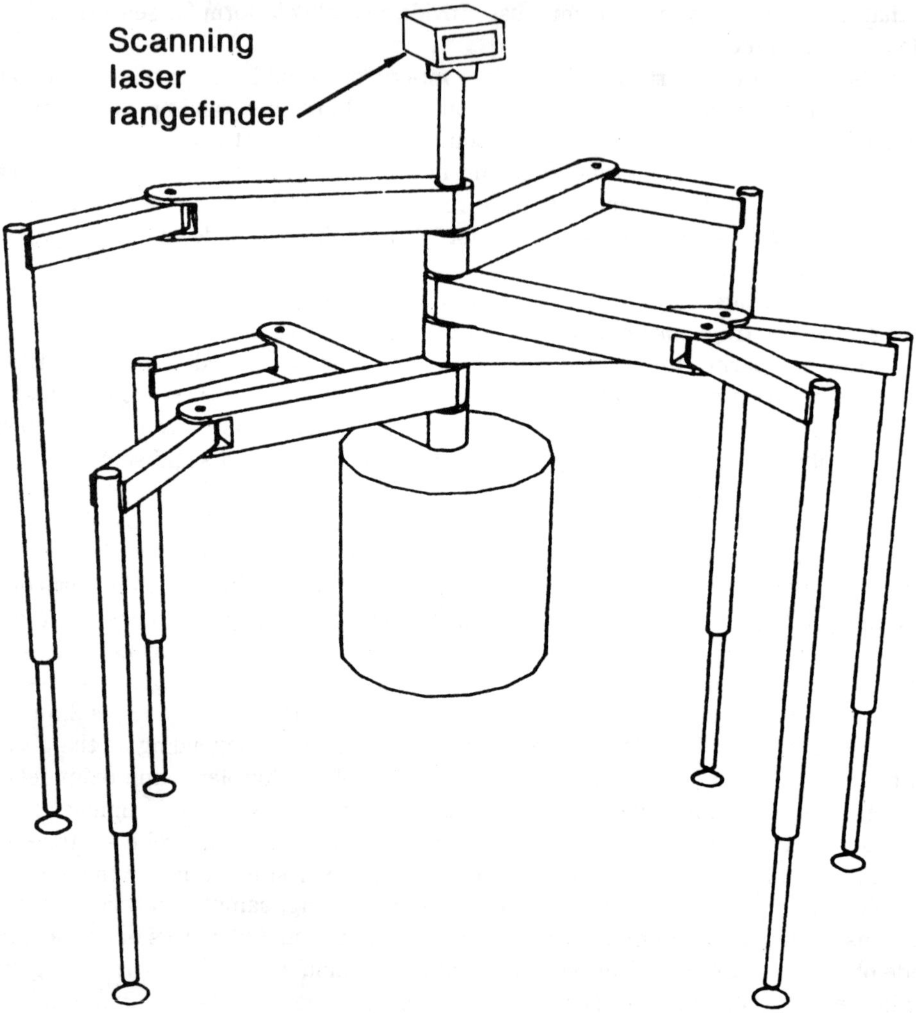

Fig. 24-1. Sketch of the Ambler.

raft. A unique result of the stacked leg configuration is that an overlapping gait is possible—that is, a gait in which a rear leg moves ahead, or "recovers," past forward supporting legs. An overlapping gait requires fewer foot placements, saving energy (energy is expended whenever a foot interacts with terrain) and reducing demands on perception and planning. While one leg is recovering, the five other legs support the body. The stability of the stance can be maximized by maintaining the center of gravity inside a conservative support polygon. Inside this region, the vehicle remains stable even if one (and possibly more) of the legs ceases to support it, either due to failure or slippage.

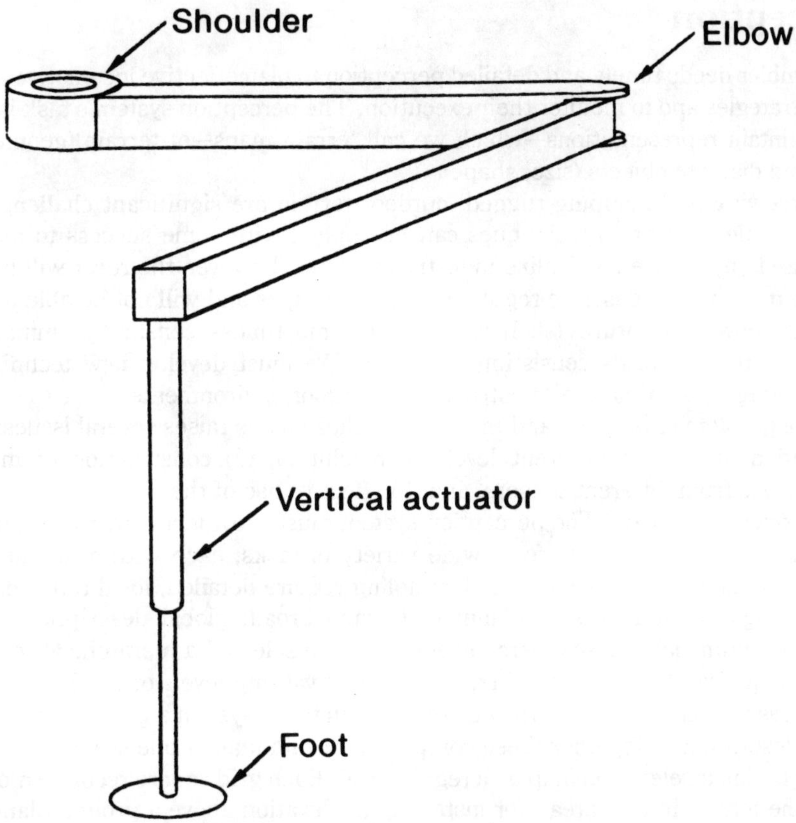

Fig. 24-2. Side view of an Ambler leg.

Experience with existing walking mechanisms (see article by McGhee [5] or Raibert [6] for an overview) suggests that they are difficult to coordinate due to their complexity, suffer large energy losses due to actuator conflict, and can be unreliable upon failure of one or more legs. We designed the Ambler to overcome these problems.

Unlike those of other walkers, the Ambler's actuator groups for body support and propulsion are orthogonal; a subset of the planar joints propels the body, while the vertical actuators support and level the body. The Ambler can level itself without propelling and propel without leveling, having no power coupling between the two motions. This should make it both easier to control and more efficient than other walking mechanisms.

The Ambler locomotor configuration is a dramatic improvement in reliability over conventional walking mechanisms. Because the legs are stacked above the body and can rotate by 2π about their shoulder joints, any leg can operate in any body sector. Thus, any functional leg can reposition itself to substitute for any failed leg, and three legs would have to fail to cause immobilization.

Perception

The Ambler needs timely and detailed perception to plan effective locomotive and sampling strategies and to monitor their execution. The perception system's task is to build and maintain representations—which we call terrain maps—of terrain (geometry, soil type) and discrete objects (size, shape).

Perceiving and mapping rugged, outdoor terrain are significant challenges. Current machine perception techniques can be applied with some success to manmade, structured, indoor scenes. Unlike industrial systems, however, the rover will have little need to recognize or describe regular geometric shapes and will not be able to capitalize on the powerful features (such as symmetry, smoothness, constant illumination) utilized to perceive worlds consisting of blocks. We must develop new techniques for constructing maps of natural, unstructured, outdoor environments.

The problem of building and maintaining those maps raises several issues: (1) representation of data at different levels of resolution, (2) construction of maps and descriptions from different sensors, and (3) effective use of the maps.

Representation The perception system must provide an environmental representation that is appropriate for a wide variety of tasks, each with different requirements. For example, locomotion and sampling require detailed, local representations, while navigation and mission planning demand broad, global descriptions. To uniformly accommodate these diverse needs, we have selected a hierarchical representation scheme that describes terrain and objects at varying levels of resolution. At each level of resolution we describe the environment in two ways: on a geometric grid and as object descriptions. Together these comprise a terrain map at one scale.

We define an elevation map on a regular grid. Each grid square records information about the terrain in that area—for instance, its elevation above a ground plane. Other terrain attributes include the following: the uncertainty of the estimated elevation; roughness; slope; labels indicating whether the terrain is unknown (has never been observed) or occluded (currently not observed because it lies in a shadow cast by another object); mineralogical composition; and a measure of traversability derived from slope, roughness, and other properties.

Object descriptions include the size, shape, and location of particular objects such as a boulder; symbolic terrain descriptions, such as hill, valley, saddle, and ridge, which may be useful for identifying promising routes or sample sites; paths the vehicle has followed; locations that have been sampled; and viewpoints from which observations have been made.

Constructing terrain maps Constructing terrain maps requires sensing and interpretation, ranging from low-level data collection to high-level scene modeling. This section first focuses on the lowest level of abstraction (sensors) and then describes an intermediate level of abstraction (local surface geometry). It does not address the highest level of object identification and semantic interpretation.

We will equip the Ambler with a battery of different sensors to collect multispectral data. Our primary sensor is a scanning laser rangefinder that measures both reflectance and range. [7] The scanner directly recovers the environment's three-dimensional structure, operating more rapidly and reliably than other vision techniques such as binocular stereo and motion. In the near future we will also use a pair of color cameras for determining material properties from color and texture, for long-range viewing, and for stereo viewing to back up the rangefinder. We also plan to incorporate an inertial reference sensor, inclinometers, tactile sensors on sampling tools, and other imaging devices. However, the perception system need not be limited to passively interpreting data; it can actively use the Ambler vehicle itself as a sensor to determine soil cohesion and friction parameters either directly, by measuring leg joint torques while walking, or indirectly, by comparing the soil in its footprints to nearby soil.

As an example of how the perception system operates, we will consider the interpretation of rangefinder signals in terms of local surface geometry (interested readers can find details in a technical report by Hebert, Kanade, and Kweon [7]). This involves creating an elevation map from a range image, matching it to another elevation map, and merging the two maps to form a composite map.

To construct elevation maps from range images, we have developed an algorithm that operates at arbitrary resolutions. It computes the locations where rays emitted by the sensor strike the terrain, and then it refers the intersection points and an estimate of their uncertainty to a reference grid, thus creating an elevation map.

To merge elevation maps from successive viewpoints, we have developed a two-stage algorithm to determine the correspondence between two elevation maps. The first stage matches a sparse set of geometric features extracted from the two maps, whose output is the estimated rigid transformation T relating the two sets of features. The second stage takes T as an initial estimate and refines it by gradient descent, iteratively minimizing an error functional defined over all the data points in the two maps. Once we know T, we can apply it to merge the maps.

Using terrain maps Once maps and descriptions of the environment have been constructed, the perception system must support and facilitate their use for a variety of tasks. For locomotion the Ambler will access elevation maps to select footfall locations that can accommodate its feet and support its mass. For navigation the Ambler will use the elevation maps to plan paths and to localize itself from landmarks. For sample acquisition the Ambler will use both elevation maps and object descriptions: the former to identify promising sampling sites based on topographic features; the latter to identify objects to be sampled, determine approach directions, and select control regimes (such as force and position).

Planning and control

We are designing and implementing a general robot architecture that addresses three important planning and control issues: (1) coordination of multiple modules and multiple goals, (2) flexibility in handling plan failures and contingencies, and (3) self-awareness of the robot's own capabilities and limitations.

A basic coordination problem is the integration of different modules. For practical reasons of efficiency and ease of implementation, the various components will use different algorithms, representations, and even languages. For example, the route planner (the software that plans routes) may use geometric algorithms, while the mission planner might use symbolic techniques. The architecture must facilitate the exchange of data between modules and flexible yet efficient control flow management.

Another important coordination issue is the handling of multiple goals. The Ambler will have multiple, often conflicting, goals, such as navigation, science, and health goals. The control architecture must prioritize and schedule goal achievement on the basis of a cost-benefit analysis that accounts for factors such as the environment, the robot's capabilities, and its past actions. For example, if the Ambler detects a potential sedimentary rock while traveling, it might decide to detour to obtain a sample if the rock is close, if the robot has no pressing deadlines, and if the robot has not already acquired sufficient sedimentary samples.

The issue of flexibility concerns how well the robot reacts to changes in its uncertain, dynamic environment. The robot must notice indications that its plans are failing, are no longer applicable, that there are unexpected contingencies, or even unexpected opportunities. The issue is complicated because, practically, the robot cannot perceive everything. Instead it must focus on those aspects it deems most important, deploying monitors to check on specified conditions.

The robot also needs flexibility in deciding how to handle problems indicated by the changes it detects. Instead of merely passing an error up the goal tree, for instance, the robot might try re-achieving the goal (for example, chipping a rock again), adding a new subgoal (detouring around an obstacle), or even attending to a different goal altogether. Once the robot decides how to handle a problem, however, the recovery processes can utilize the same algorithms that created the robot's initial plans. For example, once deciding to add a detour, the robot can use its path planner, treating the detour as if it had been planned from the start.

The issue of self-awareness is particularly important for planetary exploration robots, since they are remote from human assistance and must be largely responsible for monitoring their environment and choosing acceptable actions. The robot needs knowledge of its resources, capabilities, and limitations to make intelligent decisions about its course of action. It needs to schedule limited resources and to prioritize conflicting goals according to their relative costs and benefits. In addition, the robot should be aware of deadlines for its goals, the expected reliability of its planners, and the time necessary to execute its plans. [8]

Although our robot control architecture is being designed to provide many tools for constructing a planetary explorer, it will be open enough for easy experimentation and extension. The architecture is a distributed system with centralized control. It supports modules running on separate machines in different languages (currently, C and Lisp), communicating via coarse-grained message passing. Building on ideas from the Navlab project, [9] communication and data transfer are totally transparent to the individual modules.

Whereas planning, sensing, and actuation are distributed, control of when and how to attend to goals is centralized. The central control receives messages from other modules and routes them to the appropriate module to be handled. The control module also schedules the available computational and physical resources and maintains goal trees to help in error recovery and decision making. Although centralized control has the potential of being a bottleneck, we believe that global control is crucial for robots that have to contend with multiple goals and limited resources. At the same time, we are examining how to combine centralized control architectures with architectures that provide fast, reflexive actions (see Brooks, [10] for example).

The architecture directly supports different classes of messages for constructing robot systems. Query messages, which are used to access perceptual and internal sense data, return information and control to the requesting module. Goal messages, which plan actions by issuing other goal or command messages, are nonblocking, so that control returns before the subgoals are actually achieved. This nonblocking feature facilitates error recovery and the coordination of multiple tasks, since the central control can decide when to suspend or achieve goals.

Other message classes include (1) command messages, nonblocking messages used to control actuators, (2) constraint messages, used to add information to a database, (3) monitor messages, which check on the status of the robot or its environment, (4) decision messages, used to prioritize goals, and (5) failure messages, which indicate that either a plan-time or execution-time error has been detected.

Although the Ambler is designed to be largely autonomous, it is important that humans can intervene and operate it remotely when the situation warrants. The architecture meets this need by allowing humans to send or receive messages, at any level of abstraction, just as any other module can. This feature helps in development of the Ambler because it lets us substitute human input for as-yet-unwritten modules.

Experimental testbeds

Although simulations are often useful abstractions of the problems an autonomous robot will face, they are never as revealing as operating the actual mechanism. Our philosophy is to embed our ideas in working mechanisms that operate in natural environments. While we build the six-legged vehicle described here, we are testing our locomotion, perception, planning, and control ideas on two operational testbeds.

The first testbed is a one-legged version of the Ambler. It enables us to begin integrating the component technologies into a complete but simplified system that can demonstrate single-leg walking, using a few frames of range data, simple walk planning, and simple error recovery. A full-scale leg has been built and mounted on a carriage that travels along rails on the ceiling to simulate body motion. A scanning laser rangefinder mounted above the leg provides data for building terrain maps. A large sandbox under the testbed contains different soil types and obstacles. A rudimentary version of the planning and control architecture, running on Sun workstations, enables the leg to lift, recover, and land at a chosen position. We are also using this testbed to study foot-terrain interactions such as foot slippage and sinkage, and power consumption during footlift and footfall.

The other testbed is a Heathkit Hero 2000, a commercially available robot, which we are using to explore ideas for combining navigation and sample collection in an indoor environment. The Hero mechanism is wheeled and has an arm and gripper. For perception it has a base sonar and a rotating head sonar, and we have added a sonar on its wrist. In addition, a camera mounted in the ceiling of our lab gives the Hero a global overhead view. Using its vision system, the Hero plans paths to objects, and, once in the vicinity of an object, uses its sonars to locate and grasp the object. At present the Hero picks up and deposits plastic cups and cans, and soon we expect it to be able to retrieve printer output and to schedule the achievement of multiple, conflicting goals.

Constraints inherent in the task of autonomously exploring another planet have driven our design of a robot rover. In particular, the task demands a system that efficiently and reliably navigates over rough terrain, reliably perceives rugged terrain and irregularly shaped objects, and exhibits extreme self-reliance in performing a multitude of tasks. We have incorporated these constraints into our design for the Ambler. By pursuing the issues of locomotion, perception, planning, and control in the design of a robot that operates on another planet, we hope to find solutions for the problems involved in sending intelligent machines to Mars and beyond.

Acknowledgments

We would like to acknowledge the contributions of the entire Ambler research team at Carnegie Mellon University, whose collective efforts have produced the ideas reported here.

This research was sponsored by NASA under contract NAGW-1175. The views and conclusions contained in this article are those of the authors and should not be interpreted as representing the official policies, either expressed or implied, of NASA or the United States government.

References

1. J.R. Randolph, ed., *Mars Rover 1996 Mission Concept,* Technical Report D-3922, Jet Propulsion Laboratory, Pasadena, Calif., 1986.
2. B. Wilcox and D. Gennery, "A Mars Rover for the 1990's," *J. British Interplanetary Society,* Vol. 40, 1987, pp. 484–488.
3. D.D. Wright and R.E. Watson, "Comparison of Mobility System Concepts for a Mars Rover," *Proc. SPIE Conf. Mobile Robots II,* Vol. 852, Society of Photo-Optical Instrumentation Engineers, Cambridge, Mass., Nov. 1987, pp. 180–187.
4. J. Bares and W. Whittaker, "Configuration of an Autonomous Robot for Mars Exploration," *Proc. World Robotics Conf.*, Society of Mechanical Engineers, Gaithersburg, Md., May 1989.
5. R. McGhee, "Vehicular Legged Locomotion," in *Advances in Automation and Robotics,* G.N. Saridis, ed., Jai Press, Greenwich, Conn., 1985.
6. M. Raibert, Introduction to Special Issue on Legged Locomotion, *Int'l J. Robotics Research,* Vol. 3, No. 2, Summer 1984, pp. 2–3.
7. M. Hebert, T. Kanade, and I. Kweon, *3-D Vision Techniques for Autonomous Vehicles,* Technical Report CMU-RI-TR-88-12, Robotics Institute, Carnegie Mellon University, 1988.
8. T. Dean and M. Boddy, "An Analysis of Time-Dependent Planning," *Proc. Seventh Nat'l Conf. Artificial Intelligence,* St. Paul, Minn., 1988, pp. 49–54.
9. C. Thorpe et al., "Vision and Navigation for the Carnegie Mellon NAVLAB," *Annual Review of Computer Science,* Vol. 2, 1987, pp. 521–556.
10. R.A. Brooks, "A Robust Layered Control System for a Mobile Robot," *IEEE J. Robotics and Automation,* Vol. RA-2, No. 1, Mar. 1986, pp. 14–23.

Section F

Applied natural language

25

The natural language-database connection

David Sedlock

Editors' note *Sedlock reports on a project to build a system capable of generating full-text English summaries. The system helps with browsing and distilling a large government database in response to general and specific user queries, or "probes." The system is written in PROLOG and runs on a Sun workstation. It represents another example of problem-versus technology-driven systems engineering, where a large database problem led to a solution (rather than the other way around). (Reprinted, with permission, from the July 1988 issue of* AI Expert. *©1988,* AI Expert. *All rights reserved.)*

As part of a small team, I have been involved in giving an expert system the ability to generate full-text English summaries. The expert system acts as an intelligent front end to a large U.S. government database and is used to sift through voluminous masses of data to make certain (often complex) inferences.

The inferences may be simple (for example, finding inconsistencies in information collected in the database) or complex (for example, identifying patterns of entities and their relationships). The system allows the user to define a probe that involves many areas of interest and is developed over an extended period of time. The system is programmed in Quintus PROLOG and runs on a Sun workstation.

The natural-language-generation component of the expert system aims to give users a coherent view of their interaction with the system. It generates summaries of the basic information in the database and conclusions derived by the expert system.

The goal of our team was to make the language accurate, grammatical, and idiomatic. Unlike language-generation systems that are only able to produce sentence-size output from sentence-size input, our generation component can produce large stretches of text in response to large amounts of data.

Tree transformation

Generating text is a process of moving from a nonlinguistic to a linguistic way of representing reality. Nonlinguistic representation is what is found in the database; linguistic representation is the text that is generated. Typically, nonlinguistic representation is a relation (or relations) in a relational database.

A relation can be viewed as a tree, with the functor as the root and the attributes as subtrees. For example, the relation *connection('Smith',employs,'Jones')* can be viewed as a tree. Text can also be viewed as a tree.

Because both the input and output of the generation process are trees, generating text can be abstractly viewed as transforming trees into trees. A natural-language-generation system is, then, a program (or programs) for performing a particular class of tree transformations. In the best case, you could devise some general algorithm for transforming nonlinguistic trees into linguistic trees. In the worst case, you would have to write an ad hoc program for each transformation.

I know of no general algorithm for doing transformations. (Indeed, because so much depends on specific features of the application and of English, it is difficult to imagine what such an algorithm would look like.) Writing ad hoc programs for each transformation is obviously unacceptable.

Our team adopted a middle course. We have a few general programs and large sets of data structures. The data structures represent tree transformations and the programs use the data structures to perform the actual transformations. In effect, the data structures are written in special-purpose languages and the programs are interpreters or compilers of those languages. The system has two components: a general framework free from dependence on a particular application and a specific configuration sensitive to an application specific features.

I know of no automatic way to produce the data structures that guide the generation process. They depend on the structure of the target database, the understanding users have of the database, the data collection methods, the nature of the desired text, and the grammatical rules of English. People who understand these things have to create the data structures, so it is important that the data structures represent things people can understand and represent them in a way that is easy to use.

As might be expected, we employ the representational techniques of linguists and grammarians. These techniques, however, only suffice for the last steps of text generation. Before this point, the problem is getting information in the database into the form of a linguistic tree. Since this was uncharted territory, we invented our own techniques.

A word of caution: it is easy to contrive examples that make natural language generation look easy. Indeed, the preceding example of a database relation and the text that might be generated from it, as well as the example I'll use in walking through our process, make natural language generation look easy.

Transforming *connection ('Smith', employs, 'Jones')* into *Smith employs Jones* looks easy. The functor *connection* gets mapped into the linguistic category *clause*, while the first attribute maps into the subject *'Smith'*, the second into the verb *employs*, and the third into the object *'Jones'*. Such a simple transformation is welcome when it exists, but transformations are usually much more devious. Even this simple example hides a lot of troubling details.

An example

Our team divided the generation process into three parts: focusing on a topic (focus planner), deciding what to say about the topic (text planner), and producing the text (MUMBLE). The focusing mechanism is somewhat specific to our application. The role it plays in directly presenting the user with a choice of topics might be played by a discourse manager that keeps track of the subject and the course of speech acts and then infers a focus. Therefore, the following discussion will ignore the focus planner and concentrate on the text planner and text production component.

Suppose the focus planner and user have already determined the topic and passed it to the text planner. The text planner, then, is faced with the prospect of figuring out what to say about the topic. The topic can be represented as *topic(Entity,Slant)*, in which *Entity* is the database entity to be summarized and *Slant* gives a general indication of how the entity is to be summarized. In this example, the topic is *topic ('Smith','describe connections to persons')*. The job of the next planner is to find the information relevant to this topic in the database and format it (perhaps supplementing it somewhat) into an intermediate representation called a "message." The text planner is guided by a text plan, which determines what information is relevant and how to format and supplement it.

Text plans are written in a language called Rule Development Language [1] (RDL). Our team developed RDL for the class of expert systems we are creating. RDL was intended for use by knowledge engineers in writing the rules that direct the expert system in making inferences. However, expanded to include a library of procedures useful in text generation, RDL is also a good language for writing text plans. RDL compiles into PROLOG.

The text planner calls the RDL procedure that handles this kind of topic. The text plan first searches the database for all instances of the relation:

```
per__per__connection
    (Person1,Connection,Person2,DateFrom,DateTo)
```

which represents the fact that *Person1* is connected to *Person2* in the way specified in *Connection* from *DateFrom* to *DateTo*. The text plan finds one instance of this relation:

```
per__per__connection('Smith',employs,'Jones',
    '1/1/86','1/1/87')
```

The text plan then determines that Smith and Jones should be objects of reference and obtains gender and number information about them. It also determines that the connection is in the past and the dates should be expressed in terms of duration. The plan returns with the following message:

```
msg(
  relation(
    msg(
      proper__reference('Smith',singular,male),
      [ ]),
    employs,
    msg(
      proper__reference('Jones',singular,male),
      [ ]),
    past,
    third,
    declar),
  [msg(
      duration('1/1/86','1/1/87'),
      [ ])])
```

This is a bit complicated. A message has the form *msg (MsgProper, Adjuncts)*, where *MsgProper* is the main message and *Adjuncts* is a list of optional messages, which are eventually attached at optional points in the linguistic structure of the main message. We use this attachment process to exploit the fact that English allows certain functional structures—particularly adverbials and noun modifiers—to appear optionally in a sentence. (We also use it to add follow-on sentences to a main sentence, follow-on paragraphs to a main paragraph, and so on.)

MsgProper is a tree we represent as *RealizationClass(Slot1,Slot2,. . .,SlotN)*. The functor of this term names a realization class, which is a representation of a class of linguistic structures. The structures are the different permutations a class of message can take when it is realized in text. They are defined and used in the text-production component. The arguments of the term (slots) will be moved into positions in the linguistic structure created in the text-production phase. In this case, the form of the realization class is *Relation (Subject, Relation, Object, Tense, Person, Mood)*.

As Wittgenstein said, meaning is use, so one way to understand a message is in relation to the use the generation system makes of it. Meaning is also, as the formal semanticist says, a mapping onto a universe of discourse. The functor of the *MsgProper* of this message is *relation*. We can understand this, therefore, in terms of the processing the text-production component does with the *relation* realization class. Or we can understand it as representing a state of affairs consisting of *Smith* and *Jones*, with *Smith* standing to *Jones* in the relation of employing. Note that the message represents the same state of affairs as the original database relation, but is a bit fuller and makes explicit things the text production component needs to know to turn the nonlinguistic representation of the state of affairs into a linguistic representation.

Messages are recursive. The *MsgProper* of the message in the previous example contains two submessages, both of the *proper__reference* realization class. The production component uses the *proper__reference* realization class to form referring expressions to *Smith* and *Jones* that consist of proper nouns. The text planner has determined the number (*singular*) and the gender (*male*) of *Smith* and *Jones*. This information allows the text-production component to make subject-verb or other sorts of agreement.

The text planner has also determined which names to use to refer to *Smith* and *Jones*. In this make-believe example, determining names was easy since the persons' names were simply attributes in the relation. In real applications, naming can be much more complicated.

Next it is the turn of the text-production component, MUMBLE, to realize the message in text. MUMBLE needs to know what linguistic form to put the message into. In this example, we want to express the message as a sentence, but other possibilities exist. For example, the message might be realized as a noun phrase ("the employment of Jones by Smith"), while more complicated messages might require categories greater than a sentence.

MUMBLE first does zero or more preliminary tree transformations to determine the exact linguistic structure to use. Transformations are guided by rooted, directed, acyclic graphs (DAGs) whose nodes are trees. Each realization class has a DAG. The terminal nodes of the DAG are linguistic structures. The DAG is searched by means of a depth-first, DAG-walking algorithm. Each link has a set of conditions that determine if a node can be reached from another node and a transformation to perform if it can. The conditions are often lookups in the lexicon to determine if a certain form of a lexical item exists or checks on the values of slots in a message.

In our example, *MsgProper* is first transformed into:

```
relation svo(
  msg(
    proper__reference('Smith',singular,male),
    [ ]),
  employ,
  msg(
    proper__reference('Jones',singular,male),
    [ ]),
  past,
  third
  dec1)
```

The condition on this transformation is that the lexicon contain a verb form of *employ*. Since it does, two things occur. First, the functor has *svo* added. Because *employs* has a verb form, we know the message can be realized in an *S-V-O* clause. (This is a bit of a simplification.) Suppose the relation between *Smith* and *Jones* had been *father*. Then when the lookup for the verb form of *father* failed (we can be selective about what we put in our lexicon), we would have traversed a different link in the DAG, one that perhaps looked up the noun form of *father* and pointed us in the direction of the *S-V-C* clause *Smith is the father of Jones*.

Second, *employs* has become *employ*. The previous check in the lexicon not only showed that *employs* has a verb form, but also provided the stem of the verb. Now *employ* is ready for whatever inflection is required.

The next link in the DAG transforms the preceding example into:

```
relation svo dec1(
  msg(
    proper__reference('Smith',singular,male),
    [ ]),
  employs,
  msg(
    proper__reference('Jones',singular,male),
    [ ]),
  past,
  third)
```

This transformation has taken the mood information into account. The message will be realized by a linguistic structure in declarative form. (Our system currently handles only declarative mood and third-person sentences. We foresee the expert system using the generator to address users and command or question them. We have prepared for this possibility by allowing for messages that specify, say, second-person interrogative: "Are you sure you want to choose the DELETE SYSTEM button?")

One more link in the DAG provides the linguistic structure for the message. The leaf *A* (for "adverbial") has been designated as an attachment point. This is a place in the structure where an appropriate message from the adjuncts list can go. MUMBLE takes advantage of this and places the duration message there.

MUMBLE then realizes the messages at the leaves of the tree. The message is now fully realized, and the resulting words at terminal nodes (after having been inflected) are recursively appended along with punctuation to a binary tree whose root is a period (.)

Thus the final tree is:

```
[word('Smith'),word(employed),word('Jones'),
  word(from),word('1/1/86'),word(to),
  word('1/1/87'),punc('.'0]
```

Concatenating this word stream with white space and line breaks for output to the user produces *Smith employed Jones from 1/1/86 to 1/1/87.*

MUMBLE

The text-production component of the generation system is called, following D. McDonald, MUMBLE. [2] MUMBLE is an interpreter that recursively maps a message into a linguistic structure. As messages are processed, MUMBLE performs morphological transformations on lexical items and appends the resulting words (along with punctuation) to a word stream. MUMBLE finally formats the word stream to produce white space and line breaks. Instructions for MUMBLE's mapping are contained in realization classes that, in their linguistic aspect, resemble a combination of functional and formal grammar at the less-than-sentence level. (See Chap. 2 of R. Quirk's *A Comprehensive Grammar of the English Language*, [3] an invaluable book for text generation.)

The linguistic structure is supplemented by various instructions that indicate where certain operations should be performed, such as conjugating verbs or making predicate nouns agree with subjects. At the greater-than-sentence level (still uncharted linguistic territory), we have invented such quasifunctional and quasiformal categories as summary, discourse-unit, paragraph, sentence-group, and whatnot. These greater-than-sentence units are useful in providing formatting information. For example, paragraphs are preceded by a new line and indented five spaces.

McDonald [2] implemented a mechanism for inserting adjunct messages into optional slots in a linguistic structure. We found this useful for adding optional adverbs, noun modifiers, and follow-ons. We have not used McDonald's splicing mechanism [4] at all.

One area ignored in the MUMBLE literature was lists. To deal with a real application, the text planner must be able to plan in terms of lists. Lists raise a problem for MUMBLE since realization classes have no cycles and hence cannot represent or handle lists. We came up with a fairly clean solution to this problem by having the text planner tag lists, which the central MUMBLE interpreter catches and deals with.

We had to augment MUMBLE to handle a certain linguistic phenomenon. Because a message is processed recursively, the linguistic context of embedded messages is already determined to some extent when they are realized. Thus, in the previous example, when *msg (proper__reference ('Smith', singular, male),[ ])* came to be realized, MUMBLE knew this message had to be realized as subject. This was no big deal since the realization class *proper__reference* can only be realized as a noun phrase. But a realization class like *relation* has both clause and noun-phrase forms ("the employment of Jones by Smith"). We didn't get the noun-phrase form in the preceding example because MUMBLE was forced to realize the message as a clause. MUMBLE can therefore be described as "sensitive to linguistic context."

Sensitivity to linguistic context is a matter of degree, however. Consider the following case. We have in the database the facts that Smith employed Jones and Smith is the father of Jones. One way to make prose natural and idiomatic is to relate ideas together with certain linguistic constructions. So it might be nice to have our system generate the text "Smith employed Jones. Smith is also the father of Jones." Here "also" relates the two clauses together and contributes to an appealing flow of prose.

We do this in MUMBLE by defining a realization class, say the *also* class: *also (Msg1,Msg2)*, which generates something that schematically looks like *Fact1. Also Fact2*. The problem is this: how do we get the adverb "also" into the linguistic structure of *Fact2*? Using the standard MUMBLE structure, by the time we realize *Fact2*, we only know that it is to be realized as, say, a clause—no hint about "also."

The phenomenon exhibited in the *also* construction is quite widespread. In general, if some ideas are fitted into a larger idea, it is not enough, linguistically, to realize each smaller idea separately and concatenate the result into the larger idea. It is usually also necessary to make adjustments to the smaller ideas based on the larger idea.

We solved this problem by introducing the concept of a linguistic constraint. A realization class can create a constraint and pass it to one of its embedded realization classes. The embedded class either deals with it or passes it along to its children until some realization class can handle it. Thus, in essence, the *also* realization class would say to its *Msg2*, "Realize yourself as you would have had I not been here, but make sure you (or one of your children) include the adverb 'also' in your verb phrase." In this way, MUMBLE can pass detailed constraints arbitrarily far down a tree.

Our MUMBLE has an interesting feature that can break up monotonous patterns of prose. We allow variations on certain realization classes to be chosen randomly. Thus the *relation* realization class has versions in the active and passive voices. Lacking contrary instructions about focus from the text planner, and in situations where the passive voice is linguistically permissible, MUMBLE chooses the passive voice 20% of the time. The same mechanism also allows pronouns to occur only 80% of the time, when they are possible. This way, long stretches of active-voice sentences or repeated occurrences can be avoided.

Derived relations

So far this discussion has turned on generating text from the database. Since the generator must serve the expert system, it must also generate text from the conclusions derived from rules. This really amounts to only a slight extension of the generator. We need to distinguish between basic relations—those present in the database before the expert system goes to work—and derived relations—those asserted as the result of the expert system working.

Summarizing derived relations is just like summarizing basic relations except that to summarize a derived relation in any but the most cursory way, it is necessary to describe the relations that justify it. (This amounts to a more acute form of the fragmentation problem about to be described.) This is no problem in our system because, as a rule succeeds, both the conclusion and instantiated relations used in its derivation are asserted. A justification structure that records the relations that justify the conclusion is also asserted. So the information is all there, and it is simply a question of creating text plans and realization classes that handle the extra derived relations.

Text plans for derived relations also have different standards of relevancy from other text plans. For example, suppose the expert system finds that Smith has some attribute *F* and uses as partial justification that Smith employed Jones. Suppose the database also has Smith connected to Jones in other ways, none of which are relevant to the conclusion that Smith is *F*. In describing the fact that Smith is *F* we want to list the (relevant) ways in which Smith is connected to Jones. We only want to find the connections the expert system used in its derivation, not the other, irrelevant ones. This is no problem since the text planner can use the justification structure asserted for the conclusion that Smith is *F*.

Free text attributes

Free text attributes pose a large problem for text generation. Attribute values typically fall into three types: those that must come from some range or list of acceptable values; Those that don't, but are sure to have some consistent format; and those that can contain any string of characters (free text). An example of the first type might be the *Event-Type* attribute already mentioned. An example of the second might be the *Subject* attribute. Any string can go in this attribute, yet the string is sure to be a proper noun. An example of the third type might be a description attribute.

Suppose our database represents an entity that is vaguely defined as an item. An item can be any physical object larger than a quark and smaller than the Milky Way. The representation of an item has an attribute called *ItemDesc*, which can be any string of less than 256 characters. How can we use this attribute in generating a summary of an item? One data-entry clerk inputs the description "a television." Another inputs "television." No matter which way we plump, we'll end up generating the incorrect *Smith owns a a television* and *Jones owns television*.

The only general solution to the problem of free text attributes is to analyze the fields and extract and format what is needed from the attribute in a particular situation. We found this unacceptable because it requires building a natural-language-analysis system. Another solution is simply to dump free text attributes in some form that doesn't involve syntactic commitment. For instance, one could generate something like, "Smith owns an item. The item is described as: 'a television'."

This is probably a good solution for relatively unimportant attributes, for which summaries are not often requested or simply don't matter much. But summaries involving more important attributes suffer from this approach. Since, for example, items do not have proper names, the only way to form a referring expression to an item is with the *ItemDesc* attribute. Awkwardness here infects every summary that mentions an item.

Another solution is to examine a great number of actual values of a free text attribute in the database and try to discern some pattern in its format. Some minor editing, such as a substring operation to remove an initial occurrence of "a," might also be done. Still, free text attributes have been a thorn in our system's side, and they will cause problems for any generation system.

Data structure editors

Our generation system places a great deal of emphasis on data structures. The system has four sorts of structures: realization classes, lexical entries, punctuation/formatting information, and text plans.

It is important that these structures represent things people can understand and that the structures be easy to use (create and modify). A good way to promote these features is to provide user-friendly tools to the people who will configure the system to a particular application. Indeed, this is probably the only way the task of configuration can be done for a large, complex application. The tools must be integrated, and there should also be another tool that aids the testing and debugging of the structures with the database.

We have created one editor that graphically provides for editing realization classes, accessing libraries of realization classes, creating and modifying a lexicon, and providing punctuation and text-formatting information. The tool uses menus and other features to minimize typing and is smart about the database and MUMBLE itself. The tool automatically writes the PROLOG code that implements the data structures. Work is under way to create a graphical editor for text plans.

Nice databases

This article has presented a rather complicated system of text generation. You might question whether such complexity is necessary. Of course, to some extent, the answer depends on your requirements. If you are willing to put up with unnatural, unidiomatic prose with some grammatical mistakes, your generation system can be simpler than ours. But simpler systems have problems too.

Suppose we define a "nice" database as one in which no values are missing or unknown, and each relation in the database presents a reasonably full view of a state of affairs. A simpler generation system than ours would exploit direct correspondences between database structures and linguistic structures. While this can be successful, to some extent, in nice databases (created, perhaps, expressly to support text generation), real databases are usually more recalcitrant.

Even in a nice database, absolutely direct correspondences between a database relation and a linguistic structure are not to be found. It is true, that, in some sense, *connection ('Smith', employs, 'Jones')* directly corresponds to *Smith employs Jones*. But, in general, this direct correspondence, even in such a simple relation, will not hold.

Consider this instance of the relation *connection('Smith',complains,'Jones')*. This means that Smith complains about Jones, and it should not result in *Smith complains Jones*. The correct sentence is *Smith complains about Jones*. In addition to the problem of figuring out that a preposition is needed and that "about" is the preposition, there is also the problem that the second example has a quite different linguistic structure from the first.

Thus one relation form results in two different linguistic structures for two relation instances. The point is not that you should be a slave to the dictates of grammarians, but that the *S-V-A* form has a different behavior than the *S-V-O* form. With the incorrect analysis of *Smith complains about Jones*, your system might mistakenly produce the following attempt at the passive form: *About Jones was complained by Smith*. You might think, "so much the worse for the passive form!" But in thinking that, you limit your system's ability to handle focus and vary expression.

The simplicity of the move from *connection('Smith',employs,'Jones')* to *Smith employs Jones* is partly due to the fact that this relation instance holds true of people. People all have proper names by which they can be identified. But suppose we have to summarize *connection ('Smith', makes, complaint__497)*—in other words, *Smith* makes a complaint identified in the database as *complaint__497*. Unlike people, complaints do not usually have proper names by which they can be identified. We need recourse to some description of the complaint: *a complaint about Jones*, for example. It is impossible to ignore the structure in the object of this sentence. It directly corresponds to nothing in the relation instance.

Unknown values

Nice databases have no missing or unknown values. Real databases typically do. Consider a relation that describes events:

```
event(EventId,EventType,Subject,Object)
```

EventId is a meaningless database identifier of a particular event. *EventType* is the type of the event. *Subject* is the subject or agent in the event. *Object* is the object affected in the event. Given data collection and processing methods, *EventId* and *EventType* are required fields, but *Subject* and *Object* may contain the value *unk*, meaning "unknown." Therefore, four combinations of unknown values in instances are possible in this relation.

Notice that quite different linguistic structures result from the combinations of unknown values and each requires a different mapping of the relation's attributes into the structures. Again, you can ignore this complexity, but at the price of generating such unnatural constructions as *unk complains about unk*. This sentence could easily be improved. You can always shore up a poorly structured system with ad hoc devices, but then you are in the hopeless situation of writing ad hoc programs to do each transformation from relation to text.

Fragmented relations

Because of the requirements of normalization, a relational database tends to get fragmented into a number of relations, none of which presents a full picture of a state of affairs. Let's continue the last example and suppose, more realistically, that events can have more than one subject and object, and hence require more than one relation.

We now have the following relation forms:

```
event(EventId,EventType)
event__subj(EventId,Subject)
event__obj(EventId,Object)
```

With this database representation of an event, generating a summary of an event becomes rather complex. From the following data:

```
event)event1,complaint)
event__subj(event1,'Smith')
event__obj(evetn1,'Jones')
```

a direct correspondence scheme would only be able to generate something like, *A complaint occurred. Smith was the subject of the complaint. Jones was the object of the complaint*. This is weak.

Two things are needed here: a more flexible transformation from relation to linguistic structure (one, in particular, that allows different transformations depending on the context) and a text planner that can do more than assemble a list of relations to summarize. The text planner must be able to form subsidiary plans for other relations and knit these into the main plan. In effect, the text planner must be able to deal effectively with a forest of relations, not just the trees.

Implementation, performance

The generator runs at an acceptable speed. We circumvented the slowness of appending to the word stream (which can grow to quite a large size) by using difference lists.

We have also taken advantage of Quintus PROLOG's first argument indexing in representing realization classes. Though benchmarks can't be very useful in this context, we can report that generating short summaries occurs in a matter of a few seconds on a Sun 3/160 workstation with a user-interface programmed in Quintus' Prowindows. The natural-language-generation system requires a fair amount of work to implement, the amount of work depending on the following factors:

- Complexity of the application database's relational structure (including derived relations)
- Complexity caused by unknown values
- Size of the lexicon needed to handle the data values in the database
- Number of desired slants
- Sophistication of the text.

A lot of text plans and realization classes have to be created. We know of no way these data structures can be created automatically, so people have to do it. Creating data structures can be considerably helped by appropriate tools, as already described.

The text-generation system produces text that is acceptably accurate; that is, faithful to the relations it summarizes. Stylistically, the prose is syntactically uncomplicated and tends to be a bit flat and insipid, rather like the prose of contemporary minimalists in American fiction. Undoubtedly, much of this is due to the conceptual paucity of the database.

Good prose is driven by a lot of richly conceptualized data. The expert system, of course, is meant to raise the conceptual level of the basic database, but it only does so in patches. It cannot really approach the full and varied battery of concepts a person brings to bear on the data. Also, sometime in the foreseeable future, the expert system will lack the real-world knowledge that unquestionably plays a vital role in producing good prose. For example, if Smith were the father of Jones, our system would have difficulty coming up with *the father*. Choosing the definite referring expression *the father* over the indefinite expression *a father* depends on the fact that people have only one father.

One common way of making up for conceptual paucity is syntactic complexity. The MUMBLE system does allow you to create syntactically complex prose: you simply throw lots of messages in the adjuncts of other messages and allow MUMBLE to stuff them into optional slots in a linguistic structure. The result is often horrendous. McDonald [2] maintains what he calls an indelibility principle: once a syntactic decision is made, it cannot be retracted. He brings forward some examples of people forced into grammatical errors because earlier syntactic decisions constrained later ones, leaving them with an idea they could not grammatically express.

I believe McDonald is wrong, because acceptable syntactic complexity can be arrived at only by trial and error—generating the prose, inwardly seeing how it looks, and backtracking if it doesn't look good. Indeed, I believe it is, in principle, possible for a person to be caught in an endless loop, trying but never finding a good enough expression for an idea. In this connection, think of Flaubert's concept of the *mot juste*. McDonald's people were simply speaking before thinking.

In any case, the point is moot, for it implies that a generation system would have to try out a syntactically complex construction and analyze the result, backtracking if it found it unacceptable. We do not envision implementing this feature in our system in the near future.

Other work

We have only moderately profited from previous work in natural language generation. To a large extent, this was due to differences in purpose.

K. McKeown's work, [5] interesting and successful in its own right, is directed toward the problem of defining the structure of a database. Our problem, describing the contents of a database, is different. McKeown also did not set herself very high standards of prose, as TEXT's ubiquitous use of uncommon constructions, as *PROPULSION__TYPE of DIESEL* shows. D. Appelt's work [6] is also directed toward a different problem from ours—instructing someone how to do something.

McDonald's work [2] does not offer a complete generation system since his MUMBLE has no way of deciding what to say. We found, however, that MUMBLE provides a good structure for the last step of text generation. LOQUI, a component of a European ESPRIT project, is a natural language interface to relational databases. The natural language analysis component of LOQUI is highly developed. It provides for the querying of databases in English or German. The project claims that LOQUI has good grammatical coverage and handles such difficult phenomena as pronouns and ellipses. LOQUI also has a discourse manager that keeps track of the course of a dialogue and allows it to react intelligently to the user's actions.

Attempting to provide full natural language functionality, the LOQUI project has also developed a natural-language-generation component. Having both analysis and generation in one system is definitely an attractive idea. However, LOQUI's generation component is not up to the standards of the analysis component.

The following is an extended example of LOQUI's summary of a database that describes the LOQUI project: "The name of the project is LOQUI. The title of the project is *A Natural Language Interface to Databases*. LOQUI is described by *LOQUI-Report NLI 4711: Final Report*. LOQUI is headed by Walther Von Hahn. LOQUI begins on 15/08/84. LOQUI ends on 15/02/87. Walther Von Hahn works on LOQUI. Claudius Pyka works on LOQUI. Bill Imlah works on LOQUI. Helmut Horacek works on LOQUI. Tom Wachtel works on LOQUI. Martin Schroeder works on LOQUI. LOQUI2 follows LOQUI. LOQUI is preceded by HAM-RPM. LOQUI succeeds HAM-ANS."

This summary is not concise. The middle section could be better stated as "Walther von Hahn, Claudius Pyka, Bill Imlah, Helmut Horacek, Tom Wachtel, and Martin Schroeder work on LOQUI." Date information could be concisely stated as, "LOQUI lasted from 15/08/84 to 15/02/87."

Furthermore, the summary uses the present tense where the past tense would be more appropriate. Also, it uses no pronouns, has no variation in expression, and lacks sophisticated constructions. For example, von Hahn is mentioned twice, as head of the project and as a worker. Rather than state these facts separately, which is somewhat confusing, it would be better to say something like "Walther von Hahn leads

LOQUI. He also works on it." The "also" construction relates the two facts and forms a more sophisticated expression.

Finally, I suspect the generation component is not fully using the discourse manager; that is, the summaries produced by the system are not fully sensitive to the state of the discourse. Perhaps LOQUI is trying to use a direct transformation scheme. According to the technical description of the project, LOQUI pauses only once in the move from database to text, at an intermediate semantic representation. From there it proceeds to a word stream without any syntactic or functional representations.

It is clear why LOQUI does not use pronouns or vary expressions. You cannot form pronouns without the concept of a noun or pronoun; you cannot do simple syntactic transformations such as switching from active to passive voice without the concept of voice. LOQUI has something like our text planner since it chooses relation instances in the database and moves them into the intermediate representation for conversion to text. But this is no more than a listing operation. That is why we get a list of sentences "So-and-so worked on LOQUI." The LOQUI planner finds all the relation instances that meet the criterion *project__member('LOQUI',Member)* and then directly transforms each into text. Also, there is simply no place in the LOQUI generation process for more sophisticated constructions than the database provides.

LOQUI can do fairly well on this nice database. But I suspect performance would degrade drastically on a more fractured database containing unknown values.

The work reported in this document was conducted as part of Institute for Defense Analyses Project T-25-287. The document is not endorsed by IDA, nor should the contents be construed as reflecting the official position of this organization.

References

1. T. Swift, "RDL: A Shell for Expert Systems that Deal with Large Data Bases," Proceedings of Avignon 88—Eighth International Workshops on Expert Systems and their Applications, Avignon, France, 1988.
2. D. McDonald, "Description Directed Control: Its Implications for Natural Language Generation," in Cercone (ed.), *Computational Models of Discourse*. Cambridge, Mass.: MIT Press, 1984, pp. 209 – 266.
3. R. Quirk, *A Comprehensive Grammar of the English Language*. New York, N.Y.: Longman Inc., 1985.
4. D. McDonald, "TAGs as a Grammatical Formalism for Generation," *Proceedings of the ACL*. Chicago, Ill: University of Chicago, 1985, pp. 94 – 103.
5. K. McKeown, *Text Generation*. Cambridge, U.K.: Cambridge University Press, 1985.
6. D. Appelt, *Planning English Sentences*. Cambridge, U.K.: Cambridge University Press, 1985.

David Sedlock, *Ph.D., is currently employed at the Institute for Defense Analyses, Alexandria, Va.*

26

KID

Designing a knowledge-based natural language interface

H. Ishikawa, Y. Izumida
T. Yoshino, T. Hoshiai
and A. Makinouchi

Editors' note *KID represents a knowledge-based approach to the design of portable natural language interfaces to databases. KID "processes user queries transparently" and frees them from the usual command and query language burdens. It represents an evolutionary improvement over much previous work in the area because it focuses on transportability via the design and implementation of a world model. (Reprinted, with permission, from the Summer 1987 issue of* IEEE Expert. *©1987, IEEE. All rights reserved.)*

This article presents a knowledge-based approach to designing portable natural language interfaces to database systems—an approach called KID (knowledge-based interface to database systems). To free users from needing to know about query languages and databases, and to provide users with access to databases in natural language, KID incorporates a knowledge base called the world model containing a domain model, linguistic knowledge, and database mapping knowledge. The world model is easy for users to define and understand; to transport KID to a new domain, the user has only to build a new world model for the domain. Using the world model, KID processes user queries transparently enough to enable easy user debugging of the world model. Since we have encapsulated domain-specific knowledge into the world model, KID is portable. This article will discuss world model design, and will examine KID's knowledge-based processing of queries using the world model.

Numerous natural language interfaces to database systems have been developed in an attempt to make such systems more user friendly [1], [2]. Natural language interfaces must incorporate a knowledge base containing knowledge about a domain of discourse, databases, natural language, and a query language—thereby freeing users from needing to know about query languages and databases and enabling users to access databases in natural language. Moreover, applying natural language interfaces to new domains requires construction of new knowledge bases for those domains. Recent work focuses on portable natural language interface systems [3], [4]. However, no work has focused on the issues involved when users design knowledge bases by themselves to transport natural language interface systems to new domains—although one exception discusses some of these issues [5].

Portable natural language interface systems generally have two kinds of user—the sophisticated and the naive. Sophisticated users create knowledge bases for their systems. This article discusses a design that reduces the sophisticated user's customization efforts. Naive users apply systems after knowledge bases have been completed.

However, these two user types are not totally different. Naive users who have used a natural language interface and have read about the knowledge base editor must be able to become sophisticated without extensive training. Although you will find the word "user" throughout this article, sophisticated users more closely resemble Ballard's "superuser." [6]

Communications between natural language interface systems and users require a model for mutual comprehension, just as dialogues between human beings do. To mediate effectively between users and systems, a domain model must be represented in terms natural to concepts users would employ when thinking about a domain of discourse instead of semantically poor database schemata. Users can more easily formulate queries for conceptually natural domain models than for databases, and domain models capture more domain semantics than a database. In this respect, such models have common goals with semantic data models [7], [8]. The modeling system for a natural language interface must provide users with mechanisms for abstracting domain concepts such as classification, aggregation, generalization [9], and derivation [7], [10]. This will enable users to easily build domain models, make queries based on them, and clearly tell what queries are acceptable (that is, the natural language interface system's conceptual coverage) [5].

To guarantee its conceptual naturalness, the domain model must be independent of the database. Database schemata are subject to change for reasons unrelated to domain model semantics, such as space performance issues. To isolate such changes from the domain model, the system must provide users with a framework for describing correspondence between the domain model and underlying databases. A correspondence, referred to as a database mapping, must be understandable to users and flexible enough to buffer database schema changes and accommodate the user's view. Moreover, the database mapping must be able to express classification, aggregation, and generalization of domain concepts. Since the database mapping is used as a knowledge base to translate domain model queries into database queries, mappings must encapsulate as much domain-specific translation knowledge as possible, from the viewpoint of portability.

To customize a natural language interface system to a new domain, users must build linguistic knowledge besides domain models and database mappings. Thus, the system must provide users with a framework for describing a vocabulary; that is, a linguistic model in which to express domain model queries. Like the domain model, this linguistic model must be natural and transparent to users. The system uses the linguistic model as a knowledge base to semantically interpret user queries. Therefore, the linguistic model must be able to encapsulate as much domain-specific knowledge as possible, so that the semantic interpretation can be domain independent. Moreover, domain-specific knowledge is needed to resolve ambiguities that user queries may contain, depending on the domain. Thus, users must be able to easily define linguistic models based on the domain model.

Issues arise from the fact that the knowledge base—including the domain model, linguistic model, and database mapping—is inherently heuristic; we cannot expect users to construct complete knowledge bases from the start. Rather, a knowledge base is constructed incrementally. Users must be able to verify that their knowledge bases are correct. This can only be determined by testing knowledge bases as they are being constructed. To debug domain models and linguistic models, users must be able to foresee how changes in the models will influence semantic interpretations of their queries—because the parser uses the models. Users must be able to determine how their queries are semantically interpreted. The parser's rules must be general and clear, therefore, and rule control must be simple. Similarly, the translation mechanism must be transparent enough for users to debug database mappings. Only if all these conditions are satisfied can users know how systems understand their queries according to given knowledge bases, and refine those knowledge bases.

Finally, however sophisticated they may be, users who build knowledge bases are usually neither database experts nor linguists. Therefore, the knowledge base must be as easy for these users to write as possible. The knowledge base must be integrated; users must be able to describe all kinds of interrelated knowledge in one place, allowing easy checking for consistency. In addition, we must provide users with an environment supporting easy and flexible knowledge base construction.

A knowledge-based approach is extremely effective for constructing portable natural language interface systems that satisfy the above design criteria—a key point. In the context of our work, a knowledge-based approach makes such systems domain independent by confining the domain-specific knowledge needed to process user queries to knowledge bases that can easily be created and maintained.

KID's portability stems from its world model, a knowledge base that integrates the domain model, the linguistic model, and database mapping. Users can transport KID to a new domain simply by writing a new world model. The encapsulation of all domain-specific knowledge into the world model makes KID general.

The world model is easy for users to define and understand. KID's processing of user queries using the world model is transparent enough to users to enable easy debugging of the world model. A brief overview of KID follows. We will then examine world model design, detail the semantic interpretation of user queries using the world model, explain query translation based on the world model, and conclude by comparing our work with other related work.

A system overview

We can divide Japanese-language query processing into four phases. In the parsing phase, KID parses queries to make an intermediate meaning structure together with a parse tree. In the translation phase, KID modifies the meaning structure into a world model query, outputting a paraphrased version of the user's query. If the user confirms

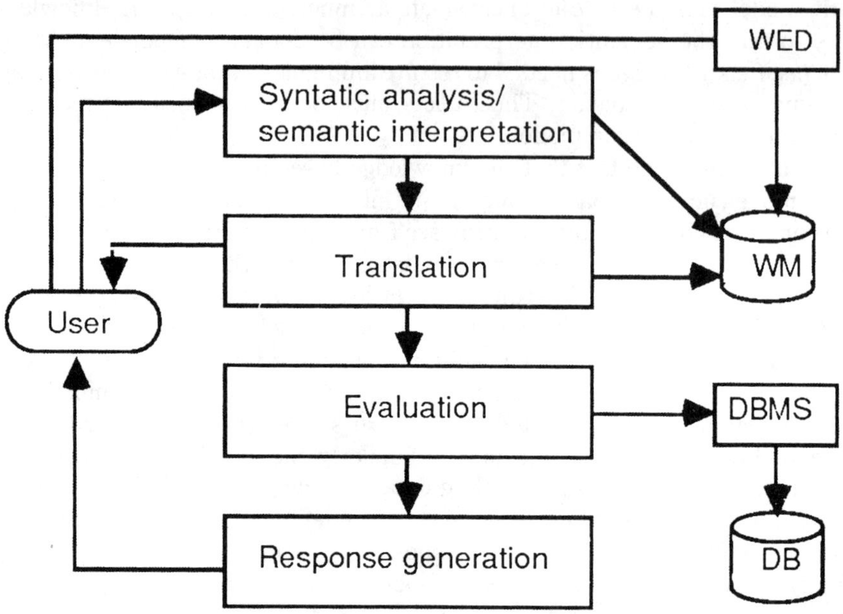

Fig. 26-1. An overview of KID.

the paraphrase, KID translates the world model query into a database query. In the evaluation phase, KID sends the database query to a relational [11] database management system (DBMS) such as RDB/V1 [12]; the DBMS evaluates the database query and sends back the tuples satisfying its conditions. In the last phase, KID displays the results. KID uses the world model in the first two phases.

We provide a flexible facility for defining domain-specific knowledge in the world model. Called the world model editor (WED), this facility makes it easier for users (using multiple windows) to build and understand the world model. We can invoke WED at any time. If KID detects undefined lexical entries in user queries, for example, we can use WED to edit the world model.

World model design

To customize KID to a new domain, users must specify domain-specific knowledge including the domain model, the linguistic model, and database mapping. The world model provides an integrated framework for describing all of these. Users have only to add new domain-specific knowledge to the world model to transport KID to a new domain.

The domain model We will now explain how to represent a domain model—that is, the model of a domain of discourse—in the world model.

Classification and aggregation To obtain a conceptually natural domain model, we decided to take an object-oriented approach [13]. We describe things and relationships among things in the domain in terms of objects and object relationships. Objects consist of substructures called attributes, which implement properties of and relationships between objects. Moreover, an attribute has several facets describing various aspects of that attribute. In particular, world model objects are called classes—classes describing properties common to individual objects called instances. Domain concepts are divided into classes. As a whole, world model classes sufficiently represent a domain model. Hence, users can see KID's conceptual coverage by browsing in the world model using WED.

The values of the attribute Attribute, as described by the values of its facet value, indicate user-defined attributes. For example, the class SALE has Retailer, Commodity, Sales, and Price as its user-defined attributes. The value of the Attribute Level distinguishes among instances, classes, and metaclasses (that is, classes of classes). For example, SALE is on a class level. The facet class of the user-defined attribute indicates the class for the attribute's value domain. As another example, the domain class of the attribute Retailer of SALE is RETAILER. Attribute names must be unique within a class; different classes may have the same attribute names (see RETAILER and FACTORY). However, we must always reference attributes by prefixing class names to avoid introducing extraneous notions such as internal and external function names [10] (that is, attribute names).

System-defined attributes also describe several characteristics of a class. First, key attributes can be specified by the attribute Key—such as Code of RETAILER. The value of the key attribute identifies class instances uniquely. Moreover, users can control the attribute value's display; the attribute Return indicates which attributes to return when referenced (see RETAILER). Furthermore, we can define the attribute's inverse (see RETAILER__NAME). We use the attribute Inverse to make inferences in semantic interpretation of user queries.

In addition to value and class, facets provide an attribute with various aspects. The facet multiple distinguishes between single-valued and multivalued attributes. For example, Sales of SALE is multivalued. The facet mandatory specifies a non-null attribute. Key attributes must be non-null. In query translation, we use knowledge specified by system-defined facets (such as multiple) and attributes (such as Key and Return).

Figure 26-2 graphically represents part of the merchandising domain model. Ovals denote classes, and arrows denote relationships between them. Solid arrows depict attribute relationships, and broken arrows depict super-sub relationships. Leaf nodes and internal nodes of the world model's graphical representation are called primitive and nonprimitive classes, respectively. They are distinguished by their metaclasses; that is, by the attribute Class. For example, SALE, RETAILER, and COMMODITY are non-primitive classes; ADDRESS, NAME, and RETAILER__NAME are primitive classes. World model classes include complex objects [14] such as SALE and they allow arbitrarily nested aggregation.

Generalization To enhance domain model naturalness, generalization enables users to easily define classes similar to existing ones with a few incremental changes. We call newly defined classes subclasses, and we call old ones superclasses. Their relationship is called a super-sub relationship. We denote superclass by the attribute Super, by which the subclass inherits all the attributes of that superclass. For example, BEER inherits Code and Name from COMMODITY. The attribute Super introduces generalization hierarchies in the world model.

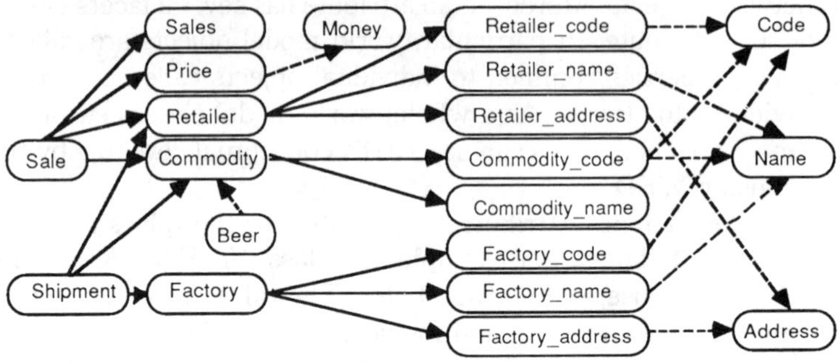

Fig. 26-2. A graphical representation of the domain model.

The need for generalization emerges naturally during model design. We adopt the heuristic method of model design, not detailed here due to space limitations. By this method, we can identify classes and their relationships, paying close attention to nouns and verbs in the user's natural language queries (collected before knowledge base design). For example, sentence fragments like "the name of the retailer" and "the name of the factory" make RETAILER→RETAILER__NAME, and FACTORY→FACTORY__NAME, parts of the world model. NAME is constructed as a common superclass of RETAILER__NAME and FACTORY__NAME (see FIG. 26-2). Furthermore, NAME is a subclass of the system-defined class JSTRING (a string of Japanese-language characters). FACTORY and RETAILER are subclasses of the system-defined class ENTITY, the superclass of all world model classes.

Derivation We provide the world model with a derivation mechanism to extend world model naturalness. Derivation enables users to see the same information in several ways, helping users define new domain model views. In KID, derivation enables users to define new attributes or classes by restricting or combining existing attributes or classes. The world model query language specifies the derivation, as our "Query translation" section will explain. Derived classes or attributes can be accessed by the same interface as basic classes; that is, classes having any database mapping. Users specify any derivation as a kind of class in the facet derivation. We derive classes or attributes not only from the basic classes or attributes, but also from other derived classes or attributes.

This is exemplified when we model the sentence fragment "sell in some place" in the merchandising domain. Suppose that the world model has no direct relationships between SALE and ADDRESS. Users can adapt their linguistic view to the world model by deriving the attribute Location for SALE, specifying Address of Retailer of SALE. BEER__DERIVATION shows that BEER can be derived as a subclass of COMMODITY by restricting its Code value.

Integration World model classes can do more than model a domain of discourse. Users can also describe database mapping and linguistic correspondence in world model classes. Integrating all relevant knowledge into one place (that is, class) enables users to easily write that knowledge and check its consistency. Database mapping can be statically described in the facet storage of the world model class attribute.

Using WED for linguistic knowledge, users can define the vocabulary based on the domain model (that is, classes) and find what lexical entries are allocated to those classes. We can also describe dynamic properties as methods in world model classes, such as a procedure to get a required value out of input text [13]. For example, the parser can put values into instances by sending them the message "GET VALUE". The world model differs significantly from semantic data models such as Hammer and McLeod's [7] in that those describe only static properties of objects.

The linguistic model To apply KID to a new domain, users must define knowledge about natural language. Such knowledge, called the linguistic model, is used when the parser semantically interprets user queries. Users express queries with the linguistic model, which contains definitions of lexical entries and relationships between them. We can define lexical entries by associating them with world model classes. Relationships between lexical entries are identical to those between associated classes. A set of all associated class attributes denotes a verb's case frame [15]. For example, the noun "retailer" and the verb "sell" refer to RETAILER and SALE classes. The case frame of the verb "sell" is a set (Retailer Commodity Sales Price). Users can express queries by looking up lexical entries allocated to classes, using WED.

Defining the linguistic model based on world model classes makes it more natural in several ways. First, the linguistic model (or case frames) can be represented succinctly by generalizing the classes. For example, when we model sentences like "sell beer" and "sell wine," usually we must define a separate case frame for each, such as (... Beer ...) and (... Wine ...). If we define BEER and WINE as subclasses of COMMODITY, however, then the case frame alone (including the Commodity case) can represent the same knowledge as the two separate case frames represent. By derivation, the linguistic model also supports a user's linguistic views that differ from the given world model classes.

Further, the linguistic model allows some ambiguity in the user's natural language queries. Ambiguities arise from the need for linguistic model naturalness. A natural language phenomenon is that generic nouns are specialized by modifications such as noun phrases and clauses; nouns themselves should be defined to correspond to classes as general as possible. For example, one naturally associates the proper noun "Tokyo" with ADDRESS, but not with RETAILER__ADDRESS or FACTORY__ADDRESS. If a user's query refers to "Tokyo," however, the noun's class must be specialized to either RETAILER__ADDRESS or FACTORY__ADDRESS (depending on the context) to answer the query clearly. These ambiguities can be resolved using the linguistic model, to be discussed in our "Semantic interpretation" section.

Mapping In KID, users define database mapping by associating world model classes with relations in the database [11]. Users can make a world model's domain and linguistic models independent of the database by encapsulating most of the domain-specific translation knowledge into the mapping. Thus, the mapping prevents database schema changes irrelevant to world model semantics from affecting world model naturalness. Moreover, the mapping enables users to flexibly express classification, aggregation, and generalization of classes.

We choose to make mapping description formalism resemble relational query language, rather than devise a new language specifically for mapping, because users can easily specify which relations to retrieve with a nonprocedural query language. This makes the mapping understandable and flexible. In addition to a one-to-one mapping between world model classes and database relations, users can specify nontrivial mappings including multiple target fields and joins [11]. The user specifies a mapping as a kind of class in the attribute's facet storage.

Although users can choose a mapping approach, we advocate the following top-down approach, in which database schemata are defined based on the given world model classes. First, consider classification and aggregation. Users should simply allocate one relation to one class. Suppose that we give relation R1 to class C1. If the domain class for an attribute A1 of C1 is primitive, then the mapping for A1 is a field F1 of R1. Otherwise, another relation R2 is given to the non-primitive domain class C2 for A1 of C1. Moreover, a field F2 of R1 is defined as a foreign key for R2 [11]. The mapping for A1 is to return fields of R2 by joining R1 and R2 with F2 or R1 and the key field of R2. For example, we define a relation SALE_TBL with a foreign key SALE_RETAILER_FLD for SALE, and a relation RETAILER_TBL with a key RETAILER_CODE _FLD for RETAILER. Moreover, we write RETAILER_NAME_MAPPING for Name of RETAILER, and SALE_RETAILER_MAPPING for Retailer of SALE.

For generalization, we recommend that users write in the class attribute Super in either of two mappings: (1) a mapping restricting some fields of the relation for the superclass, and (2) a mapping joining the relation for the superclass and another relation for the subclass including fields for subclass-specific attributes and common key fields with the superclass relation. For example, one way to define the mapping for BEER specifies the relation for COMMODITY (that is, COMMODITY_TBL) by restricting its key field (that is, COMMODITY_CODE_FLD). Another way is to join COMMODITY_TBL and the separate relation for BEER ("BEER_TBL," including a field "BEER_CAN_SIZE_FLD," including a field "BEER_CAN_SIZE_FLD" and the key field "BEER_CODE_FLD") by COMMODITY_CODE_FLD and BEER_CODE_FLD.

Semantic interpretation

In general, analyzing a sentence grammatically is called syntactic analysis; analyzing a sentence using the meanings of lexical entries is called semantic analysis [15].

Issues in parsing The parser analyzes a user's Japanese-language request to extract its meaning, and bases its analysis on modification relationships such as exist between noun phrases or verb phrases. Japanese noun phrases contain nouns followed by postpositions such as *no* or *wo*, which correspond to English prepositions. User requests often have both syntactic and semantic ambiguities [3]. Syntactic ambiguities occur when more than one possible modification relationship exists between phrases.

For example, in the request *Tokyo no biiru wo uru mise no namae wa?* (What is the name of the retailer who sells beer in Tokyo?), the noun phrase *Tokyo no* (in Tokyo) may modify either the noun phrase *biiru wo* (beer), the noun phrase *mise no* (of the retailer), or the verb phrase *uru* (sells) syntactically. Semantic ambiguities may also arise when phrases have multiple meanings; as an example, the noun phrase *Tokyo no* (in Tokyo) corresponds to a particular address, but its meaning should be either a factory address or a retailer address depending on the context. To resolve these ambiguities, we need semantic domain knowledge.

Two extremes exist when using semantics in parsing: One extreme divides syntactic and semantic analysis into two completely separate steps leading to a possible combinatorial explosion in the number of possible parses [4]. The opposite extreme—called semantic grammar—embeds semantic information in grammatical categories making no distinction between domain-specific knowledge and general knowledge; consequently, the semantic grammar-based parser is less transportable [15]. To avoid these shortcomings, we took the middle road.

Our approach Our goal is to semantically interpret user queries, keeping the parser domain independent while at the same time preventing a combinatorial explosion in the number of possible parses. Syntactic and semantic analysis proceeds incrementally. A rule in the KID parser consists of both syntactic and semantic parts, including checks and actions. The possible modification relationships between phrases must pass syntactic and semantic checks; if both checks succeed, then the syntactic and semantic actions deterministically produce the partial parse tree and the meaning for the modification, respectively. This reduces the number of possible intermediate parses drastically, thereby preventing a combinatorial explosion.

We can make the parser domain independent by encapsulating into the world model the domain-specific knowledge used by semantic checks and actions, and by restricting the parser's knowledge source to the world model; that is, semantic checks on modification relationships between phrases are based only on relationships between classes for nouns or verbs in the phrases given by the linguistic model. If the classes are connected by an attribute or super-sub relationship, then the phrases are unified into one phrase—called a unified phrase—with the meaning determined by consulting the world model only. This clarifies the parsing rules, and makes them general.

Meaning representation We use the world model not only as a knowledge base for semantic interpretation, but also as a meaning representation for user queries. Semantic interpretation identifies world model classes in the user's query, instantiates them, and makes a network of the instances isomorphic to world model classes as a meaning structure of the input. This isomorphic structure enables users to clearly verify semantic interpretation results. During processing, the parser gets values required for later processing (such as making the qualification in the world model query) from the input text, and puts them into the instances. Surface structures of phrases vary from one class to another, so users must specify individual procedures for each class. However, if users write class-specific methods under the name GET VALUE in the world model classes, then the parser performs these individual tasks uniformly by sending all instances of the GET VALUE message; this object-oriented feature of the world model keeps the parser domain independent.

The conceptual class is central in the meaning, corresponding to the root in the network. The phrase denotes the syntactic class literally. The parser integrates subtrees into a larger tree. The meaning, syntactic class, and conceptual class attach to the integrated tree by combining counterparts of the subtrees.

Principles for world model use The parser uses two general principles when it consults the world model—specialization and centralization. These help to resolve user query ambiguities naturally and efficiently.

1. The specialization principle: When two classes are given in a generalization hierarchy, the rule prefers subclass to superclass (for example, RETAILER_NAME in a NAME/RETAILER_NAME hierarchy). This principle, resolving the semantic ambiguities of phrases naturally, rests on the general language phenomenon that modifications specialize concepts.
2. The centralization principle: When two classes are given connected by an attribute relationship, the rule prefers the "whole" class to the "part" class (for example, SALE in a SALE/RETAILER attribute relationship). This helps to resolve syntactic ambiguities by determining the conceptual focus—that is, the conceptual class. From an efficiency viewpoint, semantic checks are done by using syntactic or conceptual classes that index meaning structure, rather than by searching meaning exhaustively.

Rules We classify rules into two groups according to the types of relationship between world model classes they handle: identification rules for super-sub relationships, and connection rules for user-defined attribute relationships. Rules are further specialized based on syntactic patterns to which they apply. Like identification rules, connection rules are general and domain-independent in that they treat all user-defined attributes in the same manner. Using the linguistic model, rules identify modification relationships among phrases with relationships among associated classes, enabling users to intuit clearly the semantic interpretation of queries by knowing these rules plus the above two principles. Some typical rules follow.

1. The NP-NP identification rule: This rule applies to syntactic patterns such as a noun phrase (NP) with the postposition *ga* (indicating a sentence subject or object, depending on the context) followed by a noun phrase with the postposition *no* (signifying ownership or a sentence subject). If two classes for the two noun phrases are in a hierarchy, the phrases are unified into one noun phrase. Classes of the unified noun phrase (meaning, syntactic, and conceptual classes) are the subclass according to the specialization principle. For example, consider the following:

   ...kakaku ga 300 yen no...
   (price)(300)(yen)
   (...the price is 300 yen...)

   Here the noun phrase *kakau ga* (price) and the noun phrase *300 yen no* (Japanese currency) refer to the classes PRICE and MONEY, respectively. They share a super-sub relationship, so the noun phrases are unified. The classes are all specialized as regards PRICE.

2. The NP-NP connection rule: This rule applies to syntactic patterns such as a noun phrase with the post-position *no* followed by a noun phrase with a postposition of any kind—such as *ga* or *wa* (a sentence subject or object), or *wo* (a sentence object). If an attribute relationship directly connects the associated classes (such as SALE and RETAILER) or indirectly connects them via super-sub relationships (such as RETAILER and ADDRESS), then the two noun phrases are unified into one noun phrase whose syntactic class is that of the second noun phrase (because the latter phrase is syntactically dominant in a Japanese sentence). The centralization principle determines conceptual class. Meaning is formed by merging the meanings of both noun phrases. The specialization principle modifies all these classes as required. For example, consider the following:

   ...mise no namae wa...
   (retailer)(of)(name)
   (...the name of the retailer is...)

   Here the noun phrase *mise no* (of the retailer) and the noun phrase *namae wa* (the name) correspond to RETAILER and NAME, respectively. Because RETAILER has NAME as its attribute, the two phrases are unified into one noun phrase whose syntactic class is specialized to RETAILER__NAME. The conceptual class is set to RETAILER and the merged meaning becomes RETAILER→RETAILER__NAME.
3. The PREDP connection rule: This rule applies to syntactic patterns such as a series of noun phrases followed by a predicate phrase (PREDP). If the predicate phrase class has each class for the noun phrases as its attributes, then all the phrases are unified into one predicate phrase. Moreover, if a noun phrase follows the predicate phrase—and if their classes are connected by an attribute relationship—then the two phrases are unified into one noun phrase. Classes of the unified phrase are determined as with the NP-NP connection rule above. For example, consider the following:

   ...Fujitsuya ga biiru wo uru...
   (retailer name)(beer)(sells)
   (...Fujitsuya sells beer...)

   Here the noun phrase *Fujitsuya ga* (a particular retailer's name), the noun phrase *biiru wo* (beer), and the predicate phrase *uru* (sells) refer to RETAILER__NAME, BEER, and SALE, respectively. The modification relationship between the noun phrase *biiru wo* and the predicate phrase holds, because SALE has BEER as its attribute. The relationship between the noun phrase *Fujitsuya ga* and the predicate phrase does not hold, because SALE does not have RETAILER__NAME as its attribute. However, the parser uses a heuristic at this point; the system infers that, when the user mentions the retailer's name, the user associates it with the retailer himself. The system makes this inference by knowing that the inverse class of RETAILER__NAME is RETAILER. The system takes RETAILER as the conceptual class of the noun phrase *Fujitsuya ga*. Furthermore, SALE has RETAILER as its attribute, so the modifying relationship between noun phrase and predicate phrase holds. Thus, the three phrases join into one predicate phrase—the syntactic and conceptual classes are both set to SALE—and the meaning becomes

```
SALE→RETAILER→RETAILER__NAME
  ↘
    BEER.
```

Rules control To ease world model debugging, we keep rules control simple by taking a priority-based approach [15]. We prioritize each rule according to the strength of relationships between classes for phrases handled by that rule. In general, identification rules receive higher priority than connection rules because the super-sub relationship is stronger than the attribute relationship. The parser applies rules, showing the highest priority to user utterance from left to right. If a rule's conditions are satisfied, then actions are performed; otherwise, the rules with the next highest priority are tried. This continues until the parser finds a rule whose condition is satisfied. After a rule performs an action, the parser again applies the highest priority rule from the input's beginning—continuing this process until no rules apply. If the parser has a unified tree at that time, the parsing has succeeded; otherwise, it has failed. This priority-based control results in a unique parse tree and meaning, if parsing has succeeded.

Simple rules control makes the parser robust, so it can accept even ungrammatical queries. We cannot expect users to make consistently complete and correct queries. To make the system user friendly, robustness is vital. Therefore, we write rules capable of handling patterns that standard rules cannot, and then give them lower priority than standard rules.

How the rules work To understand how the rules work, consider the following query:

Tokyo no biiru wo uru mise no namae wa?
(address)(of)(beer)(sells)(retailer)(of)(name)
What is the name of the retailer who sells beer in Tokyo?

This query contains several syntactic ambiguities. The noun phrase *Tokyo no* (in Tokyo, a particular address denoting the class ADDRESS) could modify three noun phrases: *biiru wo* (beer, BEER), *mise no* (of the retailer, RETAILER), or *namae wa* (the name, NAME). The predicate phrase *uru* (sells, SALE) could modify two noun phrases: *mise no* (of the retailer) and *namae wa* (the name). The query also contains two semantic ambiguities: *Tokyo no* (ADDRESS) and *namae wa* (NAME) could be specialized. The rules resolve all these ambiguities as explained below.

First, the predicate phrase connection rule unifies the first predicate phrase (PREDP1) *uru* (sells) and the second noun phrase (NP2) *biiru wo* (beer) into PREDP2 because SALE has BEER as its attribute. Then, the predicate phrase connection rule unifies PREDP2 and NP3 *mise no* (of the retailer) into NP5 because SALE (the syntactic class of PREDP2) has RETAILER as its attribute. This also resolves the syntactic ambiguity of PREDP1 *uru* (sells); PREDP1 modifies NP3 *miso no* (of the retailer). Next, the NP-NP connection rule unifies NP1 *Tokyo no* (in Tokyo) and NP5 into NP6, because RETAILER (the syntactic class of NP5) has ADDRESS as its attribute. This resolves both the syntactic and semantic ambiguities of NP1 *Tokyo no* (in Tokyo). NP1 modifies NP3 *mise no* (of the retailer), and ADDRESS (the class of NP1) is specialized to RETAILER__ADDRESS. Finally, the NP-NP connection rule unifies NP6 and NP4 *namae wa* (the name) into one complete sentence because RETAILER (the syntactic class of NP6) has NAME as its attribute. This resolves the semantic ambiguity of NP4 *namae wa* (the name); NAME is specialized to RETAILER__NAME.

Query translation

The meaning structure produced by semantic interpretation of the user's query is translated into a world model query; then, the world model query is translated into a database query. This section discusses the world model query language, and our approach to translation.

The world model query language Basically, the world model query language consists of the target list (specifying what data to return) and the qualification list (specifying what conditions data must satisfy). For example, "What is the name of the retailer who sells beer in Tokyo?" translates into the following world model query:

```
display SALE:Retailer:NameSALE:Beer
whereSALE:Retailer:Address = "TOKYO"
```

The keyword display is followed by the target list, and the keyword where by the qualification list. The expression consists of a class name, followed by an arbitrary number of attribute names with ":" between them. The ":" notation corresponds to the "." notation; that is, a functional join [16] or a functional composition [10]. The ":" operator can specify complex objects (that is, aggregation) to any desired detail. It can also accommodate property inheritance (that is, generalization) such as BEER:Name.

Further, users can express world model queries including joins (that is, entity-joins [16], nested queries, and aggregate functions) with "groupby" and "having" clauses [11]. For example, the user's query "Which retailer sells the most?" translates into the following world model query:

```
display SALE:Retailer
groupby SALE:Retailer:Code
HavingSUM(SALE:Sales) =
    MAX(SUM(SALE:Sales)
        groupby SALE:Retailer:Code)
```

Here, knowing that Code is the key attribute of RETAILER causes the expression in the preceding groupby clause. Moreover, knowing that Sales of SALE is multivalued puts the aggregate function SUM before SALE:Sales in the having clause. In this way, knowledge described in the world model classes is used to process user queries.

Our approach to translation Several issues arise in world model query translation. Translations must be done correctly according to domain-specific knowledge. Besides basic mapping, world model query expressions can involve any level of nested derivation, generalization, or functional joins in any combination (for example, SALE:Beer:Name). A large gap exists between the world model query including such complex expressions and the query against the "flat" relations; the gap must be bridged to correctly translate the query.

Therefore, we adopt as the translation mechanism a rule-based scheme whose advantages are naturalness, modularity, and uniformity [15]. We can divide the translation task into primitive subtasks, each performing only one function—such as generalization, derivation, or functional join—and allocate one subtask to one rule.

A second issue arises from the fact that users define mappings. The translation mechanism must be transparent enough for users to easily verify the accuracy of mappings that they build heuristically. The rule-based mechanism solves this problem also, because it is appropriate for explicitly describing behavioral knowledge—that it is modular and uniform helps users understand the translation process. To help users debug mappings, we provide trace/break functions as basic features of the rule-based mechanism. These can be invoked at any time. By employing this facility, users can follow the translation process step by step. It is also effective for rule debugging.

We want the world model to be independent of its DBMS as well as its database so that we can extend KID to a new DBMS. We make a clear separation between the rules (that is, knowledge about a particular query language) and their control (that is, the interpreter). In this way, users can control rule contents. Users have only to modify or replace the rules themselves to apply KID to a new DBMS.

In addition to mapping and derivation, we must translate based on domain-specific knowledge. A value's representation, when expressed in a world model query, does not necessarily agree with its database query counterpart. For example, while the world model represents the value of RETAILER__CODE as an integer, the corresponding value is a string in the database. The translation must take such class-specific kinds of knowledge into account. On the other hand, to maintain portability, we must provide a general framework for describing such knowledge by integrating object-oriented features with the rule-oriented scheme [13]. Users can give a common name to class-specific methods for value conversion. Then, the system can activate domain-specific translation uniformly by sending a message using the common name.

Translation rules Query translation is done cooperatively by several "rulesets" (collections of rules performing coherent tasks). We have organized rulesets for key clauses of the world model query language. Target-, groupby-, having-, and qualification rulesets process display-, groupby-, having-, and where- clauses, respectively. Each ruleset shares two workspaces, one for world model query input and one for database query output. The rulesets seek in the world model query workspace for expressions to which they apply, and translate any expressions they find to modify the workspace. Each rule transforms the ":" notation in the world model query, using relevant knowledge in the world model class such as mappings or derivations. A mapping modifies the database query workspace, and a derivation modifies the world model query workspace. Each rule is applied repeatedly until the world model query workspace is empty, at which point the translation process terminates. We describe the principal functions of each ruleset below.

The target ruleset This ruleset processes the target list in the world model query. The rules include mapping, derivation, complex object, generalization, functional join, and aggregate function.

1. Mapping: If the ":" notation includes any mapping, the contents are added to the database query workspace. The mapping's target and qualification parts are merged into corresponding parts of the database query workspace. For example,

```
(world model query                          (database query
       workspace)                              workspace)
        RETAILER: Name→
                RETAILER__TBL:RETAILER__NAME__FLD
```

2. Derivation: If the ":" notation includes any derivation (that is, derived class or attribute), then the contents are merged into the world model query workspace. For example,

```
          (world model query workspace)
                   BEER: Code
                       ↓
COMMODITY:Code where COMMODITY:CODE ≦ 103
```

3. Complex object: if a complex object whose attribute Super has neither mapping nor derivation appears with no attributes specified in the expression, then it is expanded into its component classes to merge into the world model query workspace. However, if the complex object has the attribute Return, expansion is performed according to its value. For example,

```
(world model query workspace)
         RETAILER
             ↓
RETAILER:Code RETAILER:Name
```

4. Generalization: If the ":" notation has any property inheritance, then the mapping or derivation specified in the attribute Super of the class (that is, subclass) is added to the database or world model query workspace, respectively. The mapping or derivation in the attribute of the superclass is also added. For example, suppose that the following two separate relations are given for the COMMODITY/BEER generalization, and that the mapping joining the two relations and the mapping "get COMMODITY__TBL:COMMODITY__NAME__FLD" are specified for Super of BEER and Name of COMMODITY, respectively:

```
(world model query           (database query
     workspace)                  workspace)
     BEER:Name→COMMODITY__TBL:
                COMMODITY__NAME__FLD
          where COMMODITY__TBL:
                COMMODITY__CODE__FLD
               =BEER__TBL:BEER__CODE__FLD
```

5. Functional join: A long expression including more than one ":" operator (that is, functional join) is reduced one step at a time. If the ":" notation has any map-

ping, it is merged into the database query workspace. If it has any derivation, it is merged into the world model query workspace. In the former case, the resultant class for the ":" notation (that is, the domain class for the attribute) is added to the world model query workspace. For example,

```
(world model query                                   (database query
      workspace)                                          workspace)
  SALE:Retailer:Name→where
                    ↓ SALE__TBL:SALE__RETAILER__FLD
  RETAILER:Name =RETAILER__TBL:
                          RETAILER__CODE__FLD
```

6. Aggregate function: If the expression contains an aggregate function (such as SUM or MAX), then the function's parameter is translated by recursively applying the target ruleset. For example, consider the following mapping "get SALE__TBL:SALE__SALES__FLD" for Sales of SALE:

```
(world model query        (database query
       workspace)               workspace)
SUM(SALE:Sales)→SUM
   (SALE__TBL:SALE__SALES__FLD)
```

The groupby ruleset This ruleset processes the groupby clause. Creating key fields of the database query from key expressions of the world model query resembles target list processing. For example, consider the following mapping "get RETAILER__TBL:RETAILER__CODE__FLD" for Code of RETAILER:

```
(world model query                                 (database query
   workspace)                                          workspace)
SALE:Retailer:Code→RETAILER__TBL:
                   RETAILER__CODE__FLD
where SALE__TBL:SALE__RETAILER__FLD
      =RETAILER__TBL:RETAILER__CODE__FLD
```

The having ruleset In the having clause, the aggregate function is compared with either a constant or with the result of the nested query. For the nested query, target-, groupby-, having-, and qualification rulesets are invoked recursively. For example,

```
(world model query                                   (database query
   workspace)                                            workspace)
  SUM(SALE:Sales)→SUM(SALE__TBL:SALE__SALES__FLD)
  =MAX(            =MAX(
   SUM(SALE:Sales)SUM(SALE__TBL:SALE__SALES__FLD)

   groupby          where
   SALE:Retailer:Code)SALE__TBL:SALE__RETAILER__FLD
                    =RETAILER__TBL:RETAILER__CODE__FLD
                    groupby
                    RETAILER__TBL:RETAILER__CODE__FLD)
```

The qualification ruleset This ruleset processes the where clause. Most of its functions are in common with the target ruleset—except that it must convert value and handle logical operators, comparative operators, and nested queries. The qualification ruleset always sends the predefined "NORMALIZE VALUE" message to convert value. Users optionally specify codes for this message for each class, making the translation domain independent. For example,

```
(world model query                        (database query
   workspace)                                 workspace)
RETAILER:Code=100→(send RETAILER__CODE
          "NORMALIZE VALUE" 100)

                         ↓

RETAILER__TBL:RETAILER__CODE__FLD="100"
```

A translation example The first world model query example (illustrated at the beginning of this section) is translated by the rulesets explained above into the following database query:

```
  get RETAILER__TBL:RETAILER__CODE__FLD
      RETAILER__TBL:RETAILER__NAME__FLD
      COMMODITY__TBL:COMMODITY__CODE__FLD
      COMMODITY__TBL:COMMODITY__NAME__FLD
where SALE__TBL:SALE__RETAILER__FLD
      =RETAILER__TBL:RETAILER__CODE__FLD
  and SALE__TBL:SALE__COMMODITY__FLD
      =COMMODITY__TBL:COMMODITY__CODE__FLD
  and COMMODITY__TBL:COMMODITY__CODE__FLD≦"103"
  and RETAILER__TBL:RETAILER__ADDRESS__FLD="TOKYO"
```

Related work

KID has resulted from work in different fields—natural language understanding work in the AI field, data modeling work in the database field, and object notion work in the programming language field.

There has been a major attempt to construct portable natural language interface systems such as CO-OP [3], TEAM [4], LDC [6], IRUS [17], and FRED [18]. CO-OP aims at providing cooperative responses; however, CO-OP lacks a conceptually natural model like KID's world model. TEAM incorporates a knowledge base similar to the world model; however, TEAM stresses knowledge acquisition issues rather than the knowledge base design issues discussed in this article [15]. Like KID, LDC seeks to permit customization by sophisticated users; however, LDC works with loosely structured text files rather than relational databases. IRUS and FRED resemble KID closely in design; they have conceptual database languages to gain DMBS transportability although their data models are different from KID's. Salveter's work focuses on natural language database update, which KID does not implement currently [19].

A few natural language interface systems such as Intellect [20] and Q&A [21] are commercially available. Due to its lack of detailed program description, Intellect gives users a less clear understanding of how it processes queries—thereby making it difficult to customize. Q&A has a good facility to ease vocabulary acquisition from users, but it can retrieve only one file at a time.

Researchers such as Sondheimer et al. [22] and Hayes [23] have pursued ideas on natural language understanding—ideas resembling our semantic interpretation using the world model. However, Sondheimer doesn't present general rules using the model like the identification rules in KID. Hayes' parser provides less simple rules control than does the KID parser in that he uses "multistrategy" parsing to make the parser robust.

Many ideas that the world model incorporates have been adapted from work on semantic data modeling. What is most significant about the world model is that it provides an integrated framework for describing database mapping, linguistic knowledge, and domain of discourse semantics. The world model borrows its object-oriented features from LOOPS [13].

GEM resembles our work in that it attempts to implement a semantic data model on a relational database system [16]. However, GEM's mapping is less flexible than KID's since GEM restricts generalization hierarchy implementation to one relation. EUFID resembles KID in that it aims to bridge the gap between English-like input and database query [24]. However, EUFID's mapping uses an ad hoc representation scheme.

While we originally developed KID for the Japanese language, its framework can be applied to English and other languages. KID applies a semantic data model to natural language interface design. We believe that our approach to query translation solves the problem of implementing semantic data models. Although prototypical, KID has been applied to real estate, merchandising, and medical test domains. Each world model consists of roughly 70-150 classes, 400-600 lexical entries, and 50-100 mappings.

Comprehensive evaluations of KID reveal that world models are easy to build and that KID is clearly portable. For example, one sophisticated KID user (a user we tutored) designed and created a world model for the medical test domain in two weeks, focusing mainly on the ease of the tasks. He found the domain model easier to define than the rest, which required some expertise, and he found design easier than creation. We decided that this was because the world model editor was not fully operational at that time.

We collected 400 sentences, dividing them into four groups mechanically. We performed the "blind test" and the "full-capability test" against each group of sentences in succession. In the blind test, we counted sentences that could be accepted without changing any portion of the world model. In the full-capability test, we made all necessary revisions or extensions to the world model to accept rejected sentences. We tested one group after another. As a result, the acceptance ratio (percent) of each blind test rose from 33, 60, and 76 to 84. The number of days required for the sophisticated user to attain 90 percent of acceptance for each group dropped from 10, 4, and 2 to 2. From these monotonic inclinations (not the absolute values) and a summary of user opinions, we conclude that world model definition is straightforward and that KID is easily customized. Tests have confirmed that KID understands a great variety of Japanese sentences including conjunctive, disjunctive, comparative, superlative, anaphoric, and elliptical expressions; however, they suggest that extending KID's linguistic coverage requires global knowledge about parsing rules [5].

Currently, we are improving KID's knowledge base editor and are modularizing parsing rules using objects to enable easier customizing. We have long-range plans to extend KID from handling only database queries to handling database updates, decision support, and ultimate use in expert systems.

Acknowledgment

We thank the *IEEE Expert* referees for their helpful comments.

References

1. G.G. Hendrix et al., "Developing a Natural Language Interface to Complex Data," *ACM Trans. Database Systems*, Vol. 3, No. 2, 1978, pp. 105–147.
2. D.L. Waltz, "An English Language Question Answering System for a Large Relational Database," *Comm. ACM,* Vol. 21, No. 7, 1978, pp. 526–539.
3. S.J. Kaplan, "Designing a Portable Natural Language Database Query System," *ACM Trans. Database Systems*, Vol. 9, No. 1, 1984, pp. 1–19.
4. P. Martin, D. Appelt, and F. Pereira, "Transportability and Generality in a Natural Language Interface System," *Proc. IJCAI,* William Kaufmann, 95 First Street, Los Altos, Calif., 94022, 1983, pp. 573–581.
5. J. Hendler et al., "Issues in the Development of Natural Language Front Ends," *Proc. AFIPS NCC*, AFIPS Press, Reston, Va., 1981, pp. 643–648.
6. B.W. Ballard et al., "LDC-1: A Transportable, Knowledge-Based Natural Language Processor for Office Environments," *ACM Trans. Office Information Systems*, Vol. 2, No. 1, 1984, pp. 1–25.
7. M. Hammer and D. McLeod, "Database Description with SDM: Semantic Database Model," *ACM Trans. Database Systems*, Vol. 6, No. 3, 1981, pp. 341–386.
8. J. Mylopoulos, P.A. Bernstein, and H.K.T. Wong, "A Language Facility for Designing Interactive Database-Intensive Applications," *ACM Trans. Database Systems.*, Vol. 5, No. 2, 1980, pp. 185–207.
9. M. Schrefl, A.M. Tjoa, and R.R. Wagner, "Comparison-Criteria for Semantic Data Models," *Proc. IEEE Int'l. Conf. Data Engineering*, Computer Society of the IEEE, 10662 Los Vaqueros Circle, Los Alamitos, Calif., 1984, pp. 120–125.
10. D.W. Shipman, "The Functional Data Model and the Data Language DAPLEX," *ACM Trans. Database Systems*, Vol. 6, No. 1, 1981, pp. 140–173.
11. C.J. Date, *An Introduction to Database Systems*, Addison-Wesley, Reading, Mass., 1975.
12. A Makinouchi et al., "Relational Database Management System RDB/V1," (in Japanese) *Trans. Information Processing Soc. Japan*, Vol. 24, No. 1, 1983, pp. 47–55.
13. D.G. Bobrow and M. Stefik, "The LOOPS Manual," Tech. Report KB-VLSI-81-13, Knowledge Systems Area, Xerox Palo Alto Research Center, 3333 Coyote Hill Road, Palo Alto, Calif. 94304, 1981.
14. R.L. Haskin and R.A. Lorie, "On Extending the Functions of a Relational Database System," *Proc. ACM SIGMOD Int'l Conf. Management Data*, ACM, N.Y., 1982, pp. 207–212.
15. A. Barr and E.A. Feigenbaum, *The Handbook of Artificial Intelligence*, Vol. 1, William Kaufmann, Los Altos, Calif., 1981.

16. S. Tsur and C. Zaniolo, "An Implementation of GEM—Supporting a Semantic Data Model on a Relational Back-End," *Proc. ACM SIGMOD Int'l Conf. Management Data*, ACM, N.Y., 1984, pp. 286–295.
17. M. Bates, "Accessing a Database with a Transportable Natural Language Interface," *Proc. IEEE First Conf. Artificial Intelligence Applications*, Computer Society of the IEEE, 10662 Los Vaqueros Circle, Los Alamitos, Calif., 1984, pp. 9–12.
18. G. Jakosbon et al., "An Intelligent Database Assistant," *IEEE Expert*, Summer 1986, pp. 65–79.
19. S. Salveter, "Supporting Natural Language Database Update by Modeling Real World Actions," *Proc. First Int'l Workshop Expert Database Systems*, Institute of Information Management, Technology, and Policy, College of Business Administration, University of South Carolina, Columbia, S.C. 29208, 1984, pp. 275–297.
20. L.R. Harris, "The ROBOT System: Natural Language Processing Applied to Database Query," *Proc. ACM Annual Conf.*, Vol. 1, ACM, New York, N.Y., 1978, pp. 165–172.
21. J. Walden, *Getting the Most from Q&A*, Osborne McGraw-Hill, Berkeley, Calif., 1986.
22. N.K. Sondheimer, R.M. Weischedel, and R.J. Bobrow, "Semantic Interpretation Using KL-ONE," *Proc. 10th Int'l Conf. Computational Linguistics*, Assoc. for Computational Linguistics, Bell Communications Research, 445 South Street, MRE 2A379, Morristown, N.J. 07960, 1984, pp. 101–107.
23. P.J. Hayes, "Entity-Oriented Parsing," *Proc. 10th Int'l Conf. Computational Linguistics*, Assoc. for Computational Linguistics, Bell Communications Research, 445 South Street, MRE 2A379, Morristown, N.J. 07960, 1984, pp. 212–217.
24. J.F. Burger, "Semantic Database Mapping in EUFID," *Proc. ACM SIGMOD Int'l Conf. Management Data*, ACM, N.Y. 1980, pp. 67–74.

27

The intelligent assistant Technical considerations involved in designing Q&A's natural-language interface

Gary G. Hendrix
Brett A. Walter

Editors' note *Gary Hendrix and Brett Walter describe the intelligent assistant (IA), one of the first successful natural language interfaces. The IA remains part of Symantec's Q&A integrated database management and word processing system. The design decisions that led to the IA are discussed in the paper, which contains insightful decisions about the design and development of systems that use AI tools and techniques. (Reprinted, with permission, from the December 1987 issue of* Byte *magazine.*

In 1985 Symantec introduced Q&A, an integrated database manager and word processor for the IBM PC, XT, AT, and compatibles. Q&A features a natural-language interface, called the Intelligent Assistant (IA), that lets you interact with your data through questions and commands posed in a subset of ordinary English. A variety of factors, some business-oriented and some technical, influenced its design. This article discusses the technical design decisions behind the IA. [Editor's note: *For further information on Q&A, see the product preview "Q&A" by Jon R. Edwards in the January 1986* BYTE.]

Q&A has its roots in research on natural-language processing (NLP) conducted at SRI International (formerly Stanford Research Institute) in Menlo Park, California, under the sponsorship of the Advanced Research Projects Agency of the United States Department of Defense. For many years, SRI and other laboratories have investigated how we might use computer systems to understand ordinary English, especially for practical applications such as retrieving data from large, complex databases.

Such applications are interesting because English interfaces potentially require far less training than conventional interfaces, and you can use them rapidly and accurately both in stressful situations and in situations where you may need to access data in unanticipated ways.

Design decisions

The central design requirement of the IA was that it be *usable* by untrained novices for a wide range of single-file applications. Once we decided that usability was to be its main focus, other requirements began to flow. A design decision made to address one requirement would significantly affect the others; the larger design problem became to meet the following requirements collectively.

- *Accessibility.* The IA should let you access a wide spectrum of underlying functionality.
- *Habitability.* It should allow you to express yourself through English requests that come readily and comfortably to mind.
- *Verifiability.* The IA should let you verify that its interpretation of an English request agrees with what you mean.
- *Resilience.* It should gracefully recover from anomalies in your request, ambiguous requests, and unknown words, as well as from gaps in its own linguistic knowledge.
- *Performance.* It should process requests within a reasonable length of time on an 8088-based machine with a memory limitation of 512K bytes.
- *Adaptability.* The IA should be domain-independent and should adapt easily to new databases.
- *Synchronization.* It should automatically keep its vocabulary current with database updates.

Accessibility

The central issue in creating an NLP system is encoding enough linguistic knowledge in the computer for it to understand your requests. There are two aspects to this problem: accessibility and habitability.

Having adequate accessibility means that you can access the major functionality of the underlying system through some natural-language request. That is, for every important operation that Q&A can perform, there should be at least one way to request it in English. English is particularly useful for ad hoc database query and analysis and can also be helpful in manipulating individual records and updating the database. Ultimately, we decided to provide English access to such operations as

- *Retrieving records that meet specified selection criteria.* For example, "Get the forms for programmers earning over $30,000."
- *Producing tabular reports, either detailed or summary.* For example, "Show the address and phone number of each employee," or "What's the average salary for secretaries in each department?"
- *Performing mathematical calculations.* For example, "What's Tom's salary plus Mary's?"

- *Creating new data records.* For example, "Add a new programmer to R&D whose name is "John Smith"."
- < *Updating multiple data records.* For example, "Increase the programmers' salaries by 10 percent."

To conserve space, we didn't try to provide natural-language support for word-processing operations such as "Make this paragraph bold," "Set the left margin to 2 inches," or "Send this memo to every manager in the eastern region." Also, certain Report options remained inaccessible from the IA, primarily because the English for the operations would be awkward. These options included specifying nonstandard column headings, widths, page headers, and so forth.

Habitability

Having adequate habitability means that if an operation is accessible, you can request it through natural-language sentences that come readily and comfortably to mind. For example, using a personnel database, Q&A's Report module can produce a report that lists the salaries of all female employees. This functionality is accessible with English even if there is only one way to ask for it, such as through a rather formal construction: "Print the name and the salary from the records where the sex is female." But it is quite improbable that you would express this thought in exactly these words.

You can make a natural-language system habitable in three ways. First, you can train its users to enter only those few English sentences that the system accepts. However, this approach sacrifices the key purpose of a natural-language system—naturalness. A highly restricted subset of English is merely another formal language to learn. The sentences may be easy to understand because they're in English, but they're not easy to construct because many English sentences that come naturally to mind aren't in the formal language.

Second, you can actively guide the user in creating requests. You might display a limited number of input choices and ask the user to select from a list of sentences or sentence parts.

Third, you can have the system recognize many alternative expressions of the same idea in the hope that one of them will be the one actually used. The IA uses this strategy. For example, the IA will accept hundreds of variations on the female-salary query given above. TABLE 27-1 contains a partial list of the variations that the IA will accept.

Providing access to a breadth of functionality through a wide variety of linguistic constructions requires that you approach natural-language analysis with considerable sophistication. An approach based on keywords might suffice to interpret several of the requests in TABLE 27-1 by picking out the words *female* and *salary*. However, such an approach would fail miserably on the query "Is John older than Sue?," where meaning depends critically on word order.

To achieve the accessibility and habitability necessary for the IA, we decided to use a context-free grammar expressed as a collection of augmented phrase-structure rules. Such rules are fairly easy to adapt and maintain as the grammar evolves, and you can compile them into a very efficient run-time system. The semantic augmentations to the

Table 27-1. A partial list of the variations on the female-salary query that the IA will accept

Female salaries.
Show the female salaries.
Salaries for females.
Salaries of the women.
What do we pay the women?
What are the salaries of the female employees?
What are the women paid?
Please find the earnings of our women employees and present them for me.
How much pay do women get?
Get the salaries of the employees who are women.
Get the salary data on all females.
What salaries do the female employees have?
I want to see the salaries of the females.
Let us see the salaries of the female employees.
Can I have the salaries from the records for females?
Please make a report that shows the values from the salary field from all forms where the value in the sex field is female.
For female employees, make a list of the salaries.
If an employee is female, I want to see her salary.

syntax rules are expressed as procedures in LISP; these procedures translate inputs into an internal representation language related to first-order logic. Schemes based on augmented transition networks (ATNs) or unification grammars might work equally well.

Verifiability

In a system that accepts only a narrow sliver of English or that forces you to construct requests under the guidance of the system, the meaning of inputs may always be clear. However, because the IA has been designed to accept a wide variety of inputs, and because English is often ambiguous and the system's knowledge of the language is limited, the IA will sometimes miss your intended meaning. How can you verify whether its interpretation of a request is consistent with yours?

The IA shows you its plan for dealing with each request and asks your permission before taking further action. This is not unlike the dialogues between air-traffic controllers and pilots, in which the pilot parrots back the controller's instructions. (Some systems attempt to deal with miscommunication by providing an Undo function, but Undo is inappropriate in non-RAM situations where the cost of mistakes is high.)

The IA presents its plan of action in English, but in a highly stylized manner, using indentation to clarify the meaning, as shown in FIG. 27-1. Sometimes users make requests that the underlying database can't perform or that contain language the IA doesn't understand. In such cases, the IA doesn't paraphrase the request, but presents its best efforts at understanding it.

Resilience

We designed the IA to be resilient to many types of errors in English inputs. We could have designed its grammar analyzer to flag errors in grammar. This would be appropri-

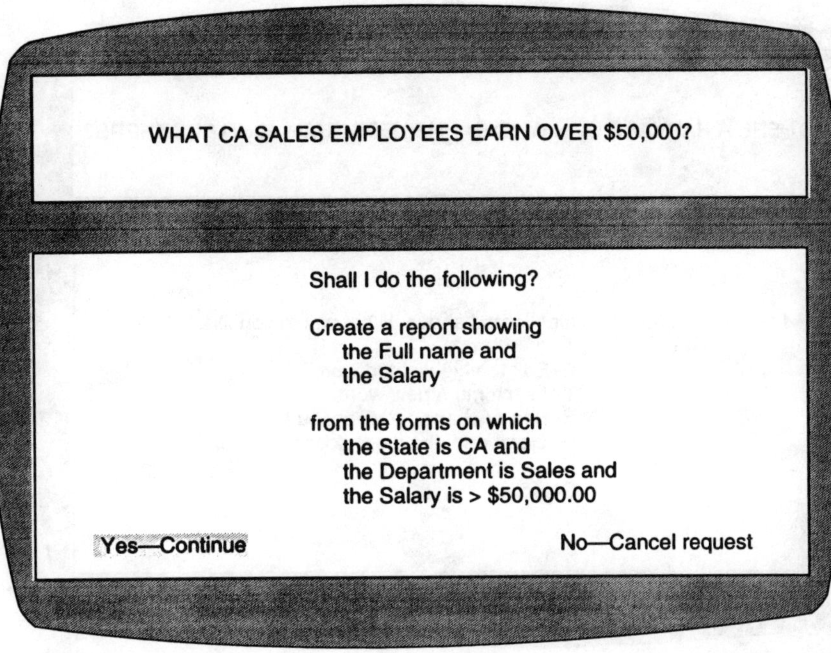

Fig. 27-1. The IA presents its plan of action in highly stylized English, clarifying its meaning with indentation.

ate in a parser for correcting the grammar and style of business letters, or for grading themes in an English course, but it's not appropriate for database users who want results, not corrections. Therefore, the IA has a forgiving response to poor English. Consider the request, "I wants you please shows me what salary's of females be?" The IA asks whether you want the full name and salary of females. (Interestingly, many foreign users have commented that the IA can understand their English when most Americans cannot.)

The question of resilience greatly influenced the IA's entire approach to language analysis. An analysis that demands strict adherence to English grammar is too brittle. An analysis that ignores syntax and relies simply on keywords is resilient but usually misses critical aspects of sentence meaning. To gain resilience without sacrificing syntactic acumen, we developed the notion of a layered relaxation grammar. The layered grammar first tries to find large, syntactically well-formed constructions, including whole sentences. If this attempt fails, the constraints on syntax are progressively relaxed, and analysis continues using progressively less demanding grammar rules.

Sometimes, however, you simply can't understand a request. For example, if you enter the request "Show the New York employees," the IA will ask for clarification: Do you mean New York City or New York state? The sequence in FIGS. 27-2, 27-3, and 27-4 shows how the IA deals with an unknown word. Although the word *man* is unknown, you can choose to define it on the fly in terms of *male*, which is already known as a value in the *sex* field. For hopelessly flawed syntax such as "Whose salaries are

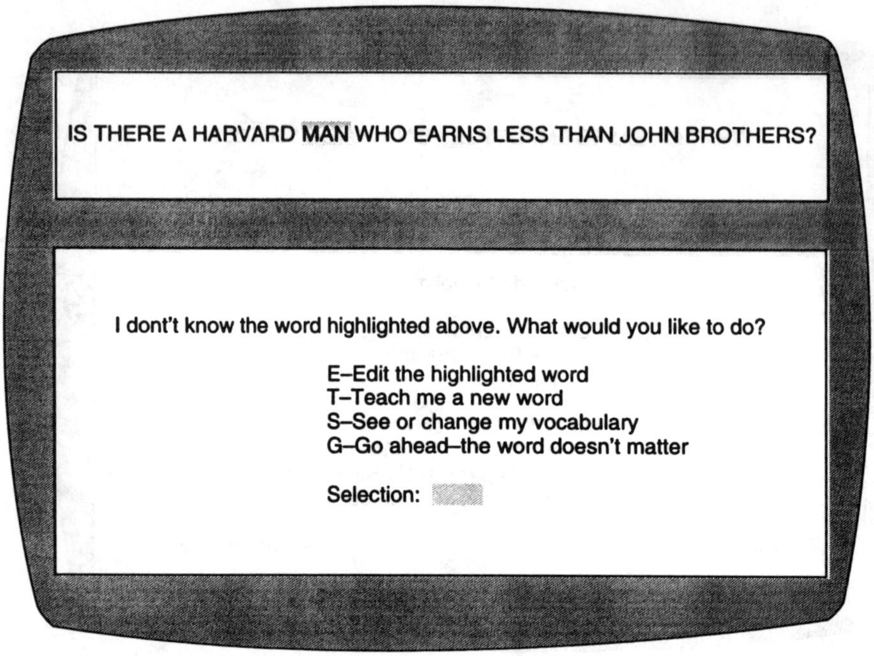

Fig. 27-2. The options that AI presents to you to define an unknown word on the fly.

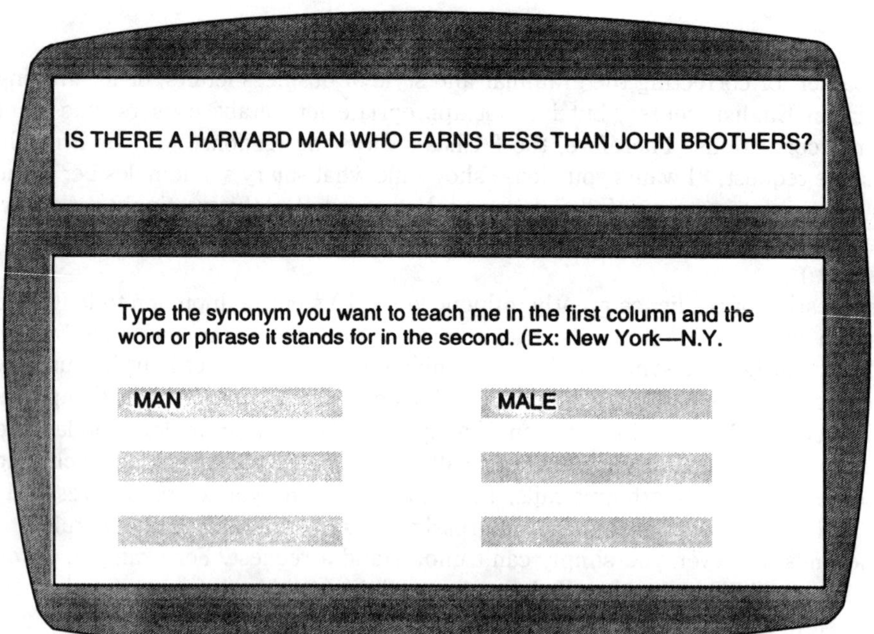

Fig. 27-3. If you select the T option in Fig. 27-2, you can define the unknown word "man" in terms of the known word "male."

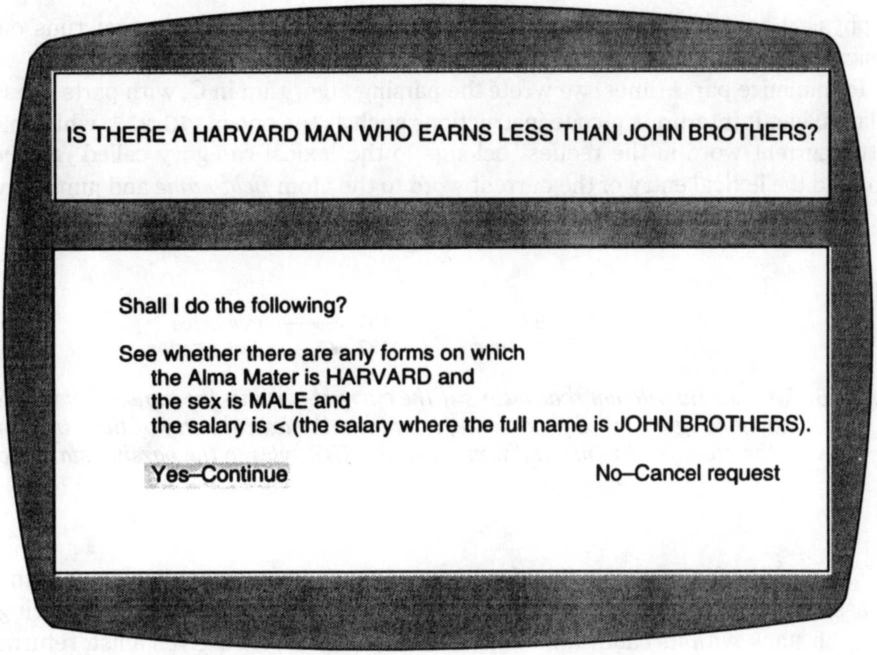

Fig. 27-4. This screen lets you approve or disapprove the IA's new understanding of the question.

between $10,000 and print them," the IA will highlight the confusing part, "between $10,000," and ask if you want to continue. If you do, it will discard the highlighted portion of the request and cope with the remainder as best it can.

Performance

The greatest engineering challenge in creating a natural-language system for Q&A was squeezing it into the IBM PC environment, which imposes two severe constraints: a relatively slow CPU and very limited addressable memory. Other natural-language systems run on $100,000 dedicated LISP machines in 10 megabytes of RAM. We needed to be able to run from a single 360K-byte floppy disk in 512K bytes of RAM. To cope with these constraints, we used several tactics.

To begin with, we recognized that we couldn't provide linguistic coverage as extensive as current theory would permit. Thus, we fashioned grammar rules that covered frequently used construction, knowingly omitting rules for less important patterns. What *not* to do became more important than what *to* do.

Both the syntax rules and the associated semantic interpretation functions begin life in LISP: the syntax rules as data structures, and the semantic functions as LISP code. For the final product, both are compiled into custom p-codes. (A p-code, or pseudocode, is a machine-language instruction, but for a virtual machine rather than the physical hardware. The p-codes are executed by an interpreter that runs on the physical hardware and emulates hardware of a different design.)

To minimize parse times, we wrote the parsing algorithm in C, with parts in assembly language. It interprets p-code instructions such as the one in FIG. 27-5, which means "if the current word in the request belongs to the lexical category called *field-name*, then bind the lexical entry of the current word to the atom *field-name* and jump forward 137 bytes to the parsing state encoded there."

5	83	137 ←	raw bytes
CAT	*field-name*	137 ←	alpha codes

Fig. 27-5. A p-code instruction that means if the current word in the request belongs to the lexical category called field-name, then bind the lexical entry of the current word to the atom field-name and jump forward 137 bytes to the parsing state encoded there.

The p-codes for semantic functions have a separate interpreter, also written in C and assembly language. An example p-code is the 1-byte instruction for replacing the top of the stack with its caddr (i.e., a LISP function that, when given a list, returns the list's third item). In writing the semantic functions, we were careful to use only about 100 LISP primitives, minimizing the size of the run-time library. Our data suggests that the p-code approach saved us a great deal of space; machine code would have been five times as costly.

Adaptability

Adapting a general-purpose natural-language interface to a new application may be the most unappreciated problem in NLP design. It's very difficult for non-linguists to provide linguistic information about a new domain. For a new database, for example, you must prime the system with hundreds, or even thousands, of new database-specific words before it becomes very useful. You must also provide structural information about the new database. If not handled properly, this priming process can create a human-factors hurdle that we call the NLP wall (see FIG. 27-6).

The essence of the problem is this: You buy a natural-language interface because it's easier to ask questions in ordinary English than to worry about syntax or the underlying database-management system. But to adapt the interface to your database, you may well have to become an expert in the DBMS and in lexicography.

We thought it was essential to shield our business-oriented users from anything requiring programming, linguistic, or database-administration knowledge. Therefore, we included a predefined base vocabulary, automatic acquisition of most data-specific terms, and a Teach system for acquiring special classes of lexical items and structural data.

The IA's base vocabulary includes over 400 words for manipulating data. This covers a broader spectrum than the number indicates, because these are the high-fre-

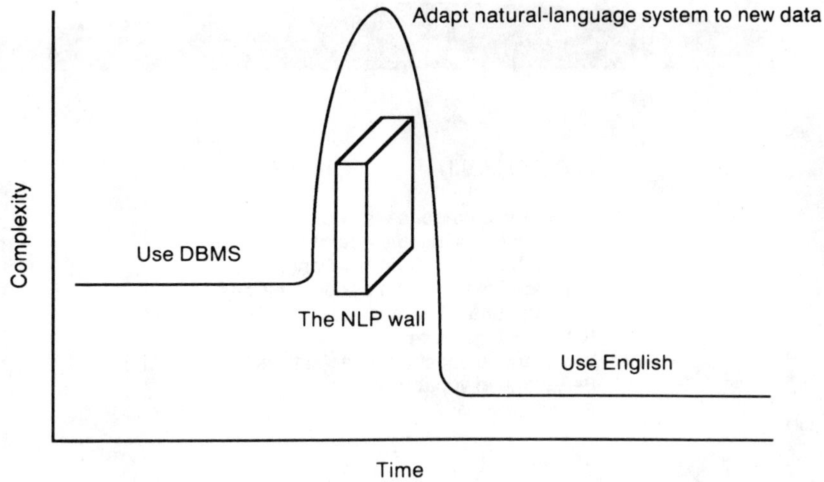

Fig. 27-6. The NLP wall, a human-factors hurdle that can occur when you try to implement a new application on your natural-language interface. The interface is meant to make interaction with the computer more natural, but in order to set up your computer to use it, you need to use a great deal of "unnatural" language.

quency words of data applications. For comparison, half the words that Shakespeare wrote come from a set of 100 high-frequency words; the King James Bible contains only 8000 words, many of them used just once. The IA automatically adds words and phrases used in labeling fields on Q&A forms to the lexicon, as well as values entered in text fields. These words represent the vast majority of the vocabulary used by an application.

Since we can't control the kinds of words and phrases you may enter as data, and since we certainly can't ask you to lexically classify every field entry and label, we used grammar rules that refer to lexical categories such as *field-name* and *text-value* instead of making full use of more convenient categories such as *noun* and *verb*.

After adding the field labels and text-field entries to the base vocabulary, the IA lets you fully access the major underlying DBMS functions. But you can greatly enhance the habitability of the system if you provide it with additional information through a Teach module.

The Teach main menu features eight lessons you can teach your IA (see FIG. 27-7). The lessons are presented roughly in the order in which they enhance the usability of the system, so if you become impatient, the most important information will generally have been acquired first.

Lesson 1 gives you the opportunity to introduce new terms for the database. For example, a personnel database might have labels for *salary* and *sex*, and data fields with the values *male* and *vice president*, so the system learns these terms automatically. But nowhere does the database actually include the words *employee* and *worker*, and they are what the database is really all about. Lessons 5 through 8 also acquire vocabulary terms.

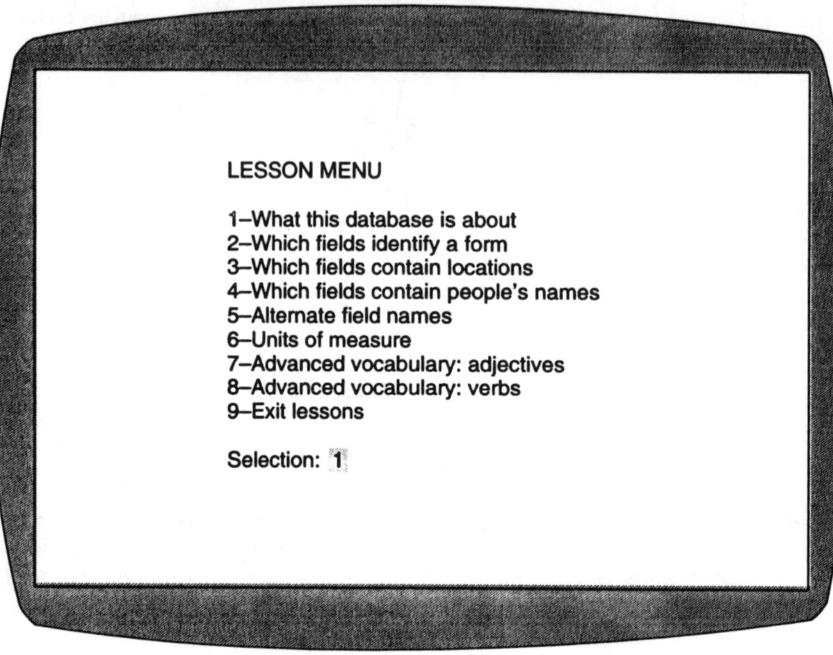

Fig. 27-7. The eight lessons (plus an exit) on the Teach main menu. These lessons enhance the usability of the system in roughly the order presented.

Acquiring structural information is a similar process. For example, Lesson 4 asks you to mark the fields that hold the names of people. This is important because personal names require special treatment in English. Lessons 2 and 3 also acquire structural information.

Synchronization

To analyze inputs, a natural-language system needs information about the words that can appear in legal sentences. This information is maintained in the system's lexicon. It is important to keep the lexicon synchronized with the database. If you don't, for example, someone could add a record for a new employee named Thelma and subsequently be told that "Thelma" is an unknown word when asking about her in English.

Full synchronization requires close cooperation between the DBMS and NLP system, and it is therefore difficult to achieve when you add NLP to an existing DBMS as an afterthought. For this reason, most natural-language systems freeze their lexicons, ignoring the problem altogether. Others scan the database hoping to find "Thelma" as a value in some field in some record, but this is highly inefficient on all but very small databases.

Because we designed Q&A as an integrated system, the requirements of the natural-language component influenced the design of the database itself. In particular, the lexicon of the IA is maintained as a database index that, like the indexes used to speed up searches on frequently queried fields, is automatically revised by all data updates.

Thus, when you use "Thelma" as a data item, the database itself automatically ensures its entry in the lexicon. Q&A's DBMS also updates the lexicon when you change the database structure, such as when you add or delete fields.

Like the other indexes in Q&A, the lexicon is stored as a disk-based B-tree and can grow arbitrarily large. Using Q&A's standard routines for searching B-trees, you can retrieve lexical items far more quickly than if you had to scan the primary data records. Thus, Q&A's IA and DBMS cooperate to let you edit live data and keep the lexicon current and fast.

Great expectations

User expectations also greatly affect the usability of NLP. In fact, unrealistic expectations pose the greatest human-factors problem in the design of a natural-language interface. Novices have few preconceived notions about an ordinary computer program, and they even blame themselves if they have difficulty learning or using it.

But people *do* have preconceived notions about using English. They use it every day with no apparent effort. It seems perfectly natural that they should be able to talk to a computer in English; they've seen it on TV for years. Thus, even a system that claims only limited understanding of English can evoke inordinately high expectations.

This problem greatly concerned us, and we devoted considerable design and engineering effort to addressing it. After making the IA as fluent as we could within the hardware limitations, we looked for ways to recalibrate user expectations to more realistic levels.

We tried to present our natural-language functionality as a concrete yet vulnerable process, with human-like imperfections. The manual, Help screens, menus, and various other parts of the system all invite you to think of the IA as a new office worker from another country who is still learning English. Like that worker, the IA tries to be helpful but sometimes makes linguistic or cultural errors.

We established Get Acquainted as the first of the three options on the IA's main menu (along with Teach and Ask). Get Acquainted introduces you to the basic capabilities of the IA and the most successful strategy for coming to "speaking terms" with it.

In each session, the first time the IA displays its query request box, it shows two example requests in a syntax it understands. In white-room tests, this dramatically improved the likelihood of success. The IA normally states its plans of action in terms that *it* can understand. After a while, a user will gradually adopt its way of "speaking" as a model for communication with it. In addition, Q&A includes an IA fast-start card that briefly states how to ask questions successfully.

We also found that foreign users wanted to use the IA in their native tongues. To accommodate them, we have adapted the IA for German, Swedish, French, Dutch, Italian, and Finnish.

Meeting the challenge

Looking back, the major challenge in designing a natural-language interface was not in understanding how to process English, but in identifying the collective needs of those who want English as an interface, and meeting them with available technology. As the microcomputer industry breaks through the 640K-type RAM barrier and migrates to faster CPUs, linguistic coverage will rise quickly to the levels supported by current linguistic theory. Other aspects of usability will remain limited only by the creative capabilities of NLP designers.

Section G

Artificial intelligence and the airline industry

28

Globe-trotter

An intelligent flight itinerary planner

Prasanta K. Bose, Gautam Biswas and Adithya M. Rao Padala

Editor's note *Globe-Trotter is an intelligent system that helps harried travelers with dynamic flight itinerary planning. Globe-Trotter is an example of an application to a "moving target" problem, the kind of problem characterized by lots of uncertainty and susceptible to small event changes. The system itself was modeled on travel agent/client interactions, where agents gather more and more information about client constraints and preferences by asking questions and testing hypotheses. In fact, Globe-Trotter mimics travel agent dialogue as it interacts with users.*

Many knowledge-based systems deal with constraint-satisfaction problems. As the name indicates, solving such problems involves consistently selecting and operating with constraint sets. We can view flight itinerary planning as constraint satisfaction. Travelers must deal with constraints including flight schedules, ticket costs, connection times, and classes of travel. Such constraints are not independent; for example, travel dates and costs are related. Satisfying one constraint (say, minimizing cost) can conflict with satisfying the others.

Helping travelers plan itineraries involves reasoning with incomplete knowledge about each traveler's constraints. Moreover, interacting with individual travelers requires reasoning with dynamic information, since constraints can change as interaction develops. We will discuss Globe-Trotter, an interactive knowledge-based system that addresses both problems by using an assumption-based reasoning mechanism with truth maintenance. Globe-Trotter dynamically reformulates constraints based on information obtained while interacting with travelers, uses those reformulated constraints to plan individual itineraries that satisfy as many constraints as possible, and generates itineraries consistent with those constraints.

When communicating with users, Globe-Trotter must reason with incomplete knowledge about user intentions. It begins with a partial specification of constraints to be met, performs default reasoning to arrive at a plausible and more complete constraint set, [1] and generates a planned itinerary. Based on the results, users can then reformulate constraints to better suit their goals. Reasoning with incomplete knowledge regarding user intentions makes inference nonmonotonic, since users can contradict initial assumptions by adding subsequent information.

Simply put, interactive constraint-based problem solvers must address two basic issues simultaneously and effectively: first, eliciting individual problem constraints; second, given the above constraint set, generating a solution. Globe-Trotter's dialogue management scheme addresses both issues. In complex constraint-based activities, presenting users with intermediate (or alternative) solutions based on incomplete knowledge and reasonable assumptions is usually more efficient and less frustrating than having to answer numerous queries before the first solution is generated. Such solutions help users to understand their requirements and reformulate previous constraints to obtain more desirable solutions. In such scenarios, the problem solver must maintain a maximal set of consistent assumptions and constraints to accommodate users who alter their requirements. To address this task, we incorporated truth maintenance techniques into the problem solver. [2] The iterative process continues until users receive results they consider satisfactory.

We will overview Globe-Trotter; describe its itinerary-planning domain; examine the system's knowledge base structure and contents, reasoning system, and the itinerary generation process; briefly discuss related work; and conclude with some parallels and future plans.

A system overview

We modeled Globe-Trotter on travel agent/client interactions. Its dialogue with travelers emulates typical travel agent behavior. The system first obtains basic information about a traveler's needs—origin and destination points, constraints governing travel dates and times, and a planned return date. Using this information, the system hypothesizes plausible traveler models (for example, business traveler, vacationer, or another model best supported by the given information). Based on that model and user-supplied information, the system makes assumptions regarding user requirements and goals, thereby producing an augmented constraint set that will more completely specify user goals. Globe-Trotter then retrieves suitable flights from its large planning database by formulating a conjunctive database query from the constraint set, accessing flight-schedule and related databases, and selecting flights that meet user requirements. At the end of each itinerary generation cycle, the system displays user-specified constraints as well as ones arrived at through default reasoning. Users, now aware of the system's current scenario, can make desired changes for the next iteration. Figure 28-1 illustrates a typical Globe-Trotter interaction window.

The system automatically maintains justifications for the validity of assumed and derived constraints that constitute its current belief set about the user. If users respecify constraints, some justifications may be invalidated, and the system will derive a new constraint set. Truth maintenance activity is necessary, since the belief database changes as user goals change and new constraints are added. For example, if travelers initially plan to leave Wednesday and return Friday—but change their minds and decide

GLOBE-TROTTER
An intelligent flight itinerary planner

More above

List of possible flights

Relation: SCHEDULES Database: AIRLINE Cardinality: 40

ORIGIN	DESTINATION	DEP	ARR	ALN	NO	COST
DENVER _CO	BOSTON_MA	1600	2328	UA	296	260
DENVER _CO	BOSTON_MA	1535	2110	CO	94	260
DENVER _CO	BOSTON_MA	1535	2110	CO	94	260
DENVER _CO	BOSTON_MA	1610	2150	UA	368	260

4 tuples retrieved

Bottom of object

Would you like to reformulate any of the information given so far? (Y or N)	ORIGIN - DENVER-CO DESTINATION - BOSTON_MA DATE OF DEPARTURE - APR 5 DATE OF RETURN - APR 6 TIME OF ARRIVAL - AFTERNOON	type_of_traveler(weekend_vacationer) important(cost_of_travel) important(time_of_travel important(town_of_origin) important(town_of_destination)
Tell me what you want.	*User specifications*	*Believed assumptions*

CHOOSE WHAT YOU WISH TO DO

Fig. 28-1. Globe-Trotter's interaction window.

to leave Friday and return Sunday—the system revises its belief that they are business travelers and assumes that they are really weekend vacationers. Thus, constraints resulting from the assumption that they are business travelers become invalid, and new constraints must be generated. A new itinerary consistent with the weekend-vacationer belief set is then retrieved. Moreover, the system must maintain alternate contexts representing different intentions that users may express. This allows users to move back and forth between plans in an incremental fashion. If users change their plans for traveling on Friday and revert to their original intention of leaving on Wednesday, the system should recall information defining the prior context, make any changes that subsequent information may cause, and continue planning from that point onward (as elaborated elsewhere). [3]

Globe-Trotter's functional architecture Figure 28-2 illustrates Globe-Trotter's overall architecture. The system's two primary functional components are ARMS (the assumption-based reason maintenance system developed by Bose [4]) and RTMS (the relational table management system). Globe-Trotter uses ARMS for assumption-based reasoning and truth maintenance. Based on deductive computation, the ARMS problem-solving component resembles a deductive retrieval system (Prolog, for instance)—but differs in that ARMS explicitly labels data as "facts" and "assumptions," and can make deductions from both. Another difference is that deductions can be goal-directed (backward chaining) or data-directed (forward chaining). When assumptions entail a fact, those assumptions must be consistent with the global set of believed facts and the context in which they are made—resulting in a restricted version of default reasoning.

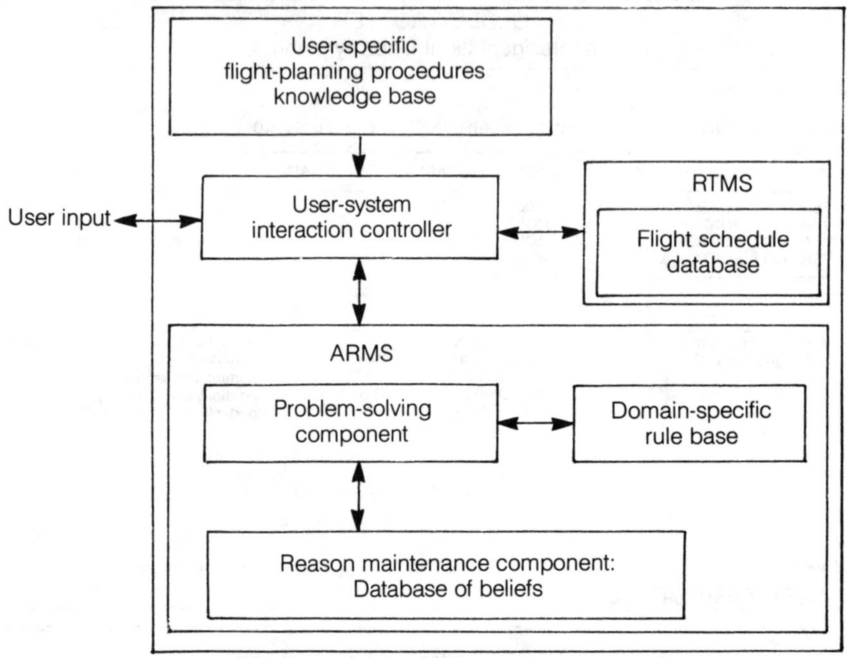

Fig. 28-2. Globe-Trotter's architecture.

Facts and assumptions that the problem solver uses to deduce a new fact are supplied to the reason maintenance component by the interface (user specified) or the problem solver (derived), which maintains dependencies and the belief status for all facts and assumptions. DeKleer details theoretical and computational aspects of an assumption-based truth maintenance system (ATMS). [5] It suffices for us to know that explicitly representing dependencies between beliefs enables the system to enforce consistency, resulting in a coherent dialogue. The reason maintenance component also provides capabilities for maintaining multiple contexts, and has the functionality to provide explanations for believed facts. ARMS runs on the TI Explorer and is implemented as an extension to the TI Explorer Prolog programming environment.

RTMS, used by the Globe-Trotter system to store flight information, is a relational database tool available on Explorer. [6] We will further describe the functions of FIG. 28-2's architectural blocks in due course.

Globe-Trotter's interface Globe-Trotter's current prototype splits the screen into four distinct panes during interaction—the interaction pane, the result pane, the display pane, and the user pane (see FIG. 28-1):

- The interaction pane is a Lisp listener (a window that runs the Lisp command loop) on the screen's lower left, where most user/system interactions take place.
- The result pane, a mouse-scrollable pane displaying a set of solution flights, enables users to scroll at their convenience through those flights. The result

pane maintains a complete history of viewed flights so that users can scroll back to an earlier set of flights. Travelers can select flights by clicking the mouse to the left of a chosen flight. They can also choose a flight from any solution set displayed, and are not restricted to choosing a flight from the current solution set.

- The display pane contains assumptions the system has used for the current solution set. Users can alter assumptions, after a solution set has been displayed, by keying in the serial number of the assumption they wish to change and then making the desired change. Currently, users cannot access fields in this window with the mouse; adding this feature will allow future users (with the mouse pointer) to click on an assumption and alter it.
- The user pane displays information that users have explicitly stated in the interaction. Users can reformulate any of this information after each solution set is presented.

The problem domain

Let's examine the travel-planning domain, constraints in that domain, and relationships between those constraints. For clarity, we will formally define our terms, their semantics in the problem domain, and their role in problem solving.

Terminology *Constraints* pertain to user requirements and intentions regarding features available on airline flights. The entire set of constraints in the domain defines the *context space* of problem-solving activity. The constraint set modeling a user's current needs is called the *active context*. A set of assumptions defines a *context*. In its entirety, the context comprises these assumptions and additional *assertions* having valid justifications in the context. Assertions in a context can be *premises, abductive premises, assumptions*, and facts deduced from them.

A premise is an assertion that is always believed to be true. For example, today's date (say, Sunday, May 14, 1989) is a premise because it holds for all interactions taking place on that day—as are propositions like "June 7, 1989 is a Wednesday," "Kennedy International and La Guardia are airports in New York City," and "Lufthansa Airlines flies out of Frankfurt, West Germany." In other words, premises are true for all contexts and do not change during interaction.

Abductive premises are valid or believed true until contradicted by users who add information to the existing set of true beliefs. They become part of the globally believed set of facts, but lose their belief status once information contradicting them is added to the global database. For example, for travelers wishing to start a journey tomorrow (given that the current date is May 14, 1989), the system generates two abductive premises: (1) "the travel date is Monday, May 15, 1989," and (2) "the date of departure is less than a week from today." The system uses the former to generate an RTMS query for extracting flights from the database, and the latter to derive further characteristics about the user.

Assumptions represent statements that are valid or believed true if they are consistent in the context of other premises and assumptions. Assumptions also represent plausible constraints that the problem solver chooses for reducing the search space. When starting an interaction, for example, Globe-Trotter makes assumptions like "the origin of travel is the same city in which the interaction is taking place" and "the month of travel is the current month." Furthermore, if travelers want to fly to New York City, choosing the destination "La Guardia Airport" would be an assumption focusing the flight selection process. Such assumptions define the current active context, and maintain their validity because no assertions exist to the contrary. The addition of further constraints to the search space reduces the computational task in selecting appropriate flights from the system's large flight database, thereby improving overall efficiency.

The system can deduce certain propositions regarding travelers from available information and previous assumptions. For example, if a traveler wants to start a trip on Monday and return on Wednesday, the system deduces that the traveler is probably a business traveler; that is, his travel is for business purposes and not a vacation.

ARMS's problem-solving component usually makes assumptions when it tries to execute rules during inference. Some rules may have one or more of their antecedents predicated by the metapredicate *assumable*, as the following example shows:

```
R-23:if (assumable(type-of-travel(business-pleasure))),
            (not(important(cost-of-travel))),
     then (class-of-travel(business-class)).
```

An individual inference is associated with an explicit set of dependencies, which are a set of premises, derived facts, and assumptions made in order to produce that inference. A valid *justification* represents supporting arguments for believing a specific assertion in the context. The justification for a fact is a 3-tuple; for example,

[<assumptions> <in-facts> <out-facts>],

where <assumptions> represents assumed predicates directly influencing this inference, <in-facts> represents facts and rules used in deriving this fact, and <out-facts> represents facts that are not believed true in the active context (but if any of them were to become true in a subsequent context, the current fact would no longer be considered true). This resembles support-list justifications used in the Doyle TMS. [2]

Given the above rule (R-23) and the following context of facts and assumptions,

P1: *assumed(type-of-travel(business-pleasure)),*
P2: *not(important(cost-of-travel)),*
P3: *important(cost-of-travel),*
P4: *class-of-travel(business-class),*

where assumption P1 and abductive premise P2 define the active context, justification for P2 is

[{ }, { }, {P3}],

whereas justification for the derived fact P4 is

[{P1}, {P2,R-23}, {P3}].

Problem-specific constraints. Travelers can make various choices when selecting flights, resulting in many possible constraints, some of which follow:

- Origin and destination,
- Departure date and time,
- Arrival date and time,
- Return date,
- Cost and class of travel,
- Preferred airline, aircraft type, meals, seating area,
- Number and location of desired stopovers.

Since most travelers do not explicitly state all this information before they request reservations, airline ticketing agents or travel agents must query travelers for relevant data and preferences.

Relationships between constraints Constraints are related to each other. The choice of certain constraints places restrictions on the choice of others. Consider a traveler who wishes to fly on a Boeing 747 from New York to Columbia, South Carolina. Clearly, the traveler would expect the problem solver to consider origin and destination constraints more important than aircraft type, and would rather see a set of non-747 flights from New York to Columbia than 747 flights to Europe. In such cases, the problem solver has the relatively easy task of making an assumption that will hold valid for all travelers—except, perhaps, a rich maverick.

However, if a traveler wishes to fly on an American Airlines Boeing 737 from Dallas to New York—and if American does not fly 737s between Dallas and New York—the agent faces a rather difficult decision. Until the agent understands why the traveler wishes to travel on a specific airline and aircraft type, the agent cannot accurately predict which constraint the traveler will choose to relax when both cannot be satisfied simultaneously. To accomplish this, one needs a mechanism for recognizing and resolving conflicts. ARMS's reason maintenance component serves this function by maintaining internally consistent contexts.

Travel agents base most of their knowledge on a clear understanding of travel domain constraints, how these constraints relate to each other, and options that must be considered when certain constraints cannot be met. If one considers all possible constraints at once, and does not place limits on how many connecting flights travelers are willing to take to get to their final destinations, flight itinerary planning falls into the class of NP-hard problems. Therefore, the system's problem-solving component must incorporate in its reasoning processes the travel agent's understanding of the domain and use it to make intelligent assumptions. These assumptions further constrain the problem, thereby reducing the solution search space.

Globe-Trotter's knowledge base

Globe-Trotter derives its intelligent behavior from its knowledge base, which models travel agent knowledge. Let's examine some representational aspects and contents of that knowledge base. Globe-Trotter contains the following types of knowledge:

- Initial knowledge about surroundings,
- Domain-specific expert knowledge,
- User-specific procedural-planning knowledge.

Globe-Trotter's initial knowledge about surroundings refers to information regarding the time and place of interaction, which helps it to assign certain default values to variables. It makes these values visible to users during interactions. The system highlights default alternatives it has chosen, making it easier for users to understand the active context (that is, the constraint set with which the system is working). In fact, if users consider system choices satisfactory, they can simply type "exit" and the system generates the flight itinerary. Internally, Globe-Trotter stores this information as abductive premise assertions.

ARMS's deductive programming language represents domain-specific expert knowledge as if-then rules based upon heuristics that travel agents use in arriving at plausible models of user intentions. A typical rule would be

```
R-8: if (type-of-travel(business)),
     then ( (important(time-of-travel)),
              (important(duration-of-travel)),
              (important(town-of-origin)),
              (important(town-of-destination)),
              (not-important(cost-of-travel)) ).
```

ARMS's problem-solving component uses such rules in a forward-chaining mode to augment the context with constraints that make user goals more explicit. The knowledge base contains rules to (1) classify travelers as belonging to a specific type, (2) associate plausible characteristic constraints pertinent to various types of travelers, and (3) characterize qualities governing particular itineraries.

Globe-Trotter applies its user-specific procedural-planning knowledge to generate appropriate plans for users. These planning procedures—called planning knowledge sources (planks)—are represented as Prolog rules and indexed by constraint sets. Planks are used to

- Generate RTMS queries from constraints in the active context,
- Resolve ambiguities with users,
- Give users additional information about travel.

For example, the procedure governing business and pleasure flights will incorporate knowledge about early ticket purchase. If the travel date is more than seven days away, the system informs users of advance-ticket-purchase advantages. If the travel date is less than seven days away, the system suggests that postponing the journey will make the trip more economical.

The following typifies a triggering rule for planks. ARMS represents the triggering rule as

```
R-33:if (important(cost-of-travel),
            travel-date(?P)
            airlines-preferred(?ALN),
            destination(?D),
            origin(?O) )
     then (planks(min-cost,travel-date(?P),origin(?O),
            dest(?D),cost(?C))).
```

Antecedent arguments prefixed by "?" represent variables; consequent goal execution leads to Prolog procedure executions attempting to minimize cost and fulfill other constraints related to the preferred airline. The above rule sets up triggering conditions for planks; that is, when all of the above rule's antecedent conditions are believed in the active context, the planks procedure is executed. The net result is the formulation and execution of a query to the relational database of flights. [7]

Reasoning with constraints The set of premises, assumptions, and deduced facts form Globe-Trotter's constraints. Each constraint is represented as a predicate clause and has a corresponding justification list. The system begins with F-0, which is the set of default assumptions initially in effect. The following exemplifies a possible F-0 subset:

P1: *place-of-origin(present-town),*
P3: *month-of-departure(present-month),*
P5: *week-of-departure(present-week).*

These predicates are stored as abductive premises; that is, they are believed true unless travelers explicitly specify otherwise. For example, the justification list for P3 would be

[{ } { } {P4}],

where P4 is the assertion *month-of-departure(other-month).*

We acquire the next constraint set—constraints asserted as abductive premises—from user specifications. Thus, if users specify that they desire a flight reservation returning on the same weekend, abductive premise P7 is added:

P7: *return(same-weekend).*

The justification for P7 is

[{ } { } {P8,P9}],

where P8 and P9 are

P8: *return(same-week),*
P9: *return(same-month).*

P8 and P9 have null justifications; therefore, they are not believed to be true. This corresponds to OUT nodes in the Doyle-style justification-based TMS system. [2]

System-generated constraints result from forward-chaining deductions based on user-supplied information and other believed facts in the active context. For example, if users specify that departure and arrival times are important, the following abductive premise is generated:

P10: *important(time-of-travel).*

Given that the following rule exists in the knowledge base—

R-6: if *(assumable(important(time-of-travel)),*
assumable(important(cost-of-travel))),
then *travel-plan(equal-priority),*
type-of-travel(business-and-pleasure)—

the system chains forward from P10 using rule R-6. But first, it makes the following assumption:

P12: *assumed(important(cost-of-travel)),*

and adds two assertions. The first states that the travel plan gives equal priority to time and cost; the second states that the trip probably includes both business and pleasure. The justification for each of these deduced assertions will then be

[{P12} {P10,R-6} {P11,P13}],

where P11 and P13 are nodes representing belief in the unimportance of travel time and cost, respectively. If either assertion becomes valid, and is added in the same context where P1 and P9 are believed, then the conclusions will no longer have valid justification and, therefore, will have to be retracted. A more detailed account of constraint formulation and reformulation appears below.

The reasoning process

When planning itineraries, travel agents constantly deal with incomplete knowledge in the form of constraints that travelers do not state explicitly. However, travelers expect travel agents to consider these constraints while constructing travel plans. Travel agents must also use their domain knowledge and develop a methodology to drive their interaction with travelers. To focus agent/traveler dialogue correctly, the active context plays an important role during their interaction. Globe-Trotter bases its reasoning process on constructing contexts as a set of user constraints and using these to choose suitable flights from the airline database.

While interacting with travel agents, travelers often alter their original requirements. Such alterations necessitate a review of prior assumptions to ensure they remain consistent with a traveler's present needs. As discussed earlier, ARMS's truth maintenance mechanism enables the system to revise its beliefs about users.

Reasoning with incomplete knowledge When solving problems with a large solution space, we must often make assumptions that lead to deductions constraining the search space. User-supplied constraints may be incompletely specified, requiring that the reasoning process make further assumptions to reduce search space to a reasonable size. Due to changes in user needs, however, some assumptions may lead to later contradictions and may have to be rejected when assimilating new information provided by users. To search and reason with incomplete knowledge in this manner, each individual fact derived from other facts and assumptions must have those facts and assumptions explicitly recorded as justification for believing that individual fact. Should assumption A1, which holds good at time T1, be found contradictory at time T2—then facts that exist based on A1 can, at time T2, be considered incorrect beliefs. Such a framework prevents the system from following fruitless search paths more than once, and also helps the system make dynamic updates to the belief database. [2], [5]

Globe-Trotter's inference process hinges on assumption-based reasoning and truth maintenance techniques. User requirements and intentions translate to constraints or assertions defining the active context. Further assumptions and deductions better define the active context, which is then used to develop a specific database query for the retrieval of appropriate flights from the flight database.

Reasoning with changing constraints As discussed earlier, user constraints may change as interaction proceeds. We can formalize this as a dynamic-belief-update problem. ARMS's reason maintenance component monitors the active context. Any information added by users (or inferred by ARMS's problem-solving component) that has a dependency relation with assertions in the active context leads to revision of the active context. The system then uses constraints in the revised context to guide interaction and generate the travel plan.

To illustrate some aspects of the above revision process, consider the following subset of rules from ARMS:

```
R-8:  if (type-of-trip(business)),
      then (important(time-of-travel)),
              important(duration-of-travel),
              not-important(cost-of-travel),
              important(town-of-origin),
              important(town-of-destination).
R-12:if (assumable(round-trip)same-week)),
              assumable(important(date-of-travel))),
      then (type-of-trip(business)).
R-21:if (assumable(round-trip(same-weekend)),
              assumable(important(date-of-travel))),
      then (type-of-trip(business-and-pleasure)).
R-21:if (assumable(round-trip(same-month)),
              assumable(important(date-of-travel))),
      then (type-of-trip(business-and-pleasure)).
R-24:if (type-of-trip(business-and-pleasure)),
      then (important(time-of-travel),
              important(cost-of-travel),
              important(town-of-destination)).
R-27:if (important(duration-of-travel)),
      then (onward-flight-stopover(minimum)).
R-29:if (round-trip(P)),
      then one-of(round-trip(same-week),
                round-trip(same-weekend),
                round-trip(same-month)).
```

Now, adding user information that a round trip is desired within the same week—that is, by Friday (the weekend is not included)—leads to the addition of abductive premise P5:

P5: *round-trip(same-week).*

Making the assumption *important(date-of-travel)* and chaining forward leads to the execution of rules R-12, R-8, R-27, and R-29. The system uses R-29 to set up a non-monotonic justification for abductive premise P5, stating that P5 is believed in the absence of belief regarding the statement that the round trip includes the weekend or is within the same month. The system makes these derived beliefs part of the active context, which now comprises the following constraint assertions:

P5: *round-trip(same-week),*
P10: *important(date-of-travel),*
P11: *type-of-trip(business),*
P12: *important(time-of-travel),*
P13: *important(duration-of-travel),*
P14: *not(important(cost-of-travel)),*
P15: *onward-flight(stopover(minimum)).*

If users now change their minds and decide to return on the weekend, abductive premise P5 loses its belief status and assertion P6 is added to the current context, as follows:

P6: *round-trip(same-weekend).*

As a result of truth maintenance, the previous active context undergoes revision. Assertions in active context defined by assumption P5 and deduced fact P11 can no longer be supported. Rules triggered because of forward chaining on P6 cause a different active context, defined by P6 and P10, with the following set of believed constraint assertions:

P6: *round-trip(same-weekend),*
P10: *important(date-of-travel),*
P21: *type-of-trip(business-and-pleasure),*
P22: *important(time-of-travel),*
P23: *important(cost-of-travel).*

The system can revisit the previous context without further recomputational effort if users change their minds and reassert P5.

Travel plan generation Globe-Trotter's main control program is implemented in ZetaLisp. As system/user interaction progresses, new facts and assumptions are constantly added to the existing belief database. ARMS monitors the active context driving the interaction process.

A user command causes active-context assertions to trigger a procedural-planning knowledge source that, upon execution, generates an action plan. The end result is a database query representing context constraints. Evaluation of the query in the flight database produces a set of flights as well as the binding of other uninstantiated constraint variables that best satisfy active-context constraints. Control is then passed back to the interaction process, which checks for further user reformulations and cycles through the complete process again. This iteration continues till users select a flight.

Database query generation RTMS (Explorer's relational database that stores flight schedules) enables control by a set of Lisp functions. [6] A typical RTMS query—generated from constraints to obtain American Airlines flights between Dallas and Columbia, South Carolina, that depart Dallas between 10 a.m. and 3 p.m. and cost less than $450—has the following form:

```
(rtms-retrieve schedules
project (origin destination dep arr cost)
where ((AND
    (=origin "DALLAS-TX")
    (=destination "COLUMBIA-SC")
    (< cost 450)
    (AND ( < dep 1500) (> dep 1000))
    (=aln "AA")))
format (15 15 5 5 10 10 ))
```

Further, the query specifies that only the attributes origin, destination, departure time, arrival time, and cost be displayed and that this display be in the prescribed format.

The *project clause* is given an attribute list that corresponds to flight information the user is interested in seeing. The *format clause* governs the manner in which this list is depicted. The *where clause*—by far the most important clause—is generated by the triggered planning-knowledge source from travel constraints that are believed within the active context. The where clause allows the composition of relational operators. The operators can be logical (AND,IMPLIES,EQ) or numeric (LESS-THAN,GREATER-THAN) comparators; they are used (1) to specify constraints on data to be retrieved, and (2) to represent the range of possible travel constraints adequately.

Conclusions

Numerous AI researchers have addressed reasoning mechanisms that aid in formulating user queries to databases. [8] However, they have emphasized natural language aspects; that is, determining user plans and goals from a natural language query made to a system. Thus, semantic interpretation of natural language queries has been a major concern.

On the other hand, we have emphasized the development of a reasoning mechanism that enables the system to handle incomplete user constraint specifications—applying default assumptions and user-supplied constraints to deduce additional constraints, thereby reducing a large search space. The net result has been the generation of an effective query that satisfies most user needs and triggers an efficient search of a large relational database. Our research has developed and implemented an integrated knowledge-based environment that applies an assumption-based reasoning mechanism for interactive knowledge-based retrieval from a large database in constraint-oriented problem domains.

Globe-Trotter is an intelligent travel planner that interacts with users, helping them find specific flights based on a set of operating constraints. Whereas many constraint-based problem-solving systems assume that all constraints accumulate before and do not change during the problem-solving process, Globe-Trotter presents an atmosphere enabling users to view and select what they actually want. The system's problem-solving process makes assumptions about users and their possible needs, and incorporates an interaction methodology enabling dynamic formulation and reformulation of constraints. The reasoning framework's use of assumption-based reasoning and truth maintenance techniques enables the system to handle incomplete knowledge of a user's travel intentions—essential for providing intelligent assistance to users in an interactive fashion.

Many problem domains exist in which a similar constraint-based approach can be applied. When buying a car, for example, most people first limit their search by using important considerations such as cost, size, and gas mileage. Next, they consider additional constraints—desired features such as sunroofs and stereos. Dealers offer many different cars and various "deals," making car selection an interesting domain for constraint-based problem solving. Similarly, we can find parallels in such tasks as purchasing homes, planning robot paths, and choosing constraints for job-shop scheduling in manufacturing processes.

We plan to address several such problems, one of which involves context evaluation. At any stage during interaction, more than one assumption can be made that will lead to the splitting of contexts; consequently, we need some means for deciding which is more specific or relevant to the active context. [9] Another important problem involves modeling constraint relaxation within the current representational framework—required because a query to the flight database may be overconstrained and, therefore, will not return a plausible travel plan.

Acknowledgments

We implemented Globe-Trotter on an Explorer Lisp machine at the Texas Instruments Computer Science Center in Dallas, Texas. In part, our work reflects Adithya M. Rao Padala's MS thesis research at the University of South Carolina.

References

1. R. Reiter, "A Logic for Default Reasoning," *Artificial Intelligence*, Apr. 1980, pp. 81 – 132.
2. J. Doyle, "A Truth Maintenance System," *Artificial Intelligence*, Nov. 1979, pp. 231 – 272.
3. A. Rao, *An Expert System for a Constraint Based Problem—Globe-Trotter: An Intelligent Personal Flight Planner*, MS thesis, Department of Computer Science, University of South Carolina, Columbia, S.C., June 1986.
4. P.K. Bose, "ARMS: An Assumption-Based Reasoning Tool in a Logic-Programming Environment," *Third Int'l Conf. Data and Knowledge Bases*, Morgan Kaufmann, Los Altos, Calif., 1988.
5. J. DeKleer, "ATMS: An Assumption-Based TMS," *Artificial Intelligence*, Mar. 1986, pp. 127 – 162.
6. S. Corey and M. Rajinikanth, "Explorer Relational Table Management System," *Proc. Advanced Systems Track Section TI-MIX Int'l Computer Symp.*, ACM, New York, N.Y., 1985.
7. M. Rajinikanth and P.K. Bose, "A Logical and Semantic Front-End to a Database System," *Proc. Int'l Symp. Methodologies Intelligent Systems*, Knoxville, Tenn., 1986, pp. 103 – 111.

8. B.L. Webber, "Questions, Answers and Responses: Interacting with Knowledge Base Systems," in *On Knowledge Base Management Systems*, M.L. Brodie and J. Mylopoulos, eds., Springer-Verlag, New York, N.Y., 1986.
9. D.L. Poole, "On the Comparison of Theories: Preferring the Most Specific Explanation," *Proc. Ninth Int'l Joint Conf. Artificial Intelligence*, Morgan Kaufmann, Los Altos, Calif., 1985, pp. 144–147.

29

GATES
An airline gate assignment and tracking expert system

Robert P. Brazile
Kathleen M. Swigger

Editors' note *GATES is a knowledge-based system that assigns gates to arriving and departing planes. It is currently in use at John F. Kennedy (JFK) airport in New York by Trans World Airlines (TWA). It represents a system concept and solution to a problem that is manually very intensive and for which heuristics do in fact exist. (Reprinted, with permission, from the Summer 1988 issue of* IEEE Expert. *© 1988, IEEE. All rights reserved.)*

We will describe GATES, an expert system that assigns gates to arriving and departing flights at New York's John F. Kennedy International Airport (JFK). GATES uses flight information and knowledge about current constraints to produce possible gate assignment schedules. System operators can modify schedules by retracting rules, adjusting tolerances, and deleting information. We developed the system for a PC, thereby providing an efficient and flexible user environment. Our approach is extensible to various engineering and industrial problems where limited resources and weakly defined constraints exist and in which scheduling must occur.

Most airline companies generate new flight schedules every quarter, and sometimes as frequently as every month. They prepare these schedules using information about airport gate configuration to ensure that valid gate assignments can be made. The flight schedules are then transmitted to individual airports that use the information to produce daily flight schedules containing flight numbers, arrival and departure times, and aircraft identification numbers.

Once daily flight schedules are prepared, ground controllers assign specific flights to specific gates. At airports having few gates and many flights, gate assignment is a nontrivial problem. Gate assignment is equally difficult where many planes arrive and depart at the same time (the hub concept). The amount of activity occurring during these specific times overloads scarce resources—congested taxiways, for instance, or service personnel and equipment. Gate assignment then becomes a task of allocating flights to gates while not violating resource constraints.

GATES captures knowledge and procedures used by an experienced ground controller who solves gate allocation problems daily. Trans World Airlines (TWA) uses this system at JFK. In its current form, GATES assists ground controllers in preparing monthly and daily gate schedules.

Related research

Bellman et al. have intensively investigated scheduling problems including job shop scheduling, project scheduling, and assembly line balancing. [1] Most often, researchers have used mathematical programming techniques to solve these problems. Mark Fox, who studied the scheduling problem more recently using constraint-directed reasoning, suggests that some scheduling problems can be solved using AI techniques. [2] His assertion has been tested in other areas, such as managing and automating process planning and scheduling functions. [3], [4]

A separate but related research area concerns using AI techniques to solve planning problems. Build [5] and Strips [6] exemplify two early planning systems. Both generated plans enabling robots to perform certain tasks. Like scheduling, planning involves opportunistic action as opposed to always following a preprogrammed, fixed operational order. [7] As researchers have suggested, [8] planning and scheduling are closely linked: Planners generate a list containing several possible operational sequences. Selecting one sequence over another, and assigning operations to specific tasks, is commonly called *scheduling*. Together, they produce acceptable solutions to problems.

Similarly, GATES combines planning and scheduling to assign planes to specific gates. As in other scheduling tasks, identifying time, cost, and personnel constraints is extremely important. We have tried to identify constraint categories that could be useful for other scheduling problems.

Problem description

Gate assignment problems can be divided into two highly related problem areas. The first involves creating quarterly (or monthly) schedules. Once a month, operators receive lists of flights for their airport, from which they prepare daily gate assignments for the month. Time is not a critical element. The average ground controller requires 10 to 15 hours to prepare a gate schedule, depending on the time of year.

The second problem area occurs when schedules are interrupted by unanticipated events such as bad weather, mechanical failure, late arrivals, and so forth. In such situations, ground controllers have only minutes to rearrange existing gate assignments that will accommodate incoming planes. Time replaces optimality as the most critical constraint whenever daily schedules must be changed in real time. Experienced ground controllers become expert at adjusting gate assignments quickly (our GATES expert has over 14 years of scheduling experience).

One gate assignment strategy attempts to formulate gate scheduling as an optimization problem using an integer linear programming model. Some airports currently use this method to produce monthly schedules. Unfortunately, linear programming proved too slow for JFK. For example, for a total of 100 flights that must be assigned to 30 gates—if a 0-1 variable is assigned to each possibility—the number of problem states is 2 to the 3000th power. Most likely, no polynomial algorithm exists for solving the general constraint satisfaction problem. [9] Moreover, the random nature of constraints and ground controller preferences makes gate problem solutions nondeterministic. Prolog's descriptive, logic-based, and nondeterministic nature—plus its ability to backtrack—enables one to obtain a deductive database using facts and rules to represent gate-scheduling constraints. Consequently, we selected the Prolog language for GATES. We developed a small prototype using Prolog and, based on its success, designed and implemented a more extensive system.

The solution process

GATES is a constraint satisfaction expert system. [10] It has production rules guiding search, can tell users why it chose specific gate assignments, and produces an audit trail of rules it used in reaching conclusions. GATES does not use confidence factors. It does have a user interface enabling clients to change rules and data and to perform "what if" analyses.

The GATES problem solver consists of two logic levels: The first produces the standard daily schedule that is used as the "initial" plan; the second adjusts the daily gate schedule in real time as information about flight delays, weather changes, and equipment failures becomes available. As input, the standard gate scheduler uses flight schedules and known constraints. Initially, flights are not assigned to gates. At the completion of the process, all flights are assigned to gates and no conflicts exist. The second-level problem solver (that is, the reassignment process) uses the current gate schedule plus any new constraints or changes to the flight schedule as input. If changes to the flight schedule result in conflicts, then GATES adjusts the gate schedule to resolve them.

First-level problem solution—the constraints

Five different constraint categories exist for gate assignment. We determined the relative importance of each, and list them below.

1. Constraints without exceptions—Some gates have physical constraints prohibiting them from servicing certain aircraft types. For example, a gate may be too small to accommodate a 747. Obviously, such restrictions cannot be relaxed under any circumstances.
2. Constraints with exceptions—These can be violated under some conditions. As a general rule, domestic flights arrive and depart at domestic gates and international flights arrive and depart at international gates. However, some service both international and domestic flights. In addition, the general rule can be

relaxed for special cases such as allowing domestic flights to arrive at international gates if they "turn" to international departures. Finally, international flights receive special priority during gate assignment because their passengers must go through customs.

3. Constraints with changing tolerances—The time required to park an incoming aircraft, service it, and ready it for departure varies for different aircraft types. To avoid conflicts between incoming and outgoing flights using the same gate, gate schedulers must consider the total time needed to perform these tasks as a constraint. However, there are "desired" times, "minimum" times, and "Well, if we have to, we'll make this assignment because everything will probably change anyway" times affecting gate assignment.
4. Guidelines—A single taxiway feeds several gates. We should avoid multiple arrivals and departures for gates served by the same taxiway within the same time frame. Clearly, relaxing this guideline can create congestion problems.
5. Convenience constraints—Most airplanes arrive and depart on the same day. Although the intervening time between arrival and departure may be several hours, every effort is made to keep a plane at its gate and to limit the number of times it must be moved from the gate and back again. Ground crews appreciate minimizing these moves; however, a plane can be moved if another plane needs that gate.

Although our final system will adapt to new knowledge and new constraints, the initial GATES version sought to implement sufficient constraints to produce an acceptable schedule. That is, its major requirement was to produce a schedule acceptable to our expert.

Production rules

To make its decisions, GATES uses two types of production rule, permissive rules and conflict rules. Permissive rules determine when it's appropriate to consider a particular gate for a particular flight and permit the system to search the next level of rules to obtain an assignment. They also rule out gates that are unacceptable choices for a flight, thereby accelerating the selection process. An example of such a rule would be—"If the flight is not continuing, then it is acceptable to consider remote gates for this flight." Simply put, this means that if no departure time is listed for the flight, we can assume the plane will "layover" at the airport. GATES then assigns the plane to overnight parking. This exemplifies rules using convenience constraints to make assignments. A Prolog version of this rule might resemble the following:

```
gateok(G,F):-not(continue(F)),
   remote__gates(L),member(G,L).
```

The symbol ":-" can be read as "if" and the commas between atoms as "and." A literal English translation of the above rule would be—"Gate G is okay for flight F if F is not continuing, if L is the set of remote gates, and if G is a member of L."

Conflict rules determine when particular flights cannot be assigned to particular gates. An example of this type of rule would be—"Gate 2 cannot service 747-type aircraft." This exemplifies rules using constraints without exceptions; as such, it cannot be set to inactive by users whenever they do "what if" analyses. An example of this type of rule would be

```
conflict(2,F):-flight__plane(F,P),ptype(P,747).
```

An English translation of this rule would be—"Gate 2 has a conflict for flight F if P is the plane used by flight F and if P is a 747-type aircraft."

Tolerances

Tolerance levels are time intervals that the schedule maintains throughout deduction. A special conflict-type-rule subcategory uses tolerance levels to determine appropriate gate assignments. For example, one tolerance level is the time interval between departing flights and arriving flights using the same gate. Airlines estimate that it takes 15 minutes to perform this interchange—that is, 15 minutes is generally enough time for a departing flight to clear the gate before an arriving flight approaches the gate. Tolerances used in conflict production rules implement constraints with changing tolerances. The following exemplifies a conflict rule using a tolerance level:

```
conflict(G,F):-
        assign(G,F1),
        depart__time(F1,T1),
        arrive__time(F,T),
        T1<T,
        dptarv(I),
        timeadd(T1,I,X),
        X>T.
```

This rule states that a conflict exists on gate G for flight F if some other flight F1, already assigned to gate G, has a departure time of T1 that is within the departure/arrival time interval tolerance of flight F's arrival.

GATES sets (or defaults to) initial tolerance levels during its first attempt to produce a gate schedule. If this first attempt is unsuccessful, or if an alternative assignment is desired, then GATES will automatically adjust tolerance levels. Tolerance levels can be set by GATES or preset by individuals using the system. Users can set tolerance levels dynamically, while the system is running, through the user interface. Users can also make other changes—they can assign flights to gates, unassign flights from gates, or specify that flights cannot be assigned to specific gates. Once tolerances are adjusted, users can either restart the entire gate assignment process or resume assignment from where the system was interrupted.

Priority operation

GATES prioritizes flights and gates by first assigning those flights and gates that have the most constraints. For example, only a few gates are equipped to service wide-bodied aircraft. Therefore, wide-bodied planes are processed first. Nearly all gates can accommodate 727-type aircraft, whereas only a few gates can accommodate 747-type aircraft. Therefore, 747s are assigned before 727s. When considering the next gate assignment, GATES seeks unassigned flights that have special characteristics limiting their assignment.

Gate assignment is also prioritized according to gate characteristics and location. For example, some gates are close together and require special attention. In most cases, aircraft using these gates cannot safely taxi to the gate but must be towed. Since towing involves additional time and resources, GATES gives these types of gate assignment lower priority.

Gate assignment

Gate assignments are made when no permissive rule, conflict rule, or tolerance level is violated. If all flights have been assigned to gates after one pass, the process terminates. If some flights cannot be assigned, then GATES deactivates optional rules or reduces noncritical tolerance levels. GATES may unassign some flights and try again to assign all flights. Thus far at JFK, GATES has successfully assigned all flights to gates.

GATES also maintains (1) a list of permissive rules allowing assignments to be made, (2) conflict rules that prevent assignments from being made, and (3) tolerance levels in effect at any given moment. At the end of deduction, operators can ask why a specific assignment was made or not made. Whenever a gate schedule is displayed, active rules and tolerance levels are also displayed.

Operators can also assign or reassign flights to gates as well as change tolerance levels and active rules. A simple window/menu interface enables operators to adjust any value at any time during scheduling. Operators can try various "what if" scenarios and note the different schedules generated under different conditions.

The GATES data representation

GATES organizes its data under two main predicates. One stores the flight schedule. The second produces actual gate assignments. We used three criteria when designing these data structures. First, they had to store and retrieve information efficiently. Second, they had to be flexible and easy to modify through a user interface. Third, they had to be in a format that could be generated from the airline's existing database. The final GATES version extracts current flight schedules and aircraft information stored on the airline's large database. It uses this information, along with updated flight information, to make ongoing assessments and changes. Based on these requirements and features available in Turbo-Prolog, we designed a pair of database predicates to store assigned and unassigned flights. A database predicate in Turbo-Prolog can be "asserted" into the database.

GATES builds the first predicate—"unsch"—from the initial flight schedule data. This predicate is defined as

```
unsch(plane,flight1,arrival.time,
   flight2,departure.time)
```

where plane is the identifier for the actual aircraft or aircraft type assigned to these flights, flight1 is the arriving flight number of a continuing aircraft, and flight2 is the flight number of the departing flight for this aircraft. Arrival time and departure time are the scheduled arrival and departure times for these flights. If an aircraft is scheduled to depart but not to arrive, or to arrive but not to depart (that is, to layover), then the flight number for the nonexistent portion is set to zero.

The data structure includes variables for flight1 and flight2 of the same aircraft because most aircraft continue to other cities (and are called continuation flights). Therefore, it is very important to assign both segments of continuation flights to the same gate. One data structure includes this information to avoid extensive search later in the program. Since only a few flights do not have a continuation portion, GATES handles these rare cases as exceptions.

The second database predicate—"adsch"—represents the arrival and departure schedules, plus their gate assignments, and is defined as follows:

```
adsch(gate1,gate2,plane,flight1,arrival.time,
   flight2,departure.time)
```

where gate1 is assigned to the arriving flight, and gate2 is assigned to the departing flight. Other parameters listed in this data structure resemble those described for the "unsch" predicate. Again, either variable for the flight numbers can be set to zero.

GATES looks through "unsch" database predicates to determine which unscheduled flight to assign. If it can assign a flight, it retracts the "unsch" entry for that flight and asserts the flight under an "adsch" entry along with its gate assignment. If it can assign a gate to only one of the flight pair, it retracts the "unsch" entry, asserts an "adsch" entry for the successfully assigned flight, and asserts another "unsch" entry for the unassigned flight. Whenever an arrival time changes, GATES can either retract the "adsch" entry for that flight and assert an entry in "unsch" with the new time, or it can rebuild the entire "unsch" data structure. Since assignment takes about 30 seconds to run, several alternative solutions may be explored before selecting the final solution.

Reassignment—the second level

GATES receives information from the airline database regarding the current status of arriving and departing flights. When a flight deviates from its schedule by some threshold value, GATES knows that the current gate assignment may require modification. If modification must occur, GATES checks the assignment to see if the change creates any new conflicts. If not, the schedule remains unchanged. GATES reassigns the questionable flight if conflict exists, using default rules and tolerances to reassign the deviant flight. For example, GATES may deduce that another gate is available at the same time and that all other assignments will be unaffected by this change. If this modification is successful, GATES makes the gate assignment and asks the user to confirm it. If GATES cannot resolve the conflict, it must take further action. It can either retract all assignments and reassign the entire schedule, or it can resolve the conflict by changing assignments minimally.

If the user decides to reschedule using minimum changes, GATES identifies the specific conflicting gate assignments where changing only one secondary (previously unchanged) flight will resolve the conflict. If such a case exists, GATES tries to reassign the secondary flight to another gate. This process continues until no conflicts exist or until all cases of this type have been examined and no single flight can be reassigned. It may then be necessary to examine combinations of two, three, or more gate changes to resolve a single conflict. The rescheduling activity occurring during this phase depends on the amount of time the operator specifies. If GATES cannot resolve the conflict within the specified time, it asks the operator to determine the new gate assignment.

The GATES reassignment process is being implemented at JFK. Tests thus far indicate the system can assign flights in five to 10 seconds that were not assigned previously due to conflicts or undesired assignments.

Prolog has proven effective and flexible in describing constraints and rules controlling schedule generation. GATES evolved from about 100 lines of Prolog code in its initial prototype to over 1000 lines of code with about 100 different Prolog predicates in the current system. TWA, handling about 100 to 115 flights per day at its JFK terminals, uses GATES to assist ground controllers. GATES accesses TWA's database for the current day's schedule and creates gate assignments in about 30 seconds. Previously, that scheduling task took an operator between 10 and 15 hours to prepare manually—and then as much as an hour to modify each morning.

As the program has grown, we have added several software engineering tools to better organize the rules and the inferencing process. Two of the more helpful tools are a data dictionary for the Prolog predicates and a special "list" function that displays predicates in the order they are used.

Thus far, the system has been well received. It presently assists ground controllers in preparing TWA's quarterly gate schedules for JFK airport. The daily scheduler will soon be fully operational and ready for test and evaluation. Future work on this project will expand the user interface to handle additional graphics. We also want to add a feature enabling us to capture daily changes the operator makes to computer-generated schedules. If these changes can be analyzed and incorporated into GATES, then—like its human counterparts—GATES can learn from experience.

Acknowledgments

Our work was supported in part by a grant from Trans World Airlines, Kansas City, Missouri. This article's preparation was supported in part by the Office of Scientific Research.

References

1. R. Bellman et al., *Mathematical Aspects of Scheduling and Applications*, Pergamon Press, Elmsford, N.Y., 1982.
2. M.S. Fox, *Constraint-Directed Search: A Case Study of Job Shop Scheduling*, PhD dissertation, Carnegie Mellon University, Pittsburgh, Pa. 15213, Dec. 1983.
3. B.R. Fox and K.G. Kempf, "Complexity, Uncertainty, and Opportunistic Scheduling," *Proc. IEEE Conf. Artificial Intelligence Applications*, Computer Society, 10662 Los Vaqueros Circle, Los Alamitos, Calif. 90720, 1985, pp. 487–492.

4. B.R. Fox and K.G. Kempf, "A Representation for Opportunistic Scheduling," *Proc. Third Int'l Symp. Robotic Research*, MIT Press, Cambridge, Mass., 1986.
5. S.E. Fahlman, "A Planning System for Robot Construction Tasks," *Artificial Intelligence*, Vol. 5, No. 1, 1972, pp. 251–288.
6. R.E. Fikes and N.J. Nilsson, "Strips: A New Approach to the Application of Theorem Proving to Problem Solving," *Artificial Intelligence*, Vol. 2, Nos. 3/4, 1971, pp. 189–208.
7. E.D. Sacerdoti, *A Structure for Plans and Behavior*, Elsevier North-Holland, New York, N.Y., 1977.
8. R. Wilensky, *Planning and Understanding*, Addison-Wesley, Reading, Mass., 1983.
9. A.K. Mackworth and E.C. Freuder, "The Complexity of Some Polynomial Network Consistency Algorithms for Constraint Satisfaction Problems," *Artificial Intelligence*, Vol. 25, No. 1, 1985, pp. 65–73.
10. B.G. Buchanan and E.H. Shortliffe, eds., *Rule-Based Systems: The MYCIN Experiments of the Stanford Heuristic Programming Project*, Addison-Wesley, Reading, Mass., 1984.

Section H

Artificial intelligence and the legal system

30

Expert systems and the law

Federal regulations and potential litigation pose dangers to a budding business

Edward Warner

Editors' note *If an expert system makes a really big mistake, who is liable for damages? The developer, the domain expert, and/or the user? There are a variety of legal questions that surround the design, development, evaluation and application of knowledge-based systems. This paper explores these thorny issues. The debate about liability and related issues has only just begun; new legal precedents are occurring frequently. Warner identifies many of the most pressing questions. (Reprinted, by permission, from the 1988 issue of* High Technology Business. *© 1988, Infotechnology Publishing Corporation. All rights reserved.)*

The stock market crash of 1987 revealed the darker side of computer automation. According to a government commission, the October free-fall was caused partly by computerized program trading, in which brokers' computer programs constantly compare the difference between the price of commodities futures and stocks. These price differences can change so fast that only computers can react quickly enough to take advantage of them. When stock prices started their dive, however, the system began feeding on itself, spinning the market out of human control and approaching what the chairman of the New York Stock Exchange later called a "meltdown."

The brokers of Black Monday readily delegated those buy/sell decisions to a computer program, but society at large is uneasy about using computers to make, or even give advice about, high-risk decisions. Nonetheless, software is becoming available which can do just that. These programs, called "expert systems," contain the knowledge of experts in a field and the logical rules those experts follow to solve a problem. Expert systems can advise a doctor on which medicine to prescribe for a patient's symptoms, tell an auditor how tax law might apply to a budgetary line-item, or decide in seconds whether a radar blip is an enemy rocket or a meteor—a task they will tackle for the Star Wars program.

No one questions the utility of spreading expert knowledge, but what happens when an expert system makes a mistake? What will be the reaction when, for example, a glitch in the software causes a prescription program to specify the wrong medicine? Unlike program-trading software, which brokerage houses developed themselves, expert systems are being produced both for internal corporate use and for sale to third parties. Sales of expert systems leaves someone to blame, and some observers say the greatest obstacle to the spread of such systems is fear of litigation.

Nowhere is the concern over product liability stronger than among companies working on expert systems for medical applications, where malpractice suits already abound. "I know of interesting endeavors that never came to light because of liability problems," says Dr. Braxton Degarmo, owner of the Medical Software Consortium, a St. Louis supplier of medical software. Degarmo participated in a U.S. Army/NASA effort to develop an "intensive-care stretcher," an unmanned emergency room for use on space vehicles. The stretcher would have monitored patients' vital signs and its expert system would have responded to changes in their condition with treatments such as drug injections. A medical-products company, he recalls, was ready to produce the stretcher's hardware, but balked at getting involved with the software because of concerns about the potential for lawsuits.

Expert systems consultant Tom J. Schwartz also knows of a medical expert system that was stalled because of legal doubts. The system's producer "sank a couple of man-years [of development time] into it and, when they looked at the cost for liability insurance, they said 'no way'," recalls Schwartz.

Litigation worries, says Degarmo, are particularly strong at universities, which are among the centers of medical expert systems development. A case in point: the Caduceus medical expert system at Carnegie-Mellon University in Pittsburgh, 17 years in development and still awaiting commercialization.

Despite these fears, the Health Industry Manufacturers Association predicts that, in the next 10 years, the biggest changes in health care will come from software. Expert systems "still haven't reached the capacity in the health-care system that their potential would indicate," says association president Frank E. Samuel, Jr.

Expert systems will also be widely used in the corporate sector. Boiler manufacturer Combustion Engineering of Stamford, Conn., for example, uses an expert system to collect the knowledge of its best designers, speeding the design process and easing the transition when designers leave the company (see "Success Story," September 1988). Coopers & Lybrand, the accounting firm, has a system that dispenses tax advice to its auditors, and Honeywell-Bull sales representatives use an expert system to configure customers' computers by simply entering the customers' needs. By one analyst's estimate, about half of the companies listed in the *Fortune* 500 are developing expert systems.

Expert systems will also be sold commercially. Louis Robinson, publisher of the *Spang Robinson Report on Artificial Intelligence* newsletter, believes expert systems will one day be so prevalent that computer companies will routinely include them with their hardware the way they bundle-in software today.

However, lawyers warn that before expert systems become commonplace they will probably become ensnared in the widening web of product-liability litigation. According to the Brookings Institution, the number of product-liability lawsuits increased eightfold from 1974 to 1986, when 13,595 such cases were filed. One reason is the increasing number of lawyers who specialize in computer-related issues, up from 100 in 1980 to 1,100 in 1985.

Mixing these numbers with a slug of hyperbole, consultant Schwartz warns, "There's 200,000 lawyers out there waiting for an expert system to kill a little old lady—and they're going to sue everybody in sight."

Of course, a suit does not automatically mean a loss in court. "The likelihood is that there would be many suits, but few judgments" against expert systems, predicts Richard Neely, a judge in the West Virginia Supreme Court of Appeals and an expert on product liability. But no expert-system producer wants to be the first to be saddled with a hefty judgment, and all expert systems producers worry that everyone's insurance rates will soar after the first company loses a suit. "A lot of people are waiting for that first test case," says Degarmo.

That first case is still over the horizon, so legal experts are looking closely at other lawsuits involving similar electronic products. In 1986, the U.S. Supreme Court upheld a $350,000 decision against Dun & Bradstreet, which provides credit information on U.S. companies, in a libel suit brought by a Vermont builder whose reputation was harmed by erroneous information from Dun & Bradstreet's computerized database. In 1982, NCR Corp. suffered a $2.3-million adverse judgment when a California court ruled that Glovatorium Inc., a dry cleaner, had been defrauded when NCR computers did not perform as promised.

Computer programs usually come with disclaimers that deny responsibility if the software fails to work as promised, but lawyers say these disavowals will offer little refuge when the summons hit the fan. Glovatorium's lawyer, Richard Perez, says he won his case despite several disclaimers in the NCR contract. One reason disclaimers carry little weight is that most software buyers never sign the enclosed license-agreement cards, notes Dan Shafer, editor of *Intelligent Systems Analyst*, a newsletter.

Eventually, something stronger than a disclaimer may be needed. In June, the House Energy and Commerce Committee approved a bill that would make companies liable if they fail to provide an adequate *warning* about hazards posed by their products.

Should an expert system user suffer damage, there will be no shortage of parties to blame. Experts say possible lawsuit targets may extend from the user to the programmer, the supplier, and even the expert whose knowledge went into the program. In determining who is at fault, lawyers say a great deal will hinge on whether the system lets the user make the final decision. Pointing to a case where an automatic radiation-therapy machine inadvertently dispensed lethal overdoses (see "Federal Rules on Expert Systems," p. 35), Ed Miller, director of the Food and Drug Administration's compliance division for radiological products, says "the reason [the overdose] could occur was an attempt to make the system more user friendly." Unfortunately, expert systems may be needed in situations where equipment is more sophisticated than the typical technician.

Another indicator of blame, lawyers say, is whether the software is found to have a "bug," or programming error. The prevalence of bugs, even in software involved in life-and-death decisions, is indicated by a recent FDA report that says bugs were behind 79 of the 84 computer-product recalls the agency initiated between 1983 and 1987. Judge Neely believes that bugs, not an expert's errors, pose the greatest potential for litigation against any type of software. Once customers come to expect a certain level of performance from any program—for instance, that it will add and subtract correctly—then a failure to meet that performance level "is like making a Buick with a wheel that falls off," he says.

No software company has yet lost a lawsuit brought over a bug, however. In 1986, Lotus Development Corp. was sued by a Florida construction company that claimed a bug in Lotus' 1-2-3 spreadsheet program caused the builder to overbid on a contract. Lotus blamed user error, and the case was settled out of court in Lotus' favor. But Boston-area lawyer Peter Marx, chairman of the New England Computer Law Forum, thinks the Lotus case is only the first in a wave of such suits. Marx warns that the courts will be increasingly inclined to hold programs to the strictest standard of liability.

Not only will expert systems need to be bug-free, they will also need to leaven their specialized knowledge with common sense. That may be very hard to do, says B. Chandrasekaran, director of the artificial intelligence research lab at Ohio State University. He points out that common sense consists of simple rules that everyone knows—such as the fact that two objects cannot occupy the same space—but also of other rules that have yet to be recognized. If we don't know all the rules of common sense, he asks, how can we program an expert system to think as intelligently as a human does?

Expert system vendors challenged in court will probably claim that their products are the equivalent of textbooks. Howard Kramer, assistant director for market regulation at the Securities and Exchange Commission, says computerized investment advisers are no different than any other research report. But consultant Schwartz disagrees. "Our society puts more stock into what a computer says than what a textbook says," he says. "Computers give interactive knowledge."

Software makers may also claim that expert systems are still an inexact science. But that defense is also not expected to hold water. Predicting the weather may seem equally inexact, but three years ago the courts ordered the U.S. government to pay $1.25 million to the survivors of four fishermen who perished in an Atlantic storm. The men had relied on an inaccurate National Weather Service forecast.

Software companies that make expert-system shells—the software used to develop an expert system—or that develop expert systems only for their own internal use, may think they don't have to worry about liability suits. But many lawyers say their sense of security may be illusory. If a product fails because it was built on a flawed structure, that structure may be held liable. Expert systems built by a company only for its own use are less vulnerable, provided they affect the company's operations alone. But corporations could be held accountable to their customers or employees. The federal government, for example, is required to maintain an accurate database of information on its employees; the Privacy Act of 1974 lets federal workers who lose out on a promotion or raise because of errors in the data sue for damages.

Apart from the liability issue, expert systems also raise the question of who owns the knowledge in them. Dennis Deutsch, a computer lawyer in Hackensack, N.J., represents a client who provided the expertise for an expert system as part of his job. The client has since lost that job, but wants to receive royalties on the system he created.

"My client is claiming the system is owned by him in the absence of a contract" to the contrary, says Deutsch.

To avoid ownership challenges, Deutsch says, "the employer must have an adequate pre-employment contract" with the expert whose knowledge is written into the program. Other steps that could help reduce the risk of litigation include

- accurately representing the system's abilities,
- creating a program that merely recommends particular actions, instead of acting on its own,
- avoiding software bugs,
- making sure disclaimers are legible, understandable, and likely to be signed,
- obtaining liability insurance.

Despite the multitude of legal issues, few observers expect expert systems to wind up in the same dog house as nuclear power. Indeed, several expert systems are already in use.

For example, the Help system at Latter Day Saints Hospital in Salt Lake City assists doctors throughout the hospital in interpreting patient data, such as lab tests. According to Dr. Homer Warner, who led the system's development, the Help software is involved in approximately 80,000 decisions a day, and has improved the medical care of half a million patients in the 20 years since it came into use.

To reduce the risk of liability, the system was thoroughly tested and makes only recommendations, says Warner. In fact, Warner believes medical "expert systems are going to be the answer to litigation," by keeping doctors from making the errors that lead to suits.

Clearly, there are times an information-bearing product is so important that its utility must be recognized, litigation or not. This was the case with Jeppesen Sanderson Inc., a Denver company that converts government data into aircraft flight charts. After Jeppesen lost a major lawsuit in which its products had been blamed for an aircraft crash, the U.S. Congress took the unusual action of promising to indemnify Jeppesen if the government's data ever proved to be at fault. The action indicated the charts' value to the nation's air-traffic system, says company president Horst Bergmann.

Lawyer Marx believes a good next step would be for the courts to endorse the benefits of expert systems by subjecting them to a more forgiving liability standard. "We want to encourage people to innovate," he says.

The trade-off between benefits and risk will probably depend on how badly an expert system is needed. In poverty-stricken parts of the Third World, points out Ellen Staelen, a senior consultant at International Data Corp., a medical expert system could provide emergency advice, even for non-doctors. "When there's such a deplorable lack of resources," in these regions, she says, "one would hate to see the lawyers hold sway."

The public, not the experts, will ultimately decide the value and risk of expert systems, through lawsuits and regulations. Such decisions may involve a willingness to accept some level of danger. As a comparison, researcher Chandrasekaran wonders what would have happened to the automobile if, at its introduction, someone had warned, "Here's a technology that's going to kill 50,000 people a year."

31

A case-based approach to modeling legal expertise

Kevin D. Ashley
Edwina L. Rissland

Editors' note *This paper describes Hypo, an expert system that helps lawyers identify and apply precedent cases. Hypo compares past cases to the present case and then assesses the degree of relevance. Hypo uses a technique known as "case-based reasoning" to make the comparisons. The paper is reprinted here because it represents a successful attempt to integrate advanced systems concepts—like case-based reasoning—into systems intended to provide intelligent support to users. (Reprinted, with permission, from the Fall 1988 issue of* IEEE Expert. *© 1988, IEEE. All rights reserved.)*

Law is an excellent domain for studying case-based reasoning. Expert system designers use case-based reasoning to capture expertise in domains where rules are ill-defined, incomplete, or inconsistent. As an indispensable supplement to reasoning deductively with legal rules, attorneys and judges reason analogically with precedent cases; rule predicates are simply not sufficiently well-defined for them to infer correct decisions deductively. In fact, one "right answer" seldom exists to legal questions. Legal experts make competing arguments instead, pitting conflicting interpretations of cases and facts against each other.

Hypo, a computer program that performs case-based reasoning in the legal domain, helps attorneys analyze and make arguments about new fact situations in terms of the most relevant precedent cases. To perform this task, indexing and retrieving relevant cases are not enough. Hypo must make factual comparisons of cases relative to the problem situation and determine the legal significance of comparisons in terms of arguments about the problem situation.

We will describe techniques that Hypo employs to compare cases, choose the best cases for evaluating, and construct arguments about a new fact situation. In particular, we will demonstrate how Hypo critically compares a problem situation (called the current fact situation, or cfs) to the most relevantly similar precedent cases (called most-on-point cases, or mopcs) to outline an argument regarding how to decide the cfs based on its significant similarities to and differences from mopcs.

Hypo's main tool for this task is the "claim lattice" mechanism. A claim lattice projects the case knowledge base (CKB) onto the problem situation to create a neighborhood of cases surrounding the problem situation in which the above comparisons become explicit. We will present a detailed example of a claim lattice actually generated by Hypo to analyze a real legal case.

Neighborhoods of cases

Hypo has a CKB of leading cases in trade secrets law and a dimension-based indexing scheme for retrieving cases that share important features with a problem situation. Beyond indexing and retrieving relevant cases, however, Hypo must also organize cases in terms of their relevance for making or responding to arguments about problem situations. Attorneys cannot adequately evaluate problem situations without drawing certain symbolic connections among relevant cases in terms of their comparative

1. Factual similarities and differences relative to the cfs: Which cases are more on point (that is, share more features with the problem situation) and which cases are less on point than other cases?
2. Outcomes: Of the cases that are most on point to the problem situation, how do their outcomes compare? If comparably on-point cases have conflicting outcomes, what are their differences relative to the problem situation?
3. Uses: In a legal argument about the cfs, which cases make stronger legal points for a party on a claim? Which are troublesome to an argument? Which distinguish other cases? And which take a point to extremes?
4. Potential relevance to the cfs: Which cases are nearly on point or most on point but for some missing facts that might jog the attorney's mind to look for and discover new facts and arguments about his cfs?
5. Significance to other parts of the legal argument: What are the cases and connections when the cfs is viewed from the slant of a different kind of legal claim?
6. Possible variations: What new cases and connections come into view when the facts of the cfs are changed hypothetically? How do the connections change when features are added, subtracted, exaggerated, or combined with those of neighboring cases?

In effect, an attorney conceptually organizes relevant cases into a neighborhood of cases more or less on point to the problem situation, some with desirable outcomes and some not, some especially useful for responding to others and some only potentially so. Within the context of the relevant-case neighborhood, small changes in problem situation facts can push the situation closer to one precedent and farther from others, with significant results in the ways that cases can be cited and responded to in arguments.

Hypo uses claim lattices to represent the conceptual neighborhood of cases. Claim lattices allow Hypo to exploit connections among relevant cases arising from comparisons relative to the cfs. A claim lattice projects the CKB onto the cfs to create the neighborhood of cases surrounding the problem situation. The case neighborhood is the CKB as seen modulo the cfs. To analyze the cfs, claim lattices (1) organize and abstract all relevant cases from the CKB, (2) place them in a graph according to their comparative similarities and usefulness as precedents for arguing how to decide the cfs, (3) focus on troublesome contrary cases, and (4) suggest fruitful combinations of facts for new hypotheticals.

Knowledge representation in hypo

Hypo uses two kinds of domain knowledge to construct claim lattices: (1) the CKB containing actual legal cases, and (2) the library of dimensions. Hypo's current CKB contains 30 or so cases on trade secrets misappropriation and a few related areas including basic contract law. Our references provide a complete description of the Hypo program. [1] Other researchers place less or no emphasis on representing and indexing cases and hypotheticals, instead employing generalized fact patterns, [2] if-then rules, [3], [4] or formal logic. [5] McCarty's early work emphasized adversarial reasoning and hypothetical reasoning. [6], [7] More recently, he has focused on deontic logic for representing permissions and obligations. [8]

Each legal case in the CKB corresponds to a real legal dispute, tried by a court, whose decision as reported in a published opinion is represented in a case representation language consisting of hierarchical clusters of frames (implemented as flavors) describing main components of the case including plaintiff (*pi*), defendant (*delta*), legal claim, prevailing party (plaintiff or defendant), holding, and facts. Some factual features are in turn expanded and represented as frames (for example, plaintiff, products, employees, disclosure events, secret information, and agreements); our references provide examples. [1], [9] A legal claim is a recognized kind of complaint for which courts will grant relief (for example, breach of contract, negligence, trade secrets misappropriation, and copyright infringement). A holding is the court's decision as to the legal effect on each claim of the case's facts, either in favor of the plaintiff or defendant.

A cfs is represented in the same case representation language as the cases in the CKB. From this basic level of a fact situation's representation, Hypo computes whether certain higher level descriptors called factual predicates are satisfied. Factual predicates state whether or not a particular legal fact is true (for example, "there exist disclosees" and "employee has switched employers") in a fact situation. Factual predicates form a language used to encode the second source of legal knowledge in Hypo; namely, the dimensions.

Dimensions capture the legal relevance of a fact cluster to a claim's merits. For a particular kind of case, dimensions generalize collections of facts that constitute strengths and weaknesses in a party's position. Each of the generalizations can be backed up by one or more cases where a court held in favor of a party, in part because of the fact cluster associated with the dimension. Dimensions allow Hypo to view the cases from various perspectives. They can be thought of as "cross sections" of a case's facts, emphasizing important features from the viewpoint of a particular legal claim.

At this point, we have implemented 13 dimensions in Hypo, although we know about 30 dimensions in all for the trade secrets and related-contracts domains. We do not compile these ourselves, but take them from scholarly analyses and treatises. [10], [11] Figure 31-1 shows examples of some potential strengths and weaknesses in a trade secrets situation and dimensions that capture them.

A dimension is also a frame-like knowledge source. It has several facets enabling Hypo to perform various tasks: First, the program can test if a dimension applies to a case or is a near miss using the dimension's prerequisites (stated in terms of actual predicates). For instance, the prerequisites of the Bribe-Employee dimension are that

The plaintiff's position is strengthened to the extent that

Brought-Tools: The plaintiff's former employees brought the plaintiff's notes, diagrams, tools to the defendant.
Competitive-Advantage: The defendant's access to the plaintiff's secret information gave the defendant a competitive advantage.
Disclose-Secrets: The plaintiff did not voluntarily disclose his secrets to outsiders.
Noncompete-Agreement: The plaintiff's employees had entered into nondisclosure agreements.
Bribe-Employee: The defendant bribed the plaintiff's employees to switch employment.
Vertical-Knowledge: The plaintiff's secrets were not simply about customer business methods.

Fig. 31-1. Sample dimensions and related factual strengths.

two corporations (plaintiff and defendant) complete with respect to a product; the plaintiff has confidential product information to which the defendant has gained access by luring the plaintiff's former employees to work for the defendant and to disclose that information. Second, Hypo compares cases along a dimension using the dimension's focal slots. The Bribe-Employee focal slot is what the defendant offered the plaintiff's employees to lure them to switch employment; its range is a set of possible enticements including salary increases, stock options, bonuses, promotions, or no enticement. To strengthen the plaintiff's position in a fact situation to which this dimension applies, add more enticements for inducing employee defection. Third, Hypo finds similar cases by retrieving cases that the dimension indexes. Bribe-Employee indexes at least two cases in the CKB: (1) Telex vs. IBM (in which the court held for plaintiff IBM's trade secrets claim where Telex had offered stock options, higher salaries, and bonuses—one for $500,000—to IBM's employees); and (2) the Midland Ross case (in which the defendant won, even though the former employee gained a modest salary increase in switching employers). Our references provide other examples of dimensions. [1], [12]–[14]

Representing case neighborhoods with claim lattices

When we present a cfs in the case representation language to Hypo for analysis, Hypo runs through the library of dimensions and produces a case analysis record containing (1) applicable factual predicates, (2) applicable dimensions, (3) near-miss dimensions, (4) potential claims, and (5) relevant cases from the CKB. Near-miss dimensions are those for which some (but not all) prerequisites are satisfied. The combined list of applicable and near-miss dimensions is called the D-list. For illustration, FIG. 31-2 describes a cds based on Telex vs. IBM, a real case in the CKB. Figure 31-3 shows the case analysis record for the cfs.

An attorney's corporate client (IBM) complains that Telex has been misappropriating trade secrets with respect to IBM's Merlin disk-drive system. Specifically, IBM complains that

• Telex offered IBM's Merlin project engineers large salaries, stock options, and bonuses (one for $500,000) as inducements to join Telex (Bribe-Employee).

• All former IBM employees had entered into nondisclosure agreements with IBM to keep IBM's trade secret information confidential (Noncompete-Agreement).

• Because of its access to IBM trade secrets, Telex developed its competing products in substantially less time and at lower expense (Competitive-Advantage).

Fig. 31-2. The cfs based on Telex vs. IBM.

Applicable factual predicates: exists-corporate-claimant, exists-confidential-info, employee-switched-employers, and so forth
Applicable dimensions: Agreed-Not-To-Disclose, Bribe-Employee, Competitive-Advantage
Near-miss dimensions: Brought-Tools, Disclose-Secrets, Vertical-Knowledge
Potential claims: Trade secrets misappropriation, breach of nondisclosure agreement
Relevant CKB citations: Midland Ross, Data General, Structural Dynamics, Raycorp vs. Tronic, Modern Controls

Fig. 31-3. A case analysis record for the cfs.

Hypo uses the case analysis record to construct the claim lattice in which (1) the root is the cfs together with its D-list, and (2) successor nodes contain pointers to cases that share a subset (usually proper) of the dimensions in the cfs D-list. Figure 31-4 shows the claim lattice actually generated by the Hypo program for analyzing FIG. 31-2's cfs from the viewpoint of a trade-secrets-misappropriation claim (a separate claim lattice exists for each possible claim.)

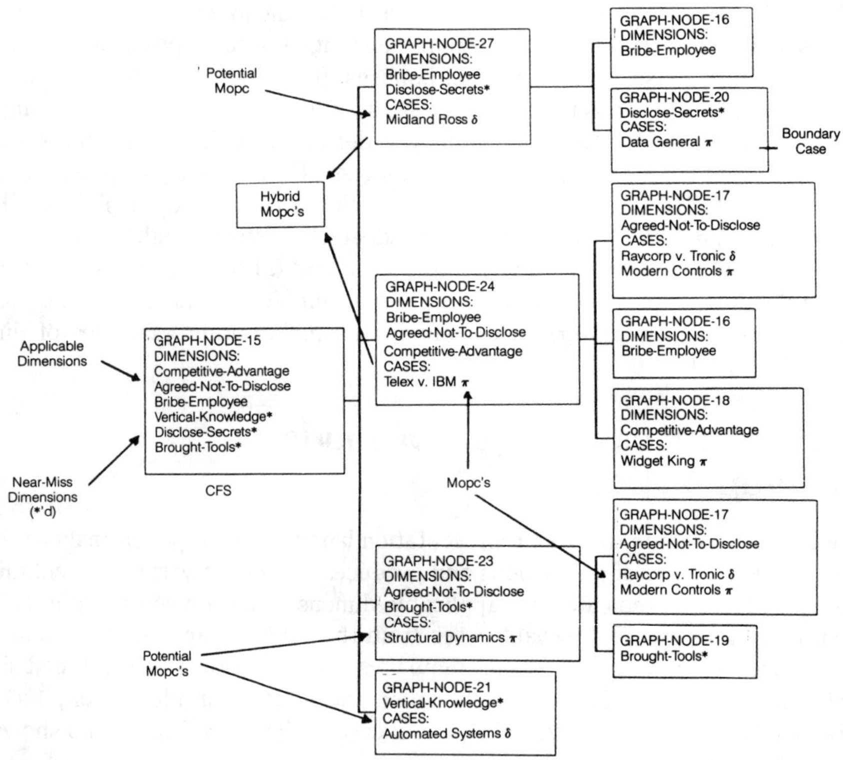

The root node represents the cfs and its D-list (asterisks indicate dimensions that are near misses as to the cfs). Successor nodes contain pro-plaintiff or pro-defendant cases, involving trade-secrets-misappropriation claims, that are on point to the cfs. Nodes closest to the root that do not have near-miss dimensions contain mopcs; otherwise, they may contain potential mopcs. Leaf nodes are least on point. Each major lattice branch that contains mopcs represents one way of arguing about the cfs. Mopcs may be counter examples to cases with opposite outcomes in successor nodes. Boundary cases exemplify extremes along particular dimensions. Hypothetical hybrid mopcs combine features of different mopcs that hold for plaintiff and defendant. Potential mopcs suggest fruitful hypothetical variants of the cfs. (Hypo generated Figure 4's graphical segments.)

Fig. 31-4. A claim lattice.

Primarily, claim lattices order relevant cases from the CKB in terms of how on point they are to the cfs, which is measured by the degree of overlap between cfs dimensions and those of retrieved cases. In other words, the claim lattice captures the extent that cases share cfs strengths and weaknesses. More specifically, of all dimensions in the cfs D-list, only those in a particular successor node's D-list (a subset of the cfs D-list) apply to each case associated with that node. Each successor node is the ancestor of all nodes whose dimensions are proper subsets of the successor node's subset. Claim lattices order these descendants according to the inclusiveness of their subsets of the cfs D-list. Each successor node may (1) contain pointers to more than one case, and (2) comprise cases won by plaintiffs and defendants.

Interpreting the claim lattice

A claim lattice's ordering scheme enables the lattice to capture a sense of closeness to the cfs of cases in the CKB, viewing relevant cases in terms of their "on-pointness" to the cfs. Computationally, this means that nodes closest to the root can be considered mopcs to the cfs (as long as their subsets of the cfs D-list do not contain near-miss dimensions); leaf nodes are the least on point. All displayed cases are relevant to the cfs because they all share some legally important strengths or weaknesses with the fact situation as represented by dimensions shared with the cfs.

Hypo judges dynamically which cases appear most on point. Even well-known landmark cases will not appear if they are not relevant to the cfs; for instance, if they don't share enough overlap of dimensions (and therefore facts), their decisions rest on factors not present in the current case. Likewise, a seemingly unimportant case might be very relevant modulo the cfs because it not only shares the same base of facts (and therefore dimensions) but it might also share more than any other case. This is shown in the claim lattice by positioning nearer to the cfs those cases sharing more dimensions.

Different major branches of the lattice correspond to different ways to argue the case, one way for each branch. Let's hypothesize that the user attorney seeks an argument for the defendant in FIG. 31-2's cfs. Hypo can argue the case for the defendant by citing a pro-defendant mopc. In the cfs claim lattice (FIG. 31-4), the mopcs are Raycorp vs. Tronic, Modern Controls, and Telex vs. IBM. (Of course, Telex vs. IBM is also the basis of FIG. 31-2's cfs. A case should be most on point on itself!) Of the three mopcs, only Raycorp vs. Tronic held for the defendant (*delta*), so Hypo cites that case in its argument. Midland Ross is not a mopc because, although it is very close to the root and was won by the defendant, the Disclose-Secrets dimension—which applies to Midland Ross and which would help the defendant if it applied to the cfs—is only a near miss for the cfs (as indicated by the asterisk next to Disclose-Secrets in FIG. 31-4).

Hypo produces the following argument, which favors the defendant as Side 1 on a claim for trade secrets misappropriation in the cfs:

[A] Side 1's point (defendant)—Cite Raycorp vs. Tronic: The defendant should win even though the employee who disclosed information signed a nondisclosure agreement with the plaintiff.

[B] **Side 2's response (plaintiff)**—Distinguish Raycorp vs. Tronic: In the cfs, the defendant's access to the plaintiff's product information saved it more time or expense than in Raycorp vs. Tronic and the defendant paid the plaintiff's former employee to switch employment.

Cite Modern Controls as counter example: This case is just as on point and held for the plaintiff where the employee who disclosed information to the defendant signed a nondisclosure agreement with the plaintiff.

In support of its point, Hypo draws the analogy between the mopc and the cfs. Since mopcs share the most legally important strengths and weaknesses with the cfs (that is, mopcs are the closest analogies to the cfs), Raycorp vs. Tronic is the most persuasive case Hypo could cite for the defendant as Side 1. Relevant similar facts are just those summarized by the dimension(s) that the mopc shares with the cfs. This case has but one shared dimension (Agreed-Not-To-Disclose). The argument point in [A] is not very strong, but it is well formed from a legal viewpoint.

Hypo also uses the claim lattice to figure out how to respond to an argument like Side 1's by citing counter examples to the cited case. In a legal argument, an attorney can discount the persuasive effect of a cited case by citing another case that is equal to or more on point but that held for the opponent. Finding such a case is a simple matter in the claim lattice; if it exists, it must be an mopc residing in one of the nodes between the root and the node containing the cited case (mopcs on other major branches of the lattice won't do—that would be like comparing apples and oranges). Mopcs in FIG. 31-4 occupying positions as counter examples are Telex vs. IBM, and Modern Controls, both of which held for the plaintiff (*pr*) and are equal to or more on point than Raycorp. In other words, Hypo makes Side 2's (the plaintiff's) response to Side 1's argument by citing the Modern Controls case as a counter example (see [B] above). It would be silly for Hypo to cite the Telex case in response because, for illustration, we have chosen Telex as the cfs. In supporting the response, Hypo underscores additional facts (if any) that make the counter example equal to or more on point than the case cited for Side 1.

The claim lattice supports other ways of responding to a point by distinguishing the cited case. Suppose Hypo cited the Midland Ross case on behalf of Side 1, as in the following exchange:

[C] **Side 1's point (defendant)**—Cite Midland Ross: The defendant should win even though the defendant paid the plaintiff's former employee to switch employment.

[D] **Side 2's Response (plaintiff)**—Distinguish Midland Ross: In the cfs, the defendant's access to the plaintiff's product information saved it more time or expense than in Midland Ross, and the Plaintiff's former employee entered into a nondisclosure agreement with the plaintiff. In Midland Ross, the plaintiff disclosed its product information to more outsiders than in the cfs.

In distinguishing, Hypo points out the "dis-analogy" between the cfs and Midland Ross by reciting unshared dimensions that help the plaintiff in the cfs or hurt the plaintiff in Midland Ross. Hypo points out that the facts associated with the Disclose-Secrets dimension obtained only in Midland Ross and not in the cfs (namely, that the plaintiff disclosed its secrets to outsiders). Also, in the cfs, the defendant gained a competitive advantage and the plaintiff's employee had entered into nondisclosure agreements. In other words, using the claim lattice, Hypo knows that (and why) the cfs presents a much stronger case for the plaintiff than does Midland Ross.

As the above examples illustrate, the claim lattice embodies (1) Hypo's knowledge of how to compare cases relative to the cfs, and (2) what the legal significance of those comparisons are in terms of arguments about the cfs. [12]

Hypo uses that knowledge to help attorneys build arguments; for example, by finding cases that, potentially, are most on point. A potential mopc closely resembles the fact situation, except that some dimensions (that is, strengths or weaknesses) that apply to it are near misses with respect to the cfs; they are located in nodes closest to the root whose subsets of dimensions contain near misses. Potential mopcs are useful (1) when fact-finding about the cfs, (2) when looking for cases to cite as counter examples to a particular mopc, and (3) when planning for the contingency that an opponent might be able to prove that missing facts are true. Figure 31-4 Midland Ross, Structural Dynamics, and Automated Systems cases are all potential mopcs. If it were true that the plaintiff in the cfs had disclosed his secrets to (let's say) 200 outsiders, Midland Ross would become a most important case to Side 1, allowing the defendant's point in [C] to be recast as follows:

[C'] **Side 1's point (defendant)**—Cite Midland Ross: The defendant should win where the plaintiff disclosed secrets to outsiders even though the defendant paid the plaintiff's former employee to switch employment.

[D'] **Side 2's response (plaintiff)**—Distinguish Midland Ross: In the cfs, the defendant's access to the plaintiff's product information saved it more time or expense than in Midland Ross and the plaintiff's former employee entered into a nondisclosure agreement with the plaintiff.

The point in [C'] is stronger than in [C] because the analogy between the cited case and the cfs is stronger. Correspondingly, the distinction in response [D'] is weaker than that in [D].

Alternatively, if the cfs were more like the potential mopc, Structural Dynamics, Side 2 would have an even stronger response to the point in [A], where it can cite the following more-on-point counterexample:

[B'] **Side 2's response (plaintiff)**—Distinguish Raycorp vs. Tronic: In the cfs, the defendant's access to the plaintiff's product information saved it more time or expense than in Raycorp vs. Tronic and the defendant paid the plaintiff's former employee to switch employment.

Cite Structural Dynamics as counter example: This case is more on point and held for the plaintiff where the employee who disclosed information to the defendant signed a nondisclosure agreement with the plaintiff and brought the plaintiff's product development tools to the defendant.

The claim lattice also focuses on another kind of extreme case; namely, boundary cases in which the plaintiff still won (or lost) despite the fact that, of all cases in the

CKB, they presented the weakest (or strongest) fact situations for the plaintiff along some dimension. A boundary case may not be as on point as a mopc, but it is still useful to Hypo as a counter. For instance, suppose in the cfs that IBM had made disclosures to 200 outsiders and that Side 1 had then cited the Midland Ross case, which would be a mopc for the defendant. In responding for Side 2, Hypo could also cite the following counter example (see FIG. 31-4):

> **[D'] (continued) Side 2's response (plaintiff)**—Cite Data General as counter example: This case held for the plaintiff even though the plaintiff disclosed to 6000 outsiders (more than in the cfs or Midland Ross).

The new response implies that, even had the plaintiff's behavior been much worse, it still should win. Here, Data General is used as an example of a much weaker case for the plaintiff along the Disclose-Secrets dimension (with disclosures to 6000 outsiders), but whose outcome still favored the plaintiff.

In the previous example, Hypo posed a hypothetical variation of the cfs (that IBM had made disclosures to 200 outsiders) to make a legal point about the connections between the Data General and Midland Ross cases. That is a natural thing for attorneys to do, and points out one of the most important uses of claim lattices: They suggest interesting hypothetical cases.

The claim lattice structure provides clues about how to "flesh out" sparse areas of the CKB, and suggests how to modify hypothetically either (1) actual cases, or (2) the cfs for constructing hypothetical cases and new connections between the cfs and its neighbors. Having located the cfs in its neighborhood of cases, Hypo uses hypothetical modifications to explore the neighborhood.

Interesting hypotheticals reside in two locales of the claim lattice: First, they reside in nodes containing potential mopcs, as the above hypothetical variant of the cfs suggests. Second, they reside between nodes containing mopcs.

Hypotheticals residing in nodes Using potential mopcs as targets, the cfs can be modified slightly to incorporate "missing" facts associated with near-miss dimensions; in FIG. 31-4, for example, (1) by adding disclosures as in Midland Ross, (2) by having former employees bring the plaintiff's product-related notes and copies of code as in the Structural Dynamics case, or (3) by making the secret information be vertical knowledge about the customer's business methods as in the Automated Systems case. Our references provide a more complete account of posing hypotheticals in Hypo. [1], [15]

Hypo uses hypothetical variants of the cfs to explain the potential mopcs' significance and to illustrate the hypothetical fact's effect on the argument. For example, if IBM did make such disclosures, not only would Midland Ross become an mopc, but Data General would also become potentially an even more on-point case that could be used to respond to an argument citing the Midland Ross case. Hypo makes these changes in possible arguments explicit by reconstructing the claim lattice around the modified cfs. Using the claim lattice to plan for contingencies in an argument is most practical. In the real Telex Corp. vs. IBM Corp., 367 F. Supp. 258, 358 (N.D. Okla. 1973), defendant Telex actually attempted to raise the issue of disclosures by IBM. In its opinion, the court cited another case involving disclosures by Midland Ross, but disposed of the defense on other grounds.

Hypotheticals between nodes Other interesting hypotheticals reside between nodes containing mopcs, and combine features of plaintiff mopcs with those of defendant mopcs. In pitting pro-plaintiff and pro-defendant features against each other, these hybrid mopcs implicitly raise the issue of which features are more important (that is, how such a case would be decided). In FIG. 31-4, an interesting hypothetical hybrid mopc combines pro-plaintiff features of the Telex case with pro-defendant disclosures of secrets as in the Midland Ross case. It happens to be the same hypothetical as above, but now we are changing the Telex case rather than the cfs.

Judges and attorneys actually use hypotheticals like this one. In his opinion in the Executive Development Center of Boston vs. Hirsch, Civ. Action 50441 (Suffolk Superior Ct. Mass. 1985), p. 28, Judge Young makes his point by constructing a similar hypothetical pitting the plaintiff's disclosures against the defendant's improper means of access. The hybrid hypothetical can be made even more interesting by pushing the number of disclosees to extremes (one disclosure or one million). [15]

Hypo can also use the claim lattice to view a fact situation from the perspective of other claim types. Figure 31-4's lattice depicts the cfs as a trade-secrets-misappropriation case. But, by virtue of the Agreed-Not-To-Disclose dimension, the cfs could also be thought of as involving a claim for breach of nondisclosure agreements entered into by employees. The claim lattice representing that claim is yet another projection of the CKB onto the cfs, this time creating a neighborhood of contracts cases organized along different dimensions like Agreement-Supported-By-Consideration but subject to the same interpretive methods as described above.

We have described a technique for dynamically viewing or reorganizing a CKB around a particular fact situation to provide a sophisticated analysis of that fact situation. Claim lattices project the fact situation through the CKB to create a neighborhood of cases, surrounding the situation, in which factual and interpretive comparisons of the cases relative to the situation become both simple and explicit. We have also described how the Hypo program uses claim lattices to (1) create skeletal legal arguments about fact situations, (2) spot troublesome contrary cases, and (3) suggest fruitful combinations of facts for new hypotheticals.

Acknowledgments

This work was supported (in part) by the Advanced Research Projects Agency of the Department of Defense, monitored by the Office of Naval Research under Contract No. N00014-84-K-0017; by University Research Initiative Award No. N00014-86-K-0764; and by an IBM Graduate Student Fellowship.

References

1. K.D. Ashley, *Modeling Legal Argument: Reasoning with Cases and Hypotheticals*, PhD dissertation (COINS Tech. Report 88-01), Computer and Information Science Dept., University of Massachusetts, Amherst, Mass., 1988.
2. A.vdL. Gardner, *An Artificial Intelligence Approach to Legal Reasoning*, PhD dissertation, Computer Science Dept., Stanford University, Stanford, Calif., 1984.

3. D.A. Schlobohm and D.A. Waterman, "Explanation for an Expert System that Performs Estate Planning," *Proc. First Int'l Conf. Artificial Intelligence and Law*, ACM, New York, N.Y., 1987.
4. D.A. Waterman and M. Peterson, "Rule-Based Models of Legal Expertise," *Proc. First Nat'l Conf. Artificial Intelligence*, AAAI, Menlo Park, Calif., 1980.
5. M.J. Sergot et al., "The British Nationality Act as a Logic Program," *Comm. ACM*, May 1986, pp. 370–386.
6. L.T. McCarty and N.S. Sridharan, "The Representation of an Evolving System of Legal Concepts: Prototypes and Deformations," *Proc. Seventh Int'l Joint Conf. Artificial Intelligence*, Morgan Kaufmann, Los Altos, Calif., 1981.
7. L.T. McCarty and N.S. Sridharan, "A Computational Theory of Legal Argument," Tech. Report LRP-TR-13, Laboratory for Computer Science Research, Rutgers University, New Brunswick, N.J., 1982.
8. L.T. McCarty, "Permissions and Obligations," in *Computing Power and Legal Reasoning*, C. Walter, ed., West Publishing Co., St. Paul, Minn., 1985.
9. E.L. Rissland, E.M. Valcarce, and K.D. Ashley, "Explaining and Arguing with Examples," *Proc. Fourth Nat'l Conf. Artificial Intelligence*, AAAI, Menlo Park, Calif., 1984.
10. M.R. Gilburne and R.L. Johnston, "Trade Secret Protection for Software Generally and in the Mass Market," *Computer Law J.*, Spring 1982.
11. R.M. Milgrim, *Business Organizations, Milgrim on Trade Secrets*, Vol. 12, Matthew Bender, New York, 1985.
12. K.D. Ashley and E.L. Rissland, "Compare and Contrast, A Test of Expertise," *Proc. Sixth Nat'l Conf. Artificial Intelligence*, AAAI, Menlo Park, Calif., 1987.
13. E.L. Rissland and K.D. Ashley, "A Case-Based System for Trade Secrets Law," *Proc. First Int'l Conf. Artificial Intelligence and Law*, ACM, New York, N.Y., 1987.
14. K.D. Ashley and E.L. Rissland, "But, See, Accord: Generating Blue Book Citations in Hypo," *Proc. First Int'l Conf. Artificial Intelligence and Law*, ACM, New York, N.Y., 1987.
15. E.L. Rissland and K.D. Ashley, "Hypotheticals as Heuristic Device," *Proc. Fifth Nat'l Conf. Artificial Intelligence, AAAI*, Menlo Park, Calif., 1986.

32

The potential of artificial intelligence to help solve the crisis in our legal system

Donald H. Berman
Carole D. Hafner

Editors' note *Berman and Hafner step back and examine the potential of AI to solve some of the problems in litigation that plague so many of us. This paper thus looks at a variety of problems, crises and opportunities. Can expert systems be used to settle disputes? Can they be used to sentence criminals? What kind of liability might we incur if we applied legal expert systems? These and a whole host of additional questions are addressed in this paper. (Reprinted with permission from the August 1989 issue of* Communications of the ACM. *© 1991, Association for Computing Machinery, Inc.)*

> The laws that govern affluent clients and large institutions are numerous, intricate and applied by highly sophisticated practitioners. In this section of society, rules proliferate, lawsuits abound, and the cost of legal services grows much faster than the cost of living. For the bulk of the population, however, the situation is very different. Access to the courts may be open in principle. In practice, however, most people find their legal rights severely compromised by the cost of legal services, the baffling complications of existing rules and procedures, and the long, frustrating delays involved in bringing proceedings to a conclusion. . . . There is far too much law for those who can afford it and far too little for those who cannot. No one can be satisfied with this state of affairs.
>
> Derek Bok [5]

The American legal system[1] is widely viewed as being in a state of crisis, plagued by excessive costs, long delays, and inconsistency leading to a growing lack of public

[1] Including legislatures, government agencies, the courts, private law firms, and the criminal justice system.

confidence. One reason for this is the vast amount of information that must be collected and integrated in order for the legal system to function properly. In many traditional areas of law, evolving legal doctrines have led to uncertainty and increased litigation at a high cost to both individuals and society. And in discretionary areas such as sentencing, alimony awards, and welfare administration, evidence has shown a high degree of inconsistency in legal decision making, leading to public dissatisfaction and a growing demand for "determinate" rules.

In this article, we consider the potential of artificial intelligence to contribute to a more fair and efficient legal system. First, using the example of a middle income home buyer who was misled by the statements of a real estate broker, we show how a predictive expert system could help each side assess its legal position. If expert systems were reasonably accurate predictors, some disputes could be voluntarily settled that are now resolved by costly litigation, and many others could be settled more quickly. We then consider the process of discretionary decision making, using the example of a judge sentencing a criminal. We describe how diagnostic expert systems developed in the medical domain could be adapted to criminal sentencing, and describe a process by which this technology could be used—first to build a consensus on sentencing norms, and then to make those norms accessible.

In the ideal case, legal decisions are made after lengthy study and debate, recorded in published justifications, and later scrutinized in depth by other legal experts. In contrast to this ideal, most day-to-day legal decisions are made by municipal and state court judges, police officers, prosecuting attorneys, insurance claims adjusters, welfare administrators, social workers, and lawyers advising their clients on whether to settle or litigate. These decisions must often be made under severe pressures of limited time, money, and information. Expert systems can provide decision makers with tools to better understand, evaluate and disseminate their decisions. At the same time, it is important to reiterate that expert systems should not and cannot replace human judgment in the legal decision making process.

Predictive legal expert systems

To assess the potential of artificial intelligence (AI) in helping to streamline the dispute resolution process, we analyze the hypothetical case of an unfortunate middle income home buyer who responds to a real estate broker's advertisement. The buyer complains to his attorney that during the broker's showing of the house the buyer asked whether "the house had water problems" and the broker replied, "Not to my knowledge." Several weeks after acquiring the house for $150,000 a heavy rain storm resulted in significant water accumulation in the basement. The buyer discovers that the flooding occurred because the land on which his house is located has serious drainage problems. To prevent a reoccurrence will cost over $20,000. After discovering that the seller had moved away, the buyer called the broker who said that since "he knew nothing about the potential water problems he felt no obligation to contribute to the cost of the repairs." After an hour's consultation with his attorney the buyer learns that his case is "complicated," the chances of obtaining redress "uncertain" and the cost of pursuing the claim will be at least $5,000. In a neighboring law office the broker hears from his attorney that the "law is in a state of flux." Therefore, even though the broker's statement was truthful, the buyer stands "a chance" and that to defend a law suit may cost "about $5,000."

Though many citizens have difficulty understanding why these parties cannot obtain a clear answer to what appears to be a relatively simple legal question, members of the legal community well understand that three potentiating factors have greatly complicated our dispute resolution processes. First, many new areas of law have emerged as society called upon its legal institutions to protect the environment, the rights of consumers, voters, minorities, the indigent, and criminals. Fifty years ago an attorney could have given this buyer a rather straightforward answer—no legal relief unless the broker lied. Today, the skilled lawyer knows that consumer protection statutes and evolving judicial doctrines might provide the basis of recovery against an honest, but uninformed broker.

Secondly, framers of legal rules have often abandoned clear directives in favor of open textured rules. Under traditional common law fraud principles the broker would not have been liable unless he knew his statement was false. Under a more modern view the broker is required "to conduct a reasonably competent and diligent inspection of the residence." [9] Litigation to determine what the broker "knew" is generally less complex than judicial attempts to fix standards for "a reasonably competent and diligent inspection" and then to decide whether the broker satisfied these amorphous norms of professional behavior.

Thirdly, procedural rules were changed from a system where the pleadings of the parties narrowly framed the issues for trial to a system where lengthy and costly pre-trial discovery is required before the contours of the litigation become known [32]. Under the earlier procedural system that relied heavily on pleadings the buyer would have alleged what transpired in considerable detail and then a trial would take place to see who was telling the truth. Today, the pleadings do not apprise the parties of the nature of the case and, therefore, lawyers must examine witnesses and documents before trial in order to learn what the case is about. In this particular case the lawyers, in addition to asking witnesses what transpired, might conduct a pre-trial examination of expert witnesses to obtain their opinions on the kind of inspection this broker should have conducted. For all practical purposes litigants now must pay for two lengthy trials, the first to find out what the witnesses will say and the second to hear them repeat it. Granted, such a system minimizes surprise but at a significant increase in cost.

A lawyer's approach to the case of the home buyer

Lawyers initially start with a factual inquiry to determine which broad area of law applies to the problem before them. After a few minutes the lawyer learns whether the problem involves a criminal or civil matter and shortly learns that he or she will need to apply legal principles applicable to the sale of houses. And in a case such as this the lawyer, relying on training and experience, would seek rather precise descriptions of what the broker said and what the client observed.

Most lawyers understand the basic principles of fraud—had the broker *expressly* and *falsely* represented that the property had no water problems then the plaintiff's chances of recovery are great. Conversely, had the broker said nothing and the buyer had seen water in the basement then his chances of victory would be nil because the law is unlikely to protect a buyer who failed totally to use his common sense. But once having sailed into the right ocean the lawyer must draw on two kinds of specialized knowledge to navigate into the narrow channels of the inner harbor. First, he must determine what published legal rules will apply to the precise facts he discovers. Secondly, after having assembled the facts and the relevant legal principles he must call upon his experience in determining whether a court, after having considered these facts and legal principles, will find in favor of his client.

As the lawyer hears the facts from the client certain legal principles are called to mind and as the lawyer delves further into the law he then becomes aware of the relevance of certain facts. In our simple example, the lawyer might initially conclude that the doctrine of *caveat emptor* ("let the buyer beware") bars recovery. But as he studies the cases he will find that the buyer might recover if the broker knew of potential water problems in the basement. Then, as the lawyer gains more factual information, he might learn that the client noticed a water line, a fact that might invoke a legal rule that would exculpate the broker since the existence of a water line should have alerted the buyer to the potential flooding. But since legal rules change, the buyer's lawyer might anticipate a court altering the legal rules to hold that since brokers are experts in real estate they have a duty to explain the meaning of the water line to a customer who lacks this kind of specialized knowledge.

The process of *finding the law* (including statutes, prior court cases, administrative rulings and procedural requirements) may involve searching a database of millions of potentially relevant documents.[2] The proliferation of legal documents is a major cause of the growing cost of legal services noted by Harvard President (and former law professor) Derek Bok. Furthermore, as the chance of missing a relevant document increases, the legal status of a case becomes increasingly difficult to determine. Although still in its infancy, there is growing interest in using artificial intelligence techniques to develop conceptual legal retrieval systems [15], [16] to assist the lawyer in more effectively utilizing this vast database.

Once having discovered the facts and found the relevant sources of law, the lawyer must predict the outcome. Unlike an engineer whose knowledge of rules and facts engenders a confident prediction that a bridge will stand, lawyers operate within an indeterminate system. Fact indeterminacy always clouds the advice one gives to clients—a jury may believe either the buyer or the broker. Or a jury may believe the broker but find for the plaintiff because they sympathize with his plight [12].

Nor can attorneys ever be sure that a court will decide that brokers who either speak truthfully or do not speak at all are liable for defects they might have discovered had they made a diligent search, because accepted modes of legal reasoning support either side of this controversy. No court would be deemed unreasonable to insist that brokers only be held liable for their intentional misrepresentations. Conversely, a court

[2] The database for LEXIS, the online legal retrieval system, currently contains more than 10 million documents, and is growing at the rate of 2.5 million documents per year.

might respond to plausible arguments that the broker should be held liable for innocent but careless representations. First, his expertise enables him to spot potential defects that would elude the eye of the inexperienced purchaser. Secondly, as businessmen brokers can better absorb the losses of the few individual buyers who sustain injury by spreading these losses evenly over all their customers.

While operating within an indeterminate system, lawyers nonetheless must regularly forecast the results of judicial proceedings. If the broker's attorney offered to settle the case for $10,000, the buyer's counsel would have to assess that offer. Few empirical studies have examined the way lawyers actually decide whether to accept settlements or proceed to litigation. Yet one can surmise that in our case of the home buyer a competent and ethical lawyer, presented with the offer described, would consider the following factors:

1. Costs of litigation. If litigation costs were equal to or greater than $10,000 settlement is clearly indicated given damages of only $20,000.
2. Amount of damages. If it appears that the plaintiff may have difficulty in proving damages in excess of $10,000 then settlement is clearly indicated.
3. Disbelief of client. Juries might not believe the buyer. After taking the depositions of the parties, attorneys predict how juries will judge the credibility of their clients. In making this prediction they will consider the demeanor of the witnesses. And given no clear indications that either party is lying, the attorney might conclude that a juror, moved by sympathy, would more readily accept the word of a first time home buyer than accept the credibility of a broker working for a large national realty company.
4. Application of an unfavorable rule of law. If, after researching the law, the attorney finds that in his jurisdiction the court presently imposes liability on only brokers who knew their representations were false then settlement is warranted unless the attorney believes that
   a. a jury will believe that the broker made statements about the condition of the property AND that he knew those statements to be false, or
   b. the court will change the law to hold brokers liable for false statements honestly made or will require brokers to make a diligent inspection of the premises.
5. Skill of the Attorney. Some lawyers have reputations for obtaining optimum results for their clients while others may be known to be less skillful. Lawyers confident of their litigating prowess or contemptuous of the abilities of opposing counsel often reject settlements that more timid counsel would readily accept.
6. Judge and Jury. Experienced lawyers realize that certain judges and juries from certain localities are prone to favor a certain class of plaintiffs or defendants.

The role of legal expert systems

Thirty years ago Layman Allen laid much of foundation for contemporary attempts to represent legal knowledge when he proposed encoding statutory law into logic as a way of reducing the syntactic ambiguity that is inherent in most statutes [2]. A decade ago computer scientists began their efforts to represent legal knowledge and model legal reasoning [15], [21], [23]. More recently, researchers have made serious efforts to translate legal rules into logic-based computer programs [30]. And now efforts are emerging to represent the unique factual and legal issues presented by individual cases [28]. Though these efforts may prove useful to lawyers and legal assistants,[3] they will not significantly impact the litigation morass that currently engulfs our courts because these systems treat the law as a set of abstract rules rather than a system manipulated by expert litigators. Lawyers do not make decisions based on what the rules "say." Rather, they base their decisions on how decision makers will apply those rules to specific factual situations.

In seminal research based on modeling the decision making of legal experts, Peterson and Waterman carefully examined how lawyers and insurance claims adjusters evaluate product liability claims [26]. From interviews with these experts they framed computer understandable rules that capture the way lawyers actually determine the settlement value of a case. For our case of the home buyer, some rules gathered from experienced litigators might read as shown in FIG. 32-1. These rules can then be organized into decision trees (illustrated in FIG. 32-2) that replicate the processes used by attorneys in estimating the settlement value of a case.

Peterson and Waterman recognize the limits of a strictly rule-based approach:

> But by themselves, the [rule-based] systems do not provide a general conceptual structure that can help us understand legal decision making. The rules are too specific, while the chains of reasoning are ad hoc products of the facts in particular cases.
>
> Peterson and Waterman [26, p. 632].

The authors then propose a general conceptual structure for evaluating civil liability claims, based on their experience in interviewing litigators and building models of product liability. In this model, the evaluation of a claim is broken down into steps, which include:

1. Analysis of loss: What damages can be claimed? In our case of the home buyer, this would include direct economic losses such as the cost of repairs and damage to personal property, if any. In the product liability cases studied by Peterson and Waterman, general damages due to pain and suffering, limitation of activity, etc., could also be claimed.
2. Analysis of liability: What is the probability of establishing that a defendant is legally liable? This may depend on the rules of the jurisdiction as well as the facts. For example, in some jurisdictions it may be necessary to show that the broker actually knew about the defect, while in others it may only be necessary to show that the broker could have discovered it.

---

[3] Such systems could aid an administrator to determine whether a claimant is entitled to a retirement benefit because he became 65 years old but could not resolve a contested issue involving the question of whether a certain illness resulted in a compensable disability.

3. Analysis of responsibility: What proportion of the responsibility should be assigned to the plaintiff for his own carelessness? This also depends on the rules of the jurisdiction, since some allow damages to be reduced by a theory of comparative negligence.
4. Analysis of characteristics: Characteristics of the litigants, judges, and attorneys are considered by legal experts when they evaluate a claim.
5. Analysis of context: Strategic considerations such as the timing of the case, the plaintiff's immediate need for money, and the effect on the defendant of publicity, etc.

The value of a case is estimated according to the following formula:

VALUE = LOSS * LIABILITY * RESPONSIBILITY
* CHARACTERISTICS * CONTEXT

R1. IF the defect is material
AND the cost of repair is greater than $1,000
THEN increase the economic loss by the cost of repair

R2. IF the defect is material
AND there is damage to personal property greater than $500
THEN increase the economic loss by the damage to personal property

R3. IF the economic loss is greater than $2,500
AND the defect existed at the time of the sale
AND the broker knew of the defect
THEN increase the loss factor by 70 percent of the economic loss

R4. IF the buyer is the first occupant
THEN increase the sympathy factor by 5 percent of the economic loss (assumption that jurors have greater sympathy for buyers of new homes who expect a dwelling with fewer defects.)

R5. IF the buyer is a first time home buyer
THEN increase the sympathy factor by 10 percent of the economic loss (assumption that jurors will feel less chance that first time home buyer knows what to look for.)

R6. IF the broker is associated with a national chain
THEN increase the sympathy factor by 10 percent of the economic loss (assumption that big companies can more easily absorb losses than an individual home buyer.)

R7. IF there were visible signs of damage
AND the buyer was not a first time home buyer
THEN decrease the sympathy factor by 30 percent of the economic loss (assumption that jurors will not be sympathetic to a buyer who could have discovered the defect himself.)

Fig. 32-1. Sample rules for a predictive expert system.

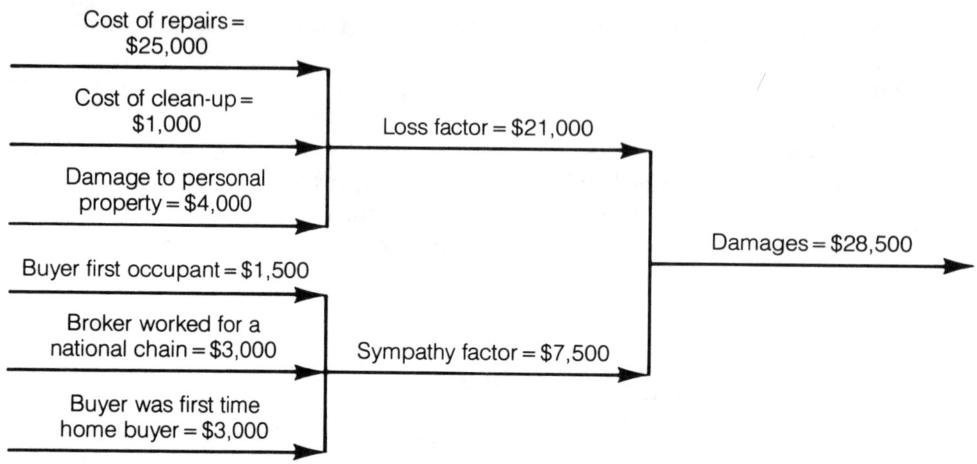

Fig. 32-2. Decision tree for a predictive expert system.

We can see how this approach helps to explain the complex effect of a single factor: the degree to which the defect was discoverable. If the defect was not discoverable at all, then the question of liability (Step 2) would probably be answered in the negative since the broker was not at fault. If the defect was very easily discoverable then the buyer's carelessness (Step 3) would probably reduce the value of the claim. However, the answer to Step 3 would depend on both the discoverability of the defect and the experience (or inexperience) of the buyer, since a very inexperienced person might not recognize a defect that an average home buyer would easily discover.

The impact of predictive expert systems

Expert systems that predict the outcome of litigation with a fair degree of accuracy, if widely available, would have a profound effect on our legal system. If a court offered litigants the option of choosing a computer-predicted settlement, many lawsuits would end. Two factors would induce litigants to accept such settlements. First, many parties to litigation are risk averse, unable to absorb total defeat, thereby pressured to accept a predictable settlement that is below their desired goal. More importantly, greatly reduced attorneys' fees would make such settlements very attractive to all parties. Not only would a litigant avoid possible defeat, he or she would also avoid the high costs of litigation. However, what is desirable in theory may be difficult to attain in practice.

Researchers who have studied the implementation of information systems in organizations and in society at large [19], [20] have found that institutional impediments may retard the development and acceptance of computerized systems, no matter how beneficial they may be in the ideal case. In the real world, a complex interplay of socio-economic, political and interpersonal incentives determine whether and how computer systems are developed and used. Morrison [25], in a study of the attitudes of private law firms toward legal expert systems, found these institutional barriers to be a major cause of the slow growth of legal expert systems in the private sector.

In law, for example, it is clear that the current practice of time billing, as contrasted with value billing, provides a disincentive for attorneys to use legal expert systems which would reduce their number of billable hours. On the other hand, the client's desire for faster and less expensive legal service provides countervailing pressure to automate, and if legal expert systems can be shown to lead to better decision making this should provide an additional incentive for clients. However, this straightforward analysis may still be too naive; an expert system that expedites the settlement of cases would not necessarily be welcomed by all branches of a client corporation. For corporate managers who see their current assignments as short term, a settlement which is chargeable to this year's budget may be less desirable than a more expensive settlement negotiated at a later time, when the manager has moved on to a new assignment.

Institutional arrangements may also result in expert systems being developed and used for the benefit of one group of clients but not for their opponents. For example, it is not surprising that Peterson and Waterman's research on expert systems for product liability was funded by the insurance industry. Industries which undertake large amounts of repetitive litigation will have strong incentives to develop predictive expert systems for their own use. It is much less likely that expert systems will soon be used by the plaintiffs' attorneys who represent individual clients in suits against insurance companies.

Another environment where legal expert systems are likely to gain acceptance can be found in institutions providing free legal services to the poor. In legal aid clinics and the public defense bar, where attorneys on fixed salaries process a myriad of cases that have similar characteristics, there are strong incentives and few disincentives for using automation. In Project Pericles at Harvard Law School, an expert system was developed for representing indigent tenants, which led to an increase in both the quantity and effectiveness of service available to the tenants, causing problems for landlords who were required to pay increased hourly fees to their attorneys.

Even in the ideal case where predictive expert systems are developed and used based solely on their contribution to a more efficient legal system, a troubling paradox emerges if *all* litigants were to accept computer-predicted settlements. Accurate predictions result from encapsulating the thinking of experts who litigate cases. Without litigation the experts would have no additional data to input—leaving the law frozen. Fortunately, the universal acceptance of such settlements is unlikely. Since an expert system could not have rules that account for all possibilities, some litigants would find the computer-predicted settlement sufficiently unsatisfactory to justify the expenses and hazards of litigation. From such newly litigated cases the experts would develop new rules to update the system's performance. In addition, changing social values would lead some litigants to reject settlements based on relatively static rules. For example, a home buyer might reject the computer-predicted settlement, recognizing the growing tendency toward consumer protection, and hoping this may lead the court to rule that brokers are liable even when they were not aware of the defect.

Normative legal expert systems

Each year our criminal justice system sentences hundreds of thousands of criminals; our family court system determines the economic future of the spouses and children in over one million divorced families [6], and administrators of social welfare programs decide what benefits millions of clients should receive. Unfortunately, many citizens similarly situated receive greatly disparate treatment from discretionary decision makers.

For example, a welfare regulation might grant an extra allowance to a person who is "substantially incapable of performing normal household duties."[4] To one administrator, this might include a person who cannot carry groceries from the store; to another it might only apply to a person who is completely bedridden. Such discrepancies in interpretation may be uncovered during an official appeal, or they may go undetected indefinitely.

When a marriage ends in divorce, the legal system is often called upon to determine the division of property and the award of alimony and child support. These awards vary greatly depending on how a judge categorizes and values property; and how he or she measures the incomes and needs of spouses and children. Some judges may allow the custodial parent to remain in the marital home until the youngest child reaches the age of majority while others require the home to be sold within a short time after the divorce. Some judges favor lengthy alimony awards while others routinely deny such requests, favoring rehabilitative alimony that lasts only a few years. Needless to say such disparate awards create dissatisfaction among litigants [35]. Indeed, the potential for inequity is so great that over a decade ago it was suggested that maintenance awards be "calculated on a computer" [8].

Criminal sentencing, in particular, is receiving increasing attention from the legal community and the public. Studies reveal that some judges place the great majority of criminals on probation while others employ probation in a small number of cases [29], and anecdotal reports have documented numerous cases of nearly-identical crimes being committed by individuals with very similar backgrounds, in which one criminal was released while the other received a long prison sentence. Critics believe that inconsistent sentencing undermines efforts to both deter and rehabilitate criminals [31].

Public dissatisfaction with inconsistent sentencing has led to a growing demand for *determinate* or fixed sentences for certain crimes; however, this solution also engenders unfairness by failing to consider the unique characteristics of the crime and the criminal. Arguably, a 15-year-old who steals a car and takes it for a ride should be treated differently than a member of a professional car theft ring who steals a car for resale. It is clear that there is a need for agreed-upon standards or norms that would provide a framework for more consistent decision making but would still allow individual circumstances to be taken into account.

One approach to developing such norms would be to maintain a database of all decisions, which could be queried to find the typical treatment of particular types of cases. Judges and administrators would then be able to find out what happened in similar cases before making a decision. This approach has been pursued by the Law and Computers Project at the University of British Columbia. A Sentencing Data Base has been created which summarizes more than 40,000 sentencing decisions of the Provincial and Supreme Courts of British Columbia during the past few years. A very simple interac-

[4] This example, taken from the British welfare law, was discussed by Bench-Capon and Sergot [3].

tive interface asks the user to enter information about five factors:

1. the crime the defendant committed,
2. the age group of the defendant,[5]
3. the sex of the defendant,
4. whether or not the defendant is married,
5. whether or not the defendant has previously been convicted of an indictable (i.e., serious) offense.

The system then displays a histogram showing the frequency of various categories of sentences, for all cases in the database that match on the five factors. It is also possible to retrieve a list of the matching cases including the exact disposition, the judge, the location, and the plea. Judges in the Provincial Court, Supreme Court, and Court of Appeals of British Columbia have been using the Sentencing Data Base since late 1987, and many find it quite useful. In addition, both prosecutors and defense attorneys have used the system and found it useful.

The frequency analysis technique applied in the British Columbia sentencing project is a valuable contribution to legal decision making. If a judge is confronted by a crime of breaking and entering that seems to be of ordinary severity, he or she will not *inadvertently* give a sentence that is extremely harsh or extremely lenient. If a judge is confronted by a crime that is very heinous, but where the criminal is a first time offender, he or she can look up the most severe sentence previously given for this crime to a first time offender. However, there are three major limitations to this technique, where a rule based approach, used in addition to databases, may be useful.

1. A system that analyzes a few factors such as age, sex, and prior convictions does not approach the true complexity of judicial decision making. In making decisions, a large number of factors with complex interactions must be taken into account in order to determine a fair sentence: the nature of the crime including mitigating and aggravating factors; the individual characteristics of the defendant including age, education, family status, reputation in the community, etc.; a complete review of the defendant's prior criminal record; and the existence of any extenuating circumstances. An attempt to model these hundreds of factors and their interactions would preclude the use of simple statistics. Even if one could enumerate them, it would be virtually impossible to collect this information for all prior cases. Existing records often do not contain this information but even if the careful perusal of these records would yield the information, society lacks the resources necessary to encode this massive amount of data.
2. If our current decision makers are behaving inconsistently, as the anecdotal evidence seems to suggest, then the mere reporting of past behavior does not ensure a meaningful pattern for judges to base their future decisions on. The mode of sentences for a particular crime may represent an accidental congruence of light sentences from some judges and severe sentences from others for a

[5] The system recognizes four age groups: under 21, 21–29, 30–59, and over 59.

collection of crimes and defendants with little in common other than the formal charge.

3. Databases cannot explain *why* a particular sentence was given, while the goal of expert systems is to model the reasoning of human experts, not only at the performance level but also at the cognitive level. One of the most important attributes of expert systems is their ability to explain why a particular analysis or recommendation was produced (in terms of their internal rule-based model). The creation and use of an expert system puts legal decision making under the microscope of precise computer specification. In areas of discretionary decision making that are believed to suffer from undesirable inconsistency, AI offers an exciting opportunity to bring more rational approaches into being.

It is possible that AI research could result in expert systems that would help judges produce an acceptable level of evenhandedness without resorting to a rigid model of fixed sentencing. The expert system would be normative rather than predictive, providing guidance based on a complex model encompassing characteristics of the crime, mitigating and aggravating circumstances, and the characteristics of the individual defendant. Although such a system might influence a judge's decisions, he or she would always be free to reject its recommendations, since no matter how many factors were included in the expert system's model, there would always be cases whose unique circumstances would justify a different result.

Modeling judgmental decisions: sentencing as diagnosis

Expert systems have achieved a high level of performance in a number of specialized domains, including mineral prospecting, computer configuration [22] and chemical analysis [11]. But perhaps the largest amount of significant expertise to be represented in expert systems is in the area of medical diagnosis and therapy [7], [10], [27], [34]. For example, according to Hayes-Roth et al. [18], the CADUCEUS system in 1982 possessed approximately 100,000 associations representing more knowledge of internal medicine than any human, and was able to correctly diagnose complex test cases missed by human experts.

Medical expert systems are based on a model of heuristic reasoning that relates symptoms of illness to suggested therapy, based on intermediate concepts of *disease states* (e.g., infectious disease organisms, conditions such as alcoholism, heart disease, etc.). The physician diagnoses the patient's symptoms by making a judgment about the disease state(s) that caused them, determines the general type of therapy required (antibiotics, surgery, special diet, etc.) and finally prescribes a specific treatment.

This model can be adapted to the sentencing of criminals by viewing the criminal acts as symptoms and the sentences as therapy. The general types of therapy correspond to various sentencing goals: specific deterrence, general deterrence, isolation of dangerous individuals, and rehabilitation [17], [24]. These in turn lead to specific recommendation: probation, a fine, a prison term, or a diversionary program such as community service or treatment for drug abuse. A relevant question that can only be answered through empirical research is: do judges use some notion corresponding to disease states to mediate between the description of a criminal act and the determination of an appropriate sentence?

The MYCIN system, [7] one of the first and best known medical expert systems, defined a basic approach to heuristic reasoning that appears to be very promising for modeling legal judgments:

1. Knowledge is represented by production rules, applied by a domain-independent inference engine. (This is now a standard approach in expert systems.)
2. A conceptual hierarchy of objects, attributes, and values is used to structure the problem, and is integrated with the inference engine. Thus, the sophistication of the rule formalism used in MYCIN is far beyond that normally found in expert system shells. Figure 32-3 shows a hypothetical context tree that might be applied in evaluating a criminal for sentencing. Using a top-down approach, first the nature of the crime would be considered, including each offense that the defendant is charged with, the defendant's actions leading to that charge, the victims of the crime, and the surrounding circumstances. Then, the characteristics of the defendant would be considered, including personal data and information on previous crimes. Finally, the existence of mitigating and aggravating circumstances would be considered.

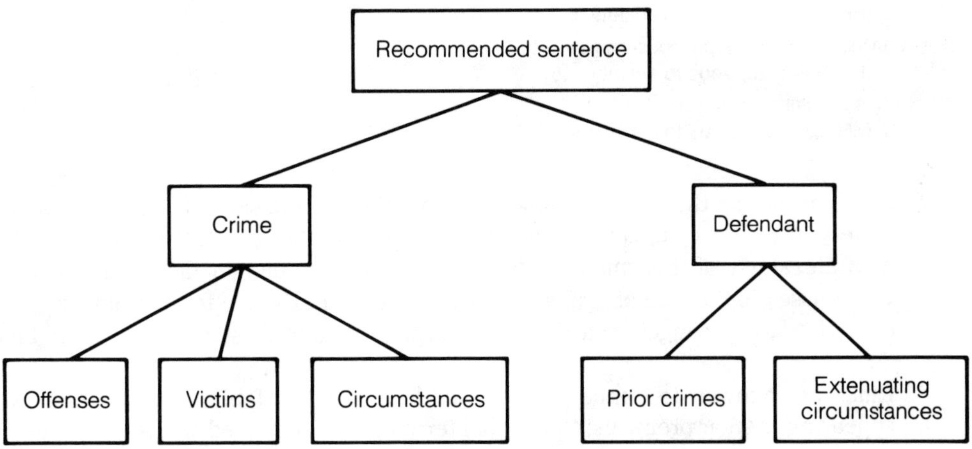

Fig. 32-3. Context tree for a diagnostic model of criminal sentencing.

3. Weights are attached to all knowledge elements in the database to indicate how strongly they are believed, and rules are also weighted to show how important they are. The system provides an algorithm for combining weights to measure the overall strength of each conclusion. The ability to represent varying degrees to which attributes apply (e.g., degrees of violence of an assault) is critical in the legal domain.

   Figure 32-4, although greatly oversimplified, shows the kinds of rules that might be included in such an expert system. The sample rules are intended to

R1. IF one of the offenses was illegal use of firearms
THEN D is dangerous to society .5

R2. IF one of the offenses was possession of illegal drugs
OR one of the offenses was sale of illegal drugs
THEN D is dangerous to society .5

R3. If one of the offenses involved bodily harm
AND D was acquainted with the victim
THEN D is dangerous to society .4

R4. IF none of the offenses involved bodily harm
AND D was acquainted with the victim
THEN D is dangerous to society −.2

R5. IF one of the offenses involved bodily harm
AND D was NOT acquainted with the victim
THEN D is dangerous to society .8

R6. IF the circumstances included the influence of alcohol or drugs
AND D's crime was driving-related
AND D's crime did not involve bodily harm
THEN D is dangerous to society .25

R7. IF the circumstances included the influence of alcohol or drugs
AND D's crime involved bodily harm
THEN D is dangerous to society .7

R8. IF D has previously spent time in prison
THEN D is dangerous to society .5

R9. IF the number of D's previous crimes = 0
THEN D is dangerous to society −.5

R10. IF D is regularly employed
THEN D is dangerous to society −.5

Fig. 32-4. Sample rules for a normative expert system.

help in weighing the evidence for and against the hypothesis, "D is dangerous to society." For example, rule R1 in FIG. 32-4 says the "danger factor" associated with illegal use of firearms is .5 and rule R2 says the danger factor associated with possession or sale of drugs is .5. Using the MYCIN rule for combining evidence [33], the "danger factor" associated with both of these offenses would be .75.

4. Rules are allowed to explicitly refer to the strength of belief in the factors appearing in their premises; thus, a jail term may be indicated when the danger factor exceeds a particular value, e.g.:

    IF there is strongly suggestive evidence (.7)
    that D is dangerous to society
    THEN the recommended sentence for D should
    include incarceration 1.0.

Experiments with medical expert systems have shown several aspects of the MYCIN model that need to be improved. One aspect is the reliance on top-down control, which frequently leads to a line of questioning that has nothing to do with the current case. Another aspect is the fact that symptoms tend to occur in meaningful clusters, so that their weights are not really independent. The CADUCEUS system [27] includes an initial *consultation* in which the user can enter the symptoms of the current case in whatever order he or she wants. CADUCEUS also employs a more complex model of medical knowledge, which takes account of the way certain combinations of symptoms provide strong evidence for particular conclusions.

Is the MYCIN model an appropriate tool for modeling the way judges evaluate criminals for sentencing? Will the described limitations of MYCIN also be relevant in the legal domain? Or will other information structures that have not yet been considered be suggested by a study of judicial decision making? As AI researchers attempt to answer these questions, they will contribute to a better understanding of how our legal system works. Whether or not expert systems are actually used in the courtroom, the exercise has potential value as a tool for jurisprudential analysis.

The impact of normative expert systems

Even if computers did not exist it would make sense for legal decision makers to carefully analyze how and why they make their decisions. To that end, some courts have formal mechanisms by which judges gather to share information. In addition, many informal mechanisms permit decision makers to exchange views about the laws they administer. However, the growing complexity of the legal system and the time pressure on decision makers makes it difficult to maintain norms through merely gathering to share information.

One solution which is gaining popularity is the development of statutory guidelines. When legislators mandate the creation of guidelines for sentencing criminals or dividing up marital property they strive to incorporate societal wisdom on how to best resolve a certain class of case. But written guidelines are of limited utility when compared to expert systems' ability to model certain kinds of decision-making problems. Most importantly, the computer can handle a far greater number of interacting rules than a person looking at a printed page; thus, the practical limitations of legislative drafting preclude the listing of the myriad of factors that ideally should be taken into account. In addition, the legislative process makes fine tuning a system most difficult while expert systems can be easily adjusted to correct errors and omissions.

Normative expert systems would never replace human judgment. Rather, they would provide decision makers with the tools to better understand, evaluate, and disseminate their ideas. No computer would ever sentence a defendant, make a child support award, or grant a housing allowance. But a computer could advise a decision maker on what factors and issues should be considered, and how his or her colleagues would be likely to view a case with similar facts.

In spite of the potential of normative expert systems to assist discretionary decision makers, there are significant barriers to their development and use. First, decision makers who are accustomed to viewing themselves as independent, judgmental thinkers may view expert systems as mechanizing or "de-skilling" their jobs. To the extent that this perception exists, the systems are likely to be strongly resisted. The best way to overcome this barrier is to make the decision makers the "owners" of the knowledge base, so that they will see it as a tool that they have created for themselves. However, most legal decision makers are not accustomed to using computers, so there is a "comfort" barrier that must be overcome, as well as the natural skepticism of professionals that computers could be an effective tool in their domain.

Second, if the use of an expert system would change the distribution of decisions, this might be unacceptable to the administering organization or to society. For example, many social entitlement programs such as workers compensation, medicaid, and social security disability, have statutory rules that determine eligibility. According to some experts,[6] the workers compensation rules are often misapplied to the detriment of the workers—resulting in a much lower cost to the government. If this view is correct, a legal expert system that accurately embodied these rules could result in a significant increase in benefits paid out, a cost which society might not be willing to pay. On the other hand, if social security disability benefits, which are determined by the states but paid by Washington, are being administered too liberally, state officials might resist the use of an expert system which would lower the overall benefits paid to their constituents.

The relationship between computer information systems and the development of norms has been studied by Kling [19], whose research shows that when norms are not taken into account, development projects are likely to fail. Kling presents several examples, including a project to upgrade the U.S. World Wide Military Command and Control System (WWMCCS), which was criticized in a 1981 report by the General Accounting Office (GAO) as follows: "DOD, despite dozens of large-scale studies, has failed to make meaningful progress . . ." [19, p. 323]. Kling traces the failure of the WWMCCS modernization to the need for field commanders in the three services to agree on precisely what data they need. He notes that different tactical battle doctrines held by officers in the three services result in different requirements for an information system, and suggests that until this problem is addressed the project cannot succeed.

Kling's research, which is focused on the organizational response to computer systems, reveals how the absence of shared norms can be an obstacle to achieving the primary goal of developing a useful computer system. On the other hand, in certain areas of law such as sentencing and child support, the development of norms is a primary goal; the use of an expert system is justified by its contribution to that objective. In either case, however, the need to agree on the behavior of the computer brings normative issues dramatically into focus. It is this focusing effect which is the primary benefit claimed here for legal expert systems.

There are potential dangers as well as benefits in the use of normative expert systems. Critics of artificial intelligence such as Weizenbaum [36] have warned about overreliance on computers; for example, a decision maker might be reluctant to vary from the computer's advice even when the facts so warranted. This is not a new problem for the legal system; the same danger exists with presumptive sentencing when the legislature suggests, but does not require, judges to sentence within certain parameters. In the same way that a judge might blindly follow a legislative guideline, a judge might ignore a directive to treat the output of a computer as merely advisory. Furthermore, it is possible that expert systems will carry greater implicit authority than legislative guidelines, due to their ability to respond to more factual variations and also due to the

---

[6] James Rowan, personal communication.

dynamic quality of computer programs. Although expert systems, if properly constructed, have the ability to explain the reasoning on which their recommendations are based, it is all too easy to just accept the recommendations without examining the reasoning behind them.

Is this a realistic scenario? Perhaps in the early 1970's when Weizenbaum was building the ELIZA program, it was more realistic than it will be in the 1990's. In a seminar on Artificial Intelligence and Law taught by the authors at Northeastern University, we have observed a growing understanding on the part of law students who take the course on the capabilities and limitations of computers. It is not unreasonable to suppose that, as computers become commonplace in schools and colleges, as youngsters grow up playing "adventure" games, and as computer programs for various tasks (for example, tax preparation and estate planning) become commonplace, expert systems will become a part of everyday life whose uses and dangers are generally recognized, just as electricity and automobiles are today. The dangers of any technology must be weighed against its benefits. The question for expert systems is whether they can contribute to making the legal system more fair and less costly than it is today.

Of all the issues surrounding the use of normative expert systems, perhaps the most significant is the possibility for review of discretionary decisions in areas where such review is now difficult to obtain. Most jurisdictions do provide for the review of criminal sentences and alimony awards. But as a practical matter such reviews rarely succeed because appellate judges routinely hold that such decisions are within the discretion of the trier of fact. Such non-reviewability is virtually dictated by the unavailability of norms. Rarely can an appellate judge find a sentence or alimony award unreasonable because standards of reasonableness do not exist. The process of knowledge engineering that would be required in order to build normative expert systems would have the desirable side effect of helping to develop such standards.

Conclusions

Weizenbaum [36] argues that computers ought not to make judicial decisions, even though they could conceivably do so. We strongly agree, and in another report [4] discuss a number of reasons why legal decisions cannot be explained by any rule-based model of law, however complex. The legal decision maker not only applies existing rules, but is often called upon to creatively modify rules, to choose among competing rules, and to create new rules [14].

But we must recognize the practical benefits as well as the theoretical limitations of technology:

a. In legal disputes where money is at stake, the cost of the dispute resolution process must be allowed to enter the moral equation. If a perfectly just award must be shared 50-50 with a lawyer, an approximate result computed by an expert system of which the petitioner keeps 90 percent may be preferable.
b. Where discretion has been shown to foster gross inconsistency and shelter discriminatory practices, it may be an improvement to have an expert system generating a range of standard alternatives, with a requirement for written justification when decisions fall outside the range. The important questions to

ask are: Would more people get a fairer result? and: Would more people understand WHY they got the result they did?

c. When citizens governed by a system of legal rules cannot ascertain the content of those rules, we must question whether we have a system of law, as that term is commonly understood [13]. Given the expanded complexity and amount of legal materials, the cost of "finding the law" has, for many citizens, rendered the law unfathomable. By making the law more accessible, conceptual retrieval systems have the potential of enhancing the legitimacy of our legal system.

The specter of a computer sentencing a criminal or forcing parties in a dispute to accept a predetermined settlement is often raised as a potential negative result of developing expert systems for law. But such things are happening even without expert systems—the emergence of no-fault insurance, proposed caps on malpractice awards, the trend toward determinate sentencing, and formal child support guidelines are all indications that, in reaction to the excessive cost and complexity of the legal system, citizens are willing to resort to an algorithmic determination of their rights. Algorithms that are written in the statute books and applied mechanically by human administrators are the paper equivalents of allowing a computer to make the decisions. Expert systems can be used in the service of such algorithmic decision making, but they can also be used to organize and present the relevant facts and issues in the service of human decision makers. The predictive and normative expert systems described in this article are intended to serve the latter function.

References

1. American Law Institute. Using Personal Computers for Decision-Making in Law Practice. ALI-ABA Invitational Conference, 1985.
2. L.E. Allen, Symbolic logic: A razor-edged tool for drafting and interpreting legal documents. *Yale Law J. 66*, (1957), 837.
3. T. Bench-Capon and M. Sergot, *Toward a rule-based representation of open texture in law*. Department of Computing, Imperial College of Science and Technology, London, England (Apr. 1985).
4. D.H. Bermán and C.D. Hafner, Indeterminacy: A challenge to logic-based models of legal reasoning. *3 Yearbook of Law Computers & Technology* (1987, to appear). Also published as Research Report NU-CCS-87-1, College of Computer Science, Northeastern University, Boston, Mass., 1987.
5. D. Bok, A flawed system. *Harvard Magazine 85*, 5 (1983), 38–40.
6. Bureau of the Census, U.S. Dept. of Commerce, *1981 Statistical Abstract of the United States*, 80.
7. R. Davis, B. Buchanan, and E. Shortliffe, Production rules as a representation for a knowledge-based consultation program. *Artif. Intell. 8*, 1 (1977), 15–45.
8. *Desk Guide to the Uniform Marriage and Divorce Act*, (BNA, Washington, D.C., 1974). Remarks of Ms. Betty Berry, past National Coordinator of NOW's Marriage and Divorce Task Force.
9. *Easton v. Strassburger*, 152 Cal. App. 3d 90 (1984).
10. L.M. Fagan et al., Representation of cynamic clinical knowledge: Measurement interpretation in the intensive case unit. *IJCAI-6* (1979), 260–262.
11. Feigenbaum et al., On generality and problem solving: A case study using the DENDRAL program." In *Machine Intelligence 6*, B. Meltzer and D. Michie, Eds. Edinburgh University Press, (1971), 165–190.
12. J. Frank, *Law and the Modern Mind* (1963), xxvii–xxviii.
13. L. Fuller, *The Morality of Law* 39 (1964).
14. A.L. Gardner, Overview of an artificial intelligence approach to legal reasoning. In Walter, C. Ed. *Computer Power and Legal Reasoning*. West Publishing Co., St. Paul, Minn. (1985), 247–74.

15. C.D. Hafner, *An Information Retrieval System Based on a Computer Model of Legal Knowledge*. Ph.D. dissertation, Univ. of Michigan, 1978. Republished by UMI Research Press, Ann Arbor, Mich. (1981).
16. C.D. Hafner, Conceptual organization of case law knowledge bases. In *Proceedings of the 1st Intelligence Conference on Artificial Intelligence and Law*. ACM, New York, 1987, pp. 35 – 42.
17. H. Hart, The Aims of the Criminal Law. *23 Law & Cont. Prob.* 401 (1958).
18. F. Hayes-Roth, D.A. Waterman, and D.B. Lenat, *Building Expert Systems*. Addison-Wesley, Reading, Mass., 1983, 9.
19. R. Kling, Defining the boundaries of computing across complex organizations. In *Critical Issues in Information Systems*, R.J. Boland and R.A. Hirscheim, Eds. John Wiley, New York, 1987, 307 – 362.
20. K.L. Kraemer, S. Dickhoven, S.F. Tierney, and J.L. King, *Datawars: The Politics of Modeling in Federal Policymaking*. Columbia University Press, New York, 1987.
21. L.T. McCarty, Reflections on TAXMAN: An experiment in artificial intelligence and legal reasoning. *Harvard Law Review 90*, (Mar. 1977), 837.
22. J. McDermott, R1: A rule-based configurer of computer systems. In *Proceedings of the 1st National Conference on Artificial Intelligence (AAAI-80)*, pp. 269 – 271.
23. J. A. Meldman, A structural model for computer-aided legal analysis. *Rutgers Journal of Computer Law 6*, (1977).
24. Model Penal Code, Sec. 1.02(2) American Law Institute, 1962.
25. R.W. Morrison, Market realities of rule-based software for lawyers: Where the rubber meets the road. In *Proceedings of the 2nd International Conference on Artificial Intelligence and Law (ICAIL 89)*. (Vancouver, Canada, June 1989). ACM, New York, pp. 33 – 36.
26. M.A. Peterson and D.A. Waterman, An expert systems approach to evaluating product liability cases. In Walter, C. Ed. *Computer Power and Legal Reasoning*. West Publishing Co., St. Paul, Minn. 1985, 629 – 59.
27. H.E. Pople Jr., Heuristic methods for imposing structure on ill-structured problems: The structuring of medical diagnostics. In *Artificial Intelligence in Medicine*. P. Szolovitz, Ed. Westview Press, Boulder Colo., 1981, 119 – 185.
28. E.L. Rissland, E.M. Valarce, and K.D. Ashley, Explaining and arguing with examples. In *Proceedings of the 1984 National Conference on Artificial Intelligence (AAAI-84)*.
29. S. Rubin, Disparity and equality of sentencing—A constitutional challenge. *Federal Rules Decision 40*, 55 (1965).
30. M. J. Sergot et al., The British Nationality Act as a logic program. *Commun. ACM 29*, 5 (May 1986), 370 – 385.
31. S. Shane-Dubow, A. Brown, and E. Olsen, *Sentencing Reform in the United States*. National Institute of Justice, U.S. Department of Justice (1985).
32. S.N. Subrin, How equity conquered common law: The federal rules of civil procedure in historical prospective. Pa. La. Rev., Vol. 135 (Apr. 1987). Manuscript on file at Northeastern Univ. School of Law, Boston, Mass. 02115.
33. W. Van Melle, A.C. Scott, J.S. Bennett, and M. Peairs, The Emycin Manual. Report No. STAN-CS-81-885, Department of Computer Science, Stanford Univ., Stanford, Calif. (1981).
34. S.M. Weiss et al., A model-based consultation system for the long-term management of glaucoma. *IJCAI-5* (1977), 826 – 832.
35. L. J. Weitzman, *The Divorce Revolution*. The Free Press, New York, 1985.
36. J. Weizenbaum, *Computer Power and Human Reason*. W.H. Freeman and Co., San Francisco, 1976.

Section I

Knowledge-based software engineering

33

KBRA
A new paradigm for requirements engineering

Andrew J. Czuchry, Jr.
David R. Harris

Editors' note *This paper describes efforts to apply AI to requirements engineering. The knowledge-based requirements assistant (KBRA) is an Air Force-funded system that "accepts informal statements and assists in incremental formalization through reusable requirement components, review, and analysis." The importance of systems like KBRA lies in the application of knowledge-based software technology to the problem of software engineering. In fact, knowledge-based software engineering assistants can be used to design and develop knowledge-based expert systems. (Reprinted, with permission, from the Winter 1988 issue of* IEEE Expert. *©1988. All rights reserved.)*

Developing requirements for hardware and software systems is challenging due to the complexity of modeling the real world in which target systems will reside, of managing many fragmentary yet interrelated requirement statements, and of coping with changing assumptions and requirement perceptions. At Sanders Associates, we are applying AI-based computer support to this difficult task.

Our knowledge-based requirements assistant (KBRA) is a component of the knowledge-based software assistant (KBSA) funded by the Rome Air Development Center [1]. KBSA seeks to create a knowledge-based life cycle paradigm spanning software development from requirements to code, and to formalize software practice so that we can use computers as active reasoning agents in developing software—thereby dividing labor so that engineers can concentrate on creative, problem-solving aspects of software development while the machine assistant handles more mundane details. Using KBSA, engineers commit to working entirely on line instead of on paper. The reward for this commitment is that decisions and their associated justifications are not lost; rather, they remain available throughout the entire software life cycle.

KBRA enables us to target several abilities missing in current tool sets; for example,

1. The ability to use the computer from the project's beginning,
2. The ability to provide multiple views on the system being specified,

3. The ability to capture and enforce ramifications of decisions,
4. The ability to handle reusability at the requirements level,
5. The ability to critique and automatically complete some requirements work.

KBRA's heritage is knowledge-based automatic programming research. KBRA relates closely in spirit to the Programmer's Apprentice [2]. While the Programmer Apprentice focuses primarily on the implementation part of the software process, a Programmer Apprentice's requirements initiative [3] (aimed at a deeper formalization of requirements than KBRA's more modest approach) has recently been started.

Recognizing the importance of supporting informality in requirement specification can be attributed to the SAFE (specification acquisition from experts) project [4]. While SAFE emphasized total automation of natural language to formal specification transformation, KBRA emphasizes intelligent assistance for incrementally refining requirements.

KBRA complements work on KBSA's specification assistant [5]. The main difference between these two efforts does not reflect different phases of the software life cycle so much as it reflects differing forms of support for requirements and specifications work. KBRA's emphasis on capturing formality from within informal modes of expression is balanced by the specification assistant's emphasis on evaluating formal specifications.

We will characterize requirements work, describe the functionality of the Lisp machine-based prototype, and examine underlying knowledge representation and reasoning approaches used in KBRA.

Requirements work

Requirements work covers acquisition, analysis, and communication.

Acquisition During acquisition, engineers "get a handle" on problem complexity and incrementally build up pieces of the requirement structure. They sketch out initial informal (fragmentary) statements, make calculations on the "back of the envelope," and draw informal box-and-arrow diagrams. Ambiguity and partially complete descriptions arise naturally during informal acquisition. However, even within a largely informal process, formal informational nuggets (requirements, dependencies, and justifications) are stated and can be placed into requirement structures.

For example, air traffic control (ATC) system description presents many requirements issues. Such systems aid human controllers in ensuring the safe movement of aircraft through controlled areas, using data from one or more radar systems to track aircraft position and velocity. Requirements clarify needs for processing controller input, displaying aircraft positions and flight plan data, reliability, fault tolerance, and other nonfunctional properties. We applied a significant knowledge-engineering effort to this domain as it was easily available and sufficiently complex (that is, reactive to the environment, a human-interface component, and based on sophisticated algorithms), which enabled us to identify important issues in supporting requirements work generally.

Requirement statements fall into the following broad knowledge categories:

1. System behavior—A description of the system's runtime behavior;
2. Boundary conditions—Properties of external objects in the system's environment;
3. Trade-off formulas—Relationships used to derive requirements from other requirements;
4. Dependencies—Indications that one requirement follows from the declaration of another;
5. Definitions—The vocabulary used in requirement statements.

Analysis Having made an initial stab at system description, engineers concentrate on interactions between requirement statements. Requirement analysis discovers these interactions and their management, taking into account what is feasible, testable, and cost effective. We contend that, in using KBRA, engineers can easily assess the requirements impact of possible design decisions and can investigate trade-off issues with substantial machine support.

Communication An engineer (and an assistant) must explain evolving requirements to end users and implementation teams. To ensure that user needs have been isolated from user wants and that engineers have arrived at an accurate requirement set, end-user validation is important (validation has not been a strong KBRA focus to date, although many presentations described below are helpful). Ultimately, requirements work seeks to develop a consistent and complete description of system needs suitable for design and implementation. In current software practice, requirements work terminates with a requirements document (often used as a contractual agreement). In advanced paradigms such as KBRA, formal representations for requirements serve as a basis for proving specification properties and machine-supported code synthesis.

The KBRA prototype

A junior-assistant theme motivates much of our research. As a first approximation, we consider KBRA the junior assistant charged with managing a system engineer's working notebook (see FIG. 33-1).

The assistant manages informally expressed knowledge entered in an on-line version of the notebook. Just as when engineers write statements in notebooks, work at one level can be incomplete while work at the next level proceeds. The assistant must piece things together and remove some of an engineer's organizing burdens. When requested to help engineers deal with problem complexity, the assistant retrieves information (about this or similar systems), notes inconsistencies between different "pages" of the on-line notebook, and generates informational presentations from different viewpoints (including dataflow, state transition, and functional breakdown). An emboldened assistant even critiques an engineer's work and completes partial descriptions. The next two sections describe specific KBRA functions designed to accomplish such junior-assistant behavior.

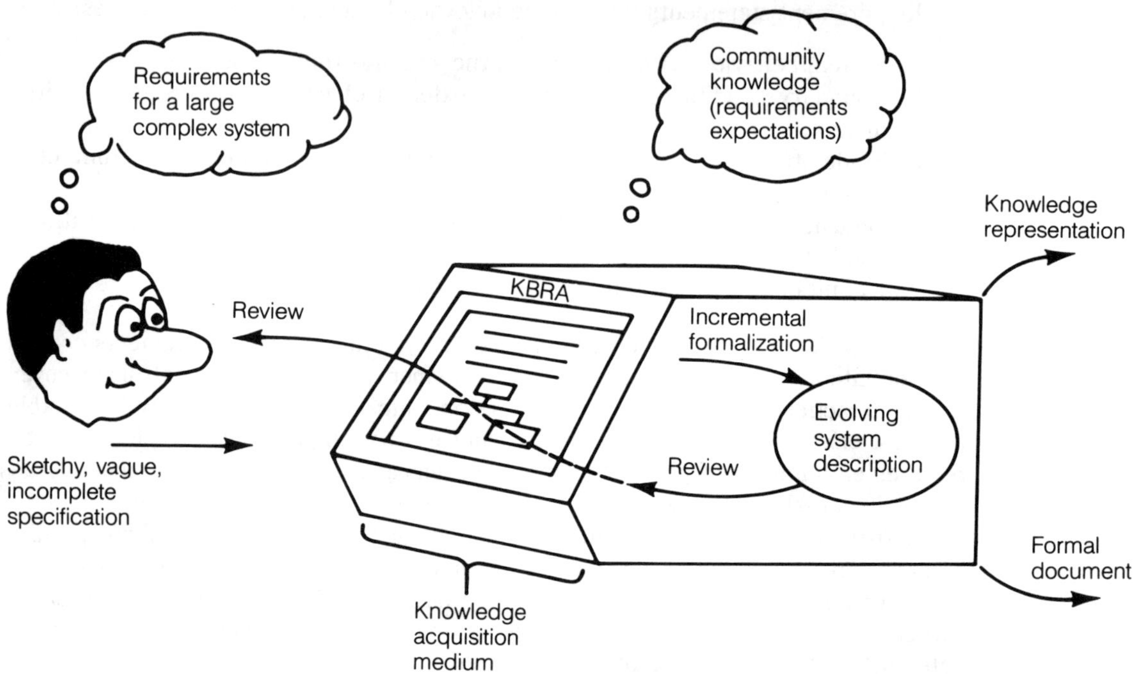

Fig. 33-1. KBRA accepts informal statements and assists in incremental formalization through reusable requirement components, review, and analysis.

The reusable-requirements library

A reusable-requirements library enables engineers to incorporate commonplace solutions into an evolving system description and provides the basis for several forms of KBRA assistance. In KBRA's current version, knowledge engineers manually encode components for physical laws, abstract descriptions of systems, requirements building blocks, typical data, and domain-specific formulas.

Choosing reusable components An ATC-tracker component brings several reusability issues into focus. We will discuss actual knowledge representation later. A tracker object type comprises a collection of subfunctions for correlation, extrapolation, smoothing, and maneuver detection. We define each function in a similar manner. Input is a state vector for the current status of a platform being tracked. Output is a record of platform position and velocity. Key discriminators for refining requirements include tracker reliability and cost (memory and processing time). If an engineer specifies discrimination properties, significant constraints (including rule-of-thumb formulas relating the number of operations per track to smoothing and correlation factors) will be imposed on evolving system descriptions. Discriminator properties can be derived from overall system-level considerations or can be entered explicitly by an engineer. We believe that a requirement (a tracker, for example) is a good candidate for reuse if (1) it is widely used, (2) it conjures up a rich set of expectations in people's minds, and (3) it interacts with other system components to constrain overall system behavior.

Cut and paste Engineers often gather, merge, and modify requirements from several existing systems. Reusable requirement components supply this activity's online version. Engineers can easily incorporate knowledge-base-object-type instances in a "cut and paste" fashion and modify them to form part of evolving system descriptions.

To simplify reuse, selection is available by explicit name through a linguistic interface. In addition, KBRA provides graphical browsing capabilities of taxonomies within the library. Engineers set a context for incorporation, select the desired object from the screen, and an instance becomes part of the system description in the declared context. We intended to investigate additional intelligent assistance for browsing and retrieval.

A source of expectations KBRA uses the library to critique and complete partial descriptions for evolving system descriptions.

Critiquing Over time, human engineers may declare system aspects containing unrealistic or conflicting statements. For example, the same information could be entered redundantly. Machine handling of redundancy can be challenging. While KBRA can detect that engineers have stated similar information, multiple instances may be redundant or intended, with refinement needed to point out key differences. An effective critic role resides in monitoring descriptions that become redundant with additions and deletions. As an illustration, KBRA will notify engineers and request clarification if no functional difference (that is, identical lists of active functions) exists between two declared states in the evolving system description.

An unreasonable requirement value, presenting a second type of detectable error, frequently results when engineers misplace a digit or incorrectly state units. KBRA checks requirements against a reasonable range (ranges are stated as part of a reusable component). KBRA cannot detect all careless errors, but assistance with even a few improves project productivity.

Finally, KBRA will critique a requirement set that has not been described in sufficient detail. This detail level may be associated with a global standard, a specific object type, or a user's explicit request. Foundations have been laid to check for data resources, object identification, and mandatory properties. For example, an engineer may request a comparison between a tracker and a new specification. If the specification does not include maneuver detection capability, but is otherwise similar to the tracker, KBRA will point out this maneuver detection omission. Such advice is generated by comparing expected discriminators and subfunction types for the generic tracker with types of declared subfunctions for the new specification.

Completing partial description KBRA can complete partial dataflow descriptions. An engineer creates the tracker and the radar message. Other items are entered automatically. KBRA notes that (1) *x-y* position can be computed from polar coordinates if a standard transformation is used, and (2) slant range (adjusted with an altitude correction) closely approximates range. This search entails using parameter approximation (for instance, slant range is an approximation for range) and typical formula knowledge (for example, polar-to-rectangular conversions and slant-range corrections).

Requirements presentation

We can describe KBRA's review and analysis capabilities by looking at knowledge acquisition goals and several available presentation types.

A knowledge acquisition medium Our goal is to provide a natural communication medium. Rather than force requirements engineers to conform to a KBRA language, we tailored KBRA's interface and environment toward various engineering expressions for problem solving. Engineers use many different methodologies [6] to capture requirements, and various approaches are useful as either precise abstractions or more loosely as aids for communicating ideas. Thus, we provide review and acquisition for many specification forms.

However, we balanced these goals for knowledge acquisition against the need to capture information in KBRA's requirements formalism. The medium need not be totally formal; a catch-as-catch-can approach—enabling us to extract formal information and piece it into the appropriate places in the requirements puzzle—is essential.

Presentation KBRA users enter and review requirements for the target system by interacting with a KBRA *presentation* (a modifiable projection of the evolving system description). All presentations display a single central evolving system description and are updated from it.

KBRA presentations encompass different modes (textual and graphic), different degrees of formality (from sketchy outline to formal methodology), and different abstractions (dataflow, state transition, and functional decomposition). A few examples suggest the variety and forms of support.

The intelligent notepad System engineers use the intelligent notepad to "jot down" requirements ideas. This presentation—an on-line analog of an engineer's textual working notebook recording the engineer's impromptu thoughts—may not reflect the evolving system description's most recent state. As requirements become formalized, uses will have many other presentations available for viewing and modifying current status. The intelligent notepad, a mechanism that might be used heavily in early phases, can also be used to review the evolution of ideas contributing to the current status.

Structured navigation provides for easy movement within outlines and editing at the logical requirements level. Engineers can shift their focus by moving into, out of, forward, and backward in outlines.

Within sentences, KBRA examines each word and responds (by underlining) when encountering specific words in a lexicon. Words in the lexicon include typical verbs used in requirements work ("update," "generate," "transfer," "evaluate," "perform," "associate") and names of reusable library items ("data," "activities," and "hardware devices"). Recognizing lexical words is important, since these words are directly linked to reusable components and other objects in the evolving system description.

The intelligent notepad includes some very crude natural-language-understanding facilities, and recognizes individual words and sentences in a catch-as-catch-can fashion. If it cannot interpret the sentence (lexical words are sparse), the sentence is still stored as a node in a text network.

Context diagrams One of several diagramming techniques available to engineers is the context diagram—the interface between the system and hardware, software, and operators in some external environment. KBRA diagram presentations can be initialized and updated from notes entered in the intelligent notepad, from information stated in other diagrams, or by starting with the diagram from scratch. Updating always occurs through modification of the central requirements repository.

State transition diagrams Finite-state machine descriptions offer a viewpoint emphasizing the states or modes of a system and events that will cause a change in state. Bubbles depict states in such diagrams, and arrows depict transitions. Arrows are marked with the event triggering state change and, in many cases, with associated actions caused by state change.

The calculator spreadsheet The calculator spreadsheet presentation is a calculator whose memory is the evolving system description displayed in spreadsheet form. As with any spreadsheet, formulas can be attached to spreadsheet cells. When using KBRA, engineers generate formulas by selecting operators, numbers, or numbers with units from the calculator, intermixed with spreadsheet cells. KBRA computes what it can as information is entered, warning of inconsistency and overspecification. When any requirement is changed, all requirements depending on that requirement are automatically revisited and tested. In addition, when engineers request explanations of cells, KBRA traces computations and dependency links.

The requirements document By interpreting document section representations, KBRA automatically generates requirements documents for system and segment specification and software requirement specification. Each document section structure contains links to other sections and explicit instructions for retrieving and modifying requirements information for document production. KBRA represents document sections in the same manner as text from the intelligent notepad.

In summary, we designed the KBRA prototype to support requirements acquisition and analysis beginning at the initial phase of "getting a handle on the problem" and continuing through to final document preparation. KBRA's reusable requirements library and presentation capabilities provide this support.

Knowledge representation

Our research has followed an architectural discipline fundamental to expert system work—namely, separating empty machine from knowledge base. The empty machine comprises structured-text mechanisms, presentation mechanisms, reasoning processes, and knowledge representation—mechanisms unified in Socle (structured object and constraint language environment), the underlying knowledge representation and reasoning system [7]. Socle (an architectural term for a column's foundation piece) is a hybrid system that merges frame-based and constraint-based programming components [8].

Socle also provides for an integrated set of inference mechanisms and inheritance of formulas that can be expressed declaratively on object types. Frame object slots are subject to inheritance, default reasoning, and procedural attachment. In addition, Socle uses constraint-based descriptions to represent formulas and dependencies. To accomplish this, Socle identifies frame slots with cells containing all information necessary for local propagation, retraction, and culprit identification.

Developing a representation for requirements acquisition and analysis presents issues associated with KBRA specifically, with informality generally, and with target system representation. We chose to parcel these issues among three basic realms: presentation, structured text, and evolving system description. Within each realm, we seek as much reuse as possible.

The presentation realm In the presentation realm, important representational issues include effective use of real estate on the screen, reusable presentation components (such as boxes and arrows), and recognition of editing commands.

Our presentation-based system uses *presenters* and *recognizers*. Presenters build presentation instances. Each presentation type contains information regarding how presentation instances should be constructed for given requirement objects. For example, the system constructs dataflow diagrams by (1) retrieving data, subfunctions, and input and output requirements, (2) creating associated boxes and arrows (the notation of dataflow methodology), and (3) organizing items for screen display. Recognizers discover syntactic properties of requested changes and create appropriate commands for modifying system description objects.

The structured-text realm Structured-text representation enables grouping and manipulation of informal text objects. Groupings can reflect requirement structure, document structure, summary, references, or loosely related text strings. Ultimately, these informal groupings may evolve into a formal requirement structure, but the roles that group objects play may not be significant at an initial requirements process stage. Structured text is a form of Hypertext [9]. In general, hypertext systems provide flexible access to underlying databases through textual and graphical objects appearing on the screen. Our structured-text approach embodies this metaphor strongly for outline processing.

Structured-text objects are tied to deeper requirement objects. A requirement declaration can occur initially as a text string. In addition, individual document sections are structured text, generated in prescribed ways from the requirements.

The evolving-system-description realm The evolving-system-description realm provides the ultimate repository for requirements. This representation approach supports three basic architectural principles. First, the state of the evolving system description is independent of the order in which requirements are entered; second, where logically possible, editing of objects is order independent; and third, a fairly fine-grained modularity of information exists within representations without enforcing completeness and consistency too early.

Reasoning process

Requirements, as entered by system engineers, are managed by KBRA's reasoning processes—inheritance, automatic classification, and constraint propagation.

Inheritance Knowledge-based systems use inheritance to infer expectations from generalizations. Within KBRA, inheritance supplies properties for requirement instances (including system activities, data items, and events). A new activity instance is created when a system activity is specified. This instance inherits default and reasonable nonfunctional requirements from the activity type. If the activity is declared to be of a more specific type, such as a coordinate transformation or a tracker, more refined expectations (including formulas that relate processing time, accuracy, and memory usage) will be inherited.

Automatic classification Automatic classification [10] places instances under the most specific taxonomy type. KBRA does not contain a general-purpose classifier; rather, it classifies by using special-purpose decision tables encoded with reusable components. Classification is important for requirement support because specialized types contain more detail and expectations than do supertypes. Consequently, KBRA can infer additional information when classification takes place.

Again, the tracker example is useful here. Cost (time and memory) and reliability are tracker discriminators. If a need exists for high reliability (with no accompanying stringent cost requirements), KBRA classifies the tracker as historical record (these trackers process historical data to smooth out possibly noisy data; hence, they are reliable but require additional processing time).

Constraint propagation Our research focuses on iterative and informal engineering problem solving. Constraint propagation—a deductive framework on top of a truth maintenance system—is our key reasoning approach [7]. The truth maintenance system manages arbitrary dependencies (for instance, requirement *b* because requirement *a*) and provides for well-founded support, retraction, explanation, and culprit identification when contradictions occur. The deductive framework provides multidirectional triggering of certain dependency types—numerical formulas, in particular.

Declaring formulas and dependencies Program control and user intervention establish formulas and dependencies. Program control establishes formulas and dependencies when instances of reusable object types are created. Such formulas tend to be physical laws and geometric formulas. Engineers establish formulas (often, very specific domain approximations) and dependencies between requirements by working interactively with the calculator spreadsheet presentation. In either case, constraint networks that link participating parameters are created. Using these constraint networks, KBRA infers related requirements and keeps track of dependency relationships.

An example Constraint propagation will enforce formulas including simple "distance = rate × time" relations within an ATC system specification. Initiation time for a tracking subsystem is the time required to properly identify and locate aircraft entering an airspace, and can be calculated by dividing an acceptable aircraft-untracked distance by aircraft maximum speed. On the other hand, clear airspace presentation to controllers requires that tracking algorithms be conservative in assigning tracks to aircraft (a slight delay can be better than mistaken identification). From this consideration, initiation time is calculated as the number of radar returns required to clearly determine target identity multiplied by the radar's sweep period.

When an engineer sets values for "sweep-period," "number-of-radar-returns-required," and "speed" to "12 seconds," "5," and "600 knots," respectively, then values of one minute and 10 nautical miles are automatically propagated to "initiation-time" and "distance."

Requirements engineers frequently try alternative solutions. Fortunately, initial decisions and derivation histories are captured in constraint networks. When a fact such as "number of radar returns = 5" is retracted, all requirement statements depending on that fact are retracted.

Contradictions may occur. Associated with a contradiction is a list of *culprits* (statements found by tracing back to the origins of calculations). KBRA identifies culprits and, if possible, automatically resolves contradictions among requirement statements. To do so, KBRA uses a *levels-of-support* concept. Engineers can affect the outcome of contradiction removal by annotating statements with different support levels. Support levels are default (use only when nothing else is available), supposition (test a possible value), belief (this value is most probable), and constant (reserved for definite constants—*pi*, for example). When results are consistent, the support level is inconsequential. However, if contradictions occur, the weakest or most tentative support level among culprits is automatically retracted. If more than one requirement has the weakest support level, engineers are prompted to make a selection.

A junior assistant charged with notebook management, KBRA plays many roles in managing the on-line working notebook of requirements information. It provides a library of reusable components that (1) can be incorporated into a system in a cut-and-paste mode, and (2) sets expectations for KBRA critiquing and completions. KBRA's review capabilities include a multipresentation mechanism that lets engineers enter information on their terms. Then, KBRA consistently propagates decisions to a central repository of requirement statements. KBRA's analysis capabilities work on this description by propagating ramifications of decisions and checking for consistency of results.

We have identified knowledge representation issues associated with requirements acquisition and analysis, and noted the three realms in which mechanisms operate to resolve knowledge issues: presentations, structured text, and evolving system description.

Finally, we have described AI techniques used to provide consistent reasoning processes for the intelligent assistant: inheritance of properties from generic object types, automatic classification based on discriminators indicating how to specialize instances, and constraint propagation for processing ramifications of requirements decisions and for supporting retraction when people change their minds.

Acknowledgments

Important contributions to KBRA's design and implementation and to the development of this article have been made by Charles Rich of MIT's AI Lab and by Patricia Ahern, John D'Addamio, J. Terry Ginn, William Hogan, and Jay Runkel of Sanders Associates. We also acknowledge the many helpful comments of *IEEE Expert* reviewers.

This research was sponsored by the Rome Air Development Center (RADC) under Contract No. F30602-85-C-0267. Views and conclusions contained herein are the authors' and should not be interpreted as representing the official opinion or policy of the RADC.

References

1. C. Green et al., "Report on a Knowledge-Based Software Assistant," in *Readings in Artificial Intelligence and Software Engineering*, C. Rich and R. Waters, eds., Morgan Kaufmann, Los Altos, Calif., 1986.

2. R. Waters, "The Programmer's Apprentice: A Session with KBEmacs," *IEEE Trans. Software Engineering*, IEEE Computer Society Press, Los Alamitos, Calif., Nov. 1985, pp. 1296–1320.
3. C. Rich, R. Waters, and H. Reubenstein, "Toward a Requirements Apprentice," *Proc. Fourth Int'l Workshop Software Specification and Design*, Monterey, Calif., Apr. 1987, pp. 79–86.
4. R. Balzer, N. Goldman, and D. Wile, "Informality in Program Specifications," *IEEE Trans. Software Engineering*, IEEE Computer Society Press, Los Alamitos, Calif., Mar. 1978.
5. W.L. Johnson, "Deriving Specifications from Requirements," *Proc. 10th Int'l Conf. Software Engineering*, IEEE Computer Society Press, Los Alamitos, Calif., 1988.
6. G. Roman, "A Taxonomy of Current Issues in Requirements Engineering," *Computer*, Apr. 1985, pp. 14–22.
7. D. Harris, "A Hybrid Structured-Object and Constraint Representation Language," *Proc. Fifth Nat'l Conf. Artificial Intelligence*, Morgan Kaufmann, Los Altos, Calif., 1986.
8. G. Steele, *The Definition and Implementation of a Computer-Programming Language Based on Constraints*, PhD dissertation, MIT/AI/TR-595, MIT, Cambridge, Mass., Aug. 1980.
9. J. Conklin, "Hypertext: An Introduction and Survey," *Computer*, Sept. 1987, pp. 17–41.
10. J. Schmolze and T. Lipkis, "Classification in the KL-ONE Knowledge Representation System," *Proc. Eighth Int'l Joint Conf. Artificial Intelligence*, Morgan Kaufmann, Los Altos, Calif., 1983.

34

Knowledge-based support for rapid software prototyping

Luqi

Editors' note *Luqi presents some ideas about how knowledge-based support can be provided for software prototyping. Like the preceding paper, as well as the one that follows, this one demonstrates how knowledge-based tools and techniques can be leveraged in the design and development of additional (conventional and knowledge-based) software. (Reprinted, with permission, from the Winter 1988 issue of* IEEE Expert. *©1988 by IEEE. All rights reserved.)*

Software prototypes are executable initial versions of software systems. Designers use prototypes to clarify requirements by demonstrating selected aspects of proposed system behavior to customers. To be useful in negotiations leading to software development projects, prototypes must be constructed and adapted to rapidly changing requirements PSDL (our prototyping system description language), and its associated computer-aided prototyping system make this possible on a large scale, as well as for embedded systems with real-time constraints. PSDL can express black-box descriptions of systems and decompositions into networks of simpler operators communicating via data streams. Associated prototyping methodology relies on reusable software components drawn from a software base to speed up prototype construction. In addition to the software base, the computer-aided prototyping system contains (1) a translator for adapting and interconnecting components, (2) schedulers for meeting real-time constraints, and (3) interfaces for entering design decisions.

Focusing on the software base, we will discuss the computer-aided prototyping system's knowledge base and show how to apply expert system technology to the software base management subsystem responsible for finding reusable software components with specified properties. We will apply rapid prototyping techniques to enable the detection and correction of requirement errors early in development. Prototyping is most useful in novel or poorly understood problem domains where designers find it impossible to anticipate every customer problem in advance. To enable more effective planning and to ensure that detailed design and implementation efforts will focus on the most important features, the prototyping effort tries to highlight unanticipated aspects of customer problems early on. We seek to automate support for analyzing new problem domains rather than automating the generation of many similar systems in well-understood problem domains. For this reason, we will address a general-purpose computer-aided prototyping system rather than specialized application generators.

Effective application generators require prior analysis of the problem domain to (1) develop a specialized problem description language, and (2) identify algorithms capable of solving all problems that language can express. This process—the easiest for narrowly defined problem domains—requires a substantial tool-building effort for each new application. The investment required to create a special-purpose application generator is justified if we plan to construct many software systems for the same problem domain [4]. The time required to construct application generators precludes their use in rapid prototyping for novel problem domains. The domain analysis required to construct an application generator for a new domain will benefit from prototyping with a computer-aided system.

Because they apply to software development generally, rather than to a fixed application area, computer-aided prototyping systems are more difficult to build than application generators. Consequently, we cannot anticipate application area problems and provide ready-made solutions (as is done in application generators). A completely automated system must solve all problems expressible in its problem statement language. Since automatically generating programs for solving problems in unconstrained domains is beyond the current state of the art, interactive systems offer practical support for prototyping.

We have designed our computer-aided prototyping system to assist human experts with software design. Our system contains knowledge comprising software components and rules describing how these components can be used and combined. Human experts provide guidance for solving problems that cannot be handled by automatically applying the expertise represented in the prototyping system's knowledge base. This structure enables us to build a useful system without requiring prior solutions to all possible problems, and supports the system's evolutionary development by allowing the addition of new components and rules to the knowledge base as we discover gaps in the system's knowledge through practical use.

Our computer-aided prototyping system functions as follows:

Designers obtain requirements from customers as written documents, with extensions and clarifications provided in response to designer questions and prototype demonstrations.

Designers propose a system interface consistent with these requirements, or make adjustments based on customer feedback, and record resulting specifications in PSDL.

Designers submit specifications to the software base management system, which attempts to retrieve or adapt available reusable components to meet those specifications. If this is impossible, then designers must decompose the system into a network of simpler components using PSDL, and repeat the process at more detailed levels until the software base can provide all components.

Component specifications have a dual role since they are used both for documenting intended prototype properties and for retrieving reusable components. Because this process is difficult to automate, designers must propose abstractions and carry out top-down design. The software base management system must find relevant components and fill in details. This is analogous to the interaction between mathematicians and an automatic theorem-proving program in which mathematicians propose lemmas as intermediate steps if the automatic procedure cannot solve the main theorem in a reasonable time; the automatic procedure takes care of fine-grained details that are tedious for the mathematician.

Our approach differs from other knowledge-based approaches to program construction by (1) the scale of its knowledge base, and (2) its computer-aided retrieval of reusable components based on specifications. The Programmer's Apprentice project [5] aims at speeding up the programming process via a library of reusable components. Reusable components implemented in the KBEmacs version of the Programmer's Apprentice—components known as "cliches"—represent algorithm fragments rather than complete modules. Using algorithm fragments, KBEmacs focuses on supporting the assembly of a module's implementation rather than assembling systems from complete modules; the scale of examples reported is a few hundred lines of code. We aim to produce software system prototypes larger by several orders of magnitude, and seek to avoid considering the internal structure of reusable components.

Programmers using KBEmacs should be familiar with library cliches (which are referenced by name) and will obtain the best results if they think in terms of these cliches. This is not a very serious problem in the prototypical version of KBEmacs, which contains only a few dozen cliches, but indicates that hundreds or thousands of cliches will probably be needed for serious applications [5].

Learning and remembering cliches can become burdensome. Our approach uses specification-based retrieval of reusable components to avoid this burden. The software base management subsystem seeks to automate the process of organizing, finding, and combining reusable components in the software base via specifications associated with components. Such capability is useful because it frees designers from having to remember what software components are currently available or from having to browse through components to discover relevant ones. This becomes especially important as available components increase in number (as they will in software bases supporting broad problem domains).

Expert system technology is appropriate for realizing the software base management system because the useful software component set is unbounded in principle and can be enormous in practice. We can view these components as instances of general patterns, with many variations on some of their properties. A practical approach is to store a representative component subset and to provide rules for generating related components (practical since it reduces the effort required to enter components into the system, conserves memory, and imposes structure on the software base).

Retrieving for the software base requires finding or constructing a program that realizes a given specification. Retrieving reusable components from a software base is a difficult search problem in a potentially infinite space. The elements of this space are pairs consisting of a specification and a corresponding executable program in which the elements of each pair are either explicitly stored or effectively constructible from explicitly stored pairs. This suggests using heuristic search methods, which are a common expert system component. Complete algorithmic solutions to the retrieval problem are unlikely because specification equivalence is an insoluble problem if the specification language is strong enough to be expressive. Our system addresses retrieval by relying on a recognizable subset of the equivalence relation on specifications.

Retrieval strategies

The software base management system retrieves reusable software components for meeting a given specification, using less designer time than it would take to code components manually. Since prototyping is most important for large problems, designer throughput provides a more appropriate measure than system delay to realize each component. Perceived time delay—an important factor in the effort required to use a system [6]—is valuable when producing answers with little perceptible delay because it avoids disturbing the designer's thought processes. Since searching a large space takes considerable time, practical designs should incorporate several search strategies ordered by speed. Those that the system can apply with little perceptible delay should be applied while the designer waits. If fast methods fail, retrieval should be spooled (thereby allowing designers to work on different aspects of the problem while the system pursues more time-consuming background search strategies).

The fastest and most superficial search strategy uses exact matches for component specifications. To facilitate retrievals based on exact matching, the system normalizes component specifications, transforming them into standard form [7]. This reduces variations when representing equivalent specifications, making syntactic matching more effective. The system normalizes specifications for retrieval requests and for each component entered into the software base. The system indexes components according to their normalized specifications; consequently, exact match searches can be performed quickly.

Retrieval strategies based on inexact matches and transformations consume more time, and are best applied off line. Checking for inexact matches and applying scribe transformations can both diverge—and both can be controlled by externally imposed time limits adjusted to match available computational resources (we will discuss transformations in detail below). Searching for inexact matches involves checking implications. If QS represents query specifications and CS represents specifications for reusable component C, then C is an inexact match for the query in case CS = > QS. Checking implications is not a decidable problem in general, but several partial decision rules exist that will correctly detect successful implications. Partial decision rules include shallow pattern matching based on the identities

$$A \text{ and } B => A$$
$$A => A \text{ or } B,$$

a propositional implication checker (based on truth tables) that ignores atomic predicate semantics and bounded-depth inference procedures sensitive to properties of common data types (for example, integers and sets) and common operations (including equality and orderings). To save time, we should apply inexact match and transformation strategies to relatively small portions of the software base; consequently, we have partitioned the software base according to the values of several categorical properties, which we detail under the "category" slot below. This structure resembles a hash table, in which categorical property values correspond to the hashing function. We identify the partition relevant to a given retrieval request based on property values, and components in the partition are subjected to a "best first" heuristic search that checks for inexact matches and attempts to create matches by applying various transformations. To realize the full potential of software use, such processing is important; exact matches can get you only so far [8]. The software base management system can find more opportunities to reuse software components created by human designers if small modifications for adapting components to a new environment can be made automatically.

An agenda mechanism resembling the one used in the AM system [9] can choose which component to analyze next. AM generates new mathematical concepts, with the most "interesting" concepts appearing first. The interpretation of "interesting" relevant to the software base management system's retrieval mechanism reflects the degree of similarity between component specification and the specification contained in the retrieval request. If a multiple-computer network is available, the system can process several of the most promising components in parallel.

The computer-aided prototyping system's knowledge base contains two kinds of information—descriptions of reusable software components, and rules for combining or adapting reusable components (the next two sections describe this knowledge in more detail).

Declarative knowledge

Primarily, the knowledge base's declarative knowledge contains reusable software components and can be organized naturally into a frame system [10]—each frame corresponding to a software component. Such organization is preferable to monolithic structures (Prolog databases, for example) because the software base can become unwieldy. The frames impose structure on the software base, which the system can use for limiting searches and for organizing secondary storage so that information units likely to be needed together can be retrieved as a single unit.

Frames in a frame system have common slots that have the same interpretation for each frame in the system. Each slot can have several facets. Each facet contains a property related to the slot. The following subsections describe slots important for managing a set of reusable software components.

Specification The specification slot contains a PSDL specification of the software component. Retrieval is based on the specification rather than on any attempt to analyze implementation code.

Implementation The implementation slot contains code for software components. Consistent with our principle of specification-based retrieval, we maintain only one implementation for each elementary specification. If a significant difference exists between two modules, module specifications should describe that difference so that retrieval mechanisms can be sensitive to it. If no significant difference exists, keeping both modules wastes space. Performance differences are sometimes important; hence, specifications must reflect these differences. The implementation slot of a nonelementary specification contains a list of other modules satisfying the specification. Nonelementary specifications help the system avoid recalculating common inexact matches, and do not affect the system's computational power in the absence of resource limits.

Category The category slot contains several properties used for partitioning the software base into disjoint subspaces. By limiting the knowledge base portion that it must search, the system uses such partitioning to improve performance. Categorical properties include the programming language used for implementation, the operating system it runs under, the component type, and maximum execution time. We have found component types of PSDL (functions, state machines, and data types) convenient for describing prototype software systems, since they provide a clear criterion for defining disjoint categories. The system uses maximum execution time to specify modules with real-time constraints, which are restricted to execute in a constant time frame. Therefore, maximum execution time can be represented as a number used to limit retrievals to only those modules capable of meeting a given real-time constraint. To efficiently generate subsets of components meeting a given bound on execution time, each partition's components are threaded together in a list kept sorted with respect to maximum execution time.

Alternatives The alternatives slot contains (1) rules for generating variations on a module, and (2) a list of related modules. The next section describes filter rules that exemplify rules for generating variations. Filter rules contain prescriptions for synthesizing composite modules by combining the current module with other modules that satisfy specified properties. Each related module is associated with a description of conditions under which the module is likely to be useful. For example, a module that finds roots by Newton's method can have a module for finding roots via the dissection method as an alternative, with the conditions that (1) derivatives are not needed, but that (2) end-points of an interval where the function reverses its sign are required as additional inputs to the module. Rules for generating variations are essential when defining the search space, while the list of related modules helps the system become more efficient by supplying heuristic advice regarding where to look next.

Transformations

It has been difficult to reuse software in practice because only rarely are two instances of the "same" software component exactly alike at a superficial level. Instead, many small variations on a theme exist. The number of small variations can be unbounded, and it can be difficult to predict which variation will be needed next (an extreme example is the set of array-sorting routines in standard Pascal). Since Pascal requires that the procedure header specify the type and bounds of the array, a different sorting procedure is needed for each array type and size.

We can provide transformations that adapt or combine components explicitly stored in the software base to accommodate a class of small variations, thereby alleviating this problem. Systems performing such transformations as part of the retrieval process have a much better chance of successfully retrieving a specified component from the software base than do systems that can only return components explicitly stored in the software base. This capability also reduces the need for designers to manually adapt reusable components after retrieval—especially important in rapid prototyping, where designer time is at a premium. The constructed implementation's efficiency is less important in prototyping, where the primary purpose is to discover system behavior acceptable to customers. Once component specifications have stabilized, identifying performance bottlenecks and reimplementing critical modules more efficiently can be justified.

A well-known approach to the small-variations problem defines parameterized generic components, thereby providing a single representation for a whole class of related components. Both the specification and implementation of generic components have one or more formal parameters that the matching process can bind to adapt components to specific applications. The retrieval mechanism must include a transformation that creates the corresponding generic-code-template instantiation. This transformation can involve some computation to expand substitutions in line for programming languages (including Pascal) that do not explicitly support generic units. Such transformations may be needed even for languages supporting generic code units (Ada, for instance) because the software base can provide a more powerful or flexible parameterization mechanism than that provided by the programming language.

Another kind of transformation involves small local rearrangements to the reusable component interface. These transformations include permuting input and output parameters, ignoring extra output parameters, and filling in values for extra input parameters. Such transformations embody general-purpose strategies encoded in knowledge base rules. The transformation for filling in extra input parameters resembles the process of determining an actual parameter value for a generic module via the matching process. For example, a query requesting a component to calculate length (**v**) (where **v** is a three-dimensional vector) can be satisfied by an operation magnitude (**v**,3) where magnitude (**v**,*n*) calculates the length of an *n*-dimensional vector.

Other transformations yield building blocks for a composite component. An important expert system function for retrieving reusable components involves a limited amount of bottom-up design, necessary if we are to free designers from having to remember all reusable components in the software base. If we limit this knowledge to the expert system, the expert system must steer decomposition in directions that match available components. One way to achieve this uses composition rules (heuristics indicating plausible ways to extend a module). Some composition rules are applicable generally, while others are associated with specific components or component classes in the software base. This kind of information fits in a module's alternatives slot.

Guard rules and filter rules form two important composition rule categories. Guard rules describe decompositions induced by case analysis, and produce conditional statements by matching reusable component specifications against part of a retrieval specification. If the retrieval specification is *S* and the reusable component specification has the form *G* = > *S*, the component can be augmented with a PSDL control constraint of the form

```
triggered if G
```

provided that the guard *G* can be expressed in a form executable in PSDL. We generate guard rules by matching parts of the retrieval specification against a component specification. If the match succeeds, the guard rule provides a partial implementation that can be completed by providing other conditional implementations applicable if *G* is false.

Guard rules are important because they enable retrieval of partial operations that satisfy query specification under a restricted set of conditions, thus providing some bottom-up guidance to designers about decomposing problems in a way that matches available components. By reporting conditions under which a known method will satisfy specification, such rules also allow useful responses for specifications not satisfiable in all cases. This helps expose and correct conceptual oversights on the part of designers who may be contemplating the most common case and fail to notice that some circumstances exist under which normally desired results cannot be achieved. Guard rules that result in partial implementations covering normal cases can help focus designer attention on abnormal cases, possibly leading to the identification of missing exception conditions or error messages in prototype design. For example, searching for a component that calculates a set's maximum element may result in a guarded operator that fulfills the specification in cases where the set is not empty. Such a response focuses designer attention on whether the set can be empty and, if it can, on identifying an appropriate response for the component being prototyped. This represents cases where bottom-up guidance from the knowledge case can identify specification faults and suggest changes to prototype design.

Filter rules provide another way to suggest decompositions based on bottom-up criteria. Filter rules factor specifications, enabling them to be met by two-component dataflow decompositions in which (1) the first component is a filter operation available in the software base, and (2) the filter rule derives the second component's specification from the query specification. For example, the filter rule associated with a sorting operator matches query specifications of the form

(x IN s <=> P(x)) & sorted(s).

The need for computer-aided rapid prototyping of software systems, particularly systems with real-time constraints, motivated our work on methods for retrieving reusable software components. While reusable components can effectively reduce designer effort, we must relieve designers of the need to remember the contents of large component libraries. We have outlined an expert system structure for retrieving reusable software components from a knowledge base that uses component specifications. Rule-based retrieval, combined with a limited ability to adapt and combine available components, is essential for making extensive software reuse practical in prototyping because standard software components appear with widely ranging variations in many practical applications. The likelihood of being able to reuse components increases if the system can provide many variations on each component that was manually constructed and entered into the software base. Rules for composing stored components are important for reducing the designer's knowledge load. We can use such rules to provide a limited amount of bottom-up design based on available components of which designers may not be aware.

We have described our approach to the automated retrieval of reusable software components in terms of the prototyping language PSDL because it supports a computer-aided prototyping system and contains several features that make our approach easier to realize—explicit black-box specifications for each component, for instance, and facilities for describing dataflow decompositions subject to nonprocedural control constraints. Our approach can be applied to other languages (including Prolog) by establishing suitable conventions and usage patterns. An essential part of our approach is the storing of a specification for each reusable software component, which can be done in the context of many different languages. However, since it contains facilities for expressing timing constraints, and since the associated execution support system contains facilities for realizing such constraints, PSDL is the language of choice for the rapid prototyping of real-time systems. Prototyping is especially important for this class of systems because their requirements are difficult to discover and understand.

Developing a complete computer-aided prototyping system is a long-range research project. We have designed and partially implemented the first version of such a system. The computer-aided prototyping system's subprogram for retrieving reusable components (still in the design stage) will require substantial effort to implement and evaluate because we must assemble an effective set of reusable software components to refine the proposed system's rules and test its effectiveness. Important areas for future research include finding more effective transformation sets and more efficient matching algorithms. We must also assemble an effective set of reusable software components for the software base. Existing components must be generalized, specified, and certified (or thoroughly tested, at least) before they can become useful members of the software base. To build up a comprehensive and effective software base, an extended incremental process is needed; experience with using initial versions of the software base will indicate the most important directions for growth.

Acknowledgments

This work was supported in part by the National Science Foundation under Grant No. CCR-8710737. We thank Henry Ayling for his careful editing and Armard Prieditis, Jack Mostow, Yuh-Jeng Lee, Robert Herndon, and Valdis Berzins for their comments and suggestions on earlier drafts of this article.

References

1. Luqi, V. Berzins, and R. Yeh, "A Prototyping Language for Real-Time Software," *IEEE Trans. Software Engineering*, Oct. 1988.
2. Luqi and M. Ketabchi, "A Computer-Aided Prototyping System," *IEEE Software*, Mar. 1988, pp. 66 – 72.
3. Luqi and V. Berzins, "Rapidly Prototyping Real-Time Systems," *IEEE Software*, Sept. 1988, pp. 25 – 36.
4. P. Freeman, "A Conceptual Analysis of the Draco Approach to Constructing Software Systems," *IEEE Trans. Software Engineering*, July 1987, pp. 830 – 844.
5. R. Waters, "The Programmer's Apprentice: A Session with KBEmacs," *IEEE Trans. Software Engineering*, Nov. 1985, pp. 1296 – 1320.
6. S. Card, T. Moran, and A. Newell, *The Psychology of Human-Computer Interaction*, Lawrence Earlbaum Associates, Hillsdale, N.J., 1983.
7. Luqi, "Normalized Specifications for Identifying Reusable Software," *Proc. ACM-IEEE Fall Joint Computer Conference*, IEEE Computer Society, 10662 Los Vaqueros Circle, Los Alamitos, Calif., Oct. 1987.
8. J. Mostow and M. Barley, "Automated Reuse of Design Plans," *Proc. Int'l Conf. Engineering Design*, American Society of Mechanical Engineers, Boston, Mass., Aug. 1987, pp. 632 – 647.
9. R. Davis and D. Lenat, *Knowledge-Based Systems in Artificial Intelligence*, McGraw-Hill, New York, N.Y., 1982.
10. M. Minsky, "A Framework for Representing Knowledge," in *Readings in Knowledge Representation*, R. Brachman and H. Levesque, eds., Morgan Kaufmann, Los Altos, Calif., 1985, pp. 245 – 262.

35

Design of knowledge-based systems with a knowledge-based assistant

Eric Schoen
Reid G. Smith
and Bruce G. Buchanan

Editors' note *Schoen, Smith and Buchanan describe yet another attempt to design and develop (in this case, intelligent) systems with the aid of knowledge-based tools and techniques. Here the emphasis is on the knowledge acquisition process, where the knowledge-based assistant plays the role of third party in the process. The paper reports on ongoing conceptual and developmental work in the area. (Reprinted, with permission, from the December 1988 issue of* IEEE Transactions on Software Engineering. *©1988, IEEE. All rights reserved.)*

I. Introduction

Intelligent assistants facilitate design and construction of complex software. In this article, we propose a model for an intelligent assistant to aid in building one kind of software—knowledge-based systems—and discuss a preliminary implementation.

The development of knowledge-based systems (KBS's) is a complex process. Often applied to poorly understood domains—for which standard programmatic solutions do not exist—successsful KBS development at present requires collaboration between *domain specialists* and *knowledge engineers*. The process is one of iterative refinement: the specialist describes domain knowledge to the engineer, who in turn encodes that knowledge using tools provided by a KBS "shell," and then elicits further knowledge from the specialist. The approach is far from ideal; difficulties can arise in any of the many steps involved in the transfer of knowledge from specialist to system (e.g., in elaborating the domain knowledge, in encoding the domain knowledge, or in verbal communication).

We view the central problem in KBS design to be knowledge acquisition—moving domain knowledge into a software system by whatever means. This is not simply a problem encountered in the initial stages of design. Rather, it extends over the complete lifetime of a system. Continuing expansion and modification of the system's knowledge base is driven by two factors: changing domain knowledge, and broadened scope of applicability. Designers of existing KBS development environments recognize this problem, and provide a wide variety of tools to reduce its difficulty. Some of these tools—such as syntax checkers—derive from conventional software engineering; others—such as multiple knowledge representation paradigms, explanation facilities, and rule debuggers—have evolved within the KBS community specifically to address the iterative and uncertain nature of knowledge acquisition.

While contemporary KBS development environments contain many tools to help manage the complexity of knowledge acquisition, they offer little or no guidance on how to *use* these tools. As a result, knowledge engineers are often faced with a bewildering set of choices: how to represent domain terminology and relations, how to determine completeness of encoded domain knowledge, how to enter additional domain knowledge without introducing inconsistencies, and so on.

The central theme of this article is a new approach to knowledge acquisition, in which an intelligent assistant joins the domain specialist and knowledge engineer. This third participant aids the engineer in using the tools of the KBS development environment to encode knowledge of the domain. Its support takes a number of forms: recognition of both incomplete knowledge and opportunities for further specialization and elaboration of domain knowledge, consistency and "style" maintenance, automatic "classification" of domain terms [11], debugging aids, explanation concerning the evolution, current status, and dependencies of the knowledge base, and validation of encoded knowledge.

We have come to view the interaction between the knowledge engineer and the engineer's interface as a discourse, albeit one carried out in the "language" of the designer's tool. All too often, system builders are forced to communicate with design aids at a syntactic level, within a vocabulary that is difficult to learn and use. By contrast, communication with a human assistant is at a high level, in which a designer can assume the assistant knows something about the design task and the system (or device) being designed, as well as about the design tools. For effective communication, each participant must be aware of the preconceptions, intentions, and specialized vocabulary of the other. Further, much is often left unstated during discourse, to be inferred by the participants. In light of this, we propose elevating the status of design tools to that of intelligent assistants, which share this "high-level communication" property with human assistants.

A. The need for intelligent assistance

Developers of early rule-based expert systems, such as MYCIN [14] and EMYCIN [36], were simultaneously attempting to understand conventions for building rule sets and editing knowledge bases (KB's) of rules. Work by Davis [21] and Suwa [56], and later Bennett [3], focused on representing such conventions so that intelligent assistance could be offered at the time of KB design or KB debugging. In particular, the programs resulting from this research encoded knowledge of the *syntax* of rules and some knowledge of the *semantics* of the domain, in order to guide acquisition and maintenance of rule sets.

Knowledge in EMYCIN-based systems was represented primarily in production rules. While constrained in format, and intended to represent independent "packets" of knowledge, these rules also proved surprisingly flexible. However, they frequently contained unforeseen interactions. Thus, it was incumbent upon the knowledge acquisition tools to prevent anomalous rules from becoming part of the rule base. To this end, the EMYCIN interface provided a number of services: syntactic analysis could discover (and often correct) typographical errors; semantic analysis could reveal subsumption or contradiction relationships between new and existing rules; statistics on rule application helped detect overly general or overly specific rule premises.

While EMYCIN was successful in these specific areas, no attempt was made to include in it more general "guidelines of *good practice*." Yet, such guidelines—concerning efficiency, clarity, and elegance in rule-based system design—were learned and communicated informally among persons using EMYCIN and similar systems.

Unfortunately, the ramifications of some of these guidelines were not totally understood at the time. For example, knowledge engineers were encouraged to add so-called "screening clauses" to rule premises; these clauses defined a narrow context within which the remaining premise clauses made sense. The primary reason for including such clauses in a rule was to prevent the consultation system from asking for specific information prior to establishing the general context for the question.

In retrospect, the use of screening clauses complicated the tasks of maintaining [2] and explaining [17] the rule base. Having no explicit concept of screening clauses, the EMYCIN knowledge acquisition interface could neither detect when one was necessary in a newly entered rule, nor could it identify the screening clauses in the existing rule base. EMYCIN was quite successful at syntactic manipulation of rule bases, but much less successful at semantic manipulation.

The EMYCIN experience provided a number of valuable lessons concerning the design of knowledge-based systems; principal of these is the need to represent information explicitly and declaratively. Since then, we have seen the power of this lesson applied in a number of different ways: Aikins' CENTAUR system [2] is a reimplementation of the rule-based PUFF system [31] in a mixed rule-and-object paradigm, replacing context-setting clauses by an explicit taxonomy of disease *prototypes* to which rules are attached; Clancey's NEOMYCIN system [16] builds on Davis' meta-rules [21] to explicitly represent diagnostic strategy, producing a system which can explain and tutor medical diagnosis at a much more detailed level than could MYCIN. When this information is made explicit in the knowledge base, the designer's assistant can use it (e.g., for explanation [57] and for knowledge base debugging [21]). Because much information was left implicit in MYCIN, a substantial amount of work was required when meningitis rules were added to the existing bacteremia rule base [1].

We believe it is now possible to construct a more powerful knowledge base designer's assistant. This assistant will act as an interface between a KBS designer (e.g., a knowledge engineer) and a KBS development environment; it will not only provide the sort of passive support provided by EMYCIN, but will also actively support encoding of domain knowledge.

B. Knowledge-intensive development environments

Key progress in two areas—representational frameworks and computing technology—has enabled us to conceive of tools like the knowledge base designer's assistant. Object-oriented programming permits us to model underlying domain principles with greater clarity and efficiency than was possible in purely rule-based formalisms. Recent advances in computing technology (e.g., powerful personal workstations) permit us the "luxury" of combining interaction and inference while retaining a reactive environment, so that usable interfaces can also perform significant amounts of deduction.

The designer's assistant forms part of a larger vision—which we call a *knowledge-intensive development environment*. This environment has two essential, interrelated components; a *representation and reasoning substrate*, and an *interaction substrate*. Extending the key principle of knowledge-based systems—separation of domain knowledge and problem-solving methods—this approach further separates problem-solving methods and interaction.

The representation and reasoning substrate integrates distinct problem-solving subsystems involving objects, rules, constraints, contexts, and explanation. This substrate has knowledge of the use of the individual subsystems, problem-solving methods, and basic knowledge of the domains in which it is applied. Our current substrate is based upon Strobe, an object-oriented language [50]. It has been augmented by a rule interpreter [48], a constraint manager, and a task configuration manager [32], [52].

The interaction substrate provides a set of tools for constructing interactive user interfaces to knowledge-based systems. It must support at least three different perspectives, corresponding to three different types of user: 1) the developer/maintainer; 2) the domain specialist; and 3) the end user. (Each of these, in turn, may require different perspectives as well.) The substrate must provide a reactive environment for developer/maintainers. It must allow domain specialists to focus on the encoded domain knowledge, hiding the underlying representational mechanisms, and provide direct expression and interaction in terms natural to the domain. Finally, the substrate must permit the construction of transparent and "easy-to-use" interfaces for end users. These three interfaces may appear as separate tools, but in fact, they all share a common, underlying software architecture. Our recent work on Impulse-86 [49], [51] indicates that it is possible to construct an interaction substrate that provides this architecture, and supports the needs of all three user groups.

The representation and reasoning substrate already contains tools well-suited to user interface design. The object-oriented paradigm used in domain knowledge base construction is equally viable for encoding and organizing interface constructs like editors, windows, menus, and views. Knowledge base construction and maintenance is itself a knowledge-based task, and thus, the interaction substrate must be a knowledge-based system. Reasoning mechanisms from the representation and reasoning substrate can be brought to bear on the management of user interaction. Rules can be used to infer missing or dependent information. The same browsing techniques used by the developer to explore the system code can support graphical explanation—for developers, domain specialists, and end users alike. Analogies to discourse can be drawn in the knowledge-intensive development environment. The interaction substrate must reason about the background, sophistication, and intentions of its user, as well as the available domain knowledge, to offer meaningful assistance. It also must often infer information left implicit by the user.

The complete knowledge-intensive development environment we describe is as yet a research goal; however, many of the individual components of the substrates do exist and are in daily use. Our first step towards integrating the components into the complete development environment is the knowledge base designer's assistant, a component of the interaction substrate. In Section II, we describe our current efforts aimed at constructing this tool. In the following sections, we describe the software technologies upon which it relies: in Section III, we discuss the role of object-oriented programming; in Section IV, we describe interaction substrates, using Impulse-86 as an example. We present samples of the sorts of interfaces it can construct and discuss its utility for knowledge-based system design. We discuss related work in Section V, and summarize our approach to knowledge acquisition in Section VI.

II. Example

In this section, we discuss the role of an *active agent*—the knowledge-based designer's assistant—in the design process. When completed, it will offer the designer a wide spectrum of assistance, ranging from instruction in use of available tools to selection of representation, reasoning, and interaction paradigms. The assistant will appear as an expert—albeit computerized—user of the KBS development environment. In this section, we describe the various services that will be provided by the assistant.

The interface between the designer and the assistant is Impulse-86. The assistant monitors knowledge base editing commands issued by the designer, and interacts by displaying suggestions in a set of windows. The assistant is aware of all changes made to an evolving knowledge base. (As with the original conception of the "Programmer's Assistant" in Interlisp [28], the assistant can be viewed as looking over the designer's shoulder.)

Throughout this section, examples are drawn from a hypothetical session in which the designer and assistant collaborate on the design of the kernel of a semiconductor fabrication knowledge base. (Information regarding VLSI technology is taken from [58].) The dialog between the designer and assistant is in reality graphical in nature, driven by interaction with customized interfaces; for clarity, we present the scenario as a transcript, in stylized natural language, of that interaction. In Section IV, we show some of the Impulse-86 editors which underlie the scenario.

Our convention is as follows: text in *italics* is commentary on the transcript; text in bold font is either input from the designer, or represents concepts related to the knowledge base under construction; text in roman font is output from the assistant. The assistant uses bold font when referring to concepts in the designer's knowledge base.

A. Assistance in building a domain model

In this example, we consider only the early phase of KBS construction. The major goal of knowledge acquisition at this point is to build a model of the domain, in terms of a vocabulary of domain-specific terms and relations. (This is a *model-based* approach to knowledge acquisition: we construct this model prior to considering specific problem cases and the knowledge needed to solve such cases. In the alternative *case-based* approach, specific problem cases are used to identify the necessary domain terms and relations.) Terms and relations from this model are used in task-specific inference and control knowledge, as well as in explanations and conclusions produced by the system. For purposes of illustration, we assume this information is represented as objects in an object-oriented language (see Section III).

During this phase, the assistant will guide acquisition of terms and relations so as to produce a model which encodes domain information in as clear, consistent, and complete a manner as possible. By this, we intend the knowledge base to contain little redundant information, so that information pertaining to any group of objects is associated with the maximally general object in the group. Further, the knowledge base should contain no contradictory information. Finally, the knowledge base should contain all terms and relations which are used by inference and control rules, as well as system-generated explanations.

Clearly, this represents an ideal, and probably unrealizable, goal. We expect inconsistencies and incomplete information to become apparent as the domain model is applied to actual problems. A designer cannot guarantee that the domain model is complete before beginning to add inference and control knowledge to the system (since unforeseen terms and relations may be necessitated by adding such knowledge). Instead, we expect the assistant to employ heuristics that judge when enough vocabulary has been acquired to begin the next phase of knowledge acquisition. Acquisition and correction of the domain model will not cease with the end of the early phase of KBS construction; rather, it will likely continue in a fashion interleaved with acquisition of inference knowledge. The assistant will be able to detect when the addition of an inference or control rule necessitates extending or correcting the domain model, and temporarily switch back to the model acquisition "mode."

Our example shows the assistant helping the designer during model acquisition by suggesting terms and relations to be specialized and/or elaborated. (The former involves defining new, more specific, subclasses of objects in the knowledge base; the latter, adding slots to existing objects.) It will do this by analyzing the evolving domain model to produce a set of *goals*, and then analyzing those goals to produce a set of knowledge base *modifications* to be made to achieve those goals. The modifications can then be communicated to the designer in a number of ways: as a description of the changes to be made to the information encoded in the knowledge base (i.e., changes to the meaning of the knowledge), as a description of the changes to be made to structures in the knowledge base (i.e., changes to the implementation of the knowledge), or as a set of editing commands to be performed to change those structures. These alternatives represent explanations of deficiencies in the model, at increasingly lower levels of abstraction; the assistant may choose the explanation which is most appropriate, given knowledge of the designer's experience.

The assistant needs to employ at least five categories of knowledge to be able to offer meaningful advice:

Type 1: Knowledge of "generic tasks," (e.g., knowledge of broad categories of application areas),

Type 2: Knowledge of knowledge base design (e.g., procedures for acquiring and elaborating knowledge, and commonly-used knowledge base structuring techniques [cliches]),

Type 3: Knowledge of the semantics of the language used to encode the domain model (e.g., general knowledge about relations, and knowledge about mapping between meanings and representation of meanings in the language),

Type 4: Knowledge of the editing tools available to the designer (e.g., available editing commands and their effects),

Type 5: Knowledge of discourse (e.g., knowledge of how to infer the goals, plans, and intentions of the user).

B. Hypothetical design session

We present an excerpt from the beginning of the hypothetical design session, in which the designer and assistant begin to encode the domain model. For each inference made by the assistant, we indicate which of the above types of knowledge has been used.

> Assistant: What sort of task will this KBS be performing? I currently know about the general characteristics of diagnosis, manufacturing, and design tasks.
> Designer: Manufacturing.

The assistant now examines its generic model of manufacturing, and finds that manufacturing can be viewed as a sequence of steps which consume raw materials to produce a finished part (Type 1 knowledge). The assistant now creates a goal of mapping terms from this particular manufacturing task—semiconductor fabrication—onto terms in the generic model (Type 2 knowledge).

> Assistant: You could now add information to the domain model to describe the sort of Finished-Part being manufactured.

These suggestions—which the designer is free to ignore—appear in a number of forms. The assistant maintains a prioritized agenda of goals, which it displays in a window. The assistant operates continuously "in the background," and reorders and redisplays its goal agenda in response to changes in the knowledge base. The assistant makes other suggestions by highlighting portions of Impulse-86 editing windows already visible on the screen.

> Designer: How?

The assistant's last suggested change was phrased in terms of a change to information encoded in the domain model. The designer asked how to implement this change, which suggests to the assistant that the designer does not understand how this information is to be encoded (Type 5 knowledge). It explains the change, in slightly less abstract terms—as changes to the structure of the knowledge base (Type 3 knowledge).

> Assistant: Create a subclass of the concept Finished-Part.
> Designer: How?

The assistant infers that the designer does not understand how to use the available editing tools (Type 5 knowledge). The assistant repeats the last suggestion, in terms of Impulse-86 editing commands (Type 4 knowledge).

> Assistant: Select the Create Object command in the KB Commands menu attached to the KB editor for the Manufacturing knowledge base. Respond to the Object Names: prompt with the name of the Finished-Part produced by this manufacturing application, to the Object Type: prompt with class, to the Generalizations: prompt with Finished-Part, and to the Groups: prompt with any symbol you choose, or simply with <return>.

The designer carries out the above steps, and names the specific kind of finished part being produced.

> Designer: Creates a subclass of Finished-Part called Integrated-Circuit.)
> Assistant: You should now add information which names the Raw-Material used to manufacture Integrated-Circuits. Create subclasses of Raw-Material using the Create Object command as you did previously.

(Types 2, 3, and 4 knowledge.)

> Designer: (Creates subclasses of Raw-Material called Silicon, Dopant, and Aluminum.)

At this point, the model contains information which indicates that silicon, dopant, and aluminum are the raw materials used to manufacture integrated circuits. Continuing in the same manner, the assistant prompts the designer to specialize *Step,* thereby defining the steps which compose the manufacturing process. As this contributes nothing new to our example, we leave out this part of the hypothetical design session.

Figure 35-1 illustrates the state of the model sometime after the end of the session excerpt. The designer has created a subclass of Manufacture, called Process, which represents the semiconductor manufacturing process. He or she has also created a number of subclasses of Step, each of which represents a distinct subtask in the manufacturing process. Figure 35-1 displays the current taxonomy of domain terms.

Knowledge of knowledge base design techniques, Strobe semantics, and Impulse-86 editing commands (Types 2, 3, and 4 knowledge) enables the assistant to translate high-level goals into concrete suggestions. For example, in order to explain its suggestion, ". . . add information to the domain model to describe the sort of Finished-Part being manufactured," the assistant refers to its knowledge regarding the representation of domain terms. The designer is being asked to provide a term which specializes the class Finished-Part for the semiconductor domain. The knowledge that classes represent domain terms, and that specialization relationships between domain terms are represented as subclass relations between corresponding classes, enables the assistant to suggest that the designer should create a subclass of Finished-Part.

When asked for further help, the assistant refers to its knowledge of Strobe and Impulse-86 to direct the designer to create a subclass of Finished-Part. From knowledge of Strobe semantics, the assistant determines that a subclass of Finished-Part will be represented as a class object whose generalization is Finished-Part. From knowl-

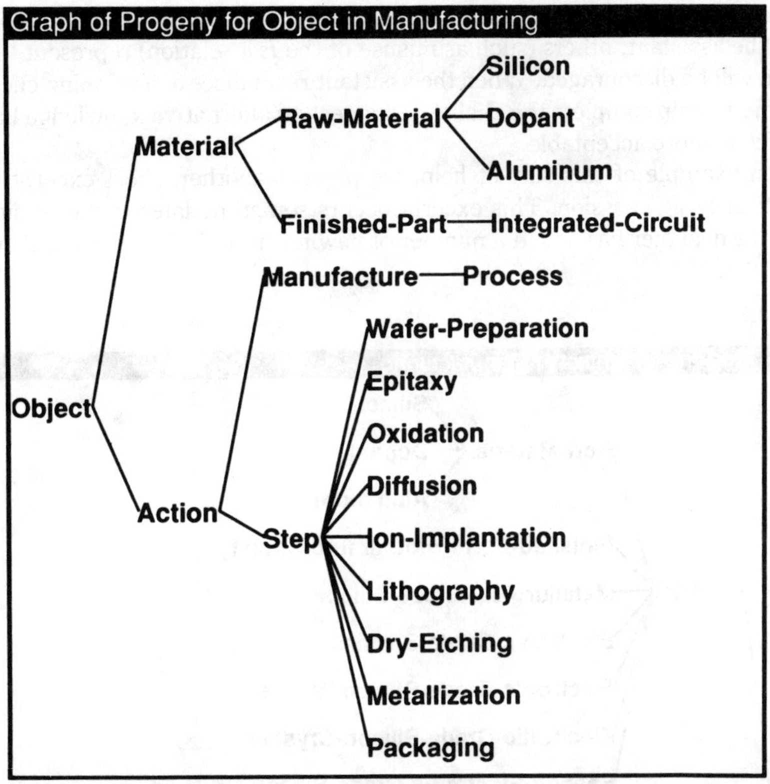

Fig. 35-1. Taxonomy of terms in the Semiconductor Manufacturing knowledge base.

edge of Impulse-86, the assistant describes the sequence of editing commands which will create the desired subclass. Note that advice is being stated in terms drawn from the evolving domain model; we believe this in itself is an important form of assistance. In-context advice is more useful than that drawn from a printed manual, or from a canned example domain. The instructions apply directly to the development task at hand; the user is freed from having to draw (possibly flawed) analogies between example and real domains. Furthermore, since the assistant knows the exact sequence of editing commands needed to implement its suggestion, it could execute the commands itself and relieve the designer of a potentially tedious task. We expect such on-line help will ease the process by which designers become experts at using the tools provided by their environments.

Another use of Type 2 knowledge we envision involves common practice in knowledge base design. We expect the assistant to know about *clichés*—common patterns of relationships between objects.[1] Some of these cliches (such as consistent refinement of

[1] We use the term *cliché* in much the same manner as in KBEmacs [60]. However, our cliches are structural—abstracting relations between concepts—while those of the Programmer's Apprentice are procedural—abstracting programs.

slot values across a subclass taxonomy) represent "good practice" and will be encouraged by the assistant; others (such as misuse of the *is-a* relation) represent "bad practice" and will be discouraged. When the assistant recognizes a developing cliche, it will either offer to help complete the cliche, or suggest an alternative knowledge base structure which is more acceptable.

As an example of this sort of help, we present another, short excerpt from our hypothetical design session. This excerpt occurs sometime later in the session; in the interim, the designer has added a number of new terms and filled in a number of slots. See FIG. 35-2.

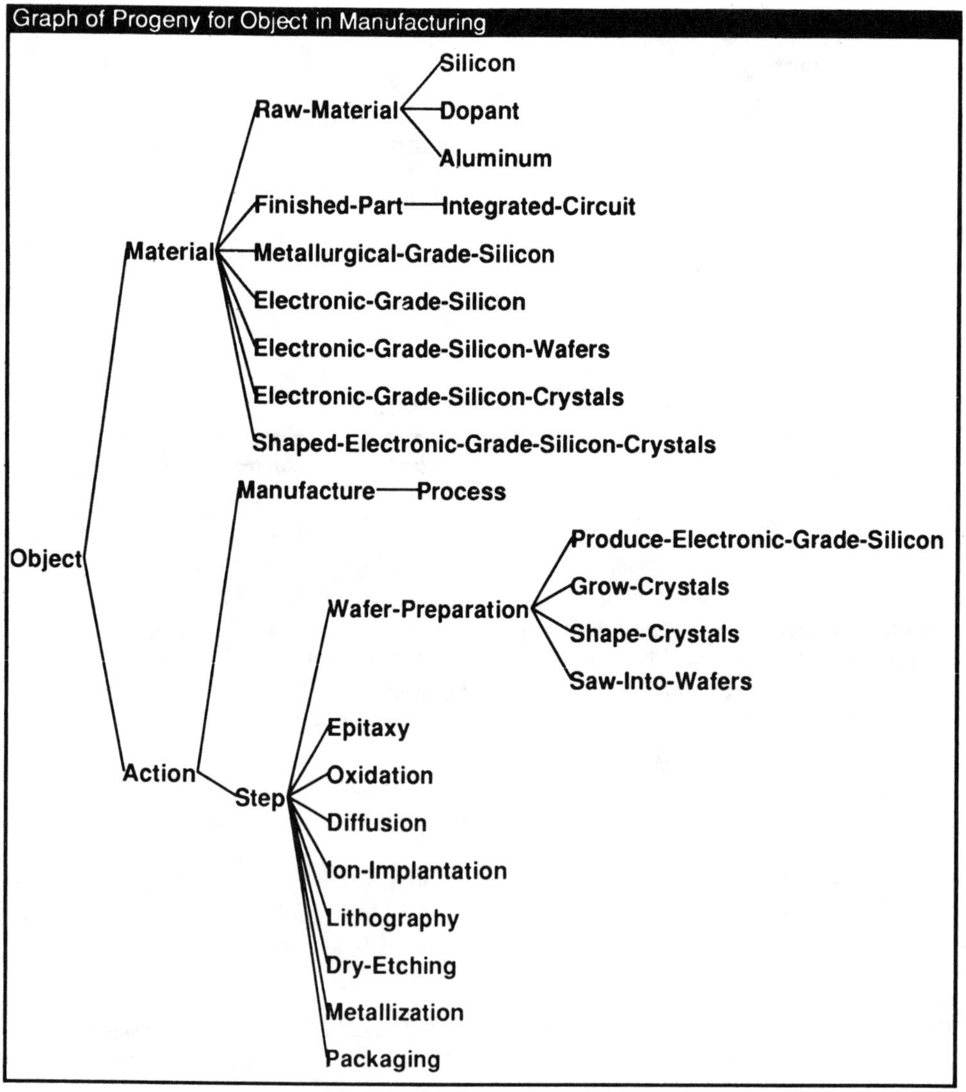

Fig. 35-2. Later taxonomy of terms in the Semiconductor knowledge base.

Assistant: I note you've created a number of subclasses of Wafer-Preparation. Let's look at Produce-Electronic-Grade-Silicon. The Output of this Step is Electronic-Grade-Silicon. Since Produce-Electronic-Grade-Silicon is a subclass of Wafer-Preparation, and Electronic-Grade-Silicon-Wafer is the out of Wafer-Preparation, I would have expected Electronic-Grade-Silicon to be a subclass of Electronic-Grade-Silicon-Wafer.

Perhaps you've incorrectly defined Electronic-Grade-Silicon, or perhaps you intended a relation other than *subclass* to hold between Wafer-Preparation and Produce-Electronic-Grade-Silicon. Since for each of the subclasses of Wafer-Preparation, the value of Output slots appears as the value of the Input slot of another subclass, I suggest each of the subclasses is actually a *substep* of Wafer-Preparation, ordered by the relation between the Input and Output slots. Is this what you meant?

A brilliant deduction by the assistant. How realistic is it? The generic manufacturing task includes information about likely relations that occur; substep relations are very common in manufacturing, so the assistant is justified in suggesting it as possible correction. Furthermore, the substep relation is a kind of *part-whole* relation; the assistant knows that in such relations, there will be a part or parts which share structure with the whole. In this case, *Wafer-Preparation* shares its input with *Produce-Electronic-Grade-Silicon*, and its output with *Saw-Into-Wafers*. Thus, the assistant concludes that *substep* is the appropriate relation.

In a narrowly circumscribed domain, like semiconductor manufacturing, it is reasonable to expect that a small number of relation types will be applicable; however, in the general case, we expect this type of inferencing to become computationally intractable. It is therefore important for the assistant to have a facility for interacting with the designer to select (or define) the appropriate relation type. For example, if the assistant is not able to suggest a single most likely replacement, or if the designer disagrees with the assistant's suggestion, the assistant displays a menu of possibilities (potentially all manufacturing relation types, or all known relation types), and allows the designer to choose.[2] We assume here that the designer has agreed with the assistant; the assistant then rearranges the knowledge base and displays the result (FIG. 35-3).

In the preceding excerpt, the assistant recognized a "misuse-of-is-a" cliché, by recognizing that the value (Electronic-Grade-Silicon) of a slot (Output) in a subclass (Produce-Electronic-Grade-Silicon) was not a subclass of the value (Electronic-Grade-Silicon-Wafer) of the same slot in the superclass (Wafer-Preparation). It further suggested a correction by finding a better cliché (step-substep), which was both a likely candidate given the domain, and a fitting correction, given the information (input-output relationships) already encoded in the knowledge base.

C. Further opportunities for assistance

The sorts of assistance we have described so far pertain largely to the acquisition of the domain model—the vocabulary of terms and relations—of a domain. However, the role

[2] The assistant could be expected to learn from its mistakes, using strategies similar to those employed in the LEAP system [38].

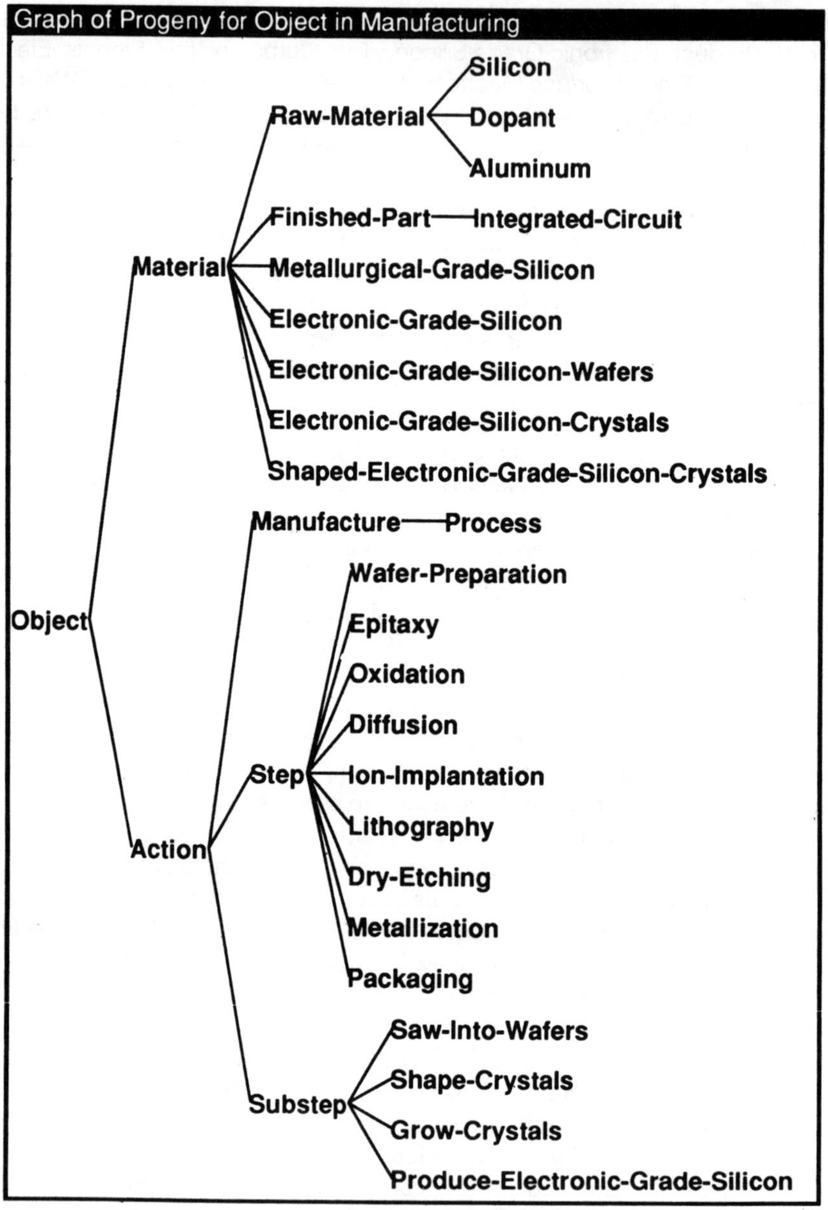

Fig. 35-3. Corrected taxonomy of terms in the Semiconductor knowledge base.

of an intelligent assistant is not limited to this aspect of knowledge acquisition. The domain model is not a complete knowledge base; it lacks necessary control and task-specific inference knowledge. Clearly, opportunities exist for an assistant to guide the knowledge engineer and domain specialist through the acquisition of these remaining classes of knowledge.[3] We intend to explore integrated acquisition of domain, control, and task-specific inference knowledge in the assistant. For these aspects of knowledge acquisition, the assistant will require knowledge about AI problem-solving methods and strategies.

The assistant can also play a role in the testing and validation of a KBS; once the knowledge base contains enough information, the assistant is able to record the results of individual tests and (perhaps) to generate test cases (by examining the encoded knowledge). As additional knowledge is acquired, the system must continue to successfully treat prior test cases. The assistant can play a useful role in checking that newly added knowledge does not conflict with existing knowledge—that the evolving knowledge base remains self-consistent. As in TEIRESIAS [21] and LEAP [38], failed test cases can identify missing and/or incorrect knowledge. Furthermore, the assistant can record dependencies between parts of the knowledge base; it is continuously involved in the evolution of the knowledge base and thus has a historical record of the development. This information can be used in two ways: the assistant can explain how a change to one part of the knowledge base will affect other parts, and can also undo changes, to allow alternate attempts at knowledge base evolution. As we have stated, maintenance of the knowledge base in this manner is likely to continue throughout the lifetime of a knowledge-based system.

In the next two sections, we discuss the two enabling technologies upon which our knowledge-intensive development environment rests: Strobe, an object-oriented programming language, and Impulse-86, a framework for constructing user interfaces. Whereas the assistant is an *active* tool, these are *passive* substrates which underlie it.

III. Object-oriented programming

Object-oriented programming is the foundation of our knowledge-intensive development environment. It contributes towards a programming methodology, which integrates diverse components of the development environment, and a representation language, which models both domain-level and development environment knowledge. The use of object-oriented programming for building expert systems and other knowledge-based applications, has been previously described [23]. In this article, we describe the role of object-oriented programming in building development environments for knowledge-based systems. In this section, we provide a brief overview of the object-oriented paradigm.

KBS's typically evolve in an incremental refinement process characterized by an exploratory programming style [27], [14], [46]. The representation and reasoning substrate is central to the KBS developer/maintainer in managing the complexity of the evolving system. A clear conceptual model of the domain of application is essential for managing this complexity.

[3] The process is most likely not a sequential ordering of phases. We believe that domain, control, and task-specific inference knowledge will be acquired in an interleaved fashion; attempts to correct deficiencies in one class of knowledge may highlight deficiencies in one or both of the other classes.

Object-oriented programming has been found by simulation specialists, cognitive psychologists, and artificial intelligence scientists to be very useful in modeling—of physical systems, human systems, and artificial systems. In constructing software systems to model complex phenomena, it is advantageous to organize computation around programming constructs whose internal structure and interrelationships explicitly reflect those of constructs in the physical world in which the resultant systems are to operate. Clarity is especially important because of the inherent complexity of the physical world—this complexity must be managed in a software system if it is to be understandable, explainable, extensible, maintainable, and reusable.

Furthermore, the object-oriented style encourages modular code and encapsulation with well-defined interfaces. Inheritance of properties simplifies code-sharing. This leads to space-efficient code and to ease of maintenance and specialization, as has been found in a variety of systems [25], [61], [6]. In addition, many traditional KBS representational entities (e.g., rules, constraints) may be encoded as objects and invoked in a uniform manner—via messages.

A clear model of the evolving system is as important to the domain specialist as it is to the KBS developer. Objects appear to be a natural and understandable knowledge organizing mechanism to humans not normally involved in computation [18]. The concept of an object as a prototype for encapsulating information—both data and procedures—is well-understood and used by humans, as are the concepts of classes and instances, taxonomies—and taxonomic inheritance of properties (along with a number of other forms of inheritance).

A. Background

In an object-oriented software system, the central construct is the *object*—a data structure similar to a record. In a medical consultation system, such as NEOMYCIN [16], we find objects that correspond to important medical concepts, like patient, drug, organism, disease, and so on. Objects are linked together in a variety of relationships in an object-oriented system. In NEOMYCIN, it is explicitly recorded that viral meningitis is a kind of meningitis, which is in turn a kind of infection. This hierarchical *a-kind-of* relation—also called the *taxonomic* relation—is carefully supported by object-oriented programming languages. Unlike the simple support provided for records by ordinary programming languages, these object-oriented languages support *inheritance of properties*. If it is recorded that meningitis is an infection situated in the CSF. This information is available—*transparently to the modeler*—via inheritance.

In object-oriented programming, the structure of the knowledge used in the software system is defined by the structure of the physical world—and not by the specific task at hand. Contrast this with the normal procedural structuring used in almost all computer programs. Because the computational structure is determined by the structure of the domain being modeled, object-oriented systems are more readily understood by both domain specialists and programmers. The objects themselves provide a natural atomic structure—a level of detail appropriate to the world being modeled. The relationships that link the objects—especially the hierarchical taxonomic relationship—lend increased structure. The collection of objects that model a particular domain, often called a *knowledge base*, captures the static knowledge of that domain. The knowledge base provides a kind of computational skeleton for a simulator, a reasoning system, or indeed any procedure that operates on it.

Over the years a number of object-oriented languages have been developed. One of the earliest was Simula, an extension to Algol designed for simulation [20], [5]. Simula defined much of the vocabulary of object-oriented programming. During the 1970's, Smalltalk was developed as a vehicle for making computers easier to use [24]. It has become the best-known object-oriented language, in large measure due to the revolutionary impact it had on integrated programming environments and user interfaces. In the artificial intelligence (AI) community, a number of object-oriented languages were developed to attack problems in vision and natural language understanding (e.g., KRL [7], FRL [44]). (The AI languages were often called *frame-based* at the time [47].) Whereas Simula and Smalltalk were independent, free-standing languages, most of the AI languages were embedded in an underlying programming language, Lisp. Commercial systems have started to become widely available in recent years (e.g., KEE [30], Loops [6]). Object-oriented programming concepts have started to appear in traditional programming languages; C++ [55] and Objective-C [19] are both object-oriented extensions to the standard C language.

B. Features of object-oriented programming languages

We devote the remainder of this section to the salient features of object-oriented programming languages. We concentrate on the features useful for modeling the static structure of a domain. We do not address the issue of messages and computation with an object-oriented skeleton. See [39], [54] for discussion of these issues.

The knowledge base designer's assistant itself is written in Strobe [50], a Lisp-based object-oriented programming language. Strobe is representative of many such languages, which provide a powerful set of tools that augment Lisp; moreover, such languages can themselves be embedded in higher-level systems that offer greater representational structure and modeling complexity. Strobe has been implemented in both Interlisp-D and Common Lisp; a subset of Strobe has been implemented in C.

Basic concepts To begin, we define the basic data structures. From largest to smallest level of granularity, the structures commonly provided by Lisp-based object-oriented languages are the following:

Knowledge base A taxonomically organized collection of objects of a domain. A knowledge base typically represents a model of some physical domain or system. Each knowledge base is a separate namespace of objects. An application may be organized around several knowledge bases.

Object A record-like structure which encapsulates a coherent set of related data *and* procedures. An object belongs to a particular knowledge base. It typically represents a single concept in the domain or system modeled by the knowledge base. An object is identified by a unique name within a knowledge base—objects of the same name may exist in different knowledge bases.

Each object has an associated *type*. Objects that represent particular, unique individual entities in the model are called *individual* or *instance* objects. Objects that represent a *set* of entities (either entities that actually exist in the model or entities that could potentially be constructed), are called *class* objects.

Slot A component of an object. A slot can represent a property or attribute of an object, a procedure that the object can execute (often called a *method*) to exhibit some behavior of the object, or a relationship between the object in which the slot resides and one or more other objects.

Facet A component of a slot—a place to encode annotations regarding the meaning of the slot with respect to its object. Many object-oriented languages define a datatype facet, which indicates what type of datum is (or can be) stored as the value of the slot. Applications can further define their own facets.

Taxonomic structure in knowledge bases Objects form the atomic structure of knowledge bases. Additional structure is imposed by relationships that exist among the objects. Object-oriented languages support a variety of relationships—some of which are hierarchical. The foremost relation supported by all object-oriented languages is the taxonomic relation, sometimes also called the *a-kind-of, is-a*, or *generalization/specification* relation.

TransitiveSymmetric-ReflexiveRelation is a kind of Relation. This is an expression of the universally quantified conditional:

$$\forall X(\text{TransitiveSymmetricReflexiveRelation}(X) \\ \rightarrow \text{Relation}(X));$$

that is, if X *is-a* TransitiveSymmerticReflexive-Relation, then X *is-a* Relation. We can also say that TransitiveSymmetricReflexiveRelation is *a-kind-of* Relation. In addition, the taxonomic relation is transitive. So, because:

$$\forall X(\text{EqualityRelation}(X) \\ \rightarrow \text{TransitiveSymmetricReflexiveRelation}(X)),$$

we can conclude that:

$$\forall X(\text{EqualityRelation}(X) \rightarrow \text{Relation}(X)).$$

Explicit representation of hierarchical taxonomic relationships is a powerful conceptual modeling tool. It has been used extensively in the physical sciences as a way of bringing order—through classification—to systems observed in the real world. For computational models, at the very least, it imposes a perspicuous structure on the domain knowledge being represented. As such, it helps to manage the complexity inherent in models of substantive real world systems.

Most object-oriented languages support taxonomic *lattices*; that is, objects may have multiple generalizations. For example, the transitive, symmetric, and reflexive characteristics of relations can be represented separately. This permits useful partitioning of information, advantageous because it fosters clarity and because it reduces the amount of information that otherwise would need to be duplicated in several classes. In the figure, transitivity information is stored in TransitiveRelation, rather than being duplicated in all transitive relations (see [54] for another example). Taxonomic lattices are often called *tangled* hierarchies. It is possible to get by without support for multiple generalizations. Many simple object-oriented languages do not support them because they increase the complexity of the implementation of the object-oriented language itself. However, if multiple generalizations are not supported, the application designer is often forced to write application-specific code that amounts to the same thing. Furthermore, the designer must spend time worrying about these situations rather than concentrating on the already difficult enough task of constructing an accurate and useful model.

Property inheritance If explicit representation of taxonomic relationships served as nothing more than a conceptual modeling tool, it would be very powerful. But, it has an additional purpose. It serves as the basis for *property inheritance*. For example, in the relation system, if we record that descendants of ReflexiveRelation are relations in which reflexivity holds, then we need not separately record that WeakPartialOrderRelation and EqualityRelation are reflexive. This fact is *transparently* accessible via the inheritance mechanisms supported by the object-oriented language. Inheritance of properties follows naturally from the universally quantified conditions noted earlier: if X is an EqualityRelation—*a-kind-of* ReflexiveRelation—then the properties of ReflexiveRelation are also properties of *all* Equality-Relations and hence are properties of X. Were we to ask the question: Are *instances of* EqualityRelation *reflexive?*, an object-oriented system would respond affirmatively.

Inheritance is not only a powerful conceptual modeling tool; it is also a powerful programming tool. It encourages modularity of design through *elision* and *refinement*. We achieve *elision* of description of objects through inheritance, which promotes a compact representation—only those properties of an object which are specific to the object itself need be explicitly stated. We *refine* properties within specializations, thus simplifying incremental knowledge base extension; properties generic to an object's class can be replaced by similar, but more specific properties, appropriate to a new subclass, independent of extensions and refinements in different branches of the taxonomic hierarchy.

Classes and instances A class object defines the generic properties of all of its specializations. Since Relation is a class object, it defines a set of properties for all subclasses and instances of Relation. A class object may also define *default* values for the properties it defines, although this is not necessary. Subclasses and instances of the classes are assumed to have those values. For example, assume Relation contains a detect slot which holds rules valid for detection of equality relations. The rules in the detect slot are by default assumed to be valid for detection of *all* subclasses and instances of Relation. If a default value is not specified for a property, nothing is assumed about its value in subclasses and instances.

In many object-oriented languages, default values may be overwritten, refined, or *canceled* in specializations. For example, the detect slot of Relation may be specified as unknown; however, it may be refined in the class EqualityRelation to (rule184 rule116 . . .). Defaults are very useful in knowledge-based systems—they can be used to make weak inferences in the absence of more specific information—and later overridden as more specific information becomes available.

Most object-oriented languages treat the *is-a* relation, defaults, and cancellation informally. For example, the *is-a* relation often conflates the notions of a prototypical member of a set and a universally quantified conditional. Further, permitting cancellation of inherited defaults can weaken the descriptive power of an object-oriented representation language (simply because an object matches the description of some class

X, it may not necessarily match the description of Y—a superclass of X—due to possible cancellation of properties in X); hence, if an object-oriented language allows cancellation, we can only use the taxonomic hierarchy for weak inferencing. See [9] and [8] for a detailed discussion of these issues.

IV. Impulse-86: support for user interaction

Impulse-86 [49] is a Strobe-based tool which supports user interface design. Responsible for the low-level "mechanics" of user interface support, it is a key component of the interaction substrate in the knowledge-intensive development environment. In this section, we present a set of requirements for user interfaces and user interface toolkits, and discuss how Impulse-86 fulfills these requirements. By way of illustration, we present four examples of Impulse-86 interfaces, each intended to support the activities of a specific class of user. We then discuss the framework in which these interfaces are constructed, using the examples to illustrate the main points.

Impulse-86 consists of an extensible kernel, providing support for the basic requirements of window-oriented user interfaces, and a set of application-specific extensions built around the kernel. It is the third in a series of systems beginning with Impulse [45]; while the first two were designed for the explicit purpose of editing Strobe knowledge bases, Impulse-86 is a general-purpose user interaction framework. It enables developers and end users to construct customized, domain-specific interfaces for their systems, without being experts in interactive graphics (knowledge base editing is a specialized extension). Our approach is to provide an extensive set of "building blocks," and a uniform framework in which to assemble them.

Although Impulse-86 has evolved from a knowledge base editor to a user interaction framework, we continue to view its kernel task as a form of editing. We take the point of view that *editing* entails many kinds of interactions between a user and a software system. The user *views* the state of the system, and *controls* or *changes* the state of the system. An editor is an entity that mediates these viewing and controlling interactions—presenting the user with a view of the system and effecting the desired control. This definition encompasses traditional text editing, browsing, program development, debugging, and end-user interaction.

Knowledge-based systems typically consist of many complex structured objects, connected by several relationships, and are intended to model richly structured domains. As a result, both the KBS developer and end user are typically interested in interacting with (i.e., understanding, changing, extending, and using) three major kinds of entities: objects and their internal structure, relationships among objects, and complete systems of objects, relationships, and code—including their dynamic behavior.

Based on the considerations thus far presented, we have been led to the following design goals for interfaces constructed with Impulse-86:

- Effective integration and use of high-resolution bit-mapped displays, pointing devices, and keyboards.
- Flexible support for varied methods of user interaction for both viewing and controlling systems (e.g., graphics, animation, menus, pointing and *smart* typein, with facilities like partial name recognition, spelling correction, and line editing).

The editor should support interaction with domain-specific information in a form natural to an end user familiar with the domain.

- Specific aids for *browsing*. A user should be able to quickly examine an evolving knowledge base, alternate hypotheses constructed by a KBS, user-defined interobject relationships, and so on.
- Unlimited interaction contexts for viewing and changing different parts of a system simultaneously.
- Programmatic access to interaction mechanisms. A user should be able to call upon building blocks in the editor in the midst of normal programs.
- Organizational support for customization and extension.[4]

There are several other useful goals that Impulse-86 itself does not address, including user modeling, assistance to a user in managing trouble, recovery from error, check-pointing, security, and so on. Extensions along these dimensions (such as the designer's assistant we discussed in Section II) are more appropriately constructed on top of the kernel environment, rather than inside it.

Many Impulse-86 interfaces follow a convention in which information is displayed in a central window, to which one or more menus are attached. For example, the small window in the upper right corner of the screen, labeled "Impulse-86," displays the names of each loaded Strobe knowledge base; the menu attached to this window contains commands related to loading, storing, and editing Strobe knowledge bases. The editor in the bottom right corner of the screen is a Strobe knowledge base editor; the central window contains information about the knowledge base, the upper menu contains knowledge-base editing commands, and the lower menu contains an alphabetized list of each of the objects in the knowledge base. Selecting an object from this latter menu provides a "focus" for some commands (e.g., the Edit Object command) in the former menu.

A. Examples of Impulse-86 editors

In this section we show a number of brief examples of specialized Impulse-86 editors. Our aim here is to demonstrate the diversity of interface styles that can be supported by the framework. Our examples depict editors applied to knowledge bases which form part of the designer's assistant, and which encode information about both relation types and management of task agendas.

The object editor The object editor is used for editing a single Strobe object and its internal structure. The object being edited encodes knowledge about relations. The object is presented to the user in a window with attached menus. The first five lines show the values of properties that are common to all objects; the remaining lines display the object's slots. The name of a property or slot is shown in boldface; if a slot has synonyms, they are enclosed in set braces; the slot's value (if any) is shown in lightface, following a color; (↑) indicates that the slot is inherited from a more general object.

---

[4] Stallman defines extensibility relative to EMACS: ". . . the user should be able to add new editing commands to change old ones to fit his needs, while he is editing" [53]. We go beyond *command* extensibility, aiming for extensibility with respect to what is viewed, how it is viewed, and how it may be changed.

We have found these conventions useful, but they are only defaults. A user can override them to customize the way this information, or other information, is presented.

The top two command menus enable a user to (for example) rename the object, change any of the slots, create new slots, delete or rename slots—standard editing operations. A small mark to the right of a command indicates the existence of subcommands that extend the functionality of that command. We have adopted the discipline that a left mouse button selection invokes the command shown, while a *middle* mouse button selection pops up a menu of subcommands (or a menu of arguments that further specify a command).

The two menus show the objects most closely related (taxonomically) to the object being edited; they can be used to invoke a new editing context in which one of those relatives is the center of attention.

Items in the display may be selected with the mouse as arguments to a command. A selection stack is maintained, with individual selections (*foci*) indicated by different styles of highlighting. As with other defaults, the highlight styles may be changed by the user.

The fast object editor—is designed for more experienced users of Impulse-86. It displays precisely the same information as does the standard object editor, but presents no command menus. Instead, these menus are available as "pop-up" menus, and appear when a mouse click occurs over the object name or any of the slot name captions. Because the fast object editor spends no time creating permanent menus, it can be displayed faster than can the standard object editor; furthermore, since it obscures less screen space, more of these editors can be made visible without occluding one another.

The object editor is used mainly by the knowledge base maintainer—typically a computer scientist—although it can also be useful to a domain specialist. It offers a view and interaction style for the domain knowledge encoded by the system—more as a computational entity than a mathematical entity (i.e., the implementation of the mathematical concept of a relation as a software object encoded in an object-oriented language). In later examples we will see other ways of interacting the domain knowledge—each appropriate to a specific task.

The rule editor The rule editor is used for editing a single Strobe rule. The rule being edited encodes a single piece of knowledge used by the designer's assistant in managing task agendas. This editor is commonly used by developers and by domain specialists. It is not intended for end-users of a knowledge-based system.

A Strobe rule is encoded as an object. As a result, the rule editor is rather similar to the object editor. In this case, however, commands specifically useful for dealing with rules replace or extend the basic object-related commands (e.g., the Translate Rule command, used to generate the English translation of the rule shown at the bottom of the figure). Furthermore, the slots of the rule are grouped together and captioned in a different manner. For example, the slots that encode left-hand side conjuncts are grouped under the IF: caption. Similarly, the slots that encode right-hand side actions are grouped under the THEN: caption.

In the figure, we see another standard attention-focusing mechanism supported by Impulse-86. Some commands in the top two menus on the left-hand side of the main window are grayed over. If a user selects a datum for which these commands are relevant, then Impulse-86 will make them visible to allow their selection.

The graph editor Graphs are a natural representation for viewing relationships between and among several objects in a system. Impulse-86 provides a simplified, object-oriented interface to a variety of graphing primitives, so users can edit interobject relationships graphically.

A graph editor displays some or all of the objects tied together by a relationship (or set of relationships). For example, the graph editor shows a taxonomic hierarchy associated of relations. Each node represents one object. More specialized objects appear to the right of their generalizations.

Graph editors enable a user to see and rearrange the overall structure of the system as implied by the graph relationship. Through pop-up menus, the user can add or delete links, and can easily invoke an interaction context that shows more detail for any object in the graph. Graph editors are like other editors with regard to defaults and foci. A user may further customize the graph editor with respect to fonts, layout (e.g., vertical versus horizontal), link types (e.g., dashed versus solid), node display (e.g., bitmaps versus names), amount of information presented, and so on. These customizations typically require no more than simple declarative changes to default values.

Impulse-86 has a number of built-in graphing relationships, such as specialization and generalization. In addition, it supports construction of customized graphs, based on user-specified functions, that, given a datum (e.g., an object), generate its successors one *graphic link* away (e.g., according to a *part-of* relationship). Impulse-86 takes care of the mechanics of computing and displaying the transitive closure of the graph generator function, making the nodes of the graph sensitive to selection with the mouse, attaching the menus, and so on.

The views offered by graph editors are useful to both developer/maintainers and to domain specialists. In addition, we will later see how some graphs can be useful to end users of systems. Such graphs are pervasive in the sciences. They help show skeletal models of physical domains.

The specification editor The forms of assistance we discussed in Section II require the assistant to understand an evolving domain model as encoded by the designer in an object-oriented framework. The assistant must "abstract" the domain model from the implementation-level data structures in the knowledge base. It depends on the designer having chosen an appropriate *grain-size* at which to represent the model.

An alternate approach we are considering involves providing an Impulse-86 editing interface customized to the task of entering terms and relations in the domain. This interface would encourage the designer to "sketch" information at an appropriate level of granularity, and would prevent him or her from entering the implementation-level knowledge base directly. Instead, the assistant would produce the knowledge base by analyzing information recorded by the custom interface.

The specification editing interface allows a designer to enter the primary terms and relations of a domain, without having to declare how the terms and relations are actually encoded in a knowledge base. The editor consists of a "workspace" (the main window), and two iconic menus. The *operations* menu selects the editor mode; from top to bottom, the available modes are select concept or relation, create concept, delete concept, create relation, and delete relation. The *link type* menu in the middle selects the type of relation to be created when the editor is in create relation mode. There are two predefined relation types—subclass (i.e., the *is-a* relation) and subpart (for encoding part-whole decompositions). The designer can define additional relation types by selecting the <New Link Type> entry in the *link type* menu; for example the successor relation was defined in this manner. The workspace depicts a collection of terms and relations.

When the designer is satisfied with the model depicted in the workspace, the assistant constructs a Strobe implementation of the model. Once again using its knowledge of KBS design techniques and of Strobe semantics (Types 2 and 3 knowledge), the assistant chooses to implement domain terms as Strobe classes, the relations between terms as slot values. Knowledge about relations (Type 3 knowledge, such as that illustrated in Section III) can help characterize new relations defined by the designer. For example, if the successor relation is seen to be transitive, irreflexive, and asymmetric, the assistant can assume the relation is a strict partial order; this information may be useful later when verifying the consistency of information encoded in the knowledge base, as well as in presenting a graphical depiction of such information.

We believe this type of interface will help the designer concentrate on specifying domain principles, rather than computational entities. The designer is not required to declare how terms and relations are implemented (i.e., which are the objects and which are the slots); the actual encoding of the domain knowledge can be performed later, at least partially by the assistant. By contrast, an interface composed of Impulse-86 object and slot editors would immediately force the designer to decide how to represent terms and relations, a decision which might have to be reconsidered later as the knowledge base evolves.

B. The Impulse-86 substrate

The Impulse-86 substrate contains five major building blocks: *Editor, EditorWindow, PropertyDisplay, Menu,* and *Operations*. Each building block, or part, is a Strobe object in the Impulse knowledge base. Each embodies special knowledge that enables it to fulfill a particular role in an interface (described below).

Editor The editor is the central object. It mediates interactions between the user and the *editee*—the domain focus—typically a part of a knowledge base (analogous to the Smalltalk *model* [24]). Together with its components, it *defines* a user interface—the way information is viewed and controlled.

Editor *instances* are built from an editor *class* by template instantiation. By instantiating a separate editor for each editee, Impulse-86 enables an unlimited number of independent interaction contexts to exist simultaneously.

Editors have components drawn from any of the five major classes (or from additional classes defined by a user). Editors are explicitly permitted to have other editors as components (and so on, in a recursive fashion). Support for recursive decomposition is important. It enables the construction of an editor whose composite structure parallels the composite structure of its editee. Knowledge about the way composites are structured in the application domain may therefore be embedded in the structure of its interfaces.

Subeditors can be dynamically added to, and removed from, an instantiated editor. Impulse-86 allows a user to specify (via a declaration or a method) a mapping between a class of objects in a domain knowledge base and an editor class to be used for them (e.g., the RuleEditor for Rule objects).

Editor window The editor window manages the screen context of a collection of editors. It is responsible for performing the usual window operations (e.g., scrolling, repainting, reshaping). It also maintains a correspondence between editees and the window regions in which the editees are displayed. This enables both data selection by mouse pointing and efficient update when parts of an overall domain structure are changed. The window also records *foci*—items selected by the user as arguments to a command.

Each editor may have at most one window among its components. When an editor has subeditors, some or all may share the same window, or utilize separate windows.

Property display The property display presents a view of an editee in a window. Impulse-86 has a number of different kinds of display, each implementing a distinctive visual style—and a user can define new types of display. A property may be *active* (i.e., have regions sensitive to mouse selection).

A property display is also responsible for setting up a correspondence between its editee and the window regions in which the editee is displayed. Impulse-86 has been designed so that property displays need not be instantiated (although it is straightforward to do so if the property display requires more context than just the correspondence between its editee and displayed window region). Editor windows, on the other hand, must be instantiated in any case—and are therefore used to maintain the correspondences set up by property display classes.

There are six displays in the object editor example. The first five are components of ObjectEditor; each display one of the five properties associated with the object itself. The sixth (ObjectSlotsDisplay) is a component of SlotEditor; it iterates over all of the slots.[5] Each of these displays prints a single datum in the ObjectEditorWindow.

The graph editor has a single specialized property display. It displays the entire graph in the editor window. (Graphical displays can also be combined with other types of property displays in editor windows.)

There is a large number of Property Display templates. For example, many property displays have a similar *caption* and *value* format. Each of these property displays has a caption, typically sensitive to selection with the mouse (*active*), followed by a region that contains a *value*. The Caption&ValuePropertyDisplay class is the common generalization. Its specializations provide alternative ways to display captions and values, such as displaying captions as bitmaps.

Menu Impulse-86 provides a large number of built-in menu styles, ranging from static menus to pop-up and pushbutton menus.

---

[5] Each property display is typically responsible for one editee. However, a property display (indeed, any component) can be iterated over a list of editees.

Menus are used to display choices to be made (*choice* menus) or operations to be invoked (*command* menus). When a selection is made in a command menu, Impulse-86 informs the editor with which the menu is associated. The responsibility for executing the selected operation lies with the editor (see below). Menus may be unique to a particular editor or shared among a collection of editors.

Menus are implemented as specialized windows. They typically have a restricted format for items (e.g., rows and columns), and a single method for handling mouse button events. In principle, they could be implemented as windows with simple property displays. However, performance considerations on current workstations and window systems often dictate a specialized implementation. Hence, analogous to the Window object, the Menu object is an interface to one or more menu packages associated with the underlying window system of the target machine for Impulse-86.

Impulse-86 provides support for different menu types. These include: StaticMenu for menus that remain on the screen, DynamicMenu for menus that pop up in response to some selections, and MultipleChoiceMenu for menus that allow a set of choices to be made before finishing an interaction and causing some action to occur. In addition, there is support for menus that contain sets of operations to be performed (CommandMenu), menus that contain a set of arguments required to *complete* specification of operations (CommandArgumentMenu), a variety of different menu styles (e.g., PushButtonMenu for control panel buttons, StatzDisplayMenu for large, scrolling *status* menus).

The separation between ObjectEditor and SlotEditor is used to advantage for indicating which commands are appropriate to a user-selected item in the editor window. For example, when an object-specific property has been selected, Impulse-86 grays over the menu of slot-related commands. This helps to focus the attention of the user on the relevant commands.

Operations Methods that perform the operations defined for an editor are grouped in operations objects. These methods are invoked by a message from the editor.

ObjectEditorOperations knows how to execute the operations listed in the ObjectEditorCommandMenu; SlotEditorOperations knows how to execute the operations listed in the SlotEditorCommandMenu. For example, when the SlotEditor receives a message that the user selected Rename Slot, it relays that message to SlotEditorOperations, which has a method that actually renames the slot.

Separating operations from menus permits the same editing operations to be invoked in a variety of ways, including menu selection, typein, function invocation, or message from a remote processor.

In addition to the five major building blocks, there are a few minor building blocks. For example, Impulse-86 provides high-level support for keyboard interaction through TTYInteractionWindows.

C. Discussion

Impulse-86 has been used to construct a wide variety of user interfaces. These range from simple "caption and value" editors (e.g., the object and rule editors described above), to graph editors (each with a specialized strategy for handling information overload). They include two-dimensional iconic graphics editors (used in program design) and data graphics editors (used in scientific data interpretation). See [49] for a complete discussion of Impulse-86.

Specialized impulse-86 interfaces typically require short development times. We attribute this to the particular set of behaviors encapsulated in Impulse-86 building blocks. The designer is insulated from the details of manipulating bitmaps, windows, mouse interactions, typein streams, and menus—I/O details which traditionally require painstaking attention. Attention can therefore be concentrated on what the customized interface should look like, what information it should show the user, and what commands the user should be able to request.

Several features of the Impulse-86 substrate contribute to this ability. The building blocks are quite general, covering a wide range of interaction styles. Implementation as an object-oriented system makes it easy to specialize and modify. A uniform, relatively fine-grain protocol is used throughout, together with a number of known methods and defaults. These characteristics ease the problem of understanding what is in the system and what mixins to use as a starting point for customized interfaces. Furthermore, no distinction is made between default methods and default values; this simplifies declarative specialization of the kernel. Finally, Impulse-86 contains a number of archetypal interfaces; modifying one of these is an effective strategy for creating a new interface.

Other groups are currently working on systems that support construction of interactive interfaces. The GUI-DON-WATCH system [43] demonstrates the utility of a user interface tuned to the operation of a particular class of consultation systems. The authors note that knowledge-base editors originally intended for use by knowledge base developer/maintainer are typically inappropriate interfaces for the end user. Impulse-86 offers a substrate that bridges the gap between the tools required by a developer/maintainer, by a domain specialist, and by an end user. Its extensibility further enables it to support the construction of specialized interfaces for each type of user.

The SIG system [35] is much closer to Impulse-86. Built on top of Smalltalk-80 [24], it too offers an extensible kernel that supports generation of interactive displays. In the terminology of [35], SIG emphasizes the *view* aspect of interaction; it addresses the *control* aspect in a less structured manner. In contrast, we have found it useful in Impulse-86 to provide a considerable amount of structure to support the control aspect of interaction as well as the view aspect. We have also found it useful to provide a relatively fine-grained structure to support user extension.

Another related effort is EZWin [33], an object-oriented editing system which provides three object classes for constructing editors. Although the two systems have similarities, there are several important differences. "EZWin systems are basically editors for graphical objects." [33, p. 186] Systems constructed in Impulse-86 are interfaces for knowledge-based systems; the interaction objects and routines are completely separate from the knowledge-base being edited. This separation allows the interface and application to be modified independently and supports the reuse of interfaces with different knowledge-based systems.

Perhaps closest to Impulse-86 is PSBase [15], a prototype system for modeling and constructing user interfaces. Like Impulse-86, PSBase separates the interface from the application. It also considers the view aspect of interaction (called presentation), and the control aspect (called recognition). Ciccarelli describes the implementation of a number of well-known text-oriented and icon-oriented interfaces in PSBase (e.g., the Xerox Star interface [47]). Impulse-86 and PSBase share much in spirit, but differ in specifics. Both systems explicitly consider composite interfaces and sharing of structure. Because Impulse-86 has been carried through to production use in a wide variety of applications, it provides a larger number of interaction styles.

Much of the recent work on graphical programming systems is relevant to Impulse-86. These systems provide iconic interfaces for creating, editing and animating programs. Program animation is triggered by application-specific events which update the display. While the interaction with and appearance of these interfaces are similar to interfaces built with Impulse-86, the underlying structure is quite different. First, most graphical programming interfaces [12], [13], [34], [40]–[42] are tightly coupled with their application: interaction and animation are managed by low-level calls from the editor and the interpreter. Impulse-86 separates the interface and application, thereby supporting reuse and modification. Second, only some of these systems [34], [40], [42] provide support for relationships such as composition and dependency. These relationships, and their explicit representation in objects, allow important structural features of the application (such as connectivity) to be maintained. The differences between Impulse-86 and these systems stem from the attempted scope of the systems. All of these systems are closely tied to the domain of programming—extension and reuse of these interfaces is limited to this domain. Impulse-86 aspires to provide interface support for a variety of applications, not just programming.

V. Related work

The philosophy embodied in this work can be traced back to the MYCIN project, described fully in [14]. The concept of an intelligent assistant derives directly from TEIRESIAS [21] system. Our conception of task models follows from TEIRESIAS's *rule models*. Its technique of "acquisition in context"—eliciting information by asking questions relevant to specific situations, rather than asking general questions—is embodied in the assistant's use of task-specific schemata to drive acquisition of domain knowledge. TEIRESIAS was designed to assist with the debugging nearly complete knowledge bases; it worked by guiding a domain specialist through a faulty reasoning trace, searching for missing and incorrect knowledge. By contrast, the designer's assistant addresses knowledge acquisition techniques for all phases of KBS development. The EMYCIN system [36] defined the concept of a KBS shell; our vision of a knowledge intensive development environment is a descendant of this approach.

Acquisition of task-specific inference and control knowledge is addressed in a number of systems. MOLE [22] acquires heuristic classification knowledge in a two-phase process. In the first phase, an initial knowledge base is constructed; the domain specialist is asked to supply common hypotheses and evidence, and then draw associations between them. In the second phase, MOLE and the specialist interact to refine the knowledge base. MOLE performs static analysis of the knowledge base to discover ambiguities and inadequacies in the knowledge base; it can recommend corrections for some knowledge base deficiencies discovered by this process. The system also performs dynamic analysis; by examining its failures on known test cases, it is able to suggest knowledge base alterations to remedy its performance. MOLE is a self-contained environment; it contains an inference component as well, allowing it to both test its knowledge, and run actual diagnostic sessions. The approach to knowledge acquisition taken by the designer's assistant differs from that in MOLE. The assistant begins by acquiring the conceptual structure of a domain, without regard for the type of problem-solving to be performed. It is our hypothesis that the conceptual structure can serve as the basis for a number of systems. In addition, the assistant is not a self-contained environment; it is a component of an extensible problem solving framework; it must be able to guide acquisition of knowledge for any number of representation languages and inference procedures.

In ROGET [3], Bennett describes a prototype knowledge-based system for acquiring the *conceptual structure*—descriptions of input evidence, inference steps, and output advice—of diagnostic expert systems. ROGET interacts with a domain specialist to acquire the structure of the new system, comparing the task requirements to abstract categories of requirements derived from previously constructed diagnostic systems. The system makes recommendations concerning the scope of the system to be constructed and the specific knowledge engineering techniques to be employed. The principal similarity to the work described in this article is the use of abstract task models to focus knowledge acquisition; however, ROGET is targeted only towards the initial phase of KBS construction. The result of a ROGET consultation is an initial EMYCIN knowledge base; additional terminology, domain-specific inference rules, and control structure must all be acquired within EMYCIN.

The Knowledge-Based Software Assistant (KBSA) is a proposed architecture to aid ". . . the development, evolution, and maintenance of large software projects" [26]. Software development and maintenance under the KBSA paradigm is fundamentally different from current practice; changes are made to the software specification, rather than to the software itself. The implementation of the software specification is rederived with each change. This is similar to the assistant's providing a concept and relation level interface for knowledge capture, deriving the computational representation of the knowledge base itself. In addition, the KBSA captures design decisions regarding the software project, and can act as an intelligent software assistant to developers, maintainers, project managers, and end-users. This parallels our goals for the KBS designer's assistant quite closely. The KBSA and the designer's assistant differ, however, in a number of important aspects. Whereas the KBSA emphasizes capturing the validating design decisions, the designer's assistant emphasizes helping the designer formulate the conceptual structure of a KBS. The KBSA creates and maintains an *executable specification* of a software system, which it assumes is simpler to debug and validate than the actual implementation. The designer's assistant, however, works with the implementation itself; in KBS development, the concept of a specification is informal, and often evolves as the KBS evolves.

KL-ONE [11] is a knowledge representation framework based on a semantic network model. It and its successors, including Krypton [10] NIKL [29], and KL-TWO [59], have made important contributions towards a formal theory of semantic network languages. Of particular relevance to the KBS designer's assistant is the notion of a *classifier*, a procedure for determining the correct place for a description in a KL-ONE network. Stated simply, the classification algorithm places a new concept in the network such that it is "above" (is an *ancestor of*) all concepts it *subsumes*, and is "below" (is a *descendant of*) all concepts that subsume it. One concept subsumes a second concept if all instances of second would also be recognized as instances of the first. KL-ONE, KL-TWO, NIKL, and Krypton knowledge bases are constructed by classification. The designer's assistant defines neither subsumption nor classification; however, by helping designers produce knowledge bases which encode information in the most general manner possible, it does offer a similar service. The assistant's library of modeling clichés is a means by which it can detect poorly structured knowledge bases; these clichés also allow the assistant to recommend a greater variety of improvements to knowledge base structure. For example, the KL-ONE classifier can only move concepts in a taxonomy; the assistant's "classifier" can in addition recommend changes in the structure of concepts, so as to make explicit generalizations not properly encoded in the knowledge base.

We expect classification to play a larger role as we experiment with larger knowledge bases. As the size of a knowledge base increases, it becomes increasingly difficult to find the appropriate concepts to be specialized and elaborated. (This is analogous to the well-known problems of *finding* and *understanding* in discussions of the software reuse [4].)

VI. Conclusion

Starting from the widespread belief that knowledge acquisition is the central problem in knowledge-based system design, we have argued that a broad spectrum of tools—ranging from powerful representation languages to sophisticated editors and debuggers—is required to manage this complex process. While contemporary KBS design environments provide many such tools, little or no support in the *use* of these tools is currently available for domain specialists and designers.

Our central thesis is that it is possible to construct an automated assistant which actively participates in the knowledge acquisition process. This assistant guides designers and domain specialists in the proper selection and use of development environment tools, and helps formulate, extend, visualize, and verify the conceptual structure of domain knowledge bases. The assistant is a knowledge-based system whose domain is the design of knowledge-based systems. Its domain knowledge includes models of various classes of knowledge-based systems (such as diagnostic, design, and simulation systems), as well as models of proper usage of both its representation language and development environment tools. The assistant is not limited to helping construct the conceptual structure of a knowledge-based system; it can also offer support throughout the lifetime of the system, in areas such as testing, validation, and knowledge base maintenance. We have partially implemented such an assistant.

Collective experience with tools for KBS development has shown us that a good development environment is critical in helping knowledge engineers produce workable, extensible, and maintainable systems. As with any complex system, poor design choices made during the beginning phase of knowledge base construction may propagate far into an evolving system, often necessitating substantial redesign after the system has grown quite large. The knowledge base designer's assistant can assist in early detection and correction of design errors, thus simplifying later debugging and extension of the knowledge base.

The designer's assistant is part of a larger vision: a knowledge-intensive development environment, which supports development and use of knowledge-based systems from the separate perspectives of developers, domain specialists, and end-users. The environment is composed of two interrelated components: a representation and reasoning substrate, which integrates various categories of problem-solving tools, and an interaction substrate, which consists of tools for constructing interactive user interfaces to knowledge-based systems. This organization reflects our view that reasoning and interaction are both knowledge-based tasks; the environment provides the "traditional" representation and reasoning support found in all KBS shells, as well as support for powerful user interfaces—such as the designer's assistant—which themselves can be knowledge-based systems.

Our emerging knowledge-intensive development environment is founded upon two key technologies: Strobe, an object-oriented programming language, and Impulse-86, a user interface framework. Strobe is useful in two ways: as a programming paradigm, it is the "glue" which joins together distinct software subsystems in a uniform manner; as a simple representation language kernel, it supports the construction of computational models which mirror the organization of the physical world in which the software systems are to operate. Impulse-86 is a key component of the interaction substrate; it implements the low-level mechanics of user-interfaces—support for windows, menus, typein, and pointing devices—as well as providing editors and browsers for domain knowledge bases. It further serves as an extensible kernel from which application-specific user interfaces can be constructed.

Strobe and Impulse-86 already contribute much to control the complexity of KBS design. These components, while passive, are the prerequisites for the more autonomous designer's assistant.

Acknowledgment

P. Patel-Schneider, H. Brown, G. Lafue, and M. Tenenbaum provided significant comments on the content and organization of this article; our thanks to them and to the reviewers. We also wish to thank our colleagues at Schlumberger-Doll Research and Schlumberger Palo Alto Research for their suggestions and contributions to the Strobe and Impulse systems.

References

1. J.S. Aikins, "Prototypes and production rules: A knowledge representation for computer consultations," Ph.D. dissertation, Stanford Univ., Tech. Rep. STAN-CS-80-814, 1980.
2. ______, "Prototypical knowledge for expert systems," *Artificial Intell.*, vol. 20, pp. 163–210, 1983.
3. J.S. Bennett, "ROGET: A knowledge-based consultant for acquiring the conceptual structure of a diagnostic expert system," *J. Automated Reasoning*, vol. 1, pp. 49–74, 1985.
4. T. Biggerstaff and C. Richter, "Reusability framework, assessment, and directions," *IEEE Software*, vol. 4, no. 2, pp. 41–49, 1987.

5. G.M. Birtwistle, O. Dahl, B. Myhrhaug, and K. Nygaard, *SIMULA BEGIN*. New York: Petrocelli/Charter, 1973.
6. D.G. Bobrow and M.J. Stefik, *The LOOPS Manual*, Xerox Palo Alto Research Center, Tech. Rep., Dec. 1983.
7. D.G. Bobrow and T. Winograd, "An overview of KRL, a knowledge representation language," *Cognitive Sci.*, vol. 1, no. 1, pp. 3–46, Jan. 1977.
8. R.J. Brachman, " 'I lied about the trees' or, defaults and definitions in knowledge representation," *AI Mag.*, vol. 6, no. 3, pp. 80–93, Fall 1985.
9. ______, "What IS-A is and isn't: An analysis of taxonomic links in semantic networks," *Computer*, vol. 16, no. 10, pp. 30–36, Oct. 1983.
10. R.J. Brachman, V.P. Gilbert, and H. Levesque, "An essential hybrid reasoning system: Knowledge and symbol level accounts of KRYPTON," in *Proc. Ninth Int. Joint Conf. Artificial Intelligence*, Aug. 1985, pp. 532–539.
11. R.J. Brachman and J.G. Schmolze, "An overview of the KL-ONE knowledge representation system," Fairchild Lab. Artificial Intell. Res., Tech. Rep. 30, 1984.
12. G.P. Brown, R.T. Carling, C.F. Herot, D.A. Kramlich, and P. Souza, "Program visualization: Graphical support for software development," *Computer*, vol. 18, no. 8, pp. 27–35, Aug. 1985.
13. M.H. Brown and R. Sedgewick, "A system for algorithm animation," *Comput. Graphics*, vol. 18, no. 3, pp. 177–186, July 1984.
14. B.G. Buchanan and E.H. Shortliffe, Eds., *Rule-Based Expert Systems: The MYCIN Experiments of the Stanford Heuristic Programming Project*. Reading, MA: Addison-Wesley, 1984.
15. E.C. Ciccarelli, IV, "Presentation Based User Interfaces," Ph.D. thesis, MIT, Tech. Rep. AI-TR-794, Aug. 1984.
16. W.J. Clancey, "The advantages of abstract control knowledge in expert system design," in *Proc. Third Nat. Conf. Artificial Intelligence*, Aug. 1983, pp. 74–98.
17. W.J. Clancey, "The epistemology of a rule-based expert system: A framework for explanation," *Artificial Intell.*, vol. 20, pp. 215–251, 1983.
18. B. Cohen and G.L. Murphy, "Models of concepts," *Cognitive Sci.*, vol. 8, pp. 27–58, 1984.
19. B.J. Cox, *Object Oriented Programming: An Evolutionary Approach*. Reading, MA: Addison-Wesley, 1986.
20. O. Dahl and K. Nygaard, "SIMULA—An ALGOL-based simulation language," *Commun. ACM*, vol. 9, no. 9, pp. 671–677, Sept. 1966.
21. R. Davis and D.B. Lenat, *Knowledge-Based Systems in Artificial Intelligence*. New York: McGraw-Hill, 1982.
22. L. Eshelman and J. McDermott, "MOLE: A knowledge acquisition tool that uses its head," in *Proc. Fifth Nat. Conf. Artificial Intelligence*, 1986, pp. 950
23. R. Fikes and T. Kehler, "The role of frame-based representation in reasoning," *Commun. ACM*, vol. 28, no. 9, pp. 904–920, Sept. 1985.
24. A. Goldberg, *SMALLTALK-80: The Interactive Programming Environment*. Reading, MA: Addison-Wesley, 1984.
25. A. Goldberg and D. Robson, *SMALLTALK-80: The Language and its Implementation*. Reading, MA: Addison-Wesley, 1983.
26. C. Green, D. Luckham, R. Balzer, T. Cheatham, and C. Rich, "Report on a knowledge-based software assistant," in C. Rich and R.C. Waters, editors, *Artificial Intelligence and Software Engineering*, C. Rich and R.C. Waters, Eds. Los Altos, CA: Morgan Kaufmann, 1986, ch. 23, pp. 377–428.
27. F. Hayes-Roth, D.A. Waterman, and D.B. Lenat, Eds., *Building Expert Systems*. Reading, MA: Addison-Wesley, 1983.
28. *Interlisp-D Reference Manual*, Xerox Artificial Intell. Syst., Pasadena, CA, Oct. 1985.
29. T.S. Kaczmarek, R. Bates, and G. Robins, "Recent developments in NIKL," in *Proc. Fifth Nat. Conf. Artificial Intelligence*, 1986, pp. 978.
30. *KEE Software Development Systems User's Manual*, 3rd ed., IntelliCorp, 1986.
31. J.C. Kunz, R.J. Fallat, D. McClung, J.J. Osborn, B.A. Votteri, H.P. Nii, J.S. Aikins, L.M. Fagan, and E.A. Feigenbaum, "A physiological rule-based system for interpreting pulmonary function test results," in *Proc. Computers in Critical Care and Pulmonary Medicine*, 1979, pp. 375–379.

32. G.M.E. Lafue and R.G. Smith, "A modular tool kit for knowledge management," in *Proc. Ninth Int. Joint Conf. Artificial Intelligence*, Aug. 1985, pp. 46 – 52.
33. H. Lieberman, "There's more to menu systems than meets the screen," *Comput. Graphics*, vol. 19, no. 3, pp. 181 – 189, July 1985.
34. R.L. London and R.A. Duisberg, "Animating programs using Smalltalk," *Computer*, vol. 18, no. 8, pp. 61 – 71, Aug. 1985.
35. D. Maier, P. Nordquist, and M. Grossman, "Displaying database objects," in *Proc. First Int. Conf. Expert Database Systems*, Apr. 1986, pp. 15 – 30.
36. W.V. Melle, A.C. Scott, J.S. Bennett, and M. Peairs, "The EMYCIN manual," Dep. Comput. Sci., Stanford Univ., Tech. Rep. STAN-CS-81-885 (HPP-81-16), Oct. 1981.
37. M. Minsky, "A framework for representing knowledge," in *The Psychology Of Computer Vision*, P.H. Winston, Ed. New York: McGraw-Hill, 1975.
38. T.M. Mitchell, S. Mahadevan, and L. Steinberg, "LEAP: A learning apprentice for VLSI design," in *Proc. Ninth Int. Conf. Artificial Intelligence*, 1985, pp. 573 – 580.
39. D.A. Moon, "Object-oriented programming with Flavors," in *Proc. First ACM Conf. Object Oriented Systems, Languages, and Application*, Sept. 1986, pp. 1 – 8.
40. M. Moriconi and D.F. Hare, "Visualizing program designs through PegaSys," *Computer*, vol. 18, no. 8, pp. 72 – 85, Aug. 1985.
41. S.P. Reiss, "Graphical program development with PECAN program development system," *Sigplan Notices*, vol. 19, no. 5, pp. 30 – 41, May 1984.
42. ______, "An object-oriented framework for graphical programming," *ACM SIGPLAN Notices*, vol. 21, no. 10, pp. 49 – 57, Oct. 1986.
43. M.H. Richer and W.J. Clancey, "GUIDON-WATCH: A graphic interface for viewing a knowledge-based system," *IEEE Comput. Graphics Applications*, vol. 5, no. 11, pp. 51 – 64, 1985.
44. R.B. Roberts and I.P. Goldstein, "The FRL manual," MIT, AI Memo 409, Sept. 1977.
45. E. Schoen and R.G. Smith, "Impulse: A display-oriented editor for Strobe," in *Proc. Nat. Conf. Artificial Intelligence*, Aug. 1983, pp. 356 – 358.
46. B.A. Sheil, "Power tools for programmers," *Datamation*, pp. 131 – 144, Feb. 1983.
47. D.C. Smith, E. Harslem, C. Irby, and R. Kimball, "The Star user interface: An overview," in *Proc. Nat. Comput. Conf.*, AFIPS Press, 1982, pp. 515 – 528.
48. R.G. Smith, "Programming with rules in Strobe," Schlumberger-Doll Res., Tech. Rep. SYS-84-12, Dec. 1984.
49. R.G. Smith, P.S. Barth, and R.L. Young, "A substrate for object-oriented interface design," in *Research Directions in Object-Oriented Programming*, B. Schriver and P. Wegner, Eds., Cambridge, MA: MIT Press, 1987, pp. 253 – 315.
50. R.G. Smith and P.J. Carando, "Structured object programming in Strobe," Schlumberger-Doll Res., Res. Note, Dec. 1986.
51. R.G. Smith, R. Dinitz, and P. Barth, "Impulse-86: A substrate for object-oriented interface design," in *Proc. First ACM Conf. Object Oriented Systems, Languages, and Applications*, Sept. 1986, pp. 167 – 176.
52. R.G. Smith, G.M.E. Lafue, E. Schoen, and S.C. Vestal, "Declarative task description as a user interface structuring mechanism," *Computer*, vol. 17, no. 9, pp. 29 – 38, Sept. 1984.
53. R.M. Stallman, "EMACS: The extensible, customizable, self-documenting display editor," in *Interactive Programming Environments*, D.R. Barstow, H.E. Shrobe, and E. Sandewall, Eds. New York: McGraw-Hill, 1984, pp. 300 – 325.
54. M.J. Stefik and D.G. Bobrow, "Object-oriented programming: Themes and variations," *AI Mag.*, vol. 6, no. 4, pp. 40 – 62, 1986.
55. B. Stroustrup, *The C+ + Programming Language*. Reading, MA: Addison-Wesley, 1986.
56. M. Suwa, A.C. Scott, and E.H. Shortliffe, "Completeness and consistency in a rule-based system," in *Rule-Based Expert Systems*, B.G. Buchanan and E.H. Shortliffe, Eds. Reading, MA: Addison-Wesley, 1984, ch. 8, pp. 159 – 170.
57. W.R. Swartout, "XPLAIN: A system for creating and explaning expert consulting programs," *Artificial Intell.*, vol. 21, pp. 285 – 325, 1983.
58. S.M. Sze, Ed., *VLSI Technology*. New York: McGraw-Hill, 1983.

59. M. Vilain, "The restricted language architecture of a hybrid representation system," in *Proc. Ninth Int. Joint Conf. Artificial Intelligence*, Aug. 1985.
60. R.C. Waters, "KBEmacs: A step towards the programmer's apprentice," MIT AI Lab, Tech. Rep. 753, 1985.
61. D. Weinreb *et al., Lisp Machine Manual*, Symbolics, Inc., 1984.

Part IV

Issues, challenges and new frontiers

AI is not without its critics and controversies. Much of the skepticism and criticism is a reaction to some overzealousness on the part of some AI researchers that led in the early years to exaggerations about what the technology could really do. There are still many who believe that efforts to recreate human problem-solving in software is misguided. The Dreyfus brothers, for example, develop an argument about "why expert systems do not exhibit expertise" in the first paper in Part IV. Andriole makes sure that everyone remembers that there are other problem-solving tools and techniques besides knowledge-based ones. Rota makes an assessment of where we are, while Hopple looks at the relationship between psychology and AI. Cohen and Howe investigate the role of evaluation in AI research, while Hecht-Nielson introduces another intelligent systems technology, neural networks. Raj Reddy completes Part IV with an assessment of where AI has been and a listing of its grandest challenges.

AI is not a "finished" technology. It is evolving, and will continue to evolve as new ideas are converted into new tools, techniques, methods and models, and as feedback from successful and unsuccessful applications is interpreted. Part IV of the sourcebook tries to provide context to Part III by leaving you with the sense that, while much has been accomplished, much more lies ahead.

36

Why expert systems do not exhibit expertise

Hubert and Stuart Dreyfus

Editors' note *Hubert and Stuart Dreyfus argue that there are clear limits to the kind of "intelligence" that our systems can ever exhibit. The paper is reprinted here because controversy is often healthy, and because there is still a great deal of debate about the nature of intelligence and our ability to incarnate it in computer software. (Reprinted, with permission, from the Summer 1986 issue of* IEEE Expert. **

Scientists who stand at the forefront of artificial intelligence have long dreamed of autonomous "thinking" machines that are free of human control. And now they believe we are not far from realizing that dream. As Marvin Minsky, a well-known AI professor at M.I.T., recently put it: "Today our robots are like toys. They do only the simple things they're programmed to. But clearly they're about to cross the edgeless line past which they'll do the things we are programmed to."

Encouraged by such optimistic pronouncements, the U.S. Department of Defense is sinking millions of dollars into developing fully autonomous war machines that will respond to a crisis without human intervention. Business executives are investing in "expert" systems whose wisdom they hope will equal, if not surpass, that of their top managers. And AI entrepreneurs are talking of "intelligent systems" that will perform better than we can—in the home, in the classroom, and at work.

But no matter how many billions of dollars the Defense Department or any other agency invests in AI, there is almost no likelihood that scientists using the conventional approach to artificial intelligence can develop machines capable of making intelligent decisions. After 25 years of research, AI has failed to live up to its promise, and there is no evidence that it ever will. In fact, rule-following, symbol-manipulating machine intelligence will probably never replace human intelligence simply because we ourselves are not "thinking machines." Human beings have an intuitive intelligence that "reasoning" machines simply cannot match.

Military and civilian managers may see this obvious shortcoming and refrain from deploying such "logic" machines. However, once various groups have invested vast sums in developing these machines, the temptation to justify this expense by installing questionable AI technologies will be enormous. The dangers of turning over the battlefield completely to machines are obvious. But it would also be a mistake to replace skilled air-traffic controllers, seasoned business managers, and master teachers with computers that cannot come close to their level of expertise. Computers that "teach" and systems that render "expert" business decisions could eventually produce a generation of students and managers who have no faith in their own intuition and expertise.

We wish to stress that we are not Luddites. There are obvious tasks for which computers are appropriate and even indispensable. Computers are more deliberate, more precise, and less prone to exhaustion and error than the most conscientious human beings. They can also store, modify, and tap vast files of data more quickly and accurately than humans can. Hence, they can be used as valuable tools in many areas. As word processors and telecommunication devices, for instance, computers are already changing our methods of writing and our notions of collaboration; expert systems, which we prefer to call competent systems, have already found a place in business and industry.

However, we believe that trying to capture more sophisticated skills within the realm of logic—skills involving not only calculation but also judgment—is a dangerously misguided effort and ultimately doomed to failure.

Acquiring human know-how

Most of us know how to ride a bicycle. Does that mean we can formulate specific rules to teach someone else how to do it? How would we explain the difference between the feeling of falling over and the sense of being slightly off-balance when turning? And do we really know, until the situation occurs, just what we would do in response to a certain wobbly feeling? No, we don't. Most of us are able to ride a bicycle because we possess something called "know-how," which we have acquired from practice and sometimes painful experience. That know-how is not accessible to us in the form of facts and rules. If it were, we could say we "know that" certain rules produce proficient bicycle riding.

There are innumerable other aspects of daily life that cannot be reduced to "knowing that." Such experiences involve "knowing how." For example, we know how to carry on an appropriate conversation with family, friends, and strangers in a wide variety of contexts—in the office, at a party, and on the street. We know how to walk. Yet the mechanics of walking on two legs are so complex that the best engineers cannot come close to reproducing them in artificial devices.

This kind of know-how is not innate, as is a bird's skill at building a nest. We have to learn it. Small children learn through trial and error, often by imitating those who are proficient. As adults acquire a skill through instruction and experience, they do not appear to leap suddenly from "knowing that"—a knowledge guided by rules—to experienced-based know-how. Instead, people usually pass through five levels of skill: novice, advanced beginner, competent, proficient, and expert. Only when we understand this dynamic process can we ask how far the rule-following computer could reasonably progress.

During the novice stage, people learn facts relevant to a particular skill and rules for action that are based on those facts. For instance, car drivers learning to operate a stick shift are told at what speed to shift gears and at what distance—given a particular speed—to follow other cars. These rules ignore context, such as the density of traffic or the number of stops a driver has to make.

Similarly, novice chess players learn a formula for assigning pieces point values independent of their position. They learn the rule: "Always exchange your pieces for the opponent's if the total value of the pieces captured exceeds that of pieces lost." Novices generally do not know that they should violate this rule in certain situations.

After much experience in real situations, novices reach the advanced-beginner stage. Advanced-beginner drivers pay attention to situational elements, which cannot be defined objectively. For instance, they listen to engine sounds when shifting gears. They can also distinguish between the behavior of a distracted or drunken driver and that of the impatient but alert driver. Advanced-beginner chess players recognize and avoid overextended positions. They can also spot situational clues such as a weakened king's side or a strong pawn structure. In all these cases, experience is immeasurably more important than any form of verbal description.

Like the training wheels on a child's first bicycle, initial rules allow beginners to accumulate experience. But soon they must put the rules aside to proceed. For example, at the competent stage, drivers no longer merely follow rules; they drive with a goal in mind. If they wish to get from point A to point B very quickly, they choose their route with an eye to traffic but not much attention to passenger comfort. They follow other cars more closely than they are "supposed" to, enter traffic more daringly, and even break the law. Competent chess players may decide, after weighing alternatives, that they can attack their opponent's king. Removing pieces that defend the enemy king becomes their overriding objective, and to reach it these players will ignore the lessons they learned as beginners and accept some personal losses.

A crucial difference between beginners and more competent performers is their level of involvement. Novices and advanced beginners feel little responsibility for what they do because they are only applying learned rules; if they foul up, they blame the rules instead of themselves. But competent performers, who choose a goal and a plan for achieving it, feel responsible for the result of their choices. A successful outcome is deeply satisfying and leaves a vivid memory. Likewise, disasters are not easily forgotten.

Intuition of experts

The learner of a new skill makes conscious choices after reflecting on various options. Yet in our everyday behavior, this model of decision making—the detached, deliberate, and sometimes agonizing selection among alternatives—is the exception rather than the rule. Proficient performers do not rely on detached deliberation in going about their tasks. Instead, memories of similar experiences in the past seem to trigger plans like those that worked before. Proficient performers recall whole situations from the past and apply them to the present without breaking them down into components or rules.

For instance, a boxer seems to recognize the moment to begin an attack not by following rules and combining various facts about his body's position and that of his opponent. Rather, the whole visual scene triggers the memory of similar earlier situations in which an attack was successful. The boxer is using his intuition, or know-how.

Intuition should not be confused with the reenactment of childhood patterns or any of the other unconscious means by which human beings come to decisions. Nor is guessing what we mean by intuition. To guess is to reach a conclusion when one does not have enough knowledge or experience to do so. Intuition or know-how is the sort of ability that we use all the time as we go about our everyday tasks. Ironically, it is an ability that our tradition has acknowledged only in women and judged inferior to masculine rationality.

While using their intuition, proficient performers still find themselves thinking analytically about what to do. For instance, when proficient drivers approach a curve on a rainy day, they may intuitively realize they are going too fast. They then consciously decide whether to apply the brakes, remove their foot from the accelerator, or merely reduce pressure on the accelerator. Proficient marketing managers may intuitively realize that they should reposition a product. They may then begin to study the situation, taking great pride in the sophistication of their scientific analysis while overlooking their much more impressive talent—that of recognizing, without conscious thought, the simple existence of the problem.

The final skill level is that of expert. Experts generally know what to do because they have a mature and practiced understanding. When deeply involved in coping with their environment, they do not see problems in some detached way and consciously work at solving them. The skills of experts have become so much a part of them that they need be no more aware of them than they are of their own bodies. Airplane pilots report that as novices they felt they were flying their planes, but as experienced pilots they simply experience flying itself. Grand masters of chess engrossed in a game are often oblivious to the fact that they are manipulating pieces on a board. Instead, they see themselves as participants in a world of opportunities, threats, strengths, weaknesses, hopes, and fears. When playing rapidly, they sidestep dangers as automatically as teenagers avoid missiles in a familiar video game. When things are proceeding normally, experts do not solve problems by reasoning; they do what normally works.

We recently performed an experiment in which an international chess master, Julio Kaplan, had to add numbers at the rate of about one per second while playing five-second-a-move chess against a slightly weaker but master-level player. Even with his analytical mind apparently jammed by adding numbers, Kaplan more than held his own against the master in a series of games. Deprived of the time necessary to see problems or construct plans, Kaplan still produced fluid and coordinated play.

As adults acquire skills, what stands out is their progression *from* the analytic behavior of consciously following abstract rules *to* skilled behavior based on unconsciously recognizing new situations as similar to remembered ones. Conversely, small children initially understand only concrete examples and gradually learn abstract reasoning. Perhaps it is because this pattern in children is so well known that adult intelligence is so often misunderstood.

This is not to say that deliberative rationality has no role in intelligence. Tunnel vision can sometimes be avoided by a type of detached deliberation. Focusing on aspects of a situation that seem relatively unimportant allows another perspective to spring to mind. Or a decision maker, after deliberation, may decide to reject a compelling intuition because changes in the environment have rendered past experiences irrelevant.

Thinking with images, not words

Experimental psychologists have shown that people actually use images, not descriptions as computers do, to understand and respond to some situations. Humans often think by forming images and comparing them holistically. This process is quite different from the logical, step-by-step operations that logic machines perform.

For instance, human beings use images to predict how certain events will turn out. If people know that a small box is resting on a large box, they can imagine what would happen if the large box were moved. If they see that the small box is tied to a door, they can also imagine what would result if someone were to open the door. A computer, however, must be given a list of facts about boxes, such as their size, weight, and frictional coefficients, as well as information about how each is affected by various kinds of movements. Given enough precise information about boxes and strings, the computer can deduce whether the small box will move with the large one under certain conditions. People also reason things out in this explicit, step-by-step way—but only if they must think about relationships they have never seen and therefore cannot imagine.

At present, computers have difficulty recognizing images. True, they can store an image as a set of dots and then rotate the set of dots so that a human designer can see the object from any perspective. But to know what a scene depicts, a computer must be able to analyze it and recognize every object. Programming a computer to analyze a scene has turned out to be very difficult. Such programs require a great deal of computation, and they work only in special cases with objects whose characteristics the computer has been programmed to recognize in advance.

But that is just the beginning of the problem. Computers currently can make inferences only from lists of facts. It's as if to read a newspaper you had to spell out each word, find its meaning in the dictionary and diagram every sentence, labeling all the parts of speech. Brains do not seem to decompose either language or images this way, but logic machines have no choice. They must break down images into the objects they contain—and then into descriptions of those objects' features—before drawing any conclusions. However, when a picture is converted into a description, much information is lost. In a family photo, for instance, one can see immediately which people are between, behind, and in front of which others. The programmer must list all these relationships for the computer, or the machine must go through the elaborate process of deducing these relationships each time the photo is used.

Some AI workers look for help from parallel processors, machines that can do many things at once and hence make millions of inferences per second. But this appeal misses the point: that human beings seem to be able to form and compare images in a way that cannot be captured by any number of procedures that operate on descriptions.

Take, for example, face recognition. People can not only form an image of a face, but they can also see the similarity between one face and another. Sometimes the similarity will depend on specific shared features, such as blue eyes and heavy beards. A computer, if it has been programmed to abstract such features from a picture of a face, could recognize this sort of similarity.

However, a computer cannot recognize emotions such as anger in facial expressions, because we know of no way to break down anger into elementary symbols. Therefore, logic machines cannot see the similarity between two faces that are angry. Yet human beings can discern the similarity almost instantly.

Many AI theorists are convinced that human brains unconsciously perform a series of computations to perceive such subtleties. While no evidence for this mechanical model of the brain exists, these theorists take it for granted because it is the way people proceed when they are reflecting consciously. To such theorists, any alternative explanation appears mystical and therefore anti-scientific.

But there is another possibility. The brain, and therefore the mind, could still be explained in terms of something material. But it does not have to be an information-processing machine. Other physical systems can detect similarity without using any descriptions or rules at all. These systems are known as holograms.

Is the mind like a hologram?

In our view, the most important property of holograms is their ability to detect similarity. For example, if we made a hologram of this page and then made a hologram of one of the letters on the page, say the letter *F*, shining a light through the two holograms would reveal an astonishing effect: a black field with bright spots wherever the letter *F* occurs on the page. Moreover, the brightest spots would indicate the *F*s with the greatest similarity to the *F* we used to make our hologram. Dimmer spots would appear where there are imperfect or slightly rotated versions of the *F*. Thus, a hologram can not only identify objects; it can also recognize similarity between them. Yet it employs no descriptions or rules.

We take no stand on the question of whether the brain functions holographically. We simply want to make clear that the information-processing computer is not the only physical system that can exhibit mindlike properties. Other devices may provide closer analogies to the way the mind actually works. The digital computer is so powerful that it already is being used to simulate holistic devices. The "new connectionists," building devices and writing programs that operate somewhat like neural nets, are creating systems that can recognize patterns and detect similarity and regularity without using inferences or isolated features at all. For example, a parallel distributed processing model developed by James McClelland and David Rumelhart has been able to learn the past tenses of both regular and irregular English verbs from repeated examples without being given or creating any general rules or lists of exceptions.

Given the above considerations, what level of skill can we expect logic machines to reach? Since we can program computers with thousands of rules combining hundreds of thousands of features, machines can become what might be thought of as expert novices. As long as digital computers' ability to recognize images and reason by analogy remains a vague promise, however, they will not be able to approach the way human beings cope with everyday reality.

Despite their failure to capture everyday human understanding in computers, AI scientists have developed programs that seem to reproduce human expertise within a specific, isolated domain. The programs are called expert systems. In their narrow areas, such systems perform with impressive competence.

In his recent book on "fifth-generation" computers, Edward Feigenbaum, a professor at Stanford, spells out the goal of expert systems: "In the kind of intelligent systems envisioned by the designers of the Fifth Generation, speed and processing power will be increased dramatically. But more important, the machines will have reasoning power: they will automatically engineer vast amounts of knowledge to serve whatever purpose human beings propose, from medical diagnosis to product design, from management decisions to education."

The knowledge engineers claim to have discovered that all a machine needs to behave like an expert in these restricted domains are some general rules and lots of very specific knowledge. But can these systems really be expert? If we agree with Feigenbaum that "almost all thinking that professionals do is done by reasoning," and that each expert builds up a "repertory of working rules of thumb," the answer is yes. Given their speed and precision, computers should be as good as or better than people at following rules for deducing conclusions. Therefore, to build an expert system, a programmer need only extract those rules and program them into a computer.

Just how expert are expert systems?

However, human experts seem to have trouble articulating the principles on which they allegedly act. For example, when Arthur Samuel at IBM decided to write a program for playing checkers in 1947, he tried to elicit "heuristic" rules from checkers masters. But nothing the experts told him allowed him to produce master play.

This checkers program is one of the best expert systems ever built. But it is no champion. Samuel says the program "is quite capable of beating any amateur player and can give better players a good contest." It did once defeat a state champion, but the champion turned around and defeated the program in six mail games. Nonetheless, Samuel still believes that checkers champions rely on heuristic rules. Like Feigenbaum, he simply thinks that the champions are poor at recollecting their compiled rules: "The experts do not know enough about the mental processes involved in playing the game."

Internist-1 is an expert system highly touted for its ability to make diagnoses in internal medicine. Yet according to a recent evaluation of the program published in *The New England Journal of Medicine*, this program misdiagnosed 18 out of a total of 43 cases, while clinicians at Massachusetts General Hospital misdiagnosed 15. Panels of doctors who discussed each case misdiagnosed only 8. (Biopsies, surgery, and postmortem autopsies were used to establish the correct diagnosis for each case.) The evaluators found that "the experienced clinician is vastly superior to Internist-1, in the ability to consider the relative severity and independence of the different manifestations of disease and to understand the . . . evolution of the disease process." The journal also noted that this type of systematic evaluation was "virtually unique in the field of medical applications of artificial intelligence."

In every area of expertise, the story is the same: the computer can do better than the beginner and can even exhibit useful competence, but it cannot rival the very experts whose facts and supposed rules it is processing with incredible speed and accuracy.

Why? Because the expert is not following any rules! While a beginner makes inferences using rules and facts just like a computer, the expert intuitively sees what to do without applying rules. Experts must regress to the novice level to state the rules they still remember but no longer use. No amount of rules and facts can substitute for the know-how experts have gained from experience in tens of thousands of situations. We predict that in no domain in which people exhibit holistic understanding can a system based on heuristic rules consistently do as well as experts. Are there any exceptions?

At first glance, at least one expert system seems to be as good as human specialists. Digital Equipment Corp. developed Xcon to decide how to combine components of VAX computers to meet consumers' needs. However, the program performs as well as humans only because there are so many possible combinations that even experienced technical editors depend on rule-based methods of problem solving and take about 10 minutes to work out even simple cases. It is no surprise, then, that this particular expert system can rival the best specialists.

Chess also seems to be an exception to our rule. Some chess programs, after all, have achieved master ratings. However, these programs have an Achilles' heel. Although designed for the world's most powerful computers, capable of examining up to 30 million possible positions in choosing each move, they can see only about four moves ahead for each player. So fairly good players, even those whose chess rating is somewhat lower than the computers, can win by using long-range strategies such as developing a queen's side pawn majority. When confronted by a player who knows its weakness, the computer is not yet a strong master-level player, although with enough speed it might someday overcome its strategic blindness by tactical accuracy and become one.

In every domain where know-how is required to make a judgment and brute force cannot substitute for understanding, rule-based computers cannot deliver expert performance, and it is highly unlikely that they ever will. Restricted to behaving like competent human beings at best, they produce performance often evaluated as being about 75 to 85 percent as good as experts.

Those who are most acutely aware of the limitations of expert systems are best able to exploit their real capabilities. Sandra Cook, vice president of expert systems at MAD Intelligent Systems, is one of these enlightened practitioners. She cautions prospective clients that expert systems should not be expected to perform as well as human experts, nor should they be seen as simulations of human expert thinking.

Cook lists some reasonable conditions under which expert, or rather "competent," systems can be useful. For instance, such systems should be used for problems that can be satisfactorily solved by human experts at such a high level that somewhat inferior performance is still acceptable. Processing of business credit applications is a good example, because rules can be developed for this task and computers can follow them as well as and sometimes better than inexperienced humans. Of course, there are some exceptions to the rules, but a few mistakes are not disastrous. On the other hand, no one should expect expert systems to make stock-market predictions because human experts themselves cannot always make such predictions accurately.

Expert systems are also inappropriate for use on problems that change as events unfold. Advice from expert systems on how to control a nuclear reactor during a crisis would come too late to be of any use. Only human experts could make judgments quickly enough to influence events.

It is hard to believe some AI enthusiasts' claim that the companies who use expert systems will dominate all competition. In fact, a company that relies too heavily on expert systems faces a genuine danger. Junior employees may come to see expertise as a function of the large knowledge bases and masses of rules on which these programs must rely. Such employees will fail to progress beyond the competent level of performance, and the company may ultimately discover that its wells of true human expertise and wisdom have gone dry.

We are in danger of becoming a society that confuses computer-type rationality with true expertise. If we fail to put logic machines in their proper place, as aids to human beings with expert intuition, then we shall end up servants supplying data to our competent machines. Should calculative rationality triumph, no one will notice that something is missing, but now, while we still know what expert judgment is, let us use that expert judgment to preserve it.

37

Artificial intelligence and computable problems

Stephen J. Andriole

Editors' note *This paper argues that, while AI is a powerful analytical methodology, there are hundreds of other tools and techniques that ought to be considered during the problems/methods matching process. The paper is useful because it makes sure we don't over-apply AI, that we don't redefine problems to fit the tools and techniques of AI.*

Introduction

This short paper suggests that artificial intelligence (AI) can evolve impressively if it assumes a role within the larger families of qualitative and quantitative methodology. Several working premises guide the following discussion. First, it is assumed that not all analytical and computational problems are amenable to computer-based solutions. Second, it assumes that AI, like operations research, decision analysis, and "conventional" computer science, all have their strengths and weaknesses; and that the misapplication of one or more of these methods classes undermines that it is possible to "match" the "right" method to explicit problem definitions.

Background

This sourcebook assumes that AI can be productively applied. The previous sections and parts of the book document successes across a wide spectrum of domains. A closer inspection of the domains, however, reveals that a great many of them are "well-bounded" and characterized by deductive inferential processes. It seems that expert systems, for example, are best used to solve problems about which we already know a great deal and whose problem-solving processes are explicit, unambiguous and—often—deductive. Is there a problem with this allocation of AI? Of course not; in fact, the matching of AI to such problem types represents a step in the right direction, a step toward the integration of AI into the larger problem-solving methods community.

Unfortunately, we often mismatch analytical methods and problems. We use heuristic solutions for mathematical problems; we use neural networks for well-bounded bank loan application evaluations, and we insist upon human information processors for air traffic control. We have few heuristics for problems/methods matching. Methods are selected often (and unfortunately) on the basis of preference, inertia, or because the color of the money is optimization, AI, or Bayesian.

AI represents one of the newest and potentially most powerful methods. But its power should be accurately targeted. This paper explores the problems/methods matching process generally; it suggests where the major methods classes can be best leveraged, and where their application is ill-advised.

Methods

There are any number of ways to classify analytical methods. Some are quantitative and some are qualitative. Some are empirical and some are subjective. Some are dynamic and some static. Zachary (1984) suggests how decision-aiding methods can be organized in FIG. 37-1. Hopple (1986) presents another taxonomy in FIG. 37-2. There are countless methods, tools and techniques. Classificatory schemes and taxonomies are extremely useful organizing devices because they categorize methods according to some consistent criteria.

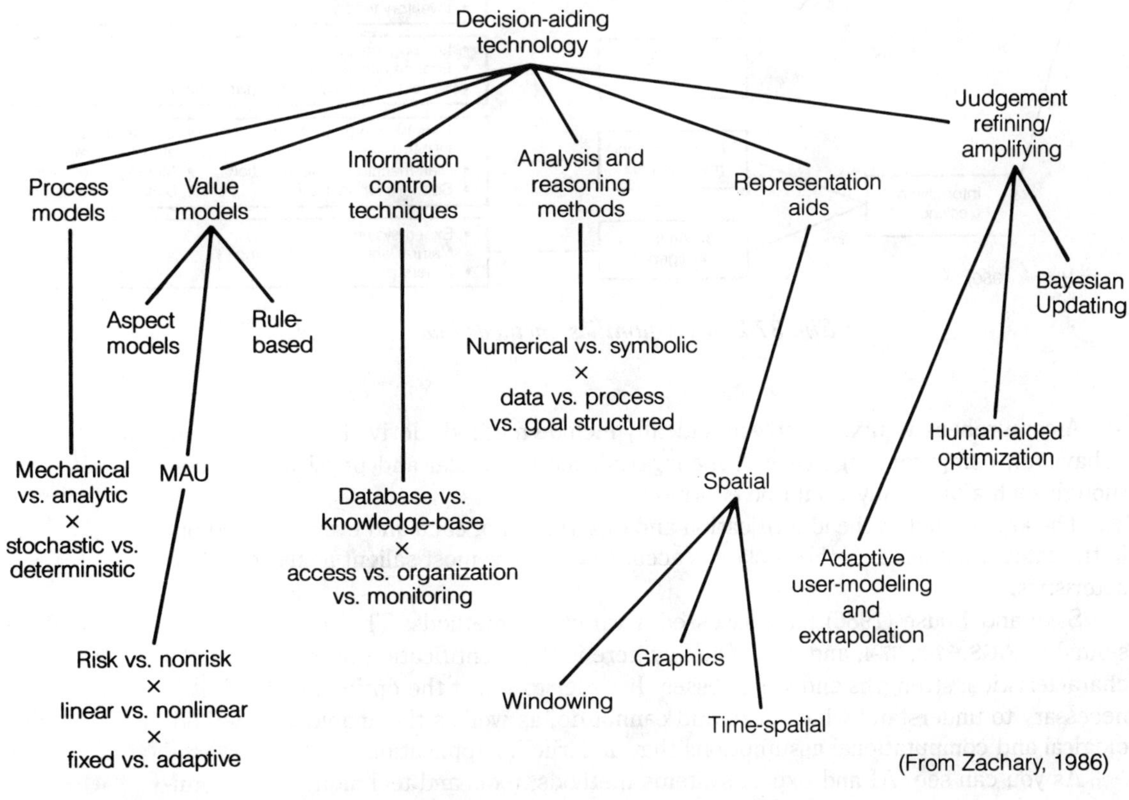

Fig. 37-1. Taxonomy of decision-aiding methods.

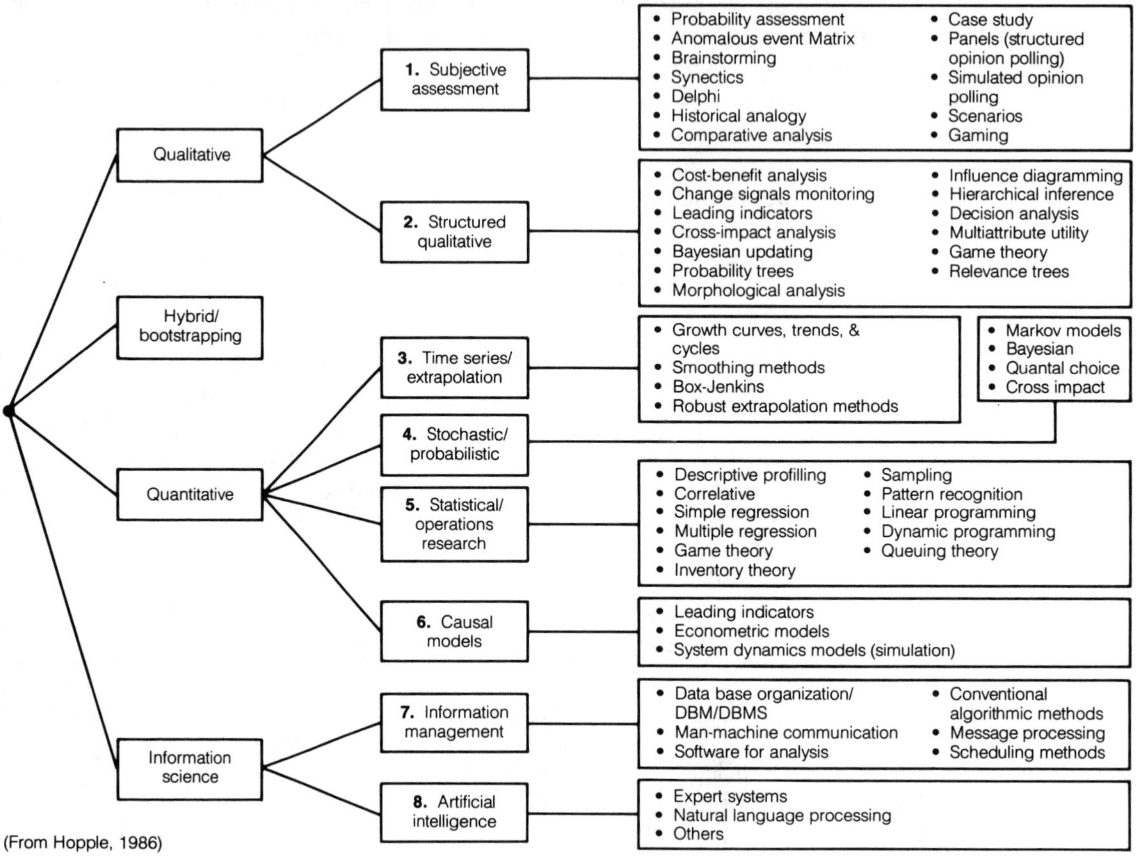

(From Hopple, 1986)

Fig. 37-2. Meta-families, methods and submethods.

A comprehensive taxonomy would ideally include methods derived from the social, behavioral, computer, engineering, managerial, mathematical and physical sciences, though such a taxonomy would be enormous.

The key lies not in the identification and description of each and every method but in the categorization of methods classes according to their most salient analytical characteristics.

Sage and Rouse (1986) have assessed a variety of methods. The results are presented in FIGS. 37-3, 37-4, and 37-5. The key here is the identification of each method's characteristics, strengths and weaknesses. In order to select the optimal method, it is necessary to understand what it can and cannot do, as well as the analytical, methodological and computational assumptions that underlie its application.

As you can see, AI and expert systems methods, tools and techniques are prominently described and assessed; it is also the case that AI sits right along side other classes of powerful methods.

Criteria	Methods			
	Artificial intelligence	Cognitive science	Decision analysis	Operations research and control theory
Objectives	Software performance	Explanation of cognition	Aiding decisions	Prediction and optimization
Methods	Symbolic; powerful software tools	Symbolic; computation-oriented	Numerical; axiomatic dec. rules	Numerical; predictive models
Products	Software and tools	Theories; training and aiding princ.	Decision prescriptions	Optimal solutions
Strength	Exploitation of context; software tools	Emphasis on process over product of behavior	Well-founded and structured	Breadth and rigor
Weaknesses	Often ad hoc; avoids engineering methodology	Often ad hoc; avoids psychological methodology	Biased toward choice; not judgement in context	Avoids context; assumption laden

(From Sage & Rouse, 1986)

Fig. 37-3. Methods Assessments.

Method / Criteria	AI & expert systems	Decision analysis & decision support	Human/system interaction
Objectives/ expectations	Design of "intelligent" systems (KBS) human-like capacities heuristics	Normative modeling, aids to option Generation Choice Selection	Effective interface—(adaptive, intelligent?) between humans and decision tools—transparent interface
Typical analytical concern or question to subject	"Models" of human processes, search & representation, symbolic processing	Decomposition, structure—elicitation of subjective judgements, evaluation of cost/benefit MAU, Bayes policy capturing	Prototyping performance modeling
Products	LISP machines, shells	Process aids (computer, other)	I/O devices, configurations
Strengths input		Structure	
Process	Explicit model, ad hoc	Normative models, face validity of models	
Output	Explanation facility	Audit trail sensitivity analysis	
Weakness input	Primitive	Often data intensive	
Process	Comprehensibility. May use unrealistic belief structures	Normative models	
Output	Comprehensibility	Sensitivity analysis	

(From Sage & Rouse, 1986)

Fig. 37-4. Methods Assessments.

Criteria \ Method	OR & control engineering	Data Base management	Cognitive science/ Psychology
Objectives/ expectations	Provide results of quantitative analysis to clients	Facilitate storage, retrieval, manipulation of data (information)	Understanding & describing human cognition
Typical analytical concern or question to subject	Linear programs, math modeling, optimization, dynamic systems analysis, statistics	Relational, hierarchical, spatial structuring, retrieval strategies	Modeling theories lens model attribution theory Empirical/experimental
Products	System model "Autopilot," etc. (control systems) aids modeling/simulation languages	DBMS software, database designs	Human models decision heuristics (validated?) Capability and/or limitation assessments
Strengths input	Can use massive real data		Experimental/empirical
Process	Rigor engr. methods		
Output	Quantification		
Weaknesses input	Requires volumes of data	Inflexible	
Process	"Artificial" lack of face validity (GIGO)		Mind reading, laboratory bound
Output	Explanation facility		Narrow domains

(From Sage & Rouse, 1986)

Fig. 37-5. Methods Assessments.

Problems

There are any number of problem types. Problem characteristics fall into many categories. Biddle (1988) has developed a list of salient problem characteristics (see TABLE 37-1), as have Hopple (1986), Andriole (1988), and Hermann (1969; see FIGS. 37-6, 37-7, and 37-8, respectively). All of these classificatory schemes illustrate the richness and complexity of problem-solving, and suggest the range of methods best suited to specific characteristics combinations.

Problems/methods matching

The decision to use AI, operations research, decision analysis, or whatever, is predicated upon the nature of the problem at hand. It should first be stated that not all problems are "computable" via the application of any individual (or sets of) method(s). Some problems are so recalcitrant that they defy modeling (and certainly quantification). Some problems can be effectively addressed via methods, tools and techniques resident in human cognitive processes and embedded in software; others are so inductive or abductive that they fall well beyond the scope of a "computable problem."

Andriole (1988) suggests how methods can be rank-ordered given certain problem types (see FIG. 37-9), and Hopple (1986) has rank-ordered his methods classes vis-a-vis his problem characteristics. Significantly, Hopple suggests that AI is potentially applicable to sets of specific problems.

Table 37-1. Biddle's task taxonomy

Level of Abstraction of the Task

Skills, Rules, Knowledge
- Does the task require explicit plan development and selection?
- Is the task solvable by application of standard operating procedures?
- Does the task require specifically identified procedures or can it be performed with little thought?

Deduction, Induction, Abduction
- Does the solution of the task require the development of new data or information (induction)?
- Does the task rely on already developed information for its solution (deduction)?
- Is it necessary to generate explanations for a series of observations?

Perceptual, Mediational, Communication and Motor
- Sensory dominant—perceptual
- Information processing and decision making tasks
- Communication dominant
- Mechanical (skill like) processes

Level of Structure to the Task

Level of Structure
- Highly structured, solution processes well understood and commonly implemented in an automated system
- Less well structured than above but solution processes still well understood and have been successfully automated previously
- Relatively unstructured problem but solution processes still tractable
- Unstructured problem, solution processes poorly understood

Bounds of the Problem
- All variables are known and understood
- Unexpected variables seldom impact solution processes
- Unexpected variables often impact results
- Currently impossible to bound the problem (impossible to separate from the environment)

Organizational Aspects of the Problem

Safety/responsibility/tradition/politics require that a human manage the process

Safety/responsibility/tradition/politics are not overriding factors

Data Aspects of the Problem

Amount of Data Required
- Massive amount of data required; beyond capability of human to absorb or manipulate
- Large amount of data required; possibly could be assimilated by dedicated human operator
- Minimal data requirements; easily mastered by operator

Accuracy of Available Data
- Available data is totally accurate or accuracy is not necessary to develop a correct solution
- Available data is generally accurate
- Available data is suspect

Precision Required of the Data
- High precision required of input data to achieve solution; precision beyond capacity of human to manipulate
- Average precision required of input data
- Precision of data not a factor in solution to problem

Table 37-1. Continued

Data Aspects of the Problem

Periodicity of Data
- Data arrives periodically in known format, and in known ranges
- Data arrives within general constraints of time and format
- Data arrives randomly and unexpectedly

Amount of Data Available vs. Amount of Data Required
- All required data is available and manipulatable
- All critical data is available and usable
- Decisions must be made without knowledge of necessary data

Fuzziness of Data
- Data sets are crisp and accepted as an accurate representation of reality
- Most data is understood and stable
- Data is not well understood and/or is unreliable

Specificity of Data
- The data is naturally or easily quantifiable
- The data is difficult to quantify without losing critical information or making difficult assumptions
- The data cannot be legitimately quantified

Storage, Recall, and Manipulation of Data Required
- Massive amounts of data are required to be stored, recalled on short notice, and manipulated
- Quantity and manipulation of data are not a factor in the problem solution

Time Requirements of the Problem

Time Requirements
- Real-time problem
- Severe time constraints
- Time constraints do not impact on problem

Computational Intensity
- Solution to problem requires unacceptable amount of time, effort, or precision to be done manually
- Problem difficult but tractable to solve manually
- Little computation involved in solving problem

	Closed	Open			Crisis
Decision process model task typology		Info input uncertainty	Conseq's of action uncertainty	Both	
Stimulus					
Hypothesis					
Options					
Response					

(From Hopple, 1986)

Fig. 37-6. Decision-making taxonomy.

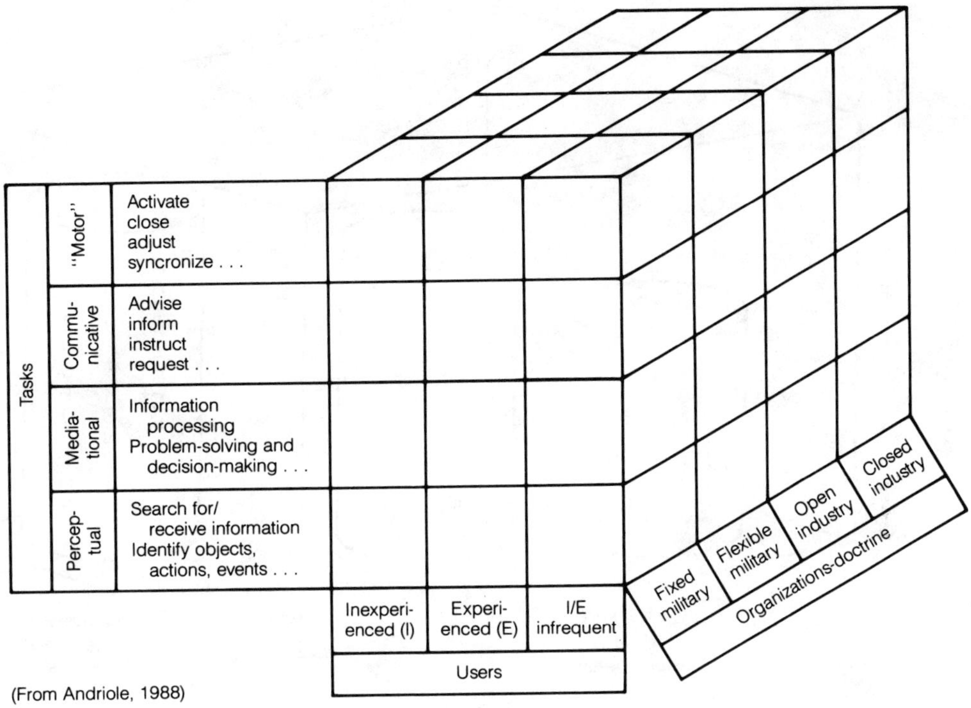

(From Andriole, 1988)

Fig. 37-7. Task/user/organization taxonomy.

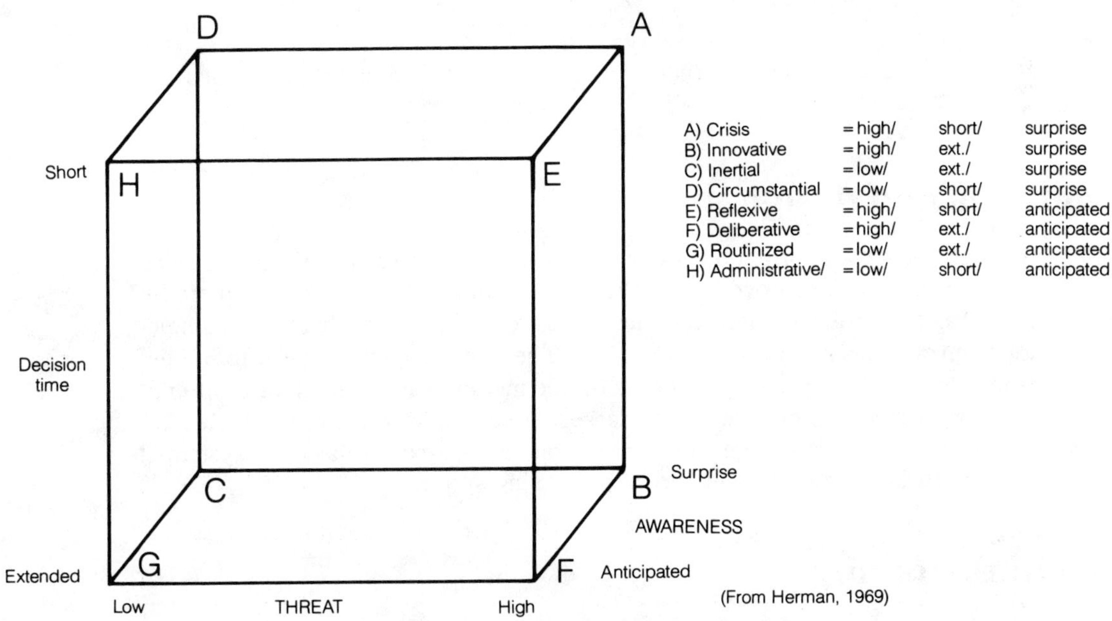

(From Herman, 1969)

Fig. 37-8. Problem taxonomy.

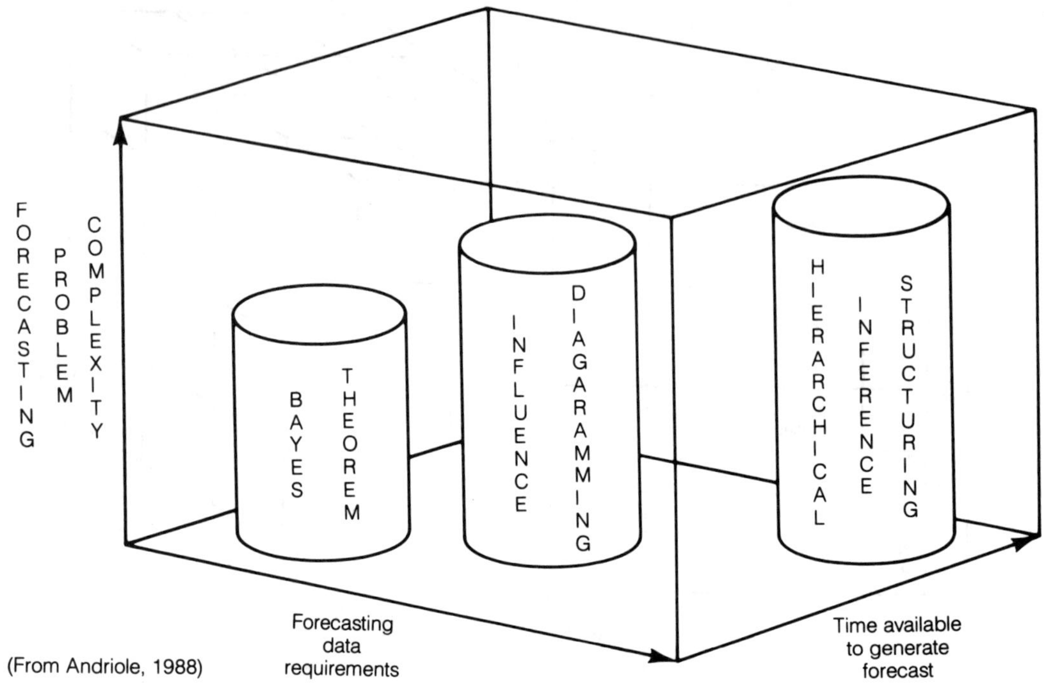

Fig. 37-9. Forecasting problems/methods matching.

The essence of the problems/methods matching process is illustrated in FIG. 37-10 (Andriole, 1988).

Methods and design

Figure 37-11 presents the information systems engineering process. The third step calls for "methods selection." Proposed here is the selection of the "right" analytical method(s) on the basis of problem characteristics. In more design cases than not, a single method seldom satisfies all of the requirements. There is frequently a need to merge methods into creative hybrids. AI might thus be one method among many, or front-end the application of quite different methods classes. We are today witnessing the use of knowledge-based natural language front-ends to databases, expert database systems, and symbolic-heuristic along side numerical processing systems.

All in the family

AI is maturing and our understanding of where and how it can be applied is growing. We now know that knowledge-based solutions are not always appropriate, and that

	Closed	Open			Crisis
		Info input unc.	Conseq's of action unc.	Both	
Qualitative	L	H	M	H	H
Subjective assessment	L	H	M	M	H
Structured qualitative	M	H	H	H	H
Quantitative	H	M	M	M	M
Time series	H	L	L	L	M
Stochastic/Probabilistic	M	H	H	H	H
Statistical//Ops Research	H	L	L	L	M
Causal Modeling	H	H*	H*	H*	H*
Hybrid	M	H*	H*	H*	H*
Info science	M	M	M	M	M
Info mgt	H	M	M	M	M
AI	L	H*	H*	H*	H*

L = Low relevance
M = Medium relevance
H = High relevance
* = Potential (rather than current) relevance

(From Hopple, 1986)

Fig. 37-10. Decision-making problems/methods matching.

sometimes the worst method is artificially intelligent-based. We also know that there are many kinds of problems uniquely suited to the tools and techniques of AI. But most importantly, AI should be regarded as a player on a larger team, a member of the methods family.

The above discussion suggests that AI has some unique capabilities and enormous potential in some specific areas. It does not suggest that those problems that have remained beyond the reach of analytical methodology are all of a sudden amenable to AI. The purpose of this short paper—appearing, as it does, at the end of a large Sourcebook of Applied Artificial Intelligence—is to broaden the methods perspective of applied problem-solvers.

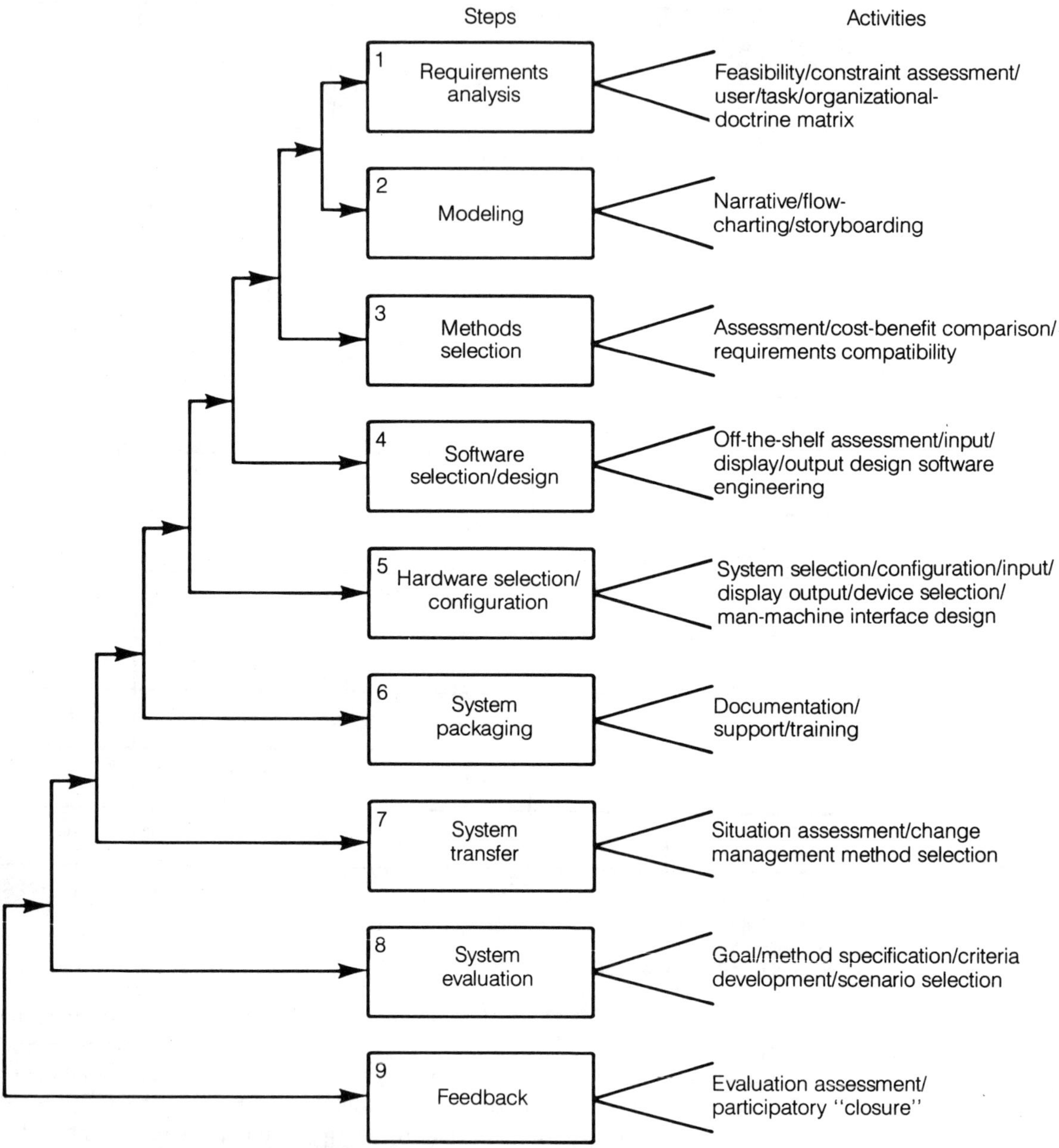

Fig. 37-11. Information systems engineering process.

References

S.J. Andriole, (1988) *Handbook of Decision Support Systems*. Princeton, NJ: Petrocelli Books/TAB Books, Inc.

J.F. Biddle, (1988) *Taxonomy of C^2 Problems*. Fairfax, VA: George Mason University.

C.F. Hermann, (1969) "International Crisis as a Situational Variable," in C.F. Hermann, ed., *International Crises*. Glencoe, NY: The Free Press.

G.W. Hopple, (1986) "Decision Aiding Dangers: The Law of the Hammer & Other Maxims." *IEEE Transactions on Systems, Man & Cybernetics*, Volume SMC-16, Number 6, November – December.

A.P. Sage and W.B. Rouse, (1986) "Aiding the Decision-Maker Through the Knowledge-Based Sciences." *IEEE Transactions on Systems, Man & Cybernetics*, Volume SMC-16, Number 4, July – August.

W. Zachary, (1986) "A Cognitively Based Functional Taxonomy of Decision Support Techniques." *Human-Computer Interaction*. Volume 2.

38

Artificial intelligence today

Gian-Carlo Rota

Editors' note *Gian-Carlo Rota looks at AI from the outside in, through the eyes of a mathematician. He assesses the field and offers a set of "lessons." The value of perspectives like Rota's is that he has no stake in AI, no overt vested interest. He is in a position to look at the field first through the eyes of a mathematician and then, generally, as a scientist.*

I am not a computer scientist, nor a specialist in AI. I am just a mathematician. I work in a branch of Mathematics that is often confused with computer science, namely, combinatorics. I would like very much to encourage such a confusion. In fact, whenever I receive an invitation to speak at a meeting on computer science or AI, an awful doubt comes to my mind: Am I being invited because the organizers are confusing combinatorics with computer science, or am I being invited because they want to meet their equal-time requirements by inviting a token mathematician?

Our subject is AI. In discussing its achievements, which are certainly indisputable, one is struck by a strange sociological phenomenon, the like of which has been seen only rarely in the sciences. Most discussions of AI are oriented towards the future, to the wonders that lie around the corner, to the radical changes in science, technology and society that lie ahead. Maybe.

There are precedents for this strange situation. In 1812, when the first organic compound, urea, was synthesized, rumors from impeccable sources began to circulate that science had at last cracked the secret code of life and that it would be a matter of a few years before scientists would duplicate living beings in the laboratory.

In 1920, at the beginning of what later came to be known as molecular biology, the civilized world was frightened by the coming clones, as they were later to be called.

And now the world is again abuzz with rumors of a similar kind. The machines that match human intelligence are coming.

From a strictly scientific viewpoint this is not wild speculation. The speed of light exceeds the speed of propagation of nerve signals in protoplasm. If and when the computer reaches molecular levels, its powers may well match or exceed those of the human brain. Whether or when this will happen is a matter of speculation; it is, in fact, one of the central questions of today's philosophy of science. Will it happen? When will it happen? A question well worth discussing. But not now. Let us instead focus on the present and briefly survey some of the features of AI as it is practiced today with a view towards singling out a few easy but sound lessons that we have learned from the past that are to be kept in mind by anyone who wants to implement AI systems today.

Here are the lessons stated in what might be called "Commandment Form".

Lesson 1 Simple mechanical devices have been invariably more successful than devices based upon general principles of self-organization.

Lesson 2 What is easy for humans is often difficult for machines. Conversely: a task that is easily performed by a machine is often difficult if not impossible to a human being.

Lesson 3 Human beings are better at analysis than they are at synthesis. For machines it is the other way around.

Lesson 4 In the crusade against wishful thinking, the machines are turning out to be our strongest allies.

Lesson 5 So far, the decisive role in solving AI problems has been played by the hard sciences and most of all by mathematics.

Lesson 6 The success of AI depends largely on the work of gifted middlemen.

Lesson 7 (and last) The Japanese problem has been seriously misstated.

Let us comment upon these lessons in turn.

Lesson 1 Simple mechanical devices have been invariably more successful than devices based on general principles of self-organization.

Last year, at Los Alamos, there was a meeting of the three experts on chess programs. It was extremely interesting, even though they met largely behind closed doors. When they came out, someone asked them: "Before you leave, why don't you give us a nutshell summary of what is common to your marvelous chess programs that work so well? Can't you give us just a snap summary on what makes them work?" They went back into their private room and came out shortly afterwards with a prepared statement they had agreed upon, which they agreed, perfectly described the three programs, different though these programs are in detail. Their answer was: "A third-rate player on a good day."

Human beings never have a perfectly good day. Chess programs are not based on any pretense of even vaguely simulating human intelligence. Their success is due to high reliability obtained by using large composite programs of great simplicity, and of great stupidity, if I may add. Here we have an instance of an old and well-known phenomenon: the victory of the idiot over the genius. Mechanical devices such as the ones that are being and will be implemented by AI research work better, because their probability of error is lower than it would be in a more sophisticated system.

This lesson has been clearly realized since the advent of expert systems. The estimation procedures used in today's expert systems are not qualitatively different from the mathematical techniques for grouping and clustering that for several years now have been used to automatically catalogue and look up journal articles and scientific citations. Crude as these procedures may appear, the evidence at the present time is that their general theory need not be significantly improved upon. Their crudity reflects the crudity of the human operator, the expert who reaches a snap judgment at the sight of familiar clues. The basic technique of expert systems is still graph search implemented by some simple scoring algorithms. To be sure, the combinatorial algorithms involved in the implementation of expert systems are becoming extremely sophisticated, but the underlying philosophy is simple.

Thus, expert systems can in no way be said to simulate intelligent processes. The program of AI has been and is that of giving machines the ability to deal with fragmented material and to integrate it by automatic means. So far, the need to implement this program by simulating intelligent human processes has not been felt; such an implementation may still be one hundred Nobel Prizes away.

Lesson 2 What is easy for humans is often difficult for machines. Conversely: a task that is easily performed by a machine is often difficult if not impossible to a human being.

Let us take an example of each. Let us recall the much-talked-about problem of building a robot that picks up an egg. At present, all we have is simple two-finger gripper-like pliers. The problems involved in building a hand-like robot are, mathematically speaking, the problems of extending control theory from one dimension to two dimensions. With their ineffable aplomb, mathematicians have pursued one-dimensional control. Why? For the simple reason that it is too hard.

In the opinion of the experts in this field, the solution of this problem is at least ten years away.

By contrast, let us consider the problem of simulating speech. This problem has proved to be simpler than was generally thought, despite the dire predictions of some philosophers.

The combinatorial theory of formal languages and formal grammars has captured far more of the grammatical constructs of human speech than might be expected a priori from the extreme simplicity of such artificial languages.

Though the problem is far from solved, we can be confident about the future. We are, to be sure, a long way from implementing an AI system which will capture meaning in speech. But who wants meaning?

What is happening now in AI can be perhaps best expressed by a thought experiment. Suppose that in the twenties, when H.G. Wells' novels were widely read and the novels of Jules Verne were still read, someone of average scientific culture had been asked the following question: "Here are two scientific problems—which one will be solved first?"

One of them might be the problem of producing the invisible man, as in the well-known novel of H.G. Wells. The other might be the problem of going to the moon, as in the well-known novel of Jules Verne. It is reasonable that a lot of people might have answered that the problem of the invisible man would be solved sooner than the problem of going to the moon. Yet it turned out to be the other way around. Nowadays no one talks seriously about the invisible man, not even when high-level DOD visitors are present with their "requirements". The situation in AI is very similar. Some of today's problems are going to be like the problem of the invisible man. Others are going to be like the problem of going to the moon. Unfortunately, we don't quite know now which is which.

Lesson 3 Human beings are better at analysis than they are at synthesis. For machines it is the other way around.

Think of the problem of learning how to speak French. It is much easier to learn to read French than to speak or write a letter in French. That is not the way it is with machines. It is easier to build a machine that will speak French than to build a machine that will understand French. A machine that eavesdrops on your telephone conversations is a much more difficult gadget to produce than one that simply answers the telephone.

Some time ago, college courses used to be subdivided into two kinds: the knowing-how courses, and the knowing-what courses. The knowing-what courses were considered by the students to be easy. Knowing-how courses were the tough ones. For machines, the knowing-what courses are the hard ones and the knowing-how courses turn out to be easier.

It is not surprising that in a great many tasks a machine's abilities turn out to be complementary to those of human beings. This puts a great premium on our being more human than we have ever been.

Lesson 4 In the crusade against wishful thinking, the machines are turning out to be our strongest allies.

Recall the controversial definition of common sense given by Albert Einstein. Common sense, wrote Albert Einstein, is the residue of all the prejudices that have been instilled in our minds before the age of seventeen.

Common sense tells us that it is easy to follow a rule. Common sense tells us that it is easy to know what it means to perform a task. That is, until you are confronted with the problem of building a machine that follows a rule, or of building a machine that learns how to perform a given task. Since we have been confronted with these problems, we have been forced to face up to what these expressions mean and to investigate processes, like following a rule or performing a task, to a degree of objectivity never thought of before. We have thereby realized that the theories of mental activity that were formulated by some of the best thinkers of our civilization—from Aristotle to Sigmund Freud—can now be exposed to be mixtures of fantasy and wishful thinking, with an occasional fact thrown in. Stimulated by the possibility, not necessarily the actuality, of simulation, psychologists are now beginning to give the first objective accounts of learning processes.

We are at last beginning to understand the process whereby an adult learns a new skill, and the common-sense views are turning out to be embarrassingly wrong. There is nothing more effective than having to build a contraption that works to make us realize what the truth is like. For example: it used to be thought that a beginner starts learning by special cases, and as he becomes more proficient he abstracts and eventually interiorizes more and more sophisticated rules. But the facts do not confirm this view. Sometimes it is the other way around. In any case, the process of learning, we now know, is much more complex than the rules-versus-special-cases description, which is now exposed as a useless oversimplification.

We are now beginning to give the first objective accounts of what it means to follow a rule. In so doing psychologists have discovered a number of striking new phenomena. Without going into details, let us mention a couple. First, if you go to an expert and ask him what the rules are that he follows in performing his task, you are not going to get anything of use. What happens is that the expert will give you what he thinks the rules ought to be, or what he learned as a child, or some such useless answer. Sometimes, it becomes apparent that the expert doesn't consciously follow any rules. The most revealing experiment in this connection is the experiment where psychologists observed the eye movements of instructor pilots. Their eye movements did not follow what they taught; they followed what they did. Similarly, after the development of expert systems (which is still the vanguard), we have realized—and a great realization it is—that not all of knowledge is inference. As soon as we found inference simulated by expert systems, we realized how many features knowledge has which are not reducible to strict logical inference. This realization is very much going on right now. This liberation from the prejudices of the past in the soft sciences is perhaps the most notable positive effect, so far, of the computer revolution. All other so-called liberations of recent years pale by comparison. At last the soft sciences can hope to achieve the standard of experimentation and verification comparable to the standards that have been reached long ago in the hard sciences.

Lesson 5 So far, the decisive role in solving AI problems has been played by the hard sciences, and most of all by mathematics.

Let me tell you a story. I have changed the names and the places, but the story is basically true. There was once a Professor Smith of Oshkosh College and there was a Professor Jones who taught at the University of Kentucky. Their specialty, their published work in mathematics, was a somewhat strange one. They investigated the theory of taking rectangles and efficiently cutting them up into smaller rectangles. Their work was not accepted by the major mathematics journals. But this is a free country, so eventually it found publication in some respectable but out-of-the-way publications such as the *Fibonacci Quarterly* and the *Rocky Mountain Journal of Mathematics*. After all, the theory was highly non-trivial, though most mathematicians at the time did not quite see what such a theory might be good for.

Last year, scientists from IBM made a pilgrimage to Oshkosh, Wisconsin. Why? Well, it turns out that masks that produce integrated chips require a fast algorithm for cutting rectangles into smaller rectangles. The implementation of such an algorithm threatened to make Hewlett-Packard chips obsolete and thus to send the company out of business. This was an unexpected application of Professor Smith's work.

At this point you may think: this sounds a little like an old Alec Guiness movie. It is a nice story, but what is this story an example of? The point is that implementing any AI project will require sophisticated combinatorial algorithms, that is, sophisticated math. It would be a mistake, however, to believe that mathematics, and more generally scientific problems, are formulated and solved in response to practical needs, such as the current needs of AI. This scenario is wrong. Such a situation happens very rarely outside science fiction novels. So rarely that when it happens we find it splashed on the front page of the *New York Times*; which proves it is rare.

What happens is quite different. Once a problem arises in AI, engineers hunt in the scientific literature for something that may hit the map. Usually, what hits the map is something that was developed elsewhere for a completely different purpose or for no purpose at all. Now those of you who work in the hard sciences are familiar with this kind of reality. Unfortunately, scientists in AI are under such heavy pressure they tend to forget this important lesson.

Recall that the Fast Fourier Transform, which is an essential component in the analysis of speech and in innumerable other analyses, was invented by a mathematician sitting at his desk who had the leisure and the serenity to do some fooling around. To take another example: Cluster analysis, which is one of the crucial problems in practical statistics today, as well as in the related field of tomography, came out of studies of stochastic geometry which were first developed for no purpose at all. And context-free grammars, which are so useful now in the invention of new computer languages, were developed by a mathematician and a linguist who wanted to spite the older linguists by showing there was some method to the madness of language.

Lesson 6 The success of AI depends largely on the work of gifted middlemen.

The basic problem of AI is the problem of integrating small components into large-scale systems exhibiting qualitatively different behavior. If we look at what happens in other sciences, we will soon realize that this problem is not an isolated one.

In physics, we find the problem of phase transition in statistical mechanics. In molecular biology (or maybe we should say in informational molecular biology), the same problem reappears as the problem of understanding how long strings of seemingly meaningless symbols in DNA can make sense and transmit genetic information.

To take a third instance, the problem of simulation of natural language is now confronted with what is known as "the semantic barrier", which is the problem of somehow reaching an explanation or understanding of how meaning comes through. Even in the recent revision that is going on of the theory of evolution a similar problem has been stated. These problems, as often happens in science, come in parallel. Their solution will require a degree of sophistication from AI specialists that cannot come out of expertise in computer science alone. This need for greater sophistication will become all the more pressing when the latest frontiers of AI will have become a reality, which will happen soon. The next frontiers of AI will be, first, the shift from digital to holographic, and second, at a more theoretical level, the implementation of algorithms that are intrinsically and constitutively random. It has recently been discovered (not quite a year ago) that in certain situations one can build an algorithm which is intrinsically random and faster than any deterministic algorithm.

Lesson 7 The Japanese problem has been seriously misstated.

It is by now evident that current advances in AI and in computing owe as much to the fact that this country is endowed by an interacting, creative, pliable and free scientific community whose results in research can be brought to bear on AI problems. As long as we have Professor Smith and Professor Jones, we do not have much to worry about. In the light of this realization, we can only be confident about the future of this country when compared to Japan or to the Soviet Union. It is good to remind ourselves from time to time of the crushing superiority of American science. I will give two anecdotes about this later on. It is good to know that there is some imperialism left in this world.

It has sometimes been stated that this country could survive with twenty first-rate universities and research institutions. Does this country have twenty first-rate universities and research institutions? It has fifty. As far as the Japanese go, it is true that the Japanese are good engineers, but when it comes to research they have fallen hook, line, and sinker for what is known as flaky AI. The Japanese problem is not one of scientific achievement, it is one of thievery. You can go very far by stealing, but I don't think you can win at the end.

In closing, let me tell you a story that some of you know quite well, about Enrico Fermi during the Second World War when he was working at the Los Alamos Lab. It happened that Fermi would often make bets about the outcome of certain events in the war, and he was winning those bets very frequently, much too frequently. At the end of the war someone asked him: "Tell us. How did you win all those bets?" Finally he gave his secret away. "Very simple. I always make the most conservative prediction." Maybe we should do that with AI.

Appendix

Story number one I was talking to a friend who is a professor of physics at a major American university. He emigrated from Holland some time ago. He frequently receives offers to go back to Holland, to Amsterdam or Leyden, one of those great old universities, but he has always turned them down. One day I asked him: Why do you turn them down? And he answered "If I went there, my career would be at an end. You see, if you take all the physics that goes on now in Holland, it is not quite as creative and as much physics as you find in the physics department at Purdue University."

Story number two I went back to Princeton to visit my philosophy professor, who was about to retire and whom I had not seen in a long time. It was very charming. At one point he said, "You know, my daughter wants to study Spanish literature. She packed her bags and went to Spain to enroll at the University of Madrid. After one month there, she met her professors and she told them that she came from America and wanted to study Spanish literature. With a strange look they answered: "You want to study Spanish literature and you came here? Why didn't you go to Yale?"

39

Psychology today and artificial intelligence tomorrow

Gerald W. Hopple

Editors' note *AI is a multidisciplinary field of inquiry. It borrows from findings, ideas, and concepts that cross-cut the social, behavioral, computer, information, managerial and engineering sciences. Psychology is one of the major contributing disciplines, and this paper describes some new initiatives in psychology that will exert a dramatic impact on the evolution of AI.*

This chapter discusses several research thrusts currently being pursued in psychology, which can be expected to feed into artificial intelligence (AI) systems of the future. The relatively new field of *cognitive science* embraces the disciplines of psychology, AI, linguistics, philosophy, and a number of other traditionally separate areas of inquiry (see, for example, Gardner, 1985). Cognitive science synergizes these separate fields to exploit the unique contributions of each in designing, developing, and fielding increasingly intelligent systems and simultaneously attempts to advance the interdisciplinary science of human, machine, and other forms of intelligent behavior.

Traditionally, AI has involved work which presumably enhances psychological theories by providing testable, computational models of human intelligence and problem solving. However, mainstream psychologists and AI experts frequently talk past each other, primarily because AI theorists emphasize the development of theories which offer plausibly sufficient accounts of mental functions while psychologists are more concerned with empirically testable predictions in the form of hypothesis tests in the context of experimental methodology—what Miller (1978) refers to as the AI emphasis on *theory development* and the contrasting psychology focus on *theory demonstration*.

Overview

This chapter takes a different tack; instead of the AI emphasis on grand theory construction, the discussion asks what it is that contemporary empirical research in psychology has to offer to AI systems of the future. How, in other words, will AI-based problem solving systems look *because of* work that is currently being conducted on how people actually perceive, make inferences and judgments, and generally think?

The rationale for this approach is twofold. First, incorporating knowledge about how people think into the system design and development process can be expected to have a significant and positive impact on the fielding of *useful* computer-based systems (that is, systems that will be compatible with the user, rather than expecting the user to be retrofitted to some alien system). Second, future sustained progress in AI will not come from a simple extrapolation of what is being done now; to achieve genuine progress—and, in particular, to overcome the omnipresent learning barrier (the fact that today's computer lacks a *general* understanding ability)—it will be necessary to pursue basic research on how people reason, solve problems, and learn or change as a result of their own experiences (see Schank, 1984). This kind of very basic research will lay the groundwork for applied progress in the future.

Two illustrations of basic research in psychology—and their implications for future AI systems—are detailed here. The first concerns alternative schemes for the representation of knowledge; mental models and other relevant cognitive structures are natural and basic interfaces or templates for perception and cognition. Computer-based mental models can serve as interface tools for AI problem solving designed to achieve genuine human-computer partnerships, an approach which also incorporates the concept of a graphic intelligent interface into interactive systems design.

The second idea exploits a large corpus of basic and applied research on the concepts of uncertainty, severe time stress, and cognitive processes in an effort to flesh out a research design for an intelligent decision aid targeted at this combination of characteristics. The design highlights two new technologies for AI-based systems: an uncertainty manager (an embedded set of algorithms and layers to minimize and reduce ambiguity and other forms of cognitive uncertainty) and intelligent templates (based on existing "unintelligent" and AI-based templating approaches but previously never applied to the vexing practical problem of ameliorating the negative effects of severe time stress).

Alternative knowledge representation schemes

How does (and should) one represent knowledge in an aiding system? Any representation of knowledge constitutes a combination of data structures and interpretive procedures that, if used in the right way, will lead to "knowledgeable" behavior. There are multiple ways to encode a fact or event in a knowledge representation scheme.

A well known cognitive science-based taxonomy features three families of representation schemes, along with a fourth—mental models—that can be distinguished from the first two in the list and features some of the characteristics of the third. All of the approaches assume that a representation is a *mapping* between the representing world and the represented world (Rumelhart and Norman, 1983).

The representation mechanisms in the typology are:

- Propositional representations:
  a. Semantic features or attributes
  b. Semantic nets;
  c. Schemas and frames;

- Analogical representations;
- Procedural representations:
  a. Demons;
  b. Productions systems;
- Mental models.

In a propositionally based representation system—the dominant scheme—knowledge is represented as a collection of symbols. The collection constitutes a list of relevant symbols or highly structured configurations of such symbols; in either case, the knowledge is explicit (declarative) rather than procedural and can be retrieved easily and quickly.

Semantic features (or attributes) are simply sets of concepts (such as, an unordered list of the elements of tactical planning, the types of defensive and offensive operations, etc.). *Semantic networks* or nets interrelate sets of concepts (nodes) by directed links (relations). In contrast, *schemas* and *frames* both exemplify higher levels of structuring. A schema is a data structure for representing generic stored concepts. A schema typically has a fixed part and a variable part; variables may take on different values, but also have schema-specified default values. Furthermore, schemas can be embedded within each other so that, for example, a more abstract schema is tagged to a more concrete one. One well known type of schema is a script, which is a schema for a frequently occurring event; another type is a plan, which represents a type of abstract schema. Hopple and Halpin (1985) and Hopple (1985) have examined the application of causal schemas to tactical planning contexts.

Whereas propositional representations are the sources of *meanings*, analogical representations are associated with *images* generally and with *visual images* in particular. Direct or analogical representations feature phenomena that can be pictorially displayed—maps, models, diagrams, and so forth. In addition to representing knowledge in very natural ways, this scheme greatly simplifies the problem of updating the representation to reflect changes in the world. An example of an analogical representation-based expert system is the General Space Planner, which has the function of arranging things in a space, given constraints that must be taken into account.

The third family consists of procedural representations, which refer to *how* to do something (the program part of an information structure) rather than the *what* of knowledge (the data or declarative component of an information structure). Generally, procedural representations are very efficient in the way they operate, provide a means for encoding heuristics (for example, in the planning domain, this could refer to "rules of thumb" that planners use to make plans), and facilitate the inclusion of both knowledge processing considerations within the same structure.

Two specific procedural representation schemes have received a lot of attention in the AI literature. First are *demons*, which are groups of active processing structures which sit "above" the database and look for patterns relevant to themselves. The appearance of a relevant pattern triggers the demon with which it is paired.

A second form of procedural knowledge is captured in the concept of *production systems*, which actually constitute a form of demon system. In such a rule-based system, all communication occurs through the working memory, which is equivalent to a common data structure. Production systems have the very valuable property of modularity in that each production is self-contained; one rule can be altered or deleted without affecting or cascading through other elements or tiers of the knowledge base. Production systems may correspond to short term memory and seem to model at least certain kinds of problem solving effectively, although we do not really know how human processing structures handle variables.

Finally, there is Johnson-Laird's (1983) work on *mental models*. Johnson-Laird maintains that the psychological core of understanding is having a working model of the phenomenon. Small-scale models of reality are not necessarily 100 percent accurate or even totally comprehensive, but can nevertheless be very useful. Images, propositions, and mental models should be regarded as three different types of representation and alternative options for encoding information. Mental model cognition (maybe along with imagery) can be contrasted with the mental representation of verbal propositions, which entails the use of explicit rules. Propositional representations are interpreted with respect to mental models. There are thus two distinct sorts of mental representation: propositional and mental model-based. Overall, images, propositions, and mental models function as follows:

- Propositional representations are strings of symbols which correspond to natural language;
- Mental models are structural analogues of corresponding states of affairs in the world (as perceived) which:
  a. Provide a basis for representing premises;
  b. Enable people to reason without formal logic;
- Images are perceptual correlates of models from a particular point of view.

The emphasis on mental models in recent work is attributable to two propositions. First, it has been known for some time that people do not perceive reality directly; some kind of "screen" intervenes between the raw data of the real world and one's perception and interpretation of reality.

Second, in research on deductive problem solving, it has been found that people can solve logical problems without the direct use of any rules of logic (Johnson-Laird, 1983). Instead, the first stage in syllogistic reasoning involves the construction of an integrated mental model that incorporates information from the premises of the syllogism. This resembles the model that would be produced if the events referred to in the premises were perceived or imagined. The validity of the conclusion suggested by constructing a mental model is assessed by searching for alternative mental models that would be compatible with that conclusion (not on the basis of the application of logical principles).

Mental models research attempts to determine how people understand some domain of knowledge. Naive mechanics, naive theories of heat, and naive theories of liquids exemplify domains that have been studied. Typically, the domains examined are simple physical or mathematical systems or devices because such systems are more tractable than complex domains like interpersonal relations and offer normative knowledge bases against which mental model-generated predictions and explanations can be compared directly and easily. For example, flowing waters and moving crowds have been analyzed as analogies employed as alternative mental models of electricity (Genter and Genter, 1983).

Mental models provide predictive and explanatory power for interacting with the environment and for understanding and using artifacts of technology (i.e., the *target system*). A *conceptual model* of the target system is invented by a scientist, engineer, designer, or psychologist to provide a representation of the system. The user has a *mental model* of the target system, and the scientist has a *conceptualization* of the user's mental model. Note that the target system, conceptual model, user's mental model, and the conceptualization of the mental model are four distinct (and potentially nonoverlapping and unique) phenomena.

Typically, mental models are naturally evolving models. In the course of using a target system, the individual formulates a mental model of the system, and it changes over time. Mental models are not necessarily technically accurate, but they must be functional. Generally, mental models are incomplete, cannot be "run" fully, are unstable, and are parsimonious. Extensive research on people's interactions with a variety of technological devices (calculators, computers, video cameras, computer text editors, the piloting of aircraft, etc.) demonstrates that the average person's understanding of the devices with which he interacts is "surprisingly meager, imprecisely specified, and full of inconsistencies, gaps, and idiosyncratic quirks (Norman, 1983: 8)."

Definition of the problem

Some empirical evidence suggests that conventional knowledge representation schemes adequately approximate knowledge representation/processing in human cognition. For example, for bodies of knowledge about how people perform a specific, real world task, rule-based systems are generally applicable; if-then rules, for example, characterize both medical diagnosis and weapon system maintenance.

However, research also implies that mental models are important mechanisms of human reasoning and problem solving and that such structures should be considered as knowledge representation schemes for at least some knowledge-based systems. Questions surface about defining mental models as they would be used in KBSs and determining systems and problem domains for which they are best suited.

A more fundamental issue concerns the full range of cognitive or mental structures which are employed in human perception and cognition. Mental models are actually a subset of the universe of cognitive structures, and standard knowledge representation schemes do not exhaust all of the types of cognitive structures.

Mental models and other relevant cognitive structures are especially important as *interfaces* or templates for perceiving, categorizing, abstracting, and explaining. Computer-based cognitive structures can be viewed as interface tools—as interfaces to processes of planning, analysis, and decision making. (This is how such structures are used in daily, unaided inference and judgment: as mechanisms which link the person to phenomena of the real world; the idea here is to exploit this fact and embed such structures in the architecture of formal aids and KBSs.) Such computer-based templates constitute a potentially very useful *graphic intelligent interface* to computer-based problem solving systems concerned with at least certain problem domains.

Design of a causal schema knowledge-based system

The technology associated with encapsulating knowledge and techniques used in AI to capture the reasoning process that human experts perform will have a significant impact on future computer systems for the military. For the man-aided machine paradigm, which characterizes such AI systems as those envisioned for robotics and autonomous expert systems, the knowledge representation scheme can be a "black box." The fully automated or man-aided machine systems can be designed or developed with knowledge representation schemes that have little or no relevance to patterns and structures characteristic of human cognition. However, for systems developed under the category of the machine-aided man paradigm (e.g., classic decision support systems and decision aids), where the human remains very much in the loop, attention must be given to the fit between the mental model of the aid and of the user. If the system and the user constitute a genuine problem solving partnership, the knowledge representation scheme of the aid must either reflect the user's "normal" modes and mechanisms of knowledge representation or be translated into a user interface which is compatible with how the human thinks and perceives. In either case, intelligent interfaces can be used productively.

The base assumption is that people's knowledge is organized in some fashion; we know hundreds and thousands of discrete facts, but impose some kind of organizational discipline on the many items of information and knowledge we carry around in our heads. For any cognitive structure which plays this role, there are *units* which make it up and *relations* which hold among the units. Mental structures include the taxonomic/categorical, the matrix type, the serial structure, and schemas and other kinds of knowledge structures (Mandler, 1984). Knowledge structures, used to store knowledge about objects, people, events, and their characteristic relationships, may be in the form of explicit propositions or networks of such propositions (Beliefs or theories, formal mental models) or schemas (knowledge structures not expressed in propositional terms, informal mental models). Schemas include scripts (event sequences extended over time) and personae (cognitive structures representing personal characteristics and typical behaviors of "stock characters").

Knowledge structures facilitate the use of strategies that allow the individual to go beyond the information contained in a stimulus—to resolve ambiguity, supplement the information "given" with a vast amount of "assumed" information, and provide an interpretive framework. Compared to other forms of cognitive organization (e.g., categorical structures, where the objects are linked only by the relations of feature similarity and class inclusion), schematic forms of organization seem to allow for more complete recall. Schemas and knowledge structures generally provide a foundation for quick, coherent, *but at least occasionally erroneous* interpretations of new experiences.

Geiselman and Samet (1980) provide a good example of the applicability and utility of the schema concept for military analysis and decision making contexts; schema theory, they point out, involves "matching the perceived material with a structured mental representation of the user's or learner's general knowledge of a topic [p. 693]." A schema thus provides a basis for categorizing, selecting, deleting, abstracting, consolidating, and organizing information. Once it is learned, the schema is employed to comprehend other situations with a similar underlying structure.

Geiselman and Samet portray a schema as a two-dimensional plot of relevant categories of information, with the dimensions being "importance" and "preferred sequence of presentation." For a scenario involving analysis of the enemy in a defensive situation, for example, 32 staff officers composed a summary of 30 enemy-situation-data messages. The ten summaries that received the highest overall evaluations (as judged by experts) were used to derive a summarizing schema or hierarchical outline. Only ten general topics were necessary to describe all of the contents of the ten "good" summaries.

In the simplest sense, a schema is an ordered checklist or analytical template, a set of categories for organizing, consolidating, and otherwise structuring information. Many analytical situations also involve causal relationships; this is true, for example, of a number of aspects of the tactical planning process. When information about a certain effect is attributed to one, two, or more possible causes, a causal schema type of knowledge structure may be activated. Extensive empirical research has been conducted on the use of causal schemas in judgments under uncertainty. Causal data have more impact than other data of equal informativeness; given data that evoke a causal schema, incidental (and diagnostic) data that do not fit the schema are given little or no weight. People rely on models or schemas to predict and explain outcomes in daily inference tasks.

Schemas and causal schemas are two particularly noteworthy cells within the knowledge structure typology. The more general typology of cognitive structures for military problem solving will provide the foundation for identifying alternative architectures for intelligent interfaces.

Given a KBS conceived as an intelligent interface, the latter will constitute a mental model of the relevant analytical process, structure the process, and provide a graphic and "smart" navigational aid to guide the user through the process. An intelligent interface system has three central subsystems: the user; the interface module; and the remaining hardware/software subsystems. The latter are the link to the real world which is being sensed or acted on. Details on the overall intelligent interface concept are provided in Halpin (1984) and Hopple and Halpin (1985). At the most general level, the concept works as follows.

The user issues a command (or set of commands) which proceed through some physical interface into the Intelligent Interface module, where they are interpreted and translated into commands for sensing or effecting the world through the hardware/software subsystems. If the Intelligent Interface is designed for tactical planning, for example, this would activate the procedures to generate plans, to replan, and to revise stored plans.

For illustrative purposes, the domain of fire support planning will be used. The fire support planner must consider a variety of causal constraints, opportunities, and determinants. The planning process features some algorithmic and/or rule-based modules (such as, target value analysis), where algorithmic operations or conventional knowledge representation schemes (such as, production rules for weapon-to-target assignment) predominate, but the process is not exclusively algorithmic. Significant parts of the fire support planning process are probabilistic (rather than deterministic), scenario-driven (linked to mentally stored scripts), and schema-like.

The fire support planning domain consists of causal factors (initially classified into the three broad clusters of *friendly, enemy*, and *the environment*) and a fire support knowledge structure or mental model in the form of a causal schema. Figure 39-1 portrays a generic, baseline fire support planning causal schema. This first-cut schema consists of the core variables in the planning process:

- The commander's concept (which evolves into the OPLAN);
- Enemy forces (a general category which is treated in more detail in later phases of the planning process);
- Friendly forces (also later broken down into its constituents);
- Assets (the fixed stock of available assets);
- The environment (composed of elements such as terrain and weather);
- The fire support concept/plan.

Scenarios enter into the schema as well, although battlefield situation scenarios are an analytical filter, not a variable per se in the model; this box is therefore set off within dotted lines.

The arrows displayed in FIG. 39-1 represent our thinking about both planning logic and causal flows in fire support planning. For example, environmental factors flow into the commander's concept and also shape (or at least set the initial parameters for) the fire support concept. The latter is also influenced (constrained) by assets available and, of course, by the evolving commander's concept.

People typically attempt to achieve a coherent interpretation of events, and sets of events are often organized by schemas of cause-effect relations. The normal tendency to use such causal schemas to provide an interpretive framework is reinforced if the individual is deluged with information (or must react rapidly under stress, as in a crisis decision situation).

Anticipated results

Use of a mental model approach to knowledge representation may be best understood in terms of a series of hypotheses about how it can be utilized most effectively—and what the payoffs would be. The central hypothesis is that causal schemas and other mental models serve as intelligent interfaces to the process of problem solving. Two other sets of hypotheses about utility and payoffs can be offered.

First, mental models are descriptive organizing devices. They are used to identify the network of relevant variables and interrelationships, to provide a capability to zoom in on any element of the model, to identify key knowledge sources and requirements, and to accelerate the interactive problem solving process by making explicit the relationships among key variables.

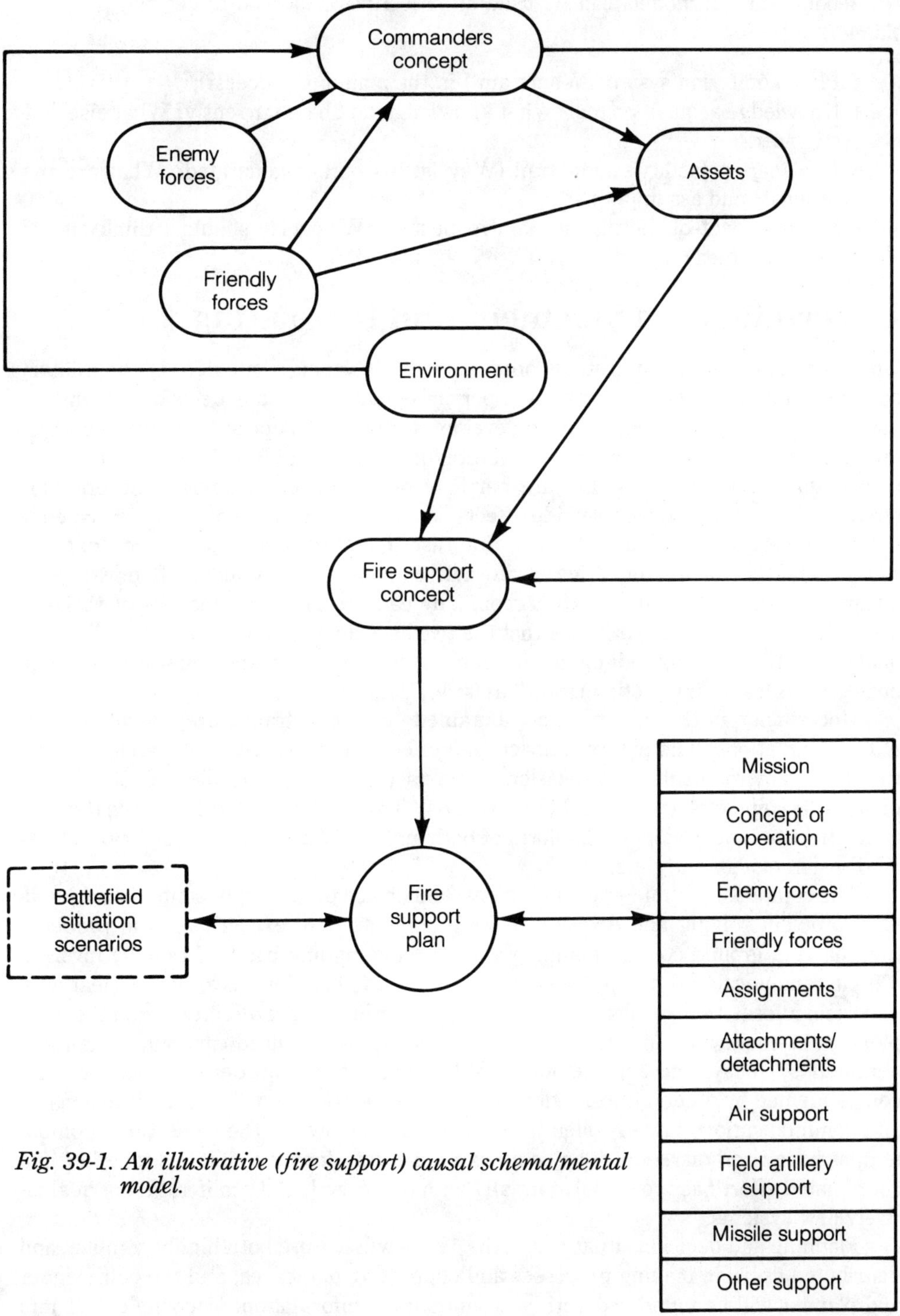

Fig. 39-1. An illustrative (fire support) causal schema/mental model.

Second, mental models can be used as prescriptive tools to direct and pace the planning process:

- Plan monitoring system (Where am I in the planning process?);
- Knowledge acquisition tool (What knowledge do I have currently? What else do I still need?);
- Explanation facility—audit trail (Why is this output generated? What are the rationale and assumptions?);
- Enhancement of the planner's introspection (What else should I think about? What am I leaving out?).

Uncertainty management and templating

Uncertainty and severe time stress pose particularly vexing challenges to the military commander and analyst. Uncertainty, a pervasive feature of many decision making situations, forces the decision maker to develop estimates and options and make choices in the face of missing, incomplete, or ambiguous information and, quite often, with respect to future outcomes that are partially or completely unknown. Severe time stress leads to such undesirable side effects as a marked decrement in performance, a sharp decrease in the ability to make fine discriminations, perceptual and cognitive rigidity, and the recognition of fewer alternatives than exist in reality. Often, extensive uncertainty and severe time stress accompany each other; in an analysis of variance sense, it is plausible to hypothesize that the two have deleterious "main effects" on the quality and timeliness of judgments, inferences, and decisions, and equally plausible to posit a significant "interaction effect" as well.

Uncertainty and severe stress attributable to time constraints are typical features of crisis situations. The nature, impact, and effects of crises have been analyzed in a variety of environments and decision contexts (see, e.g., Andriole, 1985b; Broadbent,1971; Hopple, Andriole, and Freedy, 1984). This literature clearly reveals the negative effects of uncertainty (in the form of both ambiguity and surprise) and time stress on decision quality and timeliness.

The complexity of inference, judgment, and choice processes in contemporary military problem solving and decision making contexts only exacerbates the problem. Command in ground combat planning and decision making has traditionally involved difficult analytical and choice tasks. Historically, commanders have had to deal with uncertain information, delays in receiving reports or in sending directives, and the complexities of employing units in accordance with their specialized capabilities and vulnerabilities. Today, and for the foreseeable future, these burdens remain and are complemented by others. Information continues to be uncertain, while modern sensors and communications have swollen its volume appreciably. At the same time, combat tempos have risen markedly. The complexity of fitting force capabilities together in a coordinated effort has grown substantially with the growth and proliferation of qualitatively new systems.

Planning and decision situations in the 1990s will feature both highly complex and distributed decision making processes and supporting databases, and the commander and planner will be inundated with vast amounts of information. Doctrine enters into this emerging portrait as well. The AirLand Battle concept, designed to exploit the enemy's weaknesses anywhere on the battlefield, depends for success on reacting *rapidly and effectively* to vulnerabilities as they appear. Thus, complexity, uncertainty, and very short time fuses are combined in a way which maximizes the demands on the military decision maker.

In addition to complexity, crisis conditions, and doctrine, the expectation of deception emerges as an additional source of increased uncertainty. The enemy may employ deception to either increase ambiguity (where the goal is to confuse the target) or mislead (falsely decreasing ambiguity by creating belief in the wrong alternative). The first type of deception forces the target to spread out resources to cover multiple contingencies; the second forces him to concentrate resources on a single (wrong) contingency.

Either form of deception leads to surprise. In their research on ambiguity and uncertainty in probabilistic inference, Einhorn and Hogarth (1985) posit two kinds of surprise. First, when the credibility of a source is high and the dissimilarity of signals large, one expects the distributions from which p can come to be highly skewed in both directions. However, if one highly credible sensor showed the enemy to be concentrated at location x and another showed him to be massed at location y, such a result, where $p = .5$, would be surprising given the high credibility of the sensors and the dissimilarity of the signals. In effect, the data are not good enough, given the perfectly plausible expectation about the distributions from which p could come. If the enemy is using deception, this exemplifies the route of deceiving the target by falsely increasing ambiguity.

The second case arises in the low credibility-low dissimilarity situation. If the enemy cleverly masked multiple signals to force the target to conclude that all of them indicated scenario x (e.g., an attack at point y, when the real attack comes at point z), such a result, where $p = 1$, would be surprising because one's expectation of the distributions of p would not contain such extreme values. Here, the data are "too good," rather than not good enough. This variant of deception illustrates the alternative track of misleading the target by falsely decreasing ambiguity (i.e., inducing belief in a single—and wrong—alternative).

Definition of the problem

Crisis, complexity, and deception all suggest that decision aids could be useful mechanisms for coping with and ameliorating the effects of uncertainty and time stress. Dozens of decision aids have been designed, developed, tested, evaluated, and, in some instances, fielded since 1970 in the arena of military problem solving (see, e.g., Andriole, 1983a, 1983b, 1985a, 1985c, 1986; Hopple, 1986a). Such aids have been designed and deployed for problems involving tactical and strategic intelligence, situation assessment, planning, resource allocation, weapon targeting, option identification and selection, and evaluation; the range of substantive applications, from intelligence and logistics to command and control and operations, has been extensive. The various aids have been anchored in the technologies of decision analysis, operations research/management science, artificial intelligence and other branches of computer science, statistics, and a variety of hybrids of these basic families.

Successful aiding systems can be readily identified for analytical or decision contexts which are repetitive and routine, where the cognitive processing involved requires neither the reduction of intrinsic and pervasive uncertainty nor the amelioration of the dysfunctional consequences of a highly stressed environment. Fewer aids (and fewer successful aids) have been targeted at the high uncertainty/high stress decision context.

For the decision context where high uncertainty and severe time stress intersect, it is advisable to think in terms of automated decision aids. The idea here is not to replace the analyst or commander with a machine (along the lines of the man-aided machine paradigm of decision aiding), but to exploit expertise *prior to* the onset of the decision situation by embedding such knowledge in a computer-based aiding system, thereby freeing the user to react to prestructured analytical templates and rapidly processed data (thus approaching the man-machine partnership or the machine-aided man paradigm). The man remains very much in the loop and controls the overall process, but the machine is tasked with functions that might be performed by the human *if* uncertainty were low and time stress did not impinge on the process.

It must be stressed that such a real-time advisory system does not simply issue recommendations or announce "decisions." The nature and quality of its interface with the user are absolutely crucial and must be engineered very carefully; the system must be efficient *but* user-friendly and, more importantly, the cognitive model in the aiding system should mirror the cognitive model of the user.

In addition, the explanation facilities of such a system must be unusually robust and sophisticated; this assumes not only a natural language capability and a rapid response rate to user queries, but an ability to explain its output cogently and with an awareness of inescapable subtleties and complexities. The explanation facilities will therefore be much more complex than a simple dump of relevant if-then rules; the system will be required to know when to recommend additional data collection or to stop and report partial results, and will also be aware of the frequently intractable nature of uncertainty (i.e., after the initial uncertainty has been reduced, there often remains an irreducible residual core of uncertainty in real world inference and judgment contexts).

Design of an uncertainty management/intelligent template aid

For illustrative purposes, sensor data fusion (SDF) will serve as the problem domain. Fusion involves the conversion of multiple individual sensor inputs into a single, integrated, coherent assessment of the situation; the fusion system processes all source intelligence (ranging from uncertain combat information relayed by the troops to intelligence derived from strategic systems), correlating and integrating bits of disparate information into a system or mosaic which represents the best overall snapshot of the battle picture.

SDF is a particularly appropriate candidate problem domain for a prototype aid targeted at the combination of uncertainty and severe time stress. By its very nature, sensor data fusion must confront and resolve an endemic and cascading series of uncertainties. Almost invariably, the information available to the SDF analyst is incomplete (requiring the use of plausible inferences to fill information gaps), unreliable (necessitating probabilistic reasoning and clustering to fuse reports from different sources and demanding an ability to maintain multiple and often contradictory hypotheses), and time-varying (because input data do not flow in continuously and data typically arrive out of proper time order). In addition to this network of multiple and pervasive uncertainties, the fusion process must occur in real-time or near real-time, a demanding enough requirement per se and one that is aggravated by the severe time stress associated with battlefield tempos, confusion, and crises.

The relevant literature streams are spread across a number of domains, including basic and applied psychology, decision analysis, artificial intelligence, crisis forecasting and management, computer-based systems design and development, applied problem solving, and sensor data fusion.

In particular, the literature on how people make judgments under uncertainty is large, diverse, and complex (see, e.g., Edwards, 1954, 1968; Einhorn and Hogarth, 1981, 1985; Ellsberg, 1961; Kahneman et al., 1982; Peterson and Beach, 1967). Uncertainty may involve data or appropriate mental operations and methods. Steinbruner (1974) distinguishes among risk, uncertainty, and structural uncertainty. Another dimension of variability pertains to whether the uncertainty is actual and/or perceptual. Jervis (1976) devotes considerable attention to the ways in which decisional quality is impaired when overconfident decision makers neglect *actual uncertainties*. Alternatively, decision makers could be paralyzed by *perceived uncertainties* that either do not exist or could be easily compensated for. In addition to these variegated dimensions of the concept of uncertainty, the military commander must always keep in mind the special kind of uncertainty associated with potential deception on the part of a knowledgeable opponent.

Einhorn and Hogarth (1985) differentiate uncertainty about uncertainty (ambiguity) from "simple" or first order uncertainty. If there is uncertainty about the identity of a particular case but the distributions are known (e.g., urn 1 contains 50 red and 50 black balls, but the type of ball that has just been selected is unknown), the situation is one of "simple uncertainty." If, on the other hand, urn 2 contains 100 balls, but the proportions of red and black are unknown, this constitutes uncertainty about uncertainty or second order uncertainty. Ambiguity thus characterizes a lack of knowledge of the process that generates outcomes; as Einhorn and Hogarth note, most real world generating processes are not precisely known. *Ambiguity*, the intermediate state between *ignorance* (i.e., no information is available that would allow us to rule out possible probability distributions) and *risk* (all but one distribution is ruled out), is typical of many military problem solving situations.

In addition to the conceptual and empirical work on uncertainty, there are many studies of time-related stress, both in the classical literature on stress (e.g., Milburn, 1972) and more recent work under the rubric of arousal theory (Eysenck, 1984). Extensive research demonstrates that the time pressures associated with severe stress have a number of deleterious physiological, psychophysiological, and psychological correlates and effects. Severe time stress leads in the typical instance to biased information processing, perceptions of information overload, fatigue, simpler (and often drastically simplistic) forms of behavior, a reduction in the number of cues of which the individual is aware, and numerous other adverse consequences. One of the most verified of these impacts is the association between high time stress and a premature convergence on one hypothesis or option. This premature closure syndrome reflects an artificial truncation in the range of hypotheses identified or options and alternatives delineated.

Thus, severe time stress adversely affects the decision process, with particularly negative consequences for the initial or problem identification/structuring step in the overall process. In both scientific research and real world decision making, high quality analysis results from the specification of a mutually exclusive and exhaustive set of hypotheses. This ideal is elusive enough if stress is low or nonexistent. If the analyst or commander is confronting a situation of severe time stress, the probability is minimal that the full range of hypotheses or options will even be elucidated—much less comparatively weighed.

For this reason, knowledge-based systems can be considered to be attractive solutions for this decision type. A relevant knowledge base, for example, could be comprised of prestructured hypothesis sets culled from experts and doctrine. More generally, embedded *templates* accelerate the problem solving process and compensate for the normal tendencies to experience premature convergence and make inaccurate judgments under severe time stress.

A generic and very skeletal architecture for an SDF aiding system is portrayed in FIG. 39-2. The overall system features such AI techniques as natural language processing (NLP), rule-based updating of the system database, and rule-based inferencing for tactical data fusion. Central to the design is the concept of sharing knowledge by cooperating subsystems of a command, control, and communications system.

The architecture design will flesh out the overall skeleton as a strawman, but the design task per se will concentrate on two elements of the overall system concept: the embedded templates (designed to resolve—or shortcircuit—the severe time stress aspect of the SDF process by incorporating expertise on-line into prestructured analytical templates which guide the user, fill in blanks, intelligently navigate through different aspects of the SDF process, and prompt the analyst as necessary) and the system uncertainty manager (designed to automate much of the process of uncertainty reduction and management via rules and other appropriate methodologies to handle uncertainty at various levels and in its many guises).

Templates are distilled models of activities, functions, or analytical processes. They are used to accelerate the interactive problem solving process. In one respect a template is an ordering of activities; systems engineers, to cite just one of many potential examples, have procedures that they follow for system configurations. SDF-relevant templates would serve as navigation aids, as is the case for any template; in addition, they would play the key role of filling in default values for missing items in the SDF process (a need that arises frequently because SDF input data do not always arrive in a predictable time order—and in some cases do not arrive at all).

Decision makers who subscribe to the use of explicit analytical methodology often "fill in" decision and probability tree templates in order to solve complicated analytical problems, just as evaluators often use templates to accelerate the evaluation process. Multiattribute utility (MAU) assessment is an illustrative technique. MAU permits problem solvers to evaluate complex problems via the identification and weighting of specific evaluative criteria; there are usually several levels of criteria that are organized into blocks of groups of criteria.

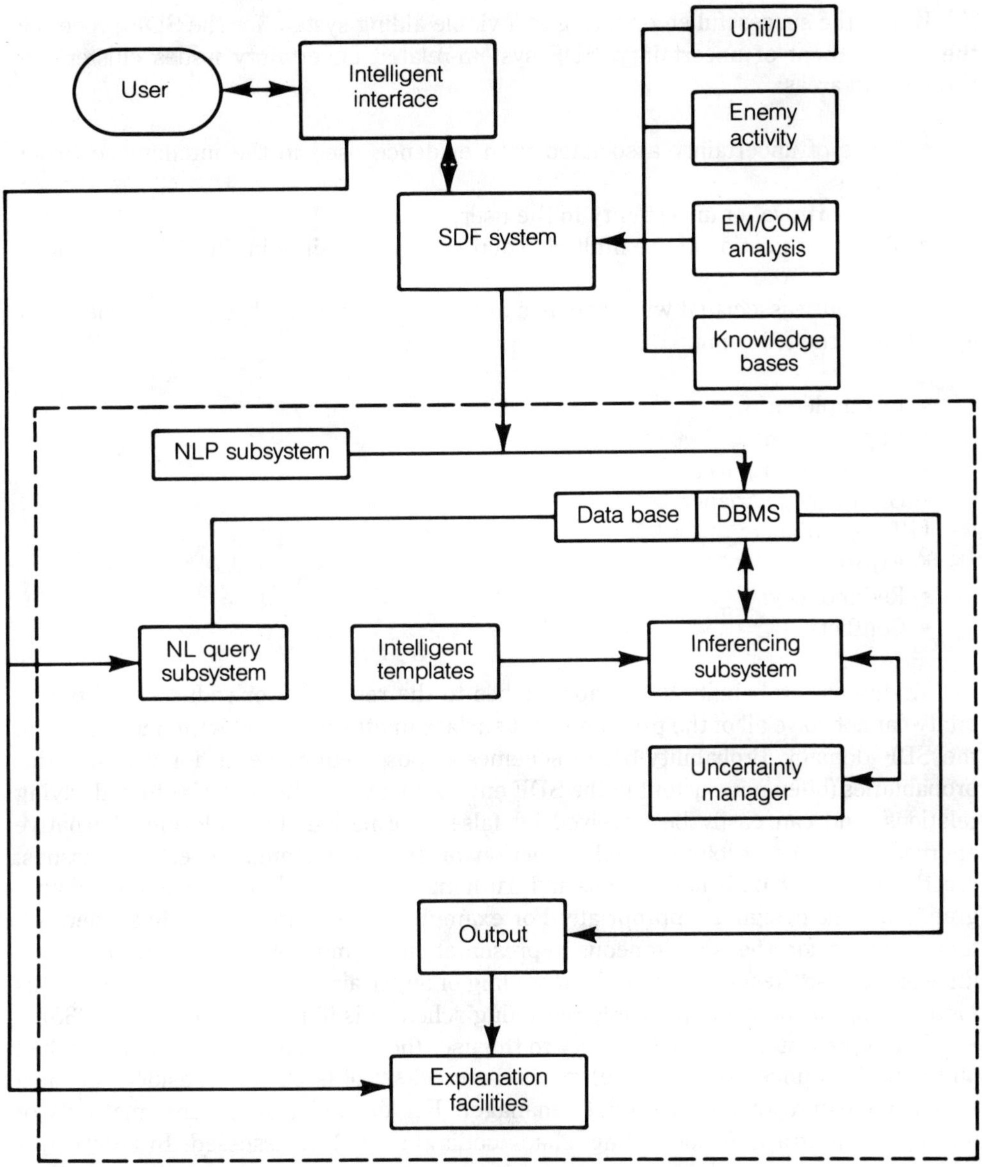

Fig. 39-2. Sensor data fusion system: architecture.

MAU and similar templates are "unintelligent" checklists or problem solving blueprints. But what if the tools and techniques of artificial intelligence were integrated into the template-building process? What if capabilities for integrating knowledge bases (fact files and rules, for example) were embedded in the template-construction process? It is in fact possible to develop a generic architecture that will accommodate the integration of knowledge bases.

Key to the successful engineering of a viable aiding system for the SDF process is the management of uncertainty. SDF system-related uncertainty issues cluster into three broad areas:

- Types of uncertainty associated with evidence used in the intelligence fusion process;
- The portrayal of uncertainty to the user;
- The identification of the multiple sources of uncertainty in the SDF process.

Uncertainty associated with evidence falls into one of a number of categories. The list includes the following:

- Incompleteness;
- Imperfection;
- Accuracy variance;
- Granularity variance;
- Time variance;
- Errors;
- Redundancy;
- Conflicts.

Traditional probability-based approaches to the resolution or reduction of uncertainty cannot solve all of the problems that surface in efforts to deal with uncertainty in the SDF domain. Probability-based schemes impose requirements for sets of prior probabilities (often nonexistent in the SDF environment), can be sensitive to underlying relations, and can easily be deceived by false information. In exploring alternative approaches to the resolution and reduction of evidence-related uncertainty issues, recent AI research on belief systems and truth maintenance will be canvassed and integrated into the design as appropriate. For example, the Multiple Belief Reasoner system provides for the simultaneous representation of multiple beliefs in the same knowledge base. Recent work on the modeling of uncertainty and precision and various kinds of approximate and plausible reasoning schemes is illustrated in Prade (1985).

The representation of uncertainty to the user (how to portray conclusions reached on the basis of uncertain evidence) raises a second set of issues for consideration as a candidate feature of an uncertainty manager. For example, alternative methods of uncertainty portrayal (color coding, shape coding) should be assessed. In addition, it will also be necessary to alert the user to situations where uncertainty cannot be eliminated or reduced any further; the question of how to accomplish this in a valid, reliable fashion must be addressed.

Finally, there are many potential sources of uncertainty that must be taken into account. Uncertainty may emanate from sensor inputs, be associated with domain knowledge, or be linked to the guidance and requirements that drive intelligence production. Uncertainty associated with sensor inputs may be in the form of accuracy or granularity variance; or it may reflect time variance, errors, redundancy, or conflicts. Typically, uncertainty associated with domain knowledge involves incompleteness.

In addition to provisions for the management of uncertainty in terms of uncertainty associated with evidence, the representation or portrayal of uncertainty, and the sources of the phenomenon, deception as a special source of uncertainty must, as noted earlier, be addressed. Deception is a unique and continuous threat to analysis and decision making in the military environment. Through deception, efforts are made to condition the target's belief, influence the target's action, or benefit from action undertaken by the target. The opponent may achieve deception by increasing ambiguity (confusing the target) or by misleading the target (falsely decreasing ambiguity). The first type achieves success by increasing the noise in the environment; the second introduces artificial certainty by making the level of noise appear to be nonexistent.

Either route allows the enemy to exploit the advantages accruing from surprise, adding another layer of uncertainty to the uncertainty stemming from one's own ignorance and internal and external attributions of ambiguity. The design of the uncertainty manager architecture will include a consideration of approaches to countering deception (e.g., evaluating evidence against an array of alternative hypotheses; event streaming, with a juxtaposition of two distinct streams, where one depicts the event pattern typical of deception; etc.).

In addition to the architecture for the uncertainty manager, methodology models should also be assessed for non-monotonic or evidential reasoning (reasoning on the basis of evidence that can be incomplete or inaccurate) and for combining evidence from multiple sources of varying degrees of reliability and accuracy (e.g., recursive Bayesian, fuzzy set calculus, Shafer-Dempster theory). Both situations are endemic to the SDF analytical process.

Anticipated results

Success in such a research endeavor would yield two interrelated and very useful sets of results. First, there would be available a stocktaking and synthesis of the available empirical and theoretical research on uncertainty, severe time stress, and cognitive processes. Both introductory discussions (such as, Charniak and McDermott, 1985) and more advanced treatments (such as, Prade, 1985; Ralescu and Ralescu, 1984) emphasize the crucial nature of uncertainty and its resolution for the intrinsic validity and—equally important—credibility to the user of expert systems. Second, basic inquiry would provide the basis for applied discussion and at least preliminary application of key issues relating to technologies, methodologies, and architectural design principles for developing decision aids to improve decision making performance under these conditions.

Conclusions

The ideas outlined in this chapter represent only two of multiple research tasks in empirically oriented psychology which could impact on future AI technology advances and fielded systems. Furthermore, it should be stressed that the military applications discussed above have analogues throughout the civilian (governmental and private) sectors.

With respect to work on mental models and the entire family of cognitive structures, the concept of KBSs with embedded mental models (as well as more conventional AI-oriented knowledge representation schemes for modules of a system where such approaches are appropriate or preferable) emerges as a system development idea worth pursuing. Clearly, rigorous, hard evidence-based models can and should be developed for certain military problem domains (much of logistics, target value analysis, and so forth). The challenge arises in the many "squishy" and dynamic domains, which account for quite a few domains (or parts of domains) in the Army, where schemas, causal schemas, scenario-based scripts, and mental models are more appropriate (and more isomorphic to the problem being dealt with) than algorithmic, rule-based, or other more formal methodologies.

More generically, for many corporate planning and decision contexts, mental models emerge as potentially viable knowledge representation schemes, especially for the realm of genuine decision support systems (as opposed to management information systems, which are more structured, bounded, and oriented around simple information and display functions—and non-AI methodologies). Many application areas, ranging from strategic planning and foreign investment to product planning and marketing, can be envisioned. The movement in this direction in the corporate decision support system/decision aid arena is discussed in Hopple (1986b).

Analogously, severe time stress and uncertainty surface as problems across the military functional areas of maneuver, fire support, intelligence/electronic warfare, air defense, and combat service support. More generically, Department of Defense decision makers will face situations of unprecedented stress and uncertainty throughout the 1980s and 1990s.

Like military analysts and commanders, corporate planners and managers frequently confront situations of high uncertainty and severe time stress. Decision support systems as conventionally configured do not generally provide systems for this class of decision contexts. The architectural principles referred to earlier would have obvious applicability to similar corporate situations.

Finally, this chapter closes with a plea for sustained basic AI research. While this volume highlights the applied reality of AI systems today, progress in the future depends critically on investments in basic R&D and academic research across a variety of disciplines and often in contexts which show little or no likelihood of immediate payoff. Schank (1984: 31) contrasts the two fundamental approaches to AI: product-directed and theory-directed; as he notes, an AI "breakthrough" often equals an advance in a particular technology.

Product-directed AI is exemplified by the many expert systems available in today's marketplace. The current systems, as Schank points out, have "expertise" but do not represent a human expert in a given field; such systems are organized, but lack self-organizational ability; they do not change or improve as the result of experience, but simply move on to the next (already programmed) if-then-rule. Only very basic research on expert system technology (and uncertainty, the human nature of expertise, and a wealth of other topics) will lead to fundamental advances in expert systems—or any other subfield of AI. Work today on psychology should lead to new AI systems tomorrow.

References

S.J. Andriole, (1986) *Handbook for the Design, Development, Evaluation, and Application of Interactive Decision Support Systems*. Marshall, VA: International Information Systems, Inc. (and forthcoming, Petrocelli Books, Inc.)

S.J. Andriole, (1985a) *Applications in Artificial Intelligence*. Princeton, NJ: Petrocelli Books, Inc.

S.J. Andriole, (1985b) *Corporate Crisis Management*. Princeton, NJ: Petrocelli Books, Inc.

S.J. Andriole, (1985c) *Decision Aids for Command and Control*. Burke, VA: Armed Forces Communications and Electronics Association/Professional Development Center.

S.J. Andriole, (1983a) *Command and Control (C2) Software Systems*. 3 vols. Washington, DC: George Washington University, School of Engineering and Applied Science.

S.J. Andriole, (1983b) *Interactive Computer-Based Systems Design and Development*. Princeton, NJ: Petrocelli Books, Inc.

D.E. Broadbent, (1971) *Decision and Stress*. London: Academic Press.

E. Charniak and D. McDermott (1985) *An Introduction to Artificial Intelligence*. Reading, MA: Addison-Wesley.

W. Edwards, (1968) "Conservatism in human information processing." in B. Kleinmuntz (ed.), *Formal Representation of Human Judgment* (pp. 17 – 52). New York: Wiley.

W. Edwards, (1954) "The theory of decision making." *Psychological Bulletin*, 51, 380 – 417.

H.J. Einhorn and R.M. Hogarth (1985) "Ambiguity and uncertainty in probabilistic inference." *Psychological Review*, 92, 433 – 460.

H.J. Einhorn and R.M. Hogarth (1981) "Behavioral decision theory: processes of judgment and choice." *Annual Review of Psychology*, 32, 53 – 88.

D. Ellsberg, (1961) "Risk, ambiguity, and the Savage axioms." *Quarterly Journal of Economics*, 75, 643 – 669.

M.W. Eysenck, (1984) *A Handbook of Cognitive Psychology*. Hillsdale, NJ: Lawrence Erlbaum Associates.

H. Gardner, (1985) *The Mind's New Science: A History of the Cognitive Revolution*. New York: Basic Books.

R.E. Geiselman and M.G. Samet (1980) "Summarizing military information: An application of schema theory." *Human Factors*, 22, 693 – 705.

D. Gentner and D.R. Genter (1983) "Flowing Waters or Teeming Crowds: Mental Models of Electricity." In D. Gentner and A.L. Stevens (eds.), *Mental Models* (pp. 99 – 130). Hillsdale, NJ: Lawrence Erlbaum Associates.

S.M. Halpin, (1984) "A Proposal for an Intelligent Interface in Man-Machine Systems." Presented at the IEEE Conference on Decision and Control. Las Vegas, Nevada.

G.W. Hopple, (1986a) "Decision aiding dangers: The law of the hammer, and other maxims." *IEEE Transactions on Systems, Man, and Cybernetics*.

G.W. Hopple, (1986b) "Psychological Issues in the Design and Development of Decision Support Systems." in S.J. Andriole (ed.), *Microcomputer Decision Support Systems: Design, Implementation, and Evaluation* (pp. 311 – 335). Wellesley, MA: QED Information Sciences.

G.W. Hopple, (1985) "Intelligent Support Systems for Command, Control, Communications, and Intelligence (C3I): A Prototype Causal Schema Knowledge-Based System." Presented at the Human Factors in Manned Systems Integration Conference. Kansas City, Missouri, July.

G.W. Hopple and S.M. Halpin, (1985) "Artificial Intelligence for C3I: The Design and Development of a Prototype Causal Schema Knowledge-Based System." In K.N. Karna (ed.), *Expert Systems in Government Symposium* (pp. 160 – 168). Washington, DC: IEEE Computer Society Press.

G.W. Hopple, S.J. Andriole and A. Freedy, (1984) *National Security Crisis Forecasting and Management*. Boulder, CO: Westview.

R. Jervis, (1976) *Perception and Misperception in International Politics*. Princeton, NJ: Princeton University Press.

P.N. Johnson-Laird, (1983) *Mental Models*. Cambridge: Cambridge University Press.

D. Kahneman, P. Slovik, and A. Tversky, (1982) *Judgment under Uncertainty: Heuristics and Biases*. New York: Cambridge University Press.

J. Mandler, (1984) *Stories, Scripts, and Scenes: Aspects of Schema Theory*. Hillsdale, NJ: Lawrence Erlbaum Associates.

T.W. Milburn, (1972) "The Management of Crisis." In C.F. Hermann (ed.), *International Crisis: Insights from Behavioral Research* (pp. 259 – 277). New York: Free Press.

L. Miller, (1978) "Has artificial intelligence contributed to an understanding of the human mind? A critique of the arguments for and against." *Cognitive Science*, 2, 111 – 127.

D.A. Norman, (1983) "Some Observations on Mental Models." In Gentner and Stevens (pp. 7 – 14).

C.R. Peterson and L.R. Beach, (1967) "Man as an intuitive statistician." *Psychological Bulletin*, 68, 29 – 46.

H. Prade, (1985) "A computational approach to approximate and plausible reasoning with applications to expert systems." *IEEE Transactions on Pattern Analysis and Machine Intelligence*, PAMI-7.

A.L. Ralescu and D.A. Ralescu, (1984) "Probability and fuzziness." *Information Sciences*, 34, 85 – 92.

D.E. Rumelhart and D.A. Norman, (1983) "Representation of Knowledge." CHIP Technical Report (no. 116). San Diego, CA: Center for Human Information Processing, University of California. Reprinted in A.M. Aitkenhead and J.M. Slack (eds.), *Issues in Cognitive Modeling*. Hillsdale, NJ: Lawrence Erlbaum Associates, 1985.

R.C. Schank with P.G. Childers, (1984) *The Cognitive Computer: On Language, Learning, and Artificial Intelligence*. Reading, MA: Addison-Wesley.

J.D. Steinbruner, (1974) *The Cybernetic Theory of Decision: New Dimensions of Political Authority*. Princeton, NJ: Princeton University Press.

40

How evaluation guides AI research

Paul R. Cohen
Adele E. Howe

Editors' note *Cohen and Howe look at how evaluation guides research and development. They also develop criteria for assessing progress. The paper appears here because it represents one of the few examples from the AI community of introspection. The paper also prescribes evaluation as a tool for cumulation and assessment. (Reprinted, with permission, from the Winter 1988 issue of* AI magazine. *© 1988, American Association for Artificial Intelligence. All rights reserved.)*

Evaluation should be a mechanism of progress both within and across AI research projects. For the individual, evaluation can tell us how and why out methods and programs work and, so, tell us how our research should proceed. For the community, evaluation expedites the understanding of available methods and, so, their integration into further research. In this article, we present a five-stage model of AI research and describe guidelines for evaluation that are appropriate for each stage. These guidelines, in the form of evaluation criteria and techniques, suggest how to perform evaluation. We conclude with a set of recommendations that suggest how to encourage the evaluation of AI research.

Evaluation means making observations of all aspects of one's research. Often, we think of evaluation only in terms of how well AI systems perform, yet it is vital to all stages of research, from early conceptualization to retrospective analyses of series of programs. Indeed, some of the most informative observations are not performance measures but, rather, describe why we are doing the research, why our tasks are particularly illustrative, why our views and methods are a step forward, how completely they are implemented by our programs, how these programs work, whether their performance is likely to increase or has reached a limit (and why), and what problems we encounter at each stage of our research. To the research community, these observations are more important than performance measures because they tell us how research should proceed.

Thus, ideally, evaluation should be a mechanism of progress both within and across individual AI research projects. Evaluation provides impetus to the research cycle. It opens new avenues of research because experiments often raise new questions as others are answered and because it identifies deficiencies and, thus, problems for further research. Evaluation provides a basis for the accumulation of knowledge. Without evaluation, we cannot replicate results. Evaluation is how you convince the community that your ideas are worthwhile, that they work and how. Because our colleagues rarely have access to run-time data and programs at various development stages, we have an unprecedented responsibility to evaluate and communicate all aspects of our research. Unfortunately, we rarely publish performance evaluations and, still less, evaluations of other research stages.

Evaluation is not standard practice in part because our methodology is vague. Where other sciences have standard experimental methods and analytic techniques, we have faith—often groundless and misleading—that building programs is somehow informative. Where other sciences expect specific aspects of research to be presented (for example, hypotheses, related research, experimental methods, and analyses and results), empirical AI has no comparable standards. Now, we do not advocate blindly adopting the empirical methods of, say, the behavioral sciences; in fact, we argue elsewhere that they are inappropriate to AI (Cohen and Howe 1988). However, we are saying that progress in AI would be amplified by a methodology which emphasizes evaluation for the overarching reason that we can do our own research better if we know, in detail, the state of our colleagues' research.

Where will this methodology—and, specifically, the evaluation criteria, experiment designs, and analytic tools—come from? The challenge is that we must develop it ourselves. Explorations along these lines have been reported in specific areas, for example, machine learning (Langley 1987), distributed systems (Decker 1988), and expert systems (Geissman and Schultz 1988; Gaschnig et al. 1983; Rothenberg et al. 1987). Discussions of a broader scope focus on the role of experiments in AI (Buchanan 1987; Newell and Simon 1976). Although these papers address different facets of evaluation, a common theme is that we must develop our own evaluation methods appropriate to AI practice. If we try to retrofit the methods of other fields, they will probably become impediments. Thus, in this article, we are motivated not by envy of "scientific method," but by the sense that we are wasting opportunities to understand, by empirical and analytic studies, the intelligent artifacts we build at great expense.

This article adopts a simple multistage model of AI research and describes the kinds of evaluation that are appropriate at each stage. (Bruce Buchanan [1987] offers a similar model.) Evaluative questions for each stage are listed in FIGS. 40-1 through 40-5 and discussed in the text. We ask these questions whenever we hear about new research—questions we want researchers to answer when they publish their work. We also describe in schematic form some common kinds of experiments with AI systems. Where possible, we offer illustrations from the AI literature. A companion paper goes one step further and presents three detailed case studies (Cohen and Howe 1988).

The tangible contribution of the article is the organization of these evaluative questions and experiment schemas into five categories that correspond with stages of research. More important, by far, is the possibility that the article will promote discussion and the development of evaluation techniques and, more broadly, AI methodology. We recognize the impediments to methodological discussions. Some might regard methodology as dangerously prescriptive, while others regard it as irrelevant: A reviewer said we are wasting our time because AI methodology is just fine. A friend dismissed this presentation as a metapaper, and not worth the time it would detract from substantive research. However, evaluation was a central issue at the recent meeting of the Program Committee of the American Association for Artificial Intelligence—not a general, perennial complaint such as bad writing but a vital, current problem in need of creative solutions. How does one evaluate AI research? This article doesn't answer the question fully; it is intended to give us a place to begin.

Evaluating each stage of research

We view empirical AI in terms of a five-stage cycle: In the first stage, a topic is refined to a task and a view of how to accomplish the task; in the second, the view is refined to a specific method; in the third, a program is developed to implement the method; in the fourth, experiments are designed to test the program; in the fifth, the experiments are run. Finally, the cycle begins again, informed by the experiments' results.

You might object that this approach isn't how AI research works. First, this superficial description seems severely top down. However, we show how evaluations can produce unexpected conclusions and, thus, iterations at each stage of the cycle. Second, the model seems idealized because it suggests that AI researchers always design, run, and analyze experiments, and we don't. However, although it is idealized, it isn't unattainable and, in fact, won't require many modifications to standard AI practice. Third, this model is probably more appropriate to individual research projects than to huge, collaborative efforts such as the Pilot's Associate or the Autonomous Land Vehicle. These projects require different models and different evaluation criteria; however, we believe the five-stage model characterizes much AI research.

Stage 1: Refine the topic to a task

Empirical AI begins when researchers find particular topics fascinating. The first stage of the research cycle involves simultaneously refining the research topic to a task and identifying a view. A task is something we want a computer to do, and a view is a predesign, a rough idea about how to do it. This stage takes a lot of effort; researchers don't simply say, "Ok, we are fascinated by discovery, so let's try mathematical discovery as a task and heuristic search as a view" (Lenat 1976). The process is iterative because if the task and view don't fare well by the evaluation questions in FIG. 40-1, you have to modify and reevaluate them.

The questions in FIG. 40-1 address two basic evaluation concerns: Can you justify the research task to yourself and the community, and is your view of how to solve the task viable? (In the questions, we sometimes refer to the problem, by which we mean the task and the view combined.) Question 1 asks us to justify the task: Why is it interesting? If it has been studied before, and you are advocating a novel view (a reformulation), why do you expect this new perspective to be an improvement? Question 2 asks whether one's view of the task will work. Perhaps the task itself is intractable or is impossible given the resources, or requires expertise or hardware that isn't available. The question is especially important if one's research method is to "build it and see what happens." The problem with this approach is not that it is relatively undirected;

1. Is the task significant? Why?
   (a) If the problem has been previously defined, how is your reformulation an improvement?

2. Is your research likely to meaningfully contribute to the problem? Is the task tractable?

3. As the task becomes specifically defined for your research, is it still representa tive of a class of tasks?

4. Have any interesting aspects been abstracted away or simplified?
   (a) If the problem has been previously defined, have any aspects extant in the earlier definition been abstracted out or simplified?

5. What are the subgoals of the research? What key research tasks will be or have been addressed and solved as part of the project?

6. How do you know when you have successfully demonstrated a solution to the task? Is the task one in which a solution can be demonstrated?

Fig. 40-1. Criteria for evaluating research problems.

all sciences have exploratory aspects. The problem is that AI is expensive. We generally cannot afford to spend months or years implementing a system unless we're pretty sure something interesting will happen. (A related question, whether the interesting stuff is obscured or observable, is discussed in the subsection on stage 4.)

Question 3 suggests reevaluating whether after narrowing the scope of a task, it still exemplifies a research topic. Most AI tasks, although specific, are designed to exemplify general tasks. For example, we built a system to design pulley systems and heat sinks, confident that they exemplified the class of mechanical design problems which can be solved without decomposition into smaller subproblems (Howe et al. 1986; Howe 1986). Question 4 asks what has been left out of research tasks. In the case of our work on mechanical design, we intentionally dropped the tasks of decomposing and reintegrating design subproblems; so, we knew in advance that we would produce a model of designing objects which required no decomposition, not a general model of mechanical design.

Questions 5 and 6 address whether we have a productive research plan. Most large projects require solutions to multiple problems, such as designing representations and control strategies and building knowledge bases. Question 5 concerns which of these solutions will be research contributions of the project. Question 6 asks whether you understand the problem well enough to recognize a solution.

Evaluations during this stage direct one's own research and also provide the AI community with carefully justified tasks, views, and reformulations. It is sometimes worth publishing work at this stage, long before anything has been implemented and demonstrated. Good contemporary examples are some early papers on reactive planning (Agre 1985; Chapman and Agre 1987) and papers related to the CYC project

(Lenat, Prakash, and Shepherd 1986; Lenat and Feigenbaum 1987). Many of the questions in FIG. 40-1 are asked and answered in these papers. Although preliminary, these evaluations can be informative, and it would be foolish to reject these papers because they don't answer the questions in FIGS. 40-2 through 40-5.

Stage 2: Design the method

At this stage, one's view is refined to a method for solving the task. The word method implies a single algorithm, such as A*, candidate elimination, or Waltz filtering. Frequently, however, the method for a task combines several algorithms and assorted knowledge structures. For example, the method in Hearsay-II involved many knowledge sources, data-driven and opportunistic control, and a novel communication structure (Erman et al. 1980). Although this complexity strains the word method, we maintain it to remind us that we don't jump immediately into building programs but first decide how we want to solve tasks.

Criteria for evaluating methods are presented in FIG. 40-2. The first two questions suggest general criteria for comparing the method with previous work. These questions are prospective because we might not be able to answer them without implementing the method. However, before we build anything, it's worth asking whether we expect our approach to be better, in some sense, than those which are already available. Question 1 documents some common interpretations of "better." Note that in the early going, a method need not necessarily be better, just different if the difference holds promise (question 1d). Question 2 asks what aspects of the method's performance will be evaluated. If the answer to question 1 is, "My method is better because it is more general," then question 2 asks, "How will this difference be demonstrated?"

Question 3 asks whether and to what extent these evaluations are qualified by the method's reliance on other factors. Sometimes, the answer is obvious; for example, one might have a method for discovering physical laws, but one's evaluations of the method should note whether it plans its own experiments or, instead, relies on a person or another method to present data in an order that facilitates discovery. However, question 3 can also be difficult to answer prospectively because the word rely is vague. Interacting components of a method rely on each other in the trivial sense that without them all, the method wouldn't work; however, other kinds of reliance are more difficult to see prospectively. Indeed, it took several years for Lenat and Brown (1983) to recognize and document the reliance of AM on its representation language.

Question 4 asks about one's assumptions. In our work on mechanical design, we initially assumed that all design variables (for example, diameter of a pulley) were continuous. Some planning algorithms assume that the state of the world is known and that the effects of all actions are predictable. Some vision algorithms assume noise is distributed uniformly. It is important to state our assumptions if only to prevent others from misstating them! For example, the uncertainty literature has suffered a decade-long debate about what the conditional independence assumption really means.

It might be difficult to answer the remaining four questions prospectively. Sometimes, one knows the scope of a method before implementing it, sometimes not (question 5). One might anticipate that a method will easily scale up, especially if it has been designed to replace one which will not, but one typically cannot prove it. Question 6 is

1. How is the method an improvement over existing technologies?

   (a) Does it account for more situations (input)?
   (b) Does it produce a wider variety of desired behaviors (output)?
   (c) Is the method expected to be more efficient (space, solution time, development time, and so on)?
   (d) Does it hold more promise for further development (for example, because of the introduction of a new paradigm)?

2. Does a recognized metric exist for evaluating the performance of your method (for example, is it normative, cognitively valid)?

3. Does it rely on other methods? (Does it require input in a particular form or preprocessed input? Does it require access to a certain type of knowledge base or routines?)

4. What are the underlying assumptions?

5. What is the scope of the method?

   (a) How extendible is it? Will it easily scale up to a larger knowledge base?
   (b) Does it exactly address the task? Portions of the task? A class of tasks?
   (c) Could it or parts of it be applied to other problems?
   (d) Does it transfer to complicated problems (perhaps knowledge intensive or more or less constrained or with complex interactions)?

6. When it cannot provide a good solution, does it do nothing or does it provide bad solutions or does it provide the best solution given the available resources?

7. How well is the method understood?

   (a) Why does it work?
   (b) Under what circumstances, won't it work?
   (c) Are the limitations of the method inherent or simply not yet addressed?
   (d) Have the design decisions been justified?

8. What is the relationship between the problem and the method? Why does it work for this task?

Fig. 40-2. Criteria for evaluating methods.

1. How demonstrative is the program?
   (a) Can we evaluate its external behavior?
   (b) How transparent is it? Can we evaluate its internal behavior?
   (c) Can the class of capabilities necessary for the task be demonstrated by a well-defined set of test cases?
   (d) How many test cases does it demonstrate?
2. Is it specially tuned for a particular example?
3. How well does the program implement the method?
   (a) Can you determine the program's limitations?
   (b) Have parts been left out or kludged? Why and to what effect?
   (c) Has implementation forced a detailed definition or even reevaluation of the method? How was this reevaluation accomplished?
4. Is the program's performance predictable?

Fig. 40-3. Criteria for evaluating method implementation.

perhaps easier to answer prospectively because it reflects an important design criterion for methods. Some methods are designed to optimize, some to satisfy, and some to simply quit when resources run out. For example, Victor Lesser and his colleagues recently described a set of approximate processing methods for real-time problem solving (Lessser, Durfee, and Pavlin 1987). By design, these methods are intended to give the best possible performance in the time available. However, lacking analytic tools, the actual performance of these methods might be impossible to predict. Then, question 6 cannot be answered prospectively. Similarly, questions 7 and 8 can rarely be answered except by empirical work. Indeed, our inability to answer these questions analytically is often the impetus for building programs.

The purpose of the questions in FIG. 40-2 is to convince oneself and the community of the utility, scope, assumptions, performance, and limitations of a method. Often, these evaluations are sufficient, and papers can be published without further evaluation. An example is DeKleer's first paper on the assumption-based truth maintenance system (ATMS), which answers many of the questions in FIG. 40-2 analytically: "[It] is possible to work effectively and efficiently with inconsistent information, context switching is free, and most backtracking (and all retraction) is avoided. These capabilities motivate a different kind of problem-solving architecture in which multiple potential solutions are explored simultaneously. This architecture is particularly well-suited for tasks where a reasonable fraction of the potential solutions must be explored" (DeKleer 1986, abstract).

Analyses of methods are rarely so thorough in AI, but even when they are, one can elect to continue to subsequent stages in the research cycle. This continuation usually involves building a program. We discern three good reasons to build programs. First, it is often worthwhile to implement the method to experiment with problematic aspects

1. How many examples can be demonstrated?
   (a) Are they qualitatively different?
   (b) Do these examples illustrate all the capabilities that are claimed? Do they illustrate limitations?
   (c) Is the number of examples sufficient to justify the inductive generalizations?
2. Should the program's performance be compared to a standard such as another program, or experts and novices, or its own tuned performance? Should the standard be normative, or cognitive validity, or outcomes either from the real world or from simulations?
3. What are the criteria for good performance? Who defines the criteria?
4. Does the program purport to be general (domain-independent)?
   (a) Can it be tested on several domains?
   (b) Are the domains qualitatively different?
   (c) Do they represent a class of domains?
   (d) Should performance in the initial domain be compared to performance in other domains? (Do you expect that the program is tuned to perform best in domain(s) used for debugging?)
   (e) Is the set of domains sufficient to justify inductive generalization?
5. Is a series of related programs being evaluated?
   (a) Can you determine how differences in the programs are manifested as differences in behavior?
   (b) If the method was implemented differently in each program in the series, how do these differences affect the generalizations?
   (c) Were difficulties encountered in implementing the method in other programs?

Fig. 40-4. Criteria for evaluating the experiment's design.

of its behavior (for example, Forbus and DeKleer [1988] recently built a couple of simple programs to explore focusing in the ATMS). Second (and more frequent), no other way exists to answer some of the questions in FIG. 40-2: Why does the method work for this particular task? Do tasks exist for which it won't work? Are the limitations of the method inherent? and so on. We eventually implemented our mechanical design method in a program and ran 125 experiments on different configurations of the program, selectively ablating components of the method because we had no other way to probe how interactions between these components affected design performance (Howe 1986).

The third role of programming is exploratory. We might try out some ideas to help us refine our method. We think it is important to distinguish this role of programming—refining a method—from programming for the purpose of experimenting with and evaluating a method. Unfortunately, exploratory programming drifts easily into building

1. How did program performance compare to its selected standard (for example, other programs, people, normative behavior)?
2. Is the program's performance different from predictions of how the method should perform?
3. How efficient is the program in terms of space and knowledge requirements?
4. Did the program demonstrate good performance?
5. Did you learn what you wanted from the program and experiments?
6. Is it easy for the intended users to understand?
7. Can you define the program's performance limitations?
8. Do you understand why the program works or doesn't work?
   - (a) What is the impact of changing the program even slightly?
   - (b) Does it perform as expected on examples not used for debugging?
   - (c) Can the effect of different control strategies be determined?
   - (d) How does the program respond if input is rearranged, noisy, or missing?
   - (e) What is the relationship between characteristics of the test problems and performance (either external, or internal if program traces are available?)
   - (f) Can the understanding of the program be generalized to the method? To characteristics of the method? To a larger task?

Fig. 40-5. Criteria for evaluating what the experiments told us.

systems, and we begin to focus on solving the task and forget that from the standpoint of empirical AI research, the purpose of building systems is to tell us something about our methods which we don't already know and can't learn by analysis. We build too many systems and evaluate too few.

Stage 3: Build a program

If our method requires programming not merely to implement it but to understand whether and why it works, then we must build a program that supports experiments. Although in practice this stage might be indistinguishable from exploratory programming in the previous stage, its purpose is different and so are the evaluations we do at this stage.

The criteria in FIG. 40-3 concern whether the program is informative. Question 1 asks whether its internal and external behavior clearly demonstrates the method. Question 2 implies that programs are rarely informative if they are designed to run on only a single example. Question 3 suggests specific ways to assess how well the program implements the method. Finally, because the purpose of building a program is to tell us something we didn't already know, question 4 asks whether we can predict performance in advance.

The questions in FIG. 40-3 (especially question 4) illustrate the iterative nature of evaluation at each stage: We don't build a program first and then throw it away if it is uninformative or utterly predictable; we develop informative, interesting programs by continuing evaluation—just as we iteratively evaluate and develop tasks, views, methods, and experiments. However, unlike the earlier evaluations of tasks, views, and methods, evaluation at this stage is primarily for the individual researcher, not for the community at large.

Stage 4: Design experiments

The fourth stage of the research cycle is to design experiments with the newly implemented system. Just as we evaluate the design and construction of systems from the standpoint of whether they are informative, so we should evaluate whether experiments with these systems will be informative. Criteria for evaluating experiments (as opposed to their outcomes) are presented in FIG. 40-4. The purpose of question 1 is to encourage us to test our programs with many, qualitatively different examples that illustrate the abilities and limitations of our programs. Questions 2 and 3 ask whether our programs should be compared with a standard (for example, an expert) and what specific comparisons will be made. Question 4 asks whether our experiments provide enough evidence to claim that a program is general, and question 5 suggests criteria for comparing programs. Both questions acknowledge that programs (and their underlying methods) are evaluated in the context of other research projects and, so, raise the methodological issues of how results accumulate and generalize over projects (see also Conclusion and Cohen and Howe [1988]).

These questions address what can be evaluated in experiments but don't say how the experiments should be conducted. AI has been evolving rudimentary, informal experiment schemas that address some of the questions in FIG. 40-4. Here, we describe six experiment schemas:

Comparison studies In the basic form of a comparison study, we select one or more measures of a program's performance; then, both the program and a standard solve a set of problems; and, finally, the solutions are compared on the measures. For example, we can compare the average number of subgoal violations generated by one planning program on a set of problems (the measure) with the same measure on another extant program (the standard). Typically, the programs implement different methods, or they can be different configurations of a single program.

Variations on the basic form depend on what you want to demonstrate. For example, if you want to measure whether the program's performance is consensual, you can compare the program to a panel of human experts. You can also include novices—an interesting control condition to ensure that successful performance requires expertise (for example, Shortliffe 1976 ran a panel of experts and novices in his studies of MYCIN). Sometimes, the performance of a program can be compared with objective, recognized standards. Normative theories, such as probability theory, provide one kind of standard; for example, some researchers argue that because human experts are incapable of integrating probabilistic information consistently, their performance should not set standards. Another kind of standard is provided by real or simulated worlds; we might evaluate a complex planner by seeing whether it generates plans that succeed in the world. All these examples suggest that our measures and standards depend heavily on what we want to demonstrate and, ultimately, on our research goals.

Direct assessment A related scheme, though not strictly a comparison study, has humans judging or scoring the program's performance. Direct assessment happens when test problems have so many acceptable solutions that a program and a standard cannot be expected to generate the same ones. For example, we built a system some years ago that generated portfolios for investors (Cohen and Lieberman 1983), none of which were identical with portfolios generated by an expert for the same problems. Our program's portfolios were not bad but, rather, there are many good ways to generate portfolios, and portfolios rarely coincide by chance. In these cases, one cannot compare the program's performance with the expert's but must instead rely on the expert's direct assessment of the program. Unfortunately, this test is weaker than a comparison because experts can be overly generous to the program. Moreover, direct assessment does not tell us whether the program is performing better than the expert.

Ablation and substitution studies We can evaluate the contribution of individual components to the performance of complex systems by removing or replacing these components. Removing components (ablation [Newell 1975]) is informative in systems that can solve problems without these components; for example, we might assess the contribution of caching by running a system without caching. It takes little insight to predict some effect; the goal is to find out whether performance on all types of problems is equally affected by the presence of a cache and, if not, what interactions between the cache and the problem type explain the variance.

Many AI systems are so brittle that they collapse when components are removed. In these cases, we might substitute dumb components for those we hope to show are smart; for example, we might substitute an exhaustive control strategy for a sophisticated, opportunistic one.

Tuning studies By tuning a system to perform as well as possible on a set of test data, we can learn how much performance can be improved, how difficult it is to achieve, and whether the resulting system can still solve other test cases. From a research perspective, it seems wasteful and potentially misleading to tune systems just to increase their performance without addressing these questions.

Limitation studies By testing a program at its known limits, we can better understand its behavior in adverse conditions—we can learn whether it is robust. We can push a program to its limits by providing imperfect data (rearranged, noisy, incomplete, or incorrect), restricted resources (computation time or available knowledge), and perverse test cases.

Inductive studies One way to support claims of generality is to solve new and different problems. If we claim that, say, a mechanical design system is general, then we might want to run problems in many areas of mechanical design—pulley systems, I beams, extrusions, and so on (Howe et al. 1986; Orelup 1987). Even if we don't claim a program is general (and we question whether inductive studies, in fact, demonstrate generality in the conclusion), we must, at least, test it on problems other than those we used to develop it.

The purpose of evaluation at this stage is to convince the researcher and the community that studies of a program (or programs) independent of their results—are well designed and complete. Experiment schemas, if we could specify them in adequate detail, would offer researchers a shorthand to describe their studies (for example, "We ran a comparison study between versions 1, 2, and 3 of the program, measuring hit rate on three data sets that were characterized by their average signal-to-noise ratio").

Stage 5: Analyze the experiments' results

Now that our method has been implemented in a fully instrumented program, and our experiments are well designed, we can ask whether the system works and why it works. The purpose of evaluation at this stage is to convince the research community that your methods are viable, and their limitations in both performance and scope, and suggest further research. The first three questions in FIG. 40-5 evaluate the program by its performance on the task. Questions 4, 5 and 6 assess the utility of the program. Questions 7 and 8 identify the program's frailties and strengths: When does it break, and what components contribute to its successful operation? Question 8e is most salient to the generalization of results because it justifies good performance for the program in terms of the task, a relationship that might be exploited in the design of other methods.

The questions in FIG. 40-5 are what most people regard as evaluation. Consequently, they neglect the earlier questions and end up with unclear or unconvincing answers at this stage. If a program hasn't been constructed in such a way that its performance is observable (FIG. 40-3), and the experiment hasn't been designed with clear or convincing criteria and control conditions (FIG. 40-4), then this stage of evaluation is not likely to be informative. Evaluation begins early in the research cycle. It can't be tacked to the end. We can't ask how a program compares with its standard (question 1) unless we have a standard, and it isn't convincing to dream one up after we have built the program! Even if you have a standard in mind, you should assure yourself that it makes sense: As noted earlier, we had a vague idea that we would compare the performance of our portfolio management program with the performance of a portfolio manager, but it turned out (too late) there was no way to make this comparison. Similarly, question 2 builds on earlier stages of evaluation: To compare a program's performance to predictions about performance, one needs predictions! One cannot simply dream up a few strawman predictions to give the impression of empiricism. Yet, we see few reports that include predictions and fewer still in which the program performs other than as predicted. The same point can be made about several other questions in FIG. 40-5: It will be difficult to determine performance limitations or why a program works or doesn't work in a post hoc manner.

Conclusion

Each stage in our simple model of research affords opportunities for evaluation; indeed, iterations at each stage and cycles throughout the model are driven by evaluation. This is the first step in what should become an ongoing discussion of AI methodology. We need to develop the model further—or alternative models as necessary—so we have a common language for discussing the stages of our research and the kinds of evaluation appropriate to each. The research cycle and the questions and experiments outlined here form only a skeleton of a methodology. One way to slowly fill out this skeleton is to carefully describe our experiments and results. Another is to publish methodological papers. For example, we want to see extensive discussions along the following lines.

First, we encourage discussions of experiment schemas, with appropriate control conditions, measures, standards, and analyses of results. We hope to see schemas that are more detailed and task specific than the few we discussed in the stage 4 subsection. We also hope to see discussions of specific evaluation criteria in the context of experiment schemas. We know that the criteria we presented in FIGS. 40-1 through 40-5 are, in some respects, a bad compromise: too general to be informative and not general enough to encompass all research in empirical AI (for example, they don't tell us how to evaluate methodological papers such as this one).

A second topic for discussion is the methodological role of programs. Why should we build programs? This topic is an important part of a broader debate on the empirical AI research cycle, which requires considerable elaboration beyond the sketch given earlier.

Third, and most important: What does it mean to replicate and generalize results? When can we claim that a particular method is general—when it has been implemented in one program and run on many test cases, or when it has been implemented in many programs in different task domains? Perhaps we should be asking, instead, how we can bound the applicability of methods. Are we obliged to claim generality on inductive grounds (for example, the program ran in several domains)? We don't say, "The run will rise because it always has." Rather, "Here's why the sun will rise." Is there a similar deductive notion of generality in AI? This methodological problem is perhaps our most difficult: How do we know that a result is general, that we don't have to build any more systems to illustrate it? How do we know, conversely, that two apparently different results are, in fact, demonstrations of the same thing? Given that AI programs are different (they have different code, algorithms, machines, domains, performance characteristics, assumptions, and underlying purposes), can we abstract any results from them that we can agree are common? (See Cohen and Howe [1988] for further discussion.)

One concrete recommendation is that editors, program committees, and reviewers should begin to insist on evaluation. Editorial policies rarely preclude evaluation—we all think it's a good idea—but neither do they require them. This is one reason that papers almost never describe an entire research cycle—a problem, a task, a view, methods, programs, experiments, and results. Editorial policy is perhaps the most effective way to guide empirical AI practice toward complete evaluation. (Lately, the machine learning community has explicitly mentioned evaluation criteria in calls for papers, and Langley (1987) has advocated evaluation in his editorials.) It can also encourage the following uncommon kinds of papers.

Short studies with extant systems Many of the experiments discussed in the subsection on stage 4, which address how and why systems work, are extensive, self-contained, publishable studies. Even after a system has been thoroughly explored, it can still serve as a test bed for studies with other methods, knowledge representations, control structures, and so on. AI systems take so long to build that we really cannot afford to drop them until we have learned all we can from them. A good model of this kind of work is a book on extensive experiments with MYCIN edited by Buchanan and Shortliffe (1984).

Negative results For example, we need to know when methods don't work as expected, when systems perform less well as they become more knowledgeable, when scaling up causes problems. When did you last read an AI paper that said something didn't work?

Progress reports We should publish progress reports throughout the development of large AI projects, not wait until they are finished. Lenat's CYC project (Lenat, Prakash, and Shepherd 1986), for example, is slated to continue throughout the 1990s. We cannot afford to wait until then to see how CYC is progressing—especially because it involves pioneering techniques and ideas that we need much sooner.

When we began writing this article, we took the view that science is not legislated, controlled, or forced upon its practitioners but is a voluntary business in which loose organizations of individuals somehow produce coherent, cumulative progress. We obviously believe evaluation and methodology will help this process; it isn't hard to do, and it suggests new research, generalizations, and hypotheses that one wouldn't discover otherwise.

Acknowledgments

This research was funded by the Office of Naval Research (ONR) under a University Research Initiative grant, contract #N00014-86-K-0764, and ONR contract AFOSR 4331690-01. We are indebted to Scott Anderson, Carole Beal, Carol Broverman, David Day, Mike Greenberg, Tom Gruber, Janet Kolodner, Pat Langley, Cynthia Loiselle, and Paul Utgoff for their comments on drafts of this paper and to Peter Patel-Schneider for sending us guidelines for reviewers.

References

P.E. Agre, 1985. *The Structures of Everyday Life, Technical Report,* Working Paper 297, Massachusetts Institute of Technology.

B.G. Buchanan, 1987. *Artificial Intelligence as an Experimental Science,* Technical Report, KSL 87-03, Knowledge Systems Lab., Dept. of Computer Science, Stanford Univ.

B.G. Buchanan and E.H. Shortliffe, 1984. *Rule-Based Expert Systems: The MYCIN Experiments of the Stanford Heuristic Programming Project.* Reading, Mass.: Addison-Wesley.

D. Chapman and P.E. Agre, 1987. *Abstract Reasoning as Emergent from Concrete Activity.* In Reasoning About Actions and Plans, Proceedings of the 1986 Workshop, eds. M.P. Georgeff and A.L. Lansky, 411 – 424. Los Altos, Calif.: Morgan Kaufmann.

P.R. Cohen and A.E. Howe, 1988. *Toward AI Research Methodology: Case Studies in Evaluation*. IEEE Transactions on Systems, Man, and Cybernetics. In press.

P.R. Cohen and M.D. Lieberman, 1983. *Folio: An Expert Assistant for Portfolio Managers*. In Proceedings of the Eighth International Joint Conference on Artificial Intelligence, 212215. Menlo Park, Calif.: International Joint Conferences on Artificial Intelligence.

K.S. Decker, E.H. Durfee, and V.R. Lesser. *Evaluating Research in Cooperative Distributed Problem Solving*. Dept. of Computer and Information Science. TR 8889, 1988. Univ. of Massachusetts.

J. DeKleer, 1986. *An Assumption-Based TMS*. Artificial Intelligence 28:127162.

L.D. Erman, F. Hayes-Roth, V.R. Lesser, and D.R. Reddy, 1980. *The HEARSAY-II Speech Understanding System: Integrating Knowledge to Resolve Uncertainty*. Computing Surveys 12:213253.

K. Forbus and J. DeKleer, 1988. *Focusing the ATMS*. In Proceedings of the Seventh National Conference on Artificial Intelligence, 193198. Menlo Park, Calif.: American Association for Artificial Intelligence.

J. Gaschnig, P. Klahr, H. Pople, E.H. Shortliffe, and A. Terry, 1983. *Evaluation of Expert Systems: Issues and Case Studies*. In Building Expert Systems, eds. F. Hayes-Roth, D.A. Waterman, and D.B. Lenat, 241280. Reading, Mass.: Addison-Wesley.

J.R. Geissman and R.D. Schultz, 1988. *Verification and Validation*. AI Expert 3(2):2633.

A. Howe, 1986. *Learning to Design Mechanical Engineering Problems*, Technical Report, EKSL Working Paper 86-01, Univ. of Massachusetts.

A. Howe, J.R. Dixon, P.R. Cohen, and M.K. Simmons, 1986. *Dominic: A Domain-Independent Program for Mechanical Engineering Design*. International Journal for Artificial Intelligence in Engineering 1(1):2329.

P. Langley, 1987. *Research Papers in Machine Learning*. Machine Learning 2(3):195198.

D.B. Lenat, 1976. *AM: An Artificial Intelligence Approach to Discovery in Mathematics as Heuristic Search*. Ph.D. diss., Dept. of Computer Science, Stanford Univ. Also, Technical Report, STAN-CS-76-570, Dept. of Computer Science, Stanford Univ.

D.B. Lenat and E.A. Feigenbaum, 1987. *On the Thresholds of Knowledge*. In Proceedings of the Tenth International Joint Conference on Artificial Intelligence, 11731182. Menlo Park, Calif.: International Joint Conferences on Artificial Intelligence.

D.B. Lenat, M. Prakash, and M. Shepherd, 1986. *CYC: Using Common Sense Knowledge to Overcome Brittleness and Knowledge Acquisition Bottlenecks*. AI Magazine 6(4):6585.

D.B. Lenat and J.S. Brown, 1983. *Why AM and Eurisko Appear to Work*. In Proceedings of the Third National Conference on Artificial Intelligence, 236240. Menlo Park, Calif.: American Association for Artificial Intelligence.

V.R. Lesser, E.H. Durfee, and J. Pavlin, 1988. *Approximate Processing in Real-Time Problem Solving*. AI Magazine 9(1):49-61.

T.M. Mitchell, *"Version Spaces: A Candidate Elimination Approach to Rule Learning."* In Proceedings of the Fifth International Joint Conference on Artificial Intelligence, 305310.

A. Newell, 1975. *A Tutorial on Speech Understanding Systems*. In Speech Recognition: Invited Papers Presented at the 1974 IEEE Symposium, ed. D.R. Reddy, 354. New York: Academic.

A. Newell and H.A. Simon, 1976. *Computer Science as Empirical Inquiry: Symbols and Search*. Communications of the ACM 19(3):113126.

M.F. Orelup, 1987. *Meta-Control in Domain-Independent Design by Iterative Redesign*. M.S. thesis, Mechanical Engineering Dept., Univ. of Massachusetts.

J. Rothenberg, J. Paul, I. Kameny, J.R. Kipps, and M. Swenson, 1987. *Evaluating Expert System Tools: A Framework and Methodology*, Technical Report, R-3542-DARPA, Rand Corporation.

E.H. Shortliffe, 1976. *Computer-Based Medical Consultations: MYCIN*. New York: American Elsevier.

41

Neurocomputing
Picking the human brain

Robert Hecht-Nielsen

Editors' note *Many believe that neural network technology represents the next phase of AI research and development. In fact, expert systems and neural networks have only a few things in common. In any case, Hecht-Nielsen explores neurocomputing and identifies some of the applications domains likely to be the most amenable to the technology. (Reprinted, with permission, from the March 1988 issue of* IEEE Spectrum.

Borrowing from biology, researchers are exploring neural networks—a new, nonalgorithmic approach to information processing

Imagine a computer that learns. Information is fed into it, along with examples of the conclusions it should be reaching or feedback on how it is doing—or the machine may even be left to its own devices. The computer simply runs through the material again and again, making myriads of mistakes but learning from them, until finally it gets itself into proper shape to carry out the task successfully. Such behavior is quite human, and naturally so; for the design of the machine's information-processing system, a neural network, was inspired by the structure of the human brain—its nerve cells, their interconnections, and their interactions—and by envy of what the brain can do.

As an alternative form of information processing, neurocomputing is fast becoming an established discipline, and some neural networks are already on the market. Neural networks are good at some things that conventional computers are bad at. They do well, for instance, at solving complex pattern-recognition problems implicit in understanding continuous speech, identifying handwritten characters, and determining that a target seen from different angles is in fact one and the same object.

Neural networks parallel-process immense quantities of information. Yet for a long time the only way to implement them was by simulating them laboriously, inefficiently, and at great expense on standard, serial computers. That situation is changing. Neurocomputers—hardware on which neural networks can be implemented efficiently—have reached the prototype stage at several companies, and some are already commercially available. All are coprocessor boards that plug into conventional machines. Developers include Hecht-Nielsen Neurocomputer Corp. (NHC), IBM Corp., Science Applications International Corp. (SAIC), Texas Instruments Corp., and TRW Inc.

Meanwhile, researchers at Boston University, the California Institute of Technology, the Helsinki University of Technology, Johns Hopkins University, the University of California at San Diego, and other universities have been investigating the theory behind neural networks and exploring their potential to solve problems that have stumped algorithmic computing for decades.

What is neurocomputing?

Nearly all automated information processing is at present based upon John von Neumann's "glorified adding machine" concept. But before such a computer can be programmed to carry out an information-processing function, some person has both to understand that function and to devise an algorithm for implementing it. For complex functions, such as computed axial tomography, development waits on the birth of geniuses capable of propounding the needed algorithm—in this case, Johan Radon and Alan Cormack.

Even worse, there may be tasks for which algorithms do not yet exist, or for which it is virtually impossible to write down a series of logical or arithmetic steps that will arrive at the answer. Yet in some of these cases it is possible to specify the tasks exactly and even develop an endless set of examples of the function being carried out. Many such tasks exist. There is no algorithmic software as yet for an automobile autopilot, a handwritten-character reader, a spoken-language translator, a system that can identify enemy airplanes or ships, or a system capable of recognizing continuous speech, regardless of who is speaking.

These tasks do have three important characteristics in common, however: humans know how to do them; large sets of examples of the tasks being carried out can be generated; and each task involves associating objects in one set with objects in another set. Such associations are known as mappings or transformations. For example, a computer than can read aloud must somehow associate groups of written letters, spaces, and punctuation with specific sounds, pauses, and intonations.

In formal terminology, neurocomputing is the engineering discipline concerned with nonprogrammed adaptive information-processing systems—neural networks—that develop associations (transformations or mappings) between objects in response to their environment. Instead of being given a step-by-step procedure for carrying out the desired transformation, the neural network itself generates its own internal rules governing the association, and refines those rules by comparing its results to the examples. Through trial and error, the network literally teaches itself how to do the task.

Neurocomputing is a fundamentally new and different information-processing paradigm—the first alternative to algorithmic programming. Wherever it is applicable, totally new information-processing capabilities can be developed, and development costs and time often shrink by an order of magnitude.

Neurocomputing does not, however, replace algorithmic programming. For one thing, neurocomputing is still in its infancy and is currently applicable to only certain classes of problems. More important, on a philosophical level, it is now suspected that neurocomputing and algorithmic programming may be conceptually incompatible. Transformations often prove impossible to describe satisfactorily in terms of an algorithm, and vice versa. This fact often unsettles people who think solely in procedural terms, since it means that neurocomputing may solve important information-processing problems without disclosing the rules used in the solution (at least in terms of present-day information-processing concepts). Neuroscience itself may run into this same problem in the future: an accurate understanding of how individual nerve cells interact in the brain may reveal virtually nothing about how brains process information.

How a neural network works

A neural network is modeled on the gross structure of the brain: a collection of nerve cells, or neurons, each of which is connected to as many as 10,000 others, from which it receives stimuli—inputs and feedback—and to which it sends stimuli. Some of those connections are strong; others are weak. The brain accepts inputs and generates responses to them, partly in accordance with its genetically programmed structure, but mainly through learning, organizing itself in reaction to input rather than by doing only by rote what it is told.

The neural networks used by engineers are only loosely based upon biology. At best, the only fair comparison is that they behave in a vaguely similar way. Since we have almost no idea how brains work, it will be a long time before we can re-create in a machine all the capabilities of the brain. Even so, neurocomputing is already offering some valuable, specialized, brain-like capabilities that in all likelihood lie beyond the reach of algorithmic programming.

A neural network consists of a collection of processing elements. Each processing element has many input signals, but only a single output signal. The output signal fans out along many pathways to provide input signals to other processing elements. These pathways connect the processing elements into a network (see FIG. 41-1).

Each processing element typically has its own small local memory, which stores the values of some previous computations along with the adaptive coefficients basic to neural-network learning. The processing that each element does is determined by a transfer function—a mathematical formula that defines the element's output signal as a function of whatever input signals have just arrived and the adaptive coefficients present in the local memory. Often a neural network is divided into layers—groups of processing elements all having the same transfer function.

Depending on the design of the neural network, the processing elements either operate continuously or are updated episodically. A scheduling function determines in which way and how often each processing element is to apply its transfer function.

Each processing element is completely self-sufficient and works away in total disregard of the processing going on inside its neighbors. In any neural network a great deal of independent parallel computation is usually under way.

At the same time, all the processing elements intimately affect the behavior of the entire network, since each element's output becomes the input to many others. The topology of the connections among processing elements influences what information-

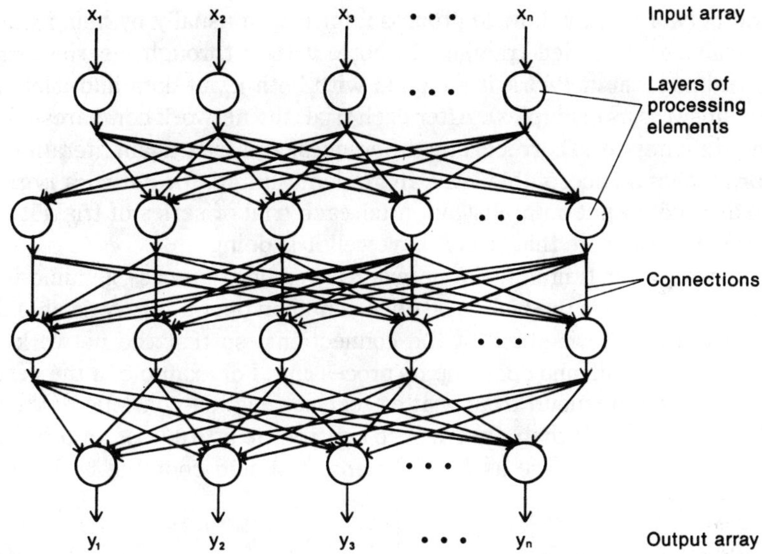

Fig. 41-1. Conceptually, a neural network consists of many processing elements (circles), each connected to many others. An input array, a sequence of numbers, is entered into the network. Each processing element in the first layer takes a component of the input array, operates on it in parallel with the other processing elements in the layer according to the transfer function, and delivers a single output to processing elements in a layer below. The result is an output array representing some characteristic associated with the input. Since inputs and adaptive coefficients (weights) can change over time, the network adapts and learns.

processing functions a neural network can carry out, as it determines what data each processing element receives and therefore the information on which it can act.

By and large, every connection entering a processing element has an adaptive coefficient called a weight assigned to it. This weight, which is stored in the local memory of the processing element, is generally used to amplify, attenuate, and possibly change the sign of the signal in the incoming connection. Often, the transfer function sums this and other weighted input signals to determine the value of the processing element's next output signal. Thus the weights determine the strength of the connections from neighboring processing elements.

Learning without programming

The weights, moreover, are not fixed but may change. Most transfer functions include a learning law—an equation that modifies all or some of the weights in the local memory in response to the input signals and the values supplied by the transfer function. In effect, the learning law allows the processing element's response to change with time, depending on the nature of the input signals. It is the means by which the network adapts itself to the answers desired and so organizes information within itself—in short, learns.

A neural network learns how to process information usually by being given either supervised training or graded training. In both, it runs through a series of trials. In supervised training, the network is supplied with both input data and desired output data (correct answers as examples). After each trial, the network compares its own output with the right answers, corrects any differences, and tries again, iterating until the output error reaches an acceptable level. In graded training, the network is given input data but no desired output data; instead, after each trial or series of trials it is given a grade or performance score that tells it how well it is doing.

In either case, after training, the network is ready to process genuine inputs. At this point, depending upon the task to be done, a human operator may disable the learning law and "freeze the weights" of the connections, so that the network will stop adapting itself to new data and speed up its processing. For example, if the network has been well trained to read aloud from written text, it need not continue to learn on real data. On the other hand, if the network is to control the attitude of an orbiting spacecraft whose mass will decrease as fuel is spent, it should continue to adapt itself to changing conditions.

From concept to hardware

Neural networks are varied. At least 50 different types are being explored in research or being developed for applications. Of these, 13 are in common use (TABLE 41-1). Although all consist of processing elements joined by a multiplicity of connections, they differ in the learning laws incorporated into their transfer functions, the topology of their connections, and the weights assigned to their connections. In fact, some neural networks that learn may not be trained (self-organizing map) and some do not even learn at all (Hopfield network). The result: a host of networks, each suited to different types of tasks.

Any neural-network architecture can take different physical forms: electronic (in which everything consists of electronic devices and circuitry), electrooptical (in which optical signals link electronic processing elements), or entirely optical (in which light signals link optical processing elements made out of some nonlinear optical material). Experimenters at various institutions are working on all of these approaches. But problems with materials make the physical hardware of a network less straightforward than the conceptual architecture ("Neural networks: the physical reality," p. 40).

A number of neurocomputers—specialized machines able to efficiently and cost-effectively implement neural networks—have been built, and a few are now becoming commercially available. All of them are configured as coprocessors to a standard serial computer, which acts as the host. The neurocomputer coprocessor, usually a board that looks much like any other circuit board, is connected to the host through a shared data bus or through a standard peripheral interconnection—PC-bus, Ethernet, or DRV-11.

As coprocessors, neurocomputers can be thought of as just another type of peripheral, like a printer or external disk drive. Data are shuffled into and out of the neurocomputer by the host computer through software routines supplied by the neurocomputer's manufacturer, even though the neurocomputer does its actual work on the data nonalgorithmically. No one has proposed a stand-alone neurocomputer—

Table 41-1. Definining Terms

Adaptive coefficients: values of the previous computations (weights) of a processing element stored in its local memory, which modify subsequent computations.
Connection: a signal transmission pathway between processing elements, corresponding to the axons and synapses of neurons in a human brain, that connects the processing elements into a network.
Learning law: an equation that modifies all or some of the adaptive coefficients (weights) in a processing element's local memory in response to input signals and the values supplied by the transfer function. The equation enables the network to adapt itself to examples of what it should be doing and to organize information within itself, and thereby learn.
Processing element: an artificial neuron in a neural network, consisting of a small amount of local memory and processing power. The output from a processing element is fanned out and becomes the input to many other elements.
Scheduling function: a function that determines if and how often a processing element is to apply its transfer function.
Transfer function: a mathematical formula that, among other things, determines a processing element's output signal as a function of the most recent input signals and the adaptive coefficients (weights) in local memory. The transfer function includes the learning law of the processing element.
Transformations: mappings or associations of objects or representations in one set (such as written words) with objects or representations in another set (such as spoken sounds) according to some rule, which is typically not known to a human programmer, but is implicit in the training data.
Weight: within a processing element, an adaptive coefficient associated with a single input connection. The weight determines the intensity of the connection, depending on the network's design and the information it has learned.

mainly because present networks do not handle input-output processing, and host computers already do that very well.

Most of the neurocomputer coprocessors built so far have been hard-wired designs optimized for implementing one type of neural network or a small selection of types. A few neurocomputers—notably those developed at IBM, Texas Instruments, and TRW—can implement several classes of networks, and a very few—such as those developed at HNC and SAIC—can implement essentially any neural network.

Such flexibility is valuable because the ability to quickly modify the neural network being used is critically important in research, application studies, and early applications. As with von Neumann machines, though, the more general-purpose a neurocomputer is, the slower it is. After the applications of neural networks are understood more fully, it may be possible to substitute specialized neurocomputers in those applications where only a particular network, or small range of networks, is needed.

For those who wish to get deeply involved in altering the structure and thus the behavior of a network, there are languages designed expressly for describing neural networks in a high-level, machine-independent way. The field is very new, and so far only four neurosoftware languages have been introduced: P3, Panspec, AnSpec, and Axon.

Neural networks applied

Several organizations are trying to apply neural networks to information-processing problems in commerce and industry that have proved intractable or far too expensive with algorithmic computers. Preliminary results have been encouraging.

Behavioristics Inc., Silver Spring, Md., has demonstrated a neural network for scheduling airline flights. Airlines sell seats at different fares depending how far in advance a reservation is made. The system, called the Airline Marketing Tactician, optimizes over time the allocation of seats between discount and standard fare classes to maximize the airline's profits. At present, several major airlines are considering the system.

Murray Smith, president of Adaptive Decision Systems Inc., Andover, Mass., has shown how accurately neural networks can score applications for bank loans. The network is given relevant data from a loan application form, and judges the applicant as a good or bad credit risk in terms of the examples on which it has been trained. The scoring system based on neurocomputing performed much more accurately than an existing operational point-scoring system based upon a combination of an expert system and a statistical model. A neurocomputer loan-scoring application has been developed for a major finance company, which plans to install it in the field around midyear.

A great challenge has been to get a computer to recognize human speech and translate it into written text—especially when a person speaks naturally, running words together in a continuous stream rather than articulating every syllable and pausing between individual words. Jeffrey Elman, associate professor of linguistics of the University of California at San Diego, has shown that neural networks can pick individual words out of connected streams and devise representations for them. The neural-network speech-recognition system with the highest accuracy and largest vocabulary was developed by Teuvo Kohonen, research professor in technical physics at the Helsinki University of Technology, under contract to Asahi Chemical Co. of Tokyo, Japan. The system has a front-end network that recognizes short, phoneme-like fragments of speech and a back-end network that recognizes strings of the fragments as words. A post-processing system uses context to distinguish between words that sound alike.

Neural networks have also broken ground in image recognition. Kohonen has shown that an associative memory network can take the image of a partially obscured face, complete it, and identify it with an image in a memory of 500 different people's faces. Kunihiko Fukushima, senior research scientist of NHK Laboratories in Tokyo, and Sei Miyake, a research director at the Automated Telecommunications Research Center in Osaka, have demonstrated a network, the neocognitron, that can identify hand-printed characters with 95-percent accuracy, regardless of shifts in position, changes in scale, and even small distortions.

Adaptive-control problems have been solved by neural networks for more than 25 years. The early demonstrations have prompted efforts to apply neural networks to the practical "eye-hand coordination" of robot arms moving in response to feedback from camera images. Remarkable progress has been made by Andres Pellionez, research associate professor of physiology and biophysics of New York University, New York City, who has demonstrated the ability to move a finger of a robot arm in a beautifully coordinated perfect straight line at any angle.

Complementary to algorithmic computing

Algorithmic computing and neurocomputing complement each other nicely. The first is ideal for accounting, aerodynamic and hydrodynamic modeling, and the like. The second is ideal for pattern recognition, fuzzy knowledge processing, and adaptive control. Neurocomputers should not be used to balance checkbooks. Algorithmic computers should not be used to recognize speech. The two can also be integrated easily in hardware.

A technology succeeds, it seems, if it fits smoothly into an existing infrastructure and important applications are developed quickly. Neurocomputing appears to fill the bill. And if the history of computing is any guide, the capabilities of neural networks are likely to grow with every successive generation.

Defining terms

Adaptive coefficients values of the previous computations (weights) of a processing element stored in its local memory, which modify subsequent computations.

Connection a signal transmission pathway between processing elements, corresponding to the axons and synapses of neurons in a human brain, that connects the processing elements into a network.

Learning law an equation that modifies all or some of the adaptive coefficients (weights) in a processing element's local memory in response to input signals and the values supplied by the transfer function. The equation enables the network to adapt itself to examples of what it should be doing and to organize information within itself, and thereby learn.

Processing element an artificial neuron in a neural network, consisting of a small amount of local memory and processing power. The output from a processing element is fanned out and becomes the input to many other elements.

Scheduling function a function that determines if and how often a processing element is to apply its transfer function.

Transfer function a mathematical formula that, among other things, determines a processing element's output signal as a function of the most recent input signals and the adaptive coefficients (weights) in local memory. The transfer function includes the learning law of the processing element.

Transformations mappings or associations of objects or representations in one set (such as written words) with objects or representations in another set (such as spoken sounds) according to some rule, which is typically not known to be human programmer, but is implicit in the training data.

Weight within a processing element, an adaptive coefficient associated with a single input connection. The weight determines the intensity of the connection, depending on the network's design and the information it has learned.

42

Foundations and grand challenges of artificial intelligence

Raj Reddy

Editors' note *Raj Reddy is one of the great pioneers in AI research and development. In this reprinted Presidential Address to the American Association for Artificial Intelligence (AAAI), he examines progress the AI community has made over the past two decades, as well as progress it is likely to make in coming years. Reddy's insights could only come from an insider, from someone who understands the technology and the events that led to its development and application. The paper constitutes a fitting close to this sourcebook. (Reprinted, with permission from the Winter 1988 issue of* AI Magazine. *© 1988, American Association for Artificial Intelligence. All rights reserved.)*

Last November, I got a call from Bob Simpson and Allen Sears, program managers for Artificial Intelligence at DARPA, which has been the major sponsor of AI research for the past twenty-five years. It was a call for help. "We are being asked some tough questions by the front office," they said. "What are the major accomplishments of the field? How can we measure progress? How can we tell whether you are succeeding or failing? What breakthroughs might be possible over the next decade? How much money will it take? What impact will it have? How can you effect technology transfer of promising results rapidly to industry?" They needed the answers in a hurry.

There was a time when we could say, "Trust us, we will accomplish great things." After twenty-five years of sustained support, it is not unreasonable to ask some hard questions. AI has become a big science, demanding a significant chunk of research dollars and accounting for over half a billion dollars of the GNP. The AI research budgets of DARPA, NSF, NASA and NIH alone account for over $100 million. In this age of huge budget deficits and many exciting ideas competing for constant research funds, it is only natural for a research manager to want to invest the research dollar wisely in activities with the potential for highest payoff. As the size of investment in AI rises above the noise level, we can no longer expect people to fund us on blind faith. We are entering an era of accountability. Rather than being concerned, I think we should view this as a challenge and lay out our vision for the future.

My first reaction to Simpson's request was, "Hey, we have nothing to worry about."

Our track record is terrific. We have created almost a billion dollar-a-year enterprise around the globe. Previously unsolvable problems are being solved. People who have never used a computer before are solving problems with one. Vision and robotics are beginning to transform manufacturing. Planning and scheduling systems are in routine use in industry. Speech and language interfaces are becoming preferred modes of communication. OK, maybe there are a lot of applications, but what about scientific progress?

AAAI is a society devoted to supporting the progress in science, technology and applications of AI. I thought I would use this occasion to share with you some of my thoughts on the recent advances in AI, the insights and theoretical foundations that have emerged out of the past thirty years of stable, sustained, systematic explorations in our field, and the grand challenges motivating the research in our field. First, let us look at some recent advances.

Advances in artificial intelligence

What can we do today that we could not do thirty years ago? It is fortunate that AI has several areas in which there has been sustained research over the past twenty to thirty years. These areas are chess, natural language, speech, vision, robotics and expert systems. I would like to illustrate the progress by providing a historical perspective on some of these areas.

Chess

Let us look at the problem of computers that play chess. Chess is an AI problem par excellence. It plays the same role in artificial intelligence that the studies of E. Coli play in biology. It illustrates and illuminates many problems that arise in AI and leads to techniques that can be generalized to work on other problems. Chess is perhaps one area which has been studied continuously since the birth of artificial intelligence in 1956. Funding agencies were afraid to support research on fun and games lest they receive a Golden Fleece award from Proxmire. In spite of lack of support, the situation is not too bleak. A $100,000 Fredkin prize awaits the system that beats the world champion.

In the mid-fifties, we had several attempts to build chess playing programs. The most notable of these was the Newell, Shaw, and Simon chess program (1958). The first published method for game tree pruning (a precursor to the alpha-beta algorithm) appeared in the NSS chess program. It was also the first system to attempt to incorporate "a practical body of knowledge about chess."

The next major landmark in chess occurred when Greenblatt's chess program (1967) won a game from a class C player in a 1966 tournament. This win revived interest in chess playing programs, and led to the annual ACM computer chess tournaments. The seventies were dominated by the Northwestern chess program (Slate and Atkin 1977). Ken Thompson of Bell Laboratories (1982) developed an application specific computer architecture for chess in the early eighties and illustrated the powerful idea that a $20,000 piece of hardware, if structured properly, could out-perform a $10 million dollar general purpose computer. Thompson's Belle program received the $5,000 Fredkin award for being the first system to achieve a master's level rating in tournament play in 1982. Hitech, a VLSI based parallel architecture created by Hans Berliner and Carl Ebeling (1986) has dominated the scene since 1985; it currently has a senior master's rating. During the last year, Hitech played 48 tournament games. It won 100% of all games played against expert-level players, 70% of all games played against master and senior-master level players, but only 15% of the games against grand masters. Just last week, a new system based on a custom VLSI design developed by two students at Carnegie Mellon University, C.B. Hsu and Thomas Anantharaman (Hsu, 1986; Anantharaman et al. 1988), called "Deep Thought," defeated the highest rated player ever in the US open chess tournament.

What did we learn from chess research? In addition to a number of insights into the nature of intelligence (which we will discuss a little later), chess research has also led to the development of a number of techniques such as the alpha-beta pruning algorithm, B* search, singular-extension-search, and hash table representation for keeping previously examined moves. The proceedings of the 1988 Spring symposium of AAAI on game playing contain a number of interesting papers which are illustrative of current research on the topic.

Speech

Speech recognition has a long history of being one of the difficult problems in Artificial Intelligence and Computer Science. As one goes from problem-solving tasks to perceptual tasks, the problem characteristics change dramatically: knowledge poor to knowledge rich; low data rates to high data rates; slow response time (minutes to hours) to instantaneous response time. These characteristics taken together increase the computational complexity of the problem by several orders of magnitude. Further, speech provides a challenging task domain which embodies many of the requirements of intelligent behavior: operate in real time; exploit vast amounts of knowledge; tolerate errorful data; use language and learn from the environment.

Voice input to computers offers a number of advantages. It provides a natural, hands-free, eyes-free, location-free input medium. However, there are many as yet unsolved problems that prevent routine use of speech as an input device by non-experts. These include cost, real-time response, speaker independence, robustness to variations such as noise, microphone, speech rate and loudness, and the ability to handle spontaneous speech phenomena such as repetitions and restarts. Satisfactory solutions to each of these problems can be expected within the next decade. Recognition of unrestricted spontaneous continuous speech appears unsolvable at the present. However, by the addition of simple constraints, such as a clarification dialogue to resolve ambiguity, we believe it will be possible to develop systems capable of accepting very large vocabulary and continuous speech dictation before the turn of the century.

Work in speech recognition predates the invention of computers. However, serious work in speech recognition started in the late fifties with the availability of digital computers equipped with A/D converters. The problems of segmentation, classification, and pattern matching were explored in the sixties and a small vocabulary connected speech robot control task was demonstrated. In the early seventies, the role of syntax and semantics in connected speech recognition was explored and demonstrated as part of the speech understanding program (Erman et al., 1980; Lowerre et al., 1980; Woods,

1980). The seventies also witnessed the development of a number of basic techniques such as blackboard models (Reddy et al., 1973; Nii, 1986), dynamic time warping [Itakura], network representation (Baker 1975), Hidden Markov models (Baker, 1975; Rabiner et al., 1986), beam search (Lowerre and Reddy 1980), and the forward-backward algorithm (Bahl et al., 1986). The early eighties witnessed a trend toward practical systems with very large vocabularies (Jelinek et al. 1985) but computational and accuracy limitations made it necessary to pause between words.

The recent speaker-independent speech recognition system called Sphinx best illustrates the current state of the art (Lee 1988). This system is capable of recognizing continuous speech without training the system for each speaker. The system operates in near real time using a 1000 word resource management vocabulary. The system achieves 94% word accuracy in speaker independent mode on a task with a grammar perplexity of 60. The system derives its high performance by careful modeling of speech knowledge, by using an automatic unsupervised learning algorithm, and by fully utilizing a large amount of training data. These improvements permit Sphinx to overcome the many limitations of speaker-dependent systems resulting in a high performance system.

The surprising thing to me was that a simple learning technique, such as learning transition probabilities in a fixed network structure, proved to be much more powerful than attempting to codify the knowledge of speech experts who can read spectrograms. The latter process of knowledge engineering proved to be too slow, too ad hoc, and too error-prone.

What did we learn from speech research? Results from speech research have led to a number of insights about how one can successfully use incomplete, inaccurate, and partial knowledge within a problem-solving framework. Speech was one of the first task domains to use a number of new concepts such as Blackboard models, Beam search, and reasoning in the presence of uncertainty, which are now used widely within AI.

Vision

Research in image processing started in the fifties with optical character recognition. What we now call computer vision started with the seminal work of Larry Roberts (1965). Roberts was the first to work on 3-D vision using gray scale images of the blocks world. Roberts used a strictly bottom up approach to vision starting with edge detection, linear feature detection, 3-D model matching, and object recognition.

Minsky and McCarthy initiated the work on robotic vision beginning with the hand-eye projects at Stanford and M.I.T. Minsky proposed the concept of heterarchical architectures for vision in which various knowledge sources interacted with one another in an opportunistic way to solve the image interpretation problem. Successful demonstrations in vision from 1965 to 1975 were limited to problems in which 3-D phenomena such as shadows, highlights, and occlusions were not too troublesome. The work of Guzman (1968), Huffman (1971), Clowes (1971), Waltz (1975), and Kanade (1981) on line drawings, Fischler et. al.'s (1973) work on image matching, Ohlander's work (1978) on natural scenes, and Binford and Agin's work (1973) on generalized cylinders are representative of the best results of that period.

The limitations and problems of the earlier approaches led Marr (1979, 1982) to propose a general framework for vision involving the primal sketch and the $2^1/_2$-D sketch. This accelerated the "back-to-basics" movement started by Horn (1975) where mathematical models reflecting constraints of physics, optics, and geometry were used to derive 3-D shape properties from 2-D images of a scene.

Barrow and Tenenbaum (1978, 1981) proposed that photometric and geometric properties are confounded in the intensity values available at each pixel, and the central problem for vision was therefore how to simultaneously recover them. Two recent results highlight the dramatic progress that has been made over the last decade. Klinker, Shafer and Kanade (1988) have been able to remove highlights from a color image to produce an intrinsic body reflection image using Shafer's dichromatic reflection model (1985). Matthies, Szeliski and Kanade (1988) have developed an algorithm for estimating depth from a sequence of N images that is N times better than stereo depth estimation.

We are beginning to see the cumulative results of the past twenty five years being applied and improved within realistic task frameworks. One of the best examples of this research is "Navlab," a navigation laboratory used for obstacle detection and navigation research at Carnegie Mellon (Thorpe et al., 1987).

The Navlab is a self-contained laboratory vehicle for research in autonomous outdoor navigation. It is based on a commercial Chevy van modified to permit an onboard computer to steer and drive the van by electric and hydraulic servos. The sensors onboard Navlab include color stereo vision, laser ranging and sonar. Onboard computers include four Sun workstations and a Warp supercomputer.

The Navlab uses a hierarchical system structure. At the lowest level, the system can sense motion and follow steering commands. The next level performs tasks such as road following, terrain mapping, obstacle detection and path planning. The high level tasks include object recognition and landmark identification, map-based prediction, and long-range route selection. The system uses a blackboard model with extensions to deal with geometry and time for communication, knowledge fusion, and spatial reasoning. The system is currently being expanded to produce better predictions through the increased use of map and model information.

Expert systems

In 1966, when I was at the Stanford AI labs, there used to be a young Ph.D. sitting in front of a graphics display working with Feigenbaum, Lederberg, and members from the Chemistry department attempting to discover molecular structures from mass spectral data. I used to wonder, what on earth are these people doing? Why not work on a real AI problem like chess or language or robotics? What does chemistry have to do with AI? That young Ph.D. was Bruce Buchanan and the system he was helping to develop was Dendral (Lindsay et al. 1980).

Now we know better. Dendral and its successor, Mycin (Shortliffe 1976), gave birth to the field of expert systems. Dendral is perhaps the single longest-lived continuous set of experiments in the history of AI from 1965–83.

The current growth rate of the expert system field is too explosive for me to do justice in a short time. Let me refer you to the book by Feigenbaum, McCorduck, and Nii on the Rise of the Expert Company (1988) and the recent view paper by Buchanan and Smith on expert systems (1988).

I would like to provide a few examples to illustrate the widespread use of expert systems in many innovative applications:

- Schlumberger is using a Dipmeter Advisor to interpret down-hole data from oil wells to assist in prospecting for oil.
- Kodak is using an Injection Molding Advisor to diagnose faults and suggest repairs for a plastic injection molding mechanisms.
- Hewlett-Packard is using a Trouble Shooting Advisor to diagnose problems in photolithography steps in semiconductor manufacturing.
- NASA is using a system to monitor data during the liquid oxygen tanking process.
- NCR is using a system for preventive maintenance of computers.
- American Express uses a credit authorization system to authorize and screen credit requests.
- AT&T uses a system to act as a software user consultant to advise users of a large statistical package.
- Federal Express uses an Inventory Control Expert to decide whether or not to store spares.
- DEC and IBM routinely use systems for configuring customer orders into shipping orders.
- Xerox uses the PRIDE system to design paper handling systems.
- Hazeltine uses the OPGEN system for planning assembly instructions for PC boards.
- IBM uses a scheduling expert system to plan the factory operations in semiconductor manufacturing. The list goes on and on.

Here are some other interesting facts:

- IBM has deployed over 100 expert systems internally.
- The return on investment at IBM on a series of expert systems costing $2.5 million was estimated at $37.5 million.
- DEC employs over 700 people in its AI division.
- A Gartner Study, released in June 1988, shows that the number of deployed expert systems increased from 50 in 1987 to 1400 in 1988, and the number of expert systems under development increased from 2500 to 8500 over the same period.

I want to digress for a moment to pay tribute to the person most responsible for widespread use of expert systems. We all know that Feigenbaum sometimes tends to overstate the case. But sometimes it takes that kind of passion, conviction, and missionary zeal to make believers out of the masses. Ed, we thank you.

Time does not permit me to review advances in many other areas of AI such as natural language, robotics, learning, discovery, planning, and problem solving. Believe me! We know a lot more about each of these areas than we did thirty years ago. I refer you to papers on these and other subjects in the AAAI proceedings of the past ten years.

Foundations of AI

"... fine examples of bricklaying for a cathedral that is beginning to take shape,"
—Simon (1980).

In an era of accountability, it is appropriate for an outsider to ask what are the intellectual concerns driving the field. What are the fundamental principles, the self evident truths so to speak, that govern our field?

As an empirical science, AI follows the classical hypothesis-and-test research paradigm. The computer is the laboratory where AI experiments are conducted. Design, construction, testing, and measurement of computer programs are the process by which AI researchers validate the models and mechanisms of intelligent action.

It is not enough to say that AI attempts to study mechanisms of intelligent action. What are the attributes of an intelligent system? Minsky (1985) in his book *The Society of Mind* provides a long and formidable list of attributes of intelligence. Newell provides us with a shorter checklist (Newell 1988). An intelligent system must:

- operate in real-time;
- exploit vast amounts of knowledge;
- tolerate errorful, unexpected and possibly unknown input;
- use symbols and abstractions;
- communicate using natural language;
- learn from the environment;
- exhibit adaptive goal-oriented behavior.

Where is AI today? What do we know now that we didn't know thirty years ago? At any given point, we can attempt to measure and evaluate the state of the art and accomplishments by assessing the capabilities of computers over the same range of tasks over which humans exhibit intelligence. These tasks range from puzzles and games at one extreme to perceptual and motor tasks at the other.

These tasks exhibit a wide variation in characteristics, such as knowledge content, data rates and amount of data, and expected response time (FIG. 42-1). As you look at tasks ranging from puzzles, chess, and theorem proving to expert systems, languages, and perceptual and motor processes, tasks go from knowledge poor to knowledge rich, low data rates to high data rates, and slow response time to instantaneous response time. The diversity of requirements in tasks involving intelligent action places significant demands on architectures for AI with respect to memory capacity, bandwidth, access times, and processor speed.

Lessons from AI experiments

The last thirty years of stable, sustained and systematic explorations have not only yielded performance systems that we saw earlier, but they have also provided us with a

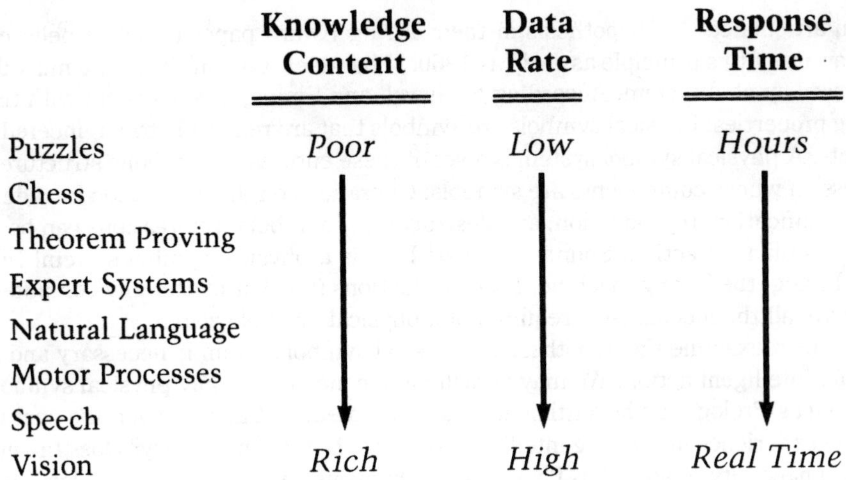

Fig. 42-1. AI problem domains and their attributes.

number of fundamental insights into the nature of intelligent action. Let us look at a few.

Bounded rationality implies opportunistic search This is the fundamental result of Simon's research on decision making in organizations leading to the Nobel Prize. It says that "computational constraints on human thinking" leads people to be satisfied with "good enough" solutions. Feigenbaum (1988) calls it the founding paradigm of AI research. Prior to Simon's work on human decision making, it was assumed that, given all the relevant facts, the human being is capable of rational choice weighing all the facts. While studying the problem of resource allocation between maintenance and salaries in the administration of public parks in the city of Milwaukee in 1935, Simon observed that the decisions made had no relationship to the expected economic utility. That, and subsequent studies of Simon (1947, 1955) on "human decision making," led to the principle of "bounded rationality." When people have to make decisions under conditions which overload human thinking capabilities, they don't give up, saying the problem is NP-complete. They use strategies and tactics of "optimal-least-computation search" and not those of "optimal-shortest-path search." By "optimal-least-computation search" here, Simon means the study of approximate algorithms for search which can find the best possible solution given certain constraints on the computation, such as limited memory capacity, limited time, or limited bandwidth. Much of the current literature on search theory completely ignores this problem. This leads Simon to observe that many of the results in search theory may be of questionable value to the real world. I believe we should keep an open mind about what search results will be relevant in the future. Silicon-based intelligence, once achieved and given its differences in memory access time and bandwidth, may indeed have different computational constraints than human intelligence.

A physical symbol system is necessary and sufficient for intelligent action The second principle of AI is the physical symbol system hypothesis, i.e., a physical symbol system is necessary and sufficient for intelligent action. Newell and

Simon articulated this hypothesis in their Turing Award paper (1976). I believe they were aware of this principle as early as 1960. What does it mean? First, we must define a physical symbol system. According to Newell and Simon, it is a system with the following properties: Physical symbols are symbols that are realizable by engineered components. A physical symbol system is a set of these entities. A symbolic structure is an expression whose components are symbols. Operations on the expression include creation, modification, reproduction, and destruction of symbols. Expressions can be interpreted as plans of action. Sounds familiar! Lisp is a physical symbol system! In fact, Lisp, Prolog, the Turing machine, Post Productions (for that matter any computer system) have all the mechanisms required of a physical symbol system.

Let us reexamine the hypothesis: a physical symbol system is necessary and sufficient for intelligent action. We may be willing to concede that any physical symbol system such as Prolog may be sufficient to achieve intelligent action given the past thirty years of experience in creating intelligent systems. But is it necessary? Does the human brain, of necessity, at some level have the mechanisms and properties of a physical symbol system? We in AI believe it is so but we cannot prove it. That is why it is a hypothesis. Not everyone believes it. Many philosophers and biologists have competing hypotheses. Nobel Prize winning biologist Edelman (1987) thinks that the brain is organized in a manner analogous to population dynamics. This view is clearly different from the information processing models of cognition and intelligent action that we in AI have come to love and cherish.

The Magic Number 70,000±20,000 The third principle of AI is that an expert knows 70,000 "chunks" of information give or take a binary order of magnitude. This is a surprising statement. Why is it 70,000? Why not a million? Why not one thousand? Several converging lines of evidence lead towards 70,000 as a rough measure of the size of an expert's knowledge base. For example, it appears that Chess Masters recognize about 50,000 chunks. Chase and Simon (1973) were able to quantify this number by constructing an experiment based on the ability of Master-level, Expert-level, and Novice-level players to recreate chess positions they have seen only for a few seconds. Based on these protocols, they were able to create an information processing model and use it to estimate the size of the knowledge base of a Masters-level player in chess. We have no comparable number for Grand Master-level play (rating of 2600 versus 2200 for a Master). It is safe to assume that 50,000 is at the low end of the size of this knowledge base as we go from Master to Grand Master to World Champion.

But is it true for experts in all domains? Indeed the evidence appears to point to the magic number 70,000±20,000. Everyone of us is an expert in speech and language. We know that vocabularies of college graduates are about that order of magnitude. As we gain more and more experience in building expert systems, we find that the number of productions begins to grow towards tens of thousands if the system is to perform more than a very narrow range of tasks in a given domain.

It is interesting that, in addition to George Miller's magic number 7±2 which is an estimate of the size of short-term memory (1956), we now have a hypothesis about the size of an expert's long-term memory for a given domain of expertise. It has been observed that no human being reaches world class expert status without at least a decade of intense full-time study and practice in the domain (Hayes, 1985 and 1987). Even the most talented don't reach expert levels of performance without immense effort.

Everyone of us is an expert in speech, vision, motion, and language. That only leaves enough time to be an expert in two or three other areas in one's life time. Indeed, most of us never get past one area of expertise.

Search compensates for lack of knowledge The fourth principle of AI is that search compensates for lack of knowledge. When faced with a puzzle we have never seen before, we don't give up: we engage in trial-and-error behavior, usually until a solution is found. Over the past thirty years of AI research, this statement has come to mean much more than the fact that we use search to solve problems. Let me illustrate the point by some examples.

During the sixties and seventies, it was believed that Masters-level performance in chess could not be achieved except by codifying and using knowledge of expert human chess players. We now know, from the example we saw earlier, that Hitech (which is able to examine over 20 million board positions in 3 minutes) is able to play at Senior Master-level, even though its knowledge is nowhere comparable to a chess master. The key lesson here is that there may be more than one way to achieve expert behavior in a domain such as chess.

This leads to the conjecture that this principle may be true for problem-solving tasks such as puzzles and games but can't be true for perceptual tasks such as speech. Even here we are in for a surprise. Earlier we saw several examples in speech where search compensates for incomplete and inaccurate knowledge. The principle is also used in language processing where words can have many meanings. For example the verb 'take' can mean many things: take a book, take a shower, take a bus, take a deep breath, take a measurement, and so on. This inherent ambiguity that you carry a book and get into a bus is often clarified by the context. Usually, uncertainty can be resolved by exploring all the alternatives until the meaning is unambiguous. When in doubt, sprout! What this principle tells us about the role of search is that we need not give up hope when faced with a situation in which all the known knowledge is yet to be acquired and codified. Often it may be possible to find an acceptable solution by engaging in a "generate-and-test" process of exploration of the problem space.

Knowledge compensates for lack of search We now come to an important insight which was not clearly understood even as late as 1970, i.e., knowledge reduces uncertainty and helps us constrain the exponential growth leading to the solution of the many otherwise unsolvable problems. Knowledge is indeed power. In the extreme case "recognition," knowledge can eliminate the need for search altogether. This principle is essentially the converse of the previous principle; search compensates for lack of knowledge and knowledge compensates for the lack of search.

We have a number of experiments that illustrate the role of knowledge. You have probably seen the Rubik's cube. The first time around, it is not uncommon for most people to take half an hour or more to solve this puzzle. With practice however, the situation improves dramatically. There have been cases where the solution was completed in less than 20 seconds. This simple example clearly illustrates the role of knowledge in eliminating the trial-and-error search behavior. The interesting unsolved question in the case of Rubik's cube is: What is the knowledge, and how is it acquired and represented?

The speech task we saw earlier also provides some quantitative data about the importance of knowledge. The Sphinx system can be run with various knowledge sources turned off. Consider the situation where one removes the syntactic knowledge source. In this case, sentences of the form "Sleep roses dangerously young colorless" would be legal. Removing the syntactic knowledge source increases the error rate of Sphinx from 4% to 30%, i.e., on the average, one out of three words would be incorrect. Removing the probabilistic knowledge about the frequency of occurrence of the words increases the error rate from 4% to 6%.

The knowledge-search tradeoff Figure 42-2, created by Hans Berliner and Carl Ebeling (1986), graphically illustrates the knowledge-search tradeoff. A human Chess Master rarely examines more than 200 positions but is able to recognize over 50,000 chess patterns. On the other hand, Hitech, which has a Senior Master rating, explores over 20 million board positions but has less than 200 rules.

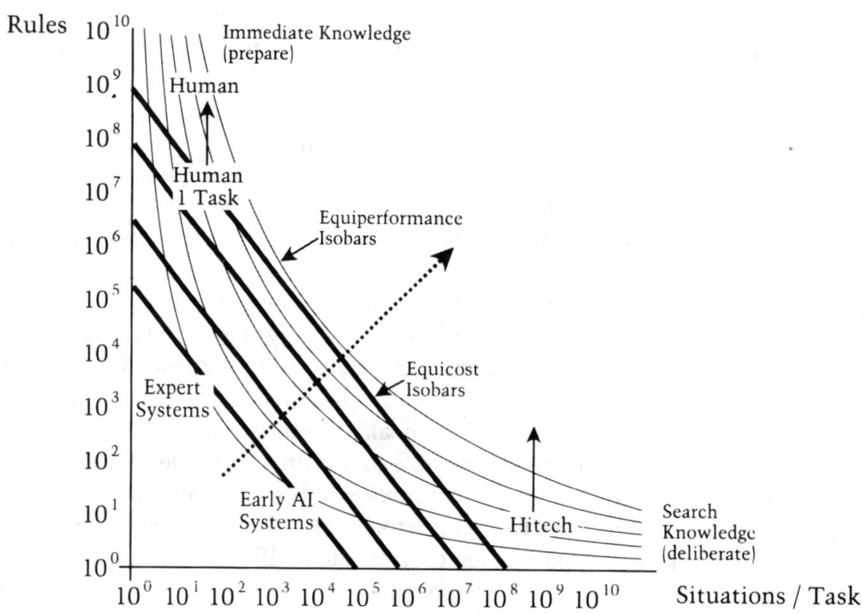

Fig. 42-2. The knowledge-search tradeoff.

This graph also shows the characteristics of various AI systems. The early AI systems had little knowledge (10 to 20 rules) and engaged in modest search. Expert systems generally have more knowledge and do little search.

Can you really trade knowledge for search and search for knowledge? Within bounds, it seems. Newell (1988) observes that Soar, which is able to learn from experience, uses more knowledge and less search with each new round of solving problems in a task domain. For example, each time Soar solves a configuration task, it discovers and adds new rules to its knowledge base which it is then able to invoke in subsequent attempts while solving other configuration problems. Conversely, even experts seem to resort to search when faced with a previously unseen problem within the domain of their expertise—for example in scientific research. Simon (1988) observes that this produces a kind of paradox—that the most "creative" problem solving may have to use "the most primitive" techniques, i.e., the weak methods such as generate-and-test, hill climbing, and means-ends analysis.

This one chart appears to provide the entire space of architectures for intelligence. When the Fredkin Prize for the World Chess Championship is won, it will probably be by a system that has neither the abilities nor the constraints of a human expert; neither the knowledge nor the limitations of bounded rationality. There are many paths to Nirvana.

In this section, we have been looking at lessons from AI research: the insights and the principles that govern our enterprise, i.e., the task of creating systems of intelligent action; the insights that we did not have as recently as thirty years ago. If there is one thing I want you to remember about this talk, it is the five fundamental principles of AI we have just discussed: bounded rationality implies opportunistic search; physical symbol systems are necessary and sufficient for intelligent action; an expert knows 70,000 things give or take a binary order of magnitude; search compensates for lack of knowledge; and knowledge eliminates the need for search. Although these may sound obvious to you now, they didn't thirty years ago! But then, Newton's Laws of Motion and the Fundamental Theorem of Calculus also appear obvious, after the fact.

Lessons from algorithm analysis

Let us now look at lessons from other disciplines that have proved to be important to AI such as Algorithm Analysis and Complexity Theory.

Of necessity, almost every problem we look at in AI is NP-complete, i.e., exponential growth and combinatorial explosion are the law of the land. Initial results from the theorists were disappointing. There was a spate of results showing that almost every interesting problem is NP-complete. It does not do any good to the "traveling salesman" to know that the "traveling salesman problem" is NP-complete. He still has to travel to do his job and find a satisfactory travel route. NP-completeness is too weak a result to provide any guidance on the choice of algorithms for real-world problems.

My favorite result from the Algorithm Analysis area is Knuth and Moore's analysis (1975) of the Alpha-Beta pruning algorithm. This is the only result I know that gives deeper, crisper and a more concise understanding of one of the major AI problems: Chess. The alpha-beta algorithm was originally articulated by John McCarthy and has been used in all chess playing programs since the early sixties. The key result here is that the use of alpha-beta reduces the exponential growth to the square root of the exponent. McCarthy's student, Mike Levin, conjectured this result as early as 1961. Slagle and Dixon (1969) proved the result for the optimal case in 1969. However, it was left up to Knuth to provide a detailed analysis of the power of alpha-beta. Let us examine the power of this result.

The selection of possible moves in chess is based on a mini-max game tree. Each ply increases the number of moves exponentially as a function of the branching factor. It has been estimated that one would have to explore over 10^{120} board positions in an exhaustive search of the chess game tree. You may know that 10^{120} is larger than the number of atoms in the universe.

On the average, in the mid-game, a player usually has the option of making any one of 35 possible moves. At a branching factor of 35, an 8-ply deep search usually requires examination of over 4 trillion board positions. This quickly increases to six million trillion positions for a 12-ply search, well beyond the capability of any current and projected computer system of the future. If one were to have a supercomputer with nanosecond cycle time, specialized to examine a node at each cycle, it would take over 200 years to make a move for a 12-ply system. The alpha-beta pruning technique effectively reduces the branching factor by the square-root leading to a branching factor of about 6. Twelve-ply search still requires evaluation of over 23 billion board positions or only 23 seconds on our supercomputer. A hash table which keeps previously examined moves, further reduces the branching factor to five, resulting in 12-ply search requiring the evaluation of over three billion board positions or just 3 seconds on our supercomputer. Since a human player usually has 3 minutes to make a move, we will only need a system that can examine about 16 million board positions to achieve Grand Master-level play! The power of alpha-beta is just awesome.

Systems such as Cray-Blitz that play chess approaching Master-level competence can examine about 25,000 board positions per second or about five million board positions in three minutes using a 25 mips equivalent scalar processor. Hitech is currently able to examine 175,000 board positions per second. Deep Thought, developed by Hsu and Anantharaman, is able to examine almost a million board positions per second. We are only a factor of 16 away from potential Grand Master-level play! With use of additional knowledge, it could even be sooner!

Coming back to Knuth's analysis, the result provides us with the ability to make concise statements about when and under what conditions we might expect to reach Grand Master-level performance. As we noted earlier, Levin, one of McCarthy's students discovered the same result in 1961, but it was left up to Knuth to provide the formal analysis and proof in 1975. There is a lesson in this to all our young scientists. If you happen to create a proof, an interesting algorithm, or an innovative data structure, don't leave it up to some future complexity theorist to re-invent it.

There have been other important results from algorithm analysis that are relevant to AI such as Karp's work on approximate algorithms, Tarjan's analysis of self-adjusting search trees, and Hopcroft and Natarajan's analysis of complexity of robot assembly tasks. While each of these provide a fundamental understanding, they have not yet been as important to AI as the analysis of alpha-beta.

Lessons from applied physics

Let us now look at some interesting insights from what I shall call "Lessons from Applied Physics." Acoustics and optics have long been studied within Physics. AI speech researchers benefited from several decades of research in models of speech and acoustics at Bell Labs and other centers. Surprisingly, there has not been equivalent formal work in vision processes. I am happy to say that rather than leaving the formal studies to some later day physicist, AI scientists in the late 70's started the "back-to-basics" movement which now provides a firm theoretical foundation for vision. I will highlight several key lessons, leading to theoretically sound computational models of vision processes based on constraints of physics, optics, and geometry:

- Marr's general framework for vision,
- Barrow and Tenenbaum's representation of intrinsic images,
- Horn, Woodham, Ikeuchi and Shafer's work on inferring 3-D shape from photometric properties such as shading and color,
- Huffman, Clowes, Waltz, Kanade, and Kender's results on inferring 3-D shape from geometrical properties and constraints,
- Ullman, Hildreth, and Waxman's results on inferring shape from motion such as optical flow.

Recently, Witkin and Tenenbaum (1983) questioned the desirability of preoccupation with recovering local surface attributes. They believe the resulting algorithms are frail and will not work well unless appropriate global constraints are simultaneously imposed on the image data. Bledsoe (1985) points out that intelligent agents of the future must be capable of reasoning at many levels. Most of the time, they may reason (like humans) at shallow qualitative levels, moving to deeper causal levels ("reasoning from basic principles of physics") only as needed. The lesson in the case of vision and applied physics is that the huge computational cost and too much precision could limit the usefulness of physics-based models even if they are superior to human vision.

Lessons from connectionism

Recent blossoming connectionist research is a result of a better understanding of computational aspects of human intelligence. There are roughly a hundred billion neural cells in the human brain. The brain operates with a cycle time of 5 ms and computes a scalar product of binary input and weight vector.

One of the intriguing aspects of this computing element is that the fan-in and fan-out is of the order of 1,000. Most of the brain's volume is occupied by wires, even though the wires themselves are of submicron cross section. A hundred billion processing elements with 1,000 connections each represent a hundred trillion connections. As many as 1% of these wires are active in a 5 ms iteration involving a trillion computations every 5 ms. Thus, one might speculate that the brain appears to perform 200 trillion operations per second give or take a few orders of magnitude.

The human brain possesses an interesting property. For tasks such as vision, language and motor control, a brain is more powerful than 1000 supercomputers. And yet, for simple tasks such as multiplication it is less powerful than a 4 bit microprocessor (Hinton, 1985). This leads us to speculate that silicon-based intelligence, when it is achieved, may have different attributes. We need not build airplanes with flapping wings.

When looking at a familiar photograph such as the Washington Monument, the brain seems to process and identify the scene in a few hundred milliseconds. This has led the connectionists to observe that whatever processing is occurring within the human brain, must be happening in less than 100 clock cycles. AI scientists such as

Jerry Feldman (1982, 1985) and Geoff Hinton (1986) want to find answers to questions about what is the nature of representation and the nature of computation taking place within the human brain? For the first time, someone is asking questions about optimal-least-computation-search. I look forward to many exciting new results from connectionist research. Some researchers worry that connectionist architectures do not provide mechanisms for understanding what the system knows, how it reasons and what it believes. Let us first get a system that works, then I am confident that someone will figure out what it knows!

Lessons from architectures

The Sphinx speech recognition system that you saw earlier achieves its real-time performance not just through the use of AI techniques such as representation, search, and learning but also through the use of efficient data structures and application specific hardware architectures. Roberto Bisiani (1988) was able to reduce the time for recognition from about 10 minutes to under 5 seconds. Any time you can make two orders of magnitude improvement, you have to sit up and take notice. How did Bisiani do this? From October 1987 through May 1988, he achieved the following:

- a speed-up of 1.5 by replacing sparse arrays with link lists
- a speed-up of 3.0 by redesigning the data structures to eliminate pointer chasing
- a speed-up of 2.0 by redesigning the beam search algorithm to use dynamic thresholds and inserting best state at the top of the list
- a speed-up of 2.5 using faster processors
- a speed-up of 1.6 using a multiple memory architecture
- a speed-up of 2.1 by using a multi-processor architecture for parallel search execution.

Note that all these speed-ups are small, independent and multiplicative (as conjectured by Reddy and Newell, 1977), resulting in a whopping speed-up by a factor of 75, i.e., 7500%. Not bad for six months of research!

The main lesson here is that serious AI scientists of the future must also be competent in other fields of computer science, i.e., algorithm analysis, data structures and software, and computer architecture.

Lessons from logic

Logic has long been used in AI as a theoretical description language for describing what the program knows and believes; used from outside for theorizing about the logical relations between the data structures before some thinking process has taken place and the data structures after the thinking process. Nils Nilsson's book (Nilsson 1971) on AI is the best example of this use of logic.

I am reminded of the time, twenty five years ago, when John McCarthy gave us an assignment in class to axiomatize the missionaries and cannibals problem. I went through the motions and I believe he gave me an "A" but I was never sure whether what I did was correct or not. There was no way to validate my axiomatization of the problem. For logic to become widely used as a theoretical description of the language of AI, we need tools and systems that help us think, formulate, and validate what we know in a concise form.

Recently, with logic programming tools, there has been an increasing use of logic as an internal representation language for AI programs for representing what it knows. This use may be good for some applications and bad for others. I don't believe a uniform representation language to solve all AI problems is either necessary or desirable at this juncture.

With advances in non-monotonic reasoning and other recent results, formal methods are enjoying a revival. From the beginning, John McCarthy has been a proponent and a major contributor to the formal theory of artificial intelligence. He is responsible for many key ideas in AI and Computer Science: the Lisp programming language, time sharing, common sense reasoning, alpha-beta pruning algorithm, circumscription in non-monotonic reasoning and so on. As my advisor at Stanford, he helped to launch my AI career as he did for many others. It gives me great pleasure to share with you the recent announcement that he has been selected to receive the prestigious $350,000 Kyoto Prize for 1988. McCarthy used to say that "To succeed, AI needs 1.7 Einsteins, 2 Maxwells, 5 Faradays and .3 Manhattan projects." Well, with Simon's Nobel prize and McCarthy's Kyoto prize, our field is making a solid beginning.

The grand challenges of AI

In an era of accountability, we cannot rest on our past accomplishments for very long. We must create a vision for the future which is exciting and challenging. Fortunately for us, any significant demonstration of intelligent systems is exciting. But we must go one step further. Whenever possible, we must identify and work on problems of relevance to the nation—bold national initiatives that capture the imagination of the public.

Let me illustrate what I mean by two examples from biology and physics: the Decoding of the Human Genome, and the Superconducting Super Collider Project. These grand challenges of science are expected to require several billion dollars of investment each. However, the expected benefits of these projects to the nation are also very high. AI is in a unique position to undertake and deliver on such nationally relevant initiatives.

What are the grand challenges of AI? Fortunately, we have several seemingly reasonable problems which are currently unsolvable, and which require major new insights and fundamental advances in various subfields of AI, and the criteria for success or failure can be clearly stated. The scope and size of these problems vary greatly—give or take an order of magnitude relative to, say, the Decoding of the Human Genome project. I would like to present a few of my favorite grand challenges here.

World champion chess machine In the early eighties, with a grant from the Fredkin Foundation, we have established a $100,000 prize for the development of a computer program which would beat the reigning world champion chess player. We saw earlier that we are already at the senior masters level. Hans Berliner says that if you plot the progress in computer chess over the past twenty years, the ratings have been growing steadily at about 45 points per year. At that rate, we should have a chess champion computer by about 1998, almost forty years after Simon's predictions. We didn't quite do it in ten years. But in the cosmic scale of time, as Carl Sagan points out, forty or even a hundred years is but a fleeting moment. We have waited billions of years for nature to evolve natural intelligence! We can certainly wait a hundred or even a thousand years to realize a human-created intelligence.

Mathematical discovery The second Fredkin prize is for the discovery of a major mathematical result by a computer. The criteria for success in this case are not as crisp as with chess. Woody Bledsoe, Chairman of the mathematics prize committee, is working with a panel of eminent mathematicians to establish the criteria for awarding the prize. For a while, we thought a successor to Doug Lenat's AM program would claim this prize. But Lenat had other plans. He is after an even greater grand challenge—i.e., to create a system called CYC which will have an encyclopedic knowledge of the world.

The translating telephone Japan recently initiated a seven year $120 million project as the first phase towards developing a phone system in which a Japanese speaker can converse with, say, an English speaker in real time. This requires solutions to a number of currently unsolved problems: a speech recognition system capable of recognizing a large (possibly unlimited) vocabulary and spontaneous, unrehearsed, continuous speech; a natural sounding speech synthesis preserving speaker characteristics; and a natural language translation system capable of dealing with ambiguity, non-grammaticality, and incomplete phrases.

Accident avoiding car In the U.S., over 40,000 people die annually in automobile accidents. It appears that a new generation automobile equipped with an intelligent cruise control using sonar, laser, and vision sensors could eliminate 80% to 90% of the fatal accidents and cost less than 10% of the total cost of the automobile. Such a device would require research in vision, sensor fusion, obstacle detection and avoidance, low cost/high speed (over a billion operations per second) digital signal processor chips, and the underlying software and algorithm design.

Self-organizing systems There has been a long and continuing interest in systems that learn and discover from examples, from observations, and from books. Currently, there is a lot of interest in neural networks that can learn from signals and symbols through an evolutionary process. Two long-term grand challenges for systems that acquire capability through development are: read a chapter in a college freshman text (say physics or accounting) and answer the questions at the end of the chapter; and learn to assemble an appliance (such as a food processor) from observing a person doing the same task. Both are extremely hard problems requiring advances in vision, language, problem-solving techniques, and learning theory. Both are essential to the demonstration of a self-organizing system that acquires capability through (possibly unsupervised) development.

Self-replicating systems There have been several theoretical studies in this area since the 1950's. The problem is of some practical interest in areas such as space manufacturing. Rather than uplifting a whole factory, is it possible to have a small set of machine tools which can produce, say, 95% of the parts needed for the factory using locally available raw materials and assemble it in situ? The solution to this problem involves many different disciplines including materials and energy technologies.

Research problems in AI include: knowledge capture for reverse engineering and replication, design for manufacturability, and robotics.

Each of the above seemingly reasonable problems would require significant breakthroughs and fundamental advances in AI and all other subfields of Computer Science and Technology. Unlike other vague statements of accomplishments, success or failure in these cases can be clearly established and appreciated by non-experts. Each of these tasks requires long-term, stable funding at significant levels. Success is by no means guaranteed and each problem represents a high-risk high-payoff investment. However, even partial success can have spinoffs to industry and have a major impact on the competitiveness of our nation.

I have tried to present several grand challenges in AI which are worthy of long-term research focus. Next, I would like to share a few thoughts on the social implications of our research.

Social implications of AI

Like any other science, AI has the potential to do a lot of good and some bad. In this talk, I would like to accent the positive and implore all of you to devote some of your time to AI applications that might help the poor, the illiterate, and the disadvantaged of our nation and the world.

By the turn of the century, it appears possible that a low cost (e.g., costing less than $1000) super computer could be accessible to every man, woman and child in the world. Using such a system, AI researchers should be able to create a personalized, intelligent assistant which would use voice and vision for man-machine communication, tolerate error and ambiguity in human interaction with machines, provide education and entertainment on a personalized basis, provide expert advice on day-to-day problems, make vast amounts of knowledge available in active form, and make ordinary mortals perform superhuman tasks leading to new discoveries and inventions at an unheard of rate. Believe it or not, such a system would help the illiterate farmer in Ethiopia as much as the scientist in U.S.A. or Japan. Let me see if I can be more convincing!

The proposal to share the wealth between north and south advocated by the Brandt Commission and the Cancun Conference never got off the ground. Share the wealth! Who are we kidding? Shipping tons of wheat and corn to feed the hungry is not a solution either. Creating mechanisms for sharing of knowledge, know-how, and literacy might be the only answer. Knowledge has an important property. When you give it away, you don't lose it.

The great Chinese philosopher Kuan-Tzu once said: "If you give a fish to a man, you will feed him for a day. If you give him a fishing rod, you will feed him for life." We can go one step further: If we can provide him with the knowledge and the know-how for making that fishing rod, we can feed the whole village.

It is my belief that the most important wealth we can share with the disadvantaged is the wealth of knowledge. If we can provide a gift of knowledge to village communities that would make them expert at what they need to know to be self-sufficient, we would then witness a true revolution.

Sharing the knowledge and know-how in the form of information products is surely the only way to reduce this ever-widening gap between the have and have-nots. The current technological revolution provides a new hope and new understanding. The computer and communication technologies will make it possible for a rapid and inexpensive sharing of knowledge.

You can make a difference in achieving this compassionate world of the future. My friends, you can have meetings, publish papers, carry placards and believe you have done your duty about social responsibility and feel good about it. My request is to take the extra step. Get involved in national and international projects, and provide your expertise to help solve problems facing people who cannot help themselves.

Conclusion

Let me conclude by first saying that the field is more exciting than ever before. Our recent advances are significant and substantial. And the mythical AI winter may have turned into an AI spring. I see many flowers blooming. There are so many successes that I never cease to be amazed with wonderment at these new and creative uses of AI.

Second, success in AI depends on advances in all of computer science. We are not, and never have been an island unto ourselves. Finally, all parts of AI belong together. Success in AI requires advances in all of its disparate parts including chess, cognitive science, logic, and connectionism. Each of these experiments yield new insights that are crucial to the ultimate success of the whole enterprise.

What can you do? I believe the time has come for each of us to become a responsible spokesman for the entire field. This requires some additional effort on our part to be articulate and be convincing about the progress and prospects of AI. Finally, choose your favorite grand challenge relevant to the nation, and work on it.

Acknowledgments

I am grateful to Hans Berliner, Bruce Buchanan, Ed Feigenbaum, Takeo Kanade, John McCarthy, Allen Newell, Herbert Simon, and Marty Tenenbaum for the fellowship, and many discussions and comments that led to this paper.

Note

Feigenbaum believes knowledge is wealth and most nations and individuals may be unwilling to share it. This is especially true of secret chemical formulae, etc. This poses a dilemma. Clearly it is necessary to create a market for knowledge to be traded as any other commodity in the world markets. At the same time, the poor nations of the world cannot afford to pay for it. There appear to be several solutions. One is to create a Knowledge Bank which pays for and acquires the rights to knowledge for distribution to third world countries. Second is to create a Free Knowledge Foundation (analogous to Free Software Foundation). Over 90% of the knowledge needed by the poor is already available in the public domain. It is just that they are not even aware of the existence and availability of knowledge relevant to their specific problem. The FKF would have to set up mechanisms analogous to the agricultural extension blocks set up by USDA for creation and communication of knowledge and know-how through expert systems technology.

References

T. Anantharaman, M. Campbell, and F. Hsu, 1988. Singular Extensions: Adding Selectivity to Brute-Force Searching. *AAAI Spring Symposium*. Stanford, CA.

L.R. Bahl, F. Jelinek, and R. Mercer, 1983. A Maximum Likelihood Approach to Continuous Speech Recognition. *IEEE Transactions on PAMI* 5(2), 179 – 190.

J.K. Baker, 1975. The Dragon System—An Overview. *IEEE Transactions on ASSP* 23(2), 24 – 29.

H.R. Barrow and J.M. Tenenbaum, 1978. Recovering Intrinsic Scene Characteristics from Images. In *Computer Vision System*, eds. A.R. Hanson and E.M. Riseman. New York: Academic Press.

H.R. Barrow and J.M. Tenenbaum, 1981. Computational Vision. *Proceedings of the IEEE*, 69: 572 – 595.

H.J. Berliner and C. Ebeling, 1986. The SUPREM Architecture. *Artificial Intelligence* 28(1).

T. Binford and G. Agin, 1973. Computer Descriptions of Curved Objects. *Proceedings of the International Joint Conference on Artificial Intelligence*.

R. Bisiani, et. al. 1988. BEAM: A Beam Search Accelerator (Tech. Rep.). Computer Science Department, Carnegie Mellon University.

W. Bledsoe, 1986. I Had a Dream: AAAI Presidential Address, 19 August 1985. *AI Magazine* 7(1):57 – 61.

B. Buchanan and R. Smith, 1988. Fundamentals of Expert Systems. In *Handbook of Artificial Intelligence*, eds. Cohen and Feigenbaum. Forthcoming.

W.G. Chase and H.A. Simon, 1973. The Mind's Eye in Chess. In *Visual Information Processing*, ed. W.G. Chase, New York: Academic Press.

M.B. Clowes, 1971. On Seeing Things. *Artificial Intelligence* 2: 79 – 116.

C. Ebeling, 1986. All the Right Moves: A VLSI Architecture for Chess. Ph.D. diss., Department of Computer Science, Carnegie Mellon University.

G.M. Edelman, 1987. *Neural Darwinism: The Theory of Neuronal Group Selection*. New York: Basic Books.

L.D. Erman, F. Hayes-Roth, V.R. Lesser, and D.R. Reddy, 1980. The Hearsay-II Speech Understanding System: Integrating Knowledge to Resolve Uncertainty. *Computer Surveys* 12(2): 213 – 253.

E.A. Feigenbaum, 1988. What Hath Simon Wrought? In *Complex Information Processing: The Impact of Herbert A. Simon*, eds. D. Klahr and K. Kotovsky, Hillsdale, NJ: Lawrence Erlbaum.

E.A. Feigenbaum, P. McCorduck, and H.P. Nii, 1988. *The Rise of the Expert Company*. Times Books.

J.A. Feldman, 1985. Connectionists Models and Parallelism in High Level Vision. *Computer Vision, Graphics, and Image Processing* 31: 178 – 200.

J.A. Feldman and D.H. Ballard, 1982. Connectionist Models and their Properties. *Cognitive Science* 6: 205 – 254.

M.A. Fischler and R.C. Bolles, 1981. Random Sample Consensus: A Paradigm for Model Fitting with Applications to Image Analysis and Automated Cartography. *CACM* 24(6): 381 – 395.

M.A. Fischler and R.A. Elschlager, 1973. The Representation and Matching of Pictorial Structures. *IEEE Transactions of Comp.* 22(1): 67 – 92.

R.D. Greenblatt, et. al. 1967. The Greenblatt Chess Program. *Proceedings of the Fall Joint Computer Conference*. ACM.

A. Guzman, 1968. Decomposition of a Visual Scene into Three-Dimensional Bodies. .*Proceedings of the Fall Joint Computer Conference*.

J.R. Hayes, 1985. Three Problems in Teaching General Skills. In *Thinking and Learning*, eds. J. Segal, S. Chipman, and R. Glaser, Hillsdale, NJ: Lawrence Erlbaum.

J.R. Hayes, 1987. Memory Organization and World-Class Performance. *Proceedings of the Twenty-First Carnegie Mellon Symposium on Cognition*. Psychology Department, Carnegie Mellon University.

M. Hebert and T. Kanade, 1986. Outdoor Scene Analysis Using Range Data. *IEEE International Conference on Robotics and Automation* 3: 1426 – 1432.

E.C. Hildreth, 1984. Computations Underlying the Measurement of Visual Motion. *Artificial Intelligence* 23(3): 309 – 354.

G.E. Hinton, 1985. Personal communication.

G.E. Hinton, J.L. McClelland, and D.E. Rumelhart, (1986). Distributed Representations. In *Parallel Distributed Processing* eds. Rumelhart et al. Cambridge, MA: Bradford Books.

J.E. Hopcroft, 1987. Computer Science: The Emergence of a Discipline. *Communications of the ACM* 30(3): 198 – 202.

B. Horn, 1977. Obtaining Shape from Shading Information. In *The Psychology of Computer Vision*, ed. P.H. Winston, New York: McGraw-Hill.

B. Horn, 1977. Understanding Image Intensities. *Artificial Intelligence* 8(2): 201 – 231.

F. Hsu, 1986. Two Designs of Functional Units for VLSI Based Chess Machines (Tech. Rep.). Computer Science Department, Carnegie Mellon University.

D.A. Huffman, 1971. Impossible Objects as Nonsense Sentences. In *Machine Intelligence* 6, eds. B. Meltzer and D. Michie, Edinburgh, Scotland: Edinburgh University Press.

K. Ikeuchi and B. Horn, 1981. Numerical Shape from Shading and Occluding Boundaries. *Artificial Intelligence* 17: 141 – 184.

F. Itakura, 1975. Minimum Prediction Residual Principle Applied to Speech Recognition. *IEEE Transactions on ASSP* 23(2): 67 – 72.

F. Jelinek, 1976. Continuous Speech Recognition by Statistical Methods. *Proceedings of the IEEE* 64: 532 – 556.

F. Jelinek, et. al. 1985. A Real Time, Isolated Word, Speech Recognition System for Dictation Transcription. *Proceedings of the IEEE* ASSP.

T. Kanade, 1981. Recovery of the Three-Dimensional Shape of an Object from a Single View. *Artificial Intelligence* 17: 409 – 460.

T. Kanade and J.R. Kender, 1983. Mapping Image Properties into Shape Constraints: Skewed Symmetry, Affine-Transformable Patterns, and the Shape-from-Texture Paradigm. In *Human and Machine Vision*, eds. J. Beck, B. Hope, and A. Rosenfeld, New York: Academic Press.

T. Kanade, C. Thorpe, and W. Whittaker, 1986. Autonomous Land Vehicle Project at CMU. *Proceedings of the 1986 ACM Computer Science Conference*, 71 – 80.

J.R. Kender, 1980. Shape from Texture. Ph.D. diss., Computer Science Department, Carnegie Mellon University.

G. Klinker, S.A. Shafer, and T. Kanade, 1988. Using a Color Reflection Model to Separate Highlights from Object Color. *International Journal of Computer Vision* 2(1): 7 – 32.

D.E. Knuth and R.W. Moore, 1975. An Analysis of Alpha-Beta Pruning. *Artificial Intelligence* 6: 293 – 326.

Y. Lamdan, J.T. Schwartz, and H.J. Wolfson, 1988. Object Recognition by Affine Invariant Matching. *Proceedings of Computer Vision and Pattern Recognition.*

P. Langley, H.A. Simon, G.L. Bradshaw, and J.M. Zytkow, 1987. *Scientific Discovery: Computational Explorations of the Creative Processes*. Cambridge, Mass: MIT Press.

K.F. Lee, 1988. Large Vocabulary Speaker Independent Continuous Speech Recognition: The SPHINX System. Ph.D. diss., Computer Science Department, Carnegie Mellon University.

K.F. Lee, H.W. Hon, and R. Reddy, 1988. An Overview of the SPHINX Speech Recognition System (Tech. Rep.). Computer Science Department, Carnegie Mellon University.

R.K. Lindsay, B.G. Buchanan, E.A. Feigenbaum, and J. Lederberg, 1980. *Applications of Artificial Intelligence for Organic Chemistry: The Dendral Project*. New York: McGraw-Hill.

B.T. Lowerre and D.R. Reddy, 1980. The Harpy Speech Understanding System. In *Trends in Speech Recognition*, ed. W.A. Lea, Englewood Cliffs, NJ: Prentice Hall.

A.K. Mackworth, 1973. Interpreting Pictures of Polyhedral Scenes. *Artificial Intelligence* 4: 121 – 137.

D. Marr, 1979. Visual Information Processing: The Structure and Creation of Visual Representations. *Proceedings of the Sixth International Joint Conference on Artificial Intelligence*. Los Altos, CA: Morgan Kaufman.

D. Marr, 1982. *Vision*. San Francisco, CA: W.H. Freeman.

L. Matthies, R. Szeliski, and T. Kanade, 1988. Kalman Filter-based Algorithms for Estimating Depth from Image Sequences (Tech. Rep.). Robotics Institute, Carnegie Mellon University.

G.A. Miller, 1956. The Magical Number Seven, Plus or Minus Two: Some Limits on Our Capacity for Processing Information. *Psychological Review* 63: 81 – 97.

M. Minsky, 1985. *The Society of Mind*. New York: Simon and Schuster.

A. Newell, J. Shaw, and H.A. Simon, 1958. Chess Playing Programs and the Problem of Complexity. *IBM Journal of Research and Development* 2: 320 – 335.

A. Newell, 1981. The Knowledge Level. Presidential Address, AAAI, 1980. *AI Magazine* 2(2): 1 – 20.

A. Newell, 1987. Unified Theories of Cognition. The William James Lectures. Psychology Department, Harvard University.

A. Newell, 1988. Putting It All Together. In *Complex Information Processing: The Impact of Herbert A. Simon*, eds. D. Klahr and K. Kotovsky, Hillsdale, NJ: Lawrence Erlbaum.

A. Newell and H.A. Simon, 1976. Computer Science as Empirical Inquiry: Symbols and Search. *Communications of the ACM* 19(3).

P. Nii, 1986. The Blackboard Model of Problem Solving and Blackboard Application Systems. *AI Magazine* 7(2&3): 38 – 53, 82 – 106.

N. Nilsson, 1971. *Problem Solving Methods in AI*. New York: McGraw-Hill.

R. Ohlander, K. Price, and D.R. Reddy, 1978. Picture Segmentation Using a Recursive Region Splitting Method. *Computer Graphics Image Process* 8: 313 – 333.

T. Poggio, V. Torre, and C. Koch, 1985. Computational Vision and Regularization Theory. *Nature* 317(26): 314 – 319.

L.R. Rabiner and B.H. Juang, 1986. An Introduction to Hidden Markov Models. *IEEE ASSP Magazine* 3(1): 4 – 16.

D.R. Reddy and A. Newell, 1977. Multiplicative Speedup of Systems. In *Perspectives on Computer Science*, ed. Anita K. Jones, New York: Academic Press.

D.R. Reddy, L.D. Erman, and R.B. Neely, 1973. A Model and a System for Machine Recognition of Speech. *IEEE Transactions on Audio and Electroacoustics* AU-21(3).

L.G. Roberts, 1965. Machine Perception of Three-Dimensional Solids. In *Optical and Electro-Optical Information Processing*, ed. J.T. Tippett, Cambridge, Mass.: MIT Press.

P.S. Rosenbloom, J.E. Laird, and A. Newell, 1987. *Knowledge-level Learning in Soar*. Menlo Park, Calif: AAAI Press.

A. Rosenfeld and R.C. Smith, 1981. Thresholding using Relaxation. *IEEE Trans. Pattern Anal. Mach. Intelligence* PAM1-3: 598 – 606.

C. Sagan, 1977. *The Dragons of Eden: Speculations on the Evolution of Human Intelligence*. New York: Random House.

S.A. Shafer, 1985. Using Color to Separate Reflection Components. *Color Research and Application* 10(4): 210 – 218.

E. Shortliffe, 1976. *MYCIN: Computer-Based Medical Consultations*. New York: American Elsevier.

H.A. Simon, 1947. *Administrative Behavior*, New York: Macmillan.

H.A. Simon, 1955. A Behavioral Model of Rational Choice. *Quarterly Journal of Economics* 69: 99 – 118.

H.A. Simon, 1988. The Scientist at Problem Solver. In *Complex Information Processing: The Impact of Herbert A. Simon*, eds. D. Klahr and K. Kotovsky, Hillsdale, NJ: Lawrence Erlbaum.

H.A. Simon, 1988. Accomplishments of Artificial Intelligence. Unpublished notes.

J.R. Slagle and J.K. Dixon, 1969. Experiments with Some programs that Search Game Trees. *JACM* 16: 189 – 207.

D.J. Slate and L.R. Atkin, 1977. Chess 4.5—The Northwestern University Chess Program. In *Chess Skill in Man and Machine*, ed. P.W. Frey, Berlin, W. Germany: Springer-Verlag.

R.E. Tarjan, 1987. Algorithm Design. *Communications of the ACM* 30(3): 205 – 212.

K. Thompson, 1982. Computer Chess Strength. In *Advances in Computer Chess III*. Pergamon Press.

C. Thorpe, M. Hebert, T. Kanade, and S. Shafer, 1987. Vision and Navigation for Carnegie Mellon Navlab. In *Annual Review of Computer Science*. Palo Alto, Calif.: Annual Reviews Inc.

J. Trogadis and J.K. Stevens, 1983. Scanning Electron Micrograph. Playfair Neuroscience Catalog, Toronto Western Hospital. Photograph.

S. Ullman, 1982. Analysis of Visual Motion by Biological and Computer Systems. *IEEE Computer* 14(8): 57 – 69.

D. Waltz, 1975. Understanding Line Drawings of Scenes with Shadows. In *The Psychology of Computer Vision*, ed. P.H. Winston, New York: McGraw-Hill.

A.M. Waxman, 1984. An Image Flow Paradigm. *Proceedings of the IEEE Workshop on Computer Vision: Representation and Control*. New York: IEEE Press.

A.P. Witkin and J.M. Tenenbaum, 1983. On the Role of Structure in Vision. In *Human and Machine Vision* eds. Beck, Hope, and Rosenfeld, San Diego, Calif.: Academic Press.

R.J. Woodham, 1981. Analyzing Images of Curved Surfaces. *Artificial Intelligence* 17: 117 – 140.

W.A. Woods and J.A. Wolf, 1980. The HWIM Speech Understanding System. In *Trends in Speech Recognition*, ed. W.A. Lea, Englewood Cliffs, NJ: Prentice-Hall.

Index

K

T